Communications
in Computer and Information Science   1918

Rationale

The CCIS series is devoted to the publication of proceedings of computer science conferences. Its aim is to efficiently disseminate original research results in informatics in printed and electronic form. While the focus is on publication of peer-reviewed full papers presenting mature work, inclusion of reviewed short papers reporting on work in progress is welcome, too. Besides globally relevant meetings with internationally representative program committees guaranteeing a strict peer-reviewing and paper selection process, conferences run by societies or of high regional or national relevance are also considered for publication.

Topics

The topical scope of CCIS spans the entire spectrum of informatics ranging from foundational topics in the theory of computing to information and communications science and technology and a broad variety of interdisciplinary application fields.

Information for Volume Editors and Authors

Publication in CCIS is free of charge. No royalties are paid, however, we offer registered conference participants temporary free access to the online version of the conference proceedings on SpringerLink (http://link.springer.com) by means of an http referrer from the conference website and/or a number of complimentary printed copies, as specified in the official acceptance email of the event.

CCIS proceedings can be published in time for distribution at conferences or as postproceedings, and delivered in the form of printed books and/or electronically as USBs and/or e-content licenses for accessing proceedings at SpringerLink. Furthermore, CCIS proceedings are included in the CCIS electronic book series hosted in the SpringerLink digital library at http://link.springer.com/bookseries/7899. Conferences publishing in CCIS are allowed to use Online Conference Service (OCS) for managing the whole proceedings lifecycle (from submission and reviewing to preparing for publication) free of charge.

Publication process

The language of publication is exclusively English. Authors publishing in CCIS have to sign the Springer CCIS copyright transfer form, however, they are free to use their material published in CCIS for substantially changed, more elaborate subsequent publications elsewhere. For the preparation of the camera-ready papers/files, authors have to strictly adhere to the Springer CCIS Authors' Instructions and are strongly encouraged to use the CCIS LaTeX style files or templates.

Abstracting/Indexing

CCIS is abstracted/indexed in DBLP, Google Scholar, EI-Compendex, Mathematical Reviews, SCImago, Scopus. CCIS volumes are also submitted for the inclusion in ISI Proceedings.

How to start

To start the evaluation of your proposal for inclusion in the CCIS series, please send an e-mail to ccis@springer.com.

Fuchun Sun · Qinghu Meng · Zhumu Fu ·
Bin Fang

Editors

Cognitive Systems
and Information Processing

8th International Conference, ICCSIP 2023
Luoyang, China, August 10–12, 2023
Revised Selected Papers, Part I

 Springer

Editors
Fuchun Sun
Tsinghua University
Beijing, China

Qinghu Meng
Southern University of Science
and Technology
Shenzhen, China

Zhumu Fu
Henan University of Science and Technology
Luoyang, China

Bin Fang
Tsinghua University
Beijing, China

ISSN 1865-0929   ISSN 1865-0937 (electronic)
Communications in Computer and Information Science
ISBN 978-981-99-8017-8   ISBN 978-981-99-8018-5 (eBook)
https://doi.org/10.1007/978-981-99-8018-5

This Springer imprint is published by the registered company Springer Nature Singapore Pte Ltd.
The registered company address is: 152 Beach Road, #21-01/04 Gateway East, Singapore 189721, Singapore

Paper in this product is recyclable.

Preface

This volume contains the papers from the Eighth International Conference on Cognitive Systems and Information Processing (ICCSIP 2023), which was held in Fuzhou during August 10–12, 2023. The conference was hosted by the Chinese Association for Artificial Intelligence and organized by Tsinghua University, Henan University of Science and Technology, the Cognitive Systems and Information Processing Society of the Chinese Association for Artificial Intelligence, and the Cognitive Computing and Systems Society of the Chinese Association of Automation, with Zhengzhou University of Light Industry, Zhongyuan University of Technology, Luoyang Institute of Science and Technology, and Luoyang Normal University as co-organizers.

ICCSIP is the prestigious biennial conference on Cognitive Systems and Information Processing, with past events held in Beijing (2012, 2014, 2016, 2018), Zhuhai (2020), Suzhou (2021), and Fuzhou (2022). Over the past few years, ICCSIP has matured into a well-established series of international conferences on cognitive information processing and related fields. Like its predecessors, ICCSIP 2023 provided an academic forum for the participants to share their new research findings and discuss emerging areas of research. It also established a stimulating environment for the participants to exchange ideas on future trends and opportunities in cognitive information processing research.

Currently, cognitive systems and information processing are applied in an increasing number of research domains such as cognitive sciences and technology, visual cognition and computation, big data and intelligent information processing, and bioinformatics and applications. We believe that cognitive systems and information processing will certainly exhibit greater-than-ever advances in the near future. With the aim of promoting the research and technical innovation in relevant fields domestically and internationally, the fundamental objective of ICCSIP is defined as providing a premier forum for researchers and practitioners from academia, industry, and government to share their ideas, research results, and experiences.

ICCSIP 2023 received 136 submissions, all of which were written in English. After a thorough reviewing process in which all submissions received three single-blind reviews, 52 papers were selected for presentation as full papers, resulting in an approximate acceptance rate of 38%. The accepted papers not only address challenging issues in various aspects of cognitive systems and information processing but also showcase contributions from related disciplines that illuminate the state of the art. In addition to the contributed papers, the ICCSIP 2023 technical program included seven plenary speeches by Qinghu Meng, Dewen Hu, Jianwei Zhang, Xuguang Lan, Jing Liang, Yongduan Song, and Xinyu Wu. We would like to thank the members of the Advisory Committee for their guidance, the members of the International Program Committee and additional reviewers for reviewing the papers, and members of the Publications Committee for checking the accepted papers in a short period of time.

Last but not least, we would like to thank all the speakers, authors, and reviewers as well as the participants for their great contributions that made ICCSIP 2023 successful and all the hard work worthwhile. We also thank Springer for their trust and for publishing the proceedings of ICCSIP 2023.

August 2023

Fuchun Sun
Qinghu Meng
Zhumu Fu
Bin Fang

Organization

Conference Committee

Honorary Chairs

Bo Zhang   Tsinghua University, China
Nanning Zheng   Xi'an Jiaotong University, China
Deyi Li   Chinese Association for Artificial Intelligence, China

General Chairs

Fuchun Sun   Tsinghua University, China
Qinghu Meng   Southern University of Science and Technology, China
Xinchang Pang   Henan University of Science and Technology, China
Xiao Zhang   Zhengzhou University of Light Industry, China
Boyang Qu   Zhongyuan University of Technology, China
Zhiquan Huang   Luoyang Institute of Science and Technology, China

Program Committee Chairs

Zhumu Fu   Henan University of Science and Technology, China
Qingtao Wu   Henan University of Science and Technology, China
Juwei Zhang   Henan University of Science and Technology, China

Organizing Committee Chairs

Bin Fang	Tsinghua University, China
Zhiyong Zhang	Henan University of Science and Technology, China
Yan Li	Zhongyuan University of Technology, China
Chao Wu	Luoyang Institute of Science and Technology, China
Youzhong Ma	Luoyang Normal University, China

Publicity Committee Chairs

Mingchuan Zhang	Henan University of Science and Technology, China
Miao Du	Zhengzhou University of Light Industry, China

Publications Committee Chair

Wenshao Bu	Henan University of Science and Technology, China

Finance Committee Chair

Meng Wang	Henan University of Science and Technology, China

Local Affairs Committee Chair

Jingtao Huang	Henan University of Science and Technology, China

Electronic Review Committee Chair

Qingduan Meng	Henan University of Science and Technology, China

Steering Committee

Qionghai Dai	Tsinghua University, China
Shimin Hu	Tsinghua University, China

Program Committee

Baofeng Ji	Henan University of Science and Technology, China
Yongsheng Dong	Henan University of Science and Technology, China
Xiaona Song	Henan University of Science and Technology, China
Ruijuan Zheng	Henan University of Science and Technology, China
Zhifeng Zhang	Zhengzhou University of Light Industry, China
Wenqing Chen	Luoyang Institute of Science and Technology, China
Jianhu Jiang	Luoyang Institute of Science and Technology, China
Lijun Song	Luoyang Institute of Science and Technology, China
Lifan Sun	Henan University of Science and Technology, China
Fazhan Tao	Henan University of Science and Technology, China
Pengju Si	Henan University of Science and Technology, China
Junlong Zhu	Henan University of Science and Technology, China
Lin Wang	Henan University of Science and Technology, China
Bin Song	Henan University of Science and Technology, China
Xuzhao Chai	Zhongyuan University of Technology, China
Deguang Li	Luoyang Normal University, China
Shijie Jia	Luoyang Normal University, China
Tongchi Zhou	Zhongyuan University of Technology, China
Baihao Qiao	Zhongyuan University of Technology, China
Jiaquan Shen	Luoyang Normal University, China

Contents – Part I

Algorithm and Control

Application

Contents – Part II

Vision

Award

Broad Learning System Based on Fusion Features

Dongmei Hu[1], Xinying Xu[1] (ID), Jiwei Xing[1] (ID), Gang Xie[1,2] (ID), Jijun Tang[3] (ID), and Rong Li[1 (✉)] (ID)

[1] Taiyuan University of Technology, Taiyuan 030024, Shanxi, China
{xuxinying,lirong}@tyut.edu.cn, xiegang@tyust.edu.cn
[2] Taiyuan University of Science and Technology, Taiyuan 030024, Shanxi, China
[3] University of South Carolina, Columbia, SC 29208, USA
jtang@cse.sc.edu

Abstract. Multimodal fusion is the integration of data from different modalities according to the principle of optimality to produce more reliable perception of objects. Deep learning has been widely used in multimodal fusion domain, but how to reduce model parameters and training time while maintaining good performance is still an academic problem. To address these issues, we design a system capable of learning and fusing features from both modalities, the Deep Residual network Broad Learning System (DR-BLS). First we use a pre-trained deep residual network (ResNet18) to extract features of different modalities separately. And then we use canonical correlation analysis to project the two obtained features in the same feature space for correlation learning and fusion of features. Finally the broad learning system is used as classifier for target recognition and classification. Experiments on target classification recognition on the University of Washington RGB-D dataset show that the method pro-posed in this paper is more stable and faster than other algorithms.

Keywords: multimodal fusion · correlation analysis · feature extraction · Board learning system

1 Introduction

In a reality where individuals navigate a diverse range of modalities, our experiences encompass sensory inputs such as sounds, textures, and scents. As the quest to enhance the intelligence of machines progresses, it becomes imperative for them to interpret and reason with multi-modal information. Additionally, in the era of big data, the availability of abundant multi-modal data introduces complexities. Recognizing the limitations of single-modal inputs to address complex tasks, the research community has seen a surge in learning algorithms focused on multi-modal fusion, making intelligent multi-modal information fusion a burgeoning field of study.

Supported by the National Natural Science Foundation of China (No. 62003233), the Shanxi Province Science Foundation for Youths (NO. 201901D211083).

F. Sun et al. (Eds.): ICCSIP 2023, CCIS 1918, pp. 3–19, 2024.
https://doi.org/10.1007/978-981-99-8018-5_1

Multi-modal fusion involves leveraging the information provided by various sensors to capitalize on the complementary strengths of different data modalities. This process aims to narrow the distribution gap within the semantic subspace, while preserving the integrity of modality-specific semantics [1]. In recent years, both domestic and international scholars have applied multi-modal fusion techniques across a spectrum of domains. For instance, in the realm of robot emotion analysis, an effective fusion of features from images, text, and speech has been achieved through a two-stage multi-modal learning framework, enabling the adaptive learning of correlations and complementarities between modalities, thus yielding superior emotional classification results compared to single-modality approaches [2]. Furthermore, human behaviors, emotions, events, and actions inherently possess multi-modal aspects. For example, multi-modal speech emotion recognition [3] has explored cross-lingual emotional recognition using languages such as Italian, English, and German. Multi-modal pedestrian detection employs a three-stage process involving multi-modal object detection, pedestrian classification, and parameter adjustment to achieve accurate pedestrian detection [4]. Multi-modal hazardous driving behavior detection extracts key information from human body key points to capture richer features and utilizes motion information from relevant objects to create a multi-modal fusion behavior recognition model for "human+object" interactions [5].

However, existing multi-modal fusion algorithms and models predominantly rely on deep learning techniques, which are plagued by issues such as substantial data and parameter requirements, challenging model setup, and the risk of converging to local optima. These challenges translate to demanding computational capabilities, prolonged training times, and difficulties in convergence, often failing to exploit their advantages in scenarios with limited sample data. Addressing these concerns, Chen et al. pioneered the concept of the Broad Learning System (BLS) [6–8], offering a solution characterized by its simple flat network structure, minimal steps, rapid learning speed, and incremental modeling. BLS ensures a certain level of accuracy while maintaining robust generalization, successfully applied in various classification and regression tasks. Researchers have proposed improved algorithms based on BLS tailored to specific tasks. Huang and Chen introduced the Bidirectional BLS (B-BLS) [9], which efficiently updates certain hidden nodes as the B-BLS network expands. Feng and Chen introduced a Fuzzy BLS for data regression and classification [10]. Li Guoqiang et al. introduced a locally receptive field-based BLS for feature extraction from images [11]. Based on the broad learning approach, this paper proposes a classification system capable of handling multi-modal information. Through parallel feature extraction of modalities and effective fusion of extracted features, the proposed system achieves classification output. Experimental results demonstrate that compared to deep learning, the fusion approach presented here circumvents time-consuming training processes, efficiently accomplishes modal fusion classification and recognition tasks with small-sample data, and enhances system accuracy and robustness.

2 Related Work

2.1 Multimodal Fusion

Multi-modal fusion refers to the integration of information from various data sources to enhance the accuracy and reliability of information. The reason for fusing different modalities is that they represent different perspectives and viewpoints on the same subject. Multi-modal fusion combines information from multiple modalities to provide a more comprehensive view than a single modality, broadening the coverage of information contained in input modalities and improving the accuracy of predictive results [12]. Effectively fusing multi-modal information to enhance perceptual capabilities is a highly appealing and challenging problem for researchers. In article [13], a novel multi-modal emotion recognition framework is proposed for classifying emotions. The model employs statistical geometric methods to learn neural appearances and key emotional frameworks as preprocessors to save computational resources and optimize the extraction of emotional features from visual and audio modalities. In article [14], a BLS model capable of learning and fusing two modalities is introduced, demonstrating improved stability and speed compared to traditional linear fusion methods when validated on an RGB-D dataset.

Despite these advancements, multi-modal fusion still faces the following challenges: different modal signals may not be temporally aligned; each modality may exhibit different types and levels of noise at different times; preprocessing data, due to variations in data format, size, quantity, and other factors, introduces complexity, all of which constrain the potential of multi-modal learning.

2.2 Transfer Learning

In machine learning, achieving a highly robust model necessitates a substantial amount of annotated samples and training and testing sets that share the same distribution while remaining mutually independent. Training a model from scratch is an exceedingly time-consuming endeavor. Transfer learning [15, 16] refers to the practice of transferring model parameters learned from other related tasks to a new model, obviating the need to start from scratch. Even when dealing with a small dataset, transfer learning can yield impressive performance, significantly reducing time costs and thereby expediting the model training process.

The ImageNet dataset contains approximately 1.2 million images spanning 1000 classes. Pre-training a network model on such an extensive dataset allows the learned feature hierarchy to serve effectively as a generalized model of the visual world, which can be efficiently transferred to a variety of different computer vision tasks. Within convolutional neural network (CNN) models, convolutional operations are designed to extract diverse features from input data. The generality of features extracted by a particular convolutional layer depends on its depth within the model. Shallow convolutional layers might primarily capture low-level features such as edges, lines, and corners, while deeper layers iteratively extract more intricate features from these lower-level representations. With this in mind, our study leverages a pre-trained ResNet18 residual network, trained on the ImageNet dataset, to facilitate image feature extraction (Fig. 1).

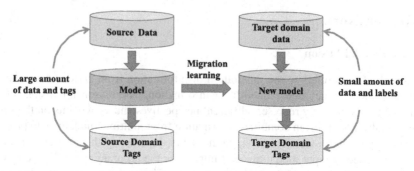

Fig. 1. Transfer learning model overview. Left: Model train with large datasets, in which process we obtain a model with strong generalization ability. Right: parameter migration is used as the corresponding parameters, and fine-tuning on a smaller datasets.

2.3   Canonical Correlation Analysis

Canonical correlation analysis (CCA) [17, 18], as shown in Fig. 2, is a classical algorithm reflecting the study of correlation between two sets of vectors. For two groups of eigenvectors, the degree of correlation between the two groups of vectors is calculated, and a representative linear combination vector is obtained to maximize the correlation between the two groups of eigenvectors. In the correlation analysis of these two sets of vectors, it can play a role in simplifying the vectors reasonably, and achieve the purpose of feature fusion by connecting or adding vectors and other strategies. The typical correlation analysis method removes the redundant features of simple concatenation and splicing fusion, improves the discriminative and robustness of feature representation, and realizes the purpose of feature dimensionality reduction and fusion.

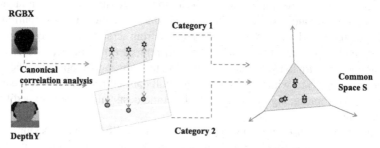

Fig. 2. Structure of CCA model. The RGB-data vector X and Depth-data vector Y map to a common space S in which they can calculate the correlation between them.

Assuming two sets of random variables belong to distinct modalities and vector spaces $X = [x_1, x_2, ..., x_n]$ and $Y = [y_1, y_2, ..., y_n]$. The purpose of CCA is to find a pair of projection axes, donate as u and v to perform linear transformation, so that the correlation $Corr(\alpha, \beta)$ between the linear combination $\alpha = u^T x$ and $\beta = v^T y$ is the largest:

$$Corr(\alpha, \beta) = \max_{u,v} \frac{u^T C_{xy} v}{\sqrt{u^T C_{xx}^T u \cdot v^T C_{yy} v}} \tag{1}$$

where C_{xx} is the covariance matrix of x, C_{xy} is the mutual covariance matrix of x and y, C_{yy} is the covariance matrix of y.

$$C_{xy} = E\left[xy^T\right] = \frac{1}{n}\sum_{i=1}^{n} x_i y_i^T \tag{2}$$

$$C_{xx} = E\left[xx^T\right] = \frac{1}{n}\sum_{i=1}^{n} x_i x_i^T \tag{3}$$

$$C_{yy} = E\left[yy^T\right] = \frac{1}{n}\sum_{i=1}^{n} y_i y_i^T \tag{4}$$

The projection axis of CCA can be obtained by solving the characteristic equation shaped as Eq. (5).

$$\begin{bmatrix} 0 & XY^T \\ YX^T & 0 \end{bmatrix}\begin{bmatrix} u \\ v \end{bmatrix} = \lambda \begin{bmatrix} XX^T & 0 \\ 0 & YY^T \end{bmatrix}\begin{bmatrix} u \\ v \end{bmatrix} \tag{5}$$

where λ is the covariance between α and β.

2.4 Broad Learning System

The Broad Learning System (BLS), proposed by Professor Junlong Chen in 2017, is structured as depicted in Fig. 3. This model is designed based on the concept of the Random Vector Functional Link Neural Network (RVFLNN) and offers an alternative approach to deep learning. Differing from RVFLNN, BLS maps input data to the feature layer before mapping it to the enhancement nodes, with the output layer connecting both the feature and enhancement layers.

In contrast to traditional learning algorithms such as perceptron [20], feedforward neural networks [21], and backpropagation [22], the BLS model can leverage random hidden layer weights to map original samples to a feature space composed of these vectors. It maintains a balance between precision, rapidity, and simplicity, along with the ability to quickly update the model through incremental learning.

The entire structure of the broad learning system consists of four components: model input, feature nodes, enhancement nodes, and model output. Input samples undergo linear transformations to map features onto the feature plane, forming feature nodes. The resultant feature nodes then pass through a non-linear activation function to generate enhancement nodes. These feature and enhancement nodes are subsequently interconnected, and their combined output is provided by the output matrix. Finally, the output matrix is directly obtained using the Ridge Regression Generalized Inverse.

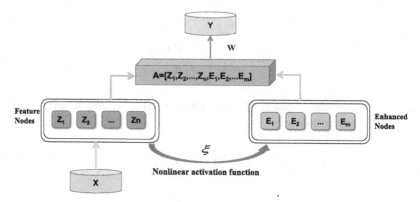

Fig. 3. Overview of Broad Learning System Architecture.

The basic structure and calculation steps of BLS are as follows: given the input sample $X \in \mathbb{R}^{N \times M}$ and output $Y \in \mathbb{R}^{N \times C}$, where N denotes the number of input samples and M denotes the feature dimension of each sample vector. First, n groups of feature mappings are generated, each group contains Z feature nodes. Thus the i-th group of mapped features is shown in Eq. (6):

$$Z_i = \varphi_i \big(X W_{ei} + \beta_{ei}, \big), \quad i = 1, 2, \ldots, n \tag{6}$$

where $\varphi(\cdot)$ is linear activation function, W_{ei} and β_{ei} are randomly initialized weights and biases.

Meanwhile, BLS uses the sparse self-coding idea to optimize the input weight W_{ei}:

$$\arg\min : \left\| Z \hat{W}_{ei} - X \right\|_2 + \lambda_1 \left\| \hat{W}_{ei} \right\|_1, \, s.t. X W_{ei} = Z \tag{7}$$

Define $Z^i = [E_1, E_2, \ldots, E_i]$ as the mapping feature of the i-th group in series, where E_j is the enhanced node of the j-th group, denoted as:

$$E_j = \xi_j \big(Z^i W_{hj} + \beta_{hj} \big), j = 1, 2, \ldots, m \tag{8}$$

where $\xi(\cdot)$ is nonlinear activation function and β_{hj} is the random initialization bias. Unlike the feature nodes, the coefficient matrix W_{hj} of the augmentation nodes is not a random matrix, but a random matrix after orthogonal normalization. The purpose of this is to "augment" the network by nonlinearly mapping the feature nodes to a high-dimensional subspace, which makes the network more expressive.

The broad learning system can be defined as follows:

$$\begin{aligned} Y &= [Z_1, Z_2, \ldots, Z_n | E_1, E_2, \ldots, E_m] W^N \\ &= \big[Z^n | E^m \big] W^N \\ &= A_n^m W^N \end{aligned} \tag{9}$$

where A_n^m represents the actual input matrix of BLS; W^N represents the output weight matrix. The output weights are calculated by solving the output weights through ridge regression as follows:

$$W = \left(\lambda_2 I + AA^{\mathrm{T}}\right)^{-1} A^{\mathrm{T}} Y \tag{10}$$

3 Broad Learning Based on Fused Features

3.1 Methodology Overview

To address the issue of multi-modal feature fusion, this paper proposes a Broad Learning System based on Fused Features (DR-BLS), which employs ResNet18 network for extracting deep features from diverse modalities and performs data fusion for classification. The network structure, illustrated in Fig. 4, comprises three main components:

- During the extraction of distinct modal features, a parallel pre-trained ResNet18 network is employed to fine-tune and extract high-dimensional features from RGB images and depth images separately.
- In the modal fusion stage, the features from the two distinct modalities are mapped to the same feature space to establish correlations. The two modal features are connected to yield correspondingly aligned feature representations in the feature subspace, facilitating feature fusion.
- In the classification recognition stage, the fundamental structure of the Broad Learning System is utilized for the classification task. The fused features are mapped to feature nodes and enhancement nodes, reinforcing the fused feature representation. The final output is computed using Ridge Regression Inverse.

The proposed DR-BLS method thus integrates the feature extraction from different modalities, modal fusion for enhanced representation, and classification recognition within the unified framework.

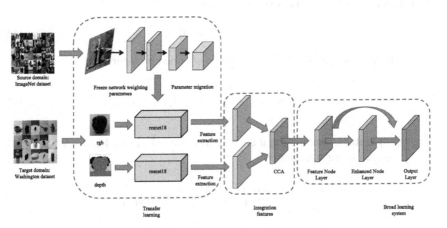

Fig. 4. DR-BLS network architecture.

3.2   ResNet Extraction of Features

The ResNet model was introduced by Microsoft Research in 2015 [23] to address the challenges of training very deep neural networks. It has since been widely applied in various fields such as autonomous driving, facial recognition, and image classification. In traditional neural networks, multiple convolutional and pooling layers are often employed, with each layer extracting features from the previous one. However, as researchers ventured into deeper convolutional networks, it was found that increasing the network depth could lead to issues like gradient explosion, vanishing gradients, performance saturation, and even degradation in network performance as training progresses, ultimately resulting in convergence issues [24, 25]. ResNet introduced a novel approach known as residual connections, depicted in Fig. 5, which to a certain extent mitigated the challenges posed by deep neural networks.

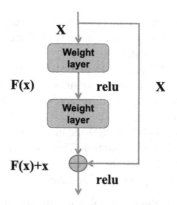

Fig. 5. Residual learning: a building block.

Equation expression for the residual structure:

$$x_{l+1} = x_l + F(x_l, W_l) \tag{11}$$

The expression of any deep i feature can be obtained by recursion:

$$x_L = x_l + \sum_{i=l}^{L-1} F(x_i, W_i) \tag{12}$$

For back propagation, assuming that the loss function is E, according to the chain rule of back propagation we can obtain:

$$\frac{\partial \varepsilon}{\partial x_l} = \frac{\partial_\varepsilon}{\partial x_L} \frac{\partial x_L}{\partial x_l} \left(1 + \frac{\partial}{\partial x_l} \sum_{i=1}^{L-1} F(x_i, \omega_i) \right) \tag{13}$$

$\partial_\varepsilon / \partial x_L$ ensures that the signal can be directly transmitted back to an arbitrary shallow layer, and this formula also ensures that there is no gradient disappearance.

This study takes into consideration both the size of the model samples and the number of model parameters, and selects the ResNet18 network as the feature extractor. The ResNet18 network consists of 18 layers, organized into four modules, each comprising several residual blocks with the same output channel number. The approach begins with transfer learning, where the pre-trained ResNet18 model parameters from the large-scale ImageNet dataset are applied to extract multi-modal features. The convolutional layers of the ResNet18 network are frozen to prevent gradient updates during model training. The parameters before the fully connected layers are transferred, and fine-tuning is performed using a small sample dataset to adjust the learned image feature network. This approach rapidly enhances and learns image features for classification recognition. The specific model and transfer learning method are illustrated in Fig. 6.

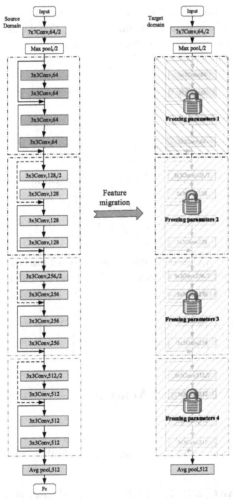

Fig. 6. ResNet18 feature migration. Left: ResNet18 pre-train on ImageNet; Right: Freeze Parameters and fine-tuning.

3.3 Fusion and Classification of Features

For the feature fusion part, it can be seen from the introduction in Sect. 3.2 and the model shown in Fig. 4 that the two modal features extracted by the ResNet18 network are two groups of random variables $H_1 = [h_{11}, h_{12}, ..., h_{1n}]$ and $H_2 = [h_{21}, h_{22}, ..., h_{2n}]$ without explicit correlation input by the CCA layer. A linear combination of two sets of variables that maximizes the correlation between the two sets of variables. Determines two n-dimensional transformation vectors $u = [u_1, u_2, ...u_n]$ and $v = [v_1, v_2, ...v_n]$ that maximize the correlation coefficient between them. The two groups of variables are uniformly mapped to the feature space generated by CCA for learning, and the shared subspace mapping feature learned through CCA is, according to the CCA feature fusion strategy, the parallel matrix $[uH_1|vH_2]$ is used as the fusion feature to achieve feature fusion and dimensionality reduction.

Based on the description of BLS in Sect. 2.4, the fusion feature $[uH_1|vH_2]$ is used as the input of the BLS classification algorithm, assuming that the initial network structure has group mapping nodes and group enhancement nodes.

Then the fused feature nodes are:

$$Z_i = \varphi_i\big([uH_1|vH_2]W_{ei} + \beta_{ei,}\big), \quad i = 1, 2, \ldots, n \tag{14}$$

The enhancement nodes are:

$$E_j = \xi_j\Big(Z^i W_{hi} + \beta_{hi}\Big), j = 1, 2, \ldots, m \tag{15}$$

Therefore, the result Y of model classification recognition is shown by Eq. (16):

$$\begin{aligned} Y &= \big[Z^n|E^m\big]\,W^N \\ &= [A_{2n}^N]W^N \end{aligned} \tag{16}$$

where $W^N = [A_{2n}^N]^+ Y$ is the output connection matrix of the DR-BLS model structure, including the total weights of the feature node layer and the enhancement node layer of the two modal fusion features. $[A_{2n}^N]^+$ is calculated by Eq. (16) as:

$$\Big[A_{2n}^N\Big]^+ = \lim_{\lambda \to 0}\Big(\lambda I + A_{2n}^N\Big[A_{2n}^N\Big]^T\Big)^{-1}\Big[A_{2n}^N\Big]^T \tag{17}$$

4 Experimental Results and Analysis

4.1 Experimental Dataset

We empirically perform experiments on two datasets, both of which are generated from real-world scenario data.

RGB-D Object Dataset [25]: The RGB-D Object dataset comprises images of 51 categories of 300 different common daily objects, captured from various viewpoints and under different lighting conditions, resulting in a total of 41,877 (color and depth) images. Color images are sized at 64 × 64 pixels, while depth images are sized at 128 × 128 pixels. Figure 7(a) illustrates four distinct instances of the "banana" category, each with its corresponding color and depth images. Partial color images of some samples are shown in Fig. 7(b). The data collection methodology involves placing each object on a turntable and using a 3D camera to record a complete rotation cycle of the turntable. Each object is captured through three video sequences, each recorded from cameras positioned at different heights.

RGB-D Scenes Dataset [26]: The RGB-D Scenes dataset is a multi-view scene image dataset provided by the University of Washington. These scenes encompass common indoor environments, including office spaces, conference rooms, and kitchens, among others. Partial color and depth images of some scenes are depicted in Fig. 7(c). The data collection process involves capturing images while walking through each scene, maintaining the RGB-D camera at a height approximate to that of human eyes. This dataset comprises 8 distinct categorized scenes, containing a total of 5972 images, all of which are of dimensions 640 × 480 pixels.

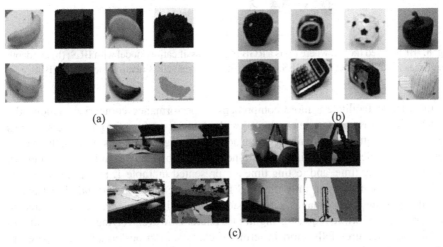

(a)   (b)

(c)

Fig. 7. Example of RGB-D Object dataset and RGB-D Scenes dataset, where (a) is four examples of bananas; (b) is a RGB image of different samples; and (c) is a scene example.

4.2 Experimental Results

RGB-D Object Dataset
In the RGB-D Object dataset, this study utilizes a total of 41,877 depth images and color images for experimentation. Prior to model training, the size of the depth images is adjusted to 64x64, as is the size of the color images. For the experimental setup, 80% of the images are selected for training purposes, while the remaining 20% are allocated for testing.

In order to evaluate the effectiveness of the proposed model for multi-modal fusion classification recognition tasks, a comparative model is designed, as illustrated in Fig. 8. The Basic Learning System (BLS) is applied individually to color images, depth images, and a concatenation of both types of images. The comparison primarily focuses on metrics such as recognition accuracy, training time, and testing time.

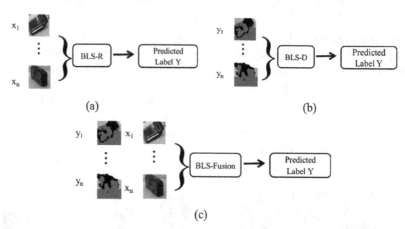

(a)　　　　　　　　　　　　　　　　　　(b)

(c)

Fig. 8. BLS-based model, where (a) is a RGB image classification model with BLS; (b) is a depth image classification model with BLS; (c) is a stitched image classification model with BLS.

In order to facilitate a more comprehensive performance comparison among the models, the experiments were conducted with identical settings for parameters such as the number of feature nodes, enhancement nodes, convergence factors, and regularization factors. The models were individually trained as described above, and the resulting test accuracy, training time, and testing time are presented in Table 1. From the table, it is evident that when utilizing only the BLS for feature extraction and individual image classification, the color images achieve superior classification accuracy compared to the depth images, while requiring slightly less time. However, relying solely on single-modal image features falls short in terms of classification performance compared to the effectiveness of combining both modalities, albeit at the cost of increased feature dimensionality and training time.

In contrast, the DR-BLS fusion algorithm outperforms the aforementioned three methods in terms of classification accuracy, demonstrating both higher accuracy and faster processing times. This highlights the effectiveness of the DR-BLS fusion algorithm in effectively learning high-dimensional features from both RGB and Depth images, significantly enhancing classification recognition accuracy. These results underscore the algorithm's efficiency and effectiveness.

Also to compare the effects of different parameters on the performance of the DR-BLS model, the experiments were performed with parameter sensitivity analysis on the model regularization factor C, convergence factor S, feature nodes and enhancement nodes. Figure 9 shows the trends of the effects of C and S on the classification accuracy of the dataset tested. Observing Fig. 9, it is found that the regularization factor C has a

Table 1. Model classification accuracy comparison on RGB-D Object dataset

Methodology	BLS-D	BLS-R	BLS-Fusion	DR-BLS
Training time/s	58.62	53.59	95.91	13.60
Test time/s	1.34	1.76	2.34	0.61
Recognition rate/%	53.07	65.32	73.62	87.19

greater impact on the recognition rate. The classification accuracy is the lowest when C = 2^10, and even the classification accuracy reaches about 30%, while the classification accuracy gradually increases as the value of C is taken decreasingly, and the classification accuracy is the highest when C = 2^−30. In contrast to the change in the value of C, the convergence factor S has little effect on the classification accuracy, and the recognition accuracy fluctuates in a gentle manner as S increases. Overall, with small values of C, DR-BLS has good robustness and can filter out noise interference.

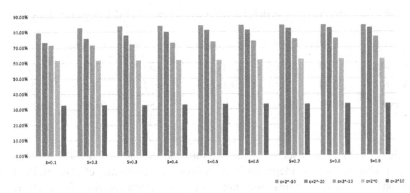

Fig. 9. The influence of correlation factors on the recognition rate of the model

Fixing C = 2^−30 and S = 0.8, the parameters of feature nodes and enhancement nodes are adjusted in the range of {500, 600, 700, 800, 900, 1100, 1200} and {900, 1000, 1100, 1200, 1300, 1400, 1500, 1600}, respectively, as shown in Fig. 10. The classification recognition rate fluctuates smoothly with the increase of enhancement and feature nodes. Therefore, overall, the regularization factor has the greatest impact on the classification recognition rate compared to the number of feature nodes and enhancement nodes.

RGB-D Scenes Dataset

The RGB-D Scenes dataset, comprising a total of 5972 images, was meticulously partitioned into distinct training and testing cohorts, adopting a balanced ratio of 8:2. Concomitantly, the image dimensions, originally presented at 640 × 480 pixels, were gracefully downsized to a more refined and intellectually resonant resolution of 128 × 128 pixels.

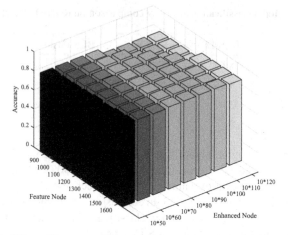

Fig. 10. Effect of feature nodes and enhancement nodes on recognition rate

Table 2. Comparison of model classification accuracy on RGB-D Scenes dataset

Methodology	BLS-D	BLS-R	BLS-Fusion	ResNet-D	ResNet-R	DR-BLS
Training time/s	17.93	17.65	22.27	4.32	7.58	10.61
Test time/s	0.34	0.51	0.45	0.17	0.12	0.22
Accuracy/%	83.21	80.07	93.00	83.56	94.05	97.52

Table 2 provides a discerning insight into the efficacy of the DR-BLS fusion algorithm, showcasing its adeptness in effectively capturing and characterizing high-dimensional nonlinear features from both color and depth images. Impressively, the classification accuracy achieved by the DR-BLS model stands at a remarkable 97.52%, representing a substantial advancement over models reliant solely on individual image feature extraction via the ResNet network, as well as the BLS model amalgamating the two image modalities.

In the context of scene classification, the elucidating confusion matrices for both the BLS and DR-BLS models are graphically depicted in Fig. 11. A careful analysis of these matrices reveals that the model employing the BLS fusion approach demonstrates enhanced performance, particularly in intricate and convoluted scenes, exemplified by cases like desk_1, desk_2, and desk_3, as well as table_small_1 and table_small_2. However, it is noteworthy that despite this improved performance, the overall classification accuracy of the BLS-based model still marginally trails the algorithm fortified by the direct utilization of the ResNet network. This study's overarching significance becomes even more pronounced when considering the broader landscape of deep architectures. It is evident that the proposed methodology not only considerably curtails model training time but also substantively enhances classification accuracy. Notably, this advancement is particularly conspicuous in more intricate and challenging scenes, emphasizing the method's robustness and applicability.

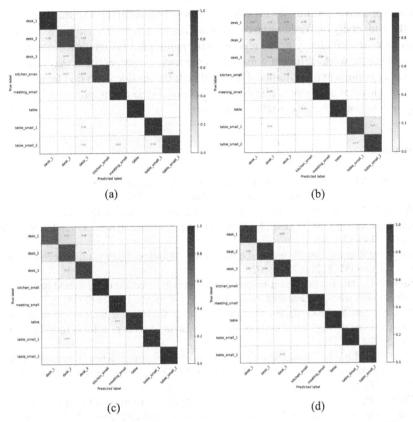

Fig. 11. The confusion matrices. Where (a) is confusion matrix pertaining to the model's application of BLS for a rudimentary fusion of the two distinct image modalities, (b) is confusion matrix corresponding to the model's utilization of ResNet for the extraction of features from depth images, (c) is confusion matrix representing the model's utilization of ResNet for feature extraction from RGB images, (d) is confusion matrix pertaining to the proposed DR-BLS model, a novel contribution of this research endeavor.

In summary, the DR-BLS proposed in this paper can effectively extract the rich information of different modal images, complete the fusion learning and classification tasks, and show very great advantages in terms of training time, testing accuracy and parameter impact, so that the system maintains good recognition performance while combining high speed, accuracy and robustness.

5 Conclusion

In order to solve the multimodal fusion problem, a novel fusion method is proposed in this paper, which combines the resnet18 network and CCA algorithm to form the DR-BLS algorithm based on the BLS. When the sample data size is small, the algorithm proposed in this paper can replace deep learning and obtain high recognition rate with less time cost.

The proposed algorithm was experimented on two different types of standard datasets from the University of Washington multimodal image disclosure, and the experimental results show the efficiency of the algorithm in multimodal fusion classification recognition. In future work, different noise interference characteristics that may exist in the complex environment of multimodal data will be fully considered to find feature extraction strategies that are more applicable to multimodal data and improve the stability of the system to obtain better classification results.

References

1. Jun, H., Caiqing, Z., Xiaozhen, L., Dehai, Z.: Survey of research on multimodal fusion technology for deep learning. Comput. Eng. **46**(5), 1–11 (2020)
2. Wang, J., Mou, L., Ma, L., Huang, T., Gao, W.: AMSA: adaptive multimodal learning for sentiment analysis. ACM Trans. Multimedia Comput. Commun. Appl. **19** (2023). https://doi. org/10.1145/3572915
3. Khan, A.: Improved multi-lingual sentiment analysis and recognition using deep learning. J. Inf. Sci. 01655515221137270 (2023)
4. Kolluri, J., Das, R.: Intelligent multimodal pedestrian detection using hybrid metaheuristic optimization with deep learning model. Image Vis. Comput. 104628 (2023)
5. Wei, X., Yao, S., Zhao, C., Hu, D., Luo, H., Lu, Y.: Lightweight multimodal feature graph convolutional network for dangerous driving behavior detection. J. Real-Time Image Proc. **20**, 15 (2023)
6. Chen, C.P., Liu, Z.: Broad learning system: an effective and efficient incremental learning system without the need for deep architecture. IEEE Trans. Neural Networks Learn. Syst. **29**, 10–24 (2017)
7. Chen, C.P., Liu, Z., Feng, S.: Universal approximation capability of broad learning system and its structural variations. IEEE Trans. Neural Networks Learn. Syst. **30**, 1191–1204 (2018)
8. Chen, C.P., Liu, Z.: Broad learning system: A new learning paradigm and system without going deep. In: Presented at the 2017 32nd youth academic annual conference of Chinese association of automation (YAC) (2017)
9. Huang, P., Chen, B.: Bidirectional broad learning system. In: Presented at the 2020 IEEE 7th international conference on industrial engineering and applications (ICIEA) (2020)
10. Feng, S., Chen, C.P.: Fuzzy broad learning system: a novel neuro-fuzzy model for regression and classification. IEEE Trans. Cybernet. **50**, 414–424 (2018)
11. Guoqiang, L., Lizhuang, X.: Application of local receptive field based broad learning system. Comput. Eng. Appl. **56**(9), 162–167 (2020)
12. Baltrušaitis, T., Ahuja, C., Morency, L.-P.: Multimodal machine learning: a survey and taxonomy. IEEE Trans. Pattern Anal. Mach. Intell. **41**, 423–443 (2018)
13. Pan, B., Hirota, K., Jia, Z., Zhao, L., Jin, X., Dai, Y.: Multimodal emotion recognition based on feature selection and extreme learning machine in video clips. J. Ambient. Intell. Humaniz. Comput. **14**, 1903–1917 (2023)
14. Jia, C., Liu, H., Xu, X., Sun, F.: Multi-modal information fusion based on broad learning method. CAAI Trans. Intell. Syst. **14**, 154–161 (2019)
15. Yosinski, J., Clune, J., Bengio, Y., Lipson, H.: How transferable are features in deep neural networks? Advances in neural information processing systems, p. 27 (2014)
16. Oquab, M., Bottou, L., Laptev, I., Sivic, J.: Learning and transferring mid-level image representations using convolutional neural networks. In: Presented at the Proceedings of the IEEE conference on computer vision and pattern recognition (2014)

17. Hotelling, H.: Relations between two sets of variates. In: Kotz, S., Johnson, N.L. (eds.) Breakthroughs in Statistics: Methodology and Distribution, pp. 162–190. Springer, New York (1992). https://doi.org/10.1007/978-1-4612-4380-9_14

18. Haghighat, M., Abdel-Mottaleb, M., Alhalabi, W.: Fully automatic face normalization and single sample face recognition in unconstrained environments. Expert Syst. Appl. **47**, 23–34 (2016)

19. Block, H.-D.: The perceptron: a model for brain functioning. I. Reviews of Modern Physics **34**, 123 (1962)

20. Schmidt, W.F., Kraaijveld, M.A., Duin, R.P.: Feed forward neural networks with random weights. In: Presented at the international conference on pattern recognition (1992)

21. Rumelhart, D.E., Hinton, G.E., Williams, R.J.: Learning representations by back-propagating errors. Nature **323**, 533–536 (1986)

22. He, K., Zhang, X., Ren, S., Sun, J.: Deep residual learning for image recognition. In: Presented at the proceedings of the IEEE conference on computer vision and pattern recognition (2016)

23. Lee, J.H., et al.: Spotting malignancies from gastric endoscopic images using deep learning. Surg. Endosc. **33**, 3790–3797 (2019)

24. Gómez-Ríos, A., Tabik, S., Luengo, J., Shihavuddin, A., Krawczyk, B., Herrera, F.: Towards highly accurate coral texture images classification using deep convolutional neural networks and data augmentation. Expert Syst. Appl. **118**, 315–328 (2019)

25. Lai, K., Bo, L., Ren, X., Fox, D.: A large-scale hierarchical multi-view RGB-D object dataset. In: Presented at the 2011 IEEE international conference on robotics and automation (2011)

26. Ren, X., Bo, L., Fox, D.: RGB-(D) scene labeling: features and algorithms. In: Presented at the 2012 IEEE conference on computer vision and pattern recognition (2012)

Multi-brain Collaborative Target Detection Based on RAP

Changjian Li, Hao Li, Gai Lu, Yang Yu$^{(\boxtimes)}$, Ling-Li Zeng, and Dewen Hu

College of Intelligence Science and Technology, National University of Defense Technology, Changsha 410073, China

3250661819@qq.com

Abstract. Brain-computer interfaces establish direct connections between the human brain and external devices, enabling information exchange. In the auditory pathway, a BCI system based on Rapid Auditory Presentation (RAP) can detect Event-Related Potentials (ERP) in electroencephalogram (EEG) signals and use machine learning or deep learning methods to achieve auditory target detection in Oddball sequences. However, due to the low amplitude of auditory evoked potential and the low signal-to-noise ratio of signals, the accuracy of target recognition is often low and this makes it difficult to meet application demands. Therefore, this paper proposes a multi-brain collaborative target detection method based on RAP. Firstly, this article designs two brain-computer interface experimental paradigms based on rapid auditory presentation for EEG signal acquisition. Secondly, a feature extraction method combining downsampling and mean filtering is used to extract time-domain features from segmented data. Then, three different classifiers are used to train and predict the experimental data, and multi-brain information fusion is performed for the predicted results as the final result. Finally, the real-time performance and target detection effect of the proposed classification discriminative model are verified from the target stimulus recall rate and information transmission rate. The experimental results show that the recognition accuracy and information transmission rate of the multi-brain information fusion strategy adopted in this paper are improved by 23.42% and 7.10 Bit/min, respectively. This indicates that the proposed approach is effective in improving the real-time performance and target detection accuracy of the RAP-BCI system.

Keywords: Brain Computer Interface · Multi-Brain Collaboration · Rapid Auditory Presentation · Event-Related Potentials

1 Introduction

In recent years, the field of computer auditory has witnessed remarkable progress, particularly in the domains of acoustic target detection, audio event detection [1, 2]. With the development of deep learning, audio target recognition through the construction of deep neural network has become the mainstream method in this field, which has the characteristics of high accuracy and strong migration ability compared with traditional audio detection [3]. However, the construction of deep learning models often requires the

F. Sun et al. (Eds.): ICCSIP 2023, CCIS 1918, pp. 20–32, 2024.
https://doi.org/10.1007/978-981-99-8018-5_2

support of a large number of high-quality data, and limited by the workload of manual annotation and the training time of large models, it is often difficult to obtain ideal results in some application scenarios. Compared with computer hearing, the human brain has the ability to understand higher levels of audio and can easily recognize target audios through short bursts of audio even in noisy environments. In addition, humans only need simple examples to complete object detection tasks, and this ability enables humans to deal with complex situations and sensitive information more effectively.

As a new way of human-computer interaction, brain-computer interface (BCI) can establish a new channel for users to exchange information with external devices and send and receive control instructions [4]. In the field of auditory, brain-computer interface based on rapid auditory presentation (RAP) is a popular method for visual object detection [5–8]. In 2004, Hill et al. improved the BCI based on P300 and explored the application of Oddball paradigm to auditory stimuli. The experiment showed that the information transmission rate of auditory paradigm was lower than that of visual information, and the motivation of subjects had a greater impact on the P300 amplitude [7]. Brain-computer interface paradigm based on rapid auditory presentation forms an audio Oddball stimulus sequence by applying the same or different audios to the same position in space, generating auditory evoked potentials (AEP) in the brain, and finally identifying targets from real-time EEG signals collected through machine learning or deep learning methods.

In the time domain analysis, pattern recognition based on EEG and event-related potential is the focus of auditory object recognition. EEG signals are very weak, often only tens of microvolts, and interference from background noise and various artifacts may even drown the ERP components in EEG signals. The collected EEG signals, therefore, have relatively low signal-to-noise ratios, and the classification of EEG signals induced by a single trial is difficult, with low recognition accuracy and poor stability. Multi-brain collaborative participation can effectively integrate the task-related features of group users and improve the decision performance of brain-computer interface systems. The study of multi-person cooperative auditory target detection methods is expected to further improve the efficiency of auditory target detection. In 2021, Zhang et al. proposed the experimental paradigm of two-brain collaboration RSVP. The fusion algorithm is shown in Fig. 1–7. The algorithm integrates data and features at two levels, and classified based on LSTM and SVM, with good classification accuracy [9].

This paper focuses on auditory target recognition using the multi-brain collaborative target detection method based on RAP, utilizing brain-computer interface and machine learning theory. Starting from the two research dimensions of target detection algorithm based on EEG and multi-brain cooperative detection method, it conducts a relatively systematic study on auditory target recognition. The multi-person auditory RAP paradigm stimulates and presents, stimulating ERP signals in the brain, collecting EEG data synchronously. After preprocessing and feature extraction, various classifiers are used for pattern recognition, and the experimental classification accuracy of various classification methods is compared. Through the research of multi-brain collaborative target detection based on the auditory RAP experimental paradigm, it supplements the auditory brain-computer interface direction experimental paradigm, enriches the use of auditory evoked potential for target discrimination research, and proposes an innovative multi-brain collaborative audio target detection method. Through the research of multi-brain collaborative object detection methods, this paper provides a new idea for realizing real-time and efficient audio target detection methods, which has important theoretical and application value.

2 Materials

2.1 Subjects

A total of 15 subjects were selected for this experiment. All subjects were college students with normal hearing, aged between 20 and 25 years old, and without any psychological disorders. Prior to the experiment, all participants were informed of the experiment's content and agreed to participate. The tasks to be completed during the experiment were also clearly stated to the participants. The subjects were divided into five groups, with three people in each group, to participate in the multi-brain collaborative experiment.

2.2 Experimental System

The RAP brain-computer interface system described in the paper utilizes the ActiCHampPlus EEG analyzer from BrainProducts of Germany as its EEG signal amplifier. This system is capable of collecting high-quality EEG signals from 32 channels simultaneously, allowing for the recording of electrical activity from multiple brain regions.

To facilitate the connection between the human brain and the EEG amplifier, wet electrodes were used along with a conductive gel during the experiment. This approach was chosen to reduce circuit impedance and improve the signal-to-noise ratio of the EEG signals recorded by the system. BP's EasyCap was used for electrode fixation.

During the experiment, a data acquisition software called Pycorder was used to record and process the EEG signals in real-time, allowing for the system to provide real-time feedback to the user.

The main parameters during data acquisition are summarized in the Table 1.

Table 1. The main parameters of the amplifier during the data collection process

Name	Parameter value
Notch filter frequency	50 Hz
Bandpass filter frequency	0.5–10 Hz
Sampling frequency	200 Hz
Reference electrode position	Posterior mastoid process of left ear
Number of lead electrodes	3 × 8 active electrodes
Data segmentation window	0–1200 ms

2.3 Experimental Paradigm

Stimuli

The experiment involves two different paradigms: Semantic-based RAP paradigm and Tone-based RAP paradigm. In the Semantic-based RAP paradigm, the audio stimuli are the numbers 1 to 8, spoken by a standard male voice. The audio stimulus sequence is generated in random order to avoid any potential order effects. In the Tone-based RAP paradigm, the target stimulus is changed to a female voice, but the other aspects of the paradigm remain the same as in the Semantic-based RAP paradigm. The auditory stimuli have been standardized to 200 ms in duration and 60 decibels in volume to ensure consistency across participants.

Experiment Procedure

In order to conduct the experiment, three participants are required to participate in each session. These participants are seated with their backs facing each other and each wears a set of earphones for audio delivery. Throughout the experiment, it is important that the participants remain relaxed and maintain their focus and attention. Participants should also avoid any unnecessary facial muscle movements and strive to minimize the number of blinks in order to reduce any potential EMG interference. These measures are necessary to ensure the accuracy and consistency of the data collected during the experiment.

The experimental flow of each trial is shown in the Fig. 1.

Once the experiment begins, the subject will hear the target stimulus number on which the current trial will focus. After a 2-s interval, a randomly generated audio sequence will be played. The stimulus duration for each audio is 200 ms, and the ISI duration is 100 ms. After the audio stimulus plays, the screen will prompt the system to predict the target. The program will automatically evaluate whether the target is the same as the correct target and provides the experimental accuracy after the end of the current experiment run.

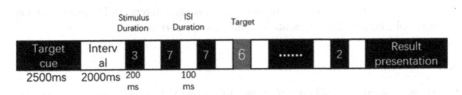

Fig. 1. The experimental process for each trial of experiments

Data Collection

The ActiCHamp Plus EEG analyzer is utilized to simultaneously capture and amplify EEG signals from three subjects. Fz, Cz, Pz, Oz, F3, F4, C3, and C4 are chosen as the active electrodes, the left auricle posterior mastoid process is selected as the reference electrode, and the forehead AFz electrode is used as the common ground electrode. The data acquisition software, Pycorder, is utilized to visualize and process EEG signals in real-time. A total of 27 electrodes (eight active electrodes and one reference electrode) are employed (Fig. 2).

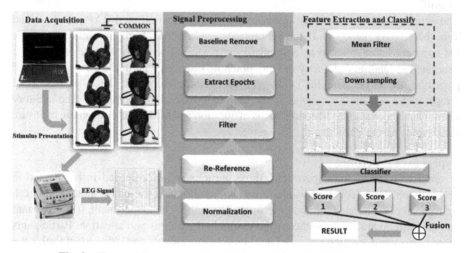

Fig. 2. The overall structure of multi brain collaborative RAP experiments

3 Methods

3.1 Data Preprocessing

Initially, the collected EEG data was standardized. Since the signals in the experiment were all referenced to the electrical pole of subject one, re-referencing the EEG signal was essential. Channel 9, channel 18, and channel 27 were chosen as the reference electrodes for the three subjects respectively. After subtracting the reference electrode signals from their EEG signals, the resulting data was re-referenced. The processed data was then subjected to data segmentation and baseline correction.

3.2 Feature Extraction

Firstly, mean filtering is applied to the signal to remove high-frequency noise by smoothing the signal. In time domain feature extraction, data downsampling is often used to extract features. By downsampling the data 10 times, the dimension of the feature is reduced, and the computational complexity is decreased. The resulting feature consists of 8 channels and 20 sample points. The channel dimension is then removed, and the two-dimensional feature is expanded by channel, resulting in 160 features for subsequent classifier construction.

3.3 Classification Method

The mean filtering and down-sampling are combined, and the down-sampled data is expanded to one dimension to obtain the time-domain characteristics of EEG signals. Then, a classifier is constructed to classify target stimulus and non-target stimulus. A variety of linear models are used for model training, and the trained model parameters are obtained, based on which new test data can be predicted. At the same time, new test data can be obtained as the possibility of target stimulus, which can be used as the target stimulus prediction basis of subjects' attention.

In this paper, we construct three linear classification models for auditory target prediction, which are Multiple Linear Regression (MLR), Logistic Regression (LR) and Stepwise Linear Discriminant Analysis (SWLDA).

3.4 Multi-brain Information Fusion Strategy

Based on the above regression classifier, three n-dimensional model parameters $[W^1, W^2, W^3]$ can be obtained, defined as:

$$W^i = (w_0^i, w_1^i, w_2^i, \cdots\cdots, w_n^i), \ for \ i \in \{1, 2, 3\} \tag{1}$$

A new data samples $[X^1, X^2, X^3]$, defined as:

$$X^i = (x_0^i, x_1^i, x_2^i, \cdots\cdots, x_n^i), \ for \ i \in \{1, 2, 3\} \tag{2}$$

then:

$$R^1 = w_0^1 + w_1^1 x_1^1 + \cdots + w_n^1 x_n^1 \tag{3}$$

$$R^2 = w_0^2 + w_1^2 x_1^2 + \cdots + w_n^2 x_n^2 \tag{4}$$

$$R^3 = w_0^3 + w_1^3 x_1^3 + \cdots + w_n^3 x_n^3 \tag{5}$$

The label predicted value of the model for the new sample can be approximately regarded as the probability estimate of the target sample. Therefore, the probability estimate size of the target sample after the fusion of the electrical data of the three regression models can be obtained by superimposing the probability of the three regression models.

$$R = R^1 + R^2 + R^3 \tag{6}$$

In the above process, the probability estimate obtained only needs to obtain the relative size without paying too much attention to its actual value. Since target stimulus is inevitable in the eight data samples of an experiment, the maximum probability estimate obtained from the eight data samples after the fusion of multi-brain information can be regarded as the target sample data, while the other seven data samples are judged as non-targets.

4 Results

4.1 Performance Evaluation Indicators

In the field of machine learning, accuracy is commonly used to evaluate a model's classification performance. However, in situations where there is an imbalance of positive and negative samples in the RAP paradigm, accuracy alone may not be sufficient to accurately reflect the classification model's performance. Therefore, additional evaluation indices should be used to achieve a better understanding of the model's true classification performance.

In order to better show the classification performance of the classifier constructed in the experiment, we introduce the recall rate as the accuracy rate. For a binary classification problem, the samples can be divided into four types, namely true positive (TP), false negative (FN), false positive (FP), and true negative (TN).

Recall rates are defined as:

$$recall = \frac{TP}{TP+FN} \tag{7}$$

In addition, information transmission rate is also a commonly used evaluation criterion to evaluate the performance of brain-computer interface systems. Defined as:

$$ITR = 60 \times \frac{B}{T} \tag{8}$$

$$B = \log_2 N + P\log_2 P + (1 - P)\log_2\left(\frac{1-P}{N-1}\right) \tag{9}$$

where T is the event selected by a single target stimulus. B is the bit rate transmitted during classification. N is the number of optional targets, for this experiment, the value of N is 8.

4.2 Signal Visualization

After feature extraction, the features after downsampling and mean filtering can be visualized. The feature visualization shows that after feature extraction, the signal classification processing time can be reduced while the information loss of EEG signals can be minimized.

Figure 3 shows the EEG time-domain maps of group 5 under the two experimental paradigms of target stimulus and non-target stimulus.

4.3 Experimental Results

In the experimentation process, the offline data from a run of experiments is first collected. The model is then trained using this data to obtain the classifier parameters for the model. These parameters can be used to predict the target. The experimental program automatically records the accuracy of the classifier and calculates the information transmission rate for the current run of experimentation after the experiment has finished.

Table 2, 3, 4 and 5 shows the differences in the accuracy rate of experiment and the size of information transmission rate under two experimental paradigms.

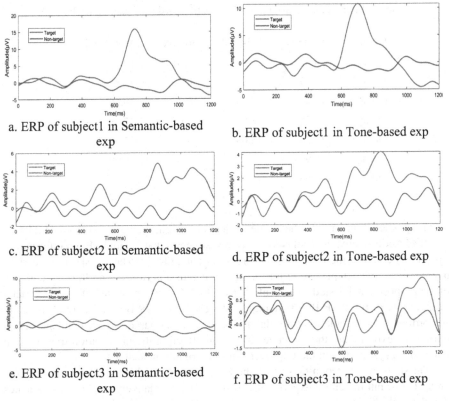

a. ERP of subject1 in Semantic-based exp

b. ERP of subject1 in Tone-based exp

c. ERP of subject2 in Semantic-based exp

d. ERP of subject2 in Tone-based exp

e. ERP of subject3 in Semantic-based exp

f. ERP of subject3 in Tone-based exp

Fig. 3. The EEG time-domain maps of group 5 under the two experimental paradigms of target stimulus and non-target stimulus.

Table 2. Accuracy of Semantic-based RAP paradigm (%)

Group	Subject1	Subject2	Subject3	Multi-Brain
Group1	50.0	46.7	40.0	73.3
Group2	43.3	76.7	26.7	76.7
Group3	83.3	63.3	73.3	93.3
Group4	53.3	46.7	86.7	90.0
Group5	83.3	80.0	65.3	90.0
Average	61.24			84.66
Std	18.81			9.00

The table above presents the results of experiments conducted using the Semantic-based RAP paradigm. These results indicate that the multi brain collaborative target detection method built upon the RAP paradigm has significantly improved the average

Table 3. Information Transfer rate of Semantic-based RAP paradigm (Bit/min)

Group	Subject1	Subject2	Subject3	Multi-Brain
Group1	4.52	3.84	2.61	10.73
Group2	3.19	11.86	0.79	11.87
Group3	14.24	7.75	10.73	18.66
Group4	5.25	3.84	15.65	17.09
Group5	14.28	13.03	8.31	17.09
Average	7.99			15.09
Std	4.95			3.54

accuracy when compared to the single subject approach, increasing it from 61.24% to 84.66%. Additionally, the analysis of variance suggests that the multi brain information fusion can enhance the robustness of the brain computer interface system to a certain degree. From the perspective of information transmission rate, the multi brain collaboration proposed in this study has resulted in an 88.86% increase in the information transmission rate of the RAP-BCI system, elevating it from 7.99 Bit/min to 15.09 Bit/min. According to the calculation formula of ITR, since other parameters remain unchanged during the experiment, the fundamental reason affecting the information transmission rate of BCI system lies in the improvement of recognition accuracy.

The single brain recognition rate of the second group of subjects in the Table 2 is poor, only 26.7%, but the entire experimental results remain relatively stable. This indicates that the multi brain information collaborative auditory target detection method adopted in this article can improve the overall stability and reliability of the BCI system to a certain extent, which is of great significance for the practicality of the brain computer interface system.

Table 4. Accuracy of Tone-based RAP paradigm (%)

Group	Subject1	Subject2	Subject3	Multi-Brain
Group1	60	36.7	46.7	80.0
Group2	42.2	33.3	24.4	57.8
Group3	95.6	66.7	51.1	93.3
Group4	73.3	57.8	53.3	84.4
Group5	76.7	26.7	40.0	80.0
Average	52.30			79.10
Std	19.88			13.09

Table 5. Information Transfer rate of Tone-based RAP paradigm (Bit/min)

Group	Subject1	Subject2	Subject3	Multi-Brain
Group1	6.88	2.09	3.85	13.04
Group2	3.00	1.59	0.58	6.33
Group3	19.87	8.71	4.77	18.66
Group4	10.73	6.32	5.26	14.71
Group5	11.87	0.80	2.62	13.04
Average	5.93			13.15
Std	5.18			4.45

According to the table above, the experimental results for the Tone-based RAP paradigm indicate a significant increase in average accuracy from 52.30% to 79.10%, as well as an increase in information transmission rate from 5.93 Bit/min to 13.15 Bit/min.

In experiment group 3, through the classifier model training, the prediction accuracy of single subject could reach 95.6%, while the overall target accuracy decreased by 2.3% through the fusion of multi-brain information. The reason for this phenomenon may be that the recognition accuracy of the other two subjects was relatively low, leading to the lower performance of the classifier in experiment 1.

In general, the Tone-based RAP paradigm had lower accuracy compared to the semantic-based RAP paradigm. When analyzed by group, the first and third groups had higher accuracy than in Experiment 1, while the other three groups had lower accuracy than in Experiment 1. It's worth noting that the experimental data variance in Experiment 2 was greater. These findings suggest that the tone-based RAP paradigm had varying effects on participants, with some being more sensitive to tone, while others being more sensitive to speech.

4.4 Factors Affecting Model Performance

To delve deeper into the factors affecting the multi-brain combined RAP auditory target detection system, this study investigates various subsampling multiples and classifier types to identify the effects on the model's performance in terms of feature extraction and classifier construction.

Downsampling Interval

In this paper, we study the effect of different subsampling intervals on the classification performance of EEG signals in time domain feature extraction. As shown in Table 6 below, the classification and discrimination accuracy of the target detection method based on multi-brain collaboration at different downsampling intervals is shown.

Under 2x, 5x and 10x sampling, multi-brain fusion strategy was used to evaluate the performance of experimental normal form 1, and the accuracy of the results were 82%, 79.98% and 84.66%, respectively. One possible reason is that the reduction of the feature dimension reduces the overfitting risk and improves the generalization ability of the model to a certain extent.

Table 6. Effect of subsampling interval on detection results of multi-brain cooperative target

Group	2 x downsampling		5 x downsampling		10 x downsampling	
	Exp1	EXP2	EXP1	EXP2	EXP1	EXP2
Group1	70.0	80.0	73.3	76.7	73.3	80.0
Group2	76.7	60.0	63.3	60.0	76.7	57.8
Group3	90.0	80.0	90.0	93.3	93.3	93.3
Group4	83.3	73.3	90.0	66.7	90.0	84.4
Group5	90.0	90.0	83.3	93.3	90.0	80.0
Average	82.00	76.66	79.98	78.00	84.66	79.10

Classifier Type The classification of EEG signals is also affected by the classifier type. This paper compares the effects of different classifiers on the performance of RAP-BCI system with multi-brain collaboration. Linear regression model, Logistic regression model and stepwise linear regression model were used respectively.

The results are shown in the Table 7 below.

Table 7. Effect of classifier type on multi-brain cooperative target detection results

Group	MLR		LR		SWLDA	
	Exp1	EXP2	EXP1	EXP2	EXP1	EXP2
Group1	83.3	56.7	83.3	56.7	73.3	80.0
Group2	76.7	66.7	83.3	66.7	76.7	57.8
Group3	90.0	93.3	90.0	93.3	93.3	93.3
Group4	86.7	90.0	86.7	76.7	90.0	84.4
Group5	83.3	93.3	83.3	93.3	90.0	80.0
Average	84	80	85.32	77.34	84.66	79.10

5   Discussion

In this paper, aiming at the shortcomings of RAP-BCI data of single subject with low signal-to-noise ratio and low target recognition accuracy, multi-brain data is used for collaborative target detection, with the purpose of improving the classification accuracy of RAP experimental paradigm of single trial, and improving the real-time, accuracy and reliability of brain-computer interface system.

The experimental results show that the multi-brain information fusion strategy is beneficial to improve the target detection accuracy and information transmission rate (ITR) of RAP-BCI system, which confirms the feasibility of the proposed multi-brain collaborative target detection method based on RAP paradigm has certain feasibility and research significance.

At the same time, there are some limitations.

First, the main method of feature extraction in this paper is the combination of down-sampling and mean filtering. The feature extraction method is relatively simple, which may not be able to complete the time-domain feature extraction well. Therefore, we can further try the commonly used feature extraction methods, such as wavelet transform. In addition, only time domain features were extracted, and frequency characteristics were not extracted and analyzed. Features could be extracted from the perspective of frequency domain, and features in time domain and frequency domain could be combined as feature vectors to better distinguish target and non-target signals.

Secondly, the three classifiers used in this paper are linear classifiers, which have poor data fitting ability. However, the use of a better classifier model, such as SVM, is expected to enhance the model classification performance of a single subject, which is a possible way to improve the performance of the RAP-BCI system.

6 Conclusion

In this study, we proposed a multi-brain collaborative BCI based RAP framework for improving the accuracy of single trial RAP by combining EEG information from multiple people. Three of the multiple linear regression models were used to evaluate the subjects' EEG data to obtain separate scores, which were combined to obtain the final results. Experiments with 15 subjects validated the proposed approach's practicability and effectiveness. The experiment results demonstrated that the proposed multi-brain collaborative RAP experiment achieved a 23.42% increase in accuracy and an average increase of 7.10 Bit/min in information transfer rate compared to single-subject BCIs. The preliminary online results indicated that the proposed multibrain collaborative BCI-based RAP framework is feasible and has a significant impact on EEG-based RAP towards practical applications.

Acknowledgement. This work was supported by the National Natural Science Foundation of China (62006239, 61722313, 62036013).

References

1. Markovinović, I., Vrankić, M., Vlahinić, S., et al.: Design considerations for the auditory brain computer interface speller. Biomed. Signal Process. Control **75**, 103546 (2022)
2. Buran, B.N., McMillan, G.P., Keshishzadeh, S., et al.: Predicting synapse counts in living humans by combining computational models with auditory physiology. J. Acoust. Soc. Am. **151**(1), 561–576 (2022)
3. Kamble, A., Ghare, P.H., Kumar, V.: Deep-learning-based BCI for automatic imagined speech recognition using SPWVD. IEEE Trans. Instrum. Meas. **72**, 1–10 (2023)
4. Prashant, P., Joshi, A., Gandhi, V.: Brain computer interface: a review. In: 2015 5th Nirma University International Conference on Engineering (NUiCONE), pp. 1–6 (2015)

5. Guo, J., Gao, S., Hong, B.: An auditory brain-computer interface using active mental response. IEEE Trans. Neural Syst. Rehabil. Eng. **18**(3), 230–235 (2010)
6. Halder, S., Rea, M., Andreoni, R., et al.: An auditory oddball brain–computer interface for binary choices. Clin. Neurophysiol. **121**(4), 516–523 (2010)
7. Hill, N.J., Lal, T.N., Bierig, K., et al.: An auditory paradigm for brain–computer interfaces. In: Advances in Neural Information Processing Systems 17 [Neural Information Processing Systems, NIPS 2004, December 13–18, 2004, Vancouver, British Columbia, Canada] (2004)
8. Jiang, L., Cai, B., Xiao, S., et al.: Semantic-based sound retrieval by ERP in rapid serial auditory presentation paradigm. In: 2013 35th Annual International Conference of the IEEE Engineering in Medicine and Biology Society (EMBC), pp. 2788–2791 (2013)
9. Zhang, H., Zhu, L., Xu, S., et al.: Two brains, one target: design of a multi-level information fusion model based on dual-subject RSVP. J. Neurosci. Methods 363 (2021). N.PAG-N.PAG

Lidar-Inertial SLAM Method for Accurate and Robust Mapping

Yuhang Wang and Liwei Zhang$^{(\boxtimes)}$

School of Mechanical Engineering and Automation, Fuzhou University, Fuzhou 350116, China
lw.zhang@fzu.edu.cn

Abstract. In recent studies on LiDAR SLAM, the achievement of robust optimized LiDAR odometry is the primary objective. For the mapping part, some studies focus on improving the processing of point cloud, while others aim to the optimization of the result deviation caused by errors. Meanwhile, in the fields of robotics and autonomous driving, multi-sensor fusion solutions based on IMUs are becoming the norm. This paper contributes to the optimization of mapping by leveraging a lightweight LiDAR-inertial state estimator. The proposed method combines information from a 6-axis IMU and a 3D LiDAR to form a tightly-coupled scheme that incorporates iterative error state Kalman filter (IESKF). Due to the continuous error accumulation, trajectory deviations can be significant. To mitigate this, an adaptive distance threshold loop closure detection mechanism is employed. Furthermore, since the algorithm primarily addresses outdoor scenes, ground features collected by sensors account for a significant portion of the computation. Improvements in the ground segmentation method lead to less disturbance during mapping on uneven terrain, enabling the method to effectively ad-dress a wider range of real-world environments. As a result, the proposed method demonstrates excellent stability and accuracy, as verified in experiments conducted on urban dataset and campus environment.

Keywords: LiDAR SLAM · Ground Segmentation · Loop Closure

1 Introduction

Mapping and state estimation pose significant challenges in the exploration of mobile robots. Thanks to the iterative optimization of multi-sensor fusion technology, the application of Simultaneous Localization and Mapping (SLAM) in outdoor environments [1–5] has been expanded in recent years. Since the development of the LOAM [2] algorithm, significant advancements have been made in the loosely-coupled LiDAR-inertial odometry system, which has demonstrated superior performance compared to the earlier direct-matching method [6]. The current approach involves the use of feature points, edge lines, and plane blocks for matching, complemented by a ground feature segmentation preprocessing step [7] which enhances both the accuracy and efficiency of the algorithm. Pure LiDAR odometry alone does not maintain robust positioning. However, when integrated with inertial measurement units (IMUs), their resistance to

© The Author(s), under exclusive license to Springer Nature Singapore Pte Ltd. 2024
F. Sun et al. (Eds.): ICCSIP 2023, CCIS 1918, pp. 33–44, 2024.
https://doi.org/10.1007/978-981-99-8018-5_3

environmental disturbances makes them favorable. The fusion solution performs better when used outdoors. In contrast to the loose-coupling method, the LiDAR-IMU tight-coupling method [8, 9] estimates parameters jointly, ensuring consistent precision. By unifying measurement data and utilizing optimization models with prediction and observation equations to practice pose information updating, the tight-coupling method yields relatively better results (Fig. 1).

Fig. 1. Example of the proposed method given in a campus environment.

In the context of the existence of many excellent tightly-coupled solutions, such as the lightweight LiDAR-inertia state estimator proposed by LINS [1], this method proposes a novel approach that tightly couples six degrees of freedom of self-motion with odometry through iterative Kalman filtering. We introduce an optimized LiDAR-inertial odometry fusion system with better performance in mapping results. The proposed system leverages the principle of achieving optimization and efficiency in mapping by fusing LiDAR and IMU data through iterative error-state Kalman filtering, and improving both ground point processing and loop closure detection.

The SOTA ground segmentation method, Patchwork [10], significantly improves the processing effect of ground points. In this paper, we adopt a similar grid structure and improve the odometry. However, the original framework cannot ad-dress large-scale drift. Thus, we use a modular design for loop detection to provide global position recognition and correct the time-associated data group with noise maps. The Scan Context global descriptor [11] accurately matches historical poses, which significantly reduces map drift caused by cumulative errors. At the same time, in large-scale mapping environment, the global descriptor may also produce mismatches. To avoid this problem, we propose a dynamic threshold decision to restrict the closed loop. Our experiments demonstrate that the proposed method is robust in complex urban environments.

The main contributions of this paper are as follows:

1) We introduce a ground segmentation method with more accurate and efficient performance in the point cloud processing part.
2) The dynamic threshold-based Scan Context is utilized for loop detection, while the adaptive distance threshold-based approach is employed to determine loop closure, thereby decreasing error recognition and improving the accuracy of positioning.

3) The experiments conducted in various scenarios indicate that our proposed work has significantly improved the accuracy of the filter SLAM framework in comparison to the original framework.

2 Related Works

2.1 Loosely-Coupled LiDAR-IMU Odometry

In loosely-coupled SLAM methods, data from sensors are applied to estimate motion separately, e.g. ([12, 13]). IMU is typically used as an aiding solution to the pose that functions as a system prior, rather than as a final optimization step. Although the calculations are fast, there are limitations in terms of accuracy.

2.2 Tightly-Coupled LiDAR-IMU Odometry

The tightly-coupled approach considers IMU data as a state prediction and employs updated measurements to rectify the predicted state. LIO-mapping [8] initially proposed a tightly-coupled LiDAR-IMU fusion strategy that utilized the error State Kalman Filter (ESKF) to facilitate the fusion process. This method enhances the performance of the system by reducing drift in degraded environments. In [14], point cloud distortion compensation and point cloud matching are integrated into a single optimization task. Moreover, IMU pre-integration was used in the back-end to improve pose optimization. Alternative tightly-coupled schemes also exist that utilize factor graph optimization, such as proposed in [15], which have shown remarkable performance.

2.3 Ground Point Constraints

Identifying ground points is crucial in determining the traffic area or segmenting the point cloud. There are numerous methods available for this purpose [16–19]. If the ground point cloud is accurately segmented from the cloud to be processed, the SLAM method with feature constraints can be significantly improved. However, in [2], only plane constraints are established, and the precision is inadequate in several other methods. The presence of redundant point clouds and constraints can adversely affect the mapping outcomes while also increasing the computational demands. To optimize the front-end efficiency of the algorithm for ground point extraction, Patchwork [11] employs an innovative piecewise grid structure for point cloud segmentation. Additionally, in the ground optimization of [20], RANSAC [21] is applied for plane fitting, which yields favorable map optimization.

2.4 Loop Closure Detection

Loop closure detection is a significant research topic that plays a crucial role in deploying a robust SLAM system. This process entails leveraging global associated map data to draw similarities between the current and historical scenes, which are later matched to achieve map convergence. The research on LiDAR SLAM has been attempting to create an effective location descriptor for loop closure matching. GLAROT [22] encodes the relative geometric positions of key-point pairs into histograms, while Scan Context [12] projects LiDAR scans into global descriptors. Additionally, BoW (Bag of Words) [23], and a scene recognition algorithm based on the bag of words model are also under investigation. By integrating loop closure detection, a substantial reduction in cumulative errors in large-scale scenarios is achievable.

3   The Framework

3.1   Overview of Proposed Framework

The paper explicates the implementation of a SLAM system for a mobile platform that employs a 3D Lidar and inertial measurement units. The system's accuracy and efficacy are optimized by incorporating a lightweight odometer. The system is composed of three principal modules, including LiDAR-inertia odometry, feature extraction, and loop closure detection (Fig. 2).

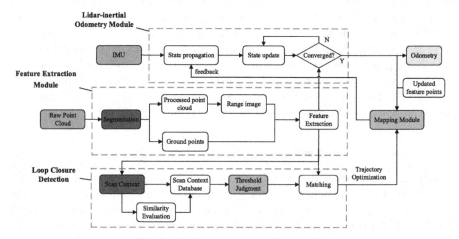

Fig. 2. Pipeline of proposed framework

The proposed method utilizes the front-end odometry to perform low-precision motion estimation at a high frequency, while the LIO module executes the filtering process to acquire an approximate estimation of the mobile platform's pose. The back-end employs an optimization method mentioned in [3] to solve the pose. The filtering method calculates a more accurate posterior value after combining the predicted value and the observed value, in which the predicted value is obtained by IMU recursion.

In this paper, the iterative error state Kalman filter is employed to iteratively converge the error quantity on the ESKF. As a variant of Kalman filter, the error state equation of ESKF is approximately linear. Since the error state is always close to 0, the calculation of Jacobian matrix and linearization during state update are more efficient, avoiding the gimbals lock problem. Under the linear Gaussian assumption, the update process involves optimizing the prior state-relative pose transformation $x_{b_{k+1}}^{b_k}$ and the observation matching residual:

$$\min F(\delta x, ^- x_{b_{k+1}}^{b_k}, w_m) \tag{1}$$

The $^- x_{b_{k+1}}^{b_k}$ represents the predicted value, w_m is the measurement noise, and $F(\cdot)$ is the loss function built in LINS[1].

The filtering process entails adjusting the state quantity, consisting of both relative pose and error components, based on comparison with predicted and current values. Once the filter model is updated, the algorithm solves for the posterior error state, based on which it iteratively updates $x_{b_{k+1}}^{b_k}$. The procedure stops the iteration when the posterior of the error state falls within a small proximity to 0.

3.2 Feature Extraction Module and Its Ground Segmentation

The feature extraction method follows the procedures developed in [2] and [3]. The main contribution of this work lies in the ground point segmentation process. The original point cloud acquired by the sensor will be projected into the range image after preprocessing and segmentation. Theoretically, the distance between the sensor and detection plane is retained within the range image, and the line and plane features are extracted from the parts marked as non-ground points in this image. These features are then integrated with the plane features in the ground points, so as to recognize the plane features separately and minimize the impact of line features on the ground plane.

The ground point segmentation may mistakenly classify the upper plane with low obstacles as ground point clouds. To address this issue, we employed Patchwork [10] for partial segmentation of the ground point cloud. The point cloud was divided into concentric zones from the sensor center outwards, which were divided into regions labeled $Z_1 \sim Z_4$. In Fig. 3, it can be observed that as the distance from the sensor increases, the number of point clouds collected at the same radial distance decreases. Hence, we adjusted the radial mesh density in concentric zones based on the radial direction, resulting in wider grids in the segments located farther from the sensor.

According to [10], over 90% of the ground points are distributed within a 20 m radius around the robot. However, the density of ground points may vary when the robot is navigating on a narrow or wide road with low obstacles on both sides. The density distribution range of the ground point will have certain changes. To enhance the effectiveness of the segmented mesh model of the original approach, an adaptive change is proposed for the radial distance of the Z_1 segmented mesh. Specifically, we obtain the segmentation of ground and non-ground points after processing the point cloud from the previous frame and set a threshold T. After subdividing the concentric area, a single grid is denoted as $bin_{r,\theta}$ and positioned in polar coordinates. The distance between the acquisition point and the origin of the sensor coordinate system is expressed as r, while the polar angle in the polar coordinate system is represented by θ.

Once non-ground points in a radial grid layer surpass a certain density threshold, and a non-ground point collection grid exceeds the predetermined threshold in a single layer for the first time, the grid layer located in the current frame becomes the outer boundary

Fig. 3. Concentric grid structure

of Z_1. The density can be calculated using the following formula:

$$\rho_{r,\theta} = 1 - \frac{n_{r,\theta}}{N_{r,\theta}} \qquad (2)$$

where $N_{r,\theta}$ is the number of ground points, $N_{r,\theta}$ is the total number of point clouds in a single bin, and $\rho_{r,\theta}$ represents the density of non-ground points of $bin_{r,\theta}$.

The regional ground plane fitting is carried out within each grid, and points undergo Principal Component Analysis (PCA) [24] to obtain height information via the dimension reduction of the point cloud data. The ground plane is estimated using the points with the lowest height value in each grid. As mentioned in [10], it was defined as a *representability issue* that the units could not be represented accurately due to the small size of the center grid. The solution provided was to increase the size of the innermost grid. However, in the plane fitting stage, there are often many irregular obstacles such as small vehicles and pedestrians in each grid area. Since the point cloud density near the center of the circle is large after expanding the grid size of the Z_1 segment, more computing power will be spent in the iteration process of fitting to deal with outliers, and the influence of this part is greater than that of other segments. Therefore, we decided to perform proportional down-sampling in the entire concentric grid region weakened the entire concentric grid region by increasing radial distance:

$$P_c = \frac{\exp(-l/10)}{2} \qquad (3)$$

where P_c is the ratio of discarded points in down-sampling and l represents the radial distance from the LiDAR to the outer boundary of the concentric region. In practice, it is simplified to gradient down-sampling. The radial distance of each grid is set to be a gradient by segmenting and setting fixed down-sampling ratios:

$$l = l_{pre} + \frac{\Delta L_m}{N_{r,m}} \qquad (4)$$

where l_{pre} represents the radial distance of the outer boundary of the region at the last down-sampling, ΔL_m represents the radial length of the Z_m segment, and $N_{r,m}$ denotes the number of radial meshes of the Z_m segment.

3.3 Loop Closure Detection Module

The previous distance-based loop closure detection strategy is simple, and suffered from mesoscale drift in practice due to the cumulative error increasing over time. This paper proposes an alternative approach using the Scan Context [11] method without initial relative pose for loop detection. The proposed method records information of each block which is divided into a grid in the form of a matrix. When the mobile platform is present in the same scene with different timestamps and different poses, Scan Context descriptor shows great deviation correction performance.

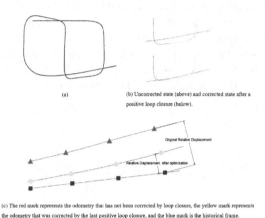

(a)   (b) Uncorrected state (above) and corrected state after a positive loop closure (below).

(c) The red mark represents the odometry that has not been corrected by loop closure, the yellow mark represents the odometry that was corrected by the last positive loop closure, and the blue mark is the historical frame.

Fig. 4. Dynamic threshold determination

The data scale will increase as the running time goes by, causing the frames of data to be judged to continually increase, thus reducing the real-time performance of mapping. It is proposed in [25] that the loop distance threshold can be determined to eliminate distant loops from the current pose. This approach can reduce wrong loop matching to some extent. In the proposed method, loop closure determination of dynamic threshold was performed before establishing loop closure. When the displacement modulus of the relative pose between the current frame and the historical frame exceeded the threshold value, thus indicating that loop closure could not be formed. As the error accumulates over time, the threshold d will also exhibit a linearly increasing form.

$$d = t_k f / 100 + w \tag{5}$$

t_k represents the current frame timestamp, f is the odometer frequency, and w is the threshold setting parameter.

At the same time, the map and trajectory are corrected after each positive loop is generated. The cumulative error is reduced, which can affect the loop decision threshold.

$$w = w_{pre} - d_{pre} \cdot \exp(-t_k f / 100) \tag{6}$$

w_{pre} is the threshold setting parameter at the time of generating the loop back, and d_{pre} is the loop back threshold at the same time. The optimized relative displacement in Fig. 4 will determine the updated threshold. The system can dynamically adjust the loop threshold to avoid the loss of the subsequent loop threshold determination link because of the continuous growth of the threshold.

4 Experiment

4.1 Results of Ground Point Segmentation Optimization

In order to better evaluate the effectiveness of this method, qualitative comparison and quantitative comparison between different algorithms will be conducted. Firstly, the ground segmentation effect of the proposed method will be compared to LINS. LINS employs the same ground segmentation module as LeGO-LOAM and exhibits satisfactory ground segmentation results. However, in case of uneven terrain or small obstacles, the ground estimation is more sensitive to some estimation noises. The proposed method has a higher tolerance for outliers. In practice, it provides better filtering performance of interference objects that are higher than the reference ground.

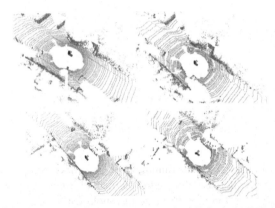

Fig. 5. Point cloud built by proposed method (left) and LINS (right).

In Fig. 5, the green point cloud consists of the ground points, whereas the red point cloud includes non-ground points. The optimized ground segmentation module introduces a significant reduction in false-positive ground point detections, correctly classifying some previously misjudged points that exist in low obstacles on both sides of the road as non-ground points.

While LINS demands an additional computational flow upon including ground segmentation, optimizing the ground segmentation could provide a boost to algorithm efficiency. Meanwhile, in scenes (such as KITTI02) with lots of low obstacles, the optimization of the point cloud grid structure could significantly elevate map processing efficiency.

The results from Table 1 indicate that, in terms of real-time performance, the proposed method outperforms LINS with optimization in efficiency, or it performs equivalently without falling behind after increasing the optimization process.

Table 1. The average processing time of the odometry per scan

method	KITTI02	KITTI05	KITTI08	DCC 01	KAIST 01	Riverside 01
LINS	6.79	5.57	5.81	5.42	3.68	3.95
Proposed	5.85	5.04	5.30	4.75	3.13	3.76

4.2 Analysis of the Trajectory Optimization Results

There are various similar streets in urban road segments, and loop detection has a great effect on the offset correction of repeated road segments, so this paper compares and analyzes the trajectory of the algorithm. The trajectory pose was recorded and the trajectory was evaluated. Firstly, the root mean square error (RMSE) was compared.

Table 2. RMSE of the ATE (meter) on Mulran dataset

Method	Sequence								
	DCC 01	DCC 02	DCC 03	KAIST 01	KAIST 02	KAIST 03	Riverside 01	Riverside 02	Riverside 03
LeGO-LOAM	36.65	29.01	28.15	52.57	43.36	40.92	113.93	129.23	192.26
LINS	54.36	45.86	40.73	74.45	68.29	61.53	182.45	232.42	301.58
SC-LINS	9.87	7.25	6.98	8.16	8.84	8.12	28.42	35.13	42.89
Proposed	6.39	4.92	4.53	5.35	5.48	5.10	21.69	28.65	34.26

We choose to test the algorithm on the Mulran dataset with many loop scenes, and it can be seen from Table 2 that the proposed method significantly improves the accuracy. In the riverside sequence lacking geometric features, the loop detection module can still obtain a large map correction effect.

Figure 6 illustrates that our approach outperforms LINS in addressing trajectory drift problems. This method provides a better fit to the ground truth trajectories provided by the dataset. The feature extraction and matching process extracts and matches relatively fewer features on open road sections, leading to a higher proportion of outliers in the corresponding results.

4.3 Experimental Results in the Campus Environment

In the real machine experiment, a mobile robot platform equipped with 16-line LiDAR and six-axis IMU is utilized to collect the data set of the campus environment. Our algorithm is executed on a computer equipped with an Intel Core i7-11800H processor, 16 GB of memory, and an NVIDIA GeForce GTX 3060 graphics card.

The experimental environment shown in Fig. 7 is a relatively simple campus road, and it can be seen that the algorithm performs well in repeated road sections. Drift and ghosting are improved with the proposed method.

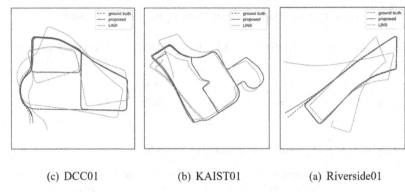

(c) DCC01   (b) KAIST01   (a) Riverside01

Fig. 6. Comparison of trajectories on different scenes

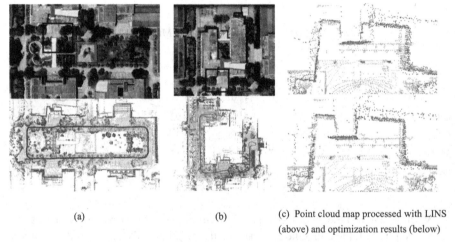

(a)   (b)   (c) Point cloud map processed with LINS
                                                   (above) and optimization results (below)

Fig. 7. The open road mapping results of the proposed method. The red boxes in (a) and (b) are the same starting and ending areas under the two maps, and the mapping results inside the red box are exhibited in (c).

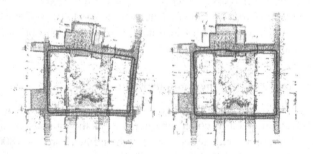

Fig. 8. Map of semi-open corridor built by LINS (left) and proposed method (right).

In the environment with less feature information, the correction of the global map by the algorithm is very obvious. The closed-loop module optimized in Fig. 8 plays a key role in the convergence of the map.

5 Conclusion

In this paper, we propose a more robust and accurate LiDAR-IMU tightly coupled SLAM method. In particular, the main work of this paper, ground optimization and loop closure detection, shows good performance improvement in the public data set and campus environment experiments. In future work, we plan to improve the front-end odometry to obtain a more stable SLAM framework.

References

1. Qin, C., Ye, H., Pranata, C.E., Han, J., Zhang, S., Liu, M.: Lins: a lidar-inertial state estimator for robust and efficient navigation. In: IEEE International Conference on Robotics and Automation (ICRA), pp. 8899–8906 (2020)
2. Zhang, J., Singh, S.: LOAM: lidar odometry and mapping in real-time. In: Robotics: Science and Systems, vol. 2, no. 9, pp. 1–9 (2014)
3. Shan, T., Englot, B.: Lego-loam: lightweight and ground-optimized lidar odometry and mapping on variable terrain. In: IEEE/RSJ International Conference on Intelligent Robots and Systems (IROS), pp. 4758–4765 (2018)
4. Kim, G., Park, Y.S., Cho, Y., Jeong, J., Kim, A.: Mulran: multimodal range dataset for urban place recognition. In: IEEE International Conference on Robotics and Automation (ICRA), pp. 6246–6253 (2020)
5. Geiger, A., Lenz, P., Urtasun, R.: Are we ready for autonomous driving? the kitti vision benchmark suite. In: IEEE Conference on Computer Vision and Pattern Recognition, pp. 3354–3361 (2012)
6. Rusinkiewicz, S., Levoy, M.: Efficient variants of the ICP algorithm. In: Proceedings Third International Conference on 3-D Digital Imaging and Modeling, pp. 145–152 (2001)
7. Himmelsbach, M., Hundelshausen, F. V., Wuensche, H. J.: Fast segmentation of 3D point clouds for ground vehicles. In: IEEE Intelligent Vehicles Symposium, pp. 560–565 (2010)
8. Ye, H., Chen, Y., Liu, M.: Tightly coupled 3d lidar inertial odometry and mapping. In: International Conference on Robotics and Automation (ICRA), pp. 3144–3150 (2019)
9. Shan, T., Englot, B., Meyers, D., Wang, W., Ratti, C., Rus, D.: Lio-sam: tightly-coupled lidar inertial odometry via smoothing and mapping. In: IEEE/RSJ international conference on intelligent robots and systems (IROS), pp. 5135–5142 (2020)
10. Lim, H., Oh, M., Myung, H.: Patchwork: Concentric zone-based region-wise ground segmentation with ground likelihood estimation using a 3D LiDAR sensor. IEEE Rob. Autom. Lett. 6(4), 6458–6465 (2021)
11. Kim, G., Kim, A.: Scan context: egocentric spatial descriptor for place recognition within 3d point cloud map. In: IEEE/RSJ International Conference on Intelligent Robots and Systems (IROS), pp. 4802–4809 (2018)
12. Tang, J., et al.: LiDAR scan matching aided inertial navigation system in GNSS-denied environments. Sensors 15(7), 16710–16728 (2015)
13. Zhen, W., Zeng, S., Soberer, S.: Robust localization and localizability estimation with a rotating laser scanner. In: IEEE International Conference on Robotics and Automation (ICRA), pp. 6240–6245 (2017)

14. Neuhaus, F., Kob, T., Kohnen, R., Paulus, D.: Mc2slam: real-time inertial lidar odometry using two-scan motion compensation. In: Pattern Recognition: 40th German Conference, pp. 60–72 (2019)
15. Sung, C., Jeon, S., Lim, H., Myung, H.: What if there was no revisit? Large-scale graph-based SLAM with traffic sign detection in an HD map using LiDAR inertial odometry. Intell. Serv. Rob. 1–10 (2022)
16. Narksri, P., Takeuchi, E., Ninomiya, Y., Morales, Y., Akai, N., Kawaguchi, N.: A slope-robust cascaded ground segmentation in 3D point cloud for autonomous vehicles. In: 21st International Conference on intelligent transportation systems (ITSC), pp. 497–504 (2018)
17. Na, K., Park, B., Seo, B.: Drivable space expansion from the ground base for complex structured roads. In: IEEE International Conference on Systems, Man, and Cybernetics (SMC), pp. 000373–000378 (2016)
18. Zermas, D., Izzat, I., Papanikolopoulos, N.: Fast segmentation of 3d point clouds: a paradigm on lidar data for autonomous vehicle applications. In: IEEE International Conference on Robotics and Automation (ICRA), pp. 5067–5073 (2017)
19. Cheng, J., He, D., Lee, C.: A simple ground segmentation method for LiDAR 3D point clouds. In: 2nd International Conference on Advances in Computer Technology, Information Science and Communications (CTISC), pp. 171–175 (2020)
20. Wang, B., Lan, J., Gao, J.: LiDAR filtering in 3D object detection based on improved RANSAC. Remote Sens. 14(9), 2110 (2022)
21. Fischler, M.A., Bolles, R.C.: Random sample consensus: a paradigm for model fitting with applications to image analysis and automated cartography. Commun. ACM 24(6), 381–395 (1981)
22. Rizzini, D.L.: Place recognition of 3D landmarks based on geometric relations. In: IEEE/RSJ International Conference on Intelligent Robots and Systems (IROS), pp. 648–654 (2017)
23. Gálvez-López, D., Tardos, J.D.: Bags of binary words for fast place recognition in image sequences. IEEE Trans. Rob. 28(5), 1188–1197 (2012)
24. Nurunnabi, A., Belton, D., West, G.: Diagnostics based principal component analysis for robust plane fitting in laser data. In: 16th International Conference on Computer and Information Technology, pp. 484–489 (2014)
25. Liao, L., Fu, C., Feng, B., Su, T.: Optimized SC-F-LOAM: optimized fast LiDAR odometry and mapping using scan context. In: 6th CAA International Conference on Vehicular Control and Intelligence, pp. 1–6 (2022)

Interictal EEG Based Prediction of ACTH Efficacy in Infantile Epileptic Spasms

Tianci Jiang[1,2], Runze Zheng[1,2], Yuanmeng Feng[1,2], Dinghan Hu[1,2], Feng Gao[3], and Jiuwen Cao[1,2(✉)]

[1] Machine Learning and I-health International Cooperation Base of Zhejiang Province, Hangzhou Dianzi University, Hangzhou 310018, China
{runzewuyu,jwcao}@hdu.edu.cn
[2] Artificial Intelligence Institute, Hangzhou Dianzi University, Zhejiang 310018, China
[3] Department of Neurology, Children's Hospital, Zhejiang University School of Medicine, Hangzhou 310018, China
epilepsy@zju.edu.cn

Abstract. Infantile epileptic spasms (IESS) are a common and refractory childhood epilepsy syndrome. Adrenocorticotropic hormone (ACTH) is one of the most effective drugs for the treatment of IESS disorder, but not effective in avoiding side effects. Therefore, improving the prognostic management of IESS by objectively predicting ACTH response is essential. To address this, this study divides patients into four groups: Normal, Mild, Moderate, and Severe, based on the effect of ACTH administration in IESS patients. The power spectral density (PSD) and Permutation entropy (PEN) of interictal EEG in IESS patients before drug administration are extracted, and the overall EEG variability between the four groups of IESS patients, as well as the variability between different brain regions, are analyzed using paired samples t-test. The PSD and PEN of five EEG brain rhythms (δ, θ, α, β, and γ) are taken as input, and support vector machine is applied to construct an ACTH drug efficacy prediction model, which achieves 96% accuracy. This study contributes to the early prediction of ACTH treatment efficacy and can help to develop appropriate treatment.

Keywords: Infantile epileptic spasms · Adrenocorticotropic hormone · Prediction

1 Introduction

Infantile epileptic spasms (IESS), also known as infantile spasms (IS), are common developmental and epileptic encephalopathy during early infancy. Its interictal electroencephalogram (EEG) shows hypsarrhythmia and the seizure EEG exhibits series and continuous discharges [1,2]. The disease often causes developmental delays or regressions, more complex co-morbidities, and even more severe epileptic syndromes.

This work was supported by the National Natural Science Foundation of China (U1909209), the National Key Research and Development of China (2021YFE0100100), the National Key Research and Development Program of China (2021YFE0205400), and the Research Funding of Education of Zhejiang Province (Y202249784).

F. Sun et al. (Eds.): ICCSIP 2023, CCIS 1918, pp. 45–56, 2024.
https://doi.org/10.1007/978-981-99-8018-5_4

The antiepileptic drug, adrenocorticotropic hormone (ACTH), effectively reduces the frequency and duration of IS seizures [3]. However, this drug has uncontrollable side effects. Therefore, objectively predicting the response to antiepileptic drugs is essential to improve the optimal treatment outcome of IS.

Scalp EEG has been widely applied in epilepsy diagnosis because of its easy acquisition, low cost, and high temporal resolution. EEG data from IS patients are categorized into interictal and seizure periods based on seizure markers. The interictal EEG of IS is characterized by hypsarrhythmia, while during seizures, the hypsarrhythmia disappears and high amplitude slow waves and extensive low voltage fast waves appear. The seizure period duration is shorter than the interictal period. Typically, clinical evaluations of the effectiveness of medication in IS rely on identifying the EEG during the interictal period. Neurologists often need to visually examine the EEG signal over a period of time to analyze it. This approach is time-consuming and singular. It requires extensive clinical experience and has significant drawbacks.

To overcome the drawbacks of visual-based detection, the prognostic assessment of EEG can be aided by computational biomarkers [4]. How to select effective biomarkers to characterize EEG comprehensively is crucial to construct relevant auxiliary systems. Time domain, frequency domain, time-frequency domain, nonlinear dynamics, and brain network features are commonly applied to evaluate the effect of IS medication [5]. Zhang et al. divided IS patients into two groups of responders and non-responders to ACTH and analyzed the differences between the two groups of IS patients by applying multiscale entropy [6]. Kanai et al. constructed brain networks employing relative power spectra (rPS), and weighted phase lag index (wPLI) and analyzed EEG changes in IS patients before and after ACTH application [7]. McCrimmon et al. distinguished normal individuals from IS patients after ACTH use by the spatial distribution and the ratio of high frequency oscillations (HFOs) in the scalp [8]. Most existing studies have assessed the effect of ACTH in IS through biomarkers, but there is a lack of predictive studies on the outcome of ACTH in IS.

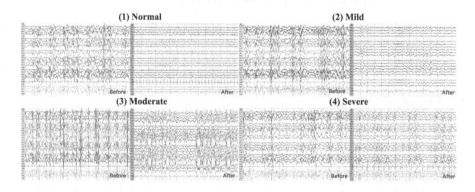

Fig. 1. Interictal EEG data of four groups of IS patients (Normal, Mild, Moderate, Severe) before and after drug treatment.

Collectively, the pathological mechanisms of IS are largely unknown, and the prediction of treatment outcomes in IS is more important and challenging for prognostic management. Here, we attempt to extract computational interictal EEG biomarkers and predict ACTH's effect on IS with statistical analysis and machine learning methods. Compared with the existing studies, the main contributions of our work are listed as follows:

1. The patients were divided into four groups: Normal, Mild, Moderate, and Severe, depending on the outcome of ACTH in IS patients. The effect after ACTH treatment was predicted only by the interictal EEG before IS medication.
2. Power spectral density and Permutation entropy were extracted, and the overall EEG signal variability between the above four groups of IS patients, as well as between different brain regions, was analyzed by paired samples t-test.
3. Based on the results of statistical analysis, the PSD and PEN of five EEG brain rhythms (δ, θ, α, β and γ) were extracted, and the four groups of patients were differentiated by support vector machine with 96% accuracy.

This study analyzed and studied EEG data before ACTH administration in 30 pediatric patients with IS at Children's Hospital of Zhejiang University School of Medicine (CHZU), and finally found that (1) the combined use of PSD and PEN could better predict the effect of ACTH administration in IS patients. (2) Energy changes in δ and θ rhythms, and nonlinear changes in γ rhythms play an essential role in constructing the prediction system.

2 Data Collection

2.1 Subject Identification

The purpose of this study was to predict the effect after drug administration by interictal EEG data before ACTH administration in IS patients. 30 IS patients' data were selected from the standard clinical EEG library of CHZU. The EEG-related information was labeled by clinical neurophysiologists with expertise in pediatric EEG. Table 1 details the basic information of the patients and the interictal EEG duration of the study. Patients were chosen based on (1) clinical diagnosis of infantile spasms (2) relatively clean EEG background with significant hypsarrhythmia in the interictal data (3) ACTH medication after the patient was admitted to the hospital. We adopted anonymous analysis in this study following the relevant ethical regulations, and only EEG data, gender, and epilepsy-related labeling were retained. The study obtained informed consent from the patient's legal guardians and also complied with the ethical regulations of CHZU and Hangzhou Dianzi University.

Based on the EEG data scores of IS patients after drug administration, we divided the patients into four groups: Normal, Mild, Moderate, and Severe. Normal means the patient's EEG becomes normal after medication, Mild means the presence of diffuse δ and θ activity with multiple multifocal spike sharp waves in EEG, Moderate means the presence of a small amount of δ and θ activity with multiple multifocal spike sharp waves in EEG, and Sever means still hypsarrhythmia after medication. Figure 1 shows

Table 1. Infantile spasms patient information

Patient	Gender	EEG(s)	Patient	Gender	EEG(s)
Normal	M	2463	Severe	M	2269
Normal	M	2463	Severe	W	2269
Normal	W	2463	Severe	M	2269
Normal	M	2463	Severe	W	2269
Normal	W	2463	Severe	W	2269
Normal	M	2463	Severe	W	2269
Mild	M	1696	Moderate	M	1309
Mild	W	1696	Moderate	W	1309
Mild	W	1696	Moderate	W	1309
Mild	M	1696	Moderate	W	1309
Mild	W	1696	Moderate	M	1309
Mild	W	1696	Moderate	M	1309
Mild	W	1696	Moderate	W	1309
Mild	W	1696	Moderate	W	1309
Mild	M	1696	Moderate	M	1309

the interictal EEG characteristics of the four types with bipolar leads before and after ACTH treatment. From the figure, we can clearly see that all four data groups before treatment show hypsarrhythmia, and the four data groups after treatment show normal, diffuse δ and θ activity with multiple multifocal spike sharp waves, a small amount of δ and θ activity with multiple multifocal spike sharp waves and hypsarrhythmia. It is very difficult to predict the effect of ACTH after medication exclusively by visual detection.

2.2   EEG Recordings

EEG data of all patients were collected in a quiet ward environment with parents. The EEG signals of IS patients were recorded for approximately 16 h, including the sleep phase, by using the 10–20 standard lead EEG system with the Fpz electrode as the reference channel and 1000 Hz sampling frequency. To reduce interference and to exclude reference lead interference, we chose bipolar leads (Fp1-F7, F7-T3, T3-T5, T5-O1, Fp1-F3, F3-C3, C3-P3, P3-O1, Fz-Cz, Cz-Pz, Fp2-F4, F4-C4, C4-P4, P4-O2, Fp2-F8, F8-T4, T6-O2), whose connections and distribution are shown in Fig. 2. Also, to avoid artifacts like eye movements and EMG interference, the interictal EEG data from the patients' sleep period were selected for the experimental analysis [9]. A 50 Hz trap filter was performed to eliminate the interference of the EEG by the industrial frequency noise. Finally, the EEG data were framed into 4 s steps with a 50% overlap rate by sliding window of 4 s, and 5292 samples were extracted from each of the four data groups described above.

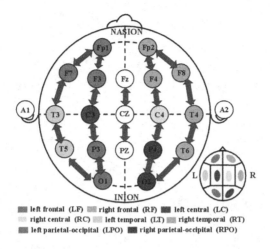

Fig. 2. 10–20 lead EEG system with bipolar leads and brain partitioning.

3 Methods

3.1 Power Spectral Density (PSD)

Power spectral density (PSD) estimation is commonly employed for frequency domain analysis of EEG signals. It describes the distribution of power along the frequency of an EEG signal, and the rhythmic distribution of the EEG signal can be observed by this method. Welch's method is a classical PSD estimation tool, which is based on the average periodogram [10]. Firstly, we set certain overlap rates for the segmented EEG data segments, then apply windows to each segmented data segment to obtain the periodogram, and finally average the periodogram of all windowed data segments to obtain the PSD estimation of EEG signals. It can be expressed by the following equation:

$$P_w\left(e^{jw}\right) = \frac{1}{K} \sum_{i=0}^{K-1} I_i(w) = \frac{1}{K \cdot M \cdot U} \sum_{i=0}^{K-1} \left| \sum_{n=0}^{M-1} x_i(n)w(n)e^{-jwn} \right|^2 \tag{1}$$

where $I_i(w)$ refers to periodogram, K denotes the number of segmented EEG segments, M indicates the length of each segment of EEG signal, $U = \frac{1}{M} \sum_{n=0}^{M-1} w^2(n)$ is the power of the window $w(n)$, and x_i refers to the signal.

We applied Welch's method to estimate the PSD for the four groups of EEG data. Figure 3 shows the PSD estimates for one sample from each of the four IS patients in the frequency range 0.5 Hz–70 Hz. We can see that there is a noticeable difference in the frequency energy distribution of the four groups. To more accurately quantify the interictal EEG signal variability of the four groups, we divided the EEG signals into five frequency bands δ(1–4 Hz), θ(4–8 Hz), α(8–13 Hz), β(13–30 Hz), and γ(30–70 Hz), and calculated the power spectral density of all channels within each band [11].

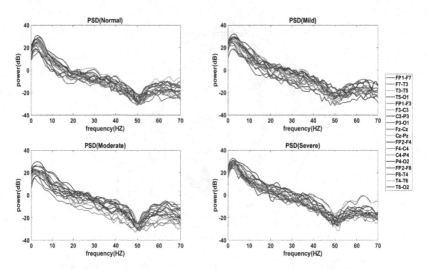

Fig. 3. Four groups (Normal, Mild, Moderate and Severe) EEG PSD estimation.

3.2 Permutation Entropy (PEN)

Permutation Entropy (PEN) is the quantitative complexity algorithm to study the local structure of dynamic time series [12, 13]. Compared with other algorithms, PEN has the features of simplicity, noise immunity, and low computational complexity. The algorithm steps are described as follows:

First, the assumed time series $\{x(i) : 1 \leqslant i \leqslant N\}$ is reconstructed:

$$X_i = \{x(i), x(i + \tau), \cdots, x(i + (m - 1)\tau)\}$$
$$i = 1, 2, \cdots, N - (m - 1)\tau \tag{2}$$

where τ is the time delay and m refers to the embedding dimension.

Secondly, incrementally sort the X_i sequence.

$$\{x(i + (j_1 - 1)\tau) \leqslant x(i + (j_2 - 1)\tau) \leqslant \cdots$$
$$\cdots \leqslant x(i + (j_m - 1)\tau)\}. \tag{3}$$

Therefore, if the embedding dimension is m dimensional, there are $m!$ kinds of sorts. In other words, each vector X_i is mapped to one of the $m!$ kinds of permutations. The j-th sort has the probability of occurrence of p_j as:

$$p_j = \frac{n_j}{\sum_{j=1}^{m} n_j} \tag{4}$$

where n_j denotes the number of occurrences of the j-th sort. The ranking entropy of the time series $\{x(i) : 1 \leqslant i \leqslant N\}$ is

$$H_x(m) = -\sum_{j=1}^{m!} p_j \ln p_j \tag{5}$$

Figure 4 reflects the PEN distribution of C3 channels in the four groups of IS. The PEN distribution was more different in the Normal and Severe groups, while the PEN distribution was similar in the Mid and Moderate groups. This shows that PEN has obvious advantages for quantifying complex dynamic changes in EEG.

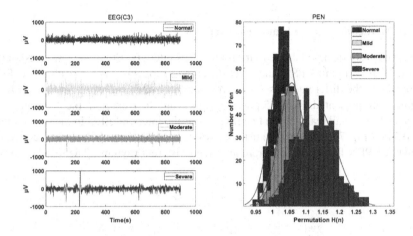

Fig. 4. PEN distribution of the C3 channels for the four IS groups.

3.3 Statistical Analysis and Models

The human brain can be divided into several functional brain regions by function, like learning, memory, cognition, and emotion. The spontaneous synergy between different regions generates different brainwave rhythms. The rhythmic activity in each frequency band has specific scalp distribution and biological significance. Meanwhile, different brainwave rhythms can reflect the activity of different functional brain regions. To characterize the interictal EEG changes in four different groups of IS patients, we chose paired samples t-test for statistical analysis of overall and different brain regions of PSD and PEN in five rhythms. The aim of this study is to distinguish four different groups of patients with different IS medication effects by machine learning models to achieve prediction of ACTH effects. Combining the characteristics of the samples and features, we chose the support vector machine (SVM) to construct the drug effect response prediction model.

4 Results and Discussions

To predict response to ACTH administration, EEG data from 30 patients with IS were screened for this study. The interictal EEG data of the patient's sleep stages were adopted, and the patients were divided into four groups of Normal, Mild, Moderate, and Severe based on their response after ACTH administration, and each EEG group was split into 5292 4 s samples. Next, the PSD and alignment entropy of the main five rhythms (δ, θ, α, β, and γ) in the EEG signal were extracted for statistical analysis, and the support vector machine was selected to construct the ACTH medication response prediction model. Precision, recall, F_score, and accuracy were employed for model performance evaluation.

4.1 IS Medication Effect Statistical Analysis

To quantitatively distinguish the four groups of IS interictal EEG, we first investigated the overall five rhythms PSD and PEN differences, together with the PSD and PEN differences in the different leads. The corresponding statistical results in Fig. 5, Fig. 6, and Fig. 7 are presented. Figure 5 presents significant differences in the distribution of PSD and PEN for all leads of the five rhythms of the interictal EEG in the four groups. Figure 6 and Fig. 7 present the statistical p-value distribution between the four groups of PSD and PEN features in different leads and different rhythms. The results showed

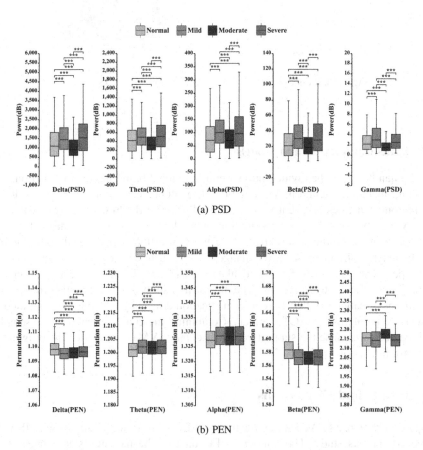

(a) PSD

(b) PEN

Fig. 5. Statistics of the distribution of PSD and PEN values for the five rhythms of the four IS groups ($*$: p $<$ 0.05, $**$: p $<$ 0.01, $***$: p $<$ 0.001).

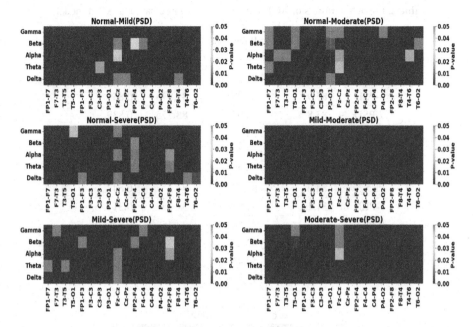

Fig. 6. Statistical p-value distribution between four groups of PSD features in different leads and different rhythms.

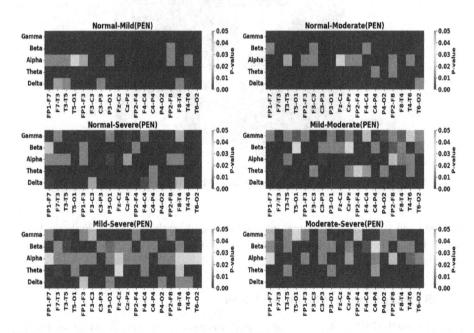

Fig. 7. Statistical p-value distribution between four groups of PEN features in different leads and different rhythms.

Table 2. Prediction results of ACTH medication response based on SVM model

Feature	Accuracy(%)	Precision(%)	Recall(%)	F_score
PSD+PEN	**96.6**	**96.5**	**96.525**	**0.96**
PSD	93.9	93.9	93.9	0.939
δ-PSD	85.9	85.925	85.875	0.859
θ-PSD	83.8	83.95	83.775	0.839
α-PSD	69.5	35	70	0.467
β-PSD	61.5	64.425	62.15	0.633
γ-PSD	43.4	60.275	44.3	0.511
PEN	84.6	84.625	84.6	0.847
δ-PEN	31.1	31.05	31.05	0.31
θ-PEN	32.6	32.55	32.45	0.325
α-PEN	32.4	32.275	32.3	0.323
β-PEN	52.1	52.45	52.1	0.523
γ-PEN	75.1	75.125	75.025	0.751

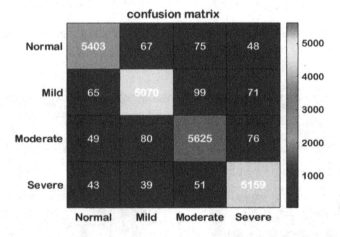

Fig. 8. Confusion matrix of the 4 groups (Normal, Mild, Moderate and Severe) of SVM.

that PSD and PEN in all brain regions differed significantly in all five rhythms. Altogether, PSD and PEN are feasible as predictive biomarkers of ACTH drug administration effects.

4.2 IS Medication Effect Prediction Model

The PSD and the PEN of δ, θ, α, β, and γ rhythms were input to the SVM for analyzing the effect of different rhythms on predicting the effect of ACTH, and the results are shown in Table 2. We can clearly see that (1) there is information complementarity between PSD and PEN features, and the combination of the two features is stronger than only a single feature. (2) The PSD of δ, θ, α and the PEN of γ play more important roles for prediction. The use of a single rhythm wave lost important information that leaded to suboptimal accuracy, while the use of all rhythms achieved the most optimal effect. Figure 8 demonstrates the PSD and PEN for all rhythms as model inputs, the confusion matrix for the four different IS groups. The above results further demonstrate the potential of PSD and PEN as biomarkers to predict the effect of ACTH on IS.

5   Conclusions

In this study, we validated that PSD and PEN can be biomarkers for predicting the effect of ACTH on the assessment of IS treatment by applying statistical analysis and machine learning methods. The experiment collected a total of 30 IS patients and divided them into four groups: Normal, Mild, Moderate, and Severe. We extracted the PSD and PEN of interictal EEG from different groups and analyzed the variability of overall and different lead PSD and PEN by paired samples t-test while inputting the features into SVM for further validation of feasibility. The study is based on offline data, how to make predictions from real-time data and avoid individual differences will be the main problem to be solved.

Ethical Statement. This study has been approved by the Children's Hospital, Zhejiang University School of Medicine, and registered in the Chinese Clinical Trial Registry (ChiCTR1900028804). All patients gave their informed consent prior to their inclusion in the study.

References

1. Pavone, P., et al.: West syndrome: a comprehensive review. Neurol. Sci. 1–16 (2020)
2. Pavone, P., Striano, P., Falsaperla, R., Pavone, L., Ruggieri, M.: Infantile spasms syndrome, west syndrome and related phenotypes: what we know in 2013. Brain Develop. **36**(9), 739–751 (2014)
3. Paprocka, J., Malkiewicz, J., Palazzo-Michalska, V., Nowacka, B., Kuźniak, M., Kopyta, I.: Effectiveness of acth in patients with infantile spasms. Brain Sci. **12**(2), 254 (2022)
4. Zheng, R., Cao, J., Feng, Y., Zhao, X., Jiang, T., Gao, F.: Seizure prediction analysis of infantile spasms. IEEE Trans. Neural Syst. Rehabil. Eng. (2022)
5. Smith, R.J., Hu, D.K., Shrey, D.W., Rajaraman, R., Hussain, S.A., Lopour, B.A.: Computational characteristics of interictal EEG as objective markers of epileptic spasms. Epilepsy Res. **176**, 106704 (2021)
6. Zhang, C.-T., Sun, Y.-L., Shi, W.-B., Yang, G., Yeh, C.-H.: Brain complexity predicts response to adrenocorticotropic hormone in infantile epileptic spasms syndrome: a retrospective study. Neurol. Therapy **12**(1), 129–144 (2023)
7. Kanai, S., et al.: Quantitative pretreatment EEG predicts efficacy of acth therapy in infantile epileptic spasms syndrome. Clin. Neurophysiol. **144**, 83–90 (2022)
8. McCrimmon, C.M., et al.: Automated detection of ripple oscillations in long-term scalp EEG from patients with infantile spasms. J. Neural Eng. **18**(1), 016018 (2021)
9. Cao, J., et al.: Unsupervised eye blink artifact detection from EEG with gaussian mixture model. IEEE J. Biomed. Health Inform. **25**(8), 2895–2905 (2021)

10. Faust, O., Rajendra Acharya, U., Adeli, H., Adeli, A.: Wavelet-based EEG processing for computer-aided seizure detection and epilepsy diagnosis. Seizure **26**, 56–64 (2015)
11. Zheng, R., et al.: Scalp EEG functional connection and brain network in infants with west syndrome. Neural Netw. **153**, 76–86 (2022)
12. Li, X., Ouyang, G., Richards, D.A.: Predictability analysis of absence seizures with permutation entropy. Epilepsy Res. **77**(1), 70–74 (2007)
13. Bein, B.: Entropy. Best Pract. Res. Clin. Anaesthesiol. **20**(1), 101–109 (2006)

CCA-MTFCN: A Robotic Pushing-Grasping Collaborative Method Based on Deep Reinforcement Learning

Haiyuan Xu⬤, Qi Wang⬤, and Huasong Min⁽✉⁾⬤

Institute of Robotics and Intelligent Systems, Wuhan University of Science and Technology, Wuhan 430081, China
mhuasong@wust.edu.cn

Abstract. Robotic grasping in dense clutter is often infeasible because of the occlusion and stacking of objects. Directly grasping the stacked objects may cause collisions and result in low efficiency and high failure rates. In practice, the lateral robotic push can separate stacked objects to create collision-free grasp affordances. Inspired by this, we devise a method called CCA-MTFCN based on deep reinforcement learning, which can learn the synergies between pushing and grasping policies to complete the task of removing all objects in a heavily cluttered environment. Specifically, a hard parameter-sharing Multi-Task Fully Convolutional Network (MTFCN) is proposed to model the action-value function, then multi-scale feature fusion mechanism is implemented in it which can enhance visual perception capability in cluttered environments. Moreover, a new reward function based on connected component analysis (CCA) is designed to effectively evaluate the quality of push actions in pushing-and-grasping collaboration. This enables us to explicitly encourage pushing actions that aid grasping thus improving the efficiency of sequential decision-making. Our approach was trained in simulation through trial-and-error, and evaluation experiments for object removal tasks in dense clutter demonstrate that our proposed method outperforms several baseline approaches in terms of task completion rate, grasp success rate, and action efficiency, which also has the capability to generalize to new scenarios.

Keywords: Robotic Grasping · Robotic Pushing · Deep Reinforcement Learning

1 Introduction

Robotic grasping is an important branch of robotics, which is the foundation and key for robots to complete various grasping tasks and has been widely used in industrial production, healthcare, exploration, military, and more [1]. In recent years, there has been extensive research on robotic grasping [2]. Although these grasping methods can achieve reasonable performance in certain organized environments, most of them are based on the premise that there is sufficient space for the end-effector gripper of the robotic arm to grasp each object. However, it is difficult to find grasping affordances without causing collisions in dense clutter due to obstacles preventing feasible grasps [3], which can lead

© The Author(s), under exclusive license to Springer Nature Singapore Pte Ltd. 2024
F. Sun et al. (Eds.): ICCSIP 2023, CCIS 1918, pp. 57–72, 2024.
https://doi.org/10.1007/978-981-99-8018-5_5

to grasping failure or even damage to the end-effector and objects. Particularly, when objects are tightly stacked in the scene, there may not be any available grasping points, making these grasping methods difficult to achieve desirable performance. Therefore, designing effective strategies for autonomous grasping in the presence of dense clutter remains a challenge.

In the practical application of human grasping in dense clutter, the list of manipulation primitives is not limited to grasping and includes non-prehensile actions such as pushing, shifting, and poking [4]. Combining non-prehensile and prehensile manipulation policies offers a very promising approach for solving this problem. Inspired by this, some recent works have used deep reinforcement learning to learn the synergies between pushing and grasping [5–8]. While there are still some problems in the synergy of two primitive actions, the first is low efficiency due to redundant pushing. To address this issue, we propose utilizing the connected component analysis (CCA) to consider stacked objects which are lack grasp affordances. Based on this, we introduce novel evaluation metrics incorporated into the reward function to improve pushing action quality and avoid useless pushes, thereby enhancing collaboration efficiency.

Besides, these methods neglect the importance of multiscale features of the objects in dense clutter, which can significantly affect the accuracy of robotic manipulation. We also find that the strong correlation between grasping and pushing can be leveraged through hard parameter sharing [9] to identify common visual representations, which can reduce the time and space complexity of the network without losing its performance. Therefore, this article proposes a Multi-Task Fully Convolutional Network (MTFCN) with hard parameter-sharing in the paradigm of multitask learning to approximate the Q-function, and an atrous spatial pyramid pooling (ASPP) [10] module is employed in it which can well fuse the multiscale features of objects in Q-network.

To sum up, we model pushing and grasping tasks into a multi-task framework to learn both tasks and the more effective synergies between them, which can address the task of removing all objects in dense clutter. The main contributions of our work are as follows:

(1) A Multi-Task Fully Convolutional Network (MTFCN) is proposed, in which the agent learns a common space representation for both pushing and grasping tasks through sharing parameters between them. Besides, the ASPP is introduced in task-specific layers of MTFCN, which can better fuse multi-scale features of objects in dense clutter.

(2) New metrics based on connected component analysis are proposed, which can reasonably evaluate the quality of pushing actions in the pushing and grasping collaboration. On this basis, a novel non-sparse CCA reward system is developed, which can explicitly encourage pushing actions that aid grasping to suppress unreasonable pushing in the collaboration.

2 Related Work

2.1 Grasping Method

Approaches to vision-based robotic grasping can be divided into geometric or data-driven [11]. Traditional geometric grasping methods rely on precise 3D models of known objects to find stable force closure, which are computationally complex, time-consuming, and difficult to generalize to unseen objects and scenarios [12]. Data-driven visual grasping detection algorithms are popular these years, which have improved the grasping detection accuracy of different objects in various scenarios and have been applied to robotic tasks. These approaches can be categorized as model-based or model-free [2]. Model-based grasp detection methods usually require pose estimation of the object before the subsequent determination of the grasp pose, which can be difficult in clutter because of the sensitivity to occlusions [11]. [13] utilized PointNet ++ [14] to perform pointwise pose regression on each pixel to predict instance-level segmentation masks and their corresponding 6D poses. Li et al. [15] trained a model-based approach using a convolutional neural network to generate 6-DOF grasp poses for unknown objects in unstructured environments from point cloud data. However, these methods rely heavily on accurate models of the object being grasped, and may not generalize well to objects that deviate from those models.

Model-free approaches are attractive due to their ability to generalize to unseen objects, which can output grasp configurations directly without a pose estimation step. Kumra et al. [16] proposed a novel Generative Residual Convolutional Neural Network model that can generate robust antipodal grasps from n-channel input for each pixel. Wang et al. [17] made the first attempt to use vision transformers [18] for grasp detection, which enabled their model to better fuse local features with global features than traditional convolutional neural network-based grasp detectors, showing better performance on popular grasp datasets. However, these supervised learning-based approaches are limited to a single grasping strategy and cannot be synergized with other strategies. Model-free reinforcement learning algorithms combined with deep neural networks can also be applied to robotic grasping, which can make the whole grasping process more natural and precise. Some scholars consider the robotic grasping process as a sequential decision-making problem and use a reward function to guide the agent's training through trial-and-error in the framework of reinforcement learning, without relying on a large dataset for training. The current research [19–21] on deep Q-network (DQN) [22] showed how deep reinforcement learning can be applied to designing closed-loop grasping strategies and achieved good generalization performance. However, these methods did not discuss the situation where the robotic arm grippers lack grasping space due to the tight arrangement of objects in dense clutter. Then, pre-grasping manipulation like pushing or poking an object becomes necessary. Unlike these methods, we propose a collaborative pushing and grasping method that can effectively solve this problem by creating grasping affordances by pushing objects to separate before grasping.

2.2 Pre-grasp Manipulation

Learning the synergies between prehensile and non-prehensile primitive actions is an effective way to perform the robotic task of removing objects in clutter [3]. Most of the early work involved hard-coded heuristics that used pre-defined sequences of actions [4, 23]. Zeng et al. [5] provided a new perspective to bridging data-driven prehensile and non-prehensile manipulation. They correspond the discrete processing action space to the simplified motion primitives in the framework of DQN. Their proposed method (named VPG) takes RGBD images as input, outputs pixel-level Q-value heatmaps of push and grasp actions, and selects the action with the largest Q-value for execution. Yang et al. [6] and Zhao et al. [7] improved the model performance by adding different attention mechanisms to weight the extracted features in the Q-network based on VPG. In [6] a non-sparse reward function was proposed which evaluated the pushing effect using the maximum Q value of the local area around the push point before and after the pushing action. In [24], a slide-to-wall strategy was proposed to address the problem that flat objects are not easy to grasp by first moving the flat object to the wall and then grasping the object with the help of the wall, but this method has limited application scenarios.

More closely related to our work is VPG [5]. Although VPG can perform autonomous complex sequences of pushing and grasping in clutter, there is no explicit encouragement for pushing tasks to assist with grasping. Their sparse reward configuration in which push gets rewarded is evaluated by whether there is a difference in the heightmap before and after pushing, which can lead to some issues. Firstly, the quality of the pushing is not stable, because the agent sometimes pushes the objects more agglomerated but also gets positive rewards, and such inappropriate pushes should not be included in the sequence decision-making of pushing and grasping collaboration. Secondly, this sometimes leads to the agent repeatedly pushing an object that already has enough grasping space to grab rewards, resulting in redundant pushing actions in the collaboration. For this reason, a new reward function is designed that uses a new metric to evaluate the quality of pushing actions, guiding the agent to perform reasonable pushes for better grasping. Besides, we improve the Q-network by introducing multi-scale fusion, which leads to better detection of objects in dense clutter. We demonstrate that our method can improve the grasping success rate and action efficiency while effectively generalizing to more cluttered scenarios.

3   Method

In this paper, we propose a DQN-based collaborative pushing and grasping framework for solving the object removal task in dense clutter which is shown in Fig. 1.

At time t, MTFCN maps a state to the Q values of all the discrete actions $Q(s_t, a_t)$ that can be taken from high-dimensional state s_t. The policy $\pi(s)$ picks the action that corresponds to the highest Q-value from the MTFCN's output, which is determined by:

$$\pi(s) = argmax(Q_{push}(s_t, a_t), Q_{grasp}(s_t, a_t)) \tag{1}$$

As the robot interacts with the environment, it learns which actions are better, based on reward that it obtains from the proposed CCA reward system.

The rest of this section introduces the selection of observation space and discretization of action space, as well as MTFCN, CCA reward system, training method in detail.

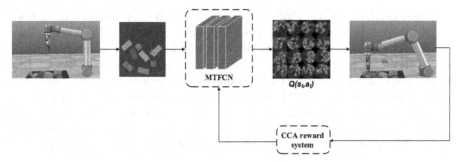

Fig. 1. Pipeline of CCA-MTFCN.

3.1 Observation Space and Action Space

The RGB-D heightmap of the cluttered environment is taken as the observation space. The heightmaps are computed by capturing RGB-D images using a fixed-mount camera, which are then projected onto a 3D point cloud. Subsequently, the data is orthogonally back-projected upwards in the direction of gravity to construct an image representation of RGB-D channels (same as in [5]). The workspace covers a $0.448^2 m^2$ manipulation surface and the input heightmap size is 224×224, which makes each pixel in the heightmap corresponds to a 2^2mm vertical column of 3D space in the workspace.

The action space is discretized by parameterizing both push and grasp actions as motion primitives. In this work, only 2D planar two-fingered parallel-jawed grasping and planar pushing are considered, a unique grasp or push pose can be determined with just four degrees of freedom (x, y, z, yaw). To simplify the action space, only $k=16$ different yaw angles are considered (different multiples of $22.5°$). The total action space is as follows:

$$a = \{(\varphi, x, y, yam)|\varphi \in \{grasp, push\}\} \tag{2}$$

If φ=grasp, the robotic arm performs a top-down grasp at (x, y) of the workspace, the grasp height z can be determined by the D channel of the heightmap after x and y are determined, and the yaw angle of the gripper is one of $k=16$ orientations. During the grasping process, the open two-finger gripper performs a vertical movement of 3cm before closing. If φ=push, the closed two-finger gripper of the robotic arm performs a 10cm straight push in one of $k=16$ directions at (x, y) in the workspace, and the push height z can also be determined by the heightmap.

With the processing mentioned above, we completely discretize the motion space. The motion planning for the kinematic primitives of the robotic arm grasping and pushing is done automatically by the stable and collision-free IK solvers.

3.2 MTFCN

We extend vanilla DQN by modeling the action-value function as a Multi-Task Fully Convolutional Network [25] (MTFCN) which is shown in Fig. 2. The low-level parameters of MTFCN are shared, while the high-level parameters are independent of each other.

We employ two DenseNet121 [26] as the backbone of MTFCN to extract features from the color channel and depth channel of the heightmap respectively. These features are then channel-wise concatenated and fed into two branch networks: one is grasping network (GNET) for learning grasping and another is pushing network (PNET) for learning pushing. PNET and GNET share the same structure, comprised of a multi-scale atrous spatial pyramid pooling (ASPP) [10] module and two blocks of concatenated layers, consisting of spatial batch normalization, rectified linear unit activation functions, and 1×1 convolutional operations. A bilinear upsampling layer is then used in both PNET and GNET to restore the feature map to the original resolution of the input heightmap.

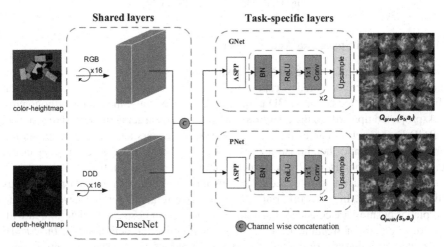

Fig. 2. Overview of MTFCN and Q-learning formulation. Before being fed into the MTFCN, the heightmap is rotated 16 times to consider 16 different yaw angles for pushing and grasping actions, which will output 16 pixel-wise Q-value heatmaps corresponding to the respective pushing and grasping actions.

Shared Layers with Hard Parameter Sharing. In our scenario, both grasping and pushing actions depend on the properties of the object (geometry, mass distribution, etc.) and require stable contact between the gripper and the object. VPG uses four Densenet121 for feature extraction for both push and grasping tasks, and we believe that some calculations are unnecessary. Considering the strong correlation and high similarity between these two tasks, we thus propose to embed them into the same semantic space for simultaneous learning. Specifically, we have shared the backbone architectures of the FCN networks for both grasping and pushing tasks, following the multi-task learning paradigm. We utilize the data sharing across tasks for better learning the parameters for visual representation, physics, and robot-specific control. Moreover, due to layer sharing, we can reduce memory usage while avoiding duplicate computation of shared layer features, improving inference speed.

Task-specific Layers with ASPP. In a cluttered environment, different objects have different shapes and they have significant differences in scale, so the multiscale features should be considered in the network. Also pooling operations in DenseNet are prone to losing location and dense semantic information. To address these issues, we introduce the ASPP module in both GNET and PNET, which performs parallel sampling on the feature maps using dilated convolutions at multiple sampling rates. Each ASPP module consists of five parallel branches, which include one 1x1 convolution and three different dilated convolutions with 3x3 kernels at varying rates, as well as a global average pooling layer to incorporate global context information. The outputs from all the branches are concatenated along the channel dimension and then passed through a 1x1 convolutional layer to adjust the channels and obtain the final output feature map. For the spatial pooling pyramid, we employed depthwise dilated separable convolutions [10] with dilation rates of 6, 12, and 18, which have increasing receptive fields to better cover multi-scale object distributions (see Fig. 3).

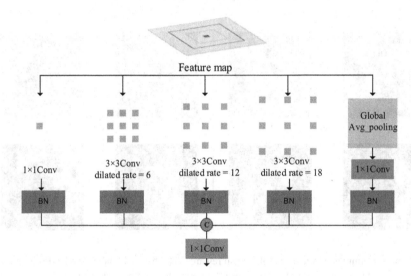

Fig. 3. The ASPP structure in GNET and PNET.

Integrating ASPP can expand the receptive field and fuse multi-scale features, thereby improving the performance of GNET and PNET from task-specific layers. This can effectively improve the problem of inaccurate grasp localization and missed detection of small objects in clutter and enhances the grasping success rate and action efficiency of the policy.

3.3 CCA Reward System

To better evaluate the quality of pushing actions in the pushing and grasping collaboration, we designed a novel reward function for pushing based on image morphology, in which the mechanism that pushing facilitates grasping is made explicit by encouraging pushing objects more discrete thus ensuring that the executed pushing actions effectively facilitate subsequent grasping during the collaboration.

We propose to utilize the connected component in the image to consider the stacking of objects in the scene and use the size of the minimum enclosing circle of each connected component to consider the dispersal degree of the stacked objects. In particular, we first binarize the image to separate objects from the background, and then apply median filtering to remove the noise. Next, a closing operation is performed on the binary image to eliminate small holes and connect narrow gaps that may exist. The purpose of this step is not only to further reduce noise but also to address situations where the distance between objects is smaller than the thickness of finger η for gripper and direct insertion is not feasible. Even if these objects are not tightly stacked together, they should also be considered as connected components since there is no space available for grasping. Finally, we perform connected component analysis on the image and find the minimum enclosing circle for each connected component (see Fig. 4).

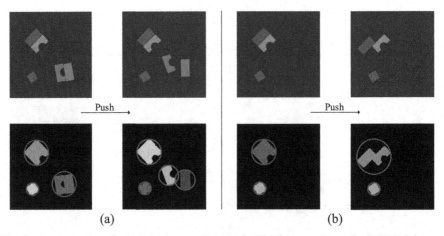

(a)   (b)

Fig. 4. Two examples of agent obtained push rewards. The first row shows the RGB heightmap, and the second row shows the visualizations after connected component analysis and finding the minimum enclosing circle, where regions with the same color represent connected components. In (a), the push action causes an increase in the number of connected components by separating clustered objects. In (b), it increases the grasp affordances. Both cases are advantageous for subsequent grasping.

If the agent selects a push action during training, we calculate the number of connected components in the images before and after pushing, denoted as C_{before} and C_{after} respectively, as well as the sum of the diameters of the minimum enclosing circles of all connected components in the images before and after pushing, denoted as Φ_{before} and Φ_{after}. If $C_{after} > C_{before}$, an increase in the number of connected components indicates that some objects have been separated from the original stacked cluster, which makes the arrangement more dispersed, and a positive reward is given to the agent. If $C_{after} = C_{before}$ and $\Phi_{after} > \Phi_{before}$, it indicates that the pushing action did not separate the clustered objects but still increased their dispersion, which also created more space for grasping, and a positive reward is given to the agent. If the push action only made detectable changes to the environment, we will give a small positive reward to the agent. Otherwise, it indicates that the push did not make contact with the object and we will give punishment to the agent. We have conducted multiple experiments and finally determined the value of the reward.

Finally, our grasp reward function and push reward function are defined as follows:

$$R(s_t, s_{t+1})_{push} = \begin{cases} 0.75 & if \ C_{after} > C_{before} \\ 0.5 & if \ C_{after} = C_{before} \& \Phi_{after} > \Phi_{before} \\ 0.25 & if \ change \ dected \\ -1 & else \end{cases} \tag{3}$$

$$R(s_t, s_{t+1})_{grasp} = \begin{cases} 1 & if \ success \\ -1 & if \ fail \end{cases} \tag{4}$$

3.4 Training Method

Our approach is based on self-supervised reinforcement learning, using Q-values generated by MTFCN as predicted values and expected rewards as label values. Since DQN is greedy and off-policy during exploration, it uses the action from the next state with the highest Q-value. The expected reward (i.e. target Q-function) at time t is:

$$Q_{target} = R(s_t, a_t) + \gamma \max_{a'} Q(s_{t+1}, a') \tag{5}$$

where $R(s_t, a_t)$ is the reward obtained according to the CCA reward system at time t. γ is the discount factor for future rewards, which is set to 0.5 in this work. $\max_{a'} Q\left(s_{t+1}, a'\right)$ Represents the maximum Q-value predicted for the next time step, where a' represents the set of all possible actions.

The loss function for both pushing and grasping tasks is identical. We employ the Huber loss function for backpropagation to train MTFCN after the agent executed each action:

$$loss = \begin{cases} \frac{1}{2} \times (Q(s_t, a_t) - Q_{target})^2 if \ |Q(s_t, a_t) - Q_{target}| < 1 \\ Q(s_t, a_t) - Q_{target})| - \frac{1}{2} otherwise \end{cases} \tag{6}$$

4 Experiments

4.1 Simulation Setup

The experimental workstation is equipped with an Intel Core i7-7700K CPU at 4.20GHz and NVIDIA 1080Ti for computing. We build a simulation environment for exploration in V-REP [28], including a UR5 robotic arm equipped with an RG2 gripper and an RGBD camera fixed on the table. MTFCN is trained by stochastic gradient descent with momentum, using fixed learning rates of 10^{-4}, momentum of 0.9, and weight decay 2^{-5}. We train with prioritized experience replay [29] using stochastic rank-based prioritization, our exploration strategy is ε-greedy [22], with ε initialized as 0.5 and then annealed over to 0.1 during training.

In the training phase, $n=10$ different toy blocks are randomly dropped into the $0.448^2 m^2$ workspace in front of the robot to construct one training task episode for self-supervised learning. The colors and shapes of which are randomly chosen. All other conditions (e.g. dynamics parameters, friction coefficients, etc.) during training are kept consistent with VPG [5]. The robot then performs data collection by trial-and-error, until the workspace is void of objects or 10 consecutive action attempts fail to complete the grasp, at which point the training task episode is reconstructed in the same way (see Fig. 5).

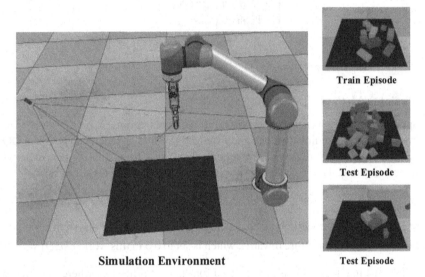

Train Episode

Test Episode

Simulation Environment   **Test Episode**

Fig. 5. Illustration of simulation setup and task episode in V-REP.

4.2 Evaluation Metrics

We primarily evaluate the performance of policy on the task of grasping and removing all objects in dense clutter using the following three metrics:

(1) Task Completion Rate: The sign of task episode completion is that all toy blocks in the workspace are grasped without failing consecutively for more than 10 attempts.
(2) Grasping Success Rate (GS): The average percentage of grasp success rate per completion.
(3) Action Efficiency (AE): The percentage of the number of objects in the test to the number of actions before completion. We hope that the agent can complete the task with as few actions as possible.

In all of above metrics, a higher value indicates better performance.

4.3 Results and Discussion

To evaluate the proposed approach, we compare CCA-MTFCN with three methods: Grasping-only method, VPG [5], ADQN-NS [6] and Ca-GPNet [7]. The Grasping-only method removes PNET from our proposed model and can only perform grasping actions while keeping other conditions constant. Therefore, GS is equivalent to AE for this method. Each test scenario in the simulation was run $N = 30$ times. Figure 6 shows the grasping performance of methods during the training, which is measured by the grasping success rate over the last $j = 300$ grasp attempts.

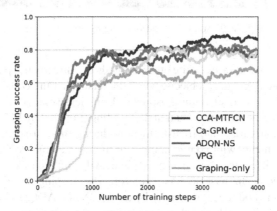

Fig. 6. Grasp success rate of CCA-MTFCN and other baselines during training.

Random Arrangements. In the random arrangements, $n = 30$ objects of random shapes and colors are placed in the workspace (see Fig. 5), which has the same setting as the training scenario except for n. This experiment is used to test the policy's generalization to more cluttered scenarios.

Challenging Arrangements. In the challenging arrangements, there are 8 challenging test cases which are shown in Fig. 7. All objects in each case are manually placed instead of being randomly generated. Objects are tightly stacked together in many of these test cases, resulting in little grasping space due to their positions and orientations, which means that the agent must use push actions to create grasping space for subsequent grasping. These configurations can reflect challenging picking scenarios of dense clutter and all of them remain exclusive from the training task episode. The Grasping-only method cannot perform pushing actions and thus, it is basically unable to complete these challenging scenarios, so we only compared our method with VPG, ADQN-NS, and Ca-GPNet.

Experimental Analysis. In both random and challenging arrangements, there are stacked objects that make grasping unfeasible. Table 1 shows that the grasping-only method performs the worst, with a grasping success rate of only 61.1%. We found that the grasping-only method requires plenty of grasping attempts to create grasp affordance

Fig. 7. Illustration of the challenging arrangements.

through collision in these cases, while other methods can directly use pushing actions to effectively separate aggregated objects, which indicates that the collaborative pushing and grasping method is effective for grasping tasks in dense clutter.

Benefiting from the stronger visual understanding provided by MTFCN, our model can perform more accurate and robust grasping during the test scenarios. Especially in random arrangements with a large number of multiscale objects, we found that our method can better detect feasible grasp points in heavily cluttered scenes, thus eliminating the need for redundant push actions. Therefore, the grasping success rate and action efficiency of our method are significantly better than VPG, ADQN-NS and Ca-GPNet as shown in Table 1. This indicates that considering multiscale features of the network is important in cluttered scenarios and is even more effective than incorporating attention mechanisms from ADQN-NS and Ca-GPNet.

Table 1. Results (%) on random arrangements.

Model	Completion	GS	AE
Grasping-only	86.6	61.1	61.1
VPG [5]	100	67.7	60.9
ADQN-NS [6]	96.7	71.6	66.2
Ca-GPNet [7]	100	73.3	71.4
CCA-MTFCN	**100**	**80.9**	**74.9**

Additionally, we found that our method is more capable to create more effective grasp points compared to other methods. In contrast, the sparse reward function in VPG and Ca-GPNet may cause the agent to push objects out of the workspace, sometimes leading to repeated pushing of an object that already has sufficient grasping space in pursuit of rewards, resulting in low task completion rates and action efficiency. This effect is more pronounced in challenging arrangements, as shown in Table 2.

All these reasons lead to our method outperforming other models across all evaluation metrics, demonstrating better generalization performance for more complex cluttered

Table 2. Results (%) on challenging arrangements.

Model	Completion	GS	AE
VPG [5]	82.9	74.2	62.6
ADQN-NS [6]	86.3	75.4	68.3
Ca-GPNet [7]	88.0	77.7	66.1
CCA-MTFCN	**98.8**	**81.0**	**71.7**

scenes. The task completion rate of our method reaches 100% and 98.8% in the two test scenarios, which shows that our method can effectively complete the task of object removal in dense clutter.

4.4 Ablation Study

To validate the effectiveness of our proposed MTFCN and CCA reward system, we conducted an ablation study. We take VPG [5] as the baseline which uses two parallel FCNs without ASPP and a sparse reward function, all other conditions remain the same. We then reconducted experiments in the challenging arrangements scenario, and the results are shown in Table 3.

We also set up a comparative experiment to investigate the effect of hard parameter sharing on the model. We replaced the shared layer in MTFCN with four Densenet121 (named as Non-sharing) without any parameter sharing and compared the floating point operations (FLOPs) and Parameters (Params) of the two models. FLOPs and Params respectively reflect the time complexity and space complexity of the model, and the lower the better. Experiments were then conducted in the challenging arrangements scenario, and the results are shown in Table 4. The results indicate that using hard parameter sharing reduces the size of model parameters while improving inference speed without significant performance loss.

Table 3. Results (%) of ablation studies for MTFCN and CCA reward system.

Model	Completion	GS	AE
baseline	82.9	76.7	62.6
baseline + MTFCN	90.0	79.5	65.2
baseline + CCA	95.1	77.6	68.9
baseline + MTFCN + CCA	**98.8**	**81.0**	**71.7**

Table 4. Results (%) of ablation studies for hard-parameter sharing.

Model	FLOPs	Params	Completion	GS	AE
Non-sharing	947.63G	34.17M	97.9	79.4	72.1
CCA-MTFCN	**474.81G**	**20.26M**	98.8	81.0	71.7

5 Conclusion

In this work, we proposed a method named CCA-MTFCN which can learn the efficient synergies between pushing and grasping in dense clutter via DQN. Specifically, a novel network MTFCN is designed to model the action-value function with the multi-scale feature fusion ASPP module and hard parameter sharing. Moreover, we introduce new metrics based on connected component analysis to better evaluate the quality of push actions in pushing and grasping collaboration and explicitly incorporate the promoting effect of push on grasp into the novel CCA reward system. The experimental results indicate that our approach outperforms the baselines in terms of all evaluation metrics, demonstrating good generalization ability and robustness. In the future, we will further test the generalization performance of our method in the real world and explore the impact of other sharing mechanisms on robotic pushing and grasping collaboration.

Acknowledgments. This work was supported by the National Key R&D Program of China (grant No.: 2022YFB4700400), National Natural Science Foundation of China (grant No.: 62073249).

References

1. Zeng, A., Song, S., Yu, K.-T., et al.: Robotic pick-and-place of novel objects in clutter with multi-affordance grasping and cross-domain image matching. Int. J. Robot. Res. 41(7), 690–705 (2022)
2. Du, G., Wang, K., Lian, S., et al.: Vision-based robotic grasping from object localization, object pose estimation to grasp estimation for parallel grippers: a review. Artif. Intell. Rev. 54(3), 1677–1734 (2021)
3. Mohammed, M.Q., Kwek, L.C., Chua, S.C., et al.: Review of learning-based robotic manipulation in cluttered environments. Sensors 22(20), 7938 (2022)
4. Dogar, M.R., Srinivasa, S.S.: A planning framework for non-prehensile manipulation under clutter and uncertainty. Auton. Robot. 33, 217–236 (2012)
5. Zeng, A., Song, S., Welker, S., et al.: Learning synergies between pushing and grasping with self-supervised deep reinforcement learning. In: 2018 IEEE/RSJ International Conference on Intelligent Robots and Systems (IROS), pp. 4238–4245. IEEE (2018)
6. Yang, Z., Shang, H.: Robotic pushing and grasping knowledge learning via attention deep Q-learning network. In: Li, G., Shen, H., Yuan, Y., Wang, X., Liu, H., Zhao, X. (eds.) Knowledge Science, Engineering and Management. KSEM 2020. LNCS, vol. 12274. Springer, Cham (2020). https://doi.org/10.1007/978-3-030-55130-8_20
7. Zhao, M., Zuo, G., Huang, G.: Collaborative learning of deep reinforcement pushing and grasping based on coordinate attention in clutter. In: 2022 International Conference on Virtual Reality, Human-Computer Interaction and Artificial Intelligence (VRHCIAI), pp. 156–161. IEEE (2022)

8. Sarantopoulos, I., Kiatos, M., Doulgeri, Z., et al.: Split deep Q-learning for robust object singulation. In: 2020 IEEE International Conference on Robotics and Automation (ICRA), pp. 6225–6231. IEEE (2020)

9. Crawshaw, M.: Multi-task learning with deep neural networks: a survey. arXiv preprint arXiv: 2009.09796 (2020)

10. Chen, L.C., Zhu, Y., Papandreou, G., et al.: Encoder-decoder with atrous separable convolution for semantic image segmentation. In: Ferrari, V., Hebert, M., Sminchisescu, C., Weiss, Y. (eds.) Computer Vision – ECCV 2018. ECCV 2018. LNCS, vol. 11211. Springer, Cham (2018). https://doi.org/10.1007/978-3-030-01234-2_49

11. Kleeberger, K., Bormann, R., Kraus, W., et al.: A survey on learning-based robotic grasping. Curr. Robot. Rep. **1**, 239–249 (2020)

12. Sahbani, A., El-Khoury, S., Bidaud, P.: An overview of 3D object grasp synthesis algorithms. Robot. Auton. Syst. **60**(3), 326–336 (2012)

13. Dong, Z., Liu, S., Zhou, T., et al.: PPR-Net: point-wise pose regression network for instance segmentation and 6D pose estimation in bin-picking scenarios. In: 2019 IEEE/RSJ International Conference on Intelligent Robots and Systems (IROS), pp. 1773–1780. IEEE (2019)

14. Qi, C.R., Yi, L., Su, H., et al.: Pointnet++: deep hierarchical feature learning on point sets in a metric space. In: Advances in Neural Information Processing Systems 30 (2017)

15. Li, H., Qu, X., Ye, B.: Six-degree-of-freedom robot grasping based on three-dimensional point cloud features of unknown objects. Control Theory Appl. **39**(06), 1103–1111 (2022)

16. Kumra, S., Joshi, S., Sahin, F.: Antipodal robotic grasping using generative residual convolutional neural network. In: 2020 IEEE/RSJ International Conference on Intelligent Robots and Systems (IROS), pp. 9626–9633. IEEE (2020)

17. Wang, S., Zhou, Z., Kan, Z.: When transformer meets robotic grasping: exploits context for efficient grasp detection. IEEE Robot. Autom. Lett. **7**(3), 8170–8177 (2022)

18. Dosovitskiy, A., Beyer, L., Kolesnikov, A., et al.: An image is worth 16x16 words: transformers for image recognition at scale. arXiv preprint arXiv:2010.11929 (2020)

19. Kalashnikov, D., Irpan, A., Pastor, P., et al.: QT-Opt: scalable deep reinforcement learning for vision-based robotic manipulation. arXiv preprint arXiv:1806.10293 (2018)

20. Quillen, D., Jang, E., Nachum, O., et al.: Deep reinforcement learning for vision-based robotic grasping: a simulated comparative evaluation of off-policy methods. In: 2018 IEEE International Conference on Robotics and Automation (ICRA), pp. 6284–6291. IEEE (2018)

21. Breyer, M., Furrer, F., Novkovic, T., et al.: Comparing task simplifications to learn closed-loop object picking using deep reinforcement learning. IEEE Robot. Autom. Lett. **4**(2), 1549–1556 (2019)

22. Mnih, V., Kavukcuoglu, K., Silver, D., et al.: Playing atari with deep reinforcement learning. arXiv preprint arXiv:1312.5602 (2013)

23. Gupta, M., Sukhatme, G.S.: Using manipulation primitives for brick sorting in clutter. In: 2012 IEEE International Conference on Robotics and Automation, pp. 3883–3889. IEEE (2012)

24. Liang, H., Lou, X., Yang, Y., et al.: Learning visual affordances with target-orientated deep Q-network to grasp objects by harnessing environmental fixtures. In: 2021 IEEE International Conference on Robotics and Automation (ICRA), pp. 2562–2568. IEEE (2021)

25. Long, J., Shelhamer, E., Darrell, T.: Fully convolutional networks for semantic segmentation. In: Proceedings of the IEEE Conference on Computer Vision and Pattern Recognition, pp. 3431–3440 (2015)

26. Huang, G., Liu, Z., Van Der Maaten L., et al.: Densely connected convolutional networks. In: Proceedings of the IEEE Conference on Computer Vision and Pattern Recognition, pp. 4700–4708 (2017)

27. Sifre, L., Mallat S.: Rigid-motion scattering for texture classification. arXiv preprint arXiv: 1403.1687 (2014)
28. Rohmer, E., Singh, S.P.N., Freese, M.: V-REP: a versatile and scalable robot simulation framework. In: 2013 IEEE/RSJ International Conference on Intelligent Robots and Systems, pp. 1321–1326. IEEE (2013)
29. Schaul, T., Quan, J., Antonoglou, I., et al.: Prioritized experience replay. arXiv preprint arXiv: 1511.05952 (2015)

6-DoF Grasp Planning on Point Cloud for Human-to-Robot Handover Task

Chunfang Liu$^{(\boxtimes)}$, Weifan Wang, Ruitian Pang, Chenxin Li, and Yan Shang

Faculty of Information and Technology, Beijing University of Technology, Beijing, China
cfliu1985@bjut.edu.cn, wangweifan@emails.bjut.edu.cn

Abstract. Human-to-robot handover is a key task in the human-robot collaboration. However, the diversity in object shapes and poses makes it extremely challenging for robots to ensure safe and successful grasping. To overcome these challenges, we present a method for generating 6-Degree-of-Freedom (6-DoF) grasp poses for human-to-robot handover tasks. The method performs grasp planning on 3D point cloud, which mainly consists of two stages: scene understanding and 6-DoF grasp pose prediction. In the first stage, for safe interaction, the Faster R-CNN model is utilized for accurate detection of hand and object positions. Then, by combining with segmentation and noise filtering, the safe handover points on objects can be extracted. In the second stage, a 6-DoF grasp planning model is built based on GraspNet for handover tasks. The experiments evaluate the developed model by performing grasp planning on several objects with different poses in the handover scenes. The results show that the proposed method not only predicts secure 6-DoF grasp postures for handover tasks, but also be capability to generalize to novel objects with diverse shapes and sizes.

Keywords: Handovers · 6-DoF grasp planning · Human-robot interaction

1 Introduction

Object handover is a typical collaborative manipulation task, which comes naturally to people. In contrast, it is challenging for robot systems to execute handovers as smoothly and safely as humans do. This disparity can be attributed to differences in the level of perception, uncertainty handling, and responsiveness to previously unseen situations between humans and robots [1].

The topic of object handovers between humans and robots is an active area of research thanks to the interest in collaborative robots [2]. Human-to-robot handover (H2R) can not only assist patients or disabled individuals in delivering items but delegate dangerous or tedious tasks to robots, thereby enhancing workplace safety and efficiency [3]. Successful handover possesses two crucial attributes: safety and generalizability. In terms of safety, the robot must avoid making contact with the human hand to prevent potential harm [4]. The second attribute is generalizability, where the robot should be capable of performing handovers for any physically graspable object.

F. Sun et al. (Eds.): ICCSIP 2023, CCIS 1918, pp. 73–86, 2024.
https://doi.org/10.1007/978-981-99-8018-5_6

In recent years, significant progress has been made in the field of human-robot handovers. [5] presents a vision-based system for reactive human-to-robot handovers of unknown objects. It employs real-time grasp generation and a closed-loop motion planning algorithm to ensure reactive and smooth robot motion. Similarly, [6] proposes a dynamic switching method that enables the robot to continue tracking the object by maintaining its end effector close to potential pre-grasp positions throughout the object's motion. [7] proposes a framework for learning control policies for vision-based human-to-robot handovers, utilizing a novel mixed approach that combines imitation learning (IL) and reinforcement learning (RL). [8] presents an approach for safe and object-independent human-to-robot handovers using real time robotic vision and manipulation. This approach utilizes a modified Generative Grasping Convolutional Neural Network (GG-CNN) [9] to generate grasps during object handover. However, due to the limited information from images, it is only suitable for grasping from a single direction. Compared to the pixel information from images, point cloud representation provides richer 3D information for 6D grasping and enables better generalization to different objects.

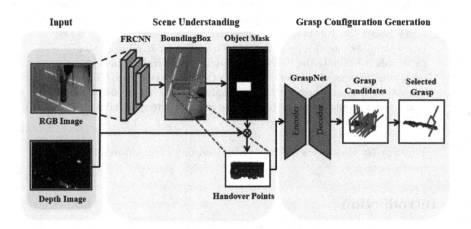

Fig. 1. The overview of our proposed method.

In this paper, we propose a method for generating 6-DoF grasp planning in the context of human-to-robot handover tasks (Fig. 1). This approach takes RGB image and depth images as input. Then, in order to realize safety interaction, a Faster R-CNN model is employed to accurately detect both hands and objects within the handover scene. Meanwhile, by combining with segmentation algorithms and filtering techniques, candidate handover point clouds are extracted. Furthermore, we build a 6-DoF grasp planning model based on Grasp-Net, an end-to-end 6D grasp pose planning network, which effectively predicts grasp posture on the extracted handover points. Our proposed method offers two key advantages. Firstly, it facilitates secure grasping for human-robot handover tasks. Secondly, it performs to generate viable 6-DoF grasp poses from single-view point cloud and has good generalization capability for diverse shapes and sizes of new objects. The experimental results for handing over different objects verify the effectiveness of the proposed method for real-timely planning the suitable 6-DoF grasp postures for human-robot handover tasks.

2 Related Work

Human-robot handover is one of the fundamental challenges in the field of human-robot collaboration. This section focuses on two essential challenges encountered in H2R handovers: object perception and grasp planning.

2.1 Object Detection

Object detection networks are commonly applied to locate objects for perceiving the objects involved. The Region-based Convolutional Neural Network (R-CNN) was introduced in [10] for object detection. Building upon R-CNN, [11] proposed the Fast R-CNN detector, while [12] presented the Faster R-CNN detector, which was the first end-to-end and near real-time deep learning detector. YOLO [13] emerged as the first one-stage detector in the deep learning era. In [8], YOLO V3 [14] trained on the COCO dataset was employed for object detection in the context of handover. [15] applies object detection to simultaneously recognize objects and hands.

2.2 Grasp Planner

Detecting a graspable rectangle based on RGB-D images input has gained popularity in the field [16–18]. Nevertheless, the grasp poses generated by these methods are constrained in 2D plane which limits the degree of freedom of grasp poses. In contrast, point cloud-based 6D grasp planning is not restricted by the direction of the grasp, offering greater flexibility and freedom in generating grasp poses.

The methods for generating grasp configurations on object point clouds can be divided into model-based and learning-based. Model-based approaches [19–21] require 3D models of objects to generate grasp planning, thus they cannot handle unseen objects. However, in real-world application scenarios, objects are often partially occluded and not fully observable, especially due to occlusions caused by human hands. Recently, researchers have made efforts to tackle the issue by employing learning-based methods, which infers grasping strategies from partially observed objects. In clutters, [22–24] predict 6/7-DoF grasp configurations on single-view RGB-D images or point cloud. Furthermore, these approaches exhibit robust generalization to different environments and objects.

The rest of this paper is organized as follows. Section 3 describes the proposed method. Experimental evaluation is shown in Sect. 4. The conclusions and future work are summarized in Sect. 5.

3   Proposed Method

In this section, we provide a detailed description of our approach for generating safety-oriented 6-DoF grasp poses during handover interactions. As illustrated in Fig. 1, our method consists of three main components: Input, Scene Understanding, and Grasp Configuration Generation. The Input component accepts RGB-D images captured by a camera as its input. The Scene Understanding component focuses on accurately extracting handover points from the input images. On the other hand, the Grasp Configuration Generation component directly predicts a set of 6-DoF grasp candidates based on the input handover point cloud and outputs the most feasible grasp pose.

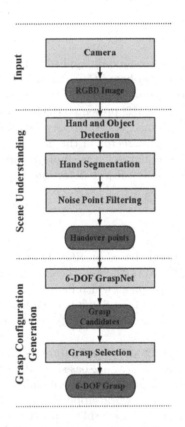

Fig. 2. The modular flowchart of the method.

The modular flowchart of the method, as shown in Fig. 2, consists of six modules. It begins with the Input module, which captures the handover scene using a RGB-D camera. The Hand and Object Detection module ensures precise recognition of relevant entities within the scene. The Hand Segmentation module outputs pixel-level masks, filtering out potential grasping points belonging to the user's hand. The handover points are processed and selected by the Noise Point Filtering module, with noise and irrelevant points being removed to ensure the accuracy of the handover points. The 6-DoF GraspNet module predicts grasp quality estimation, grasp pose, grasp depth and grasp width information for the handover points. To ensure the feasibility of execution, the Grasp Selection module is used to filter out unviable grasp poses. All modules are executed in sequence.

3.1 Scene Understanding

In this subsection, we present the modules utilized in the Scene Understanding component. Scene Understanding plays a important role in ensuring the safety of grasp planning. Its primary objective is to accurately perceive and understand the scene, enabling informed decision-making for grasp planning.

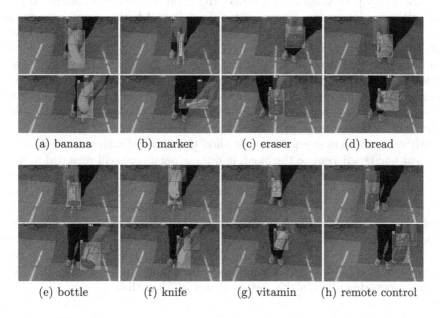

| (a) banana | (b) marker | (c) eraser | (d) bread |

| (e) bottle | (f) knife | (g) vitamin | (h) remote control |

Fig. 3. Recognition performance of hand and object detection.

Hand and Object Detection

This module is employed to locate the pixel coordinates of the human giver's hand and held objects, providing a prerequisite for accurate hand segmentation. We employ the hand-object detection method proposed in [25], which was trained on the 100 Days of Hands (100DOH) dataset, a new large-scale hand video interaction dataset. The method is constructed based on the widely adopted Faster-RCNN [12] (FRCNN) framework, which is a standard object detection system in the field. It takes RGB images as input and outputs bounding boxes for the detected hands and objects in the image. In addition, it predicts hand side $s \in \mathbb{R}^2$, contact state $c \in \mathbb{R}^5$ and correlation vectors that capture the contact relationship between the hand and the object via additional fully connected layers. The outputs represent the hand side (right/left), the contact state (portable/non-portable/self/other/none), the hand and object boxes, as well as the vectors that connect the hand to the object boxes.

Our selection of this model is based on its superior performance in simultaneously detecting hands and unseen objects. As illustrated in Fig. 3, the model demonstrates excellent robustness, regardless of variations in hand size and object shape.

Hand Segmentation

When the point clouds of both the object and the hand are simultaneously fed into the grasp pose generation module, the hand itself is also considered as a potential grasping region. To guarantee the safety of human hands during the handover process, the segmentation of the hand is essential. In [5], a full convolutional network is introduced, which generates a binary segmentation mask indicating whether each pixel belongs to the hand or the background. Nevertheless, the upsampling layers in this network contribute to an unsatisfactory inference speed. [15] proposed the utilization of the YCbCr color space [26] for skin detection. However, significant performance fluctuations in skin detection arise from variations in lighting conditions.

Although the skin segmentation method has shown effectiveness, it does not segment points adjacent to the hand, and these points are still regarded as non-graspable points. Instead of employing a skin detection algorithm, we directly utilize the hand bounding box and the object bounding box to segment the hand and adjacent points. The area inside the object bounding box is considered graspable, but if there is an overlap with the hand bounding box, that overlapping region is deemed non-graspable. Moreover, the area inside the hand bounding box is also considered non-graspable. This method enables the generation of a graspable region mask, which is simple and computationally efficient. The algorithm process described in this part is shown in Algorithm 1.

Noise Point Filtering

The Noise Point Filtering module is employed to address the presence of noise in the point cloud generated from the graspable region mask, which includes background points and outliers. The presence of such noise can significantly impact the accuracy of grasp prediction. To mitigate this, a two-step approach is adopted. Firstly, the Random Sample Consensus(RANSAC) [27] algorithms is utilized to segment the plane and effectively filter out the background points in the point cloud. Subsequently, a statistical filtering technique is applied to eliminate obvious outliers. By implementing these steps, the module achieves the objective of obtaining more accurate handover points, thereby enhancing the overall precision.

Algorithm 1. The generation of a graspable region mask

Input: hand bounding box top-left point (hx_1, hy_1), and the bottom-right point (hx_2, hy_2), object bounding box top-left point (ox_1, oy_1), and the bottom-right point (ox_2, oy_2).

Output: *mask* represents an array with the pixel dimensions of an image.

1: **for** $i = 0 \rightarrow row$ **do** //*row* refers to the number of rows in an *mask*
2:     **for** $j = 0 \rightarrow clos$ **do** //*clos* refers to the number of clos in an *mask*
3:         **if** $(oy_1 <= i <= oy_2) and (ox_1 <= j <= ox_2)$ **then**
4:             **if** $hy_1 <= i <= hy_2$ **then**
5:                 $mask[i][j] = 0$ //The grayscale value is set to 0.
6:             **else**
7:                 $mask[i][j] = 255$ //The grayscale value is set to 255.
8:             **end if**
9:         **else**
10:             $mask[i][j] = 0$
11:         **end if**
12:     **end for**
13: **end for**
14: **return** *mask*

3.2   Grasp Configuration Generation

In this subsection, we introduce the modules employed in the Grasp Configuration Generation component. Grasp Configuration Generation plays a crucial role in achieving 6-DoF grasp planning. Its primary objective is to generate suitable grasp configurations that are specifically tailored to the requirements of handover tasks.

6-DoF GraspNet

GraspNet [22] is a learning-based framework that can generate a set of diverse 6-DoF grasps given a partial point cloud of an object. It was trained on the GraspNet-1Billion grasp dataset [22], which contains 97,280 RGB-D images with over one billion grasp poses. In this paper, the objective is to make predictions about the orientation and translation of the parallel gripper in the camera frame, as well as the width and depth of the gripper. However, due to the explicit constraint issues associated with rotation matrices, it becomes difficult for neural networks to effectively learn. As a solution, GraspNet tackles this challenge by decoupling the orientation into two components: viewpoint classification and in-plane rotation prediction. The 6-DoF grasp poses defined by GraspNet are illustrated in Fig. 4.

GraspNet mainly consists of three components: Approach Network, Operation Network, and Tolerance Network. Approach Network is used to estimate the approach vector and feasible grasp points. It adopts the PointNet++ [28] backbone network, taking an original point cloud as input. For M points, the output of the network is $M \times (2 + V)$, where 2 represents the binary classes indicating graspable or non-graspable, and V represents the number of predefined

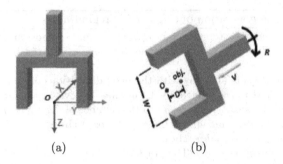

(a)   (b)

Fig. 4. (a) The reference frame of the gripper. (b) The representation of grasp pose. *obj* denotes object point. D denotes the approaching distance from grasp point to the origin of gripper frame. W denotes the gripper width. V denotes the approaching vector. R denotes denotesthe in-plane rotation around approaching axis.

approach vectors. The loss function of the Approach Network is defined as (1):

$$L^A\left(\{c_i\},\{s_{ij}\}\right) = \frac{1}{N_{cls}}\sum_i L_{cls}\left(c_i, c_i^*\right)$$

$$+ \lambda_1 \frac{1}{N_{reg}}\sum_i\sum_j c_i^* \mathbf{1}\left(\left|v_{ij}, v_{ij}^*\right| < 5°\right) L_{reg}\left(s_{ij}, s_{ij}^*\right) \quad (1)$$

Here, c_i denotes the binary prediction of whether point i is graspable or not. s_{ij} denotes the predicted confidence score for viewpoint j for point i . v_{ij} denotes the approximate vector prediction of the jth virtual view for graspable point i. $\left|v_{ij}, v_{ij}^*\right|$ denotes the angular difference, which is the loss term in the first indicator function $\mathbf{1}()$ that constrains the loss of the approximation vector. L_{cls} denotes a two class softmax loss, while L_{reg} denotes the smooth L_1 loss.

Operation Network further predicts in-plane rotation, approaching distance, gripper width and grasp confidence. The loss function of the Operation Network is defined as (2):

$$L_R\left(R_{ij}, S_{ij}, W_{ij}\right) = \sum_{d=1}^{K}\left(\frac{1}{N_{cls}}\sum_{ij}L_{cls}^d\left(R_{ij}, R_{ij}^*\right) + \lambda_2\frac{1}{N_{reg}}\sum_{ij}L_{reg}^d\left(S_{ij}, S_{ij}^*\right)\right.$$

$$\left. + \lambda_3\frac{1}{N_{reg}}\sum_{ij}L_{reg}^d\left(W_{ij}, W_{ij}^*\right)\right) \quad (2)$$

where R_{ij} represents the binned rotational angle, ranging from 0 to 180°. S_{ij}, W_{ij}, and d represent the grasp confidence score, grasp width, and approach distance respectively. L^d means loss for the dth binned distance. The sigmoid cross-entropy loss function is used to handle the multi-class binary classification of L_{cls}.

Tolerance Network proposes a representation called grasp affinity fields(GAFs) to predict the tolerance of each grasp pose to disturbances. Given a ground truth grasp pose, the Tolerance Network searches its neighbors in the sphere space to see the farthest distance where the grasp score $s > 0.5$, indicating that the grasp is still reliable, and sets it as the target for the GAFs. The loss function of the Tolerance Network is defined as (3):

$$L^F(A_{ij}) = \frac{1}{N_{reg}} \sum_{d=1}^{K} \sum_{ij} L_{reg}^d \left(T_{ij}, T_{ij}^* \right) \tag{3}$$

where T_{ij} denotes the maximum perturbation that the grasp pose can resist.

During training, the parameters of GraspNet are optimized by minimizing (4):

$$L = L^A \left(\{c_i\}, \{s_{ij}\} \right) + \alpha L^R \left(R_{ij}, S_{ij}, W_{ij} \right) + \beta L^F \left(T_{ij} \right) \tag{4}$$

We have adopted GraspNet as the grasp planner for our method, owing to its model-free nature and its capacity to generate robust grasp plans even for unfamiliar objects. Nonetheless, it is important to mention that the original GraspNet was primarily designed for grasping objects placed on tabletop surfaces. To adapt GraspNet for generating grasps on arbitrary objects using the hand, it becomes imperative to acquire the segmented point cloud specifically corresponding to the target object. The 6-DoF GraspNet takes the handover points as input and computes a candidate set as shown in Fig. 5.

Fig. 5. The grasp set predicted by GraspNet based on point cloud.

Grasp Selection

Despite GraspNet estimates a score for each predicted grasp to measure grasp stability, not all generated stable grasps are feasible for execution by the robot. In addition, although we have applied noise filtering techniques to the point cloud data, certain candidate grasp poses deviate from the underlying distribution of the object's point cloud. A common characteristic among these poses is the presence of abnormally large z-values for their respective center points. In order to deal with this issue, we have introduced a filtering mechanism based on the z-values of the grasp configurations, employing a threshold of 0.6m. Grasp configurations exceeding this threshold are discarded. This refined approach effectively addresses the aforementioned challenge.

Moreover, while hand segmentation helps to some extent in predicting grasp planning only on the object, there can be instances where the approach direction of the grasp planning aligns with the direction in which the person is handing over the object. For the safety of the handover process, we calculate the angle between the approach direction of the grasp and the y-axis and any grasps that have an angle exceeding $105°$ are discarded. Finally, the remaining grasp candidates are ranked based on their confidence scores, and the grasp with the highest score is selected for execution by the robot.

4 Experiments

4.1 Experimental Preparation

For this work, we demonstrate the process of data collection by simulating a handover scenario. The scenario involves an experimenter positioned in front of the robot, transferring an object to it. Concurrently, RGB-D images are captured by a camera throughout the handover process (Fig. 6(a)). In particular, the experimental setup includes a RM75-B robot arm affixed mounted on a rail system, providing $7°$ of freedom and a maximum reach of 610 mm. The robot's end effector is equipped with an Intel RealSense D435 RGB-D camera, which has a resolution of 1280×720 at 30 fps. To collect data, the robot starts from a predefined home pose that is carefully positioned to ensure both the human interaction partner and the object are within the camera's field of view.

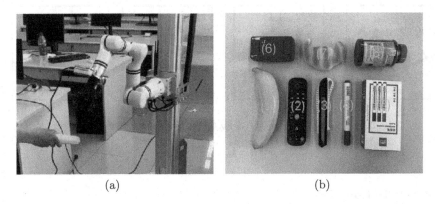

(a)   (b)

Fig. 6. (a) The assumed handover scenario during data collection. (b) Test objects: (1) banana, (2) remote control, (3) knife, (4) marker, (5) pen case, (6) eraser, (7) bread, (8) bottle.

The objective of the experiment is to accurately predict the pose of objects provided by human givers. A set of 8 test objects was chosen (shown in Fig. 6(b)), consisting of items from the YCB object set [29] as well as unseen items compatible with the robot gripper. Each object is consecutively handed over by the user for a total of 10 times, allowing the user to adjust their handover behavior accordingly.

4.2   Experimental Results

We evaluate the grasp poses based on the outputs provided by the Grasp Selection module. The results of the experiment can be categorized into two scenarios: planning success and planning failure. The successful handover prediction refers to the ability of our method to generate a safe and feasible grasp plan for objects held in the human hand. Conversely, it is considered a failure if the grasp pose does not meet these criteria. An experimental observer labeled the result of each trial.

Table 1. Grasp prediction experiment outcomes, in times. Each object was handed 10 times.

	Banana	Eraser	Marker	Bottle	Bread	Pen case	Remote control	knife
Planning Success	9	8	6	9	6	7	9	8
Planning Failure	1	2	4	1	4	3	1	2

Fig. 7. The scenarios of handovers with different objects.

According to the data presented in Table 1, the frequency of successful grasp predictions was higher for objects such as banana, bottle, and remote control, whereas marker and bread exhibited comparatively lower rates of success. Based on the experiments, it was observed that cylindrical or elongated objects such as the banana and knife, retained a larger quantity of high-quality point cloud after hand segmentation, resulting in a higher success rate of grasp predictions. In comparison, the smaller objects, like bread, had fewer points in the point cloud after segmentation, leading to a lower success rate. Hence, the failure can be ascribed to the constrained availability of point cloud data, thereby impeding the generation of appropriate grasp configurations through the 6-DoF GraspNet module. Furthermore, the excessive occlusion of the object by the hand and the inherent variations in the object's pose during the handover process can further contribute to a diminished quantity of point cloud acquired by the camera. Figure 7 shows the scenarios of handovers with different objects, serving as the input for our proposed method. Figure 8 illustrates the predicted viable grasp poses based on point cloud in the corresponding handover scenarios.

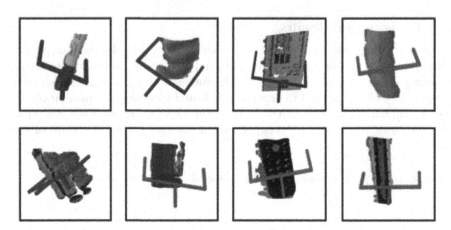

Fig. 8. The predicted viable grasp poses based on point cloud in the corresponding handover scenarios.

5 Conclusions

In this paper, we present a method for generating 6-DoF grasp planning in the context of human-robot handover tasks. The method takes camera-captured images to accomplish hand-object detection, segmentation, target point extraction, and precise grasp proposal prediction, facilitating the planning of 6-DoF grasps for handover scenarios. Through conducting 80 grasp prediction experiments on 8 different objects, we have demonstrated the safety and effectiveness of our proposed method, even when applied to previously unseen objects.

Future work spans two directions: (1) The grasp planner should generate more optimal grasp plans for objects, thereby enhancing the efficiency and effectiveness of downstream operational tasks. (2) We can integrate the proposed method with a trajectory planning algorithm to enable accurate and smooth object transfer on the robotic arm.

Acknowledgement. The work was jointly supported by Beijing Natural Science Foundation (4212933), Scientific Research Project of Beijing Educational Committee (KM202110005023) and National Natural Science Foundation of China (62273012).

References

1. Ortenzi, V., et al.: Robotic manipulation and the role of the task in the metric of success. Nat. Mach. Intell. 340–346 (2019)
2. Ajoudani, A., et al.: Progress and prospects of the human-robot collaboration. Auton. Robot. 957–975 (2018)
3. Edsinger, A., Kemp, C.C.: Human-robot interaction for cooperative manipulation: handing objects to one another. In: RO-MAN 2007 - The 16th IEEE International Symposium on Robot and Human Interactive Communication (2007)

4. Salem, M., Lakatos, G., Amirabdollahian, F., Dautenhahn, K.: Would you trust a (faulty) robot?: effects of error, task type and personality on human-robot cooperation and trust. In: Proceedings of the Tenth Annual ACM/IEEE International Conference on Human-Robot Interaction (2015)
5. Yang, W., Paxton, C., Mousavian, A., Chao, Y.-W., Cakmak, M., Fox, D.: Reactive human-to-robot handovers of arbitrary objects. In: 2021 IEEE International Conference on Robotics and Automation (ICRA) (2021)
6. Marturi, N., et al.: Dynamic grasp and trajectory planning for moving objects. Auton. Robot. **43**(5), 1241–1256 (2019)
7. Christen, S., Yang, W., Pérez-D'Arpino, C., Hilliges, O., Fox, D., Chao, Y.-W.: Learning human-to-robot handovers from point clouds. In: Proceedings of the IEEE/CVF Conference on Computer Vision and Pattern Recognition (CVPR) (2023)
8. Rosenberger, P., et al.: Object-independent human-to-robot handovers using real time robotic vision. IEEE Robot. Autom. Lett. 17–23 (2021)
9. Morrison, D., Leitner, J., Corke, P.: Closing the loop for robotic grasping: a real-time, generative grasp synthesis approach. In: Robotics Science and Systems XIV (2018)
10. Girshick, R., Donahue, J., Darrell, T., Malik, J.: Region-based convolutional networks for accurate object detection and segmentation. IEEE Trans. Pattern Anal. Mach. Intell. **38**, 142–158 (2016)
11. Girshick, R.: Fast R-CNN. In: 2015 IEEE International Conference on Computer Vision (ICCV) (2015)
12. Ren, S., He, K., Girshick, R., Sun, J.: Faster R-CNN: towards real-time object detection with region proposal networks. IEEE Trans. Pattern Anal. Mach. Intell. 1137–1149 (2017)
13. Redmon, J., Divvala, S., Girshick, R., Farhadi, A.: You only look once: unified, real-time object detection. In: 2016 IEEE Conference on Computer Vision and Pattern Recognition (CVPR) (2016)
14. Redmon, J., Farhadi, A.: Yolov3: an incremental improvement. arXiv: Computer Vision and Pattern Recognition (2018)
15. Duan, H., Wang, P., Li, Y., Li, D., Wei, W.: Learning human-to-robot dexterous handovers for anthropomorphic hand. IEEE Trans. Cogn. Dev. Syst. 1–1 (2022)
16. Mahler, J., et al.: Dex-net 2.0: deep learning to plan robust grasps with synthetic point clouds and analytic grasp metrics. In: Robotics: Science and Systems XIII (2017)
17. Zhang, H., Lan, X., Bai, S., Zhou, X., Tian, Z., Zheng, N.: Roi-based robotic grasp detection for object overlapping scenes. In: 2019 IEEE/RSJ International Conference on Intelligent Robots and Systems (IROS) (2019)
18. Chu, F.-J., Xu, R., Vela, P.A.: Real-world multiobject, multigrasp detection. IEEE Robot. Autom. Lett. 3355–3362 (2018)
19. Bicchi, A., Kumar, V.: Robotic grasping and contact: a review. In: Proceedings 2000 ICRA. Millennium Conference. IEEE International Conference on Robotics and Automation. Symposia Proceedings (Cat. No.00CH37065) (2002)
20. Bohg, J., Morales, A., Asfour, T., Kragic, D.: Data-driven grasp synthesis-a survey. IEEE Trans. Robot. 289–309 (2014)
21. Miller, M., Allen, A.: Graspit! a versatile simulator for robotic grasping (2004)
22. Fang, H.-S., Wang, C., Gou, M., Lu, C.: Graspnet-1billion: a large-scale benchmark for general object grasping. In: 2020 IEEE/CVF Conference on Computer Vision and Pattern Recognition (CVPR) (2020)

23. Gou, M., Fang, H.-S., Zhu, Z., Xu, S., Wang, C., Lu, C.: RGB matters: learning 7-dof grasp poses on monocular RGBD images. In: 2021 IEEE International Conference on Robotics and Automation (ICRA) (2021)
24. Wang, C., Fang, H.-S., Gou, M., Fang, H., Gao, J., Lu, C.: Graspness discovery in clutters for fast and accurate grasp detection
25. Shan, D., Geng, J., Shu, M., Fouhey, D.F.: Understanding human hands in contact at internet scale. In: 2020 IEEE/CVF Conference on Computer Vision and Pattern Recognition (CVPR) (2020)
26. Garcia, C., Tziritas, G.: Face detection using quantized skin color regions merging and wavelet packet analysis. IEEE Trans. Multimedia 264–277 (1999)
27. Fischler, M.A., Bolles, R.C.: Random sample consensus: a paradigm for model fitting with applications to image analysis and automated cartography. Commun. ACM 381–395 (1981)
28. Qi, C.R., Yi, L., Su, H., Guibas, L.J.: Pointnet++: deep hierarchical feature learning on point sets in a metric space. arXiv preprint arXiv:1706.02413 (2017)
29. Calli, B., Walsman, A., Singh, A., Srinivasa, S., Abbeel, P., Dollar, A.M.: Benchmarking in manipulation research: using the yale-cmu-berkeley object and model set. IEEE Robot. Autom. Mag. **22**(3), 36–52 (2015)

Leg Detection for Socially Assistive Robots: Differentiating Multiple Targets with 2D LiDAR

Hanchen Yao[1,2,3] (ID), Jianwei Peng[1,2,3] (ID), Zhelin Liao[2,3] (ID), Ran Zhao[4] (ID), and Houde Dai[1,2,3(✉)] (ID)

[1] Fujian College, University of Chinese Academy of Sciences, Jinjiang 362216, China
{yaohanchen21,pengjianwei20}@mails.ucas.ac.cn
[2] Fujian Institute of Research on the Structure of Matter, Chinese Academy of Sciences, Fuzhou 350002, China
dhd@fjirsm.ac.cn
[3] Quanzhou Institute of Equipment Manufacturing, Haixi Institutes, Chinese Academy of Sciences, Jinjiang 362216, China
3211239023@fafu.edu.cn
[4] Zhongyuan-Petersburg Aviation College, Zhongyuan University of Technology, Zhengzhou 451191, China
zhaoran@zut.edu.cn

Abstract. While socially assistive robots working in environments with a lot of people walking and obstructions, LiDAR-based detectors may have trouble locating the target person. The lack of identifying information is a drawback of the 2D range data obtained by a LiDAR sensor. Consequently, when applying the traditional technique of clustering 2D laser dots with geometric properties, modern LiDAR-based leg detectors typically fail. To recognize and identify the target individual in real time, an improved leg detector based on density-weighted support vector data description (DW-SVDD) is presented. The suggested DW-SVDD leg detector in this study incorporates density weight, width, and girth features into the support vector data description. Socially assistive robots that follow humans may quickly and accurately identify items from vast quantities of 2D laser point data with this detector. To evaluate detection accuracy, the proposed leg detector is tested on a mobile robot both indoors and outdoors. Field experiment results show that the proposed DW-SVDD leg detector enables socially assistive robots to detect partial occlusions and similar obstacles effectively. Additionally, the results indicate that the proposed leg detector achieves an MOTA of 34.96% and MOTP of 39.17%, demonstrating its efficacy in practical applications.

Keywords: Leg detection · Socially assistive robot · Multiple target detection

This work was supported in part by the Central Government Guides Local Special Funds for Science and Technology Development under Grant 2020L3028 and 2021L3047.

F. Sun et al. (Eds.): ICCSIP 2023, CCIS 1918, pp. 87–103, 2024.
https://doi.org/10.1007/978-981-99-8018-5_7

1   Introduction

Is there a solution to specifically identify the target in a multi-person scenario without the use of wearable sensors? Human-robot interaction (HRI) requires socially assistive robots to detect, identify, and track the behavior of the target person [1]. There is an urgent requirement for socially assistive robots [2–4] to serve a congested workspace due to the acceleration of aging process and the rise in labor costs (e.g., hospital, supermarket, restaurant, or warehouse). In multi-person and cluttered scenarios, identifying interactive targets without the use of wearable sensors remains an unresolved challenge.

Camera sensors have gained popularity in the robotics market. However, they lose the ability to recognize pedestrians at night. Compared to RGB-D cameras require advanced computational power and violate personal privacy [5], Light Detection And Ranging (LiDAR) is a high-accuracy range sensor that provides 2-dimensional (2D) range information at high rates for dynamic environments. The usage of RGB-D cameras is constrained by the COVID-19 pandemic since masks hide a significant amount of RGB information about the face. Additionally, RGB-D cameras are rarely useful in environments with inadequate or excessive lighting when used outside.

A LiDAR-based socially assistive robot, which can serve as a logistical help, doesn't need active markers or optical reflection markers. For instance, the human-following robot EffiBOT (Effidence Inc., Romagnat, France) uses LiDAR sensors [7]. EffiBOT can follow a picking operator due to its "Follow-me" functionality. The efficiency of logistics in factories and warehouses is increased because picking operators no longer need to manually push or pull carts.

The majority of researches concentrated on leg detection with LiDAR because of the height restrictions of mobile robots. Compared to waist detection [8] and shoulder detection [9], leg detection does not require adjusting the measurement range based on the person's height. Leg detection at a lower height can simultaneously detect human legs and obstacles, while waist detection and shoulder detection at a higher height are considered to be prone to overlooking potential obstacles. Generally speaking, investigations [8–12] aim to build a classifier based on the leg's geometry constraints. The circle fitting [9] and bounding box [8] are traditional methods for obtaining leg characteristics. However, neither of the two approaches is sufficient to keep the leg detecting stable. Arras et al. [10] created a ground-breaking work in the AdaBoost approach to develop a robust classifier, which collected 14 characteristics to learn the shape of legs, to address the issue brought on by the sparsity of the LiDAR data. The drawback is that the situation with the occluded legs was not taken into account. Li et al. [11] added extra characteristics to an AdaBoost-based detector to increase the detection accuracy when legs are partially occluded. Additionally, Beyer et al. [12] used the leg features to create a deep learning (DL) detector. This DL method's lengthy run-time makes it impossible to employ online with a robot that follows people. In conclusion, these methods are prone to false positives brought on by ambient noises, such as chair and table legs. Due to the poor information quality

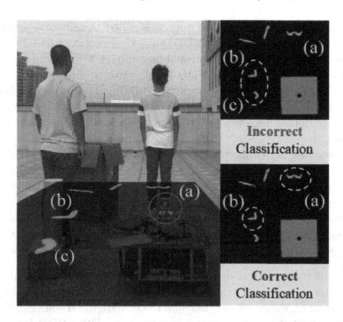

Fig. 1. In multi-person environments, leg detection may experience recognition errors due to insufficient features. The test dataset is divided into incorrect classification and correct classification. (a) Laser data where both legs are connected is difficult to recognize as a single person. (b) Side-standing leg data is obstructed by the other leg. (c) Obstacles resembling cylinders are often mistakenly identified as human legs.

of 2D range data, it is difficult for these conventional classifiers to categorize the target person's leg in the crowd.

Recently, to solve the classification issue in 2D range data, some researchers used the support vector data description (SVDD) as a one-class classification (OCC) [13]. Chung *et al.* [14] used an SVDD-based classifier to choose leg clusters without presuming that human legs have any particular geometric shapes. As a result, even though more complicated leg forms were supported for searching, the accuracy of leg detection decreased. Cha *et al.* [15] addressed this problem by modifying the SVDD-based classifier to learn the classification boundary in 3D feature space using a 2D LiDAR. Jung *et al.* [16] used an SVDD algorithm to detect the shoulder using a marathoner service robot in order to assess the outside performance. Despite the great performance of these SVDD algorithms for detecting the target person's legs, it was challenging to distinguish a specific target from other objects and occlusions. The SVDD-based leg detector could identify hallways and human legs for side-by-side following in our prior investigation [17] (Fig. 1).

This paper suggests an enhanced leg detector based on density-weighted support vector data description (DW-SVDD) to locate the target person in a crowded environment with obstacles and occlusions. The proposed DW-SVDD leg detector offers the following benefits over the leg detectors discussed above:

- In this paper, we propose a novel approach called Density-Weighted Support Vector Data Description (DW-SVDD) that leverages 2D LiDAR data to create a 3D density representation, enabling robust leg detection in complex scenarios. The proposed DW-SVDD leg detector inputs girth G_i, width W_i characteristics and density weight $\rho(x_i)$ into support vector data description. As a result, it is possible to obtain dynamic leg data with a more reliable detecting performance, even in situations with similar obstacles and partial occlusions.

- The density weight parameter for the density distribution of LiDAR data is calculated by comparing the k-NN distance of each data point with the maximum k-NN distance of the dataset. One of the main advantages of the k-NN algorithm is its simplicity and intuitive nature. It does not assume any underlying statistical distribution of the data and can be applied to both numerical and categorical data. Therefore, our suggested DW-SVDD leg detector may be incorporated into the robot platform's low-cost embedded system.

The rest of this paper is organized as follows. Section 2 is about the DW-SVDD leg detector proposed in this paper and its application for socially assistive robots. Different experiments are designed to evaluate the traditional SVDD and DW-SVDD in Sect. 3. In this section, our proposed DW-SVDD leg detector is compared with other leg detectors in a real-time robot platform. Also, indoor and outdoor datasets are self-collected for real-time evaluation of the DW-SVDD leg detector. Additionally, all leg detectors are evaluated in CLEAR MOT metrics for multi-object tracking. Finally, Sect. 4 concludes the paper.

2   DW-SVDD Leg Detector

Support Vector Data Description (SVDD) is a powerful machine learning technique widely used for anomaly detection, novelty detection, and one-class classification tasks [18]. As an improved version of the support vector machine, SVDD generates a minimum-volume hypersphere that encircles the positive samples in feature space and identifies abnormalities of leg characteristics. By giving the density weight of each data point during the search process, the description favors data points in high-density areas. Eventually the optimal description shifts toward these dense regions. Therefore, the high-level confidence of leg data is described as a positive cluster with similar obstacles and partial occlusions.

2.1   Density Weighted Support Vector Data Description

Given the 2D range data as $x_i = \{x_1, x_2, \ldots, x_m\}$, where $x_i \in \mathbf{R}^m$, $i = 1, 2, \ldots, m$. In the proposed DW-SVDD human leg detector, the density weight $\rho(x_i)$ depends on the k-nearest neighbor (k-NN) distance [19–21], which denotes $d\left(x_i, x_i^k\right)$ as the distance between x_i and the k-th nearest neighbor of x_i^k.

In k-NN, a query x_i^k is labeled by a majority vote y_i^k of its k-nearest neighbors in the training set. To weigh close neighbors more heavily, Fig. 2 is arranged in

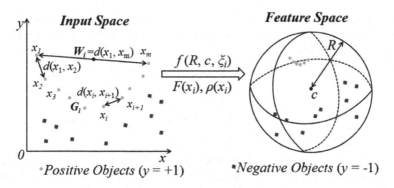

Fig. 2. Laser point in 2D range data is detected by using the DW-SVDD leg detector. DW-SVDD transforms 2D laser data into 3D density relationships, making it more suitable for leg detection in multi-person scenarios. Leg data description depends on $F(x_i)$ and $\rho(x_i)$.

increasing order in terms of Euclidean distance $d\left(x_i, x_i^k\right)$, such as:

$$\begin{cases} d\left(x_i, x_i^k\right) = \sqrt{\left(x_i - x_i^k\right)^T \left(x_i - x_i^k\right)} \\ y_i = argmax \sum_{\left(x_i^k, y_i^k \in T\right)} \delta\left(y = y_i^k\right) \end{cases} \tag{1}$$

where x_i is the training vector in the feature space, y_i is the corresponding class label in the training set $T = \{x_i, y_i\}_{i=1}^N$, x_i^k is the query for the i-th nearest neighbor among its k nearest neighbors, y_i^k is the class label for the i-th nearest neighbor among its k nearest neighbors. Also, $\delta\left(y = y_i^k\right)$ is the Dirac delta function [13].

As shown in Fig. 2, by measuring the k-NN distance, density weight $\rho(x_i)$ is set as:

$$\rho\left(x_i\right) = 1 - \frac{d\left(x_i, x_i^k\right)}{d\left(x_j, x_j^k\right)} \tag{2}$$

where $d\left(x_j, x_j^k\right)$ is the maximum k-NN distance of the dataset.

Density weight $\rho\left(x_i\right)$ measures the relative density based on the density distribution of the target data by comparing the k-NN distance of each data point with the maximum k-NN distance of the dataset. Moreover, density weight falls within the range $\rho\left(x_i\right) \in (0, 1)$.

To define attributes of legs, girth G_i, width characteristics W_i and density weight $\rho\left(x_i\right)$ are utilized to build the proposed DW-SVDD-based leg detector. The DW-SVDD optimization objective is to seek a tight data description:

$$\begin{cases} \min L\left(R, c, \xi_i\right) = R^2 + C \sum_{i=1}^n \rho\left(x_i\right) F\left(x_i\right) \xi_i \\ s.t. \|x_i - c\| \leq R^2 + \xi_i, \xi_i \geq 0, F\left(x_i\right) = \left(G_i, W_i\right) \\ G_i = \sum_{j=1}^{m-1} d\left(x_j, x_{j+1}\right), W_i = d\left(x_1, x_m\right) \end{cases} \tag{3}$$

where R is the hypersphere radius, c is the center of the sphere, ξ_i is the relaxation variable for reducing the influence of singular points, and C is the penalty factor that weighs the hypersphere volume and misclassification rate. $F(x_i)$ is a function that maps data from the original space to the feature space through nonlinear transformation.

To describe the LiDAR data, the Lagrange function can be further derived as:

$$
\begin{aligned}
L(R, c, \xi_i) = R^2 + C \sum_{i=1}^{N} \rho(x_i) \xi_i \\
- \sum_{i=1}^{N} \alpha_i \left(R^2 + \xi_i - \|F(x_i) - c\|^2 \right) - \sum_{i=1}^{N} \eta_i \xi_i
\end{aligned}
\tag{4}
$$

where α_i and η_i are the Lagrange multipliers.

The original training data are not spherically distributed for the LiDAR data that a nonlinear data relationship exists. Accordingly, anomalies cannot be isolated effectively by a hypersphere. Since partial differentiation should equal zero [13], the new equation and constraints are denoted as:

$$
\begin{cases}
L = \sum_{i=1}^{m} \alpha_i k(x_i, x_i) \\
- \sum_{i=1}^{m} \sum_{j=1}^{m} \alpha_i \alpha_j k(x_i, x_j) \\
s.t. 0 \leq \alpha_i \leq C, \sum_{i=1}^{m} \alpha_i = 1
\end{cases}
\tag{5}
$$

where $k(x_i, x_i)$ is an inner product, and $k(x_i, x_j)$ is the Kernel function.

By seeking the solution of Eq. (3), we could get the center c and radius R of the hypersphere:

$$
\begin{cases}
c = \sum_i \alpha_i x_i \\
R = |x_k - c|
\end{cases}
\tag{6}
$$

where x_k is the support vector, whose distance to the center of the hypersphere is the radius R.

2.2   DW-SVDD Leg Detection Algorithm

To find and save the candidate leg cluster C_k, Algorithm 1 is proposed to describe the leg detection scheme. The DW-SVDD leg detection algorithm not only takes geometric features (e.g., the girth G_i and width W_i) into consideration, but also the density weight $\rho(x_i)$. As the algorithm should be executed in real-time on a socially assistive robot, short computing time and high recognition accuracy are the advantages of the proposed Algorithm 1. According to the training 2D range data x_i input, candidate leg clusters are obtained with the proposed leg detection algorithm. Besides, the central position of the LiDAR is the position of the hypersphere center c in Eq. (6).

In this paper, we present a novel leg detector for pedestrian tracking based on DW-SVDD (Density-Weighted Support Vector Data Description). The proposed approach leverages the benefits of DW-SVDD to accurately and robustly detect and distinguish human legs in complex and crowded environments. By transforming 2D laser data into 3D density relationships, our leg detector exhibits enhanced performance in multi-person scenarios, where multiple legs are present within the sensing range.

Algorithm 1: DW-SVDD Leg Detection Algorithm

Input: x_i: the training 2D range data
Output: C_k: the candidate leg cluster
1 **for** $j = 1$ to N **do**
2    $d\left(x_i, x_i^k\right) \rightarrow$ Eq.(1);
3   **if** a query $d\left(x_i, x_i^k\right)$ is labeled by a majority vote $d\left(y_i, x_i^k\right)$ **then**
4       $x_i^k = x_{sorted(i)}, y_i^k = y_{sorted(i)}$;
5   **end**
6 **end**
7 **foreach** $k = 1$ to N **do**
8   **if** $x_i > x_{i+1}$ **then**
9   [index, dist] = sort $[d\left(x_i, x_i^k\right)$, ascend];
10   **end**
11 **end**
12 **for** $i = 1$ to k **do**
13    $y_i \rightarrow$ Eq.(1);
14    $\rho(x_i) \rightarrow$ Eq.(2);
15    $G_i, W_i, F(x) \rightarrow$ Eq.(3);
16    $k\left(x_i, x_j\right), L \rightarrow$ Eq.(5);
17    $c, R \rightarrow$ Eq.(6);
18   **if** $d\left(c, x_i^k\right) \in (0, \mathrm{R})$ **then**
19       $C_K \rightarrow$ Save;
20   **end**
21 **end**

2.3 Socially Assistive in Multiplayer Scenarios

As shown in Fig. 3, a socially assistive robot equipped with LiDAR, which collects the clustering of multiple pedestrians. To distinguish the tracking target $C_k\left(x_k, y_k, \theta_k\right)$ from interfering target $C_{k+1}\left(x_{k+1}, y_{k+1}, \theta_{k+1}\right)$, the robot locks the tracking target by updating the relative change angle $\Delta\theta < \delta_c$ between the robot and the followed target at each time interval, and the moving distance $L_p < \delta_f$ of the following target in real-time.

Algorithm 2: Socially Assistive Algorithm

Input: C_k: the candidate leg cluster
Output: v_l, v_r: speed input to the left and right wheel motor
1 **for** $k = 1$ to N **do**
2 | min $d(c, C_k)$; **if** $\Delta\theta < \delta_c, L_p < \delta_f$ **then**
3 | | $a_v, a_\omega, v_l, v_r \rightarrow$ Eq.(9);
4 | **end**
5 **end**

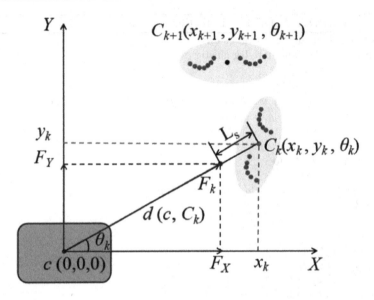

Fig. 3. Motion control in the robot coordinate system. The LiDAR is installed on the center of the robot for simplifying the coordinate system, which is set as c (0, 0, 0).

The relative angle variation $\Delta\theta$ between the following target and the robot in time interval Δt is always within the range of $\Delta\theta < \delta_c$, which is described as:

$$\begin{cases} \theta = \arctan\left(\frac{y_{k+1}-y_k}{y_{k+1}-y_k}\right) \\ \Delta\theta = \frac{(\theta_{k+\Delta t}-\theta_k)}{\Delta t} \end{cases} \quad (7)$$

The distance with the following target in Δt is always within the range of $L_p < \delta_f$, which is described as:

$$L_p = \sqrt{(x_{k+\Delta t} - x_k)^2 + (y_{k+\Delta t} - y_k)^2} \quad (8)$$

According to the dynamic model of socially assistive robots [17], the dynamic equation of the robot in the X-axis and Y-axis is denoted as:

$$\begin{cases} F_X = F_k \cos\theta_k = ma_v \\ F_Y = F_k \sin\theta_k = \frac{Ja_\omega}{(d(c,C_k)-L_s)} \end{cases} \quad (9)$$

where F_X and F_Y are the component of the force on the X-axis and Y-axis, respectively. F_k is the force that pulls the robot to follow the target. m is the weight of the robot, J is the rotational inertia of the robot, a_v and a_ω are linear acceleration and angular acceleration, respectively. L_s is the safe distance that the robot would not collide with the following target.

Algorithm 2 defines how the socially assistive robot maintains a safe distance L_s between the robot and the following target. More than one cluster may be available in a cluttered environment [22]. For the safety of the following target, the robot should follow the nearest cluster.

3   Self-collected Dataset

The majority of datasets are only able to gather 2D range information while a single target is moving. Despite the fact that Beyer *et al.* [12] made their LiDAR dataset-a 10-h record for an aged care facility-available for download. The users probably live in a relatively clean area because there aren't many impediments in this dataset. Because labelling is so expensive, it is hard to discover datasets with several people or obstacles. Additionally, data from the Leon@Home Testbed [25], which includes location estimates determined by two human trackers, has been gathered to assess service robots in a realistic home context. Obviously, the aforementioned data is insufficient to train the suggested detector.

3.1   Overview

Table 1 contains self-collected OpenField and MessyIndoor datasets for comparing and evaluating the DW-SVDD leg detector. Additionally, because our team is dedicated to using open-source datasets, this data will be posted on the GitHub website along with any supporting materials, such as movies and rosbag data.

Table 1. Overview of Self-Collected Datasets

Dataset Topics	OpenField	MessyIndoor
Running Time	46.2 s	38.2 s
Humans Number	5	5
Obstacles Number	0	5
Topics: /scan	933 msgs	898 msgs
Topics: /odom	469 msgs	449 msgs
Topics: /leg_clusters	926 msgs	885 msgs

3.2 Training Dataset

Experiments in a multi-person setting are split into detection experiments and following experiments in order to validate the DW-SVDD approach for socially assistive tasks. As shown in Fig. 4, the man wearing a white shirt is the target being followed, and the man wearing a black shirt is the target being interfered with. As shown in Figs. 4a and 4b, the interfering target frequently creates a barrier between the robot and the target being pursued in a multi-person environment. When legs are too close together, the mobile robot interprets the grouping of several legs as an incorrect goal and sets misleading data (Fig. 4c). A control group of real data was also established (Fig. 4d).

4 Experiments of Leg Detection

4.1 SVDD Leg Detector vs DW-SVDD Leg Detector

SVDD and DW-SVDD leg detectors are evaluated on the Redmi laptop computer, which is equipped with an Intel Core i5-10300H processor, 16 GB RAM, an Nvidia GTX 1650 GPU, and an Ubuntu 20.04 operating system. All the contrastive methods are implemented in the ROS (Robot Operating System) and do not employ any parallel acceleration optimization techniques.

The data in 3200 laser data samples was discovered to objectively examine the recognition and detection of targets by mobile robots in a multi-person scene. The training set from Fig. 4 is used to test the SVDD leg detector in Fig. 5. It is obvious that the SVDD method's excessive reliance on leg characteristics is the reason why the detection results are inadequate.

Figure 5(a) shows that the robot only detects one human leg information because the followed target is completely blocked. The robot only detects part of the human leg information in Fig. 5(b). In Fig. 5(c), the distance between the followed target and the interfering target is very close, detectors have difficulty clustering these features into the following target. The control group in Fig. 5(d) also demonstrated successful detection.

Figure 6 demonstrates how much more accurate and efficient our suggested strategy is. The identification of laser point sequences in close proximity is made easier since density information is taken into account. Figure 6(a) demonstrates that the robot only picks up information about one human leg because all other target information was lost. The DW-SVDD approach in Fig. 6(c) obviously outperforms the SVDD method since it recognizes two targets as opposed to one in Fig. 5(c). Additionally, Fig. 6(d) more clearly illustrates the test's outcome.

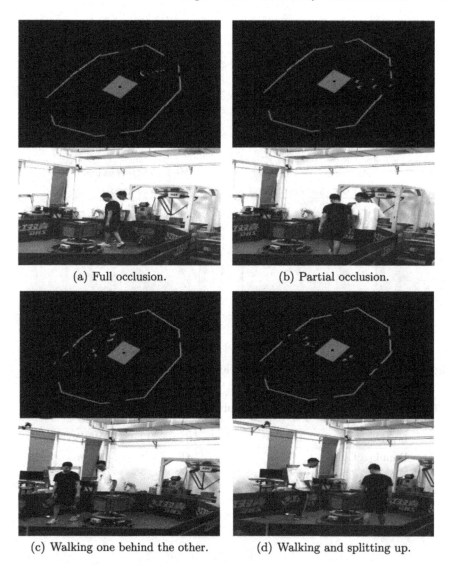

(a) Full occlusion.   (b) Partial occlusion.

(c) Walking one behind the other.   (d) Walking and splitting up.

Fig. 4. Training dataset: In a setting with multiple people, following and interfering targets are moving about at various positions.

The quantitative evaluation results are shown in Table 2. We could conclude that DW-SVDD leg detector has advantages over SVDD-based leg detector in terms of multi-target classification. As for Area Under the Curve (AUC), the

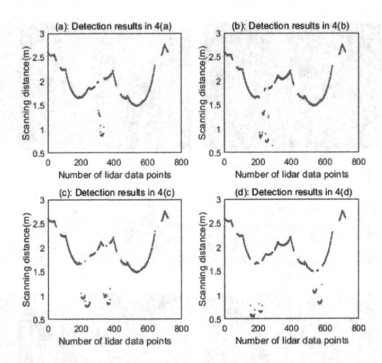

Fig. 5. The detection results of the SVDD leg detector for the four scenarios in Fig. 4.

Table 2. Comparing the Detection Results of SVDD and DW-SVDD Detectors

Leg Detector	SVDD [14, 17]	DW-SVDD
Running Time	41.2 ms	47.0 ms
Number of Iterations	9	15
Average Lost Points	15	6
AUC	60.36%	73.41%
Variance of Distance and Radius (s_{d-r}^2)	19.21	12.30

DW-SVDD leg detector is 73.41%, which shows the higher accuracy of the detector. To describe the variance between the distance and radius, s_{d-r}^2 is defined to reflect the fluctuation of data:

$$s_{d-r}^2 = \frac{\sum_{i=1}^{n} \left(d\left(x_i, x_i^k\right) - r \right)^2}{n} \tag{10}$$

where the distance $d\left(x_i, x_i^k\right)$ and the radius r are described in Algorithm 1 and Eq. (6), respectively.

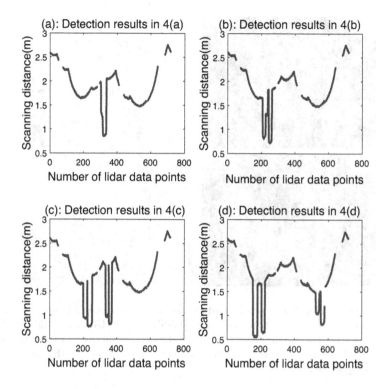

Fig. 6. The detection results of the DW-SVDD leg detector for the four scenarios in Fig. 4.

4.2   DW-SVDD Leg Detector in Real-Time Robot Platform

This detector is practically implemented with a 2-wheeled mobile robot in order to test the effectiveness of the DW-SVDD-based leg detector in a real-world setting. To gather 2D range data, a LiDAR with a 360° measurement angle (R2000, Pepperl+Fuchs GmbH, Germany) was put in the middle of the mobile robot. It has a 360° scanning angle and a measurement range of up to 30 m. With a measurement speed of 250 kHz and a scanning rate of 10 m/s, laser data on the leg can be detected.

Leg Detection for Partial Occlusions. One interference target was intended to pass through the target person and the robot in Fig. 7. The detector can easily be shown to discriminate between the two targets despite the interference target and the target after it being so close together that they are even partially obscured. It should be noted that if a person's legs are totally hidden, they cannot be recognized. In this situation, the LiDAR is deprived of all knowledge on the features of the human leg.

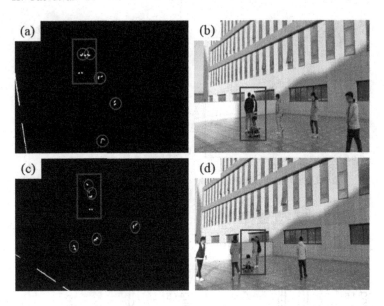

Fig. 7. The DW-SVDD leg detector could be used by socially assistive robots to identify partial occlusions. (a)(b) In blue box, the DW-SVDD leg detector could be able to recognize both people in real-time if they are standing adjacent to the target. (c)(d) The DW-SVDD leg detector also functions when someone passes by the target in blue box. (Color figure online)

Leg Detection with Similar Obstacles. In Fig. 8, despite the close proximity of the interference target and the target, even partially obscuring the target, the detector can be seen clearly differentiating between the two targets. The density weighting, which considers the distance between the legs and attempts to separate legs with similar obstacles, makes this detection successful.

Table 3. Evaluation Results of Three Leg Detectors

Leg Detector	LegDetector [24]	SVDD [14,17]	DW-SVDD
ID Switch	115	137	155
Miss	2371 msgs	2113 msgs	1474 msgs
FP	2294 msgs	2110 msgs	1890 msgs
MOTA	18.70%	27.41%	34.96%
MOTP	26.97%	37.02%	39.17%

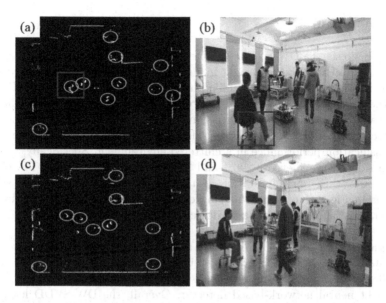

Fig. 8. The DW-SVDD leg detector could be used by socially assistive robots to identify similar obstacles. (a)(b) In the blue box, the DW-SVDD leg detector might be able to recognize both people in real-time if they are seated in similar obstacles. (c)(d) MessyIndoor Dataset detection results. (Color figure online)

4.3   Leg Detection in CLEAR MOT Metrics

Due to a scarcity of publicly available code, we could only find an open-source ROS-enabled leg detector package [23], which is based on the geometric constraints of legs.

The CLEAR MOT metrics [24] are adopted for the quantitative evaluation of socially assistive robots. These metrics are commonly utilized for multi-object tracking, and provide scorings of ID switches (ID_k), misses ($Miss_k$), false positives (FP_k), valid assignments, and precision of matchings cumulated from every frame. These scores can be aggregated in multi-object tracking accuracy (MOTA) score and multi-object tracking precision (MOTP):

$$\begin{cases} MOTA = 1 - \frac{\sum_k (I_k + Miss_k + FP_k)}{\sum_k g_k} \\ MOTP = \frac{\sum_{i,k} d(x_i, x_k)}{\sum_k c_k} \end{cases} \tag{11}$$

where g_k is the ground truth annotations, c_k is the number of matchings between the estimated person and ground truth positions at time k. The distance $d(x_i, x_k)$ is described in Algorithm 1.

As shown in Table 3, results indicate that the MOTA and MOTP of the proposed DW-SVDD leg detector achieved 34.96% and 39.17%, respectively.

5 Conclusion

This study presents a DW-SVDD leg detector to detect, track, and follow human targets using a LiDAR at leg height in a socially assistive robot. To improve the leg detection performance for partial occlusions and similar obstacles in 2D range data, the proposed leg detector integrates k-NN distance, density weight, and support vector data description. Experimental results show that the DW-SVDD leg detectoroutperforms the other two detectors, exhibiting superior clustering and classification performance in a cluttered environment. Specifically, the proposed leg detector achieved 34.96% and 39.17% for MOTA and MOTP, respectively. However, there are limitations to the detector, as it falsely detects similar obstacles in Fig. 8 due to not filtering out noise from distant laser points. In addition, this leg detector fails to detect the target person who wears a long skirt.

In future works, we plan to develop a stable and dependable socially assistive system for mobile robots. This will involve using a high-performance robot controller to test out a sensor fusion strategy, which will include running a lightweight neural network-based detector. Overall, the DW-SVDD leg detector shows promising results and has the potential to be integrated into a more comprehensive socially assistive scenario in the future.

References

1. Hu, Y., Abe, N., Benallegue, M., et al.: Toward active physical human-robot interaction: quantifying the human state during interactions. IEEE Trans. Hum. Mach. Syst. **52**(3), 367–378 (2022)
2. Yuan, J., Zhang, S., Sun, Q., et al.: Laser-based intersection-aware human following with a mobile robot in indoor environments. IEEE Trans. Syst. Man Cybern. Syst. **51**(1), 354–369 (2018)
3. Xue, G., Yao, H., Zhang, Y., et al.: UWB-based adaptable side-by-side following for human-following robots. In: 2022 IEEE International Conference on Robotics and Biomimetics (ROBIO), pp. 333–338, IEEE, Jinghong, China (2022)
4. Liu, P., Yao, H., Dai, H., et al.: The detection and following of human legs based on feature optimized HDBSCAN for mobile robot. J. Phys: Conf. Ser. **2216**(1), 012009 (2022)
5. Zhou, G., Zhao, R., Yao, H., et al.: A low-cost conductive-textile based multifunctional flexible capacitive sensor for human motion tracking. In: 2021 IEEE International Conference on Robotics and Biomimetics (ROBIO), pp. 317–321, IEEE, Sanya, China (2021)
6. Su, S., Cheng, S., Dai, H., et al.: An efficient human-following method by fusing kernelized correlation filter and depth information for mobile robot. In: 2019 IEEE International Conference on Robotics and Biomimetics (ROBIO), pp. 2099–2104, IEEE, Dali, China (2019)
7. EffiBOT (AGV/AMR). https://www.effidence.com/en/effibot/. Accessed 1 Oct 2022
8. Li, H., Dong, Y., Li, X.: Object-aware bounding box regression for online multi-object tracking. Neurocomputing **518**, 440–452 (2023)

9. Nurunnabi, A., Sadahiro, Y., Laefer, D.F.: Robust statistical approaches for circle fitting in laser scanning three-dimensional point cloud data. Pattern Recogn. **81**, 417–431 (2018)

10. Arras, K.O., Mozos, O.M., Burgard, W.: Using boosted features for the detection of people in 2D range data. In: Proceedings 2007 IEEE International Conference on Robotics and Automation, pp. 3402–3407, IEEE, Rome, Italy (2007)

11. Li, D., Li, L., Li, Y., et al.: A multi-type features method for leg detection in 2-D laser range data. IEEE Sens. J. **18**(4), 1675–1684 (2017)

12. Beyer, L., Hermans, A., Linder, T., et al.: Deep person detection in two-dimensional range data. IEEE Robot. Autom. Lett. **3**(3), 2726–2733 (2018)

13. Tax, D.M., Duin, R.P.: Support vector domain description. Pattern Recogn. Lett. **20**(11–13), 1191–1199 (1999)

14. Chung, W., Kim, H., Yoo, Y., et al.: The detection and following of human legs through inductive approaches for a mobile robot with a single laser range finder. IEEE Trans. Industr. Electron. **59**(8), 3156–3166 (2011)

15. Cha, D., Chung, W.: Human-leg detection in 3D feature space for a person-following mobile robot using 2D LiDARs. Int. J. Precis. Eng. Manuf. **21**, 1299–1307 (2020)

16. Jung, E.J., Lee, J.H., Yi, B.J., et al.: Development of a laser-range-finder-based human tracking and control algorithm for a marathoner service robot. IEEE/ASME Trans. Mechatron. **19**(6), 1963–1976 (2013)

17. Yao, H., Dai, H., Zhao, E., et al.: Laser-based side-by-side following for human-following robots. In: 2021 IEEE/RSJ International Conference on Intelligent Robots and Systems (IROS), pp. 2651–2656, IEEE, Prague, Czech Republic (2021)

18. Nguyen, X.T., Kim, H., Lee, H.J.: An efficient sampling algorithm with a K-NN expanding operator for depth data acquisition in a LiDAR system. IEEE Trans. Circuits Syst. Video Technol. **30**(12), 4700–4714 (2020)

19. Cha, M., Kim, J.S., Baek, J.G.: Density weighted support vector data description. Expert Syst. Appl. **41**(7), 3343–3350 (2014)

20. Wu, X., Liu, S., Bai, Y.: The manifold regularized SVDD for noisy label detection. Inf. Sci. **619**, 235–248 (2023)

21. Sung, Y., Chung, W.: Hierarchical sample-based joint probabilistic data association filter for following human legs using a mobile robot in a cluttered environment. IEEE Trans. Hum. Mach. Syst. **46**(3), 340–349 (2015)

22. Standard Classification (Banana Dataset). https://www.kaggle.com/saranchandar/standard-classification-banana-dataset. Accessed 15 Sep 2018

23. ROS Leg_Detector. http://wiki.ros.org/leg_detector. Accessed 10 Sep 2017

24. Bernardin, K., Stiefelhagen, R.: Evaluating multiple object tracking performance: the clear mot metrics. EURASIP J. Image Video Process. **2008**, 1–10 (2008)

25. Álvarez-Aparicio, C., Guerrero-Higueras, Á.M., Olivera, M.C.C.: Benchmark dataset for evaluation of range-based people tracker classifiers in mobile robots. Front. Neurorobot. **11**, 72 (2017). https://www.frontiersin.org/articles/10.3389/fnbot.2017.00072/full

Image Compressed Sensing Reconstruction via Deep Image Prior with Feature Space and Texture Information

Zhao Peng, Wang Jinchan$^{(\boxtimes)}$, Peng Huanqing, Xiang Fei, and Zhang Liwen

College of Information Engineering, Henan University of Science and Technology, Luoyang 471023, China
wjc@haust.edu.cn

Abstract. Deep learning has yielded remarkable achievements in compressed sensing image reconstruction in recent years. However, when the sampling rate is low, the reconstruction image is blurred and lacks texture details. In this paper, we design a dual-path compressed sensing reconstruction network based on image feature space information flow and texture information, which can solve the above problems to a certain extent. The feature space information flow path employs proximal gradient descent algorithms to map essential structural information from the pixel space to the feature space, effectively reducing data dimensionality and redundancy. On the other hand, after combining the attention mechanism, the texture information path restores the texture details of the image in the frequency domain, which can effectively enhance the quality and visual effects of the reconstruction image. During training, a unified loss function guides the alternating optimization of both paths. Evaluation of prominent benchmark datasets, including Set5, Set11, and BSD68, reveals that our proposed method outperforms traditional iterative approaches and existing deep learning-based methodologies in terms of both reconstructed image quality and network robustness under low sampling rates.

Keywords: Image feature space information · Texture information · Deep learning · Compressed sensing

1 Introduction

Image Compressed sensing (CS) is an emerging technology [1]. Based on the theory of compression perception, through non-traditional sampling methods and sparse representations, it can achieve efficient compression of signals on the premise of ensuring high-quality reconstruction. CS technology integrates the sampling and compression of the two traditional steps, which selectively measures the important information of the image, thereby greatly reducing the number of samples and storage space for the required samples [2].

CS technology has brought many advantages to the image field but faces multiple problems such as signal sampling design, sparse representation, and image reconstruction [3].Among them, the problem of reconstruction is the core problem of compressed sensing technology, and solving this problem is the key to achieving high-quality image reconstruction [4]. The current reconstruction methods are roughly divided into two categories, which are traditional compression sensing reconstruction methods and deep learning-based reconstruction methods.

Traditional CS reconstruction methods can usually be divided into two categories: methods based on sparse representation and methods based on optimization. Based on the sparse representation method, the signal is expressed as a sparse vector with the sparse properties of the signal, and it samples it by measuring the matrix. The method based on optimization issues is to restore the original signal by optimizing a specific target function. Common methods based on optimization include ordinary least squares [5], TVAL3 [6], STD-CS [7], etc. Among them, Li et al. combined the augmented Lagrangian method with two-stage optimization techniques to achieve total variation minimization by introducing transformation variables and penalty terms [6]. This method is capable of maintaining high reconstruction quality while having a lower computational complexity. STD-CS is a denoising method proposed by Dabov et al., which utilizes the sparsity in the 3D transform domain of images and the characteristics of collaborative filtering to reduce noise by exploiting the correlation and similarity between neighboring pixels [7].

In recent years, the development of deep learning technology provides a new solution for image CS, which can learn the prior knowledge of the image from a large number of training data, so as to improve the reconstruction performance [8–11]. There are many Compressed sensing reconstruction methods based on deep learning, among which the method based on sparse representation is more widely used. This method regards CS reconstruction as a sparse representation problem and uses a Convolutional neural network (CNN) to learn the sparse representation of signals [12–15]. These methods train a deep neural network to learn sparse representation models of signals from observed data. When the network training is completed, the network can be used to reconstruct the new CS data. For example, the CSNet [16] proposed by Shi et al. uses the observation data as input to learn the sparse representation of images and extract features using the depth Convolutional neural network. Yao et al. proposed the DR2-Net, a deep residual reconstruction network, to achieve high-quality image reconstruction by training the network to learn the sparse representation and reconstruction process of images. Zhang et al. proposed ISTA-Net [18], a deep network that incorporates the optimization algorithm ISTA (Iterative Shrinkage-Thresholding Algorithm) into a deep learning framework to construct an end-to-end network structure for reconstructing sparse signals. This network is capable of adaptively learning sparse representation and the reconstruction process while maintaining good interpretability.ReconNet [19] is an iterative applied convolutional layer network proposed by Kulkarni et al. for learning sparse representation and residual information of images.

Moreover, prior information about the image plays a crucial role in CS reconstruction [20], providing additional constraints, promoting sparsity, preserving the structure and details of the image, and improving the robustness of the reconstruction network [21]. Based on these advantages, numerous researchers have developed various reconstruction methods. Cui et al. proposed an improved image CS method using the non-local neural network structure (NL-CSNet) [22], which utilizes non-local self-similarity priors and global feature representations. This approach enhances reconstruction quality and facilitates the understanding and utilization of image prior knowledge.Sun et al. introduced DPA-Net [23] based on structural and texture paths, which produces superior reconstruction quality at low sampling rates. However, there is room for further improvement in terms of interpretability for each channel.

Furthermore, in the process of compressive sensing signal reconstruction, it is desirable to achieve high-quality reconstruction using as few measurements as possible. In scenarios with limited resources, such as sensor networks, airborne platforms, and embedded mobile devices, there is a critical need to achieve higher-quality reconstructions under low measurement rates. To address these challenges, We design a compressed sensing reconstruction network based on feature information flow and texture information(Dubbed FSITM-Net). Processing image information in the feature space contributes to reducing data dimensionality and eliminating redundancy, thereby better restoring the dominant structure of the image and enhancing the accuracy of the reconstructed image. Texture information, as a vital characteristic of images, captures local and global features, and when combined with attention mechanisms, effectively enhances the quality and visual effects of the image. In summary, incorporating image feature space information flow and texture information helps solve some of the issues associated with sparse representation methods, thereby improving the reconstruction quality and robustness of the image.

2 Compressed Sensing Theory

In compressive sensing, let $x \in R^n$ be a sparse signal and $y \in R^m$ be the observation vector obtained by sampling x through a linear transformation $y = Ax$, where $A \in R^{m \times n}$ represents the measurement matrix, typically a Gaussian matrix, with $m \ll n$. Compressive sensing theory suggests that signal x can be reconstructed by solving the optimization problem of Lasso regression as given in Eq. (1) [24].

$$\min_{x \in R^n} \frac{1}{2} \| y - Ax \|_2^2 + \lambda \| x \|_1 \tag{1}$$

where $\| y - Ax \|_2^2$ is the data fidelity term, measuring the difference between the predicted values and the observed data in terms of squared Euclidean distance. $\lambda \| x \|_1$ is the regularization operator used to measure the sparsity transformation of signal x, which can be achieved through predefined sparse operators such as Discrete Cosine Transform (DCT), wavelet transform, curvelet transform, etc. Various methods have been proposed to solve the problem in Eq. (1), such as sparse regularization methods [25], Alternating Direction Method of Multipliers (ADMM) [26], Matching Pursuit [27], etc. Although these methods have achieved certain effectiveness in solving the signal reconstruction problem, they often have high computational complexity and are sensitive to parameters, which greatly limits the practical application of CS.

3 Dual-Path Deep Compressive Sensing Image Reconstruction Network

Based on the principles of iterative optimization algorithms, we propose an FSITM-Net model. It comprises three components: a sampling sub-network, an initial reconstruction sub-network, and a deep reconstruction sub-network. The sampling sub-network and the initial reconstruction sub-network are responsible for linear sampling and reconstruction operations in the pixel domain and measurement domain respectively. The deep reconstruction network, divided into two paths based on feature and frequency domains, focuses on reconstructing image features and texture information. The model consists of k modules, representing iterations, and after completing both paths, the final reconstructed image is obtained by combining the two path images (Fig. 1).

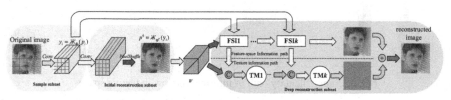

Fig. 1. The compressed sensing network structure of FSITM-Net

3.1 Sampling and Initial Reconstruction of the Network

In this paper, Block Compressed Sensing (BCS) technique is employed to divide the image $P \in R^{H \times W}$ with height H and width W into non-overlapping image blocks of size B × B, resulting in $(H/B) \times (W/B)$ blocks. Each image block is reshaped into a vector $p \in R^B$. With a measurement rate of α, a learnable sampling matrix $\Phi \epsilon R^{\times (B^2 \times \alpha) B^2}$ is used to sequentially sample each small I mage block p_i, resulting in a measurement matrix Y. The sampling process is implemented using an unbiased convolution layer without bias terms. The size of the convolution kernel is $B \times B \times 1$, with the stride of B = 32. The convolution layer is followed by no activation function. The weight of the convolution layer is denoted as W_Φ. The sampling process is represented by Eq. (2) and denoted as the operation $\mathcal{K}_\Phi(\cdot)$.

$$y_i = \mathcal{K}_\Phi(p_i) = W_\Phi * p_i \qquad (2)$$

In the initial reconstruction sub-network, the sampling matrix $\Phi \epsilon R^{(B^2 \times \alpha) \times B^2}$ is reshaped into $B^2 \times \alpha$ filters, where each filter has a size of $1 \times 1 \times B^2$. Then the tensor of size $B^2 \times 1 \times 1$ is reshaped to $1 \times B \times B$ by Pixelshuffle, and the initial reconstruction image is obtained. The process of initial reconstruction can be summarized as follows:

$$p^0 = \mathcal{K}_{\Phi^T}(y_i) = \text{Pixelshuffle}(W_{\Phi^T} * y_i) \qquad (3)$$

where P^0 denotes the initial reconstructed image block. Pixelshuffle is a pixel shuffling operation commonly used in super-resolution, which is a technique for enlarging images and feature maps.

3.2 Feature Space Information Flow and Texture Path Construction Module

The deep reconstruction network consists of the Feature Space Information Flow Supplementary Module and the Texture Path Construction Module, each containing multiple building blocks along two pathways. The initial reconstructed image is further deep reconstructed based on its prior information in the feature space. Additionally, in the frequency domain, texture building blocks are utilized to supplement the details of the image, resulting in a higher-quality reconstruction.

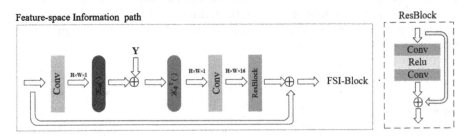

Fig. 2. Supplementary path of information flow in feature space

The Feature Space Residual Information Supplementary Module, as shown in Fig. 2, is inspired by the architecture presented in the reference 28. In this structure, the convolved output of the initial reconstruction, denoted as W, is fed into this module. By performing operations between the measurement matrix and the convolved structure, the information difference for each stage of image construction is calculated to further enhance the weight of the information difference for the next step of construction. The advantage of this approach lies in manipulating the residual information in the feature space, thereby obtaining better feature correlation and expression capabilities. By appropriately manipulating and processing this differential information, it is possible to accurately restore lost details and information, thereby improving the quality and fidelity of the reconstructed image. Additionally, residual blocks are employed in this module to suppress artifacts caused by block reconstruction during the initial reconstruction process.

The structure of the Texture Information Module is shown in Fig. 3. In this structure, the information from the initial reconstruction and the feature space reconstruction is jointly inputted into the texture block structure. In this module, an attention mechanism is introduced. A global average pooling (GAP) structure is employed to aggregate attention weights in a certain way. Subsequently, the weights are allocated through two convolutional layers and an activation function layer. These weights are then multiplied with input A to obtain the output result B of the attention mechanism. Next, the data Z undergoes Fourier transformation and is processed in the frequency domain. Two residual blocks are used to extract features at different scales. These features are then fused and transformed back through inverse Fourier transformation at the output end, and finally merged with Z features to be outputted to the next texture information module.

In the Texture Path Structure, the attention mechanism is introduced to dynamically allocate weights to the input information, enabling the texture path to pay more attention to texture information. Moreover, most of the texture information in an image consists of high-frequency components. Extracting high-frequency information in the spatial domain is often affected by low-frequency interference. However, in the frequency domain representation after Fourier transformation, low-frequency, and high-frequency components are separated, making it easier to extract high-frequency information. Therefore, in the paper, the image is transformed from the spatial domain to the frequency domain to extract texture details. By combining consistency in the compression and reconstruction processes, we are able to reconstruct the original data more accurately and provide a more advanced and precise image reconstruction algorithm.

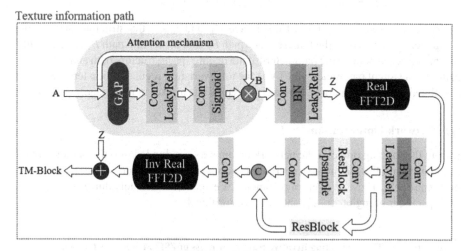

Fig. 3. Texture information path

4   Network Learning and Optimization

The FSITM-Net decomposes the image reconstruction problem into subtasks of image texture component and prior component. Specific pathways are designed for each subtask, allowing each pathway to focus on specific features in the image. Simultaneously, the pathways for these two subtasks are jointly trained to reconstruct the entire image under the supervision of a shared loss function.

4.1   Loss Function

The prior information block of an image contains a smooth background, while the texture block contains rich details. It is worth considering incorporating smooth constraints and texture blocks into the image reconstruction process to eliminate noise and discontinuities in the image while enhancing the richness of image details. We design a loss function of the form to recover the image, where $\{X\} = \{x_1, x_2, ..., x_N\}$ represents a set of training data pairs, and $x \in X$ represents a training image. In Eq. (4), two fidelity terms are defined: the difference between the predicted output image and the input ground truth image, as well as the difference between Φ and Φ^T to optimize the measurement data. Additionally, in order to promote the recovery of feature space components, total variation is applied to them, while the remaining texture details are restored in the texture path. By minimizing the loss function in the equation, optimal weight parameters w_S and w_T can be obtained.

$$
\begin{cases}
\min\limits_{w_s, w_T, w_A} \sum\limits_{i=1}^{N} \{||x_i - f_i - t_i||_1 + \beta \mathrm{TV}(f_i) + ||\Phi\Phi^T - I||_F^2\} \\
f_i = P_S(x_i, w_s),\, t_i = P_T(x_i, w_T),\, i = 1, \cdots, N
\end{cases}
\tag{4}
$$

where x_i represents the ground truth image, f_i, and t_i are the structure and texture components predicted by the feature space path P_F and the texture path P_T, respectively. w_S and w_T correspond to the parameters of the feature space structure path and the texture path. β is a weight parameter, and TV is the total variation regularization term, which is calculated using the equation, where (r, c) represents a pixel in the image.

4.2 Network Optimization

During the training process, the network parameters are divided into the parameters w_S associated with the feature space structure path and the parameters w_T associated with the texture path. These two sets of parameters are updated alternately during the training. The specific training process is shown in Algorithm 1.

Algorithm 1   The alternating iterative training process of FSITM-Net is as follows.

Input: The learning rate α, mini-batch size s, maximal iteration number Emax, parameter β, and input image X, the number of iterations k

1: Initialize the network parameter w and iteration number i=1.

2: while i≤Emax do

3:    Input a batch of training images{X}={$x_1, ..., x_N$}

4:    Fix the weight parameters w_T^{i-1} of the texture path and update the parameters w_S^i of the feature space path in this loop:

   $g_{wS} \leftarrow \nabla_{wS}(\sum_{i=1}^{N} l_1(x_i, w_S) + \beta f_2(w_S))$

   $w_S^i \leftarrow w_S^{t-1} - \alpha \cdot Adam(w_S, g_{wS})$

   Where $l_1(x_i, w_S)=||x_i - P_S(x_i, w_S) - t_i||_1 + ||\Phi\Phi^T - I||_F^2, f_2(w_S)=\mathrm{TV}(P_S(x_i,w_S))$, and= $P_T(x_i, w_T^{i-1})$;

5:    Fix the structure path parameters w_S^i and update the texture path parameters w_T^i following the following loop.

   $g_{wT} \leftarrow \nabla_{wT}(\sum_{i=1}^{N} l_1(x_i, w_T))$

   $w_T^i \leftarrow w_T^{t-1} - \alpha \cdot Adam(w_T, g_{wT})$

   Where $l_1(x_i, w_S)=||x_i - P_S(x_i, w_S) - t_i||_1 + ||\Phi\Phi^T - I||_F^2$ and $t_i = \mathrm{PT}(x_i, w_T^{i-1})$;

6:    Increase the number of iterations i=i+1;

7: end While

8 Update and adjust the network through joint training of both paths.

Output: Output the trained network parameters w_S and w_T.

5 Experimental Results and Analysis

We used the same training dataset, BSD400, consisting of 400 images [28–30]. Before training, each image was segmented into multiple 96 × 96 image patches and subjected to flipping and rotation transformations to enhance the diversity of the training data. FSITM-Net was compared with seven networks proposed by researchers, including TVAL3, STD-CS, RenonNet, DR2-Net, ISTA-Net, ISTA-Net +, DPA-Net, and NL-CSNet. The first two methods are based on iterative optimization, while the latter six are based on deep learning approaches.

5.1 Experimental Setup

The proposed algorithm was implemented using PyTorch and optimized using the Adam optimizer. The two pathways of FSITM-Net were alternately optimized. During the optimization process, the initial learning rate was set to 0.0002, β was set to 0.0008, k was set to 5, and the number of iterations was set to 100. The learning rate was scheduled using the CosineAnnealingLR method, which decayed the learning rate in a cosine function form to ensure smoother convergence during training. The reconstruction experiments compared the peak signal-to-noise ratio (PSNR) and the structural similarity index (SSIM) of the reconstructed images at sampling rates of 0.01, 0.04, 0.10, 0.25, 0.30, 0.40, and 0.50 using three widely used datasets: SET5, SET11, and BSD68.

5.2 Evaluation of FSITM-Net

The main strengths of FSITM-Net for compressive sensing reconstruction lie in its dual-path construction and texture construction module in the frequency domain. To evaluate the benefits of these two strengths, two sets of ablation experiments were conducted in the study.

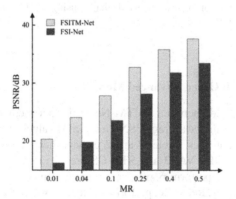

Fig. 4. PSNR comparison of reconstructed images using FSITM-Net and FSI-Net at different measurement rates in the Set11 dataset.

In the first set of ablation experiments, a structure called FS-Net was created by using only the feature space module path. FS-Net was trained under the same conditions as

FSITM-Net and tested on the Set11 dataset. The experimental results, as shown in Fig. 4, reveal that FSITM-Net outperforms FS-Net in terms of image reconstruction quality across various sampling rates. This indicates that the proposed dual-path network excels at reconstructing the structural and textural details of the images, thereby enhancing the overall quality of the reconstructed images.

In the second set of ablation experiments, we constructed the texture path module in the spatial domain without performing Fourier transformation and referred to this structure as FST-Net. It was trained with the same loss function. By conducting experiments on the SET11 dataset with a sampling rate of 0.25, we evaluated the contribution of the frequency-domain block in FSITM-Net to the reconstruction quality. The experimental results, as shown in Fig. 5, demonstrated that all the data values of the validated FSITM-Net reconstructed images were superior to those of FST-Net. This validates the effectiveness of constructing the texture module in the frequency domain for improving the reconstruction quality.

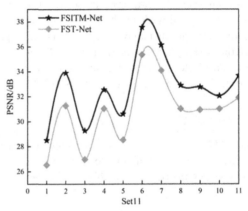

Fig. 5. The PSNR comparison of reconstructed images using FSITM-Net and FST-Net in the Set11 dataset (MR = 0.25)

5.3 Comparison with Other Advanced Methods

The comparison was made between FSITM-Net and other methods on the SET5 and SET11 datasets, evaluating the average PSNR and SSIM values of reconstructed images at multiple measurement rates. Tables 1 and 2 present these results, with the best performance marked in bold. TVAL3 and STD-CS are two iterative optimization-based algorithms that typically perform poorly at low measurement rates. Among the deep learning-based algorithms, ReconNet performs better at lower measurement rates. However, the reconstruction quality of ReconNet does not significantly improve when the measurement rate is increased from 0.1 to 0.5. On the Set11 dataset, FSITM-Net consistently outperforms other networks in terms of PSNR and SSIM for measurement rates of 0.01, 0.04, 0.1, and 0.25, particularly excelling in SSIM. At measurement rates of 0.4 and 0.5, while the PSNR of the reconstructed images by FSITM-Net is lower than that of the ISTA-Net$^+$ network, it still achieves the best SSIM. On the Set5 dataset, although the reconstructed images by FSITM-Net exhibit the highest PSNR only at a measurement rate of 0.5, its SSIM is the highest across all measurement rates. The experimental results demonstrate that the proposed texture path module has a better effect on recovering image details and performs optimally in SSIM performance testing.

In addition, we compare FSITM-Net, DPA-Net, ReconNet, ISTANet, and ISTA-Net+ on a larger BSD68 dataset, evaluating the PSNR and SSIM of reconstructed images at measurement rates of 0.5, 0.4, 0.3, 0.1, and 0.04. The research results are shown in Table 3. In terms of PSNR and SSIM performance, FSITM-Net outperforms all other methods at all measurement rates. Based on the experimental results from Tables 1–3, the proposed FSITM-Net performs optimally in terms of PSNR, except for lower PSNR performance on the Set5 dataset, where FSITM-Net performs the best overall across both Set11 and Set5 datasets. Typically, at higher measurement rates, where the measurement vectors contain sufficient information, simpler single networks can reconstruct high-quality images. FSITM-Net predicts the prior information component and texture component of the test image separately in the feature space information flow and texture path and then merges them through summation. Although summation may introduce some pixel value bias, which is unfavorable for PSNR measurement, qualitative observations from Figs. 6–9 indicate that the images reconstructed by FSITM-Net at lower sampling rates exhibit excellent visual quality.

Table 1. Average PSNR (dB) and SSIM performance comparison on Set5 at multiple measurement rates

Algorithm	MR = 0.04		MR = 0.1		MR = 0.3		MR = 0.4		MR = 0.5	
	PSNR	SSIM	PSNR	SSIM	PSNR	SSIM	PSNR	SSIM	PSNR	SSIM
TVAL3 [6]	22.14	0.6076	27.07	0.7865	32.75	0.9107	34.89	0.9363	36.75	0.9540
ReconNet [19]	22.99	0.6069	25.95	0.7228	29.79	0.8329	30.78	0.8579	32.54	0.8893
ISTA-Net [18]	24.23	0.6749	29.75	0.8457	36.09	0.9432	38.23	0.9610	40.28	0.9719
ISTA-Net + [18]	24.71	0.6933	29.87	0.8490	36.69	0.9474	38.77	0.9630	40.73	0.9737
DPA-Net [23]	**26.63**	**0.7767**	**30.32**	0.8713	**36.17**	0.9495	**38.05**	0.9632	39.57	0.9716
FSITM-Net	26.39	0.7673	30.21	**0.8811**	35.91	**0.9550**	37.92	**0.9672**	**39.58**	**0.9745**

In Figs. 6 and 7, the reconstructed Foreman and House images of all methods on the Set11 dataset are shown with sampling rates of 0.04 and 0.1, respectively. In Fig. 6, even at a sampling rate of 0.04, FSITM-Net reconstructed Monarch images with more detailed patterns of butterflies, which were closer to the original image. From Fig. 7, it can be seen that FSITM-Net performs the best in reconstructing Foreman images at a sampling rate of 0.1, while FSITM-Net performs the best in reconstructing house images, and can effectively reconstruct details of eaves. This is mainly because FSITM-Net reconstructs images through two paths: feature space information flow and texture, resulting in better visual quality in its reconstruction. This also clearly demonstrates the effectiveness of the proposed FSITM-Net.

Table 2. Average PSNR (dB) and SSIM performance comparison on Set11 at multiple measurement rates

Algorithm	MR = 0.01		MR = 0.04		MR = 0.1		MR = 0.25		MR = 0.4		MR = 0.5	
	PSNR	SSIM	PSNR	SSIM	PSNR	SSIM	PSNR	SSIM	PSNR	SSIM	PSNR	SSIM
TVAL3 [6]	14.90	0.0646	17.88	0.1997	22.45	0.3758	27.63	0.6238	31.21	0.7531	33.39	0.8157
STD-CS [7]	15.52	0.4008	20.43	0.5487	23.81	0.6715	28.77	0.8191	31.61	0.8891	33.32	0.9054
ReconNet [19]	17.27	0.4084	20.63	0.5259	24.28	0.6406	25.60	0.7589	27.26	0.8097	29.04	0.8502
DR2-Net [17]	17.44	0.4294	20.80	0.5806	24.32	0.7175	28.66	0.8432	-	-	-	-
ISTA-Net [18]	17.30	0.4082	21.23	0.5961	25.80	0.7961	31.53	0.9161	35.36	0.9533	37.43	0.9675
ISTA-Net + [18]	17.34	0.4131	21.31	0.6240	26.64	0.8036	32.57	0.9237	36.06	0.9579	38.07	0.9706
DPA-Net [23]	18.05	0.5011	23.50	0.7205	26.99	0.8354	31.74	0.9238	35.04	0.9565	36.73	0.9670
NL-CSNet [22]	19.59	**0.5229**	23.74	0.7097	27.24	0.8386	-	-	-	-	-	-
FSITM-Net	**20.34**	0.5025	**24.09**	**0.7213**	**27.83**	**0.8545**	**32.72**	**0.9357**	**35.81**	**0.9624**	**37.66**	**0.9728**

Table 3. Average PSNR (dB) and SSIM performance comparison on BSD68 at multiple measurement rates

Algorithm	MR = 0.04		MR = 0.1		MR = 0.3		MR = 0.4		MR = 0.5	
	PSNR	SSIM	PSNR	SSIM	PSNR	SSIM	PSNR	SSIM	PSNR	SSIM
ReconNet[19]	21.66	0.4994	24.15	0.5969	25.87	0.7280	26.71	0.7660	28.01	0.8150
ISTA-Net[18]	22.12	0.543	25.02	0.6958	29.93	0.8722	31.85	0.9128	33.60	0.9401
ISTA-Net + [18]	22.17	0.5573	25.33	0.7001	30.34	0.8782	32.21	0.9158	34.01	0.9421
DPA-Net [23]	23.27	0.6096	25.57	0.7267	29.68	0.8763	31.33	0.9127	32.86	0.9373
FSITM-Net	**24.28**	**0.6439**	**26.78**	**0.7784**	**31.28**	**0.9113**	**33.10**	**0.9389**	**34.86**	**0.9586**

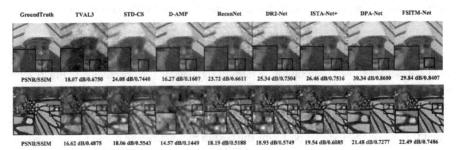

Fig. 6. Reconstructed images of foreman and Monarch in the Set11 dataset (MR = 0.04)

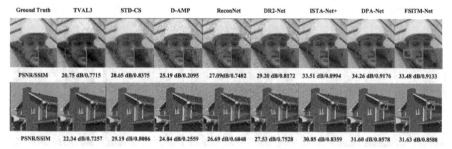

Fig. 7. Reconstructed images of foreman and house in the Set11 dataset (MR = 0.1)

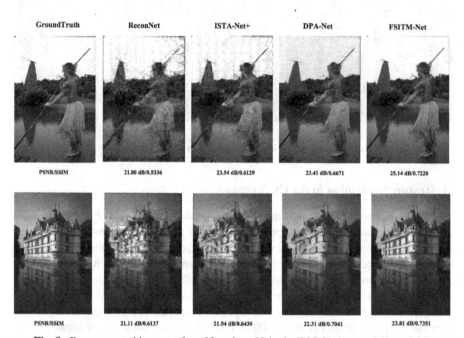

Fig. 8. Reconstructed images of test02 and test03 in the BSD68 dataset (MR = 0.04)

Figures 8 and 9 display the reconstructed images of ReconNet, ISTA-Net, DPA-Net, and FSITM-Net on the BSD68 dataset at measurement rates of 0.04 and 0.1, respectively. By zooming in on the images, it can be observed that FSITM-Net preserves more reasonable contours and finer texture details during the reconstruction process. In contrast, ReconNet and ISTA-Net, which employ block-based reconstruction methods, exhibit artifacts in the images. The images reconstructed by DPA-Net do not possess the same level of structural refinement as FSITM-Net, indicating the superior performance of FSITM-Net in suppressing artifacts using residual blocks during the reconstruction process.

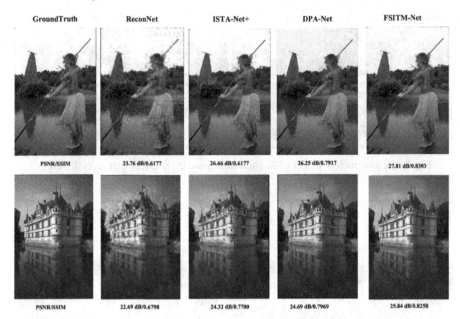

Fig. 9. Reconstructed images of test02 and test03 in the BSD68 dataset (MR = 0.1)

5.4 Texture Separation in the CS Domain

The FSITM-Net proposed not only improves the reconstruction quality but also separates images into prior information and texture information. Figure 10 demonstrates the results of separating image prior information and texture information at a sampling rate of 0.1 using different weight parameters β. It can be observed that when β is small, more information is distributed to the feature information flow path, whereas when β is large, more information lies in the texture path. Therefore, a balanced parameter needs to be set to construct a more ideal image on both paths. According to the experimental results, when the weight parameter is set to 0.0008, FSITM-Net can effectively separate texture and structural path information, leading to better reconstruction performance.

Figures 11 and 12 showcase the reconstructed Barbara and Flintstones images at a sampling rate of 0.25 using the STD-CS, DPA-Net, and FSITM-Net networks. Both images exhibit rich texture details. STD-CS utilizes a pre-selected sparse dictionary to represent the texture, DPA-Net learns texture decomposition adaptively using the texture path and texture attention module, while FSITM-Net constructs the texture using the feature space information flow and texture path. The experiments show that FSITM-Net recovers more texture details compared to the other two methods and produces higher image quality when reconstructing the Flintstones image.

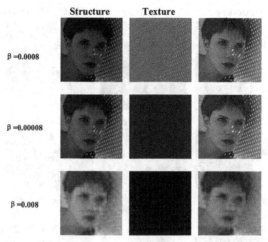

Fig. 10. The influence of weight parameter β on image structure information and texture information(MR = 0.1)

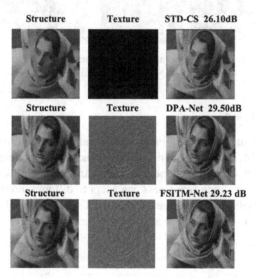

Fig. 11. The structure and texture components of Barbara images are separated by variational methods STD-CS, DPA-Net and FSITM-Net in CS domain(MR = 0.25)

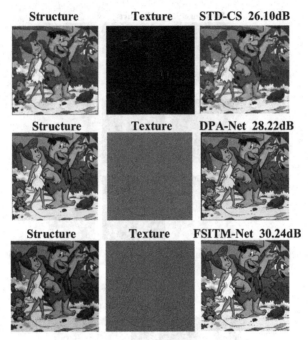

Fig. 12. The structure and texture components of Flinstones images are separated by variational methods STD-CS, DPA-Net and FSITM-Net in CS domain (MR = 0.25)

5.5 Sensitivity to Noise

The robustness assessment of detection networks under noise interference in compressive sensing is crucial for addressing noise interference and data integrity in real-world environments, as well as improving the practicality and applicability of the methods. A detection network with strong robustness can adapt to different noise levels and types, making it widely applicable in various scenarios. This is essential for enhancing the reliability and effectiveness of compressive sensing methods.

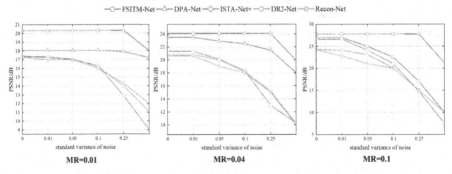

Fig. 13. Comparison of PSNR of multiple deep learn-based methods in reconstructed images with different proportions of Gaussian noise

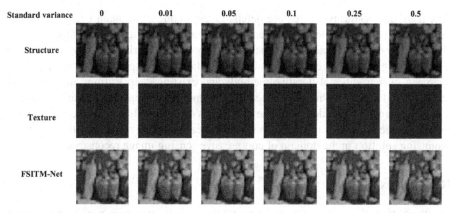

Fig. 14. The reconstructed image of FSITM-Net is obtained under the destruction of five different standard variance noises (MR = 0.01)

To evaluate the robustness of the FSITM-Net network in handling noise, we conducted a series of experiments. Firstly, five types of Gaussian noise with mean 0 and standard deviations of 0.01, 0.05, 0.1, 0.25, and 0.5 were added during testing. The noisy test set was then inputted, and the PSNR of the reconstructed images from five deep learning networks was compared at sampling rates of 0.01, 0.04, and 0.1, as shown in Fig. 13. From the graph, it can be observed that FSITM-Net is only affected and shows decreased PSNR in the reconstructed images when the noise standard deviation is 0.5, while it is hardly affected when the noise intensity is lower. On the other hand, the other four networks are more susceptible to noise, resulting in a decrease in the PSNR of the reconstructed images. This indicates that the FSITM-Net network exhibits strong robustness.

Figure 14 presents the reconstructed peppers image by FSITM-Net at a sampling rate of 0.01 under the degradation of 5 different standard deviation noises. From the image, it can be observed that there are noticeable noise artifacts in the reconstructed image when the noise standard deviation is 0.5, while the quality of the reconstructed image is not significantly affected under the other four standard deviations of Gaussian noise. Moreover, at a low sampling rate of 0.01, the contribution of the texture path is smaller than that of the structure path. Due to total variation regularization, the structure path demonstrates strong robustness against noise degradation. Therefore, as the standard deviation of noise increases, FSITM-Net exhibits relatively minor performance degradation compared to other competing methods, indicating its strong resistance to noise.

6   Conclusion

In summary, we present an advanced solution in the field of compressive sensing image reconstruction. The proposed method introduces a dual-path compressive sensing reconstruction network that leverages image feature space information flow and texture information. By effectively reconstructing the main structural information through the application of the proximal gradient descent algorithm in the image feature space information flow path, and restoring the texture details in the frequency domain using the texture information path combined with attention mechanisms, the method achieves remarkable improvements in both reconstruction quality and network robustness, even under low sampling rates. The experimental results validate the superiority of the proposed approach over traditional iterative methods and existing deep learning methods. The reconstructed images exhibit enhanced quality and visual appeal, making the method a viable alternative for addressing the challenges of low-quality image reconstruction. Its effectiveness and practicality in various applications are evident, positioning it as a promising solution in the domain of compressive sensing image reconstruction.

References

1. Zhang, Y., et al.: A review of compressive sensing in information security field. IEEE Access **4**, 2507–2519 (2016)
2. Wen, W., Hong, Y., Fang, Y., Li, M., Li, M.: A visually secure image encryption scheme based on semi-tensor product compressed sensing. Signal Process. **173**, 107580 (2020)
3. Yang, J., Wright, J., Huang, T.S., Ma, Y.: Image super-resolution via sparse representation. IEEE Trans. Image Process. **19**, 2861–2873 (2010)
4. Deka, B. & Datta, S. Compressed Sensing Magnetic Resonance Image Reconstruction Algorithms. Springer (2019). https://doi.org/10.1007/978-981-13-3597-6
5. Dismuke, C., Lindrooth, R.: Ordinary least squares. Methods Des. Outcomes Res. **93**, 93–104 (2006)
6. Li, C., Yin, W., Jiang, H., Zhang, Y.: An efficient augmented Lagrangian method with applications to total variation minimization. Comput. Optim. Appl. **56**, 507–530 (2013)
7. Dabov, K., Foi, A., Katkovnik, V., Egiazarian, K.: Image denoising by sparse 3-D transform-domain collaborative filtering. IEEE Trans. Image Process. **16**, 2080–2095 (2007)
8. Ni, R., Wang, F., Wang, J., Hu, Y.: Multi-image encryption based on compressed sensing and deep learning in optical gyrator domain. IEEE Photonics J. **13**, 1–16 (2021)
9. Qiao, M., Meng, Z., Ma, J., Yuan, X.: Deep learning for video compressive sensing. Apl Photonics **5**, 030801 (2020)
10. Yang, G., et al.: DAGAN: deep de-aliasing generative adversarial networks for fast compressed sensing MRI reconstruction. IEEE Trans. Med. Imaging **37**, 1310–1321 (2017)
11. Islam, S.R., Maity, S.P., Ray, A.K., Mandal, M.: Deep learning on compressed sensing measurements in pneumonia detection. Int. J. Imaging Syst. Technol. **32**, 41–54 (2022)
12. Taha, A., Alrabeiah, M., Alkhateeb, A.: Enabling large intelligent surfaces with compressive sensing and deep learning. IEEE Access **9**, 44304–44321 (2021)
13. Adler, A., Boublil, D., Elad, M., Zibulevsky, M.: A deep learning approach to block-based compressed sensing of images. arXiv preprint arXiv:160601519 (2016)
14. Yang, Y., Sun, J., Li, H., Xu, Z.: ADMM-CSNet: a deep learning approach for image compressive sensing. IEEE Trans. Pattern Anal. Mach. Intell. **42**, 521–538 (2018)
15. Sun, B., Feng, H., Chen, K., Zhu, X.: A deep learning framework of quantized compressed sensing for wireless neural recording. IEEE Access **4**, 5169–5178 (2016)
16. Shi, W., Jiang, F., Liu, S., Zhao, D.: Image compressed sensing using convolutional neural network. IEEE Trans. Image Process. **29**, 375–388 (2019)
17. Yao, H., et al.: Dr2-Net: deep residual reconstruction network for image compressive sensing. Neurocomputing **359**, 483–493 (2019)
18. Zhang, J., Ghanem, B.: ISTA-Net: interpretable optimization-inspired deep network for image compressive sensing. In: Proceedings of the IEEE conference on computer vision and pattern recognition, pp. 1828–1837 (2018)

19. Kulkarni, K., Lohit, S., Turaga, P., Kerviche, R., Ashok, A.: ReconNet: non-iterative reconstruction of images from compressively sensed measurements. In: Proceedings of the IEEE Conference on Computer Vision and Pattern Recognition, pp. 449–458 (2016)
20. Elad, M., Aharon, M.: Image denoising via sparse and redundant representations over learned dictionaries. IEEE Trans. Image Process. **15**, 3736–3745 (2006)
21. Protter, M., Elad, M., Takeda, H., Milanfar, P.: Generalizing the nonlocal-means to super-resolution reconstruction. IEEE Trans. Image Process. **18**, 36–51 (2008)
22. Cui, W., Liu, S., Jiang, F., Zhao, D.: Image compressed sensing using non-local neural network. IEEE Trans. Multimed. **25**, 816–830 (2021)
23. Sun, Y., Chen, J., Liu, Q., Liu, B., Guo, G.: Dual-path attention network for compressed sensing image reconstruction. IEEE Trans. Image Process. **29**, 9482–9495 (2020)
24. Candès, E.J., Romberg, J., Tao, T.: Robust uncertainty principles: exact signal reconstruction from highly incomplete frequency information. IEEE Trans. Inf. Theory **52**, 489–509 (2006)
25. Grasmair, M., Haltmeier, M., Scherzer, O.: Sparse regularization with lq penalty term. Inverse Probl. **24**, 055020 (2008)
26. Boyd, S., et al.: Distributed optimization and statistical learning via the alternating direction method of multipliers, vol. 3, pp.1–122. Foundations and Trends® in Machine Learning (2011)
27. Wang, J., Kwon, S., Shim, B.: Generalized orthogonal matching pursuit. IEEE Trans. Signal Process. **60**, 6202–6216 (2012)
28. Chen, W., Yang, C., Yang, X.: FSOINet: feature-space optimization-inspired network for image compressive sensing. In: ICASSP 2022 - 2022 IEEE International Conference on Acoustics, Speech and Signal Processing (ICASSP), pp. 2460–2464 (2022).
29. Wu, Y., Sun, J., Chen, W., Yin, J.: Improved image compressive sensing recovery with low-rank prior and deep image prior. Signal Process. **205**, 108896 (2023)
30. Ye, D., et al.: CSformer: bridging convolution and transformer for compressive sensing. IEEE Trans. Image Process. **32**, 2827–2842 (2023)

Multi-objective Optimization Energy Management Strategy for Fuel Cell Hybrid Electric Vehicles During Vehicle Following

Bo Chen[1], Mingrui Liao[2], Fazhan Tao[1,3], Haoxiang Ma[1(✉)], and Longlong Zhu[1]

[1] School of Information Engineering, Henan University of Science and Technology, Henan, China
9906398@haust.edu.cn
[2] Aerospace System Engineering Shanghai, Minhang District, Shanghai, China
[3] Longmen Laboratory, Luoyang, Henan, China

Abstract. With the advancements in automotive automation and network connectivity technologies, achieving optimal co-optimization of driving safety, driving comfort, fuel economy and energy sources durability remains a great challenge for fuel cell hybrid electric vehicles (FCHEV). However, in most existing studies, power source durability is often disregarded, and there is an urgent need to address the trade-off between different targets. In the paper, a multi-objective optimization energy management strategy (EMS) for FCHEV in the following vehicle scenarios is proposed. Specifically, fuel cell voltage attenuation and lithium battery capacity attenuation are utilized to characterize the degradation level of the fuel cell and battery, respectively. Subsequently, a degradation model for the fuel cell and battery within the on-board power system of the controlled vehicle is established. On this basis, a multi-objective cost function integrating driving safety, driving comfort, fuel economy and energy sources durability is constructed. Then, the model predictive control (MPC) method was used to solve the above multi-objective functions. The results highlight that the MPC-based strategy can reduce equivalent fuel consumption cost by up to 10.49% compared with the traditional strategies.

Keywords: Fuel cell hybrid electric vehicles · Energy management strategy · Model predictive control

1 Introduction

With the advancement of economy, the problem of energy shortage is spreading, and the national awareness of green environmental protection is increasing, which fuel cell hybrid electric vehicles (FCHEV) have been chosen by more and more people due to its high efficiency and zero pollution characteristics [1, 2]. The energy management system (EMS) serves as the core of hybrid electric vehicles, playing a crucial role in shaping their reliability, control, economy, and emission performance.

The current research on EMS can be broadly categorized into two groups: rule-based strategies and optimization-based strategies [3]. Rule-based strategies have found wide-ranging applications in the engineering field due to their advantageous characteristics,

F. Sun et al. (Eds.): ICCSIP 2023, CCIS 1918, pp. 122–133, 2024.
https://doi.org/10.1007/978-981-99-8018-5_9

such as their simplicity in design, low computational complexity, and robustness. Nevertheless, these strategies may not exhibit satisfactory performance in scenarios with limited expert experience owing to their inherent lack of adaptability.

The optimization-based EMS is utilized to determine the optimal power distribution among various power sources. This approach can be divided into two categories: global optimization strategies and local optimization strategies [4, 5]. Global optimization strategies are commonly employed as they guarantee global optimality. However, these methods require extensive prior knowledge and involve lengthy computations, limiting their adaptability to real-time driving conditions. To address this limitation, an online EMS based on local optimization is proposed, which offers the advantages of requiring less prior knowledge, shorter computation time, and lower computational complexity. Examples of commonly used real-time optimization energy management strategies include Model Predictive Control (MPC) etc.

There have been studies both domestically and internationally that have used MPC algorithm to achieve fuel economy and driving safety goals. In [7], the MPC method effectively reduces the fuel consumption during the following process and ensuring safety. Considering the impact of SOC trajectory on fuel economy of hybrid electric vehicles, a comprehensive MPC method was proposed in [8] to optimize vehicle speed trajectory and plan SOC while simultaneously considering fuel economy and driving safety. Another MPC method with optimized frequency was proposed in [9] that aims to minimize vehicle energy consumption while adhering to traffic and speed constraints. With the growing maturity of automotive connectivity and automation technologies, future behaviors of preceding vehicles can be easily predicted. In [10], a MPC scheme is proposed that utilizes forward-looking traffic information to minimize fuel consumption in connected hybrid electric vehicle (HEV), achieveing fuel efficiency improvements by estimating the speed of preceding vehicles within the range of anticipation. In [11], fuel economy of HEV was improved while maintaining the desired inter-vehicle distance from the preceding vehicle. To preemptively mitigate the risk of traffic accidents during car-following scenarios, an optimal method based on forward prediction was proposed. For connected hybrid electric vehicles, an optimized power system energy consumption scheme based on the distance between the preceding and current vehicles was proposed in [12]. In [13], a MPC method based on EMS was implemented for car-following scenarios of parallel hybrid electric vehicle (PHEV), effectively improving total energy consumption and safety of the vehicle. Although the above-mentioned studies have made progress in improving fuel economy, driving safety, and emissions, the driving comfort has not been fully considered in [12, 13], directly impacting the fatigue level of drivers and passengers [14, 15] addressed the conflicting goals between fuel economy and safety and proposed a multi-objective framework to significantly optimize EMS system parameters to address the safety, fuel saving, and emission reduction issues of the PHEV. These methods were designed for HEV or PHEV, rather than FCHEV. Therefore, this paper uses MPC algorithm to solve the above multi-objective optimization problem for FCHEV in the following scenarios, while optimizing driving safety, driving comfort, fuel economy and energy source durability. Two main contributions are listed as follows:

1) To address the difficulty in observing the degree of internal degradation of energy sources, the external parameters (FC voltage and BAT capacity) are utilized as degradation characterization variables to construct FC and BAT degradation models.
2) To address the neglect of the impact of power source degradation on overall vehicle durability in multi-objective energy optimization for FCHEV, the power source degradation models are incorporated into the multi-objective energy optimization, aiming to further enhance the overall vehicle performance of FCHEV.

The remainder of this paper is organized as follows. In Sect. 2, the longitudinal dynamics and energy sources degradation model of FCHEV is modeled. In Sect. 3, the multi-objective optimization function in the following vehicle scenarios is constructed and the MPC method is used to solve the above multi-objective functions. In Sect. 4, a comparative simulation experiment is carried out and the simulation results are discussed. In Sect. 5, the conclusions are drawn.

2   Modelling of Longitudinal Dynamics and Power Sources

The model of the FCHEV is shown in Fig. 1. FC as a primary energy source, transmits the power to the motor through a unidirectional DC/DC converter. Both the BAT and the SC serve as energy storage system, in which BAT provides auxiliary power for FC, and SC connects to the bidirectional DC/DC to provide/absorb peak power. These three energy sources provide power for FCHEV.

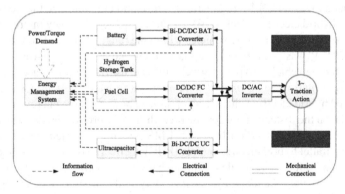

Fig. 1. The power structure of FCHEV.

2.1   Vehicle Longitudinal Dynamics Model

The longitudinal dynamics model of FCHEV is defined as follows:

$$\begin{cases} \dot{x}_t = v_t \\ \dot{v}_t = \dfrac{1}{m_t}\left(u - F_a - F_r - F_g\right) \end{cases} \tag{1}$$

where x_t represents the longitudinal position, v_t represents speed of the vehicle; m_t represents mass of the vehicle; u represents traction force, F_a represents atmospheric drag, F_r represents rolling resistance; F_g represents ramp resistance. The expression for F_a, F_r and F_g are outlined as follows:

$$\begin{cases} F_a = 0.5\varepsilon CAv_t^2 \\ F_r = fm_tg\cos\theta \\ F_g = m_tg\sin\theta \end{cases} \tag{2}$$

where ε represents air density; C represents air drag coefficient; A represents vehicle effective frontal area; f represents rolling resistance coefficient; g represents the gravitational constant; θ represents the road slope.

2.2 Fuel Cell Degradation Model

The output voltage of the FC is given as follows:

$$V_{fc} = V_o - V_\Omega - V_a - V_c \tag{3}$$

where V_{fc} represents output of the FC, V_o represents open circuit voltage of FC, V_Ω represents potential losses caused by ohmic, V_a represents potential losses caused by activation, V_c represents potential losses caused by concentration.

The above parameter formulas are as follows:

$$\begin{cases} V_o = E - 0.85e^{-3}(T - 298) + \dfrac{RT}{zF}In(P_{H_2}\sqrt{Po_2}) \\ V_\Omega = R_eI_{fc} \\ V_a = \dfrac{RT}{\beta zF}In(\dfrac{I_{fc}}{I_0}) \\ V_c = \dfrac{RT}{zF}(\dfrac{I_{fc}}{I_L - I_{fc}}) \end{cases} \tag{4}$$

where E represents the voltage generated at standard atmospheric pressure; T represents operating temperature; R is universal gas constant; z represents the number of electrons transferred; F represents Faraday constant; P_{H_2} and Po_2 represent partial pressure of hydrogen-oxygen, respectively; R_e represents internal resistance; I_{fc} represents the current of the FC; β represents Tafel constant; I_0 represents exchange current; I_L represents limiting current.

The hydrogen consumption of the FC is defined as follows:

$$\begin{cases} m_{H_2} = \displaystyle\int_0^t \dfrac{P_{fc}}{\eta_{fc}\rho_{H_2}}dt \\ P_{fc} = V_{fc}I_{fc} \end{cases} \tag{5}$$

where m_{H_2} represents the mass of hydrogen consumption; P_{fc} represents output power of the FC; P_{H_2} represents low heating value of hydrogen; η_{fc} represents efficiency of the FC, defined by:

$$\eta_{fc} = \frac{V_{fc}}{1.254}\left(\frac{P_{fc} - P_{aux}}{P_{fc}}\right) \tag{6}$$

where P_{aux} represents input power of auxiliary equipment.

The voltage decay of the FC is used to characterize the degradation degree of the FC and the degradation model of FC is established. The ratio of the voltage attenuation of the FC to the maximum allowable voltage attenuation is defined as the degradation rate of the FC, as shown in the formula:

$$C_{fc} = \frac{k_r(n_s V_a + V_b t_a + V_c t_b + V_d \int_0^t |\Delta P_{fc}| dt)}{\Delta V} \tag{7}$$

where C_{fc} represents degradation rate of the FC; k_c represents the correction coefficient of driving cycles; n_s represents the number of start/stop cycles; t_a represents time durations of low power; t_b represent time durations of high power operation conditions; ΔP_{fc} represents transient power changes of the FC; ΔV represents maximum allowable voltage attenuation; V_a represents voltage attenuation rates of star-stop cycling, V_b represents voltage attenuation rates of low power operation; V_c represents voltage attenuation rates of high power operation; V_d represents voltage attenuation rates of transient power changes.

Considering the degradation degree of the FC, the output voltage expression of the FC is as follows:

$$V_{fc} = V_o - I_{fc}R_e(1 + C_{fc}) - \frac{RT}{\beta z F}\ln\left(\frac{I_{fc}}{I_0}\right) - \frac{RT}{zF}\ln\left(\frac{I_{fc}}{I_L(1 - C_{fc}) - I_{fc}}\right) \tag{8}$$

2.3 Lithium Battery Degradation Model

The lithium-ion batteries have been chosen as the energy storage system for hybrid power systems. The output voltage of the BAT is defined as follows:

$$V_{bat} = V_o' - I_{bat}R_{bat} \tag{9}$$

where V_{bat} represents the output of the BAT; V_o' represents open circuit voltage; I_{bat} represents the current of the BAT; R_{bat} represents internal resistance; V_o' is related to the maximum capacity and current of the BAT, which is defined as follows:

$$V_o' = \begin{cases} V - K\dfrac{Q_{bat}}{Q_{bat} - I_{bat}t}(I_{bat}t + I_{bat}') + Ee^{(-BI_{bat}t)}, I_{bat} \geq 0 \\ V - \dfrac{KQ_{bat}I_{bat}'}{I_{bat} - 0.1Q_{bat}} - \dfrac{KQ_{bat}I_{bat}t}{Q_b - I_b t} + Ee^{(-BI_{bat}t)}, I_{bat} < 0 \end{cases} \tag{10}$$

where V represents reference voltage value; K represents polarization resistance; Q_{bat} represents maximum capacity; I_{bat}' represents filtered current; E represents exponential voltage; B represents the reciprocal of time constant.

The SOC of BAT can be calculated based on the current of BAT and charge and discharge efficiency η_{bat}, from 0 to 1 as follows:

$$SOC_{bat} = SOC_i - \eta_{bat} \int \frac{i_{bat}}{3600Q_{bat}} dt \tag{11}$$

where SOC_i represents the initial SOC of BAT.

Similar to the FC, the capacity decay of the BAT is used to characterize the degradation level, constructing the degradation model for the BAT. The degradation model of the BAT defines the ratio of the actual consumed energy from t = 0 to the present to the total energy consumed until end-of-life as the BAT degradation rate.

$$C_{bat} = \frac{\int_0^t |I_{bat}| dt}{2 \times 3600 N_{bat} Q_c} \tag{12}$$

where C_{bat}, Q_c and N_{bat} represent the degradation rate of BAT, nominal capacity and the number of charging/discharging cycles until end-of-life, respectively.

Considering the degree of degradation of BAT, the remaining capacity of BAT is expressed as:

$$Q_{bat} = (1 - 0.2C_{bat})Q_c \tag{13}$$

3 Construction of Multi-objective Optimization Function in the Following Vehicle Scenarios

Aiming at the construction of multi-objective optimization function in the following vehicle scenarios, the influence mechanism of each parameter of following vehicle control and EMS on driving safety, comfort, fuel economy and energy source durability was analyzed, and the corresponding evaluation index and cost function of each objective were established. Multi-objective optimization of EMS based on MPC is shown in Fig. 2. The meaning of the symbol is at the end of this chapter.

3.1 Driving Safety Function

The driving safety function is established, and the braking distance can be estimated as:

$$S_{brk} = v_{veh}\tau_{brk} + \frac{v_{veh}^2}{2a_{brk}} \tag{14}$$

where τ_{brk} represents the brake response time, v_{veh} is the speed of the following vehicle, and a_{brk} is the brake deceleration.

The braking reaction time of the minimum following distance is set at 0.5 s and the braking deceleration is 8 m/s^2. The braking reaction time of the maximum following distance is set to 1 s, and the braking deceleration speed is set to 6 m/s^2. From which

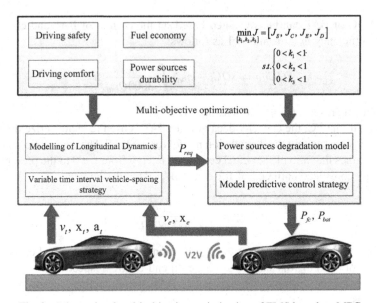

Fig. 2. Schematic of multi-objective optimization of EMS based on MPC

the minimum following distance $\Delta S_{\min}$ and maximum following distance $\Delta S_{\max}$ can be obtained as:

$$\Delta S_{\min} = 2 + 0.5 v_{veh} + 0.0625 * v_{veh}^2$$
$$\Delta S_{\max} = 10 + v_{veh} + 0.0825 * v_{veh}^2 \tag{15}$$

Additionally, an optimal following zone is defined as:

$$\Delta S_{ub} = \alpha * \Delta S_{\max} + (1 - \alpha) * \Delta S_{\min}$$
$$\Delta S_{lb} = \alpha * \Delta S_{\min} + (1 - \alpha) * \Delta S_{\max} \tag{16}$$

where ΔS_{ub} and ΔS_{lb} are the upper and lower bounds of the best following region respectively, and α are the adjustment coefficients.

The objective function of driving safety J_S is as follows:

$$J_S = \begin{cases} +\infty & \Delta s < \Delta s_{\min} \\ 0.2 * \tan(\frac{\pi}{2} * \frac{\Delta s - \Delta s_{lb}}{\Delta s_{\min} - \Delta s_{lb}}) & \Delta s_{\min} \leq \Delta s < \Delta s_{lb} \\ \left| \Delta s - \frac{\Delta s_{up} + \Delta s_{lp}}{2} \right| & \Delta s_{lb} \leq \Delta s \leq \Delta s_{ub} \\ 2 * (\Delta s - \Delta s_{ub})^2 & \Delta s_{ub} \leq \Delta s \leq \Delta s_{\max} \\ 2 * (\Delta s - \Delta s_{ub})^2 + 100 * (\Delta s - \Delta s_{\max})^2 & \Delta s > \Delta s_{\max} \end{cases} \tag{17}$$

3.2 Driving Comfort Function

Based on the dynamics model of the vehicle above, by calculating the speed at each moment, thus minimizing the speed change of the self-driving vehicle, the objective function of driving comfort is as follows:

$$J_C = \frac{1}{t_s} \sum_{k=2}^{n} |v_i(k) - v_i(k-1)| \tag{18}$$

where J_C represents the objective function of driving comfort; t_s represents the total time of driving conditions.

3.3 Fuel Economy Function

Taking into account the health of BAT, it is essential to restrict the SOC of the battery within the range of 0.5 to 0.75. Therefore, the objective function for achieving optimal fuel economy can be formulated as follows:

$$J_E = \sigma_{H_2} \sum_{k=1}^{n} (\frac{1}{\eta_{fc}\rho_{H_2}} P_{fc}(k) + \lambda_{bat}P_{bat}(k)) \tag{19}$$

where J_E represents the objective function of fuel economy function; σ_{H_2} represents hydrogen price.

3.4 Power Sources Durability Function

The degradation models based on FC and BAT, the objective function of energy sources durability is as follows:

$$J_D = \sigma_{fc}P_{nfc}C_{fc} + \sigma_{bat}P_{nbat}C_{bat} \tag{20}$$

where J_D represents the objective function of energy sources durability; σ_{fc} represents unit power price of FC; σ_{bat} represents unit power price of BAT; P_{nfc} represents the nominal power of FC; P_{nbat} represents the nominal power of BAT.

3.5 Optimizing Algorithm for MPC

Among the main control parameters of EMS system, the weight factors of multi-objective optimization are set k_1, k_2, k_3, where k_1 and k_2 affect vehicle following performance, k_3 affects fuel economy and power source durability. Therefore, $X = [k_1, k_2, k_3]$ is chosen as the weight factor. In this paper, the multi-objective optimization problem involving weight factor X is defined as follows:

$$\min_{[k_1,k_2,k_3]} J = [J_S, J_C, J_E, J_D] \tag{21}$$

$$s.t. \begin{cases} 0 < k_1 < 1 \\ 0 < k_2 < 1 \\ 0 < k_3 < 1 \end{cases} \tag{22}$$

The composite index J is used to evaluate the overall performance between driving safety, driving comfort, fuel economy and energy source durability. The cost function with time step k is expressed as:

$$J(k) = J_S + k_1 \cdot J_C(k) + k_2 \cdot J_E(k) + k_3 \cdot J_D(k) \tag{23}$$

The formula for solving the multi-objective optimization problem using the MPC with time step k is as follows:

$$J(k) = \sum_{t=k}^{k+N_p-1} J_S + k_1 \cdot J_C(k) + k_2 \cdot J_E(k) + k_3 \cdot J_D(k), \ k = 0, 1, 2\ldots \tag{24}$$

where N_p is the length of the scroll optimization. Each objective is described in details as follows:

1) Driving safety function J_S: minimizing the tacking error of desired following distance.
2) Driving comfort function J_C: minimizing the speed variation of current vehicle to avoid rapid acceleration and deceleration.
3) Fuel economy function J_E: minimizing the sum of equivalent hydrogen consumption cost via fuel cell and battery.
4) Power sources durability function J_D: minimizing the degradation rate of power sources to prolong their lifespan.

4 Simulation and Analysis

This paper proposed a multi-objective optimization based on EMS for FCHEV in the following vehicle scenarios. In order to demonstrate the effectiveness of this method in achieving a balance between various performance metrics during vehicle following, simulations were performed using Matlab/Simulink.

4.1 Simulation Results and Analysis

As shown in Fig. 3, under the real-time working conditions of Urban Dynamometer Driving Schedule (UDDS), the real-time positions of the preceding and current vehicles can be seen. It is evident that despite various instances of rapid acceleration and deceleration, the speed of the current vehicle is basically the same as that of the preceding vehicle, which can greatly ensure the performance indicators of driving comfort. As shown in Fig. 4, it can be observed that the tracking error curve remains within the range of -1 to 1, ensuring a strict evaluation of driving safety metrics.

The data reveals clear discrepancies between MPC-based strategy and traditional strategies into account in Fig. 5, which demonstrates the initial alignment of the battery SOC curves under both strategies, lasting for 90 s. This can be attributed to the fact that within the initial 90 s, power is solely supplied by the BAT and SC, while the fuel cell remains inactive. However, after the initial 90 s, divergences in the battery SOC curves between the two strategies become noticeable, which verified that MPC-based strategy ensured a low battery discharge depth, thereby safeguarding the internal structure of the battery and effectively extending its service life.

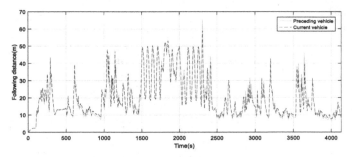

Fig. 3. Following distance of preceding vehicle and current vehicle in UDDS.

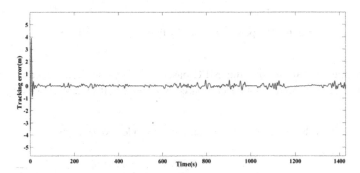

Fig. 4. Tracking error of preceding vehicle and current vehicle in UDDS.

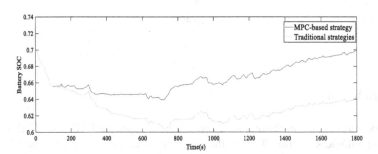

Fig. 5. The variation of battery SOC between two strategies in UDDS.

As shown in Fig. 6, the power distribution of FC, BA and SC in EMS based on MPC under UDDS driving conditions. As the main energy source among the three energy sources, the output power of FC is always maintained in the range of 4.5–20 kW, providing a continuous and stable output power for the vehicle. The output power of BAT is mostly kept in the range of (-10)-12 kW, which not only reflects the stability of BAT to the power output, but also helps to prolong the service life of BAT. Furthermore, the output power of SC is mainly in the range of (-5)-10kW, which reflects its advantages of providing transient high power.

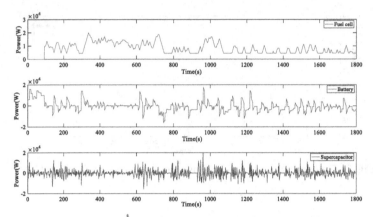

Fig. 6. The power provided by three sources in UDDS.

The results highlight that the MPC-based strategy can reduce equivalent fuel consumption cost by up to 10.49% compared with the traditional strategies in Table 1.

Table 1. The hydrogen consumption under two strategies.

Strategy	Hydrogen consumption(gal)
MPC-based strategy	7.34
Traditional strategies	8.2
Improvement	10.49%

5   Conclusion

This paper proposed a multi-objective optimization based on EMS for FCHEV in the following vehicle scenarios. Firstly, the degradation models for the FC and BAT are established in the on-board power system of the controlled vehicle, utilizing voltage attenuation of the FC and capacity attenuation of the BAT to characterize their degradation levels. Secondly, based on the constructed degradation models of the FC and BAT, a multi-objective cost function is developed, integrating driving safety, driving comfort, fuel economy, and energy source durability. Finally, a multi-objective energy management method based on MPC is adopted to solve the multi-objective functions and obtain the optimal energy allocation results. The results highlight that the MPC-based strategy can reduce equivalent fuel consumption cost by up to 10.49% compared with the traditional strategies.

Acknowledgments. Supported in part by the National Natural Science Foundation of China under Grant (62301212), Major Science and Technology Projects of Longmen Laboratory under

Grant (231100220300), the Program for Science and Technology Innovation Talents in the University of Henan Province under Grant (23HASTIT021), the Scientific and Technological Project of Henan Province under Grant (222102210056, 222102240009), China Postdoctoral Science Foundation (2023M730982), the Science and Technology Development Plan of Joint Research Program of Henan underGrant (222103810036), the Open Fund of InnerMongoliaKeyLaboratory of ElectromechanicaControl under Grant (IMMEC2022001, IMMEC2022002).

References

1. Fathabadi, H.: Combining a proton exchange membrane fuel cell (PEMFC) stack with a Li-ion battery to supply the power needs of a hybrid electric vehicle. Renewable Energy **130**, 714–724 (2019)
2. Sun, H., Fu, Z., Tao, F., Zhu, L., Si, P.: Data-driven reinforcement learning-based hierarchical energy management strategy for fuel cell/battery/ultracapacitor hybrid electric vehicles. J. Power. Sources **455**, 227964 (2020)
3. Chen, J., Xu, C.F., Wu, C.S., et al.: Adaptive fuzzy logic control of fuel-cell-battery hybrid systems for electric vehicles. IEEE Trans. Industr. Inf. **14**(1), 292–300 (2018)
4. Li, G., Gorges, D.: Ecological adaptive cruise control and energy management strategy for hybrid electric vehicles based on heuristic dynamic programming. IEEE Trans. Intell. Transp. **20**, 3526–3535 (2018)
5. Hovgard, M., Jonsson, O., Murgovski, N., Sanfridson, M., Fredriksson, J.: Cooperative energy management of electrified vehicles on hilly roads. Control. Eng. Pract. **73**, 66–78 (2018)
6. Zhang, H., Peng, J., Tan, H., Dong, H., Ding, F.: A deep reinforcement learning-based energy management framework with lagrangian relaxation for plug-in hybrid electric vehicle. IEEE Trans. Transp. Electrification **7**(3), 1146–1160 (2021)
7. Li, L., Wang, X., Song, J.: Fuel consumption optimization for smart hybrid electric vehicle during a car-following process. Mech. Syst. Signal Process. **87**, 17–29 (2017)
8. Xie, S., Hu, X., Liu, T., Qi, S., Lang, K., Li, H.: Predictive vehicle following power management for plug-in hybrid electric vehicles. Energy **166**, 701–714 (2019)
9. Maamria, D., Gillet, K., Colin, G., Chamaillard, Y., Nouillant, C.: Optimal predictive eco-driving cycles for conventional, electric, and hybrid electric cars. IEEE Trans. Veh. Technol. **68**(7), 6320–6330 (2019)
10. Zhang, F., Xi, J., Langari, R.: Real-time energy management strategy based on velocity forecasts using V2V and V2I communications. IEEE Trans. Intell. Transp. Syst. **18**(2), 416–430 (2017)
11. Xiong, H., Tan, Z., Zhang, R., He, S.: A new dual axle drive optimization control strategy for electric vehicles using vehicle-to-infrastructure communications. IEEE Trans. Industr. Inf. **16**(4), 2574–2582 (2020)
12. Nguyen, V.-L., Lin, P.-C., Hwang, R.-H.: Enhancing misbehavior detection in 5G vehicle-to-vehicle communications. IEEE Trans. Veh. Technol. **69**(9), 9417–9430 (2020)
13. Xu, F., Shen, T.: Look-ahead prediction-based real-time optimal energy management for connected HEVs. IEEE Trans. Veh. Technol. **69**(3), 2537–2551 (2020)
14. He, Y., et al.: Multi-objective co-optimization of cooperative adaptive cruise control and energy management strategy for PHEVs. IEEE Trans. Transp. Electrification **6**(1), 346–355 (2020)
15. Wang, Y., Moura, S.J., Advani, S.G., Prasad, A.K.: Power management system for a fuel cell/battery hybrid vehicle incorporating fuel cell and battery degradation. Int. J. Hydrogen Energy **44**(16), 8479–8492 (2019)

Pointwise-Measurement-Based Event-Triggered Synchronization of Reaction-Diffusion Neural Networks

Danjing Zheng and Xiaona Song$^{(\boxtimes)}$

School of Information Engineering, Henan University of Science and Technology,
Luoyang 471023, China
xiaona_97@163.com

Abstract. In this paper, the synchronization issue of reaction-diffusion neural networks (RDNNs) is addressed based on a dynamic event-triggered mechanism (DETM). First, pointwise measurement is used to balance system design cost and system performance, and DETM is employed to reduce the utilization of communication resources. Subsequently, the pointwise control is performed at certain specific points to save the number of actuators. In addition, the stability criteria for a closed-loop error system with less conservativeness are derived by using a time-dependent Lyapunov-Krasovskii functional and integrating some inequalities. Finally, a numerical example is provided to illustrate the validity of the proposed synchronization scheme.

Keywords: Reaction-diffusion neural networks · Dynamic event-trigger- ed mechanism · Pointwise measurements · Pointwise control · Synchronization

1 Introduction

In recent years, neural networks (NNs) have gradually become a research hotspot because of their rapid development in various fields such as chemistry, physics, medicine, and biology [1]. Up to now, many excellent results have been obtained on the stability analysis and synchronization of NNs [2,3]. However, it should be noted that the reaction–diffusion phenomenon is ignored in the aforementioned papers. In fact, the reaction–diffusion phenomenon is unavoidable when the electrons are moving in a non-uniform electromagnetic field [4]. Therefore,

This work was supported in part by the National Natural Science Foundation of China under Grants 61976081, in part by the Natural Science Fund for Excellent Young Scholars of Henan Province under Grant 202300410127, in part by Key Scientific Research Projects of Higher Education Institutions in Henan Province under Grant 22A413001, in part by Top Young Talents in Central Plains under Grant Yuzutong (2021) 44, and in part by Technology Innovative Teams in University of Henan Province under Grant 23IRTSTHN012.

F. Sun et al. (Eds.): ICCSIP 2023, CCIS 1918, pp. 134–148, 2024.
https://doi.org/10.1007/978-981-99-8018-5_10

to describe the nature of material movement more vividly in subsequent studies, the reaction–diffusion neural networks (RDNNs) are proposed. Recently, many excellent results on the dynamical analysis of such NNs have been presented, including stability [5,6], synchronization [7], and state estimation [8], etc.

In the aforementioned papers, all the measured data are transmitted and all the control signals are continuous, which is almost impossible in practice. Moreover, some new problems inevitably occur with data transmission in the system because of the limited network transmission resources, such as packet loss and time delay. Therefore, to improve the utilization of the network, the alternative control methods are proposed, such as quantization control [9], sampled-data control [10,11], and event-triggered control [12], and so on. More recently, to avoid Zeno behaviors, the sampled-data-based event-triggered mechanism (ETM) has received increasing attention, where sampled-data is sent out only when the event-triggered condition is met. To date, ETM has become a core concept in industrial information technology, especially in dealing with complex network dynamic systems. Therefore, the study of event-triggered techniques is becoming increasingly relevant when dealing with networks with limited bandwidth.

Based on the above method, to further save design costs, pointwise measurement and pointwise control (PMPC) are adopted to reduce the number of actuators and sensors. In actual engineering applications, controlling all points will improve system performance, but it will also increase system design costs. Therefore, PMPC are proposed to further balance the system performance and design cost, such as [13] investigated the fuzzy state observer with guaranteed cost by pointwise measurement, and the problem of exponential stability for parabolic partial differential equation systems was studied in [14]. Thus, one goal of this paper is to further reduce system design costs by using PMPC methods. After reducing the design cost and alleviating channel pressure by the above methods, it is also meaningful to reduce the conservativeness of the system analysis.

This article aims to enhance the communication efficiency of the RDNNs, reduce system design costs, and save the number of actuators by integrating pointwise measurement, ETM, pointwise control, and relaxed Lyapunov-Krasovskii functional (LKF) technology. The main contributions included in this paper are as follows:

(i) While modeling NNs, the reaction–diffusion term is introduced to make the system model more general and practical [15,16]. Moreover, the PMPC [17] are introduced to reduce the design cost. In contrast to the traditional full-domain measurement and control [18,19], PMPC only measure and control by sensors and actuators at selected points, which achieves the desired control effect while reducing the number of sensors and actuators.

(ii) To reduce channel pressure and relieve computing burden while maintaining a desirable closed-loop performance, the ETM is employed in many existing results (see [20,21]). Inspired by [22,23], to further reduce the number of triggers, a dynamic event-triggered mechanism (DETM) based on pointwise measurement is introduced. Compared with the traditional ETM, it can adjust the trigger frequency by changing the corresponding parameters according to the actual situation.

(iii) A time-dependent LKF (see [24,25]) is constructed to get a synchronization criterion with less conservativeness. Meanwhile, a representative interval $[t_k, t_{k+1}]$ is used instead of the whole time in this work, thus simplifying the analysis. Moreover, the LKF for each time interval is relaxed, and in contrast to [26,27], our results do not require any additional conditions to guarantee that each component of the LKF is positive definite, but the conditions of the Lyapunov method can still be satisfied.

Notations: In this paper, diag $\{\cdot\}$ represents a diagonal matrix, col $\{\cdot\}$ denotes a column vector, $\vartheta_j = \begin{bmatrix} 0_{n,(j-1)n} & I_n & 0_{n,(8-j)n} \end{bmatrix}$, $(j = 1, 2, ..., 8)$; sym $\{S\}$ represents the expression $S + S^T$. In addition, for expression convenience, define $\perp = \perp(z,t)(\perp = m_r, s_r, v_r, v), \Im_j = \Im(z, t - j(t))(\Im = m_r, s_r, v, v_r, j = \eta, \sigma)$.

2 Problem Description and Preliminaries

2.1 System Description

In this section, we consider the drive system as:

$$\frac{\partial m_r}{\partial t} = d_r \frac{\partial^2 m_r}{\partial z^2} - a_r m_r + \sum_{\kappa=1}^{n} c_{r\kappa} g_\kappa(m_\kappa) + \sum_{\kappa=1}^{n} d_{r\kappa} g_\kappa(m_{\kappa\sigma}), \qquad (1)$$

where m_r is the state vector of the r_{th} neuron, $r = 1, 2, ..., n$; $d_r > 0$ is the transmission diffusion coefficient; z represents the space vector, $a_r > 0$ is a constant; $c_{r\kappa}$ and $d_{r\kappa}$ represent the feedback connection strength and delayed feedback connection strength, correspondingly. $m_{\kappa\sigma}$ is the state vector with delay. Furthermore, provided that the activation function $g_\kappa(\cdot)$ and time delay σ have the following characteristic:

$$|g_\kappa(\bar{\tau})| \le \bar{G}_\kappa, \ \varepsilon_\kappa^- \le \frac{g_\kappa(\bar{\tau}_1) - g_\kappa(\bar{\tau}_2)}{\bar{\tau}_1 - \bar{\tau}_2} \le \varepsilon_\kappa^+,$$
$$0 \le \sigma_1 \le \sigma \le \sigma_2, \ \frac{d\sigma}{dt} \le \bar{\sigma} < \infty,$$

where $\sigma_1, \sigma_2, \bar{\tau}, \bar{\tau}_1, \bar{\tau}_2, \varepsilon_\kappa^-, \varepsilon_\kappa^+, \bar{\tau}_1 \ne \bar{\tau}_2$, and $\bar{\sigma}$ are arbitrarily given constants.

Besides, the boundary and initial conditions of (1) are given in the following forms:

$$m_r(z,t) = 0, (z,t) \in \partial\Omega \times [-\sigma_2, +\infty),$$
$$m_r(z,\zeta) = \varpi_r(z,\zeta), (z,\zeta) \in \Omega \times [-\sigma_2, 0),$$

where $\varpi_r(z,\zeta)$ is bounded and continuous.

For the drive system (1), the corresponding response system can be written as follows:

$$\frac{\partial s_r}{\partial t} = e_r \frac{\partial^2 s_r}{\partial z^2} - a_r s_r + \sum_{\kappa=1}^{n} c_{r\kappa} g_\kappa(s_\kappa) + \sum_{\kappa=1}^{n} d_{r\kappa} g_\kappa(s_{\kappa\sigma}) + \epsilon(z)u_r, \qquad (2)$$

where u_r is the controller, the space is divided into M subdomains, $\epsilon(z) \triangleq [\epsilon_0(z)\,\epsilon_1(z)\,\cdots\,\epsilon_\rho(z)\,\epsilon_{M-1}(z)]$, $\bar{z}_\rho \triangleq (z_{\rho+1}+z_\rho)/2, \epsilon_\rho(z) \triangleq \delta(z-\bar{z}_\rho)\epsilon_\rho, z_{\rho+1}-z_\rho = g_m$, $\delta(z)$ is a Dirac delta function, and $\bar{z}_\rho$ presents a certain specific spatial point. Additionally,

$$s_r(z,t) = 0, (z,t) \in \partial\Omega \times [-\sigma_2, +\infty),$$
$$s_r(z,\zeta) = \omega_r(z,\zeta), (z,\zeta) \in \Omega \times [-\sigma_2, 0),$$

where $\omega_r(z,\zeta)$ and $\varpi_r(z,\zeta)$ have the same characteristic.

Define the error $v_r = s_r - m_r$, then the error system is shown as follows:

$$\frac{\partial v_r}{\partial t} = d_r \frac{\partial^2 v_r}{\partial z^2} - a_r v_r + \sum_{\kappa=1}^{n} c_{r\kappa} f_\kappa(v_\kappa) + \sum_{\kappa=1}^{n} d_{r\kappa} f_\kappa(v_{\kappa\sigma}) + \epsilon(z)u_r, \qquad (3)$$

where $f_\kappa(v_\kappa) = g_\kappa(s_\kappa) - g_\kappa(m_\kappa)$, $f_\kappa(v_{\kappa\sigma}) = g_\kappa(s_{\kappa\sigma}) - g_\kappa(m_{\kappa\sigma})$, and clearly, $\varepsilon_\kappa^- \leq \frac{f_\kappa(\bar{\tau})}{\bar{\tau}} \leq \varepsilon_\kappa^+$ for $\bar{\tau} \in \mathbb{R}$.

For convenience, the compact form of the error system can be expressed as

$$\frac{\partial v}{\partial t} = D\frac{\partial^2 v}{\partial z^2} - \tilde{A}v + \tilde{C}f(v) + \tilde{D}f(v_\sigma) + \epsilon(z)u, \qquad (4)$$

where $v = (v_1, v_2, ..., v_n)^T, u = (u_1, u_2, ..., u_n)^T, D = \mathrm{diag}\{d_1, d_2, ..., d_n\}, \tilde{A} = \mathrm{diag}\{a_1, a_2, ..., a_n\}, \tilde{C} = (c_{r\kappa})_{n\times n}, \tilde{D} = (d_{r\kappa})_{n\times n}$, and $f(\cdot) = (f_1(\cdot), f_2(\cdot), ..., f_n(\cdot))$.

2.2 Event-Triggered Mechanism

In practical systems, the traditional periodic sampling mechanism usually transmits much unnecessary information, resulting in a waste of limited communication resources. Therefore, a DETM is adopted in this section to effectively save communication resources. The form is as follows:

$$t_{k+1} = \min\{t > t_k | \beta v^T(\bar{z}_\rho, t_k)\Pi v(\bar{z}_\rho, t_k) + \mu\bar{\chi}_{\bar{z}_\rho, t} - (v(\bar{z}_\rho, t) - v(\bar{z}_\rho, t_k))^T \Pi$$
$$\times (v(\bar{z}_\rho, t) - v(\bar{z}_\rho, t_k)) \leq 0, t \in \{\lambda_n\}_{n\in\mathbb{N}}\}, \qquad (5)$$

where t_k is denoted as the release instants of the event generator, $\beta \in [0,1)$ implies the traditional event-triggered threshold, Π is a symmetric weighting matrix to be determined, $\bar{\chi}_{\bar{z}_\rho, t} \triangleq \bar{\chi}(\bar{z}_\rho, t)$ is the introduced internal dynamic variable, the scalar $\mu > 0$ is to be designed, and $\lambda_n = nh$ denotes the sampling period.

We define $\lambda_{n_\lambda+i} = t - \eta(t), 0 \leq \eta(t) \leq \eta_M, e_{\bar{z}_\rho} = v(\bar{z}_\rho, t_k) - v(\bar{z}_\rho, \lambda_{n_\lambda+i}), t \in [\lambda_{n_\lambda+i}, \lambda_{n_\lambda+i+1})$. Then, from the DETM (5), we have

$$\beta(v(\bar{z}_\rho, t - \eta(t)) + e_{\bar{z}_\rho})^T(v(\bar{z}_\rho, t - \eta(t)) + e_{\bar{z}_\rho}) + \mu\bar{\chi}_{\bar{z}_\rho, \eta} - e_{\bar{z}_\rho}^T \Pi e_{\bar{z}_\rho} \geq 0, \qquad (6)$$

where $\bar{\chi}_{\bar{z}_\rho, \eta} = \bar{\chi}(\bar{z}_\rho, t - \eta(t)), t \in [t_k, t_{k+1})$, and $\bar{\chi}_{\bar{z}_\rho, t}$ satisfies the following condition:

$$\frac{\partial \bar{\chi}_{\bar{z}_\rho, t}}{\partial t} = -a\bar{\chi}_{\bar{z}_\rho, t} - \mu\bar{\chi}_{\bar{z}_\rho, \eta}, \qquad (7)$$

with $\bar{\chi}(\bar{z}_\rho, 0) = \bar{\chi}_0 \geq 0$. Based on the above consideration, to ensure that the systems (1) and (2) can still keep synchronized in the presence of interference, we design an event-triggered pointwise controller, which is described as follows:

$$u = Kv(\bar{z}_\rho, t_k), t \in [t_k, t_{k+1}), \tag{8}$$

where $v(\bar{z}_\rho, t_k) = v(\bar{z}_\rho, t - \eta(t)) + e_{\bar{z}_\rho}$, and $v(\bar{z}_\rho, t - \eta(t)) = v(z, t - \eta(t)) - \int_{\bar{z}_\rho}^{z} \frac{\partial v(\varepsilon, t-\eta(t))}{\partial \varepsilon} d\varepsilon = v_\eta - \int_{\bar{z}_\rho}^{z} \frac{\partial v(\varepsilon, ih)}{\partial \varepsilon} d\varepsilon$.

Therefore, the system (4) can be rewritten as

$$\begin{aligned}
\frac{\partial v}{\partial t} =& D\frac{\partial^2 v_r}{\partial z^2} - Av + \tilde{C}f(v) + \tilde{D}f(v_\sigma) + \epsilon(z)K \\
& \times [v_\eta + e_{\bar{z}_\rho} - \int_{\bar{z}_\rho}^{z} \frac{\partial v(\varepsilon, ih)}{\partial \varepsilon} d\varepsilon].
\end{aligned} \tag{9}$$

Lemma 1 [28]. For a given matrix $O \in \mathbb{R}^{n \times n}, O = O^T$ and $O > 0$, for all continuously differentiable function $\bar{d}(\varrho)$ in $[b_1, b_2] \to \mathbb{R}^n$. Then

$$\int_{b_1}^{b_2} \dot{\bar{d}}^T(\varrho)O\dot{\bar{d}}(\varrho)d\varrho \geq \frac{1}{b_2 - b_1}(w_1^T O w_1 + 3w_2^T O w_2),$$

where $w_1 = \bar{d}(b_2) - \bar{d}(b_1), w_2 = \bar{d}(b_2) + \bar{d}(b_1) - \frac{2}{b_2-b_1} \int_{b_1}^{b_2} \bar{d}(\varrho)d\varrho$.

Lemma 2 [29]. Suppose there exist positive constants $a, \alpha, a > \alpha$, the function $V(t) \in [t_0 - \sigma, +\infty)$ is a non-negative function, and $\bar{V}(t) \overset{\Delta}{=} \sup_{\sigma \leq s < 0} V(t+s), (t > 0)$, such that the derivative of $V(t)$ satisfies

$$\dot{V}(t) + aV(t) \leq \alpha\bar{V}(t), t \geq t_0,$$

then $V(t) \leq e^{-\xi(t-t_0)}\alpha\bar{V}(t), t \geq t_0$, where ξ is the only positive solution of $\xi = a - \frac{\alpha e^{\xi\sigma}}{2}$.

3   Main Result

In this section, the synchronization criterion of the drive system (1) and the response system (2) is obtained under sufficient conditions. Before presenting the main results, to further simplify the content, the following notations are given:

$$\partial_t v = \frac{\partial v}{\partial t}, \epsilon = \epsilon(z), \eta = ih, \gamma = \text{col}\{v_\eta \; \hbar\}, \hbar = \begin{cases} \frac{1}{\eta(t)} \int_\eta^t v(z, \theta)d\theta, t \neq \eta \\ v_\eta, \quad\quad\quad\quad t = \eta, \end{cases}$$

$$\psi_1 = v - v_\eta, \psi_2 = v + v_\eta - 2\hbar, \Upsilon^T = \begin{bmatrix} v^T \; f^T(v) \end{bmatrix}, \Upsilon_\sigma^T = \begin{bmatrix} v_\sigma^T \; f^T(v_\sigma) \end{bmatrix},$$

$$\phi = \text{col}\begin{bmatrix} v \; \partial_t v \; v_\eta \; \hbar, \end{bmatrix}, \text{ and } \nabla = \text{col}\{v \; \partial_t v \; f(v) \; v_\sigma \; f(v_\sigma) \; \hbar \; v_\eta \; e_{\bar{z}_\rho} \}.$$

Theorem 1. For given scalars $\beta > 0$, $\eta_M > 0$, and $g_m > 0$, the synchronization of systems (1) and (2) is realized under the controller (8), if there exist matrices $\bar{P}$, $\bar{Q}$, $\bar{U}$, $\bar{H} \in \mathbb{R}^{n \times n} > 0$, and $\bar{\Pi} \in \mathbb{R}^{n \times n} > 0$, diagonal matrices $\bar{\Theta}_1$, $\bar{\Theta}_2 \in \mathbb{R}^{n \times n}$, symmetric matrices $\bar{G}$, $\bar{\Psi} \in \mathbb{R}^{n \times n}$, and $\bar{T}' \in \mathbb{R}^{2n \times 2n}$, and arbitrary matrices $\bar{D}_1$, $\bar{D}_2 \in \mathbb{R}^{n \times 4n}$, such that the following constraints hold:

$$\bar{\Xi}(1,0,0) < 0, \tag{10}$$

$$\bar{\Xi}(1,\eta_M,0) < 0, \tag{11}$$

$$\begin{bmatrix} \bar{\Xi}(0,\eta_M,\eta_M) & \sqrt{\eta_M}\phi^T\bar{F}^T \\ * & -\bar{\Sigma} \end{bmatrix} < 0, \tag{12}$$

$$\begin{bmatrix} -\alpha(\bar{\Psi}D + \beta\bar{\Pi}) & (v\bar{K})^T & (\beta\bar{\Pi})^T \\ * & -\frac{\pi^2}{g_m}\bar{H} & 0 \\ * & * & -\frac{\pi^2}{g_m}\bar{Q} \end{bmatrix} < 0, \tag{13}$$

where

$$\bar{F} = \mathrm{col}\left[\bar{D}_1 \ \bar{D}_2\right], \bar{\Sigma} = \mathrm{diag}\{\bar{U}, 3\bar{U}\},$$

and

$$\begin{aligned}
\bar{\Xi}_0 =& \bar{\Xi}_1 + \bar{\Xi}_2 + \bar{\Xi}_3, \bar{\Xi}_i = \bar{\Xi}_i(\varepsilon, \eta_k, \eta(t)), (i = 0,1,2,3), \\
\bar{\Xi}_1 =& \vartheta_1^T(a\bar{P} - 2\varphi^T\bar{\Psi}\tilde{A})\vartheta_1 + 2\vartheta_1^T\bar{P}\vartheta_2 + (\varphi\vartheta_1 + \vartheta_2)^Tg_m^{-1}\varepsilon_p\bar{H}(\varphi\vartheta_1 + \vartheta_2) \\
& + [\vartheta_1, \vartheta_3]^T(\bar{T}')[\vartheta_1, \vartheta_3] + (a - 2\varphi)\vartheta_1^T\bar{\Psi} \times \mathrm{D}\vartheta_1 - 2\vartheta_1^T\varphi^T - 2\vartheta_3^T\bar{\Theta}_1\vartheta_3 \\
& - (1 - \bar{\sigma}) \times e^{-a\sigma}[\vartheta_4, \vartheta_5]^T(\bar{T}')[\vartheta_4, \vartheta_5] + \vartheta_7^T\bar{Q}\vartheta_7 - 2\vartheta_2^T\bar{\Psi}\tilde{A}\vartheta_1 \\
& \times \bar{\Psi}\vartheta_2 + 2\vartheta_1^T(E^-)^T\bar{\Theta}_1\vartheta_3 + 2\vartheta_3^T\bar{\Theta}_1 E^+\vartheta_1 - 2\vartheta_5^T\bar{\Theta}_2\vartheta_5^T - 2\vartheta_2^T\bar{\Psi}\vartheta_2 \\
& - 2\vartheta_1^T(E^-)^T\bar{\Theta}_1 E^+\vartheta_1 + 2\vartheta_5^T\bar{\Theta}_2 E^+v_4 + 2\vartheta_1^T\varphi^T\bar{\Psi}\bar{D}\vartheta_5 + 2\vartheta_1^T\varphi^T\bar{\Psi}\tilde{C}\vartheta_3 \\
& - 2\vartheta_4^T(E^-)^T\bar{\Theta}_2\vartheta_4 + 2\vartheta_4^T(E^-)^T\bar{\Theta}_2\vartheta_5 + 2\vartheta_2^T\bar{\Psi}\bar{D}\vartheta_5 + 2\vartheta_2^T\bar{\Psi}\tilde{C}\vartheta_3, \\
\bar{\Xi}_2 =& 2\vartheta_1^T\varphi^Tvg_m^{-1}\varepsilon_p\bar{K}\vartheta_7 + 2\vartheta_2^Tvg_m^{-1}\varepsilon_p\bar{K}\vartheta_7 + 2\vartheta_1^T\varphi^Tvg_m^{-1}\varepsilon_p\bar{K}\vartheta_8 + 2\vartheta_2^Tvg_m^{-1}\varepsilon_p\bar{K}\vartheta_8, \\
\bar{\Xi}_3 =& a\eta(t)(\eta_k - \eta(t))[\vartheta_7^T\bar{X}\vartheta_7 + \vartheta_6^T\bar{X}\vartheta_6] + (\eta_k - 2\eta(t))[\vartheta_7, \vartheta_6]^T\bar{X}[\vartheta_7, \vartheta_6] \\
& + (\eta_k - \eta(t))\vartheta_2^T\bar{U}\vartheta_2 + 2(\eta_k - \eta(t))\{[\vartheta_7, \vartheta_6]^T\bar{X}[0, \vartheta_1^T - \vartheta_6^T]\} - \vartheta_8^T\bar{\Pi}\vartheta_8 \\
& - \mathrm{sym}\{\psi_1^T\bar{D}_1[\vartheta_1, \vartheta_2, \vartheta_7, \vartheta_6]\} + \vartheta_7^T\beta\bar{\Pi}\vartheta_7 + \varepsilon\eta(t)[\vartheta_1, \vartheta_2, \vartheta_7, \vartheta_6]^T\bar{D}_1^T \\
& \times \bar{U}^{-1}\bar{D}_1^T[\vartheta_1, \vartheta_2, \vartheta_7, \vartheta_6] - 3\mathrm{sym}\{\psi_2^T\bar{D}_2[\vartheta_1, \vartheta_2, \vartheta_7, \vartheta_6]\} + 3[\vartheta_1, \vartheta_2, \vartheta_7, \vartheta_6]^T \\
& \times \psi\eta(t)\bar{D}_2^T\bar{U}^{-1}\bar{D}_2^T[\vartheta_1, \vartheta_2, \vartheta_7, \vartheta_6] + a(\eta_k - \eta(t)) \times \mathrm{sym}\{\psi_1^T\bar{D}_1[\vartheta_1, \vartheta_2, \vartheta_7, \vartheta_6]\} \\
& - a(\eta_k - \eta(t)) \times \varepsilon\eta(t)[\vartheta_1, \vartheta_2, \vartheta_7, \vartheta_6]^T\bar{D}_1^T\bar{U}^{-1}\bar{D}_1^T[\vartheta_1, \vartheta_2, \vartheta_7, \vartheta_6] \\
& + a(\eta_k - \eta(t)) \times 3\mathrm{sym}\{\psi_2^T\bar{D}_2[\vartheta_1, \vartheta_2, \vartheta_7, \vartheta_6]\} \\
& - a(\eta_k - \eta(t)) \times 3\varepsilon\eta(t)[\vartheta_1, \vartheta_2, \vartheta_7, \vartheta_6]^T\bar{D}_2^T\bar{U}^{-1}\bar{D}_2^T[\vartheta_1, \vartheta_2, \vartheta_7, \vartheta_6].
\end{aligned}$$

Proof: We consider a new LKF as follows:

$$V(t) = \sum_{\iota=1}^{5} V_\iota(t), \tag{14}$$

where

$$V_1(t) = \int_0^l \left\{ v^T P v + (\frac{\partial v}{\partial z})^T \Psi \times \mathrm{N}(\frac{\partial v}{\partial z}) \right\} dz,$$

$$V_2(t) = \int_0^l e^{a(\theta - t)} \int_{t-\sigma(t)}^t \Upsilon(z,\theta) T' \Upsilon^T(z,\theta) d\theta dz,$$

$$V_3(t) = \int_0^l \eta(t)(t_{k+1} - t) \begin{bmatrix} v_\eta \\ \hbar \end{bmatrix}^T X \begin{bmatrix} v_\eta \\ \hbar \end{bmatrix} dz,$$

$$V_4(t) = \int_0^l (t_{k+1} - t) \int_\eta^t (\frac{\partial v(z,\theta)}{\partial \theta})^T U(\frac{\partial v(z,\theta)}{\partial \theta}) d\theta dz,$$

$$V_5(t) = \int_0^l \bar\chi_{\bar z_\rho, t} dz.$$

The time derivative of $V(t)$ is derived directly as follows:

$$\dot V(t) = \sum_{\iota=1}^5 \dot V_\iota(t). \tag{15}$$

According to (4), for the matrix $\Phi = \varphi v + \partial_t v$, the following equality holds:

$$0 = 2\Phi\Psi \sum_{\rho=0}^{M-1} \int_{z_\rho}^{z_\rho+1} [-\partial_t v + \mathrm{D}\frac{\partial^2 v}{\partial z^2} - \tilde A v + \tilde C f(v)$$

$$+ \tilde D f(v_\sigma) + \epsilon K v(z, ih) + \epsilon e_{\bar z_\rho} - \epsilon K \int_{\bar z_\rho}^z \frac{\partial v(\varepsilon, ih)}{\partial \varepsilon} d\varepsilon].$$

Furthermore, taking the boundary conditions into consideration, we get

$$2\sum_{\rho=0}^{M-1} \int_{z_\rho}^{z_\rho+1} (\partial_t v)^T \Psi (\mathrm{D}\frac{\partial^2 v}{\partial z^2} dz) = -2 \int_0^l \frac{\partial v^T}{\partial z \partial t} \Psi (\mathrm{D}\frac{\partial v}{\partial z} dz),$$

and

$$2\sum_{\rho=0}^{M-1} \int_{z_\rho}^{z_\rho+1} (\varphi v)^T \Psi (\mathrm{D}\frac{\partial^2 v}{\partial z^2} dz) = -2\varphi \int_0^l \frac{\partial v^T}{\partial z} \Psi (\mathrm{D}\frac{\partial v}{\partial z} dz).$$

Moreover, we note that

$$-2 \sum_{\rho=0}^{M-1} \int_{z_\rho}^{z_\rho+1} (\varphi v + \partial_t v)^T \epsilon \Psi K (\int_{\bar z_\rho}^z \frac{\partial v(\varepsilon, ih)}{\partial \varepsilon} d\varepsilon) dz$$

$$\leq \int_0^l (\varphi v + \partial_t v)^T \epsilon H (\varphi v + \partial_t v) dz + \epsilon \sum_{\rho=0}^{M-1} \int_{z_\rho}^{z_\rho+1}$$

$$(\int_{\bar z_\rho}^z \frac{\partial v(\varepsilon, ih)}{\partial \varepsilon} d\varepsilon)^T Z (\int_{\bar z_\rho}^z \frac{\partial v(\varepsilon, ih)}{\partial \varepsilon} d\varepsilon) dz, \tag{16}$$

by Wirtingers inequality [30], we have

$$\sum_{\rho=0}^{M-1} \int_{z_\rho}^{z_\rho+1} (\int_{\bar{z}_\rho}^z \frac{\partial v(\varepsilon, ih)}{\partial \varepsilon} d\varepsilon)^T Z(\int_{\bar{z}_\rho}^z \frac{\partial v(\varepsilon, ih)}{\partial \varepsilon} d\varepsilon) dz$$

$$\leq \frac{g_m^2}{\pi^2} \int_0^l (\frac{\partial v(z, ih)}{\partial z})^T Z(\frac{\partial v(z, ih)}{\partial z}) dz,$$

where $Z = (\Psi K)^T H^{-1}(\Psi K)$, $\int_0^l \epsilon dz = g_m^{-1} \int_0^l \epsilon_\rho dz$.
Based on Lemma 1, it yields

$$-\int_0^l \int_\eta^t (\frac{\partial v(z, \theta)}{\partial t})^T U(\frac{\partial v(z, \theta)}{\partial t}) d\theta dz$$

$$\leq -\int_0^l \frac{1}{\eta(t)} \times (\psi_1^T U \psi_1 + 3\psi_2^T U \psi_2) dz. \tag{17}$$

For (17), on the basis of Wirtinger's inequality [30], if there exist any matrices $D \in \mathbb{R}^{n \times 4n}, E \in \mathbb{R}^{n \times 4n}$, it follows that

$$-\int_0^l \frac{1}{\eta(t)} \psi_1^T U \psi_1 dz \leq \int_0^l -6\psi_2^T D_2\phi + 3\eta(t)\phi^T D_2^T U^{-1} E^T \phi dz. \tag{18}$$

Next, we need to prove that $\bar{\chi}_{\bar{z}_\rho, t} \geq 0$. By considering (5) and (7), one has

$$\frac{\partial \bar{\chi}_{\bar{z}_\rho, t}}{\partial t} + a\bar{\chi}_{\bar{z}_\rho, t} \leq \beta v^T(\bar{z}_\rho, ih)\Pi v(\bar{z}_\rho, ih) - e_{\bar{z}_\rho}^T \Pi e_{\bar{z}_\rho}.$$

In addition, by referring to [22], we note that $\bar{\chi}_{\bar{z}_\rho, t} \geq 0$.
Then, the first part on the right side of the equal sign in the above equation can be further addressed as

$$\int_0^l v^T(\bar{z}_\rho, ih)\beta\Pi v(\bar{z}_\rho, ih) dz$$

$$= \int_0^l v_\eta^T \beta\Pi v_\eta dz - 2\int_0^l v_\eta^T \beta\Pi \int_{\bar{z}_\rho}^z \frac{\partial v(\varepsilon, ih)}{\partial \varepsilon} d\varepsilon dz$$

$$+ \int_0^l (\int_{\bar{z}_\rho}^z \frac{\partial v(\varepsilon, ih)}{\partial \varepsilon} d\varepsilon)^T \beta\Pi(\int_{\bar{z}_\rho}^z \frac{\partial v(\varepsilon, ih)}{\partial \varepsilon} d\varepsilon) dz. \tag{19}$$

Referring to (16), we have

$$2\sum_{\rho=0}^{M-1} \int_{z_\rho}^{z_\rho+1} v_\eta^T \beta\Pi \int_{\bar{z}_\rho}^z \frac{\partial v(\varepsilon, ih)}{\partial \varepsilon} d\varepsilon dz$$

$$\leq \int_0^l v_\eta^T Q v_\eta^T dz + \frac{g_m^2}{\pi^2} \int_0^l (\frac{\partial v(z, ih)}{\partial z})^T$$

$$\times (\beta\Pi)^T Q^{-1}(\beta\Pi)(\frac{\partial v(z, ih)}{\partial z}) dz. \tag{20}$$

Moreover, by virtue of the definition of (1), we can deduce that

$$0 \le 2\big[f(v) - E^- v\big]^T \Theta_1 \big[E^+ v - f(v)\big], \tag{21}$$

$$0 \le 2\big[f(v_\sigma) - E^- v_\sigma\big]^T \Theta_2 \big[E^+ v_\sigma - f(v_\sigma)\big]. \tag{22}$$

By combining (15)-(22), one can acquire that

$$\dot{V}(t) + aV(t) - \alpha \sup_{-\sigma \le s < 0} V(t+s)$$

$$\le \sum_{p=0}^{M-1} \int_{z_p}^{z_{p+1}} \nabla^T \big(\frac{t_{k+1} - t}{\eta_M} \Xi_0(1, \eta_M, 0) + \frac{t - ih}{\eta_M} \Xi_0(1, \eta_M, \eta_M)$$

$$+ \frac{\eta_M + ih - t_{k+1}}{\eta_M} \Xi_0(1, 0, 0)\big) \nabla dz + \int_0^l \frac{\partial v_{ih}^T}{\partial z} (-\alpha \Psi \times \mathrm{D} + \beta \Pi)$$

$$+ \frac{g_m}{\pi^2} (\Psi K)^T H^{-1} (\Psi K) + \frac{g_m}{\pi^2} (\beta \Pi)^T Q^{-1} (\beta \Pi)) \frac{\partial v_{ih}}{\partial z} dz. \tag{23}$$

Then, we can derive

$$\dot{V}(t) + aV(t) - \alpha \sup_{-\sigma \le s < 0} V(t+s) < 0, t \in [t_k, t_{k+1}). \tag{24}$$

Hence, it is easy to see that $V(t)$ is a monotonically decreasing function whose minimum value will be at t_{k+1} instant, which implies that

$$\lim_{t \to t_{k+1}} V_4(t) = 0, \tag{25}$$

then, we can define the value of $V(t)$:

$$V_{\min}(t) = \lim_{t \to t_{k+1}} (V_1(t) + V_2(t) + V_3(t) + V_5(t)). \tag{26}$$

Furthermore, let $\bar{\Psi} = \nu \bar{Y}, \varpi = \mathrm{diag}\underbrace{(Y, ..., Y)}_{8}$, where $Y = \bar{Y}^{-1}$, afterwards, pre- and post multiplying both sides of the matrixes in (23) by ϖ^T and ϖ, respectively. Then, define $\bar{P} \triangleq YPY; \bar{\Theta}_1 \triangleq Y\Theta_1 Y; \bar{\Theta}_2 \triangleq Y\Theta_2 Y; \bar{X} \triangleq YXY; \bar{U} \triangleq YUY; \bar{D}_1 \triangleq YD_1Y; \bar{D}_2 \triangleq YD_2Y; \bar{H} \triangleq YHY; \bar{\Pi} \triangleq Y\Pi Y;$ and $\bar{K} \triangleq KY^{-1}$, moreover, the feedback gain can be expressed as

$$K \triangleq \bar{K}Y^{-1}. \tag{27}$$

According to the above analysis, we can conclude that the synchronization of the drive system (1) and the response system (2) is realized. This completes the proof. The algorithm for the design of the event-triggered pointwise controller is given in Algorithm 1.

Algorithm 1: Event-triggered Pointwise Controller Design

Input   : Give scalars $\beta > 0, \eta_M > 0, and\ g_m > 0$, and the matrices $D, A, \tilde{C}, \tilde{D}$;
Output: $u(\bar{z}_\rho, t_k) = Kv(\bar{z}_\rho, t_k)$,
1 **for** $i = 0 : N$ **do**
2 $\quad$ **if** *(5) holds;* **then**
3 $\quad\quad$ | update the data of t_{k+1}, $t_{k+1} = t_k$ at the certain spatial point;
4 $\quad$ **else**
5 $\quad\quad$ | t_{k+1} maintains the value of the previous sampling moment;
6 $\quad$ **end**
7 $\quad$ Update i $(i = i + 1)$ with the obtained parameters, use the LMI toolbox in MATLAB to solve *(10)–(13)*, then determine whether exists solutions;
8 $\quad$ **if** *the solutions are not obtained ;* **then**
9 $\quad\quad$ | back to **Input** ;
10 $\quad$ **else**
11 $\quad\quad$ | obtain K based on *(27)*;
12 $\quad$ **end**
13 **end**

---

4   Simulation Analysis

In this section, a numerical simulation is provided to prove the feasibility of the theoretical analysis.

Consider the drive system as follows:

$$\frac{\partial m_r}{\partial t} = d_r \frac{\partial^2 m_r}{\partial z^2} - a_r m_r + \sum_{\kappa=1}^{n} c_{r\kappa} g_\kappa(m_\kappa) + \sum_{\kappa=1}^{n} d_{r\kappa} g_\kappa(m_{\kappa\sigma}), \tag{28}$$

with initial conditions

$$m_1(z, o) = 1.2 \sin(z), (z, o) \in \Omega \times [-0.35, 0],$$
$$m_2(z, o) = -1.4 \sin(z), (z, o) \in \Omega \times [-0.35, 0].$$

The corresponding model of the response system is as follows:

$$\frac{\partial s_r}{\partial t} = d_r \frac{\partial^2 s_r}{\partial z^2} - a_r s_r + \sum_{\kappa=1}^{n} c_{r\kappa} g_\kappa(s_\kappa) + \sum_{\kappa=1}^{n} d_{r\kappa} g_\kappa(s_{\kappa\sigma}) + \epsilon(z) u_r, \tag{29}$$

with initial conditions

$$s_1(z, o) = -1.1 \sin(z), (z, o) \in \Omega \times [-0.35, 0],$$
$$s_2(z, o) = 1.3 \sin(z), (z, o) \in \Omega \times [-0.35, 0],$$

where $v_1 = v_2 = 0.01, a_1 = 13.3, a_2 = 14.6, c_{11} = 1.19, c_{12} = 1.29, c_{21} = -1.11, c_{22} = 1.35, d_{11} = 1.3, d_{12} = 1.4, d_{21} = -1.39, d_{22} = 1.4, q = 1, g_\kappa(\cdot) = \tanh(\cdot)$. In addition, we suppose that $\sigma(t) = 2e^t/(15 + 5e^t), a = 0.872, \varphi = 7, \alpha = 0.87, g_m = 0.1$.

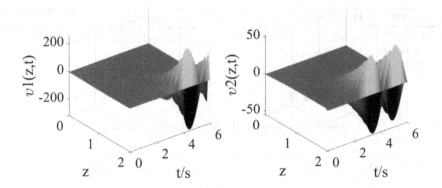

Fig. 1. The error system without controller.

The dynamic state trajectories of the error system without controller are depicted in Fig. 1, which means that the error system is unbounded in the absence of the control effect. Furthermore, the gain matrix can be obtained in terms of Theorem 1, meanwhile, the threshold is given as $\beta = 0.02$:

$$K = \begin{bmatrix} -11.8474 & -0.0764 \\ 0.0840 & -12.8829 \end{bmatrix}.$$

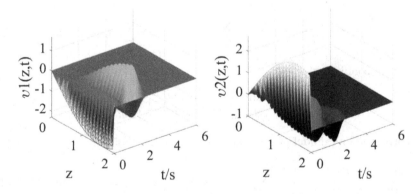

Fig. 2. The error system with controller.

Fig. 2 shows the state trajectories of the controller gains obtained above. Furthermore, we clearly see that the systems (28) and (29) are synchronized with the designed controller, which indicates the effectiveness of our proposed method.

Figures 3 and Figs. 4 illustrate the release intervals and instants under the pointwise-measurement-based ETM and DETM, respectively, where β represents the threshold, and it is clear to see the number of data transmissions for different

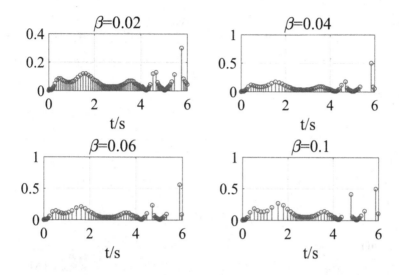

Fig. 3. Transmit instants and transmit interval of ETM.

thresholds ($\beta = 0.02, 0.04, 0.06, 0.1$). Moreover, Fig. 5 gives the event-triggered instants under DETM and ETM. From Fig. 3-5, we intuitively see that DETM can further reduce the number of network data transmissions under the same conditions.

Furthermore, by various thresholds, the number of transmitted data (NTD) is listed in Fig. 6. From the Fig. 6, we find that NTD= $174, 126, 107, 95$ and 87 when the threshold $\beta = 0.02, 0.04, 0.06, 0.08, 0.1$ under ETM, respectively.

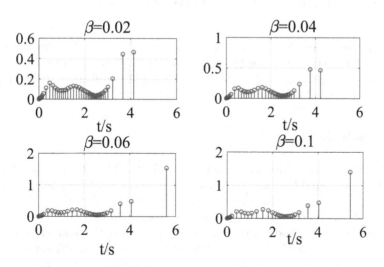

Fig. 4. Transmit instants and transmit interval of DETM.

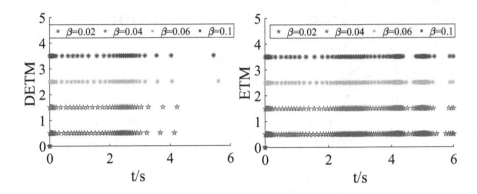

Fig. 5. Event-triggered instants of DETM and ETM.

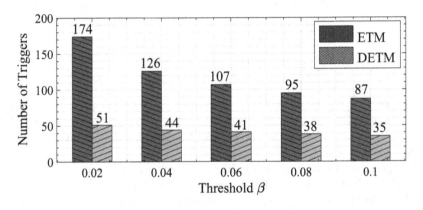

Fig. 6. Event-triggered number of ETM and DETM.

Similarly, there are NTD= $51, 44, 41, 38$ and 35 when the threshold $\beta = 0.02, 0.04, 0.06, 0.08, 0.1$ under DETM, respectively. It is shown that the threshold is inversely proportional to NTD, and DETM can further reduce channel resources compared with ETM.

5   Conclusion

In this work, a pointwise-measurement-based DETM is devised for RDNNs. First, the considered NNs are subject to the reaction–diffusion phenomenon. On this basis, pointwise measurement is adopted to reduce the system design cost. Then, a DETM is constructed to further save channel resources. Moreover, the pointwise control method is employed to further reduce the number of actuators while maintaining satisfactory control performance. Next, the drive and response systems are synchronized under a dynamic event-triggered pointwise controller by choosing a time-dependent Lyapunov functional under relaxed conditions.

Finally, the validity of the main results and the superiority of the DETM are confirmed by a numerical example. In the future, to further reduce the number of sensors and actuators, we will consider the synchronization of RDNNs through boundary control based on boundary measurements.

References

1. De Lacy Costello, B., Ratcliffe, N., Adamatzky, A., Zanin, A.L., Liehr, A.M., Purwins, H.G.: The formation of Voronoi diagrams in chemical and physical systems: experimental findings and theoretical models. Int. J. BifurcationChaos **14**(07), 2187–2210 (2004)
2. Wei, Y., Park, J.H., Karimi, H.R., Tian, Y.C., Jung, H.: Improved stability and stabilization results for stochastic synchronization of continuous-time semi-Markovian jump neural networks with time-varying delay. IEEE Trans. Neural Netw. Learn. Syst. **29**(6), 2488–2501 (2017)
3. Lin, H., Zeng, H., Zhang, X., Wang, W.: Stability analysis for delayed neural networks via a generalized reciprocally convex inequality. IEEE Trans. Neural Netw. Learn. Syst. **34**(10), 7491–7499 (2023)
4. Wu, K., Sun, H., Shi, P., Lim, C.C.: Finite-time boundary stabilization of reaction-diffusion systems. Int. J. Robust Nonlinear Control **28**(5), 1641–1652 (2018)
5. Wu, X., Liu, S., Wang, H., Sun, J., Qiao, W.: Stability analysis of fractional reaction-diffusion memristor-based neural networks with neutral delays via Lyapunov functions. Neurocomputing **550**(14), 126497 (2023)
6. Lv, T., Gan, Q., Xiao, F.: Stability for a class of generalized reaction-diffusion uncertain stochastic neural networks with mixed delays. Int. J. Mach. Learn. Cybern. **10**(5), 967–978 (2019)
7. Cao, Z., Li, C., He, Z., Zhang, X., You, L.: Synchronization of coupled stochastic reaction-diffusion neural networks with multiple weights and delays via pinning impulsive control. IEEE Trans. Neural Netw. Learn. Syst. **9**(2), 820–833 (2022)
8. Zhang, X., Han, Y., Wu, L., Wang, Y.: State estimation for delayed genetic regulatory networks with reaction-diffusion terms. IEEE Trans. Neural Netw. Learn. Syst. **29**(2), 299–309 (2016)
9. Liu, K., Wang, R.: Finite-time synchronization of networks via quantized intermittent pinning control. IEEE Trans. Cybernet. **48**(10), 3021–3027 (2017)
10. Song, S., Park, J.H., Zhang, B., Song, X.: Fuzzy sampled-data control for synchronization of T-S fuzzy reaction-diffusion neural networks with additive time-varying delays. IEEE Trans. Cybernet. **51**(5), 2384–2397 (2020)
11. Song, X., Zhang, Q., Zhang, Y., Song, S.: Fuzzy event-triggered control for PDE systems with pointwise measurements based on relaxed Lyapunov-Krasovskii functionals. IEEE Trans. Fuzzy Syst. **30**(8), 3074–3084 (2021)
12. Li, X., Zhang, W., Fang, J., Li, H.: Event-triggered exponential synchronization for complex-valued memristive neural networks with time-varying delays. IEEE Trans. Neural Netw. Learn. Syst. **31**(10), 4104–4116 (2019)
13. Wu, H., Zhu, H.: Guaranteed cost fuzzy state observer design for semilinear parabolic PDE systems under pointwise measurements. Automatica **85**, 53–60 (2017)
14. Wang, Z., Wu, H.: Fuzzy control for nonlinear time-delay distributed parameter systems under spatially point measurements. IEEE Trans. Fuzzy Syst. **27**(9), 1844–1852 (2019)

15. Huang, Y., Chen, W., Ren, S., Zhang, Z.: Passivity and synchronization of coupled reaction-diffusion Cohen-Grossberg neural networks with fixed and switching topologies. Neural Process. Lett. **49**(3), 1433–1457 (2019)
16. Song, X., Man, J., Song, S., Ahn, C.K.: Gain-scheduled finite-time synchronization for reaction-diffusion memristive neural networks subject to inconsistent Markov chains. IEEE Trans. Neural Netw. Learn. Syst. **32**(7), 2952–2964 (2021)
17. Wang, Z., Wu, H., Wang, J., Li, H.: Quantized sampled-data synchronization of delayed reaction-diffusion neural networks under spatially point measurements. IEEE Trans. Cybernet. **51**(12), 5740–5751 (2020)
18. Wang, J., Liu, Y., Sun, C.: Pointwise exponential stabilization of a linear parabolic PDE system using non-collocated pointwise observation. Automatica **93**, 197–210 (2018)
19. Wu, W., Zhou, W., Chen, T.: Cluster synchronization of linearly coupled complex networks under pinning control. IEEE Trans. Circuits Syst. I Regul. Pap. **56**(4), 829–839 (2008)
20. Wang, A., Dong, T., Liao, X.: Finite/fixed-time bipartite consensus for networks of diffusion PDEs via event-triggered control. Inf. Sci. **609**, 1435–14507 (2022)
21. Zhang, H., Qiu, Z., Cao, J., Abdel Aty, M., Xiong, L.: Event-triggered synchronization for neutral-type semi-Markovian neural networks with partial mode-dependent time-varying delays. IEEE Trans. Neural Netw. Learn. Syst. **31**(11), 4437–4450 (2019)
22. Wang, X., Fei, Z., Wang, T., Yang, L.: Dynamic event-triggered actuator fault estimation and accommodation for dynamical systems. Inf. Sci. **525**, 119–133 (2020)
23. Liu, D., Yang, G.: Observer-based dynamic event-triggered control for multiagent systems with time-varying delay. IEEE Trans. Cybernet. **53**(5), 3376–3387 (2022)
24. Xu, S., Lam, J., Zhang, B., Zou, Y.: New insight into delay-dependent stability of time-delay systems. Int. J. Robust Nonlinear Control **25**(7), 961–970 (2015)
25. Lin, H., Zeng, H., Wang, W.: New Lyapunov-Krasovskii functional for stability analysis of linear systems with time-varying delay. J. Syst. Sci. Complexity **34**(2), 632–641 (2021)
26. Lee, T.H., Park, J.H., Xu, S.: Relaxed conditions for stability of time-varying delay systems. Automatica **75**, 11–15 (2017)
27. Kwon, W., Koo, B., Lee, S.M.: Novel Lyapunov-Krasovskii functional with delay-dependent matrix for stability of time-varying delay systems. Appl. Math. Comput. **320**, 149–157 (2018)
28. Kwon, W., Koo, B., Lee, S.M.: Wirtinger-based integral inequality: application to time-delay systems. Automatica **49**(9), 2860–2866 (2013)
29. Shen, Y., Wang, J.: Almost sure exponential stability of recurrent neural networks with Markovian switching. Automatica **20**(5), 840–855 (2009)
30. Fridman, E., Blighovsky, A.: Robust sampled-data control of a class of semilinear parabolic systems. Automatica **48**(5), 826–836 (2012)

An Improved Image Super-Resolution Algorithm for Percutaneous Endoscopic Lumbar Discectomy

Xue Li[1], Zihan Zhou[1], Kaifeng Wang[2], Haiying Liu[2], Yalong Qian[2], Xingguang Duan[1(✉)], and Changsheng Li[1(✉)]

[1] Beijing Institute of Technology, 5 South Zhong Guan Cun Street, Haidian District, Beijing, China
{duanstar,lics}@bit.edu.cn
[2] The Department of Spinal Surgery, Peking University People's Hospital, No. 11 Xizhimen South Street, Xicheng District, Beijing, China

Abstract. High-resolution (HR) spinal endoscopic images are essential to enhance the surgeon's visual presence for the guidance of surgical procedures. However, available image super-resolution methods, especially deep learning methods, are mostly trained with open-source life scene datasets which possess limited medical image features. To address this issue, we have proposed an improved SRGAN model for the visual enhancement of percutaneous endoscopic lumbar discectomy (PELD) surgical images. Specifically, a residual dense block (RDB) and a dynamic RELU function are introduced. We validate the proposed method on PELD datasets. Quantitative and qualitative comparisons are carried out by comparing methods. The method proposed in this paper improves PSNR by 2.8% and SSIM by 6% compared with the original SRGAN, which proves the superiority of this methods.

Keywords: Single Image Super-Resolution · Generative Adversarial Network · Medical images processing · Percutaneous Endoscopic Lumbar Discectomy

1 Introduction

With the rapid development of robotic technologies, minimally invasive technology is being paid more and more attention [1,2], among which percutaneous endoscopic Lumbar discectomy (PELD) as one of its typical representatives [3]. The procedure of PELD is to establish a surgical channel and remove the nucleus pulposus under the microscope with the help of natural anatomical gap [4]. It has numerous advantages including less trauma, less cost, and quick disappearance

X. Duan and C. Li—Supported by organization the National Key R&D Program of China (2022YFB4703000), and the Beijing Institute of Technology Research Fund Program for Young Scholars.

F. Sun et al. (Eds.): ICCSIP 2023, CCIS 1918, pp. 149–160, 2024.
https://doi.org/10.1007/978-981-99-8018-5_11

of postoperative pain. However, the field of vision is limited by the narrow bony cavity filled with water. Important tissues such as nerves around the target area increases the operational risks. Therefore, clear endoscopic images are essential for surgeons during the operation.

Single image super-resolution (SISR) refers to restoring a given low-resolution image to a corresponding high-resolution image, which is widely used in medical imaging, military, and video surveillance fields. Currently, the mainstream algorithms include interpolation-based algorithms [5], reconstruction-based algorithms, and learning-based algorithms. Linear and nonlinear interpolation methods possess the advantages of high calculation rates and simple operations, but suffers from the limitation of edge-blurring. The reconstruction-based algorithms utilize the prior information of image to reconstruct a high-resolution image, which can suppress noise and preserve image edge information. When the scale factor increases, the speed of image reconstruction decreases significantly, and the quality of preliminary information affects the reconstruction results.

With the rapid development of computer technologies, learning-based algorithms have been proposed in recent years. Convolutional neural networks (CNN) are used for reconstruction, such as SRCNN [6], DCSCN [7]. The limitations mainly include smoothed outputs, and high-frequency information loss. To address these issues, researchers have proposed generative adversarial networks (GAN) [8] to achieve reconstruction tasks, using pixel extraction instead of feature extraction to obtain more realistic reconstructions. Super-resolution using a generative adversarial (SRGAN) [9] adopts the sub-pixel convolution to upsample low-resolution images to high-resolution ones, and the similarity of them is analyzed by discriminator networks. The perceptual loss is used to replace the least mean squares so that the high-level information obtained by the generator networks is close to the original image.

In this paper, we propose an SRGAN based end-to-end deep learning framework, and an improved residual dense block (RDB) is proposed to enhance the image reconstruction performance. To improve the accuracy of the image reconstruction, the dynamic ReLU (Dy ReLU)is introduced in generator networks. The experimental results show that our method has higher PSNR and SSIM than Bicubic [10], SRGAN, and the reconstruction quality is significantly improved.

2   Related Works

This section reviews related works in image resolution, and generative adversarial networks.

2.1   Image Super-Resolution

There are many single-image super resolution (SISR) methods already in existence. Among them, the interpolation method is the simplest and most widely used method. However, its implementation is very poor which often produces blurry hyper-images. To enhance linear models with rich image priors, sparse-based techniques was introduced, along with many sophisticated models for mapping LR to HR spaces, including neighbor embeddings, random forests, and convolutional neural networks. In order to reduce the manual intervention process required for super-resolution, Chao et al. firstly introduced convolutional neural network into image super-resolution (SRCNN). SRCNN can directly use the existing image datasets for training without preprocess the original image data, which greatly improves the reconstruction efficiency and the reconstruction effect is more ideal. Due to the high computational cost and slow running speed of the original SRCNN, FSRCNN [11], ESPCN [12], SR Resnet [9] and others appeared to improve the detection efficiency. FSRCNN has the advantages of real-time, and the reconstruction efficiency of the ESPCN model has been greatly improved. However, when the magnification is too large, the high-frequency features of the reconstructed image will not be obvious, and the details will be too smooth to have a large gap with the real image. SRResNet can obtain a higher PSNR value, but there is a big gap between the visual effect and the real image.

2.2   GAN

Goodfellow et al. [13] first designed a Multilayer Perceptron (MLP) structure, which included a generator network and a discriminator network to confront each other and train intervals to get better images. The generator network generates SR images highly similar to the ground truth (GT) images, while the discriminator network distinguishes the true images and SR images. Ideally, it is difficult for the discriminator network to identify the difference between the true images and SR images. GAN can be used to learn to transform data from one domain data into another without labels [14] to train other machine learning models when real data is unavailable [15]. Despite the remarkable progress for GANs in image generators, recent studies have shown [16,17] that the traditional GAN network is still limited to realistic tasks, including mode collapse, hyperparametric sensitivity, and training models.

2.3   SRGAN

SRGAN networks firstly access GANs into simple image super-resolution tasks [9] which achieve more reconstruction details with a larger up-scale factor. Supervised SR algorithms optimize the mean squared error (MSE) between the recovered HR image and the ground truth obtaining optimal results. Although a high peak signal-to-noise ratio (PSNR) can be achieved, MSE captures perceptually relevant differences and smoothes the detail of the images. Inherently, a new loss function is proposed for SRGAN named perceptual-loss consisting of adversarial-loss and content-loss. Perceptual-loss is used to train generator networks consisting of ResNet blocks to generate high perceptual quality images.

2.4   Dense Convolutional Networks

In deep learning networks, gradient disappearance and gradient dispersion tend to increase with the number of network layers. To cope with these issues, the general concepts of shortcut connectivity and residual connectivity were proposed by ResNet emerged [18]. Subsequently, DenseNet presented the idea of densely connected layers [19], which was more intensive than residual networks. The output of each layer can be stitched with the previous ones so that the subsequent convolutional layer can adaptively fuse the previous feature. DenseNet can also alleviate gradient disappearance with the output layer directly connecting to each layer where only one derivation is required to reach reverse derivation. The above operations effectively utilize the features and enhance the transfer between layers. The DenseNet can reduce the number of parameters to a certain extent.

2.5   Activation Functions

Activation functions introduce non-linear in deep neural networks. Among various activation functions, ReLU [20–22] is widely used. Although ReLU has the advantages of reducing the amount of calculation, solving the problem of gradient disappearance, and overfitting, it would emerge as a dead node. Therefore, numerous improvements to the Relu function have appeared, which are based on negative inputs with a nonzero slope α. LeakyReLU fixes α to a small value [23], while PReLU treats α as a learnable parameter with limitations that the output is not smooth [24]. RReLU randomizes its trainable parameters [25]. Different from these static activate functions, dynamic ReLU can make good use of the input to dynamically adjust the activation function. The calculation parameters are reduced by compressing the global feature through pooling. After ReLU processing, a constraint value within $[-1, 1]$ will be obtained to determine the appropriate activation function.

3   Network Structure

Since the generator networks contains several residual block to preserve image information integrity that is insufficient details generated, deep networks and multi-level connection is used in this paper to improve the expressiveness of the generator networks. The residual dense block contains dense connected layers, local feature fusion (LFF), and local residual learning, establishing a contiguous memory mechanism [26] as shown in Fig. 1.

F_{d-1} and F_d are defined as the input and the output of the d-th RDB, through the dense connected layers, featured in F_{d-1}, $F_{d,1}$, and $F_{d,c}$ will be fully exploited. The characteristics in c-th layer of the d-th RDB can be recorded as

$$F_{d,c} = RReLU(W_{d,c}[F_{d-1}, F_{d,1}, ..., F_{d,c}]) \tag{1}$$

where $[F_{d,1}, ..., F_{d,c}]$ represents all features in the d-th RDB. Local feature fusion fuses the previous RDB and all Conv layers in the current RDB. Then, 1×1

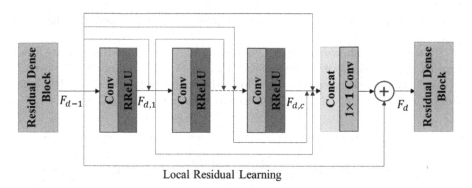

Fig. 1. Residual dense block (RDB) network structure.

convolution reduces the channels and the feature number. The residual dense block (RDB) is deeper than the traditional residual block. RDB has encouraged the flow of information and gradients and directed access to each layer of the next RDB, which could fully use hierarchical features to generate more accurate high-resolution images.

Rectified Linear Units (ReLU) is one of the most commonly used activation functions that can improve the performance of the neural networks. However, ReLU and its generalizations(non-parametric or parametric) are static, and perform the same operation on all input samples. To improve the feature expression for our model, this paper has introduced a dynamic piecewise function named dynamic ReLU (DY-ReLU) [27]. It encodes the input global context information through an auxiliary function, adaptively constructing a piece linear activation function. Traditional static ReLU can be expressed by

$$y = max(x, 0) \tag{2}$$

where $\mathbf{x}$ is the input vector, For the $c - th$ channel of the input x_c, $y_c = max(x_c, 0)$. Dynamic ReLU can be expressed by

$$y_c = f_{\theta(\mathbf{x})}(x_c) = max a_c^x(\mathbf{x}) x_c + b_c^k(\mathbf{x}) \tag{3}$$

The output of the hyper $\theta(\mathbf{x})$ with the coefficient (a_c^k, b_c^k) is expressed by

$$[a_1^1, ..., a_C^1, ..., a_1^K, ..., a_C^K, b_1^1, ..., b_C^1, ..., b_1^K, ...b_C^K]^T = \theta(\mathbf{x}) \tag{4}$$

where K is the number of functions, C is the number of channels. (a_c^k, b_c^k) is related to the corresponding input element x_c and other elements $x_{j \neq c}$.

An input tensor $\mathbf{x}$ with dimension$C \times H \times W$ through the pooling layer and the fully connected layer, finally outputs 2KC elements. It is denoted as the $\Delta a_{1:C}^{1:K}$ and $\Delta b_{1:C}^{1:K}$.

$$a_c^k(\mathbf{x}) = \alpha^k + \lambda_a \Delta a_c^k(\mathbf{x}) \tag{5}$$

$$b_c^k(\mathbf{x}) = \beta^k + \lambda_b \Delta a_c^k(\mathbf{x}) \tag{6}$$

where α^k and β^k are the initial values of a_c^k and b_c^k. λ_a and λ_b indicates the value of the error range.

To sum up, as shown in Fig. 2, Dynamic ReLU can change the activate function (K values) as the input parameters change, which can improve the overall network framework efficiency. Therefore, this paper introduced the Dynamic ReLU in generator networks to improve the accuracy of reconstruction.

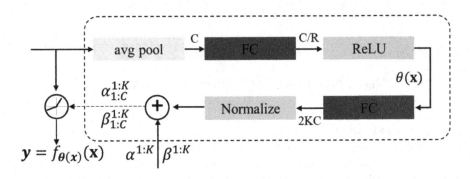

Fig. 2. Dynamic ReLU structure schematic.

the pixel-wise MSE loss is used to minimize the distance between the corresponding high-resolution image $I^H R$ and a super-resolved image. It is defined by

$$l_{pixel}^{SR} = \frac{1}{r^2 WH} \sum_{x=1}^{rW} \sum_{y=1}^{rH} (I_{x,y}^{HR} - G(I^L R)_{x.y})^2 \tag{7}$$

where W and H denote the size of I^{LR}, and r is the upsampling factor. While MSE loss achieve particularly high PSNR, but lack high-frequency hlcontent. Hence, the perceptual loss is proposed, which is based on the pre-trained 19-layer VGG network described by Simonyan and Zisserman. We define the loss as the euclidean distance between the feature representations of a reconstructed image and the reference image.

$$l_{percep}^{SR} = \frac{1}{W_{i,j} H_{i,j}} \sum_{x=1}^{W_{i,j}} \sum_{y=1}^{H^{i,j}} (\Phi_{i,j}(I^{H,R})_{x,y} - \Phi_{i,j}(G(I^{H,R}))_{x,y})^2 \tag{8}$$

where $W_{i,j}$ and $H_{i,j}$ describe the dimensions of the respective feature maps within the VGG network. i represents the feature map obtained by the j-th convolution before the i-th maximum pooling layer in the VGG19 network. We also use hinge loss proposed in spectral normalization GAN, which is given by

$$V_D(G, D) = E_{I^{HR} \sim P_{train(IHR)}}[log D(I^{HR})] + E_{I^{LR} \sim p_G(I^{LR})}[log(1 - D(G(I^{LR})))] \tag{9}$$

The generative loss is defined based on the probabilities of the discriminator D over all the training samples as

$$l_{Gen} = \sum_{n=1}^{N} -logD(G(l^{LR})) \tag{10}$$

Based on the above motivations, Fig. 3 illustrates the image super resolution reconstruction.

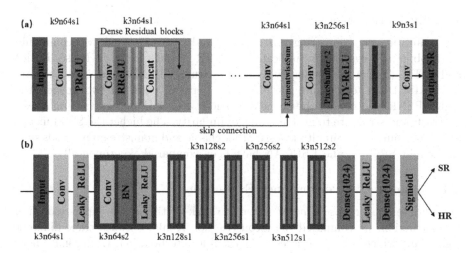

Fig. 3. Improved Network Structure. (a) Generator Network, (b) Discriminator Network

4   Experiments Verification

4.1   Datasets and Pre-processing

To evaluate our improved algorithms using percutaneous endoscopic lumbar discectomy (PELD) surgical datasets, which were intercepted by Peking University People's Hospital in China. The following images were acquired during lumbar disc herniation syndrome endoscopic operation in patients. All studies were performed in compliance with the use committee policies. Specifically, we collected endoscopic surgery videos and extracted image frames from them, eliminating image frames with surgical instruments. Finally, a total of 5665 images were selected as the training set and 300 images as the test set.

4.2 Implementation Details

The programs of reconstruction algorithm and other algorithms ran on the computer with Nvidia Graphics Cards 3090, Intel®-CoreTM i7-8550 U CPU @ 2.00 GHz, 8GB RAM. The experimental training process is as follows: Set the learning rate to $2 * 10^{-4}$, and the batch size to 8. The Adam algorithm is used during the training process, while the cosine annealing is used to optimize the objective function. The generator and discriminators alternate updates until the network model converges.

4.3 Evaluation Metrics

For quantitatively comparing different methods, we employed two commonly used objective evaluation indicators: PSNR (Peak Signal-to-Noise Ratio) and SSIM (Structure Similarity Index Measure). PSNR uses Mean Square Error(MSE) loss to measure the difference between pixels in two images, the higher PSNR, the smaller the image distortion [28]. SSIM integrates brightness, contrast, and structure to evaluate image similarity. The higher the SSIM means the higher similarity. Simultaneously, other classic and mainstream methods such as Bicubic, SRCNN, and ESRGAN have been compared experimentally.

4.4 Quantitative Performance Evaluation

To validate the proposed methods for the task of the image super-resolution reconstruction, we compared the reconstruction results between three different algorithms which are open access: (1) Bicubic interpolation, traditional linear interpolation algorithm; (2) SRCNN, the first application of a convolutional neural network to SISR; (3) SRGAN, Generative Adversarial Network (GAN) introduced in SISR. In the comparative experiments of each algorithms, the same training dataset, testing dataset, and training iterations are set for all algorithms.

Table 1. Quantitative comparison between our method and others.

Images		Bicubic	SRCNN	SRGAN	OURS
Dataset-1	PSNR	32.894	37.993	38.342	8.955
	SSIM	0.796	0.952	0.882	0.937
Dataset-2	PSNR	32.642	36.140	37.453	38.5989
	SSIM	0.784	0.946	0.869	0.929
Dataset-3	PSNR	32.876	38.917	38.658	39.722
	SSIM	0.7931	0.9594	0.8943	0.938
Average	PSNR	32.878	37.683	38.151	39.249
	SSIM	0.7907	0.9523	0.8820	0.935

Table 1 illustrates reconstruction results compared within objective qualitative indicators. From the Table 1, We have found that almost all of the selected images has the best objective performance for the proposed method.

Figure 4 demonstrates that the our method produces superior quality images compared to mainstream super-resolution techniques like bicubic, SRCNN, and SRGAN. Compared with the original SRGAN, the improved algorithm proposed in this paper has an average PSNR increase of 2.8%, and an average SSIM increase of 6%. The higher the Avg-PSNR and Avg-SSIM values, the greater the image quality achieved by this approach.

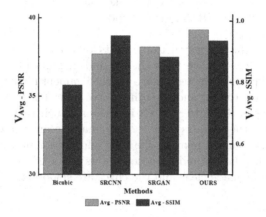

Fig. 4. Super-resolution results of the Avg-PSNR and the Avg-PSNR.

4.5 Ablation Study

To validate how each part of the proposed method affect the renderings, we modify the base models one at a time and compared the results. Table 2 summaries the quantitative result.

Table 2. Ablation experiment of the algorithm

Images		Aboriginal	+RDB	+RDB +Dy-ReLU
Dataset-1	PSNR	38.342	39.452	39.427
	SSIM	0.882	0.931	0.937
Dataset-2	PSNR	37.453	38.204	38.5989
	SSIM	0.869	0.900	0.929
Dataset-3	PSNR	38.658	39.609	39.722
	SSIM	08943	0.924	0.938
Average	PSNR	38.151	39.088	39.249
	SSIM	0.8820	0.918	0.935

Table 2 shows the PSNR and SSIM of the image super-resolution reconstruction algorithm under different conditions. It can be seen that the above measures can improve the super-resolution reconstruction performance of the algorithm, and the three measures have the best effect when used in combination.

4.6 Qualitative Performance Evaluation

To compare the effects more easily, we take four representative images in our dataset and use different SR algorithm models for super-resolution reconstruction.

Figure 5 shows the reconstruction results of each SR algorithm after we extract a representative image from the set and magnify it by two times. The partially enlarged parts of the test image are the ligamentum flavum at the upper joint, the nerve root, the fat and the other nerve root. The image reconstructed with bicubic interpolation and SRCNN is very hazy, neither the outline nor the edge information of the tissue is obvious. The image reconstructed by SRGAN is very smooth with a blurred texture, the edge information of nerve roots and fat is not clear enough. The method proposed in this paper has some improvements, the reconstructed image is clear and the edges are smoother.

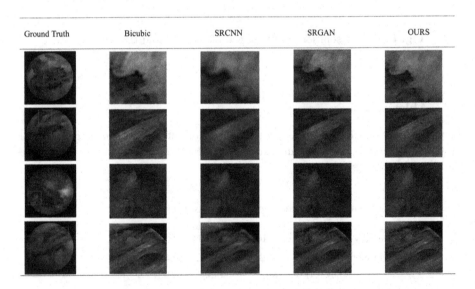

Fig. 5. Comparision of the reconstruction effect of each algorithm.

5   Conclusion

A generative adversarial network with improved dense residual modules is proposed to address the unrecoverable image details and feature information in low-resolution images. In particular, the residual dense block continuously transmits the state of each layer, so that the effective features of the image can be directly transferred to the deep layer and fused, which improves the way of information exchange and reduces the information loss during feature extraction. In addition, replacing the activation function in the generator networks with the Dynamic-ReLU function strengthens the network fitting ability without increasing the depth and width of the network to improve the reconstruction performance of the network on super-resolution tasks and deblurring tasks. Experimental results show that the method can extract deeper feature information from low-resolution images to generate high-resolution images that can improve texture clarity and quality. The proposed method outperforms previous methods in terms of PSNR, and SSIM with well visual quality.

References

1. Li, C., et al.: A miniature manipulator with variable stiffness towards minimally invasive transluminal endoscopic surgery. IEEE Robot. Autom. Lett. **6**(3), 5541–5548 (2021)
2. Li, C., Gu, X., Xiao, X., Lim, C.M., Ren, H.: Flexible robot with variable stiffness in transoral surgery. IEEE/ASME Trans. Mechatron. **25**(1), 1–10 (2019)
3. Zhang, X., Du, J., Yeung, A.: Development of percutaneous endoscopic lumbar discectomy (peld) technology in china. J. Spine **6**(374), 2 (2017)
4. Pan, M., Li, Q., Li, S., Mao, H., Meng, B., Zhou, F., Yang, H.: Percutaneous endoscopic lumbar discectomy: indications and complications. Pain Physician **23**(1), 49 (2020)
5. Zhang, L., Wu, X.: An edge-guided image interpolation algorithm via directional filtering and data fusion. IEEE Trans. Image Process. **15**(8), 2226–2238 (2006)
6. Dong, C., Loy, C.C., He, K., Tang, X.: Image super-resolution using deep convolutional networks. IEEE Trans. Pattern Anal. Mach. Intell. **38**(2), 295–307 (2015)
7. Yamanaka, J., Kuwashima, S., Kurita, T.: Fast and accurate image super resolution by deep cnn with skip connection and network in network. In: Neural Information Processing: 24th International Conference, ICONIP 2017, Guangzhou, China, November 14-18, 2017, Proceedings, Part II 24, pp. 217–225. Springer, Cham (2017). https://doi.org/10.1007/978-3-319-70096-0_23
8. Creswell, A., White, T., Dumoulin, V., Arulkumaran, K., Sengupta, B., Bharath, A.A.: Generative adversarial networks: an overview. IEEE Signal Process. Mag. **35**(1), 53–65 (2018)
9. Ledig, C., et al.: Photo-realistic single image super-resolution using a generative adversarial network. In: Proceedings of the IEEE Conference on Computer Vision and Pattern Recognition, pp. 4681–4690 (2017)
10. Keys, R.: Cubic convolution interpolation for digital image processing. IEEE Trans. Acoust. Speech Signal Process. **29**(6), 1153–1160 (1981)
11. Passarella, L.S., Mahajan, S., Pal, A., Norman, M.R.: Reconstructing high resolution esm data through a novel fast super resolution convolutional neural network (fsrcnn). Geophys. Res. Lett. **49**(4), e2021GL097571 (2022)
12. Zadeh, L.A.: Fuzzy sets as a basis for a theory of possibility. Fuzzy Sets Syst. **1**(1), 3–28 (1978)
13. Goodfellow, I., et al.: Generative adversarial networks. Commun. ACM **63**(11), 139–144 (2020)

14. Fedus, W., Goodfellow, I., Dai, A.M.: Maskgan: better text generation via filling in the_. arXiv preprint arXiv:1801.07736 (2018)
15. Zhu, J.-Y., Park, T., Isola, P., Efros, A.A.: Unpaired image-to-image translation using cycle-consistent adversarial networks. In: Proceedings of the IEEE International Conference on Computer Vision, pp. 2223–2232 (2017)
16. Mao, X., Li, Q., Xie, H., Lau, R.Y., Wang, Z., Smolley, S.P.: Least squares generative adversarial networks. In: IEEE International Conference on Computer Vision (ICCV) 2017, pp. 2813–2821 (2017)
17. Hinton, G.E., Osindero, S., Teh, Y.W.: A fast learning algorithm for deep belief nets. Neural Comput. **18**, 1527–1554 (2006)
18. He, K., Zhang, X., Ren, S., Sun, J.: Deep residual learning for image recognition. In: Proceedings of the IEEE Conference on Computer Vision and Pattern Recognition, pp. 770–778 (2016)
19. Huang, G., Liu, Z., Van Der Maaten, L., Weinberger, K.Q.: Densely connected convolutional networks. In: Proceedings of the IEEE Conference on Computer Vision and Pattern Recognition, pp. 4700–4708 (2017)
20. Hahnloser, R.H., Sarpeshkar, R., Mahowald, M.A., Douglas, R.J., Seung, H.S.: Digital selection and analogue amplification coexist in a cortex-inspired silicon circuit. Nature **405**(6789), 947–951 (2000)
21. Nair, V., Hinton, G.E.: Rectified linear units improve restricted Boltzmann machines. In: Proceedings of the 27th International Conference on Machine Learning (ICML-10), pp. 807–814 (2010)
22. Jarrett, K., Kavukcuoglu, K., Ranzato, M., LeCun, Y.: What is the best multi-stage architecture for object recognition? In: 2009 IEEE 12th International Conference on Computer Vision. IEEE, pp. 2146–2153 (2009)
23. Maas, A.L., Hannun, A.Y., Ng, A.Y., et al.: Rectifier nonlinearities improve neural network acoustic models. In: Proceedings of ICML, vol. 30, no. 1. Atlanta, Georgia, USA, p. 3 (2013)
24. He, K., Zhang, X., Ren, S., Sun, J.: Delving deep into rectifiers: surpassing human-level performance on imagenet classification. In: Proceedings of the IEEE International Conference on Computer Vision, pp. 1026–1034 (2015)
25. Xu, B., Wang, N., Chen, T., Li, M.: Empirical evaluation of rectified activations in convolutional network. arXiv preprint arXiv:1505.00853 (2015)
26. Zhang, Y., Tian, Y., Kong, Y., Zhong, B., Fu, Y.: Residual dense network for image super-resolution. In: Proceedings of the IEEE Conference on Computer Vision and Pattern Recognition, pp. 2472–2481 (2018)
27. Chen, Y., Dai, X., Liu, M., Chen, D., Yuan, L., Liu, Z.: Dynamic ReLU. In: Vedaldi, A., Bischof, H., Brox, T., Frahm, J.-M. (eds.) ECCV 2020. LNCS, vol. 12364, pp. 351–367. Springer, Cham (2020). https://doi.org/10.1007/978-3-030-58529-7_21
28. Hore, A., Ziou, D.: Image quality metrics: Psnr vs. ssim. In: 2010 20th International Conference on Pattern Recognition, pp. 2366–2369. IEEE (2010)

Algorithm and Control

KGRL: A Method of Reinforcement Learning Based on Knowledge Guidance

Tingting Xu[1,2], Fengge Wu[1,2(✉)], and Junsuo Zhao[1,2]

[1] Institute of Software, Chinese Academy of Sciences, Beijing 100190, China
fengge@iscas.ac.cn
[2] University of Chinese Academy of Sciences, Beijing 100049, China

Abstract. Reinforcement learning usually starts from scratch. Due to the characteristic of receiving feedback from interactions with the environment, starting from scratch often leads to excessive unnecessary exploration. In contrast, humans have a lot of common sense or prior knowledge when learning. The existence of prior knowledge accelerates the learning process and reduces unnecessary exploration. Inspired by this, in this article, we propose a knowledge-guided approach to learning reinforcement learning policies. We use prior knowledge to derive an initial policy and guide the subsequent learning process. Although prior knowledge may not be completely applicable to new tasks, the learning process is greatly accelerated because the initial policy ensures a fast start to learning and guidance in the middle allows for avoiding unnecessary exploration. This is a new framework that combines human prior suboptimal knowledge with reinforcement learning. We refer to it as KGRL - Knowledge-Guided Reinforcement Learning. The KGRL framework includes defining fuzzy rules based on prior knowledge, learning an initial policy based on fuzzy rules, and guiding the new policy through knowledge-guided encoding. We conducted experiments on four tasks in OpenAI Gym and PLE, and the results show that our algorithm combines prior knowledge and reinforcement learning effectively. By utilizing knowledge-guided encoding, it improves the performance of reinforcement learning, trains faster, and increases rewards by approximately 12.7%.

Keywords: Reinforcement learning · Knowledge Guidance · Policy based Reinforcement learning

1 Introduction

Reinforcement learning has shown great applications in fields [1–4] such as the game of go, which has led to increased attention on its performance in various domains of daily life. Currently, research on reinforcement learning in areas such as intelligent driving [5], healthcare [6], and robot control [7] is in full swing. However, due to its interactive nature with the environment, efficiency in initial interaction with the environment is low, and most of the time is spent in ineffective exploration, making it difficult to apply reinforcement learning to various fields.

© The Author(s), under exclusive license to Springer Nature Singapore Pte Ltd. 2024
F. Sun et al. (Eds.): ICCSIP 2023, CCIS 1918, pp. 163–175, 2024.
https://doi.org/10.1007/978-981-99-8018-5_12

Similarly, humans learn through interactive feedback, but rarely start from scratch. Humans have a lot of prior knowledge, such as common sense and accumulation from predecessors. When humans begin to learn a new skill, they often use existing knowledge to form a rough idea and build on it. This rough idea corresponds to the initial policy of the reinforcement learning agent, which guides the subsequent learning process. Although these existing knowledge may not fully match the new task, humans can adjust their strategies in the following learning process. Therefore, this article draws on human learning ideas to guide reinforcement learning agents, obtain an initial policy based on existing knowledge, and continuously adjust them to accelerate the learning process of reinforcement learning agents.

In supervised learning, the combination of human knowledge has been studied [8–11]. An important area of work that uses human knowledge in sequential decision-making problems is imitation learning [12–15]. Imitation learning uses human knowledge to learn from expert trajectories collected from the same task we want to solve. Demonstration data is a specific example of human knowledge in a task and can be viewed as a low-level representation of human knowledge. We hope to use advanced knowledge (such as common sense) to help us learn in unseen tasks (therefore, there is no demonstration data). In addition, high-level knowledge can be easily shared with other similar tasks.

There are some previous works that study how to guide or improve reinforcement learning with knowledge [16–22]. Some works use knowledge-based sub-goal policies in hierarchical RL [23,24], but the instruction representation used lacks the required diversity, unable to benefit from the compositionality of knowledge, and is not a popular target representation. In a concurrent work, Wu et al. [25] showed that existing knowledge can help learn difficult tasks, where more naive target representations lead to poorer performance, even with post hoc target relabeling. Andreas et al. [26] utilized structured policy search with knowledge descriptions to quickly adapt to unseen environment using existing knowledge to describe each environment. Another series of works focused on RL in text adventure games, where state is represented as a knowledge description and action is either a textual action available in each state [27], or all possible actions [28] (although not every action is applicable to every state). Generally speaking, these works focus on text-based games with discrete 1-bit actions, while we consider continuous actions in physics-based environments, which can be seen as a high-level policy with typical low-level policies tailored to each state; the discretization of these games limits the complexity of the interaction with the environment.

To utilize human knowledge, a major challenge is to obtain a representation of the provided knowledge. In most cases, the provided knowledge is imprecise and uncertain, and may only cover a small part of the state space. Therefore, traditional methods, such as classical bivalent logic rules, cannot provide sufficient model for approximate reasoning patterns instead of precise ones [29,30]. In contrast, fuzzy logic can be seen as an extension of classical logic systems, providing an effective conceptual framework for representing knowledge in uncertain and imprecise environments. The contributions of this article are as follows:

1. We propose a new framework that combines human prior suboptimal knowledge with reinforcement learning. We call it KGRL - Knowledge-Guided Reinforcement Learning.
2. We propose defining fuzzy rules based on prior knowledge to learn initial policies using fuzzy rule learning.
3. We propose guiding new policies through knowledge-guided encoding, encoding vectors using embedding networks, and capturing different state changes, thereby mapping them to different preference vectors.

2   Preliminary

2.1   Policy Based Reinforcement Learning

The typical Reinforcement learning problem considers a Markov decision process (MDP) defined by the tuple (S, A, T, R, γ) where S is the state space, A is the action space, the unknown transition probability $T : S \times A \times S \rightarrow [0, \infty)$ represents the probability density of reaching $s_{t+1} \in S$ from $s_t \in S$ by taking the action $a \in A$, $\gamma \in [0, 1)$ is the discount factor, and the bounded real-valued function $R : S \times A \rightarrow [rmin, rmax]$ represents the reward of each transition. We further denote $\rho_\pi(s_t)$ and $\rho_\pi(s_t, a_t)$ as the state marginal and the state-action marginal of the trajectory induced by policy $\pi(a_t|s_t)$. The objective of reinforcement learning is to find a policy $\pi(a_t|s_t)$ such that the expected discounted future reward $\Sigma_t E_{(s_t, a_t) \sim \rho_\pi}[\gamma^t R(s_t, a_t)]$ is maximized.

Policy based Reinforcement learning is to parameterize the policy itself and obtain the policy function π_θ:

$$\pi_\theta(s, a) = P(a|s, \theta) \tag{1}$$

Then directly train the policy function to obtain the optimal policy. The probability of taking any possible behavior under a given state and certain parameter settings is determined as a probability density function π_θ. The specific form of the policy is determined by the parameters θ, so it is necessary to use the objective function $J(\theta)$, solving for optimal parameters θ. Thus determining the optimal policy. $J(\theta)$ is related to the received reward, and therefore the higher the value, the better. Gradient ascent is used to solve it.

There are three ways to represent the policy function: initial state value, average value, or average reward per time step. The first method involves maximizing the cumulative reward from state s1 to the terminal state by adopting a certain policy:

$$J_1(\theta) = V^{\pi_\theta}(s_1) = E_{\pi_\theta}[v_1] \tag{2}$$

The second method applies to continuous environments, starting from a certain intermediate state. If there is no initial state, the probability of an individual being in a certain state at a certain moment, i.e., the state distribution at that moment, is calculated for each possible state. Then, the reward that can be obtained by continuously interacting with the environment from that moment onwards is calculated for each possible state and summed according to the probability distribution of each state at that moment:

$$J_2(\theta) = \sum_s d^{\pi_\theta}(s) V^{\pi_\theta}(s) \tag{3}$$

$d^{\pi_\theta}(s)$ represents a static distribution of the Markov chain over states under the current policy. The third method involves considering the possibility of an individual being in all possible states within a certain time step, and then calculating the instantaneous reward that can be obtained by taking all actions in each state:

$$J_3\theta) = \sum_s d^{\pi_\theta}(s) \sum_a \pi_\theta(s, a) R_s^a \tag{4}$$

Several effective policy-based algorithms have been proposed in the literature. TRPO [7] and ACKTR [32] both update the policy subject a constraint in the state-action space (trust region). Proximal policy optimization (PPO) [31] designs a clipped surrogate objective that approximates the regularization.

2.2   Fuzzy Logic and Fuzzy Rules

Fuzzy logic is based on fuzzy set theory [29]. The concept of fuzzy sets is an extension of classical or crisp set concepts, and in comparison, fuzzy sets are actually more extensive. Classical sets only consider a limited number of membership degrees, such as "0" or "1," or data ranges with a limited number of members. For example, if a temperature is defined as a crisp high, its range must be between 80 °F and higher, and it has nothing to do with 70 or even 60 °F. However, fuzzy sets enlarge this high temperature range. In other words, fuzzy sets consider a larger temperature range, such as from 0 °F to higher as a high temperature. The exact contribution of 0 °F to this high temperature depends on the membership function. This means that fuzzy sets use a linguistic universe as their basis and consider an infinite number of memberships in a set. Therefore, classical sets or crisp sets can be seen as subsets of fuzzy sets.

Fuzzy rules are a summary of expert knowledge in various application domains. Generally represented by a sequence in the form of IF-THEN, such rules guide algorithms to take actions or produce outputs based on observed information, and can include closed-loop control systems with inputs and feedback. Designing or building a set of fuzzy rules requires personal knowledge and experience, and specific practices may vary depending on the application. Fuzzy IF-THEN rules link conditions described by linguistic variables and fuzzy sets with outputs or conclusions. The IF part is mainly used to collect knowledge of flexible conditions, while the conclusion or output part is expressed in linguistic variable form. IF-THEN rules are widely used in fuzzy inference systems to calculate the degree of match between input data and rule conditions.

Fuzzy mapping rules provide a function mapping between inputs and outputs using linguistic variables, based on a fuzzy graph that describes the relationship between fuzzy inputs and fuzzy outputs. Sometimes, it is difficult to determine a certain relationship between inputs and outputs in practical applications, or the relationship between these inputs and outputs is very complex, even if this relationship has developed gradually. Fuzzy mapping rules are a good solution for these situations.

3   Method

Human common sense knowledge often exhibits imprecision and uncertainty. Traditional knowledge representation methods, such as hard rules based on classical bivalent logic, are ill-suited for representing this type of knowledge [Zadeh, 1996]. Fuzzy logic is largely applicable to the representation of human imprecise knowledge because it relies on a conceptual framework to address issues of uncertainty and lexical imprecision. Therefore, fuzzy logic is well-suited for the representation of imprecise human knowledge.

To illustrate how human knowledge can be transformed into fuzzy rules, we consider the example of learning to fly a kite. During the learning process, when the learner observes the kite sinking, they instinctively tighten the kite string to maintain its flight. However, the learner does not know exactly what speed or how many turns to rotate the kite string inwards. The only thing they know for sure is that if the kite continues to sink, they need to rotate the kite string inwards and tighten it faster. As the learning process continues, the learner gradually acquires the best policy for flying a kite. The prior knowledge of keeping the kite in the air can be expressed in the form of "if...then..." statements, such as "if the kite starts to sink, then the kite string should be rotated inwards and tightened to a greater degree". However, the definition of "greater degree" is not precise. Therefore, we can use fuzzy sets to represent "greater degree".

To clarify how human knowledge can be transformed into fuzzy rules, the next step is to define what fuzzy rules are. On the other hand, how can we learn the initial policy from fuzzy rules? How can we guide the reinforcement learning agent's learning through the initial policy derived from the fuzzy rules? In the following, we will introduce our knowledge-guided reinforcement learning algorithm from these aspects.

In this section, we propose a novel end-to-end framework that utilizes existing knowledge, where prior knowledge is continuously optimized through the entire policy. The proposed policy framework is referred to as Knowledge-Guided Reinforcement Learning (KGRL), and the overall architecture of KGRL is illustrated in Fig. 1. KGRL is a process that guides the reinforcement learning agent's learning by interpreting human knowledge into fuzzy rules. In Sect. 3.1, we describe how to define fuzzy rules, which will integrate human knowledge into the reinforcement learning framework in an end-to-end manner. In Sect. 3.2, we introduce how to learn an initial policy from fuzzy rules and how to guide the reinforcement learning agent's learning through the initial policy derived from knowledge translation. It fine-tunes the prior knowledge because rule-based knowledge is often suboptimal and even covers only a small portion of the prior space.

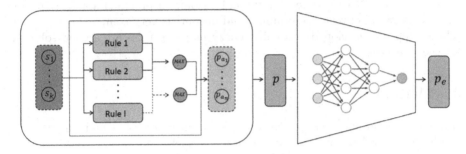

Fig. 1. The algorithm framework diagram of KGRL shows the process of using fuzzy rules to train initial strategies and using initial strategies for knowledge guidance. The process of knowledge guidance is achieved through encoder encoding.

3.1   Defining Fuzzy Rules

Extracting some fuzzy rules from human knowledge as knowledge representation provides "experience". When defining fuzzy rules, since the policy selects the corresponding action based on the existing state, we take the state information as input and output the action preference vector p, which represents the trend of the current state. Each rule selects a corresponding action based on the state's belonging to a fuzzy set of states, in the form of:

Rule l: IF S_1 is M_{l_1} and S_2 is M_{l_2} and ... and S_k is M_{l_k} THEN Action is a_j

Here, S_i represents variables that describe different parts of the system state. M_{l_i} corresponds to the fuzzy set of S_i. The conclusion of this rule indicates the corresponding action a_j.

Fuzzy rules are typically stated in the form of "if X is A and Y is B, then Z is C". "X is A" and "Y is B" are referred to as the premise conditions of the fuzzy rule, while "Z is C" is the conclusion of the rule. X, Y, and Z are variables, while A, B, and C are fuzzy sets, often called linguistic values. A fuzzy rule takes the observation values of X and Y as input and outputs the value of Z. To obtain the inference conclusion of a fuzzy rule, we first calculate the truth value T for each premise condition. Then the conjunction operator is applied to these truth values, resulting in the strength w of the conclusion (w can also be seen as the degree of satisfaction of the rule).

$$w = min(T_1, T_2) = min[u_A(x_0), u_B(y_0)] \tag{5}$$

In the above process, x0 and y0 respectively represent the observation values of X and Y; T1 and T2 represent the truth values of the premise conditions X is A and Y is B. The minimum operator is used as the conjunction operator.

Finally, we need to match the strength of the inference conclusion on the domain of Z, and here we adopt the inverse membership function applied to C as the matching method.

$$z = u_C^{-1}(w) \tag{6}$$

Assuming we have observation values $s_1...s_K$ for $S_1...S_K$, we can obtain the truth value of each premise condition by applying the membership function $u_{l_i}(s_i)$, where u_{l_i} is the membership function of M_{l_k}. Therefore, the strength of the rule l can be calculated according to the above method. For discrete action spaces, the strength of a rule can be seen as its preference towards the corresponding action. Different rules cover different parts of the state space. Therefore, for multiple rules concerning the same action a_i, their relationship is an "or" relationship. To calculate the preference value for action a_i, the maximum operator can be used to extract the maximum strength value from the rule set corresponding to a_i. Finally, we obtained the action preference vector p:

$$w_l = min[u_{l_1}(s_1), u_{l_2}(s_2), ..., u_{l_k}(s_k)] \tag{7}$$

Vector p represents the preference of all actions corresponding to the rules in a certain state.

For continuous action spaces, we need to further map the strength of rules to a continuous action value. As described in the above method, a commonly used method for matching strength is to apply the inverse membership function of the conclusion. Taking an n-dimensional continuous action space as an example, in this paper each rule is designed only for d dimensions. The reasoning result of rule l can be calculated by the following method:

$$p_d = u_{a_j}^- 1(w_l) \tag{8}$$

If there are multiple rules for the same action dimension, we use the weighted average of the action values of these rules, weighted by their individual strengths, as the final output of these rules.

3.2   Knowledge Guidance Module

Some fuzzy rules converted from human-provided knowledge serve as the representation of human knowledge, forming an initial policy. However, this initial policy is only a very rough one and cannot cover the entire state space completely. In order to obtain an optimal or near-optimal policy, the original policy needs to be extended and further refined. We use a knowledge-guided module g(.) to refine and complete the rough rule-based policy. The knowledge-guided module g(.) takes the preference vector p as input and outputs the action preference vector p_e after being guided by knowledge.

The improvement process can be viewed as a correction and supplementation of the rough rule-based policy. The initial policy may only cover a part of the entire state space. After further learning, it can learn the whole state space more quickly and accurately obtain the optimal policy based on the existing foundation. The knowledge-guided process is based on the current state s. A direct approach is to use a neural network to approximate the knowledge-guided module g(.), i.e., using the state and preference vector as inputs to the neural network:

$$p_e = g_\theta(s, p) \tag{9}$$

Here, θ represents the parameters of the neural network. However, the correction process of the knowledge-guided module may differ at different states. This means that the mapping from the action preference vector p to the refined preference vector p_e may vary during state transitions. Consequently, the knowledge-guided module $g_\theta(.)$ needs to adapt to the varying states. Therefore, we use an embedding network to encode the vectors and capture different state changes, thereby mapping to different preference vectors.

$$p_e = g_\theta(\tau_{i,K}^{pre}(s), p) \tag{10}$$

we create an encoder that takes the past trajectory $\tau_k = (s_0, a_0, ...)$ as input, and gets a new action preference vector $p_e = g_\theta(\tau_{i,K}^{pre}(s), p)$ with the original action preference vector p.The first network takes the state as input and generates weights for the second network. The second network takes the action preference vector p as input, refines it, and finally outputs the refined action preference vector p_e. This is completely consistent with the semantic relationship between refining action preference based on state in the refinement module.

4   Experiment

4.1   Experiment Setup

we firstly evaluate our algorithm on four tasks: CartP ole, LunarLander and LunarLanderContinuous in OpenAI Gym and FlappyBird in PLE. CartPole is an experimental environment in reinforcement learning, proposed by Barto and Sutton in 1982. It is a simple problem that involves balancing a stick-like object on a cart by moving the cart left or right. The goal is to keep the pole balanced for as long as possible. This environment is commonly used as a benchmark in reinforcement learning research.LunarLander and LunarLanderContinuous are two other experimental environments in the OpenAI Gym. LunarLander is a discrete control problem where the goal is to safely land a lunar lander on the surface of the moon by controlling its thrust and orientation. LunarLanderContinuous is a continuous control problem where the goal is the same but the control inputs are continuous rather than discrete. FlappyBird is an experimental environment in PLE (PyGame Learning Environment), proposed by Tasfi in 2016. In this environment, the player controls a bird that must fly through a series of pipes without hitting them. The game is over if the bird hits a pipe or falls off the screen. FlappyBird is commonly used as a benchmark for testing reinforcement learning algorithms due to its simple yet challenging nature.

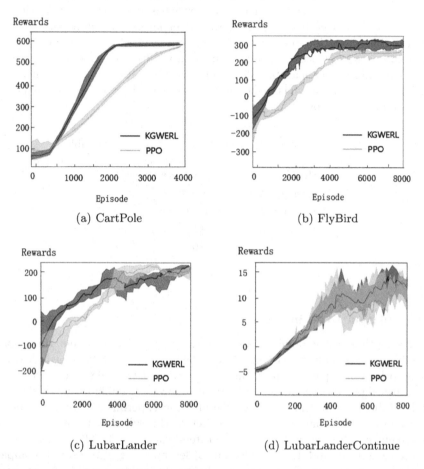

(a) CartPole

(b) FlyBird

(c) LubarLander

(d) LubarLanderContinue

Fig. 2. Comparison results between PPO and KGWERL, a knowledge-based Reinforcement learning algorithm in this paper, in four experimental environments.

Table 1 provides the hyperparameter settings for this experiment. We optimized the model's parameters using the Adam optimizer with a learning rate of 1×10^{-4}. As the training process involved softmax, we set the softmax temperature parameter to 0.1 and the decay factor to 0.99. The policy was updated every 128 time steps. In the PPO model that did not adopt the knowledge guidance framework proposed in this paper, we used a neural network with two fully connected hidden layers as the policy approximator. For the KGMF

(Knowledge Guidance Module with Feedforward Neural Network) that approximated the knowledge guidance module using a feedforward neural network, we employed an additional neural network with two fully connected hidden layers for knowledge refinement. For the KGME (Knowledge Guidance Module with Encoder) that approximated the knowledge guidance module using an encoder, we leveraged the encoder to generate a knowledge refinement module with one hidden layer, where each encoder had two hidden layers of 32 units per layer. The Figure 2 illustrates that the proposed algorithm achieved promising experimental results in all four tasks. The experimental results show that the knowledge guided Reinforcement learning algorithm has faster Rate of convergence than the PPO algorithm, and has higher cumulative rewards, with an average performance improvement of 12.7%.

Table 1. Table captions should be placed above the tables.

Heading level	Font size and style
learning rate	1×10^{-4}
discounted factor γ	0.99
temperature τ	0.1
GAE λ	0.95

4.2   Ablation Experiment

In this section, we conducted ablation experiments to examine the impact of different experimental conditions on the proposed reinforcement learning framework in this paper. Specifically, we examined the rule-based initial policy, knowledge-guided module, and various knowledge guidance methods separately. Table 2 shows the results of the ablation experiment. The first item in the experimental table verified the impact of the rule-based initial policy on reinforcement learning, while the second item examined the effect of having no knowledge-guided module on reinforcement learning. We also tested the impact of using a neural network approximate knowledge-guided module on reinforcement learning in the third item, and the influence of using an encoder approximate knowledge-guided module was investigated in the last item. The results showed that removing the initial policy and knowledge-guided module both led to a decline in performance, indicating that the proposed knowledge-guided method can effectively improve the exploration efficiency of reinforcement learning and enhance its performance. Among the different knowledge guidance methods, the encoder approximate knowledge-guided module had the best performance based on the experimental results, generating higher cumulative rewards. This finding suggests that the encoder can more effectively guide the mapping of action preference vectors and better integrate the original policy into the reinforcement learning policy.

Table 2. Ablation experiments on CAMPE.

	CartPole	FlappyBird	LunarLander
Remove initial policy	$357.4\pm_{11.3}$	$-3.3\pm_{1.6}$	$114.2\pm_{23.5}$
KGM	$344.74\pm_{30.7}$	$-3.8\pm_{2.5}$	$120.2\pm_{29.1}$
KGMF	$466.25\pm_{47.2}$	$6.7\pm_{1.1}$	$169.1\pm_{16.8}$
KGME	$497.34\pm_{20.7}$	$9.4\pm_{1.5}$	$195.9\pm_{23.1}$

5   Conclusion

This paper proposes a knowledge-guided reinforcement learning method called KGRL, which aims to leverage human prior knowledge to accelerate the learning process of reinforcement learning (RL) agents and reduce the phenomenon of "taking detours". The method consists of a fuzzy rule module and a knowledge guidance module. Specifically, fuzzy rules are first generated to represent human prior knowledge, and then the knowledge guidance module refines and further learns these imprecise prior knowledge. This policy framework is end-to-end and can be combined with existing policy-based algorithms. We evaluate this method on both discrete and continuous tasks, and experimental results show that even with very low-performing human prior knowledge, this method can significantly improve the learning efficiency of RL agents. In future work, we will further investigate the contribution of knowledge representation to reinforcement learning and explore its interpretability.

References

1. Mnih, V., et al.: Human-level control through deep reinforcement learning. Nature **518**(7540), 529 (2015)
2. Justesen, N., Torrado, R., Bontrager, P., Khalifa, A., Togelius, J., Risi, S.: Illuminating generalization in deep reinforcement learning through procedural level generation. arXiv:1806.10729 (2018)
3. Zhang, C., Vinyals, O., Munos, R., Bengio, S.: A study on overfitting in deep reinforcement learning. ArXiv, abs/1804.06893 (2018)
4. Silver, D., et al.: Mastering the game of go with deep neural networks and tree search. Nature **529**(7587), 484–489 (2016)
5. Li, J., Yao, L., Xu, X., et al.: Deep reinforcement learning for pedestrian collision avoidance and human-machine cooperative driving. Inf. Sci. **532**, 110–124 (2020)
6. Yu, C., Liu, J., Nemati, S., et al.: Reinforcement learning in healthcare: a survey. ACM Comput. Surv. (CSUR) **55**(1), 1–36 (2021)
7. Schulman, J., Levine, S., Abbeel, P., Jordan, M., Moritz, P.: Trust region policy optimization. In: International Conference on Machine Learning, pp. 1889–1897 (2015)
8. Collobert, R., et al.: Natural language processing (almost) from scratch. J. Mach. Learn. Res. **12**(Aug), 2493–2537 (2011)

9. Fischer, M., Balunovic, M., Drachsler-Cohen, D., Gehr, T., Zhang, C., Vechev, M.: DL2: training and querying neural networks with logic. In International Conference on Machine Learning, pp. 1931–1941 (2019)
10. d'Avila Garcez, A.S., Broda, K.B., Gabbay, D.M.: Neural-symbolic learning systems: foundations and applications, 1st edn. Springer, London (2012). https://doi.org/10.1007/978-1-4471-0211-3
11. Hu, Z., Ma, X., Liu, Z., Hovy, E., Xing, E.: Harnessing deep neural networks with logic rules. arXiv preprint arXiv:1603.06318 (2016)
12. Gordon, G.J., Dunson, D.B., Dudík, M. (eds.): Proceedings of the Fourteenth International Conference on Artificial Intelligence and Statistics, AISTATS 2011, Fort Lauderdale, USA, 11–13 April 2011, volume 15 of JMLR Proceedings. JMLR.org (2011)
13. Ho, J., Ermon, S.: Generative adversarial imitation learning. In: Advances in Neural Information Processing Systems, pp. 4565–4573 (2016)
14. Pomerleau, D.: Efficient training of artificial neural networks for autonomous navigation. Neural Comput. 3(1), 88–97 (1991)
15. Hester, T., et al.: Learning from demonstrations for real world reinforcement learning. CoRR, abs/1704.03732 (2017)
16. Luketina, J., et al.: A survey of reinforcement learning informed by natural language. arXiv preprint arXiv:1906.03926 (2019)
17. Fried, D., et al.: Speakerfollower models for vision-and-language navigation. In: Advances in Neural Information Processing Systems, pp. 3314–3325 (2018)
18. Kaplan, R., Sauer, C., Sosa, A.: Beating Atari with natural language guided reinforcement learning (2017)
19. Bahdanau, D., Hill, F., Leike, J., Hughes, E., Kohli, P., Grefenstette, E.: Learning to understand goal specifications by modelling reward (2018)
20. Fu, J., Korattikara, A., Levine, S., Guadarrama, S.: From language to goals: inverse reinforcement learning for vision-based instruction following. In: International Conference on Learning Representations (2019). https://openreview.net/forum?id=r1lq1hRqYQ
21. John D Co-Reyes, Abhishek Gupta, Suvansh Sanjeev, Nick Altieri, John DeNero, Pieter Abbeel, and Sergey Levine. Meta-learning language-guided policy learning. In International Conference on Learning Representations (2019). https://openreview.net/forum?id=HkgSEnA5KQ
22. Chevalier-Boisvert, M., et al.: BabyAI: First steps towards grounded language learning with a human in the loop. In: International Conference on Learning Representations (2019). https://openreview.net/forum?id=rJeXCo0cYX
23. Das, A., Gkioxari, G., Lee, S., Parikh, D., Batra, D.: Neural modular control for embodied question answering. arXiv preprint arXiv:1810.11181 (2018)
24. Shu, T., Xiong, C., Socher, R.: Hierarchical and interpretable skill acquisition in multi-task reinforcement learning. arXiv preprint arXiv:1712.07294 (2017)
25. Wu, Y., Chan, H., Kiros, J., Fidler, S., Ba, J.: ACTRCE: augmenting experience via teacher's advice (2019). https://openreview.net/forum?id=HyM8V2A9Km
26. Andreas, J., Klein, D., Levine, S.: Learning with latent language (2017)
27. He, J., et al.: Deep reinforcement learning with a natural language action space. arXiv preprint arXiv:1511.04636 (2015)
28. Narasimhan, K., Kulkarni, T., Barzilay, R.: Language understanding for textbased games using deep reinforcement learning. arXiv preprint arXiv:1506.08941 (2015)
29. Zadeh, L.A.: Fuzzy sets. Inf. Control 8(3), 338–353 (1965)

30. Zadeh, L.A.: Knowledge representation in fuzzy logic. In: Fuzzy Sets, Fuzzy Logic, And Fuzzy Systems: Selected Papers by Lotfi A Zadeh, pp. 764–774. World Scientific (1996)
31. Schulman, J., Wolski, F., Dhariwal, P., Radford, A., Klimov, O.: Proximal policy optimization algorithms. arXiv preprint arXiv:1707.06347 (2017)
32. Wu, Y., Mansimov, E., Grosse, R.B., Liao, S., Ba, J.: Scalable trust-region method for deep reinforcement learning using kroneckerfactored approximation. In: Advances in Neural Information Processing Systems, pp. 5279–5288 (2017)

Terminal Sliding Mode Control of DC-DC Buck Converter Based on Disturbance Observer

Dexin Fu, Leipo Liu$^{(\boxtimes)}$, and Qiaofeng Wen

College of Information Engineering, Henan University of Science and Technology, Luoyang 471023, Henan, China
liuleipo123@163.com

Abstract. This paper proposes a terminal sliding mode control of DC-DC buck converter based on disturbance observer. At first, a disturbance observer is devised to estimate disturbances with unknown disturbance structure. And a novel terminal sliding function incorporated with disturbance estimation is constructed, which can not only reduce the chattering effectively but also make the state converge to the equilibrium point in a finite time. Then a terminal sliding mode controller is designed to make the system state can reach the sliding surface in a finite time. Finally, an experimental platform is established, and the simulation and experimental results verify the effectiveness of the control method.

Keywords: Finite time stable · Terminal sliding mode · Disturbance observer · DC-DC buck converter

1 Introduction

DC power supplies have become a ubiquitous and indispensable equipment in daily life, because of their simple structures, low cost and high efficiency. DC-DC converters have been widely applied in many fields, such as DC motor drives, computers, automobiles, photovoltaic systems [1,2,13,26], etc. Therefore, many control methods for DC-DC converter have been proposed, such as initial PID control [4,9,11], fuzzy control [12,19,27], sliding mode control (SMC) [5,18,24], neural network control [3,10,25], etc. Among these control strategies, sliding mode control has received extensive attention due to its robustness against parameter variations, fast dynamic response and insensitivity to disturbances.

There are many different forms of SMC strategies because of different sliding functions, such as integral sliding mode control [19,22], terminal sliding mode control (TSMC) [8], high-order sliding mode control [6,7,16,23,28], etc. The sliding function is designed to be linear or nonlinear. Linear sliding function only guarantees the asymptotic stability, that is, the system state can not converge to zero in a finite time. However, in the practical engineering process, we always want to stabilize the system as quickly as possible. Though the convergence speed

F. Sun et al. (Eds.): ICCSIP 2023, CCIS 1918, pp. 176–190, 2024.
https://doi.org/10.1007/978-981-99-8018-5_13

can become faster by adjusting the sliding mode parameters in the linear sliding function design, this will increase the control gain. As a result, a big chattering may be caused and then the system performance will deteriorate. Therefore, an approach to solving this problem is to design nonlinear sliding function-terminal sliding mode function [15,31,32], which can achieve finite-time stabilization.

At the same time, the influence of disturbance can not be ignored in the process of designing TSMC. There are two methods to deal with the influence of disturbance on DC-DC converter. One way is to use the upper bound of disturbance, but it will increase the chattering of the system when the bound is large. The other way is to estimate the disturbance by establishing a disturbance observer (DO) [17,21,22,29,30]. The author in [22] proposed an integral sliding mode control strategy for DC-DC boost converter based on state and disturbance observer. In [17] a control strategy based on a nonsingular terminal sliding mode for DC-DC buck converter with disturbances was proposed. It is worth noting that most of the above results are involved in the known model of disturbance, such as [17,21,22]. But in practice, the structure of the disturbance is often unknown, such as [29], a disturbance observer is designed, and the gain of the disturbance observer can be obtained by Lyapunov method. However, this method is only feasible when the first-order differential of the disturbance is slowly changing.

Based on the above discussion, in order to improve the tracking accuracy of output voltage, a TSMC for DC-DC buck converter based on DO is proposed in this paper. Firstly, for the system with an unknown disturbance structure, a DO is constructed to estimate the disturbance, and the first-order differential of the disturbance is assumed to be bounded. By using a matrix transformation, the exponential convergence speed of the disturbance error can easily be obtained, this method extends the results in [29]. And then, a terminal sliding mode function combined with disturbance estimation is designed, which not only avoids the singular problem of terminal sliding mode design, but also introduces a continuous term to replace the discontinuous term in [20]. So the chattering of the system is reduced and the performance is improved. In addition, a terminal sliding mode controller is designed to make the state of DC-DC buck converter finite-time stable. Finally, the effectiveness of the scheme is verified by simulation. Furthermore, the experimental platform for DC-DC buck converter is built. In this platform, the output voltage is measured by series voltage divider, and the inductance current is measured by a hall-sensor. In the end, the experimental results also verify the effectiveness.

The paper is organized as follows. In Sect. 2, the dynamic model of buck converter is described. Section 3 designs the disturbance observer for the buck converter. In Sect. 4, a novel terminal sliding surface and controller are designed for the buck converter. In Sect. 5, the simulation and experimental results are presented. Finally, the conclusion is addressed in Sect. 6.

2   Mathematical Model of DC–DC Buck Converter System

As shown in Fig. 1, the dynamic model of the synchronous DC-DC buck converter is composed of a DC power supply (V_{in}), controlled switches (Q_1, Q_2), a diode (D), a filter inductor (L), capacitor (C), and load resistor (R). Considering the converter operates in continuous conduction mode (CCM) and switch Q_1 is ON and Q_2 is OFF, the following differential equation can be obtained from KVL and KCL.

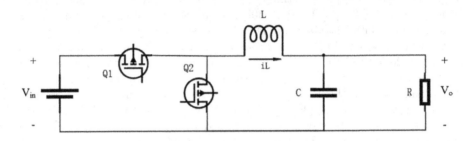

Fig. 1. Mode of DC-DC converter.

$$\begin{cases} \frac{di_L}{dt} = \frac{V_{in}}{L} - \frac{V_o}{L} \\ \frac{dV_o}{dt} = \frac{i_L}{C} - \frac{V_o}{RC} \end{cases} \tag{1}$$

When Q_1 is OFF and Q_2 is ON, we obtain that

$$\begin{cases} \frac{di_L}{dt} = -\frac{V_{in}}{L} \\ \frac{dV_o}{dt} = \frac{i_L}{C} - \frac{V_o}{RC} \end{cases} \tag{2}$$

Introducing the control variable ν, where $\nu \in [0, 1]$ represents a PWM signal. By combining (1) with (2), we obtain

$$\begin{cases} \frac{di_L}{dt} = \frac{\nu V_{in}}{L} - \frac{V_o}{L} \\ \frac{dV_o}{dt} = \frac{i_L}{C} - \frac{V_o}{RC} \end{cases} \tag{3}$$

Let output voltage error be $V_o - V_r = x_1(t)$, where V_r is reference output voltage. The Eq. (3) can be rewritten as $\dot{x}_1(t) = \frac{i_L}{C} - \frac{V_o}{R_o C} + d_1(t)$, where $d_1(t) = \frac{V_o}{R_o C} - \frac{V_o}{RC}$. Let $x_2(t) = \frac{i_L}{C} - \frac{V_o}{R_o C}$. We have

$$\begin{cases} \dot{x}_1(t) = x_2 + d_1(t) \\ \dot{x}_2(t) = \frac{\nu V_{in} - V_r}{LC} - \frac{x_1}{LC} - \frac{1}{R_o C}(\frac{i_L}{C} - \frac{V_o}{RC}) \end{cases} \tag{4}$$

Let $u = \frac{\nu V_{in} - V_r}{LC}$, $d_2(t) = -\frac{1}{R_o C} d_1(t)$, R_0 is nominal value of R. The model is further rewritten as

$$\begin{cases} \dot{x}_1(t) = x_2 + d_1(t) \\ \dot{x}_2(t) = u - \frac{x_1}{LC} - \frac{x_2}{R_o C} + d_2(t) \end{cases} \tag{5}$$

3 Design of Disturbance Observer

For system (5), $d_1(t)$ is disturbance with unknown structure, so a disturbance observer is designed as follows

$$
\begin{cases}
\dot{\hat{x}}_1(t) = \hat{d}_1(t) + x_2 + l_1(x_1 - \hat{x}_1) \\
\dot{\hat{d}}(t) = l_2(x_1 - \hat{x}_1)
\end{cases}
\tag{6}
$$

Let the disturbance observer error and state observer error be $\tilde{d}_1(t) = d_1(t) - \hat{d}_1(t)$ and $\tilde{x}_1(t) = x_1(t) - \hat{x}_1(t)$, respectively, where $\hat{d}_1(t)$ is estimation of $d_1(t)$ and $\hat{d}_2(t)$ is estimation of $d_2(t)$. From (5) and (6), the error equation can be got as

$$
\begin{bmatrix} \dot{\tilde{x}}_1(t) \\ \dot{\tilde{d}}_1(t) \end{bmatrix} = \begin{bmatrix} -l_1 & 1 \\ -l_2 & 0 \end{bmatrix} \begin{bmatrix} \tilde{x}_1(t) \\ \tilde{d}_1(t) \end{bmatrix} + \begin{bmatrix} 0 \\ \dot{d}_1(t) \end{bmatrix}
\tag{7}
$$

In this paper, we assume that $\dot{d}_1(t)$ satisfies $|\dot{d}_1(t)| \le \theta$, $\theta \ge 0$.

It is worth noting that the stability of system (7) can not be obtained directly by Lyapunov stability theory. So we use a new method of matrix transformation to address this problem. Choose $l_1 = -m_1 - m_2$ and $l_2 = m_1 m_2$. $m_1 < 0$, $m_2 < 0$.

Let us define the matrix $Z(t) = \begin{bmatrix} Z_1(t) \\ Z_2(t) \end{bmatrix} = P \begin{bmatrix} \tilde{x}_1(t) \\ \tilde{d}_1(t) \end{bmatrix}$, where P is a transformation matrix. P is set as $P = \begin{bmatrix} 1 & 0 \\ -m_1 & -1 \end{bmatrix}$. So, $P^{-1} = \begin{bmatrix} 1 & 0 \\ -m_1 & -1 \end{bmatrix}$. System (7) can be converted into

$$
\dot{Z}(t) = AZ(t) + B
\tag{8}
$$

where $A = \begin{bmatrix} m_2 & -1 \\ 0 & m_1 \end{bmatrix}$, $B = \begin{bmatrix} 0 \\ -\dot{d}_1(t) \end{bmatrix}$.

We can choose m_1 and m_2 such that A has expected eigenvalues. There are positive constants m and a such that $\|e^{At}\| \le ae^{-mt}$, $m = \min\{-m_1, -m_2\}$.

Solving (8), we obtain

$$
\begin{aligned}
Z(t) &= e^{At}Z(0) + \int_0^t e^{A(t-\tau)} B(\tau) d\tau \\
\|Z(t)\| &\le ae^{-mt}\|Z(0)\| + \theta \int_0^t e^{\|A(t-\tau)\|} d\tau \\
&\le ae^{-mt}\|Z(0)\| + \frac{a\theta}{m}(1 - e^{-mt})
\end{aligned}
\tag{9}
$$

From (9) it is obvious that $\lim\limits_{t \to +\infty} \|Z(t)\| \le \dfrac{a\theta}{m}$, that is, since $\begin{bmatrix} \tilde{x}_1(t) \\ \tilde{d}_1(t) \end{bmatrix} = P^{-1}Z(t)$, system (7) is exponentially bounded stable.

Remark 1. For system (6), we use the matrix transformation method to obtain the convergence of observer error, which can deal with the case that the first-order differential of the disturbance is bounded. When d_1 undergoes a step change, the special case of $\theta = 0$ includes the hypothesis proposed in [29]. And under the condition of $\theta = 0$, system (7) is exponentially stable.

Remark 2. In order to improve the observation accuracy, we can choose the appropriate parameters m_1 and m_2 to make $\frac{a\theta}{m}$ smaller.

4   Terminal Sliding Function Design

Firstly, the following assumption is vital to conduct our research.

Proposition 1. *For system (5), suppose that lumped disturbances $d_1(t)$, $d_2(t)$ are bounded such that $|d_1 - \hat{d}_1| < \lambda_1$, $|d_2 - \hat{d}_2| < \lambda_2$, where $\lambda_1 > 0$, $\lambda_2 > 0$.*

A terminal sliding function is designed as

$$s = cx_1(t) + x_2(t) + \alpha \frac{x_1(t)}{|x_1(t)| + \delta} + \hat{d}_1(t) \tag{10}$$

where $c > 0$, $\alpha > 0$, $\delta > 0$.

Remark 3. The traditional terminal sliding functions are designed as $s = c_1 x_1(t) + c_2 x_2(t) + x_1^{\frac{q}{p}}(t), p > 0, q > 0$, such as [14,15] this will lead to singular problem. Obviously, the structure of the proposed design avoids this problem.

Remark 4. The proposed terminal sliding function replaces discontinuous functions $sgn(x_1)$ in [20] with continuous term $\frac{x_1(t)}{|x_1(t)| + \delta}$. It reduces the chattering of the system. Furthermore, the added estimation of the disturbance will bring better disturbance rejection ability.

When the desired sliding motion is achieved on the sliding surface, $s = 0$. From (10) and (5) we have

$$\dot{x}_1(t) = -cx_1(t) - \alpha \frac{x_1(t)}{|x_1(t)| + \delta} + d_1(t) - \hat{d}_1(t) \tag{11}$$

Theorem 1. *Suppose there exists a positive constant γ that satisfies $\alpha > \gamma > \lambda_1$ and let $\rho = \frac{\gamma\delta}{\alpha - \gamma}$. If Proposition 1 holds, that sliding mode dynamics (11) will reach the neighborhood of $\{x_1 | x_1| < \rho\}$ in a finite time. And the time is $t_f = \frac{|x_1(0)|}{\gamma - \lambda_1}$.*

Proof. We choose the Lyapunov function as

$$V_{x_1}(t) = \frac{1}{2} x_1^2(t) \tag{12}$$

The time derivative of (12) results in

$$\dot{V}_{x_1}(t) = \dot{x}_1(t)x_1(t) = -cx_1^2(t) - \alpha \frac{x_1^2(t)}{|x_1(t)| + \delta} + x_1(d_1(t) - \hat{d}_1(t)) \tag{13}$$

Since $\rho = \frac{\gamma\delta}{\alpha-\gamma}$, when $|x_1| \geq \rho$, we have $\alpha\frac{x_1^2(t)}{|x_1(t)|+\delta} \geq \gamma|x_1|$, from (13) we obtain

$$
\begin{aligned}
\dot{V}_{x_1}(t) &\leq -\alpha\frac{x_1^2(t)}{|x_1(t)|+\delta} + |x_1(t)||d_1(t) - \hat{d}_1(t)| \\
&\leq -\gamma|x_1| + |x_1(t)||d_1(t) - \hat{d}_1(t)| \\
&\leq -|x_1|(\gamma - |d_1(t) - \hat{d}_1(t)|) \\
&\leq -2^{\frac{1}{2}}(\gamma - \lambda_1)V_{x_1}^{\frac{1}{2}}
\end{aligned}
\tag{14}
$$

From the inequality (14), it can be obtained that the time t_f when $V_{x_1}(t)$ converges from $V_{x_1}(0)$ to 0, that is, the time required for $x_1(t)$ to converge from the initial state $x_1(0)$ to equilibrium point is

$$
\begin{aligned}
t_f &= \int_{V_{x_1}(0)}^{0} \frac{1}{-2^{\frac{1}{2}}(\gamma - \lambda_1)V_{x_1}^{\frac{1}{2}}}dV_{x_1}(t) \\
&= \int_{0}^{V_{x_1}(0)} \frac{1}{2^{\frac{1}{2}}(\gamma - \lambda_1)V_{x_1}^{\frac{1}{2}}}dV_{x_1}(t) \\
&= \frac{(2V_{x_1}(0))^{\frac{1}{2}}}{\gamma - \lambda_1}
\end{aligned}
\tag{15}
$$

The proof is completed.

Remark 5. In the above proof, for $\rho = \frac{\gamma\delta}{\alpha-\gamma} = \frac{\delta}{\frac{\alpha}{\gamma}-1}$, we can make ρ small enough by reducing γ and δ so that the neighborhood of $|x_1|$ holds in a small range.

Next, a TSMC law is designed as follows

$$
\begin{aligned}
u = {}& \frac{x_1(t)}{LC} + \frac{x_2(t)}{R_oC} - cx_2(t) - c\hat{d}_1 - \hat{d}_2 - \frac{\alpha(x_2(t)+\hat{d}_1(t))\delta}{(|x_1(t)|+\delta)^2} - \dot{\hat{d}}_1(t) \\
&- a_1|s|^k sgn(s) - a_2 sgn(s) - \beta\frac{s}{|s|+\varepsilon}
\end{aligned}
\tag{16}
$$

where $a_1 > 0$, $a_2 \geq \lambda_2 + (\frac{\alpha}{\delta}+c)\lambda_1 > 0$, $1 > k > 0$, $\beta > 0$, $\frac{k}{k+3} > \varepsilon > 0$.

Theorem 2. *System (5) will converge to the sliding surface $s = 0$ in a finite time if TSMC law (16) is used and the time can be estimated by t_{sf}.*

Proof. Choose the following Lyapunov function

$$
V(t) = \frac{1}{2}s^2(t)
\tag{17}
$$

$V(0)$ is initial value of $V(t)$, taking derivative of $V(t)$, we obtain

$$
\dot{V}(t) = s\dot{s} = s(c\dot{x}_1(t) + \dot{x}_2(t) + \alpha\frac{\dot{x}_1(t)\delta}{(|x_1(t)|+\delta)^2} + \dot{\hat{d}}_1(t))
\tag{18}
$$

Substituting (16) and (5) into (18) yields

$$
\begin{aligned}
\dot{x}_2(t) = {}& \frac{x_1(t)}{LC} + \frac{x_2(t)}{R_oC} - cx_2(t) - c\hat{d}_1(t) - \hat{d}_2(t) - \frac{\alpha(x_2(t)+\hat{d}_1(t))\delta}{(|x_1(t)|+\delta)^2} \\
&- \dot{\hat{d}}_1(t) - \frac{x_1(t)}{LC} - \frac{x_2(t)}{R_oC} + d_2(t) - a_1|s|^k sgn(s) \\
&- a_2 sgn(s) - \beta\frac{s}{|s|+\varepsilon}
\end{aligned}
\tag{19}
$$

Substituting (19) into (18) yields

$$
\begin{aligned}
\dot{V}(t) = s\,&\Big(c(x_2(t)+d_1(t)) + \tfrac{x_1(t)}{LC} + \tfrac{x_2(t)}{R_oC} - cx_2(t) - c\hat{d}_1(t) - \hat{d}_2(t) \\
&-\alpha\tfrac{(x_2(t)+\hat{d}_1(t))\delta}{(|x_1(t)|+\delta)^2} - \hat{d}(t) - \tfrac{x_1(t)}{LC} - \tfrac{x_2(t)}{R_oC} + d_2(t) \\
&+\alpha\tfrac{(x_2(t)+d_1(t))\delta}{(|x_1(t)|+\delta)^2} + \hat{d}(t) - a_1|s|^k sgn(s) - a_2 sgn(s) - \beta\tfrac{s}{|s|+\varepsilon} \Big) \\
= s\,&\Big(cx_2(t) - cx_2(t) + c(d_1(t)-\hat{d}_1(t)) + \tfrac{x_1(t)}{LC} + \tfrac{x_2(t)}{R_oC} \\
&-\tfrac{x_1(t)}{LC} - \tfrac{x_2(t)}{R_oC} + \alpha\tfrac{(x_2+d_1)\delta}{(|x_1(t)|+\delta)^2} - \alpha\tfrac{(x_2(t)+\hat{d}_1(t))\delta}{(|x_1(t)|+\delta)^2} \\
&+d_2(t) - \hat{d}_2(t) - a_1|s|^k sgn(s) - a_2 sgn(s) - \beta\tfrac{s}{|s|+\varepsilon} \Big) \\
= s\,&\Big(c(d_1(t)-\hat{d}_1(t)) + \alpha\tfrac{(d_1(t)-\hat{d}_1(t))\delta}{(|x_1(t)|+\delta)^2} + d_2(t) - \hat{d}_2(t) \\
&-a_1|s|^k sgn(s) - a_2 sgn(s) - \beta\tfrac{s}{|s|+\varepsilon} \Big)
\end{aligned}
\tag{20}
$$

In (20), inequality $\tfrac{\alpha\delta}{(|x_1|+\delta)^2} < \tfrac{\alpha}{|x_1|+\delta} < \tfrac{\alpha}{\delta}$ obviously holds, so we easily obtain

$$
\begin{aligned}
\dot{V}(t) =\ & cs(d_1(t)-\hat{d}_1(t)) + s(d_2(t)-\hat{d}_2(t)) + s\alpha\tfrac{(d_1(t)-\hat{d}_1(t))\delta}{(|x_1(t)|+\delta)^2} \\
& -s(a_1|s|^k sgn(s) + a_2 sgn(s) + \beta\tfrac{s}{|s|+\varepsilon}) \\
\le\ & c|s||d_1(t)-\hat{d}_1(t)| + |s||d_2(t)-\hat{d}_2(t)| + |s|\alpha\tfrac{|d_1(t)-\hat{d}_1(t)|\delta}{(|x_1(t)|+\delta)^2} \\
& -a_1|s|^{k+1} - a_2|s| - \beta\tfrac{s^2}{|s|+\varepsilon} \\
\le\ & |s|(\lambda_2 + (\tfrac{\alpha}{\delta}+c)\lambda_1 - a_2) - a_1|s|^{k+1} - \beta\tfrac{s^2}{|s|+\varepsilon} \\
=\ & -|s|(a_2 - (\lambda_2 + (\tfrac{\alpha}{\delta}+c)\lambda_1)) - a_1|s|^{k+1} - \beta\tfrac{s^2}{|s|+\varepsilon} \\
\le\ & -a_1|s|^{k+1} - \beta\tfrac{s^2}{|s|+\varepsilon} \\
=\ & -a_1(2V)^{\frac{k+1}{2}} - \tfrac{2\beta V}{(2V)^{\frac{1}{2}}+\varepsilon}
\end{aligned}
\tag{21}
$$

From (21), we can get reaching time by the following equation.

$$
\begin{aligned}
t_{sf} =\ & \int_{V(0)}^{0} -\frac{2^{\frac{1}{2}}V^{\frac{1}{2}}+\varepsilon}{a_1 2^{\frac{k}{2}+1}V^{\frac{k}{2}+1} + a_1\varepsilon 2^{\frac{k+1}{2}}V^{\frac{k+1}{2}} + 2\beta V}\,dV \\
\le\ & \int_{V(0)}^{1} -\frac{2^{\frac{1}{2}}V^{\frac{1}{2}}+\varepsilon}{(a_1 2^{\frac{k}{2}+1} + a_1\varepsilon 2^{\frac{k+1}{2}} + 2\beta)V^{\frac{k+1}{2}}}\,dV \\
& -\int_{1}^{0} \frac{2^{\frac{1}{2}}V^{\frac{1}{2}}+\varepsilon}{(a_1 2^{\frac{k}{2}+1} + a_1\varepsilon 2^{\frac{k+1}{2}} + 2\beta)V^{\frac{k}{2}+1}}\,dV \\
=\ & \frac{1}{a_1 2^{\frac{k}{2}+1} + a_1\varepsilon 2^{\frac{k+1}{2}} + 2\beta}\left(\frac{2^{\frac{3}{2}}(V(0)^{\frac{2-k}{2}}-1)}{2-k} \right. \\
& \left. +\frac{2(V(0)^{\frac{1-k}{2}}-1)}{1-k} + \frac{2k-2\varepsilon(k+3)}{k(k+3)} \right)
\end{aligned}
\tag{22}
$$

The proof is completed.

Remark 6. From (15) and (22), we can conclude the state of system (5) will converge to equilibrium point in a finite time t_s, furthermore, $t_s = t_f + t_{sf}$.

5   Simulation and Experimental Results

5.1   Simulation Results

The component parameters of the DC-DC buck converter are shown in Table 1. The purpose of this experiment is to verify the control effectiveness of the proposed method through simulation. By adjusting the parameters, the output voltage can quickly track the reference value when the reference voltage and load change. According to (5), we construct a simulation model as shown in Fig. 2 by Simulink. The mode of DO and controller is established by (6) and (16), respectively. The parameters of the experiment are $a_1 = 3 \times 10^4$, $a_2 = 5 \times 10^4$, $k = 0.72$, $\beta = 640$, $\varepsilon = 0.001$, $c = 2500$, $\delta = 0.007$, $\alpha = 1088$, $l_1 = 660$, $l_2 = 1.8 \times 10^4$, $Ro = 50\Omega$.

Table 1. Component values of DC-DC converter

Descriptions	parameters	nominal values
Input voltage	V_{in}	24(V)
Desired voltage	V_o	8-16(V)
Inductance	L	220 μH
Capacitance	C	470 μF
Load resistance	R	50-100Ω

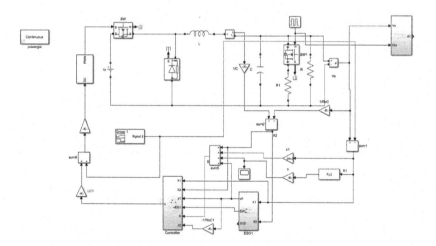

Fig. 2. Simulation mode of DC-DC buck converter.

Figure 3 displays the response of the output voltage of the converter during the periodic changes in load from 50Ω to 100Ω and back to 50Ω. When the

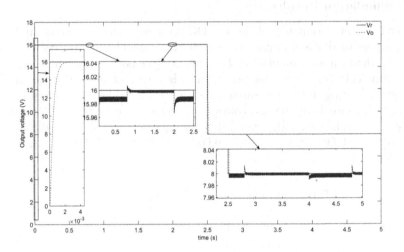

Fig. 3. The curve of V_o during periodic changes in load.

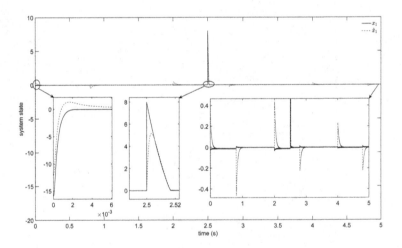

Fig. 4. State trajectories of x_1 and $\hat{x}_1$ with d_1 and V_r change.

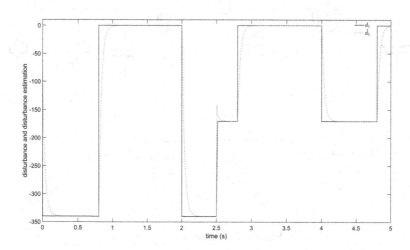

Fig. 5. The estimation effectiveness of $\hat{d}_1$ on d_1.

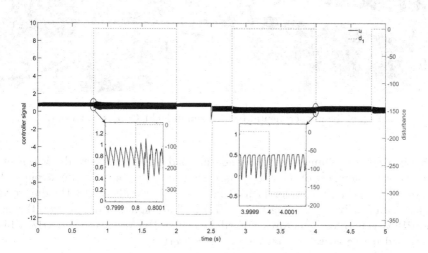

Fig. 6. The duty cycle signal under disturbance.

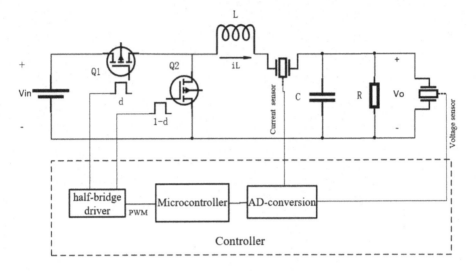

Fig. 7. The control strategy.

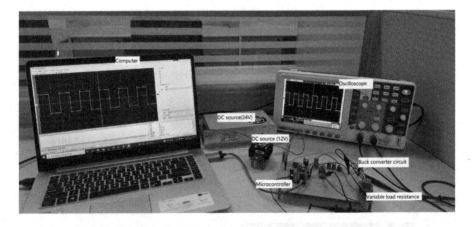

Fig. 8. The experimental test system of DC-DC buck converter.

reference voltage changes at $2.5s$ and the load undergoes periodic variations, the state trajectories of $\hat{x}_1$ and x_1 are shown in Fig. 4. Figure 5 depicts the curve of $\hat{d}_1$ tracking d_1 under such variations. Figure 6 illustrates the duty cycle signal obtained by processing the control u. This signal, after passing through the PWM generator, generates a fixed frequency PWM wave at 40 kHz, which is applied to the switching devices of the converter.

5.2   Experimental Results

To further verify the effectiveness of the proposed scheme, we build an experimental test system of synchronous buck converter in Fig. 8 according to the

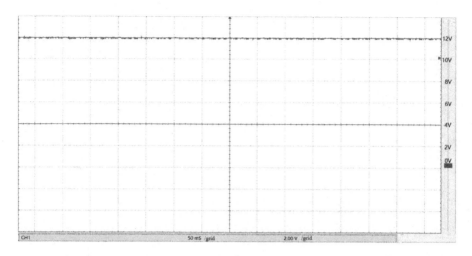

Fig. 9. The experimental test output voltage under no disturbance.

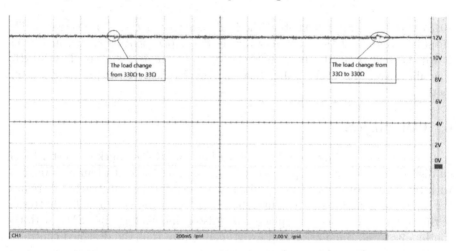

Fig. 10. The experimental test output voltage under disturbance.

control strategy shown in Fig. 7. The experimental environment is similar to the simulation environment, and the experimental waveform is transmitted to the computer through the USB interface. The main components are MOSFET: FHP110N8F, half-bridge driver IC: IR2104S, inductance: 220 μH and capacitor: 470 $\mu F/16~V$. The DO controller combination is realized by STM32F103 to control the output voltage of the converter.

The main purpose is to maintain output voltage of the DC-DC buck converter stability. Figure 9 shows the output voltage waveform when the load remains constant. Figure 10 shows the curve that the output voltage can converge to the reference voltage after a short fluctuation when the load changes in the range of

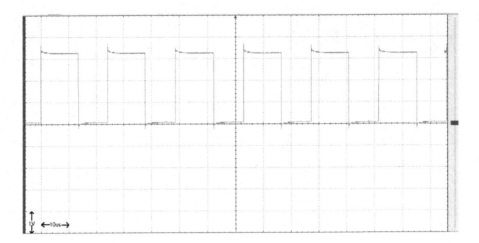

Fig. 11. The control waveform output during the experimental test.

$50\,\Omega$ to $100\,\Omega$, no matter whether the load suddenly increases or decreases. The output waveform of the controller during the experiment as shown in Fig. 11. It can be seen that the frequency of the waveform is maintained at $40\,\text{kHz}$. The above experimental results show the effectiveness of the proposed control method.

6   Conclusion

A novel terminal sliding mode control method for DC-DC buck converter based on disturbance observer is proposed. By combining the disturbance estimation with the sliding function, a new sliding mode manifold is constructed to reduce the influence of unknown structural disturbances on the system. The chattering of the system is reduced by replacing the discontinuous term in TSMC with the continuous term. Simulation and experiment prove that the designed controller not only makes the output voltage error of the system converge to zero in a finite time, but also has good disturbance rejection ability.

Acknowledgements. We extend our heartfelt gratitude to the esteemed reviewers for their invaluable feedback, as it has significantly enhanced the quality and substance of our paper.

References

1. Bayat, F., Karimi, M., Taheri, A.: Robust output regulation of zeta converter with load/input variations: LMI approach. Control. Eng. Pract. **84**, 102–111 (2019)
2. Bensaada, M., Stambouli, A.B.: A practical design sliding mode controller for DC-DC converter based on control parameters optimization using assigned poles associate to genetic algorithm. Int. J. Electr. Power Energy Syst. **53**, 761–773 (2013)

3. Chen, J., Chen, Y., Tong, L., Peng, L., Kang, Y.: A backpropagation neural network-based explicit model predictive control for DC-DC converters with high switching frequency. IEEE J. Emerg. Select. Top. Power Electr. 8(3), 2124–2142 (2020)
4. Cheng, C.H., Cheng, P.J., Xie, M.J.: Current sharing of paralleled DC-DC converters using GA-based PID controllers. Expert Syst. Appl. 37(1), 733–740 (2010)
5. Chincholkar, S.H., Jiang, W., Chan, C.Y.: An improved PWM-based sliding-mode controller for a DC-DC cascade boost converter. IEEE Trans. Circuits Syst. II-Exp. Briefs 65(11), 1639–1643 (2018)
6. Dehkordi, N.M., Sadati, N., Hamzeh, M.: A robust backstepping high-order sliding mode control strategy for grid-connected DG units with harmonic/interharmonic current compensation capability. IEEE Trans. Sustain. Energy 8(2), 561–572 (2017)
7. Di Gennaro, S., Rivera Dominguez, J., Antonio Meza, M.: Sensorless high order sliding mode control of induction motors with core loss. IEEE Trans. Industr. Electron. 61(6), 2678–2689 (2014)
8. Feng, Y., Zheng, J., Yu, X., Truong, N.V.: Hybrid terminal sliding-mode observer design method for a permanent-magnet synchronous motor control system. IEEE Trans. Industr. Electron. 56(9), 3424–3431 (2009)
9. Guo, L., Hung, J.Y., Nelms, R.M.: Evaluation of DSP-based PID and fuzzy controllers for DC-DC converters. IEEE Trans. Industr. Electron. 56(6), 2237–2248 (2009)
10. Khleaf, H.K., Nahar, A.K., Subhi, A.: Intelligent control of dc-dc converter based on PID-neural network. Int. J. Power Electron. Drive Syst. 10(4), 2254 (2019)
11. Houreh, A.B., Ershadi, M.H.: Fuzzy control of the push-pull fly-back three-phase DC-DC converter. MMC_A 92(1), 1–6 (2019)
12. Hsu, C.F., Chung, I.F., Lin, C.M., Hsu, C.Y.: Self-regulating fuzzy control for forward DC-DC converters using an 8-bit microcontroller. IET Power Electron. 2(1), 1–13 (2009)
13. Huangfu, Y., Zhuo, S., Rathore, A.K., Breaz, E., Nahid-Mobarakeh, B., Gao, F.: Super-twisting differentiator-based high order sliding mode voltage control design for DC-DC buck converters. Energies 9(7), 494 (2016)
14. Komurcugil, H.: Adaptive terminal sliding-mode control strategy for DC-DC buck converters. ISA Trans. 51(6), 673–681 (2012)
15. Komurcugil, H.: Non-singular terminal sliding-mode control of DC-DC buck converters. Control. Eng. Pract. 21(3), 321–332 (2013)
16. Li, J., Yang, Y., Hua, C., Guan, X.: Fixed-time backstepping control design for high-order strict-feedback non-linear systems via terminal sliding mode. IET Control Theory Appl. 11(8), 1184–1193 (2017)
17. Lin, H., Liu, J., Leon, J.I., Marquez, A., Luo, W., Franquelo, L.G.: Observer-based sliding-mode control of a DC/DC buck converter for railway systems. IET Renew. Power Gener. 14(18), 3579–3588 (2020)
18. Naik, B.B., Mehta, A.J.: Sliding mode controller with modified sliding function for DC-DC buck converter. ISA Trans. 70, 279–287 (2017)
19. Noh, B.-U., Choi, H.H.: Fuzzy integral sliding mode controller design for boost converters. Nonlinear Dyn. 78(3), 1863–1875 (2014). https://doi.org/10.1007/s11071-014-1576-x
20. Pan, H., Zhang, G., Ouyang, H., Mei, L.: A novel global fast terminal sliding mode control scheme for second-order systems. IEEE Access 8, 22758–22769 (2020)

21. Pandey, S.K., Patil, S.L., Chaskar, U.M., Phadke, S.B.: State and disturbance observer-based integral sliding mode controlled boost DC-DC converters. IEEE Trans. Circuits Syst. II-Exp. Briefs 66(9), 1567–1571 (2019)

22. Pandey, S.K., Patil, S.L., Phadke, S.B.: Regulation of nonminimum phase DC-DC converters using integral sliding mode control combined with a disturbance observer. IEEE Trans. Circuits Syst. II-Exp. Briefs 65(11), 1649–1653 (2018)

23. Rath, J.J., Defoort, M., Karimi, H.R., Veluvolu, K.C.: Output feedback active suspension control with higher order terminal sliding mode. IEEE Trans. Industr. Electron. 64(2), 1392–1403 (2017)

24. Shen, L., Lu, D.D.C., Li, C.: Adaptive sliding mode control method for DC-DC converters. IET Power Electron. 8(9), 1723–1732 (2015)

25. Shoja-Majidabad, S., Hajizadeh, A.: Decentralized adaptive neural network control of cascaded DC-DC converters with high voltage conversion ratio. Appl. Soft Comput. 86, 105878 (2020)

26. Shtessel, Y.B., Zinober, A.S., Shkolnikov, I.A.: Sliding mode control of boost and buck-boost power converters using method of stable system centre. Automatica 39(6), 1061–1067 (2003)

27. Torres-Pinzon, C.A., Paredes-Madrid, L., Flores-Bahamonde, F., Ramirez-Murillo, H.: LMI-fuzzy control design for non-minimum-phase DC-DC converters: an application for output regulation. Applied Sci.-Basel 11(5), 2286 (2021)

28. Utkin, V.: Discussion aspects of high-order sliding mode control. IEEE Trans. Autom. Control 61(3), 829–833 (2016)

29. Wang, J., Li, S., Yang, J., Wu, B., Li, Q.: Extended state observer-based sliding mode control for PWM-based DC-DC buck power converter systems with mismatched disturbances. IET Control Theory Appl. 9(4), 579–586 (2015)

30. Wang, Q., Yu, H., Wang, M., Qi, X.: An improved sliding mode control using disturbance torque observer for permanent magnet synchronous motor. IEEE Access 7, 36691–36701 (2019)

31. Yazici, I., Yaylaci, E.K.: Fast and robust voltage control of DC-DC boost converter by using fast terminal sliding mode controller. IET Power Electron. 9(1), 120–125 (2016)

32. Zhou, K., Yuan, C., Sun, D., Jin, N., Wu, X.: Parameter adaptive terminal sliding mode control for full-bridge DC-DC converter. Plos One 16(2), e0247228 (2021)

Distributed Dynamic Process Monitoring Based on Maximum Correlation and Maximum Difference

Lin Wang, Shaofei Zang, Jianwei Ma$^{(\boxtimes)}$, and Shengqiao Ding

College of Information Engineering, Henan University of Science and Technology,
Luoyang 471000, China
wlin151388@163.com

Abstract. In order to solve the problem of dynamic characteristics caused by the autocorrelation of different measurement variables and the cross-correlation of variables reflected at different sampling times in industrial processes, a dynamic monitoring method of distributed latent variable model based on maximum correlation maximum difference (MCMD) is proposed. Firstly, delay measurements are introduced into each measurement variable to form an augmented matrix, which is used to establish sub-blocks for each measurement variable, and MCMD is used to describe the influence of delay variables on the current measurement value. This operation can not only eliminate redundant fault information, but also describe the dynamic characteristics of industrial processes more comprehensively. Secondly, dynamic principal component analysis (DPCA) is used to establish a monitoring model for each sub-block. Then, the Bayesian inference mechanism is used to convert the statistical indicators of different sub-blocks into posterior probabilities, and the fusion strategy is used to obtain a more comprehensive monitoring indicator, so that the indicator can indicate the process state more comprehensively. Finally, the effectiveness and feasibility of the proposed method are verified by the Tennessee-Eastman (TE) process.

Keywords: Principal Component Analysis · Maximum Correlation Maximum Difference · Distributed Monitoring

1 Introduction

With the development of industrial sensing and control technology, many process monitoring data have emerged. These data contain essential process information. By analyzing its characteristics and mining its essence, industrial economic benefits can be improved, and the dependence on traditional monitoring methods on mathematical models and prior knowledge can be eliminated. Therefore, data-driven monitoring methods are becoming a research hotspot [1, 2]. The common methods are principal component analysis (PCA) [3], partial least squares (PLS) [4], independent component analysis (ICA) [5], and canonical variate analysis (CVA) [6]. Among them, PCA is widely used because of its effective data dimension reduction and feature extraction ability.

F. Sun et al. (Eds.): ICCSIP 2023, CCIS 1918, pp. 191–205, 2024.
https://doi.org/10.1007/978-981-99-8018-5_14

The actual industrial process data often has a strong time-series correlation. The traditional PCA is not suitable for the actual industrial process with dynamic characteristics because of the assumption that the process samples are independent of each other. References [7], a dynamic principal component analysis (DPCA) model was constructed by introducing delay measurements to achieve dynamic correlation between data. The above method assumes that all variables form an augmented matrix with the same dynamic amplitude, which improves the dynamic detection performance while eliminating the problem of information redundancy and insufficient dynamics. Moreover, a single centralized model ignores local information and is unsuitable for large-scale industrial process fault detection.

In order to effectively reveal the complex and diverse variable correlations in large-scale complex industrial processes and effectively use local information, distributed modeling strategies have become a hot topic in large-scale industrial monitoring. Recently, references [8, 9] proposed a multi-block PCA based on weighted copula correlation (WCMBPCA) to monitor large-scale correlation processes and used the weight matrix formed by copula correlation to block to achieve the description of data correlation pattern and correlation degree. Based on WCMBPCA [10], a non-parametric rank-based weight calculation method WDSMBPCA is proposed. The new weight strategy realizes the simultaneous estimation of the correlation and skewness of the data. Kullback Leibler divergence (KLD), which considers the difference in probability distribution between variables, can effectively measure the slight difference between variables and is used to solve the fault detection problem [11, 12]. Reference [13] used KLD to describe the correlation between variables and put variables with similar statistical characteristics into the same block to establish a multi-block PCA model. Reference [14] combined KLD with Bayesian inference and applied it to the electric drive system of high-speed trains, which proved the effectiveness of KLD. The above-refined block strategy has achieved good detection results but cannot solve the monitoring problem of dynamic processes. Recently, literature [15] proposed a distributed fault detection method based on mutual information (MI) and DPCA (MI-DPCA), which can deal with the problems of linear, nonlinear and dynamic characteristics of data. In [16], the DPCA weighted distributed fault detection method (mRMR-WDPCA) based on minimal redundancy maximal relevance (mRMR) reduces the redundancy problem caused by MI criterion through mRMR and weighting strategy and achieves better fault detection effect. However, the above MI-based variable selection method and redundancy judgment criterion will cause local information to be too strong and lead to global information loss. In addition, the algorithm does not consider the influence of historical samples.

Through the above analysis, this paper proposes a maximum correlation maximum difference (MCMD) algorithm combined with MI and KLD to describe the influence of delay variables on the current measured values. It uses this value to establish a DPCA model for each sub-block selection variable. Bayesian reasoning and appropriate weighting strategies are used for fusion to achieve large-scale industrial process monitoring. The main innovations of this paper are as follows: (1) This method combines MI and KLD to propose an MCMD algorithm. Unlike mRMR using MI for redundancy judgment, MCMD uses the KLD probability difference rule to judge redundancy, which avoids the loss of information caused by too strong local information, thus providing the optimal sub-block variable. (2) This method integrates the posterior probability of the past sample and the current posterior probability of each sub-block, eliminates the harmful effect of noise, and more comprehensively reflects the difference between the fault state and normal state. (3) This method designs a distributed modeling framework that integrates the MCMD algorithm, Bayesian weighting strategy and DPCA model and achieves better detection results, which provides a new idea for the dynamic detection of large-scale complex industrial processes.

2 Related Work

2.1 Dynamic Principal Component Analysis

PCA is a typical latent variable model, which extracts irrelevant latent variables through orthogonal transformation to eliminate redundant information. The PCA statistical model is established by $X \in R^{N \times M}$ decomposition of a raw data matrix containing M variables and N samples. The mathematical expression is as follows:

$$X = TP^T + \tilde{T}\tilde{P}^T = \sum_{i=1}^{k} t_i p_i^T + E \tag{1}$$

$$T = XP \tag{2}$$

where, T and P are principal component score matrix and load matrix respectively, $\tilde{T}$ and $\tilde{P}$ are residual score matrix and residual load matrix respectively, t_i is the i th principal component, p_i is the corresponding load vector, k is the number of retained principal components, and E is the residual matrix.

Compared with the conventional PCA model, DPCA shows the process dynamics by introducing the first h delay measurements to X. The dynamic augmented matrix is as follows:

$$X(h) = \begin{bmatrix} x(t) & x(t-1) & \cdots & x(t-h) \\ x(t+1) & x(t) & \cdots & x(t-h+1) \\ \vdots & \vdots & \ddots & \vdots \\ x(t+N-h-1) & x(t+N-h-2) & \cdots & x(t+N-2h-1) \end{bmatrix} \tag{3}$$

where $X(h) \in R^{(N-h) \times (h+1)M}$, N represent the available process samples, the input dimension of the DPCA model becomes $(h+1)M$. When applied to process monitoring, the DPCA model is first established using conventional PCA decomposition for $X(h)$. Then, the test sample Y is expanded to $Y(h)$ according to Eq. (3). Finally, the statistical indicators are constructed for monitoring. The statistical indicators T^2 and Q are:

$$T^2 = Y(h)^T P \Lambda P^T Y(h) \tag{4}$$

$$Q = Y(h)^T (I - PP^T) Y(h) \tag{5}$$

where T^2 and Q statistics define squared Mahalanobis distance and squared Euclidean distance, respectively. Λ is a diagonal matrix composed of eigenvalues of the covariance matrix of $X(h)$. The calculation method of its control limit can be referred to [17].

2.2 Kullback Leibler Divergence and Mutual Information

KLD is an asymmetric measure of the difference between two probability density distributions in information theory. In practical applications, the symmetric form of this method is usually used to measure the distribution difference. For two continuous probability distributions $k_1(x)$ and $k_2(x)$, the KLD distance is expressed as [18]:

$$D_{KL}(k_1 \| k_2) = \int k_1(x) \log \frac{k_1(x)}{k_2(x)} dx + \int k_2(x) \log \frac{k_2(x)}{k_1(x)} dx \tag{6}$$

For the variables x_i and x_j under normal distribution, the KLD component is further constructed by mean and variance [19]:

$$D_{KL}(x_i, x_j) = \frac{1}{2} \left[\frac{\sigma_i}{\sigma_j} + \frac{\sigma_j}{\sigma_i} + (\mu_i - \mu_j)^2 \left(\frac{1}{\sigma_i} + \frac{1}{\sigma_j} \right) - 2 \right] \tag{7}$$

$$\mu_i = \frac{1}{N} \sum_{N=1}^{i} x(i) \tag{8}$$

$$\sigma_i = \frac{1}{N} \sum_{N=1}^{i} (x(i) - \mu_i)^2 \tag{9}$$

where μ_i and σ_i are the mean and variance of variable x_i, respectively. N is the number of samples. The smaller the difference between x_i and x_j is, the closer the value of $D_{KL}(x_i, x_j)$ is to 0, and vice versa.

MI measures the interdependence of random variables. Given two random variables x_i and x_j, whose joint density is $p(x_i, x_j)$, edge density is $p(x_i)$ and $p(x_j)$, respectively. MI is defined as [16]:

$$I(x_i, x_j) = \iint_{x_i, x_j} p(x_i, x_j) \lg \frac{p(x_i, x_j)}{p(x_i) p(x_j)} dx_i dx_j \tag{10}$$

3   Proposed Method

In order to solve the problem of dynamic process monitoring of large-scale industrial processes, this section will describe the proposed process monitoring method in detail. Firstly, MCMD algorithm is introduced to realize the selection of variables. Based on MCMD, each sub-block is modeled separately. Finally, the statistics of each sub-block are weighted and fused to realize dynamic process monitoring.

3.1   Maximum Correlation Maximum Difference

In order to evaluate the influence of each element in a set on a variable, an MCMD algorithm is proposed based on mRMR. Unlike mRMR, this method can consider both the correlation between variables and the difference in probability distribution. Suppose a set Z is given, then the maximum correlation between the element and the variable v in the set can be defined as [16]:

$$\max C(Z, v), \quad C = \frac{1}{|Z|} \sum_{x_i \in Z} I(x_i, v) \tag{11}$$

where $|Z|$ represents the number of variables in the set Z, it can be seen that only considering the maximum correlation between variables and variables v in set Z, ignoring the difference between variables in set Z will produce redundancy and loss of crucial information. Therefore,the maximum difference rule is proposed to select mutually exclusive variables:

$$\max D(Z), \quad D = \frac{1}{|Z|^2} \sum_{x_i, x_j \in Z} D_{KL}(x_i, x_j) \tag{12}$$

Finally, in order to consider the maximum difference and the maximum correlation rule at the same time, the MCMD method is designed, which combines Eq. (11) and Eq. (12), then optimizes C and D at the same time by incremental search:

$$\max_{x_j \in X - S_{m-1}} \left[I(x_i, v) - \frac{1}{M-1} \sum_{x_i \in Z_{M-1}} D_{KL}(x_i, x_j) \right] \tag{13}$$

3.2 Monitoring Scheme

MCMD can realize the measurement of each element in a set to a single variable, which is convenient for describing the influence of the delay variable on the current measurement value. In order to better solve the problem of dynamic characteristics caused by the complex correlation between variables in large-scale industrial processes, a sub-block partitioning method shown in Fig. 1 is proposed to describe the dynamic characteristics of each measurement variable. The method consists of two processes, offline modeling and online monitoring. The specific steps are as follows:

Offline Modeling:

Step 1. An augmented matrix $X(h)$ is constructed by introducing h time measurements into the original matrix X.

Step 2. The MCMD values between each measurement variable $X_t^i (i = 1, 2, \cdots, m)$ of X_t and all variables $X_l^i (i = 1, 2, \cdots, m, l = t, t-1, \cdots, t-h)$ in $X(h)$ are calculated.

Step 3. According to the formula (13), variables u are selected to form a sub-block X_i.

Step 4. The DPCA fault detection model is established for the obtained m different sub-blocks.

Online Monitoring:

Step 1. The test sample Y is augmented to obtain the augmented matrix $Y(h)$.

Step 2. According to the results of the sub-block division in the offline phase, the sub-block Y_i is obtained by the corresponding division of $Y(h)$, and the statistical index of the sub-block is obtained:

$$X_i = T_i P_i^T + E_i \tag{14}$$

$$T_i^2 = Y_i^T P_i \Lambda_i P_i^T Y_i \tag{15}$$

$$Q_i = Y_i^T (I - P_i P_i^T) Y_i \tag{16}$$

From the above division method, it can be seen that compared with the conventional variable selection method for all $(h+1)M$ variables or other variable selection methods that only use correlation (difference), the variable selection method used in this paper strengthens local information through correlation, while the difference rule effectively eliminates redundant information and avoids information loss caused by excessive local information, thus providing the optimal sub-block variables.

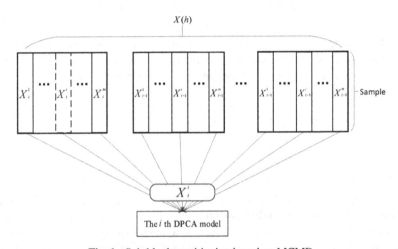

Fig. 1. Sub-block partitioning based on MCMD

3.3 Fusion Strategy

According to the MCMD-based modeling method in Sect. 3.2, m sets of statistics will be obtained, making the monitoring model more sensitive to random disturbances and increasing the false alarm rate. To this end, Bayesian inference converts the statistics from online monitoring into a probability form, integrated into a comprehensive index through a weighting strategy.

Taking the statistical index T_i^2 of the i th model as an example, the probabilities of the test sample x_i under normal condition N and fault condition F are expressed as follows:

$$P_{T_i^2}(x_i|N) = \exp\left(\frac{-\theta T_i^2}{T_{CL}}\right) \tag{17}$$

$$P_{T_i^2}(x_i|F) = \exp\left(\frac{-\theta T_{CL}}{T_i^2}\right) \tag{18}$$

where θ is an adjustable parameter, which reduces the sensitivity to abnormal data by selecting the appropriate value. T_{CL} is the control limit corresponding to T_i^2. Using Eq. (17) and Eq. (18), the occurrence probability $P_{T_i^2}(x_i)$ of sample x_i can be obtained:

$$P_{T_i^2}(x_i) = P_{T_i^2}(x_i|N)P_{T_i^2}(N) + P_{T_i^2}(x_i|F)P_{T_i^2}(F) \tag{19}$$

where $P_{T_i^2}(N)$ is the prior probability of the system under normal conditions with confidence α and the value of $P_{T_i^2}(F)$ is $1 - \alpha$. The statistical index T_i^2 is converted into a posteriori failure probability in the following way:

$$P_{T_i^2}(F|x_i) = \frac{P_{T_i^2}(x_i|F)P_{T_i^2}(F)}{P_{T_i^2}(x_i)} \tag{20}$$

Bayesian inference formula (20) provides the probability statistical information of different sub-blocks, each statistical value is between 0 and 1, and has the same confidence limit α. The probability statistics information of each sub-block is collected and combined according to the appropriate rules, that is, formula (21) ~ formula (24). The combination result BIC_{T^2} is defined as:

$$BIC_{T^2} = \sum_{i=1}^{M} \left(\frac{\omega_i P_{T_i^2}(x_i|F)P_{T_i^2}(F|x_i)}{\sum_{i=1}^{M} P_{T_i^2}(x_i|F)} \right) \tag{21}$$

where ω_i is the weight coefficient. In order to reduce the impact of excessive local information, the weight coefficient should also consider the state of the past sample. Therefore, the average failure probability of the past Y samples is defined by the following formula:

$$\overline{BI} = \frac{\sum_{j=new-Y+1}^{new} BI_j}{Y} \tag{22}$$

$$BI_i = \frac{P_{T_i^2}(x_i|F)P_{T_i^2}(F|x_i)}{\sum_{i=1}^{M} P_{T_i^2}(x_i|F)} \tag{23}$$

where BI_i is the fault probability based on the current moment, and $\overline{BI}$ is the judgment criterion for the past Y samples. When these two probability values exceed $1 - \alpha$, it can show that the current fault state is more accurate and can give a larger weight coefficient. Otherwise, a smaller weight coefficient is given, the specific form is as follows:

$$\omega_i = \begin{cases} \frac{1}{\varepsilon}, BI_i \geq 1 - \alpha \& \overline{BI} \geq 1 - \alpha \\ \varepsilon, \text{otherwise} \end{cases} \tag{24}$$

where ε is a smaller positive number and α is the confidence limit.

It is worth noting that the values of ε and Y are closely related to the final monitoring effect. Too large ε will weaken the difference between the fault and normal states, resulting in a lower fault detection rate (FDR). On the contrary, excessive emphasis on fault information will lead to a higher false alarm rate (FAR). Similarly, considering the state of the past sample can eliminate the influence of local noise on the overall state, but too large Y will introduce too much unnecessary information to cover up the fault information. By selecting the appropriate ε and Y, the balance between FDR and FAR (i.e. high FDR and appropriate FAR) is achieved.

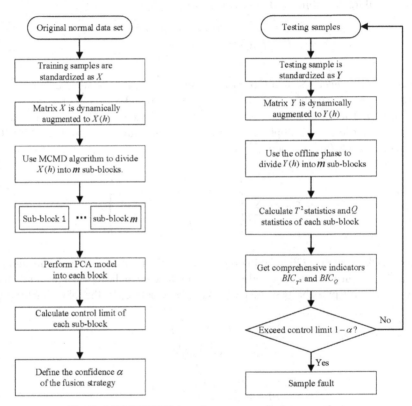

Fig. 2. MCMDWPCA based process monitoring procedures

Similarly, the comprehensive probability index BIC_Q of the statistic Q_i can be obtained. The current sample is considered faulty when any probability index is greater than $1 - \alpha$. Otherwise, it is considered to be in a normal state. Combining the sub-block division in Sect. 3.2 and the Bayesian fusion strategy in Sect. 3.3, the monitoring process, including offline and online parts, is shown in Fig. 2.

4   Case Study

In order to verify the performance of the proposed method, Tennessee-Eastman (TE) industrial process is used. TE has become a standard experimental platform for verifying control methods and fault detection methods. The TE process mainly comprises five production units: reactor, condenser, separation tower, stripper and compressor. There are two variable blocks in the whole process: the XMEAS block of 41 measurement variables and the XMV block of 12 operation variables. Twenty-one faults are set, and each fault is introduced from the 160th sampling time. The process variables and fault types can be found in Reference [21]. In this study, XMV (1–11) and XMEAS (1–22) were selected as input variables according to the Reference [22].

Table 1. The FDRs in TE process by different methods

Fault no	DPCA	MI-DPCA	WDSMBPCA	mRMR-WDPCA	MCMDWDPCA
	T^2/Q	BIC_{T^2}/BIC_Q	BIC_{T^2}/BIC_{SPE}	BIC_{T^2}/BIC_Q	BIC_{T^2}/BIC_Q
1	0.999	0.999	**1.000**	0.997	**1.000**
2	0.985	0.986	0.986	0.985	**0.994**
4	**1.000**	**1.000**	**1.000**	**1.000**	**1.000**
5	0.450	0.269	**1.000**	**1.000**	0.279
6	**1.000**	**1.000**	**1.000**	**1.000**	**1.000**
7	**1.000**	**1.000**	**1.000**	**1.000**	**1.000**
8	0.974	0.975	0.981	0.982	**0.986**
10	0.511	0.745	0.767	**0.811**	0.650
11	0.940	**0.954**	0.849	0.865	0.947
12	0.991	0.994	0.990	**0.999**	0.995
13	0.954	0.954	0.952	0.946	**0.957**
14	**1.000**	**1.000**	**1.000**	**1.000**	**1.000**
16	0.520	0.765	0.772	**0.852**	0.608
17	0.977	0.979	0.972	0.966	**0.981**
18	0.906	0.906	0.908	**0.910**	**0.910**
19	0.666	0.624	**0.720**	0.350	0.620
20	0.636	0.666	0.654	0.675	**0.685**
21	0.505	**0.574**	0.565	0.529	**0.574**

In the offline modeling stage, the monitoring model of MCMDWDPCA is established with 500 data under normal working conditions as the training set. The delayed measurement value h is determined to be 2 according to Reference [23], the confidence level α is 0.99, the number of variables in each sub-block is 23, and the number of retained principal components is set by the cumulative variance contribution rate $CPV \geq 85\%$.

Through repeated tests, the adjustable parameter θ is set to 1.45, the weighting coefficient ε is set to 0.55, and Y is set to 3.

The results of model DPCA, MI-DPCA [15], mRMR-WDPCA [16], WDSMBPCA [10] and MCMDWDPCA are shown in Table 1. Faults 3,9 and 15 have a small degree of failure, resulting in a weak impact on the process, and most detection schemes cannot detect them. Therefore, only the remaining 18 faults are considered this time, and the best fault detection rate is displayed in bold to facilitate identification. The proposed method obtains the highest fault detection results in most fault types. Specifically, when dealing with faults 1, 4, 6, 7, and 14, all methods have achieved fault detection results close to 1. In particular, when faults 2, 8, 13, 17, 18, 20, 21 are detected, the proposed MCMDWDPCA is superior to the other four methods and has the highest fault detection results. The main reason is that the MCMDWDPCA model considers the linear and nonlinear correlation between variables. The maximum difference rule retains the variables with the largest difference while selecting the delay variables most relevant to the current measured value, which reduces the redundancy between variables and avoids the local information in distributed modeling. Too strong and cover up faulty information. In addition, to better observe, the effectiveness of the variable selection method and the weighting strategy is further analyzed.

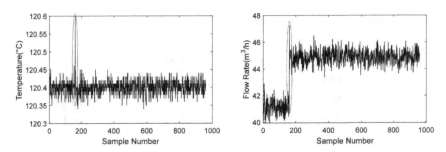

Fig. 3. Reactor temperature and cooling water flow in fault 4

MCMD, KLD and MI are modeled using the sub-block partitioning method in Sect. 3.2, respectively, and a Bayesian fusion strategy is used. The test results are shown in Table 2. Notably, KLD-PCA eliminates redundancy between variables while weakening local information in the sub-blocks, resulting in a failure rate of 4 and 11 close to 1. In addition, MI-DPCA strengthens local information, but produces a large amount of redundant information. MCMD-DPCA uses both correlation and difference rules to enhance local information and eliminate redundant information to provide optimal dynamic variable sub-blocks. The results show that, except for faults 10, 16, 19 and 21, MCMD-DPCA has achieved the lowest failure rate, which is better than the other two methods. In order to better illustrate the superiority of the algorithm in this paper, the monitoring details of fault 4 are given.

Fault 4 causes the reactor cooling water inlet temperature to change step by step, and a cascade controller controls the reactor temperature to control the reactor cooling water flow. The variable changes are shown in Fig. 3. When the disturbance occurs, the reactor temperature suddenly rises, and the control loop rapidly responds by increasing the reactor cooling water flow, so the reactor temperature is pushed to the set value soon. It can be seen from Fig. 4 that KLDDPCA loses the monitoring effect, and MIDPCA still has a few samples under the control limit. Only MCMDDPCA achieves 0 fault missing alarm rate and can be monitored timely and accurate.

Table 2. The MARs of variable selection methods

Fault no	MCMDDPCA	KLDDPCA	MIDPCA
	BIC_{T^2}/BIC_Q	BIC_{T^2}/BIC_Q	BIC_{T^2}/BIC_Q
1	0.000	0.000	0.000
2	0.005	0.006	0.013
4	0.000	0.969	0.010
5	0.657	0.657	0.679
6	0.000	0.000	0.000
7	0.000	0.000	0.000
8	0.010	0.013	0.024
10	0.336	0.384	0.313
11	0.043	0.911	0.406
12	0.003	0.006	0.006
13	0.043	0.464	0.043
14	0.000	0.251	0.000
16	0.361	0.881	0.323
17	0.018	0.442	0.209
18	0.083	0.230	0.103
19	0.301	0.092	0.851
20	0.290	0.330	0.392
21	0.406	0.402	0.430

The MCMDDPCA uses the weighting strategy in Sect. 3.3, and the fault false alarm rate is shown in Table 3. It can be seen from the table that the weighting strategy effectively eliminates the dynamic local noise by considering the past sample state. Except for fault 5, MCMDWDPCA has achieved the lowest fault false alarm rate. For further analysis, the monitoring details of fault 0 are given.

Table 3. The FARs of weighted strategies

Fault no	MCMDDPCA BIC_{T^2}/BIC_Q	MCMDWDPCA BIC_{T^2}/BIC_Q
0	0.050	0.025
1	0.000	0.000
2	0.031	0.013
4	0.013	0.013
5	0.006	0.013
6	0.013	0.013
7	0.013	0.013
8	0.000	0.000
10	0.006	0.000
11	0.013	0.013
12	0.000	0.000
13	0.000	0.000
14	0.013	0.013
16	0.088	0.044
17	0.013	0.006
18	0.006	0.000
19	0.000	0.000
20	0.000	0.000
21	0.031	0.019

Fault 0 is 960 test samples obtained from 48 h of normal operation, and the monitoring details are shown in Fig. 5. In engineering practice, the monitoring process is considered faulty when six continuous sampling points exceed the control limit. Different from the MCMDDPCA statistics continuously exceeding the control limit, the MCMDWDPCA after using the fusion strategy does not continuously.

exceed the control limit and the false alarm rate of a single sampling point is only 2.5%, which is half of the MCMDDPCA. The proposed method is also effective in monitoring normal working conditions.

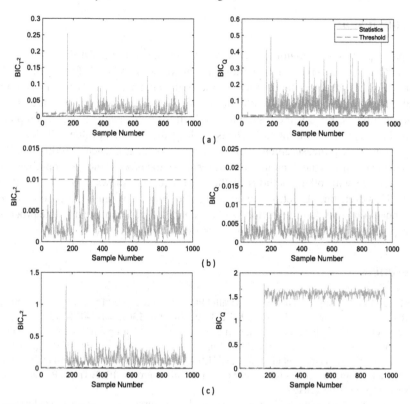

Fig. 4. Monitoring results of fault 4: (a) MIDPCA, (b) KLDDPCA, (c) MCMDDPCA

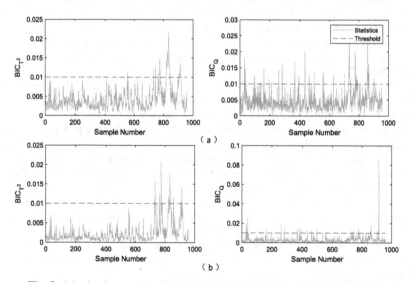

Fig. 5. Monitoring results of fault 0: (a) MCMDDPCA, (b) MCMDWDPCA

5 Conclusion

This paper proposes a dynamic process monitoring method of a distributed latent variable model based on maximum correlation and maximum difference. Firstly, the MCMD method describes the correlation between the augmented matrix and each measurement variable, forming the optimal variable sub-block. Then, the statistics of PCA are obtained in each sub-block. Finally, the Bayesian weighted fusion strategy obtains a comprehensive probability index. This method selects the delay measurement value with the greatest correlation for each measurement variable, eliminates the influence of redundant information, and describes the dynamic characteristics of the process more comprehensively. By comparing with other methods in the TE process, it shows good fault detection results. However, this detection cannot judge the impact of faults on product quality and cannot cope with fault detection in multi-condition and non-steady-state processes. Corresponding research work needs to be carried out in the future.

References

1. Zhu, J., Ge, Z., Song, Z.: Distributed parallel PCA for modeling and monitoring of large-scale plant-wide processes with big data. IEEE Trans. Ind. Inf. **13**(4), 1877–1885 (2017)
2. Jiang, Q., Yan, X., Huang, B.: Review and perspectives of data-driven distributed monitoring for industrial plant-wide processes. Ind. Eng. Chem. Res. **58**(29), 12899–12912 (2019)
3. Wang, T., Xu, H., Han, J., et al.: Cascaded H-bridge multilevel inverter system fault diagnosis using a PCA and multiclass relevance vector machine approach. IEEE Trans. Power Electron. **30**(12), 7006–7018 (2015)
4. Xie, X., et al.: An advanced PLS approach for key performance indicator-related prediction and diagnosis in case of outliers. IEEE Trans. Ind. Electron. **63**(4), 2587–2594 (2015)
5. Zhang, Y., Yang, N., Li, S.: Fault isolation of nonlinear processes based on fault directions and features. IEEE Trans. Control Syst. Technol. **22**(4), 1567–1572 (2014)
6. Li, X., Duan, F., Loukopoulos, P., et al.: Canonical variable analysis and long short-term memory for fault diagnosis and performance estimation of a centrifugal compressor. Control. Eng. Pract. **72**, 177–191 (2018)
7. Ku, W., Storer, R.H., Georgakis, C.: Disturbance detection and isolation by dynamic principal component analysis. Chemom. Intell. Lab. Syst. **30**(1), 179–196 (1995)
8. Tian, Y., Hu, T., Peng, X., et al.: Decentralized monitoring for large-scale process using copula-correlation analysis and Bayesian inference–based multiblock principal component analysis. J. Chemom. **33**(8), e3158 (2019)
9. Tian, Y., Yao, H., Li, Z.: Plant-wide process monitoring by using weighted copula–correlation based multiblock principal component analysis approach and online-horizon Bayesian method. ISA Trans. **96**, 24–36 (2020)
10. Hsu, C.C., Shih, P.C., Tien, F.C.: Integrate weighted dependence and skewness based multiblock principal component analysis with Bayesian inference for large-scale process monitoring. J. Taiwan Inst. Chem. Eng. **119**, 6–22 (2021)
11. Gautam, S., Tamboli, P.K., Roy, K., Patankar, V.H., Duttagupta, S.P.: Sensors incipient fault detection and isolation of nuclear power plant using extended Kalman filter and Kullback-Leibler divergence. ISA Trans. **92**, 180–190 (2019)
12. Cai, P., Deng, X.: Incipient fault detection for nonlinear processes based on dynamic multiblock probability related kernel principal component analysis. ISA Trans. **105**, 210–220 (2020)

13. Wang, B., Jiang, Q., Yan, X.: Fault detection and identification using a Kullback-Leibler divergence based multi-block principal component analysis and Bayesian inference. Korean J. Chem. Eng. **31**(6), 930–943 (2014)

14. Chen, H., Jiang, B., Ding, S.X., et al.: Probability-relevant incipient fault detection and diagnosis methodology with applications to electric drive systems. IEEE Trans. Control Syst. Technol. **27**(6), 2766–2773 (2018)

15. Tong, C., Lan, T., Shi, X.: Fault detection by decentralized dynamic PCA algorithm on mutual information. CIESC J. **67**(10), 4317–4323 (2016)

16. Zhong, K., Han, M., Han, B.: Dynamic feature characterization based variable-weighted decentralized method for fault detection. Acta Automatica Sinica **47**(9), 2205–2213 (2021)

17. Joe, Q.S.: Statistical process monitoring: basics and beyond. J. Chemometr. J. Chemometr. Soc. **17**(8–9), 480–502 (2003)

18. Harmouche, J., Delpha, C., Diallo, D.: Incipient fault detection and diagnosis based on Kullback-Leibler divergence using principal component analysis: Part I. Signal Process. **94**, 278–287 (2014)

19. Chen, H., Jiang, B., Lu, N.: An improved incipient fault detection method based on Kullback-Leibler divergence. ISA Trans. **79**, 127–136 (2018)

20. Kong, X., Ge, Z.: Deep learning of latent variable models for industrial process monitoring. IEEE Trans. Ind. Inf. **18**(10), 6778–6788 (2021)

21. Downs, J.J., Vogel, E.F.: A plant-wide industrial process control problem. Comput. Chem. Eng. **17**(3), 245–255 (1993)

22. Lee, J.M., Yoo, C.K., Lee, I.B.: Statistical process monitoring with independent component analysis. J. Process Control **14**(5), 467–485 (2004)

23. Ku, W., Storer, R.H., Georgakis, C.: Disturbance detection and isolation by dynamic principal component analysis. Chemometr. Intell. Lab. Syst. **30**(1), 179–196 (1995)

Simplification of Extended Finite State Machines: A Matrix-Based Approach

Chao Dong[1], Yongyi Yan[1(✉)], Huiqin Li[1], and Jumei Yue[2]

[1] College of Information Engineering, Henan University of Science and Technology,
Luoyang 471000, China
yyyan@mail.nankai.edu.cn
[2] College of Agricultural Equipment Engineering, Henan University of Science and
Technology, Luoyang 471000, China
yjm@mail.nankai.edu.cn

Abstract. Extended Finite State Machines play a crucial role in capturing complex behaviors and interactions in the field of system modeling and analysis. However, as the complexity of systems increases, so does the size and complexity of extended finite state machines. This poses challenges in terms of understanding, analyzing, and computing efficiency. Simplification is an effective method for complex systems in the field of system modeling and analysis. In this paper, we investigate the simplification problem of extended finite state machines using the semi-tensor product of matrices. Firstly, based on the semi-tensor product of matrices, we dynamically model the state transitions of extended finite state machines, successfully bridging the gap between extended finite state machines and control theory. Secondly, utilizing the state transition model of extended finite state machines, we introduce the concept of supervisors and provide a definition for supervisors. We propose a simplification algorithm that effectively reduces the complexity level of extended finite state machine systems. Finally, through examples demonstration we validate our conclusions' correctness as well as demonstrate effectiveness our proposed algorithm.

Keywords: Semi-tensor product · STP approach · STP method · matrix approach · algebraic method · finite-valued systems

1 Introduction

Extended finite state machines (EFSMs) play a crucial role as an important modeling tool in the fields of automation and computer science. EFSMs effectively describe system behavior and state transitions, and are widely applied in areas such as data structures, state networks, and test data [1, 4, 10]. However, in practical applications, EFSMs often face the challenge of excessive complexity, which poses difficulties in system design and analysis.

This work was supported by the National Natural Science Foundation of China (Grant Nos. U1804150, 62073124).

Simplification is a key method to address the issue of high complexity in EFSMs. By transforming complex EFSM models into simpler and more analyzable and manageable forms, system design efficiency can be improved and the probability of errors reduced [14, 18, 20]. Therefore, focusing on how to effectively simplify EFSMs holds significant importance during the research process.

In order to address the simplification problem of EFSMs, the semi-tensor product (STP) of matrices has been introduced as a powerful mathematical tool [6]. STP is capable of automatically discovering hierarchical structures in data and effectively handling multidimensional arrays. In [7], the principles and fundamental techniques of finite games are described using the STP of matrices, along with several issues and recent results on the theory and applications of finite games using STP, as well as its potential uses in artificial intelligence. In reference [11], utilizing the matrix-based STP, subsets and complements of finite sets are proposed, along with an algebraic representation for corresponding structure matrices. The relationships between intersections and unions of structure matrices are then studied separately. Finally, an algorithm based on these theorems is provided for enumerating topological numbers on finite sets. By employing STP, reference [13] investigates reachability and controllability in time-varying k-valued logical control networks and finite memory k-valued logical control networks. For finite memory k-valued logical control networks, they transform them into time-varying k-valued logical control networks and provide necessary and sufficient conditions for their controllability as well as control methods. Additionally, STP has been widely applied in various fields such as Boolean networks [8, 15, 17], nonlinear systems [2, 5, 21], information systems [3, 12, 19], etc.

This paper aims to conduct in-depth research on the simplification problem of EFSMs based on the STP framework. Firstly, we utilize STP to dynamically model the state transitions of EFSMs, obtaining a dynamic model of state transitions that allows for convenient analysis and research by introducing relevant concepts from the control domain. Secondly, based on the dynamic system model of EFSMs, we propose a simplification algorithm that greatly reduces the complexity of the models, laying a foundation for further research on EFSMs.

In this paper, Sect. 2 provides some background knowledge to facilitate understanding of the subsequent content. In Sect. 3, we mainly study the dynamic model of state transitions in EFSMs and propose a simplification algorithm based on this model, effectively reducing the complexity of EFSM systems. In Sect. 4, an example is provided to validate the main conclusions of this paper. Finally, Sect. 5 concludes the entire paper.

2 Preliminaries

2.1 Extended Finite State Machine

Definition 1 (Extended Finite State Machine) [16]. An EFSM is a seven-tuple: $A = (L, D, \Sigma, A_s, L_0, D_0, L_m)$, where L is a finite set of positions; $D = D_1 \times \cdots \times D_p$ is a domain of p one-dimensional data variables; Σ is a finite set of events; $L_0 \subseteq L$ is a set of initial positions; $D_0 = D_0^1 \times \cdots \times D_0^P$ is a set of initial data values; $L_m \subseteq L$ is a set of marked (final) positions; and A_s is a finite set of edges (or transitions), each edge $\alpha \in A_s$ being a 5-tuple $\alpha = (o_\alpha, t_\alpha, \sigma_\alpha, g_\alpha, f_\alpha)$ where:

- $o_\alpha \in L$ is the origin position of α;
- $t_\alpha \in L$ is the terminal position of α;
- $\sigma_\alpha \in \Sigma$ is the transition label;
- $g_\alpha \subseteq D$ is the enabling guard of e;

- $f_\alpha : D \to D$ is the data update function.

Transfer $\alpha = (o_\alpha, t_\alpha, \sigma_\alpha, g_\alpha, f_\alpha)$ occurs when the current state is o_α and g_α is judged to be true. When a transfer occurs, both the current state and the current data value are updated. At the same time, t_α is reachable and f_α should be used in the process.

Given two EFSMs, G and G_s, we call G_s a submachine of G, and G_s is obtained from G by removing certain positions of G and transitions connected to those positions, or by replacing certain guards of the edges of G, or by removing certain transitions of G, denoted as $G_S \leq G$.

The state of an EFSM consists of its current position and the current values of its data variables, therefore, the set of states of an EFSM is given by $L \times D$.

Example 1 [16].

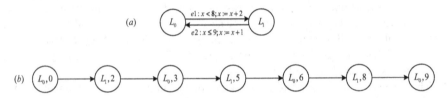

Fig. 1. An EFSM (a) and its equivalent FSA (b)

As shown above, we can see EFSM with two states L_0 and L_1, and the two states are connected by two edges. In our example, we have used a single variable x to constitute the data variable d, i.e., $D = D_1 = \{1, 2, 3, 4, 5, 6, 7, 8, 9\}$; L_0 is the only initial position. At the initial position L_0, the value of L_0 is 0, that is $D_0 = \{0\}$. Starting at position L_0, the EFSM executes $e1$, then it determines whether $e1$ is satisfied. If satisfied, the state is transferred from L_0 to L_1 and the state value is executed $x := x + 2$. Next, the EFSM executes $e2$ and determines whether $e2$ is satisfied. If satisfied, the state is transferred from L_1 to L_0 and the state value is executed $x := x + 1$. For ease of understanding, we define the discriminatory process g_α to be $x \geq 0$.

Starting from state L_0, the value of x is 0, g_α is judged to be true and $e1$ is satisfied, the state is transferred from L_0 to L_1 and the state value is executed $x := x + 2$. At this point the value of x is 2, g_α is judged to be true and $e2$ is satisfied, the state is transferred from L_1 to L_0 and the state value is executed $x := x + 1$. At this point the value of x is 3, g_α is judged to be true and $e1$ is satisfied, the state is transferred from L_0 to L_1 and the state value is executed $x := x + 2$. At this point the value of x is 5, g_α is judged to be true and $e2$ is satisfied, the state is transferred from L_1 to L_0 and the state value is executed $x := x + 1$. At this point the value of x is 6, g_α is judged to be true and $e1$ is satisfied, the state is transferred from L_0 to L_1 and the state value is executed $x := x + 2$. At this point the value of x is 8, g_α is judged to be true and $e2$ is satisfied, the state is transferred from L_1 to L_0 and the state value is executed $x := x + 1$. At this point the value of x is 9, g_α is judged to be true, but $e1$ is not satisfied, therefore the state and state value transfer is terminated. The above process is shown in b of Fig. 1.

2.2 The Semi-Tensor Product (STP)

High-dimensional arrays come up frequently in our mathematical and engineering problems. When using high-dimensional arrays to solve some problems, the matrix form is very inconvenient and the high-dimensional arrays are too complex to operate and more difficult to define operations. To solve this problem, Daizhan Cheng and Hongsheng Qi, inspired by the hierarchy of data handled by pointers in the C program language, proposed a matrix multiplication method called the semi-tensor product of matrices or STP for short.

The STP can actively find different levels of data, which makes it possible to handle multidimensional arrays more efficiently, because the STP of matrices can be combined with ordinary matrix multiplication, allowing the latter to be extended to any two matrices without changing the main properties. This makes it extremely convenient to work with multidimensional arrays in a logical dynamic space system.

Definition 2 (The semi-tensor product) [9]. For $M \in R^{m \times n}$ and $N \in R^{p \times q}$, their semi-tensor product is expressed as $M \ltimes N$, defined as:

$$M \ltimes N := (M \otimes I_{s/n})(N \otimes I_{s/p}) \tag{1}$$

where s is the least common multiple of n and p, $\otimes$ is the Kronecker product.

Remark 1. The STP of a matrix is an extension of traditional matrix multiplication, when n is equal to p, it becomes traditional matrix multiplication. In this paper, all matrix products are semi-tensor products, and we omit the sign $\ltimes$ unless other-wise specified. Although STP breaks through the dimension limitation of traditional matrix multiplication, it still retains the basic properties of the traditional matrix.

3 Main Results

3.1 EFSMs State Transition Dynamic System Model

The following preparations are needed to model the bilinear dynamic model of an EFSM using the algebraic state space method of logical dynamic systems.

An EFSM is a 7-tuple $A = (L, D, \Sigma, A_s, L_0, D_0, L_m)$, $\alpha = (o_\alpha, t_\alpha, \sigma_\alpha, g_\alpha, f_\alpha)$, where $L = \{l_1, l_2, \cdots, l_n\}$, $\Sigma = \{e_1, e_2, \cdots, e_m\}$, $D = \{d_1, d_2, \cdots, d_p\}$, identify $l_i (1 \leq i \leq n)$ with $\delta_n^i (1 \leq i \leq n)$, expressed as $l_i \sim \delta_n^i$, for simplicity, δ_n^i is the vector form of l_i. Then L can be denoted as Δ_n, that is, $L = \{\delta_n^1, \delta_n^2, \cdots, \delta_n^n\}$. Similarly, for Σ, identify e_j with $\delta_m^j (1 \leq j \leq m)$(denoted as $e_j \sim \delta_m^j$), δ_m^j is the vector form of e_j, and use Δ_m to denote Σ, i.e., $\Sigma = \{\delta_m^1, \delta_m^2, \cdots, \delta_m^m\}$. We do the same things to $d_z (1 \leq z \leq p)$, that is, identify

d_z with δ_p^z, denoted as $d_z \sim \delta_p^z$, so δ_p^z is the vector form of d_z, then D can be denote as Δ_p, i.e., $D = \{\delta_p^1, \delta_p^2, \cdots, \delta_p^z\}$.

In the EFSM, a transition $\alpha = (o_\alpha, t_\alpha, \sigma_\alpha, g_\alpha, f_\alpha)$ is enabled if the current position is O_α and the value of guard condition g_α is judged to be true. When the transition α is executed, position t_α is reached and the variables are updated by applying f_α. Then the essence of g_α is the judgment of the input sequence. In our bilinear dynamic model, when the judgment is false, the system output is 0; otherwise, the system output is normal. Identify g_α with $\delta_2^k (k = 1$ or $k = 2)$, denoted as $g_a \sim \delta_2^k (k = 1$ or $k = 2)$, that is, $\delta_2^k (k = 1$ or $k = 2)$ is the vector form of g_α, i.e., $g_\alpha = \{\delta_2^1, \delta_2^2\}$.

At the same time, because δ_2^k is the judgment of the transition matrix of the dynamic system, the judgment result can be true or false. If $k = 1$, it is true; If $k = 2$, it is false, and the output is 0.

In $\alpha = (o_\alpha, t_\alpha, \sigma_\alpha, g_\alpha, f_\alpha)$ of an EFSM, f_α is the update function of data $D \to D$. Similarly, for the convenience of modeling, we define f to represent the transition function of the state transition matrix.

Definition 3 (Transition structure matrix). $F = [F_1...F_m]$ is called the transition structure matrix of an EFSM $A = (L, D, \Sigma, A_S, L_0, D_0, L_m)$, which is defined as:

$$F_{j(s,t)} := \begin{cases} if \delta_2^k = \delta_2^1 \begin{cases} 1 \ if \ \delta_n^s \in f(\delta_n^t, \delta_m^j) \\ 0 \ Otherwise \end{cases} \\ if \delta_2^k = \delta_2^2 \ 0 \end{cases}$$

The following is a traditional finite state machine to compare the EFSM studied in this paper.

An finite state machine is a seven-tuple $A = (X, E, Y, f_1, g_1, x^0, X^m)$, in which X, E and Y are finite sets of states, input symbols, and outputs, respectively, $x^0 \in X$ is the initial state, $X^m \in X$ is the set of accepted states, f_1 and g_1 are transition and output functions, which are defined as

$$f_1 : X \times E \to X,$$

$$g_1 : X \times E \to Y.$$

For a finite state machine $A = (X, E, Y, f, g, x^0, X^m)$, where $X = \{x_1, x_2, \cdots, x_z\}, E = \{e_1, e_2, \cdots, e_c\}, Y = \{y_1, y_2, \cdots, y_v\}$, identify $x_f (1 \le f \le z)$ with $\delta_z^f (1 \le f \le z)$, expressed as $x_f \sim \delta_z^f$, and $\delta_z^f (1 \le f \le z)$ is the vector form of $x_f (1 \le f \le z)$. Then X can be denoted as Δ_z, that is, $X = \{\delta_z^1, \delta_z^2, \cdots, \delta_z^z\}$. Similarly, for E, identify e_g with $\delta_c^g (1 \le g \le c)$ (denoted as $e_g \sim \delta_c^g$), $\delta_c^g (1 \le g \le c)$ is the vector form of e_g, we use Δ_c to denoted E, i.e., $E = \{\delta_c^1, \delta_c^2, \cdots, \delta_c^c\}$. We do the same things to $y_h (1 \le h \le v)$, that is, identify y_h with $\delta_v^h (1 \le h \le v)$, denoted as $y_h \sim \delta_v^h$, δ_v^h is the vector form of y_h, then Y can be denote as Δ_v, i.e., $Y = \{\delta_v^1, \delta_v^2, \cdots, \delta_v^v\}$.

Remark 2. Matrix $F' = [F_1 \ldots F_m]$ is called the transition structure matrix of finite state machine $A = (X, E, Y, f, g, x^0, X^m)$, which is denoted as:

$$F'_{i(s,t)} = \begin{cases} 1 & \delta_z^s \in f_1(\delta_z^f, \delta_c^i) \\ 0 & Otherwise \end{cases}$$

Remark 3. According to Definition 3, F_i is jointly determined by e_j and g_a. This is the characteristic of EFSMs. According to Remark 2, in a traditional finite state machine, F'_i is uniquely determined by e_i. Essentially, F'_i is the adjacency matrix of the subgraph identified by e_i in the state transition graph of the traditional finite state machine, called the transpose of the transition matrix.

Through the above examples, we can clearly understand the differences between the EFSMs and the traditional finite state machine.

Theorem 1 (State transition dynamic model). Let $F = [F_1 \ldots F_m]$ be the state transition matrix of an EFSM $A = (L, D, \Sigma, A_s, L_0, D_0, L_m)$, $L = \{l_1, l_2, \cdots, l_n\}$, $\Sigma = \{e_1, e_2, \cdots, e_m\}$, $g_\alpha = \{\delta_2^1, \delta_2^2\}$. Then, after the EFSM read input e_j at any l_i, the new state is

$$l_{i+1} = F \ltimes \delta_m^j \ltimes \delta_n^i \ltimes \delta_2^k \tag{2}$$

where δ_m^j is the vector form of the input e_j, δ_n^i is the vector form of state $l_i(1 \leq i \leq n)$, δ_2^k is the judgment of transition matrix of dynamic system in EFSMs.

Proof. The transition function of an EFSM A is $f : L_0 \times \Sigma \to L_m$, which can be expressed as $f(\delta_n^i, \delta_m^j) = F \times \delta_m^j \times \delta_n^i$. Where δ_n^i and δ_m^j are vector forms of state $l_i(1 \leq i \leq n)$ and finite event set $e_j(1 \leq j \leq m)$ respectively.

In fact, the EFSM A reads input $e_j(1 \leq j \leq m)$ at state l_i and moves to state l_{i+1} after being judged to be "true", i.e., $f(l_i, e_j) = l_{i+1}$.

According to Definition 3, the column judged "true" by $col_i(F_j)$ contains one element equal to 1, all the other elements are 0.

Now, we could just calculate $F \times \delta_m^j \times \delta_n^i$, but we should be careful, according to Definition 3, $F \times \delta_m^j \times \delta_n^i$ contains the vectors under two different decisions between state l_i and state l_{i+1} after reading input $e_j(1 \leq j \leq m)$, i.e., state l_i through state l_{i+1} are judged to be "true" and "false". To make clear the state after reading the input, the true state after reading the input can be obtained by multiplying the judgment vector after $F \times \delta_m^j \times \delta_n^i$, i.e., $F \times \delta_m^j \times \delta_n^i \ltimes \delta_2^k$.

Then, after the EFSM reads input $e_j(1 \leq j \leq m)$ at any state l_i, the new state is $l_{i+1} = F \ltimes \delta_m^j \ltimes \delta_n^i \ltimes \delta_2^k$.

By establishing the state transition output expression function for EFSMs, we have successfully incorporated advanced research methods from the control theory domain into EFSMs. With the aid of this expression function, we can describe the system's possible transitions more accurately under different states and specify the corresponding output behaviors for each transition. This enables us to thoroughly investigate various scenarios that may occur in the system under different conditions and propose targeted strategies. This innovative approach provides a superior foundation for our in-depth study of EFSMs. The integration of control theory and EFSMs allows us to analyze and optimize system behavior more effectively.

3.2 Simplification of Extended Finite State Machines

When we utilize the conclusions from the previous section to establish the state transition model of EFSMs and conduct in-depth system research, we realize that the scale of the system is excessively large. In such cases, we need to find a method that can reduce the complexity of EFSMs without affecting the overall system.

Based on these considerations, we adopt a supervisor to regulate the state transition behavior of EFSMs. Through this approach, we can identify and retain valid information while filtering out irrelevant or invalid information, thereby reducing the complexity of EFSM systems. The supervisor plays a crucial role in this method. It is responsible for monitoring and evaluating state transitions in EFSMs and deciding whether specific transitions are allowed based on predefined rules and strategies. By introducing a supervisor, we can filter out transitions that do not meet system requirements or are insignificant, only retaining valid transitions that have significant impacts on system behavior. To achieve this goal, we propose the following definition.

Definition 4 (supervisor S). Given an EFSM $G = (L, D, \Sigma, A_s, L_0, D_0, L_m)$, if and only if $g_a \sim \delta_2^1$, a supervisor S is called a supervisor of G. Where $\alpha \in A_s$ and $\alpha = (o_\alpha, t_\alpha, \sigma_\alpha, g_\alpha, f_\alpha)$. In the bilinear dynamic model, g_a is the judgment of state transition, and δ_2^1 is vector form when the judgment is "true".

Remark 4. In connection with Definition 3 above, we can see that F includes all transferred cases of EFSMs, and that when the supervisor S appears, it excludes all cases in which g_a is judged to be "false" and retains only those in which g_a is judged to be "true". This means that supervisor S acts as a "filter", returning 0 for cases where g_a is judged to be "false" and the rest of the input proceeds normally.

Definition 5 (Submachine G_s). Given an EFSM $G = (L, D, \Sigma, A_s, L_0, D_0, L_m)$, a submachine G_s of G under supervisor S can be obtained from G.

Remark 5. G_s represents the EFSM obtained from G under the supervision of supervisor S. In essence, it reduces the number of redundant state transition matrices, which means that each remaining edge has stronger supervised control. Here we should note that when G_s receives input characters, only the characters judged as $g_a \sim \delta_2^1$ are normally output, and the rest characters are output as 0.

By introducing a supervisor, we are able to reduce the complexity of EFSMs without compromising the overall system functionality and performance. The supervisor has the capability to filter out invalid state transitions, thereby reducing redundant information and unnecessary complexity in the system. This approach not only enhances the comprehensibility and maintainability of the system but also contributes to optimizing system behavior and improving overall performance. This method holds significant importance in practical applications, providing an effective approach for us to conduct in-depth research and optimization of EFSMs.

Next, based on the above definitions, we simplify the EFSM model with the supervision of supervisor S and propose Algorithm 1.

Algorithm 1 (Simplification of an extended finite state machine)

Given an EFSM $G = (L, D, \Sigma, A_s, L_0, D_0, L_m)$, where: $L = (l_1, l_2, \ldots, l_n)$ is a finite set of positions; $D = D_1 \times \cdots \times D_P$ is a domain of P one-dimensional data variables; $\Sigma = (e_1, e_1, \cdots\cdots e_m)$ is a finite set of events. Let F be the state transition structure matrix of an EFSM. Now the supervisor S is used to supervise the EFSM, and the EFSM model is simplified by the supervision of supervisor S. Then, we have the following algorithmic steps.

- Step 1: The state transition structure matrix F of an EFSM is obtained.
- Step 2: Find the supervisor S using Definition 4.
- Step 3: Use supervisor S to find the corresponding G_s of G.
- Step 4: Get the state transition structure matrix of G_s, let's call it N.
- Step 5: Compute the desired state according to the state transition structure matrix N.

Algorithm 1 adopts supervisor S to simplify the EFSM model. This simplification is not a simple problem, but the EFSM under the whole STP bilinear system model, which provides a basis for further research in the established bilinear system model.

4 Illustrative Example

In this section, we use an example to verify the correctness of the main conclusions and the effectiveness of the algorithm.

Example 2. As shown in Fig. 2, given an EFSM $G = (L, D, \Sigma, A_s, L_0, D_0, L_m)$, IN represents the input signal, $\emptyset$ represents $g_a \sim \delta_2^2$. When $g_a \sim \delta_2^2$, the system feedback is 0. Otherwise, all signals enter l_1, where l_1, l_2, l_3, l_4, l_5 is the state expressed at corresponding time, that is, $L = \{l_1, l_2, l_3, l_4, l_5\}, e_1$ and e_2 are two input events, i.e., $\Sigma = \{e_1, e_2\}$. When the state starts at l_1, reads input e_1, gets result l_2, l_1 receives signal e_2 and gets result l_3, l_2 receives signal e_1 and gets result l_4, l_2 receives signal e_2 and gets result l_3, l_3 receives signal e_1 and gets result l_5, l_3 receives signal e_2 and gets result l_4, l_4 receives signal e_1 and gets result l_3, l_4 receives signal e_2 and gets result l_5, l_5 receives signal e_1 and gets result l_1, l_5 receives signal e_2 and gets result l_2.

From the conclusion in part 3 we have: $L = \{l_1, l_2, l_3, l_4, l_5\} \sim L = \{\delta_5^1, \delta_5^2, \delta_5^3, \delta_5^4, \delta_5^5\}, \Sigma = \{e_1, e_2\} \sim \Sigma = \{\delta_2^1, \delta_2^2\}$ and now we use step 1 and step 2 of Algorithm 1.

Step 1. We can obtain the state transition structure matrix shown here, i.e.,

$$F = \begin{bmatrix} 0 & 0 & 0 & 0 & 0 & 0 & 0 & 1 & 0 & 0 & 0 & 0 & 0 & 0 & 0 & 0 & 0 & 0 \\ 1 & 0 & 0 & 0 & 0 & 0 & 0 & 0 & 0 & 0 & 0 & 0 & 0 & 0 & 0 & 1 & 0 \\ 0 & 0 & 0 & 0 & 0 & 1 & 0 & 0 & 0 & 1 & 0 & 1 & 0 & 0 & 0 & 0 & 0 \\ 0 & 0 & 1 & 0 & 0 & 0 & 0 & 0 & 0 & 0 & 0 & 0 & 1 & 0 & 0 & 0 & 0 \\ 0 & 0 & 0 & 0 & 1 & 0 & 0 & 0 & 0 & 0 & 0 & 0 & 0 & 0 & 1 & 0 & 0 & 0 \end{bmatrix}$$

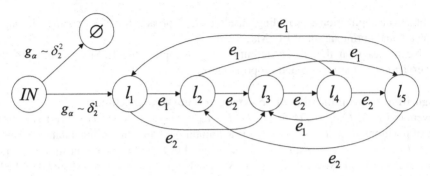

Fig. 2. State transition diagram

Step 2. If and only if $g_a = \delta_2^1$, the submachine G_s of an EFSM G under the supervision of supervisor S is obtained, and the state transition diagram is shown below (Fig. 3).

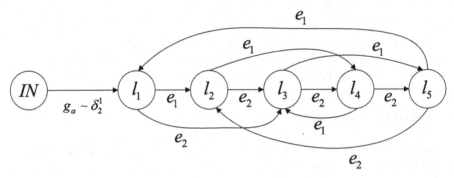

Fig. 3. A simplified diagram of an EFSM

At this time, we can obtain the new state transition structure matrix of G_s, i.e.,

$$
N = \begin{bmatrix}
0 & 0 & 0 & 0 & 1 & 0 & 0 & 0 & 0 & 0 \\
1 & 0 & 0 & 0 & 0 & 0 & 0 & 0 & 0 & 1 \\
0 & 0 & 0 & 1 & 0 & 1 & 1 & 0 & 0 & 0 \\
0 & 1 & 0 & 0 & 0 & 0 & 0 & 1 & 0 & 0 \\
0 & 0 & 1 & 0 & 0 & 0 & 0 & 0 & 1 & 0
\end{bmatrix}
$$

By observing matrix N, it is evident that the state transition matrix of the system has been reduced by half compared to the original system. This change greatly enhances the simplicity of the system and effectively reduces computational complexity. By reducing the size of the state transition matrix, we are able to eliminate redundant information and unnecessary state transitions, making the system more streamlined and efficient. These optimization measures contribute to improving system performance and reducing computational resource requirements.

5 Conclusion

By utilizing the STP, we have successfully established the dynamic equations for state transitions in the EFSM, providing a powerful tool for in-depth research on this topic. This innovative approach not only enriches the modeling and analysis methods of EFSMs but also promotes cross-fertilization between control theory and systems engineering. Furthermore, based on the dynamic equations of state transitions in the EFSM, we introduce supervisors and propose a simplification algorithm that simplifies the understanding and analysis process of system behavior. By reducing the number of possible state combinations, we can more easily infer potential paths of state transitions under specific input conditions. Additionally, in practical applications, a smaller state transition matrix implies faster and more efficient operations such as model checking and formal verification. With reduced computational complexity, we are able to obtain critical results more quickly and make corresponding decisions.

References

1. Turlea, A.: Testing extended finite state machines using NSGA-III. In: 10th ACM SIGSOFT International Workshop on Automating TEST Case Design, Selection, and Evaluation (A-TEST), Tallinn, Estonia, pp. 1–7 (2019)
2. Gao, B., et al.: Stability of nonlinear feedback shift registers with periodic input. Cmc-Comput. Mater. Continua **62**(2), 833–847 (2020)
3. Wang, B., Feng, J.E.: On detectability of probabilistic Boolean networks. Inf. Sci. **483**, 383–395 (2019)
4. Rivas, D., Das, P., Saiz-Alcaine, J., Ribas-Xirgo, L.: Synthesis of controllers from finite state stack machine diagrams. In: 23rd IEEE International Conference on Emerging Technologies and Factory Automation (ETFA), pp. 1179–1182. Politecnico Torino, Torino (2018)
5. Cheng, D., Xiaoming, H., Wang, Y.: Non-regular feedback linearization of nonlinear systems via a normal form algorithm. Automatica **40**(3), 439–447 (2004). https://doi.org/10.1016/j.automatica.2003.10.014
6. Cheng, D.Z., Qi, H.S., Zhao, Y.: An introduction to semi-tensor product of matrices and its applications. World Scientific (2012)
7. Cheng, D.Z., Wu, Y.H., Zhao, G.D., Fu, S.H.: A comprehensive survey on STP approach to finite games. J. Syst. Sci. Complex. **34**(5), 1666–1680 (2021)
8. Cheng, D.Z., Zhang, L., Bi, D.: Invariant subspace approach to boolean (control) networks. IEEE Trans. Autom. Control **68**(4), 2325–2337 (2023)
9. Cheng, D.Z.: Semi-tensor product of matrices and its application to Morgen's problem. China Sci. **44**(3), 195–212 (2001)
10. Ipate, F., Gheorghe, M., Lefticaru, R.: Fundamental results for learning deterministic extended finite state machines from queries. Theor. Comput. Sci. **862**, 160–173 (2021)
11. Guo, H.F., Xing, B., Ming, Z.W., Feng, J.E.: Algebraic representation of topologies on a finite set. Mathematics **10**(7), 1143 (2022)
12. Li, H.T., Zhao, G.D., Meng, M., Feng, J.E.: A survey on applications of semi-tensor product method in engineering. Sci. China-Inf. Sci. **61**(1), 1–17 (2018)
13. Zhao, J.T., Chen, Z.Q., Liu, Z.X.: Reachability and controllability of time-variant k-valued logical control network and finite memories k-valued logical control network. In: 36th Chinese Control Conference (CCC), Dalian, Peoples R China, pp. 2379–2386 (2017)

14. Bermingham, L., Lee, I.: A framework of spatio-temporal trajectory simplification methods. Int. J. Geogr. Inf. Sci. **31**(6), 1128–1153 (2017)
15. Li, L.L., Zhang, A.G., Lu, J.Q.: Disturbance decoupling problem of delayed boolean networks based on the network structure. IEEE Trans. Circuits Syst. Ii-Exp. Briefs **70**(3), 1004–1008 (2023)
16. Ouedraogo, L., Kumar, R., Malik, R., Akesson, K.: Nonblocking and safe control of discrete-event systems modeled as extended finite automata. IEEE Trans. Autom. Sci. Eng. **8**(3), 560–569 (2011)
17. Li, X., Liu, Y., Cao, J.D., Abdel-Aty, M.: Minimal reconstructibility of boolean control networks. IEEE Trans. Syst. Man Cybern.-Syst. **53**, 4944–4949 (2023)
18. Zhou, Y.J., Rathore, A., Purvine, E., Wang, B.: Topological simplifications of hypergraphs. IEEE Trans. Vis. Comput. Graph. **29**(7), 3209–3225 (2023)
19. Wang, Y.H., Cheng, D.Z., Liu, X.Y.: Matrix expression of Shapley values and its application to distributed resource allocation. Sci. China-Inf. Sci. **62**(2), 1–11 (2019)
20. Yoon, Y., Kim, B.C.: CAD model simplification using feature simplifications. J. Adv. Mech. Des. Syst. Manuf. **10**(8) (2016)
21. Li, Z.Q., Qiao, Y.P., Qi, H.S., Cheng, D.Z.: Stability of switched polynomial systems. J. Syst. Sci. Complex. **21**(3), 362–377 (2008)

Lane Change Decision Control of Autonomous Vehicle Based on A3C Algorithm

Chuntao Zhou[1], Mingrui Liao[3], Longyin Jiao[1], and Fazhan Tao[1,2(✉)]

[1] School of Information Engineering, Henan University of Science and Technology, Henan, China
taofazhan@haust.edu.cn
[2] Longmen Laboratory, Luoyang, Henan, China
[3] Aerospace System Engineering Shanghai, Minhang District, Shanghai, China

Abstract. Coordinating the lateral and longitudinal control of vehicles during lane changing, while considering the vehicle's operational state and the surrounding environment, poses a highly challenging task. In recent years, deep reinforcement learning (DRL) technology has experienced rapid development and has found widespread applications in the traditional automatic control industry. With the improvement of driving safety requirements, DRL technology provides a new research direction and an effective way for the development of vehicle autonomous lane change. This paper investigates automated decision control for lane changing in autonomous vehicles using the Asynchronous Advantage Actor-Critic (A3C) algorithm, while also proposing reasonable multi-objective performance evaluation metrics. Nevertheless, the traditional A3C algorithm frequently encounters convergence oscillation or degradation issues, hindering agents from attaining the highest reward. To address the mentioned issues, an improved parameter updating method based on a weighted average of advantage value is proposed. The simulation results on the highway simulation platform demonstrate that the enhanced A3C algorithm offers increased stability in comparison to the traditional A3C algorithm. Moreover, in comparison to the Deep Q-Network (DQN) algorithm and the Deep Deterministic Policy Gradient (DDPG) algorithm, the enhanced A3C algorithm showcases faster convergence speed and a higher success rate, hence confirming the superiority of the proposed improvement.

Keywords: Deep reinforcement learning · Asynchronous advantage actor-critic · Lane change

1 Introduction

In recent years, the issue of traffic safety and congestion has become increasingly grave due to the steady rise in car ownership. Research indicates that the surge in traffic accidents and urban congestion can predominantly be attributed to human factors such as drivers' limited driving skills and distracted driving. Consequently, in the present context, there is a growing need to explore intelligent vehicles capable of replacing human drivers to achieve autonomous driving. This has emerged as a crucial research area for the future

© The Author(s), under exclusive license to Springer Nature Singapore Pte Ltd. 2024
F. Sun et al. (Eds.): ICCSIP 2023, CCIS 1918, pp. 217–229, 2024.
https://doi.org/10.1007/978-981-99-8018-5_16

advancement of the automotive industry. During the act of driving, a driver typically demonstrates three fundamental driving behaviors: car-following, lane-changing, and free driving [1]. Among these, the lane-changing maneuver demands the driver to be attentive to both the vehicles in the current lane and the target lane simultaneously. Consequently, the lane-changing decision is more intricate compared to other driving behaviors. It is considered one of the driving behaviors that most significantly showcases autonomous driving technology.

Currently, research on intelligent vehicle decision-making algorithms primarily relies on rule-based design methods [2, 3]. These methods utilize advanced "expert systems" to establish behavior rules that govern the driving process. Subsequently, these rules are tested and validated in specific scenarios. However, in complex scenarios and under challenging driving conditions, such as sudden accidents, this method fails to yield satisfactory outcomes [4]. With the rapid advancements in machine learning, the integration of reinforcement learning and deep learning has witnessed significant progress. The introduction of the DQN by the Google DeepMind team has played a pivotal role in enhancing agent performance, as illustrated by Alpha Go's triumph over professional Go players. In comparison to traditional rule-based control algorithms, DRL exhibits superior self-learning capabilities when confronted with novel situations. Moreover, DRL offers notable advantages such as heightened precision, rapid response time, and enhanced generalizability in tackling diverse scenarios. Regarding lane changing, it is a common temporal sequence problem in which the completion of the task requires a series of actions. The successful execution of each action directly impacts the ultimate goal of the task, which is to achieve a successful lane change. This type of problem is well suited to be solved by DRL techniques. Therefore, DRL has become another feasible scheme for automatic lane change of intelligent vehicles [5].

DRL algorithms can be categorized based on the type of action space they utilize. These categories include discrete action space, which stores a predefined set of discrete actions as control commands, and continuous action space, which allows for sampling any real number within a specified threshold. The DQN algorithm serves as a representative DRL algorithm that operates within a discrete action space. By utilizing discrete action spaces, the challenge of searching for the optimal action within a finite space is mitigated, but this approach may also result in reduced control accuracy. On the other hand, the A3C algorithm adopts a continuous action space, enabling better control accuracy. However, it is important to note that the A3C algorithm encounters challenges with regards to poor convergence during the training process. Given that the lane change process prioritizes safety, achieving better control accuracy is of utmost importance. To address this requirement, we take A3C as the framework, use an improved parameter updating method based on a weighted average of advantage value to solve the problem of poor convergence effect of A3C algorithm.

The remaining sections of this article are arranged as follows: Sect. 2 encompasses a literature review of the relevant literature. Section 3 outlines the methodology and provides comprehensive details of our algorithm. The simulation results are then presented in Sect. 4. Finally, the concluding remarks are provided in Sect. 5, accompanied by a discussion regarding potential future research directions.

2 Related Works

The existing automatic lane changing methods depend on predefined rules and meticulously crafted models. Several of these methods employ virtual lane trajectories or a sequence of trajectory points to facilitate the lane changing process. Nonetheless, these methods are inadequate for managing unforeseeable situations that may occur during real-time driving processes.

RL techniques have proven to be effective in addressing the decision-making and control challenges encountered in autonomous driving systems. When making decisions, the set of actions available is usually defined discretely and reflects the current state of the vehicle. Using the Q-learning method, You et al. trained a model that successfully achieved decision control of autonomous driving vehicles in a highway driving scenario [6]. Within this framework, the agent learns to execute actions including acceleration, braking, overtaking, and turning. Mukadam et al. devised more sophisticated strategies by employing the Q-mask technique [7]. They decomposed the decision-making process into five discrete actions: no action, acceleration, deceleration, lane change to the left, and lane change to the right. In order to tackle the control decision problem in autonomous driving vehicles, certain researchers discretized the action space to streamline the complexity of driving behaviors and enhance the efficiency of model learning. Zhang et al. proposed the use of double Q-learning as an extension to Q-learning for training vehicle speed control [8]. The experiment entails controlling the vehicle's acceleration, deceleration, and maintenance by manipulating the degree of pedaling of the accelerator pedal. Jaritz et al. employed the A3C algorithm to develop a comprehensive framework aimed at learning vehicle control in rally games [9]. The control commands were discretized into 32 values to attain precise vehicle control. Hoel et al. utilized the DQN algorithm to implement lane change decision control for autonomous vehicles in a simulated 3-lane environment [10].

While discrete action spaces can effectively control decision-making in autonomous vehicles, the outputs in real-world environments are continuous. Thus, addressing the issue of vehicle control in continuous space is essential. Wang et al. employed quadratic Q-function approximators to derive optimal actions by solving functional equations [11]. Furthermore, the model learns from the driving behavior of professional drivers prior to training, thereby enhancing the algorithm's convergence speed. Liang et al. introduced the Controllable Imitative Reinforcement Learning (CIRL) method, which employs the DDPG algorithm as a framework to facilitate vehicle learning utilizing expert knowledge. Simultaneously, motion exploration is constrained within a predetermined range to promote more efficient learning by the agent [12]. Kaushik et al. employed the DDPG algorithm to enable vehicles to learn overtaking actions within a continuous action space [13]. Their approach involves initially training agents on simpler tasks, such as lane keeping, before progressing to more complex tasks like overtaking. Sallab et al. compared the accomplishment of the agent's lane keeping task, in both discrete and continuous action spaces, using the DQN algorithm and deep deterministic Actor Critic (DDAC) algorithm [14]. The simulation results indicated that both methods were able to successfully complete the lane keeping behavior. However, the DDAC algorithm yielded smoother reward values and exhibited superior performance.

The studies mentioned above often employ simplistic reward function designs, which adversely impact the agent's learning efficiency. For instance, [10] utilizes a reward function that solely consists of rewarding the agent for reaching the end and punishing it for colliding. Likewise, [12] divides the reward function into four parts, but three of them are simplistic two-valued piecewise functions, while the remaining part remains constant. Although simple reward functions can allow agents to accomplish control tasks, this approach is inefficient and time-consuming. Simple reward functions fail to adequately assess the quality of actions, potentially impeding the agent's acquisition of valuable knowledge. The use of sparse rewards poses another issue. As mentioned in [14], sparse rewards necessitate extensive random exploration, increasing the difficulty of exploration and consuming significant memory resources.

In order to facilitate efficient learning for the agent, the use of an effective reward function is crucial. This function serves to guide and evaluate the agent's actions, enabling the acquisition of valuable knowledge and ensuring the agent's adherence to the desired course of action. In this study, we propose the development of a "heuristic" reward function derived from the A3C algorithm, specifically designed to enable lane change control in a continuous state space. By enhancing the parameter update mode, we observe a significant improvement in the convergence speed of the algorithm when compared to traditional methods.

3 Methods

3.1 A3C Algorithm

The problem of RL can be viewed as a Markov process, where the agent learns through continuous interaction with the environment. The agent receives the current state from the environment, selects an action A_t based on the state S_t, and transitions to a new state S_{t+1}, thereby receiving a reward R_t. Once the agent reaches the end point, the interaction with the environment ceases, signaling the completion of a episode. The objective of the agent is to maximize the cumulative reward by following the optimal policy π^*.

RL methods can be categorized into two main types based on the different iteration methods: value function based methods and strategy gradient based methods. The A-C algorithm utilizes both the value function method for action selection and the strategy gradient method for action evaluation. Figure 1 displays the structural diagram of the A-C algorithm.

The A-C algorithm encounters issues of inefficient agent learning and slow algorithm convergence due to the randomness of agent detection. Currently, two methods are employed to address this issue: the priority experiential replay mechanism (EP) and asynchronous reinforcement learning (ARL). In comparison to the other two methods, the ARL method can more effectively eliminate data correlation, leading to significantly improved convergence efficiency of the algorithm. Additionally, the ARL method's multi-thread operation mechanism allows efficient utilization of computer memory. Hence, the ARL method is often the preferred choice for addressing the issues faced by the A-C algorithm.

A key aspect of the A3C algorithm for enhancing convergence speed is the simultaneous operation of multiple threads to asynchronously update each local network agent.

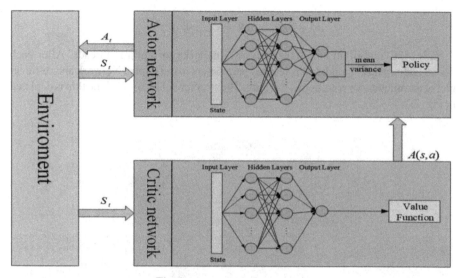

Fig. 1. Actor-Critic framework.

Consequently, this approach results in a further weakening of the data correlation and optimizes the utilization of computing resources. The policy and value function of each subnetwork are denoted as $\pi(a_t|s_t; \theta')$ and $V(s_t; \theta'_v)$, respectively; similarly, the total network is represented by $\pi(a_t|s_t; \theta)$ and $V(s_t; \theta_v)$. Once the maximum number of steps t_{max} is completed, the main network gathers the parameters of each subnetwork to perform an update on $\pi(a_t|s_t; \theta)$ and $V(s_t; \theta_v)$.

The action network employs gradient descent to compute the loss function a_{loss}:

$$a_{loss} = \nabla_{\theta'} \log \pi(a_t|s_t; \theta')A(s_t, a_t; \theta, \theta_v) \tag{1}$$

Among the various functions, $A(s_t, a_t; \theta, \theta_v)$ serves as the dominant function.

$$A(s_t, a_t; \theta, \theta_v) = \sum_{i=0}^{k-1} \gamma^i r_{t+i} + \gamma^k V(s_{t+k}; \theta_v) - V(s_t; \theta_v) \tag{2}$$

We decided to incorporate the entropy $H(\pi)$ of strategy π into the objective function in order to broaden the algorithm's search scope:

$$\nabla_{\theta'} \log \pi(a_t|s_t; \theta')A(s_t, a_t; \theta, \theta_v) + \beta H(\pi(s_t; \theta')) \tag{3}$$

The evaluation network utilizes the time difference error (TD-error) to compute the network loss function c_{loss}. The loss function at the i-th time step is defined as follows:

$$c_{loss} = \partial(R - V(s_i; \theta'_v))^2 / \partial\theta'_v \tag{4}$$

For algorithm optimization, we employ the RMSPropOptimizer method, where each local network maintains individual gradients to update parameters:

$$d\theta \leftarrow d\theta + \nabla_{\theta'} \log \pi(a_t|s_t; \theta')(R - V(s_i; \theta'_v)) + \beta H(\pi(s_t; \theta')) \tag{5}$$

$$d\theta \leftarrow d\theta + \partial(R - V(s_i; \theta'_v))^2 / \partial\theta'_v \tag{6}$$

The A3C algorithm simultaneously assigns tasks to multiple threads. After each thread learns a task, it updates its learned parameters to the Global Network and retrieves global parameters for continuous learning. The structure of the A3C algorithm is depicted in Fig. 2.

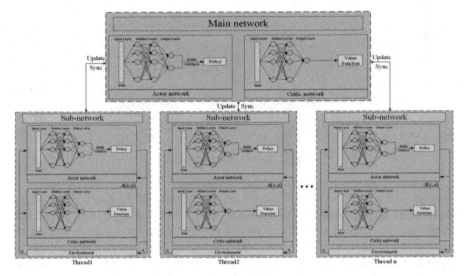

Fig. 2. A3C algorithm principle.

3.2   A3C Algorithm Improvement

To update the vector parameters θ and θ_v, the A3C algorithm requires collecting the parameters from each thread at the end of a round. However, this can lead to significant changes in the main network's parameters during the update due to parameter accumulation, which hampers algorithm convergence. To address this issue, we propose a novel method called prepond-weighted average. The parameters can be updated using the following approach:

$$\theta \leftarrow \theta + \lambda_a waa(d\theta) \tag{7}$$

$$\theta_v \leftarrow \theta_v + \lambda_c waa(d\theta_v) \tag{8}$$

Here, $waa(d\theta) = \sum_1^n \frac{A_i}{A} d\theta'$ represents the weighted average of each component during the calculation period, determined by its dominant value. Similarly, $waa(d\theta_v) = \sum_1^n \frac{A_i}{A} d\theta'_v$ represents the weighted average of each component during the calculation period, determined based on its dominance value. In contrast to the parameter updating rules of the original A3C algorithm, our proposed modification guarantees iterative updates of the neural network vector in the optimal direction. This is accomplished by elevating the weighted average of parameter increments within the A3C algorithm. Moreover, this modification effectively alleviates potential oscillations during neural network convergence.

3.3 Parameter Setting

State Space. Agents can obtain more accurate vehicle and road information through good state space design and make decisions with higher accuracy. Consequently, we selected seven state values as state variables: current horizontal position x, vertical position y, lateral velocity V_x, longitudinal velocity V_y, trigonometry of the Angle with the lane line $\sin \omega$ and $\cos \omega$, and distance dis_h from the front car. Therefore, the state space is defined as:

$$State = \{x \; y \; V_x \; V_y \; \sin \omega \; \cos \omega \; dis\_h\} \tag{9}$$

Action Space. To accurately represent the agent's complete motion behavior, the actions chosen are acceleration a and steering wheel angle θ. Here $a \in [-1, 1]$. In this context, a negative value indicates deceleration, a zero value indicates constant speed, and a positive value indicates acceleration. Therefore, the action space is defined as:

$$Actions = \{\theta \; a\} \tag{10}$$

Reward Function. During the lane change process, it is crucial to consider both the change in speed and angle. A well-designed reward function can promote network convergence and enhance the success rate of lane changing. Taking into account various scenarios, the reward function is formulated as follows:

Speed Reward. The lane change process necessitates the vehicle to accelerate and surpass the vehicle ahead, thereby requiring a significant increase in lateral speed. Additionally, the agent must be provided with a longitudinal speed to facilitate the transition into a lane free of obstacles. As a result, the speed reward is defined as follows:

$$R_v = \partial \times V_x + \beta \times V_y \tag{11}$$

where $\partial = 0.1, \beta = 0.06$.

Angle Reward. When the vehicle runs straight, $\omega = 0$. At this time, $\sin \omega = 0$ and $\cos \omega = 1$. If the vehicle wants to implement lane change strategy, ω will be larger. Therefore, we can give $\sin \omega$ a larger reward and $\cos \omega$ a smaller reward. The angle reward is as follows:

$$R_\theta = \gamma \times \sin \theta + \nu \times \cos \theta \tag{12}$$

$$\theta = \begin{cases} \omega & \text{if } \theta < \frac{\pi}{2} \\ \omega - \frac{\pi}{2} & \text{else} \end{cases} \tag{13}$$

where, $\gamma = 2, \nu = 0.1$.

Distance Reward. The proximity between the agent and the obstructing vehicle is pivotal in determining the occurrence of a lane change behavior. It is desirable for the agent to execute a lane change within a relatively close yet safe distance. To quantify this, the distance reward is established as:

$$R_d = \eta \times (50 - dis\_h) \tag{14}$$

where, $\eta = -0.3$.

Collision Reward. In order to ensure safe lane changes, it is crucial to avoid collisions. To address this, we impose penalties on collisions that occur during the lane change procedure. This penalty, referred to as the collision reward, is formally defined as follows:

$$R_c = \varphi \times C_{flag} \tag{15}$$

$$C_{flag} = \begin{cases} 1 \text{ if collision} \\ 0 \text{ else} \end{cases} \tag{16}$$

where, $\varphi = 0.1$.

To sum up, the total reward function is as follows:

$$R = R_v + R_\theta + R_d + R_c \tag{17}$$

4 Results

In this study, we built the physical environment on the highway simulation platform. In the simulation environment, we return the relative distance between the agent and the obstacle car through the built-in sensor. In addition, collision detection between the agent and the obstacle vehicle has been added. We stipulated that the episode would end if the agent collided with the obstacle car, and that the episode is successful if the target car reaches the end of the road. In the end, we designed a straight two-lane map. The road length is 1000 m, the width is 3.5 m, the vehicle length is 5 m, the width is 2 m.

Table 1 shows the software and hardware environments that agents rely on during the training process.

Table 1. Software and hardware environment.

Hardware and software	Model/Version
CPU	Intel Core i5-12400f
RAM	16.0GB
Operating system	Windows Server 2019 64-bits
Python	3.8
Deep learning framework	Pytorch-1.5
Visualization tool	highway-1.15

The quality of neural network parameters will determine the convergence speed of the model. Table 2 lists some specific parameters of the improved A3C algorithm used in the training process, such as the learning rate, the maximum number of episodes and the maximum number of steps.

Table 2. Improved A3C network parameters

Parameter Name	Parameter Value	Parameter Name	Parameter Value
MAX_EPIOSDES	500	MEMORY_CAPACITY	5000
MAX_EP_STEPS	100	BATCH_SIZE	64
Actor-network learning rate	0.0001	Critic-network learning rate	0.001
Gamma	0.99	Tau	0.001

4.1 Verification of Universality

Different Speed Comparison. Different initial speeds have an impact on the success rate of automatic lane change in autonomous vehicles. In this study, we conducted a simulation experiment where we tested three different initial speeds for the target vehicle: 20 km/h (low speed), 40 km/h (medium speed), and 80 km/h (high speed). Additionally, we included five obstacle vehicles in the simulation. The experiment took place in a two-lane environment using the enhanced A3C algorithm. We present the findings of this simulation in Fig. 3.

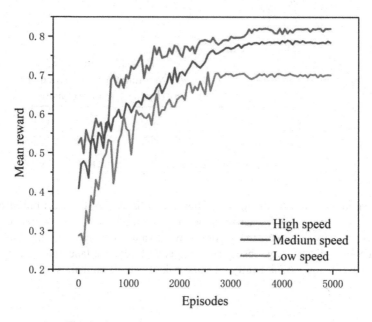

Fig. 3. Average reward value under different speed.

The simulation results demonstrate that the improved A3C algorithm is capable of converging under varying initial speeds. The average reward value is directly proportional to the initial speed, as indicated by the speed reward in our reward function. Furthermore, agents with slower initial speeds exhibit faster convergence, reflecting the algorithm's smoothness.

Different Traffic Flow Densities Comparison. The success rate of automatic lane change in autonomous vehicles can be affected by different traffic flow densities. For low traffic flow density, we set the initial speed of the target vehicle to 40 km/h and include 1 obstacle vehicle. For medium traffic flow density, the initial speed of the target vehicle is also set to 40 km/h, but there are 5 obstacle vehicles. Lastly, under high traffic flow density, the initial speed remains the same, but there are 10 obstacle vehicles. Figure 4 displays the simulation results of the improved A3C algorithm on the straight dual carriageway.

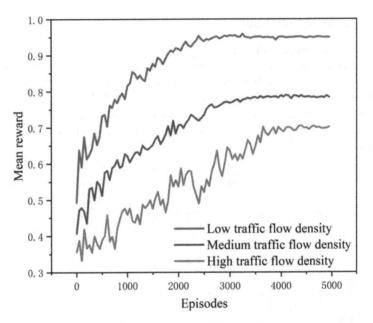

Fig. 4. Average reward value under different traffic flow density.

The simulation results demonstrate that the enhanced A3C algorithm effectively achieves lane change control across three different traffic densities. Moreover, as the traffic flow density increases, the average reward value decreases and the convergence speed becomes slower. This observation aligns with real-life lane change patterns, as frequent lane changes significantly raise the risk of vehicle collisions.

4.2 Verification of Superiority

To validate the superiority of the proposed algorithm, a realistic traffic scene was set up to simulate the environment. In this scenario, both the agent and obstacle vehicles have an initial speed of 40 km/h, the number of obstacle vehicles is 5, and the road is a two-lane lane with a length of 1000 m and a width of 3.5 m. The movement of the obstacle car is random, while its speed remains fixed. Subsequently, we employ three algorithms for conducting simulation experiments in this environment. Figure 5 illustrates the simulation results.

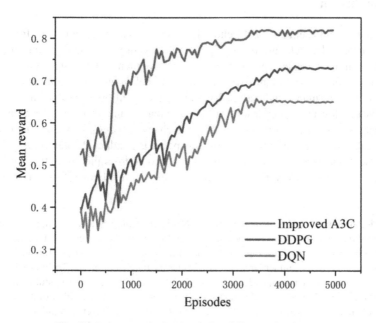

Fig. 5. Average reward value under different algorithms.

The simulation results demonstrate that the average reward value of the improved A3C algorithm exhibits smoother changes and converges faster compared to the DQN and DDPG algorithms due to the updated parameter mode. Upon algorithm convergence, the average reward value of the improved A3C algorithm significantly surpasses the other two algorithms. Therefore, based on a consideration of convergence speed and average reward, the improved A3C algorithm proves to be the optimal solution in this environment.

The trained model was tested using 100 episodes. Table 3 displays the average speed and collision rate of the agent when using different algorithms.

Based on the average speed and collision rate data presented in the table above, the improved A3C algorithm exhibits an average speed of 62.2 km/h, surpassing the other two algorithms. Moreover, it exhibits a significantly lower collision rate of 3% compared to the other two algorithms. Consequently, the improved A3C algorithm proves to be advantageous in a suburban environment.

Table 3. Performance index

Algorithm	Average velocity	Collision rate
Improved A3C	62.2 km/h	3%
DDPG	58.8 km/h	10%
DQN	55.3 km/h	18%

5 Conclusion

In this study, we present an end-to-end reinforcement learning framework for the automatic control of lane change in intelligent vehicles, utilizing the A3C algorithm. We construct a multi-threaded, parallel running environment for the algorithm, allowing for asynchronous and random exploration, while balancing the optimization strategy for multiple performance indicators. To improve the stability of the algorithm's convergence, we employ a weighted average of the dominant values. This enhancement further enhances the overall performance of the lane change process. It is important to note, however, that the verification process in this paper is conducted solely in a simulation environment and lacks real-world experiments. To address this limitation and ensure the safety of real vehicle verification, future work can involve verification on a model vehicle.

Acknowledgments. Supported in part by the National Natural Science Foundation of China under Grant (62301212), Major Science and Technology Projects of Longmen Laboratory under Grant (231100220300), the Program for Science and Technology Innovation Talents in the University of Henan Province under Grant (23HASTIT021), the Scientific and Technological Project of Henan Province under Grant (222102210056, 222102240009), China Postdoctoral Science Foundation (2023M730982), the Science and Technology Development Plan of Joint Research Program of Henan underGrant (222103810036), the Open Fund of InnerMongoliaKeyLaboratory of ElectromechanicaControl under Grant (IMMEC2022001, IMMEC2022002).

References

1. Yang, Q., Koutsopoulos, H.N.: A Microscopic traffic simulator for evaluation of dynamic traffic management systems. Transp. Res. Part C Emerg. Technol. **4**, 113–129 (1996)
2. Gipps, P.: A model for the structure of lane-changing decisions. Transp. Res. Part B Methodol. **20**, 403–414 (1986)
3. Kesting, A., Treiber, M., Helbing, D.: General lane-changing model MOBIL for car-following models. Transp. Res. Rec. **1**, 86–94 (1999)
4. Urmson, C., et al.: Autonomous driving in traffic: boss and the urban challenge. AI Mag. **30**, 17 (2009)
5. Yu, A., Palefsky-Smith, R., Bedi, R.: Deep reinforcement learning for simulated autonomous vehicle control. Course Project Reports: Winter (2016)
6. You, C., Lu, J., Filev, D., Tsiotras, P.: Highway traffic modeling and decision making for autonomous vehicle using reinforcement learning. In: IEEE Intelligent Vehicles Symposium (IV) (2018)

7. Mukadam, M., Cosgun, A., Nakhaei, A., Fujimura, K.: Tactical decision making for lane changing with deep reinforcement learning. In: 31st Conference on Neural Information Processing Systems (NIPS) (2017)

8. Zhang, Y., Sun, P., Yin, Y., Lin, L., Wang, X.: Human-like autonomous vehicle speed control by deep reinforcement learning with double q-learning. In: 2018 IEEE Intelligent Vehicles Symposium (IV) (2018)

9. Jaritz, M., Charette, R., Toromanoff, M., Perot, E., Nashashibi, F.: End-to-end race driving with deep reinforcement learning. In: 2018 IEEE International Conference on Robotics and Automation (ICRA) (2018)

10. Hoel, C., Wolff, K., Laine, L.: Automated speed and lane change decision making using deep reinforcement learning. In: The 21st International Conference on Intelligent Transportation Systems (ITSC) (2018)

11. Wang, P., Chan, C., Fortelle, A.: A reinforcement learning based approach for automated lane change maneuvers. In: The 29th Intelligent Vehicles Symposium (IV) (2018)

12. Liang, X., Wang, T., Yang, L., Xing, E.: CIRL: controllable imitative reinforcement learning for vision-based self-driving. arXiv:1807.03776 (2018)

13. Kaushik, M., Prasad, V., Krishna, K.M., Ravindran, B.: Overtaking maneuvers in simulated highway driving using deep reinforcement learning. In: The 29th IEEE Intelligent Vehicles Symposium (IV) (2018)

14. Sallab, A., Abdou, M., Perot, E., Yogani, S.: Deep reinforcement learning framework for autonomous driving. Electron. Imaging **2017**, 70–76 (2017)

Image Encryption Algorithm Based on Quantum Chaotic Mapping and Wavelet Transform

Zheng Jinyu[1,2(✉)] and Xiang Fei[1,2]

[1] Henan University of Science and Technology, Luoyang 471023, Henan, China
Zhengjinyu_1119@163.com
[2] Henan International Joint Laboratory of Cyberspace Security Applications, Luoyang 471023, Henan, China

Abstract. Aiming at the problems of low security and slow encryption speed of traditional chaotic system, this paper designs a wavelet domain image encryption algorithm which combines quantum chaotic mapping and Lorenz hyper chaotic mapping. Firstly, the SHA-256 hash algorithm is used to generate the initial key, and the quantum chaotic sequence and Lorenz hyper chaotic sequence are generated iteratively. Then, the plaintext image matrix is decomposed by discrete wavelet, and the sub-band coefficient matrix of each component after decomposition is scrambled by quantum chaotic sequence, and then it is reconstructed by discrete wavelet to complete the scrambling. Finally, Lorenz hyper chaotic sequence is used to diffuse the scrambled images, and the cipher text images after secondary encryption are obtained and analyzed for security. The simulation results show that the chaotic sequence combined with quantum chaos and used for encryption can be associated with the plaintext image through SHA-256, and the way of wavelet domain scrambling can get a better encryption effect, good performance against all kinds of attacks, and has the characteristics of high security and fast computing speed.

Keywords: Quantum Chaotic Mapping · Image Encryption · Discrete Wavelet Transform

1 Introduction

In the rapidly evolving environment of the internet, the diversification of communication methods, such as text, images, videos, and voice, has made information more varied [1]. Compared to other types of information transmission, digital images are more convenient and occupy less memory. However, they are also vulnerable to threats such as copying, unauthorized access, and tampering, which poses risks to personal privacy. Therefore, there is an urgent demand for ensuring the privacy of image transmission. Image encryption technology can effectively enhance the security of image information and provide protection for the privacy of images.

In nonlinear dynamics, chaotic systems possess unique cryptographic properties such as unpredictable motion trajectories, pseudo-randomness, ergodicity, and sensitivity to initial conditions. The connection between chaotic systems and cryptography, as well as their structural similarities, endow chaotic systems with inherent advantages in the field of image encryption [2–6]. Reference [7] proposes an image encryption algorithm based on two-dimensional Logistic and Arnold mappings, which has the advantage of a large key space. However, the algorithm shows a significant deviation between the generated information entropy and the theoretical value. In reference [8], an improved image encryption algorithm in the wavelet transform domain is introduced, which enhances robustness and key sensitivity to a certain extent. However, this algorithm lacks the ability to resist differential attacks, and the correlation between adjacent pixels is not ideal. Reference [9] proposes an image encryption algorithm, which combines chaotic encryption in the wavelet domain with compressive encryption to enhance the security of the encryption key and reducing the correlation between the plaintext and cipher text images. However, this algorithm exhibits poor randomness in the cipher text images. In reference [10], an image encryption algorithm that combines two high-dimensional hyper chaotic systems is presented, which increases the key space and significantly reduces the correlation. However, the information entropy value of this algorithm is not ideal, and it lacks strong resistance against differential attacks. In reference [11], AKHSHANI A *et al.* first propose the use of quantum chaotic mapping in the field of image encryption, which provides a new direction for image encryption. However, the lack of advanced encryption technology at that time resulted in insufficient security for image encryption. Reference [12] proposes an image encryption algorithm that combines quantum chaotic mapping and Chen hyper-chaotic mapping, which significantly reduces the correlation coefficient of the cipher text image. However, this algorithm is vulnerable to differential attack analysis. In reference [13], an image encryption algorithm combining quantum Logistic mapping and fractional Fourier transform is proposed, which enhances key sensitivity and reduces the correlation between adjacent pixels. However, this algorithm exhibits poor resistance against differential attacks.

The simulation results demonstrate that the proposed algorithm not only performs excellently in terms of information entropy, key space, and correlation, but also exhibits strong resilience against various attack methods. Moreover, it achieves faster encryption speed.

2   Theoretical Foundation

2.1   Quantum Chaotic Mapping

Chaos systems can exhibit various properties of quantum chaos when quantified using different quantization criteria [14]. The quantum logistic mapping is obtained by quantizing the classical logistic system through the recoil rotor model [15]. Due to the presence of a perturbation term at the end and its variation with initial values, quantum chaos exhibits better non-periodicity and randomness. Its expression is given by:

$$\begin{cases} x_{n+1} = \gamma(x_n - |x_n|^2) - \gamma y_n \\ y_{n+1} = -y_n e^{-2\beta} + e^{-\beta}\gamma[(2 - x_n - x_n^*)y_n - x_n z_n^* - x_n^* z_n] \\ z_{n+1} = -z_n e^{-2\beta} + e^{-\beta}\gamma[2(1 - x_n^*)z_n - 2x_n y_n - x_n] \end{cases} \tag{1}$$

In the equation, γ, β are system parameters, x_n, y_n, z_n are the state values of the system and x_n^*, y_n^*, z_n^* are their complex conjugates. Akhshani A *et al.* [17] have demonstrated that the system exhibits good chaotic properties when $\gamma = 3.99$, $\beta \geq 6$. Therefore, we set $\gamma = 3.99$, $\beta = 6$ in this paper, and the initial parameters x_n, y_n, z_n, x_n^*, y_n^*, z_n^* are real numbers. The ranges of these parameters are as follows: $0 \leq x_n \leq 1$, $0 \leq y_n \leq 0.1$, $0 \leq z_n \leq 0.2$.

2.2 Lorenz Hyper Chaos

The Lorenz hyper chaotic system is an evolution of the classical Lorenz chaotic system, and its defining equation is given by:

$$\begin{cases} \dot{x} = a(y - x) + w \\ \dot{y} = cx - y - xz \\ \dot{z} = xy - bz \\ \dot{w} = -yz + rw \end{cases} \tag{2}$$

In the equation, a, b, c, r are system parameters and x_n, y_n, z_n are the state values of the system. The system is in a hyper chaotic state when $a = 10$, $b = \frac{8}{3}$, $c = 28$, $-1.52 \leq \gamma \leq -0.06$ (we set $\gamma = -1$). In this paper, the fourth-order Runge-Kutta method is used to discretize the Lorenz hyper chaotic system. The definition of the Runge-Kutta discretization is as follows:

$$\begin{cases} y_{i+1} = y_i + \dfrac{h}{6}(k_1 + 2k_2 + 2k_3 + k_4) \\ k_1 = f(x_i, y_i) \\ k_2 = f(x_i + \dfrac{h}{2}, y_i + \dfrac{h}{2}k_1) \\ k_3 = f(x_i + h, y_i + hk_3) \end{cases} \tag{3}$$

2.3 Discrete Wavelet Transform

The Discrete Wavelet Transform (DWT) is a localized analysis method for time or spatial frequency [16]. When given a scaling function $\varphi(x)$ and wavelet function $\psi(x)$, it is possible to combine them to form a two-dimensional scaling function and three two-dimensional wavelet functions.

$$\begin{cases} \varphi(x, y) = \varphi(x)\varphi(y) \\ \psi^H(x, y) = \psi(x)\varphi(y) \\ \psi^Y(x, y) = \varphi(x)\psi(y) \\ \psi^D(x, y) = \psi(x)\psi(y) \end{cases} \tag{4}$$

The approximate coefficients and detail coefficients obtained after performing a 2D Discrete Wavelet Transform (2-DDWT) on an image matrix are as follows. The approximate coefficients correspond to the low-frequency subband coefficients, while the detail coefficients correspond to the high-frequency subband coefficients.

$$W_\varphi(0, m, n) = \frac{1}{\sqrt{MN}} \sum_{x=0}^{M-1} \sum_{y=0}^{N-1} f(x, y) \varphi_{0,m,n}(x, y) \tag{5}$$

$$W_\psi^i(j, m, n) = \frac{1}{\sqrt{MN}} \sum_{x=0}^{M-1} \sum_{y=0}^{N-1} f(x, y) \psi_{j,m,n}^i(x, y) \tag{6}$$

In the equation, $i = \{H, V, D\}$. The decomposed components obtained after wavelet transformation can be reconstructed into a linear combination of four functions (2-DIDWT).

$$f(x, y) = \frac{1}{\sqrt{MN}} \sum_m \sum_n W_\varphi(0, m, n) \varphi_{0,m,n}(x, y)$$

$$+ \frac{1}{\sqrt{MN}} \sum_{j=0}^{\infty} \left\{ \begin{array}{l} \sum_m \sum_n W_\psi^H(j, m, n) \psi_{j,m,n}^H(x, y) \\ + \sum_m \sum_n W_\psi^V(j, m, n) \psi_{j,m,n}^V(x, y) \\ + \sum_m \sum_n W_\psi^D(j, m, n) \psi_{j,m,n}^D(x, y) \end{array} \right\} \tag{7}$$

In the equation, $\varphi_{j,m,n}(x, y)$ and $\psi_{j,m,n}^i(x, y)$ are the scaling functions and wavelet functions at different scales and positions, which are defined as:

$$\begin{cases} \varphi_{0,m,n}(x, y) = 2^{\frac{j}{2}} \varphi(2^j x - m, 2^j - n) \\ \psi_{j,m,n}^i(x, y) = 2^{\frac{j}{2}} \psi^i(2^j x - m, 2^j - n) \end{cases} \tag{8}$$

3 Encryption Algorithm

This algorithm proposes a wavelet domain image encryption algorithm that combines quantum chaotic systems and Lorenz hyper chaotic systems. The plaintext image is scrambled using the wavelet domain permutation algorithm and the diffusion algorithm based on modular addition and using chaotic sequences initialized by a key generator. This process produces the cipher text image. The overall encryption algorithm is illustrated in Fig. 1.

3.1 Initialization of the Chaotic System

The initialization of the chaotic system is done using SHA-256 as the key generator. The plaintext image is passed through SHA-256 to generate a 64-bit character hash sequence,

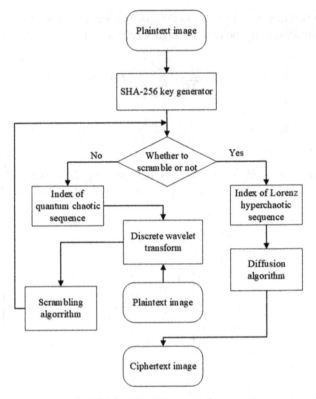

Fig. 1. Algorithm Flowchart

which serves as the chaotic key K. Then, the sequence is divided into 8 segments, each consisting of 8 bits, resulting in 8 segment keys k_i namely:

$$K = k_1, k_2, ..., k_8 \tag{9}$$

In the initialization of the quantum chaotic system, the key stream is processed according to the following formulas to obtain the initial values associated with the plaintext:

$$\begin{cases} x_0 = k_2 \oplus k_3 \times \sum_{j=1}^{9} \frac{k_j \times 2^{j-1}}{2^{27}} \\ y_0 = k_5 \oplus k_6 \times \sum_{j=1}^{9} \frac{k_j \times 2^{j-1}}{2^{27} \times 10} \\ z_0 = k_1 \oplus k_8 \times \sum_{j=1}^{9} \frac{k_j \times 2^{j-1}}{2^{27} \times 5} \\ h = k_4 \oplus k_7 \end{cases} \tag{10}$$

In the equation, x_0, y_0, z_0 is the initial value of the quantum chaotic mapping, and the initial values of the quantum chaotic system must satisfy $0 \leq x_n \leq 1, 0 \leq y_n \leq 0.1$, $0 \leq z_n \leq 0.2$.

Taking x_0 as an example, from the equation $\sum_{j=1}^{9} \frac{k_j \times 2^{j-1}}{2^{27}} < \sum_{j=1}^{9} \frac{2^9 \times 2^{j-1}}{2^{27}} < \frac{1}{2^9}$, we can deduce that $0 \leq x_n \leq 1$, thus y_0, z_0 meeting the requirements of the quantum chaotic system. h is the discarded interference term in the key stream of the quantum chaotic system.

In the Lorenz hyper chaotic system, the key stream is processed according to the following formulas to obtain the initial values associated with the plaintext:

$$
\begin{cases}
x_0 = k_2 \oplus k_3 \times \sum_{j=1}^{9} \frac{k_j \times 2^{j-1}}{2^{24}} \\
y_0 = k_5 \oplus k_6 \times \sum_{j=1}^{9} \frac{k_j \times 2^{j-1}}{2^{24}} \\
z_0 = k_1 \oplus k_8 \times \sum_{j=1}^{9} \frac{k_j \times 2^{j-1}}{2^{24}} \\
w_0 = k_4 \oplus k_7 \times \sum_{j=1}^{9} \frac{k_j \times 2^{j-1}}{2^{24}}
\end{cases}
\tag{11}
$$

In the equation, x_0, y_0, z_0, w_0 is the initial value of the Lorenz hyper chaotic system. Simulation results confirm that when the above initialization formulas are used, the Lorenz hyper chaotic system exhibits improving randomness.

3.2 Encryption Process

1. Read the target image to be encrypted and use the dwt2 function in MATLAB to perform a two-dimensional discrete single-scale wavelet transform on the target image. Afterwards, the image is decomposed into four frequency components containing the corresponding subbands of wavelet coefficients.
2. The matrices of the low-frequency subband coefficients (LL) and high-frequency subband coefficients (HL, LH, HH) are unfolded into one-dimensional row vectors and perform non-repetitive scrambling of the vector positions. Specifically, preserve only one occurrence of repeated index values in the initialized quantum chaotic sequence S1 and append missing elements in ascending order at the end of S1. Then, the positions of each element in the one-dimensional vectors are performed non-repetitive scrambling. After scrambling, the one-dimensional vectors are restored to two-dimensional matrices.
3. The four newly generated two-dimensional frequency subband coefficient matrices after scrambling are performed wavelet reconstruction using the idwt function, which is the two-dimensional inverse wavelet transform with a single scale. As a result, the cipher text image after the first round of scrambling encryption is obtained.
4. Use the initialized Lorenz hyper chaotic sequence S2 to perform diffusion algorithm based on modular addition on the scrambled encrypted image. Specifically, divide the pseudo-random sequence S2 into S21 and S22, ranging from 1 to M * N and from M * N + 1 to 2 * M * N. Respectively, S21 is used for forward diffusion (i from 1 to M * N) and S22 is used for reverse diffusion (i from M*N to 1). The specific

expressions are as follows:

$$\begin{cases} C_i = (C_{i-1} + S_i + P_i) \bmod 256 \\ P_i = (2 \times 256 + C_i - C_{i-1} - S_i) \bmod 256 \end{cases} \quad (12)$$

$$\begin{cases} C_i = (C_{i+1} + S_i + P_i) \bmod 256 \\ P_i = (2 \times 256 + C_i - C_{i+1} - S_i) \bmod 256 \end{cases} \quad (13)$$

Where C, P and S represent the cipher text image, the scrambled cipher text image and the pseudo-random vector, respectively. The final encrypted image is obtained by performing two rounds of iterative diffusion on the scrambled cipher text image.

4 Simulation Results and Analysis

The simulation testing of the encryption algorithm in this paper is conducted on a 64-bit Windows10 system using the MATLAB 2016b platform. Three grayscale images of size 512×512 are used as the objects for simulation, and the results of the simulation are analyzed.

4.1 Simulation Results

The initial values of the quantum chaotic mapping after algorithm iterations for the Lena image are: $x_0 = 0.0209$, $y_0 = 0.0029$, $z_0 = 0.0234$; for the Baboon image: $x_0 = 0.1116$, $y_0 = 0.0527$, $z_0 = 0.1092$; and for the Peppers image: $x_0 = 0.0613$, $y_0 = 0.0063$, $z_0 = 0.0014$. The simulation results of Lena, Baboon and Peppers are shown in Fig. 2.

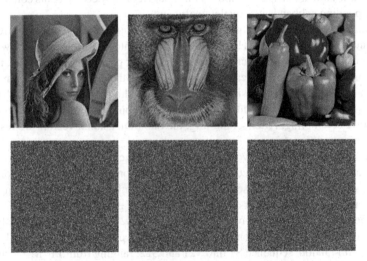

Fig. 2. Simulation Results.

4.2 Histogram Analysis

A histogram reflects the distribution of pixel values in an image. The more uniform the histogram distribution of the cipher text image compared to the plaintext image, the higher the security level of the algorithm and the better its resistance to statistical attack analysis. The histograms of the Lena image before and after encryption using this algorithm are shown in Fig. 3.

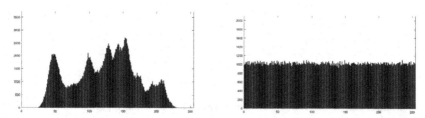

Fig. 3. Comparison of Histograms of Lena before and after Encryption.

The simulation results demonstrate that the cipher text image generated by this algorithm exhibits a uniform distribution in its histogram, which indicates its ability to effectively resist statistical attack analysis.

4.3 Correlation Analysis of Adjacent Pixels

Pixel correlation indicates the level of correlation between adjacent pixels in an image. The smaller the correlation between neighboring pixel values in the cipher text image, the better its performance in resisting statistical information attacks. The formula for calculating correlation is as follows:

$$E = \frac{1}{N} \sum_{i=1}^{N} x_i \tag{14}$$

$$D(x) = \frac{1}{N} \sum_{i=1}^{N} (x_i - E(x))^2 \tag{15}$$

$$Cov(x, y) = \frac{1}{N} \sum_{i=1}^{N} (x_i - E(x))(y_i - E(y)) \tag{16}$$

$$r_{xy} = \frac{Cov(x, y)}{\sqrt{D(x)}\sqrt{D(y)}} \tag{17}$$

In the equation, x_i and y_i represent the values of adjacent pixels and r_{xy} represents the correlation between adjacent pixels. The pixel correlations in different directions for the Lena image in this paper are shown in Fig. 4.

The simulation results show that the correlation coefficients of adjacent pixel values in the plaintext image are close to 1 in the row, column, and diagonal directions, which

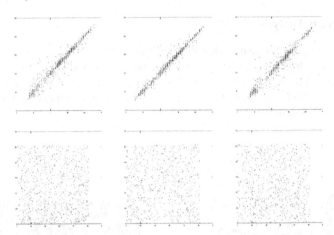

Fig. 4. Comparison of Correlations of Lena between Plaintext and Cipher text in row, column, and diagonal.

indicates a high degree of correlation between adjacent pixels. On the other hand, the correlation coefficients of adjacent pixel values in the cipher text image are close to 0 in all three directions, which indicates that this algorithm effectively reduces the correlation between adjacent pixels in the image resulting in a good encryption effect.

4.4 Differential Attack Analysis

Differential attack analysis is an important method for measuring the extent to which small changes in plaintext images affect the corresponding changes in cipher text images. The performance indicators commonly used to evaluate the resistance of an algorithm to differential attacks are the Number of Pixel Changes Rate (NPCR) and the Unified Average Changing Intensity (UACI). The formulas for calculating NPCR and UACI are as follows:

$$D(i,j) = \begin{cases} D(i,j) = 0, C(i,j) = C'(i,j) \\ D(i,j) = 1, C(i,j) = C'(i,j) \end{cases} \tag{18}$$

$$NPCR = \frac{\sum_{i,j} D(i,j)}{N \times N} \times 100\% \tag{19}$$

$$UACI = \frac{\left[\sum_{i,j} \frac{|C(i,j) - C'(i,j)|}{255}\right] \times 100\%}{N \times N} \tag{20}$$

$N \times N$ represents the size of the encrypted image and $C(i,j)$, $C'(i,j)$ represent the pixel values at coordinates (i,j) in the cipher text image and the cipher text image obtained by changing 1 bit in the corresponding pixel of the plaintext image, respectively. Under ideal conditions, the NPCR is 99.6093% and the UACI is 33.4635%. The parameters of the target encrypted image and the comparison results with Lena image from other literature are shown in Table 1.

Table 1. Comparison of Pixel Change Rate and Unified Average Change Intensity

	Lena	[12]	[18]	[20]	Baboon	Peppers
NPCR/%	99.6094	99.61	99.57	99.65	99.6059	99.6109
UACI/%	33.4819	33.13	33.42	33.49	33.4939	33.4393

Now we set:

$$\begin{cases} \eta = |\eta' - \eta_0| \\ \Gamma = |\Gamma' - \Gamma_0| \end{cases} \tag{21}$$

In the equation, η' and η_0 represent the actual value of NPCR and the theoretical value of NPCR, respectively. Γ' and Γ_0 represent the actual value of UACI, the theoretical value of UACI, respectively. The relative differences in cipher text parameters are shown in Table 2.

Table 2. Comparison of relative differences in NPCR and UACI.

	Lena	[12]	[18]	[20]	Baboon	Peppers
NPCR/%	0.0001	0.0007	0.0393	0.0407	0.0034	0.0016
UACI/%	0.0184	0.3335	0.0435	0.0265	0.0304	0.0242

The data comparison indicates that this algorithm produces cipher text images with pixel change rate and uniform average change intensity closer to the theoretical values when changing the plaintext image by 1 bit, compared to similar algorithms. This demonstrates that the algorithm has strong key sensitivity and better performance in resisting differential attacks.

4.5 Information Entropy Analysis

Information entropy is one of the indicators used to measure the randomness of a signal. The closer the information entropy value is to the theoretical value, the higher the security of the algorithm. In a grayscale image with 256 levels of gray, according to the calculation formula of information entropy, its theoretical value is $H_0 = 8$. The specific calculation formula is:

$$H(m) = -\sum_{i=0}^{M} p(m_i) \log_2 p(m_i) \tag{22}$$

$$H = \frac{H(m) - H_0}{H_0} \tag{23}$$

In the equation, $H(m)$ represents the information entropy, M is the grayscale level of 256 and $p(m_i)$ is the probability of pixel occurrence. H_0 and H is the theoretical value and the relative error of information entropy, respectively. The information entropy of the proposed encrypted image Lena is 7.9994, Baboon is 7.9993, and Peppers is 7.9992. The relative error of information entropy for Lena image and the comparison with other references are shown in Table 3.

Table 3. Comparison of information entropy relative error

	ours	[18]	[19]	[20]
Lena	0.0006	0.0024	/	0.0027
Baboon	0.0007	/	0.0974	/
Peppers	0.0008	/	0.0973	/

The data comparison shows that this algorithm has higher information entropy values compared to similar algorithms and is closer to the theoretical value. Therefore, this algorithm can effectively resist information entropy attacks and has higher security.

4.6 Key Space Analysis

Key space analysis is conducted to prevent an attacker from performing a brute-force attack by exhaustively trying all possible keys. The larger the key space, the higher the time cost for the attacker. A secure encryption algorithm should ensure a key space of at least 2^{128} to resist exhaustive key search attacks.

In this paper, SHA-256 is used as the key generator, which theoretically provides a key space of $S_1 = 2^{256}$. The sensitivity of the initial value and parameter $x_0, y_0, z_0, \beta, \gamma$ of the quantum chaotic mapping is 10^{-16}. The key space potentially offered by the theory of quantum chaotic mappings is $S_2 = 10^{16} \times 10^{15} \times 10^{15} \times 4 \times 10^{16} \times 6 \times 10^{16} \approx 2 \times 10^{78}$. The sensitivity of the initial values and parameter $x_0, y_0, z_0, a, b, c, r$ in the Lorenz hyper chaotic system is 10^{-16}, then the key space potentially offered by the Lorenz hyper chaos is $S_3 = (10^{16})^8 = 10^{128}$. Therefore, the theoretical key space provided by the image encryption algorithm proposed in this paper is $S = S_1 \times S_2 \times S_3 = 2 \times 10^{462} \gg 2^{128}$. The key space of the image to be encrypted in this study is compared with the encryption time of similar algorithms, as shown in Table 4.

Table 4. Key Space Comparison

	ours	[12]	[18]	[19]	[20]
Key space	2×10^{462}	2^{527}	2^{172}	2^{356}	10^{84}

As can be seen from the table, the paper algorithm can provide larger key space and higher security against the exhaustion key attack. This proves that the algorithm can effectively withstand brute-force key attacks.

4.7 Encryption Speed Analysis

The computation time of the image encryption algorithm is primarily consumed by the iterative multiplication operations during the encryption process. In this algorithm, $\Theta(\frac{N}{2} \times \frac{N}{2} \times 4)$ iteration is performed on the image after discrete wavelet transform in the scrambling phase, and $\Theta(2 \times N \times N)$ iteration is performed on the scrambled cipher text image in the diffusion phase. Therefore, the encryption algorithm involves a total of $\Theta(3 \times N \times N)$ rounds of multiplication operations. The encryption time of the image to be encrypted in this study is compared with the encryption time of similar algorithms, as shown in Table 5.

Table 5. Encryption Speed Comparison

	Lena	[19]	[20]	Baboon	Peppers
Speed/s	0.0269	0.0995	4.0340	0.0205	0.0287

The data comparison shows that this algorithm has a faster encryption speed when encrypting 512*512 grayscale images compared to similar encryption algorithms.

5 Conclusions

This paper presents a wavelet domain image encryption algorithm based on quantum Logistic mapping and Lorenz hyper-chaotic system. The algorithm takes full advantage of the non-periodicity and strong randomness of quantum chaotic mapping, and addresses the limitations of traditional encryption algorithms, such as small key space and low security. It proposes a method that utilizes SHA-256 as a generator to generate initial keys, iteratively generates quantum chaotic sequences and Lorenz hyper-chaotic sequences, and encrypts the image in the wavelet domain.

The proposed algorithm overcomes the limitations of classical encryption methods in terms of limited parameter variability and poor sensitivity in spatial domain encryption. The presence of perturbations in the quantum chaotic system makes its nonlinear dynamical characteristics more complex, resulting in better randomness of the generated chaotic sequences. Encrypting the image in the transform domain further enhances the security of the encryption algorithm.

Simulation results demonstrate that the proposed algorithm performs well in various metrics. It exhibits the capability to resist statistical attacks, differential attacks, brute-force attacks, and other attack methods, while maintaining excellent encryption speed.

References

1. Yang, N.: Research on improvement of digital image encryption algorithm based on chaotic mapping. Sci. Technol. Innov. Appl. **25**, 9+12 (2017)
2. Ghosh, D., Singh, J.: Spectrum-based multi-fault localization using chaotic genetic algorithm. Inf. Softw. Technol. **133**, 106512.1–106512.16 (2021)

3. Ahmad, L.: A Lyapunov-based direct adaptive controller for the suppression and synchronization of a perturbed nuclear spin generator chaotic system. Appl. Math. Comput. **395**, 125858 (2021)
4. Paknejad, P., Khorsand, R., Ramezanpour, M.: Chaotic improved PICEA-g-based multiobjective optimization for workflow scheduling in cloud environment. Fut. Gener. Syst. **117**, 12–28 (2021)
5. Conejero, J.A., Martínez-Giménez, F., Peris, A., Rodenas, F.: Sets of periods for chaotic linear operators. Revista de la Real Academia de Ciencias Exactas, Físicas y Naturales. Serie A. Matemáticas **115**, 63 (2021). https://doi.org/10.1007/s13398-020-00996-z
6. Zheng, J., Hanping, Hu.: A symmetric image encryption scheme based on hybrid analogdigital chaotic system and parameter selection mechanism. Multimedia Tools Appl. **80**(14), 20883–20905 (2021). https://doi.org/10.1007/s11042-021-10751-0
7. Hu, C., Chen, X., Chen, X.: Multi-chaotic image encryption algorithm based on improved generalized Arnold mapping. Packag. Eng. **38**(3), 144–149 (2017)
8. Bao, L., Liu, W.: Improved image encryption algorithm based on chaotic encryption in wavelet transform domain and circular shift. J. Comput. Appl. Res. **33**(10), 3074–3077, 3108 (2016)
9. Shen, C., Du, J.: An image encryption algorithm based on hybrid super chaotic system. Comput. Knowl. Technol. **14**(20), 186–189 (2018)
10. Al-Maadeed, S., Al-Ali, A., Abdalla, T.: A new chaos-based image-encryption and compression algorithm. J. Electr. Comput. Eng. **2012**(1), 1–11 (2012)
11. Akhshani, A., Akhavan, A., Lim, S.-C., Hassan, Z.: An image encryption scheme based on quantum logistic map. Commun. Nonlinear Sci. Numer. Simul. **17**(12), 4653–4661 (2012)
12. Zhang, X., Zhang, J.: Image encryption algorithm based on quantum chaotic mapping and chen hyper chaotic mapping. J. Chin. Acad. Electron. Inf. Technol. **16**(6), 582–586 (2021)
13. Xie, G., Deng, H.: Image encryption algorithm based on quantum chaos and fractional Fourier transform. Comput. Eng. Appl. **54**(17), 214–220 (2018)
14. Berry, M.V., Balazs, N.L., Tabor, M., et al.: Quantum maps. Ann. Phys. **122**(1), 26–63 (1979)
15. Goggin, M.E., Sundaram, B., Milonni, P.W.: Quantum logistic map. Phys. Rev. A **41**(10), 5705 (1990)
16. Zhang, J., Wang, W.: Fourier implementation method of wavelet transform. Sci. Technol. Vis. **25**, 164 (2013)
17. Akhshani, A., Akhavan, A., Mobaraki, A., et al.: Pseudo random number generator based on quantum chaotic map. Commun. Nonlinear Sci. Numer. Simul. **19**(1), 101–111 (2014)
18. Zhao, G., Li, J., Ma, Y., et al.: Anti-degradation chaotic image encryption algorithm based on wavelet transform. Comput. Appl. Softw. **37**(4), 290–296 (2020)
19. Shen, Z., Wang, W., Rong, X., et al.: Multi-image encryption algorithm based on integer wavelet transform and 2D chaotic system. Comput. Eng. Des. **43**(3), 624–631 (2022)
20. Xi, X., Xie, S., Zhang, J.: Image encryption algorithm based on multiple chaotic systems. Sens. Microsyst. **41**(9), 140–143, 155 (2022)

Physics-Informed Neural Network Surrogate Modeling Approach of Active/Passive Flow Control for Drag Reduction

Longyin Jiao, Dongkai Zhang$^{(\boxtimes)}$, Juntao Shang, and Gefei Yang

Henan University of Science and Technology, 263, Kaiyuan Avenue, Luoyang 471023, China
fengmituzi@163.com

Abstract. This paper presents a novel surrogate modeling method with physics constraints that is specifically designed for optimal design in flow control systems. The governing partial differential equations describing these flows are presented, considering a simplified fluid confined within a channel bounded by two parallel walls. Boundary conditions and flow control are introduced through geometric grooves and transpiration effects. The discretization of the governing equations and boundary conditions is also discussed. For numerical simulations, a Galerkin-based PDE solver is employed, utilizing spectral methods. The separation of Fourier components results in a system of ordinary differential equations for the modal functions. The effectiveness of transpiration in inducing flow control is evaluated by comparing the computed values with the reference pressure gradient required to drive the flow in the channel without transpiration. Data for the physics-informed neural network optimization is sampled using the Latin hypercube sampling method. The dataset, generated by direct numerical simulation, is divided into training and validation datasets. A deep neural network, consisting of multiple hidden layers, is utilized for constructing the surrogate model. The optimization process involves the use of Genetic Algorithms to search for acceptable local optimal values. The integration of GAs with the surrogate model involves several steps. Numerical experiments are conducted to validate the effectiveness of the PINN-based surrogate model approach. The results demonstrate an average acceptable error when comparing the test dataset with the predictions of the PINN surrogate model. Furthermore, the effectiveness of the proposed approach is demonstrated through a comparison between the results obtained from direct numerical simulation (DNS) and the predictions generated by the surrogate model. This comparative analysis serves to validate the accuracy and reliability of the surrogate model in capturing the key characteristics and behaviors of the flow control system.

Keywords: Surrogate model · Physical Constrain · Neural Network; Flow Control · Optimization

© The Author(s), under exclusive license to Springer Nature Singapore Pte Ltd. 2024
F. Sun et al. (Eds.): ICCSIP 2023, CCIS 1918, pp. 243–255, 2024.
https://doi.org/10.1007/978-981-99-8018-5_18

1 Introduction

The design and optimization of aerospace vehicles require accurate and efficient aerodynamic analysis. Traditional methods involve conducting computational fluid dynamics (CFD) simulations, which are computationally expensive and time-consuming [1, 2]. To overcome these challenges, surrogate models, also known as response surface models, approximation models, or metamodels, have gained attention due to their ability to approximate complex relationships and provide rapid predictions [3]. These mathematical models are employed as efficient substitutes for complex and computationally intensive numerical analyses in various fields, including analysis, optimization, and design processes. By utilizing surrogate models, researchers can greatly enhance the efficiency of optimization and design tasks while reducing the computational complexity [4] associated with the original numerical models. Additionally, surrogate models effectively filter out numerical noise and facilitate parallel optimization designs.

The development of surrogate model methods can be traced back to the utilization of polynomial response surfaces in structural optimization design during the 1970s [5]. Since the emergence of multidisciplinary design optimization (MDO) in the 1980s, surrogate model methods have emerged as a crucial research branch within the MDO field. Over time, these methods have been applied to diverse domains, such as aerodynamic optimization design in the late 20th century. Notably, various surrogate model techniques have been developed, including response surface models (RSM) [6], Kriging models [7], radial basis functions (RBFs) [8], support vector regression (SVR) [9],artificial neural networks (ANN) [10], multivariate interpolation [13] and regression (MIR) [11, 12], and polynomial chaos expansions (PCE) [14, 15]. These surrogate models offer promising alternatives for accurately approximating complex numerical analyses while significantly improving computational efficiency [16].

Artificial neural network surrogate models have gained significant popularity in various fields due to their ability to approximate complex functions and systems. These models offer a flexible and data-driven approach to surrogate modeling, enabling efficient and accurate predictions.

One of the key strengths of ANN surrogate models is their capability to capture nonlinear relationships and high-dimensional interactions. ANNs can learn from large and diverse datasets, allowing them to model complex systems with multiple input variables and intricate relationships. This flexibility makes ANN surrogate models well-suited for applications in engineering, finance, optimization, and many other domains. The architecture of ANNs, including the number of layers and nodes, can be customized to suit the specific requirements of the problem, further enhancing their adaptability.

However, ANN surrogate models also come with some considerations. They require a sufficient amount of high-quality training data to ensure accurate predictions. Overfitting, where the model performs well on the training data but poorly on unseen data, is a potential challenge that needs to be addressed through appropriate regularization techniques and validation procedures.

Traditional machine learning approaches, such as ANN excel at learning patterns and making predictions from data. However, they often lack the ability to explicitly enforce physical laws and constraints, limiting their effectiveness in systems governed by well-defined equations. Physics Informed Neural Networks (PINNs) address this limitation by seamlessly integrating physical equations or constraints into the learning process, enabling the model to respect fundamental laws and utilize prior knowledge.

PINNs are a class of machine learning models that integrate physics-based knowledge and data-driven learning. They aim to leverage the power of neural networks to capture complex relationships while respecting the underlying physical laws governing a system. By incorporating domain-specific information and constraints, PINNs offer a promising approach for predictive modeling in scientific and engineering domains.

Furthermore, the surrogate modelling approaches have been adopted in many studied in flow control. Some researchers provide valuable insights into the development and application of a surrogate model for predicting aerodynamic responses in aircraft conceptual design. However, further elaboration on the data processing methodologies and a more robust evaluation of the surrogate model's performance would enhance the scientific rigor and practical applicability of the study. A physics-informed neural network-based surrogate framework is proposed by Haghighat, E [17] to predict moisture concentration and shrinkage during the drying process of a plant cell. The PINN model achieves high accuracy in predicting these variables, showcasing the potential of PINNs as a valuable tool in understanding and modeling complex drying mechanisms.

Some research focus on surrogate modeling [18] for fluid flows using physics-constrained deep learning without simulation data. By incorporating physics-based knowledge into the deep learning framework, the authors demonstrate accurate predictions of flow behavior even with limited or no simulation data. This highlights the potential of physics-constrained deep learning in capturing the underlying dynamics of fluid flows. Introduces a physics-informed deep learning framework for inversion and surrogate modeling in solid mechanics. By incorporating momentum balance [20], constitutive relations, and multi-network models, the authors achieve improved accuracy and convergence in predicting field variables. This framework shows promise in solid mechanics applications and offers potential advancements in component and system design.

Sun [19], etc. presents physics-aware deep neural networks for surrogate modeling of turbulent natural convection. The authors combine deep neural networks with physics-based constraints to accurately capture the underlying physics of turbulent flows. This approach demonstrates improved accuracy and predictive capabilities compared to traditional surrogate models, suggesting its usefulness in engineering simulations and optimization.

Collectively, some papers demonstrate the effectiveness and potential of PINNs and physics-constrained deep learning in various fields, including drying processes, fluid flows, solid mechanics, and thermos-fluid systems modeling. The integration of physics-based knowledge into the deep learning frameworks improves accuracy, convergence, and predictive capabilities, offering valuable insights and advancements in these domains.

The paper is organized into three main chapters. Section 2 focuses on modeling and discretization, covering the governing partial differential equations, boundary conditions, flow control, and the discretization process. Section 3 discusses the numerical method used for solving the equations, such as the Galerkin-based PDE solver, and the acquisition or generation of datasets. Finally, Sect. 4 introduces the physics informed neural network surrogate modeling approach, including the design of the physics constrained artificial neural network, the optimization process, and the experiments conducted to validate the methodology.

2 Modeling and Discretization

2.1 Governing Partial Differential Equations

This section focuses on presenting the governing partial differential equations (PDEs) that describe the steady channel flows. The simplified fluid is confined in a channel bounded by two parallel walls extending to $\pm\infty$ in the x-direction and placed a distance 2h apart as shown in Fig. 1. The flow is driven in the positive x-direction by a pressure gradient. The fluid is incompressible and Newtonian with kinematic viscosity v, dynamic viscosity μ and density ρ. The governing equations are defined as the following PDEs:

$$\begin{cases} \nabla \cdot \boldsymbol{u} = 0 \\ (\boldsymbol{u} \cdot \nabla)\boldsymbol{u} + \dfrac{1}{\rho}\nabla p - \upsilon\nabla^2\boldsymbol{u} = 0 \end{cases} \tag{1}$$

where ∇^2 denotes the Laplace operator. The velocity and pressure fields and the flow rate have the form:

$$\begin{cases} \boldsymbol{u}(x, y) = [\text{Re}(1 - y^2) + u_{x1}(x, y), u_y(x, y)] \\ p(x, y) = -2x/\text{Re} + const \end{cases} \tag{2}$$

where $\boldsymbol{u}$ denotes the velocity vector scaled with the maximum of the x-velocity U_{max}, p stands for the pressure scaled with ρU_{max}^2, h has been used as the length scale and $Re = U_{max}h/v$ stands for the Reynolds number.

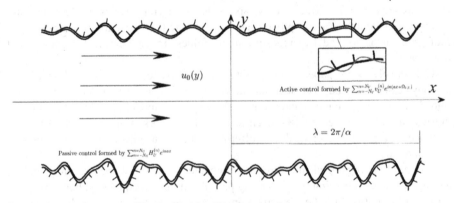

Fig. 1. Sketch of the flow configuration.

2.2 Boundary Conditions and Flow Control

The flow control is introduced by both geometric groove and transpiration effects. The suction/blowing distributed on the periodic grooved wall combined active flow control and passive flow control, which can be described by Fourier expansion. Equip the walls with periodic grooves with the conduit geometry described by Fourier expansions of the form:

$$
\begin{cases}
y_L(x) = -1 + B_L \sum_{n=-N_G}^{n=+N_G} \tilde{H}_L^{(n)} e^{in\alpha x} \\
y_U(x) = 1 + B_U \sum_{n=-N_G}^{n=+N_G} \tilde{H}_U^{(n)} e^{in(\alpha x + \Omega_G)}
\end{cases}
\tag{3}
$$

where the subscripts L and U refer to the lower and upper walls, respectively, $\tilde{H}_L^{(n)}$ and $\tilde{H}_U^{(n)}$ are the coefficients of the Fourier expansions describing shape of corrugations at the lower and upper walls, respectively, N_G is the number of Fourier modes required to describe geometry, Ω_G stands for the phase shift between both corrugation systems, α and λ denote their wave number and wavelength, respectively, and stars denote dimensional quantities. Where B_L and B_U provide measures of the heights of the corrugations while the sums describe their shapes. The expansion coefficients satisfy the reality conditions, i.e.

Equip both walls with the x-periodic transpirations of the form:

$$
\begin{cases}
v_{N,L}(x) = \text{Re}_L \sum_{n=-N_V, n\neq 0}^{n=+N_V} v_L^{(n)} e^{in(\alpha x + \Omega_{V,L})} \\
v_{N,U}(x) = \text{Re}_U \sum_{n=-N_V, n\neq 0}^{n=+N_V} v_U^{(n)} e^{in(\alpha x + \Omega_{V,U})}
\end{cases}
\tag{4}
$$

where $v_{L,N}(x)$ and $v_{U,N}(x)$ are the wall-normal velocities at the lower and upper walls, respectively, $Re_L = V_L h / v$ and $Re_U = V_U h / v$ are the lower and upper transpiration Reynolds numbers, respectively, V_L and V_U are the differences between the maximum and minimum of $v_{N,L}$ and $v_{N,U}$, respectively.

2.3 Discretization of Governing Equations and B.C.

The stream function $\psi(x, y)$ is introduced with the fixed flow rate constraint. Then $u_1 = \partial \psi / \partial y$, $v_1 = -\partial \psi / \partial x$, and eliminate pressure bringing the governing equations to the following form:

$$
\begin{aligned}
&\nabla^4 \psi - \text{Re} \cdot u_0 \frac{\partial}{\partial x}(\nabla^2 \psi) + \text{Re} \frac{\partial^2 u_0}{\partial y^2} \frac{\partial \psi}{\partial x} \\
&= \frac{\partial}{\partial y}\left(\frac{\partial \langle u_1 u_1 \rangle}{\partial x} + \frac{\partial \langle u_1 v_1 \rangle}{\partial y}\right) - \frac{\partial}{\partial x}\left(\frac{\partial \langle u_1 v_1 \rangle}{\partial x} + \frac{\partial \langle v_1 v_1 \rangle}{\partial y}\right)
\end{aligned}
\tag{5}
$$

∇^4 denotes the biharmonic operator and $\langle .. \rangle$ denotes products. The solution is assumed to be in the form of Fourier expansions, i.e.

$$
\begin{cases}
\psi(x, y) = \sum_{n=-\infty}^{n=+\infty} \varphi^{(n)}(y) e^{in\alpha x} \\
u_1(x, y) = \sum_{n=-\infty}^{n=+\infty} u_1^{(n)}(y) e^{in\alpha x} \\
v_1(x, y) = \sum_{n=-\infty}^{n=+\infty} v_1^{(n)}(y) e^{in\alpha x} \\
p_1(x, y) = Ax + \sum_{n=-\infty}^{n=+\infty} p_1^{(n)}(y) e^{in\alpha x}
\end{cases}
\tag{6}
$$

3   Numerical Method and Datasets

3.1   Galerkin-Based PDEs Solver

The numerical method to solve the PDEs' problem is spectral direct numerical simulation. Separation of Fourier components result in a system of ordinary differential equations for the modal functions of the form:

$$
\begin{aligned}
& D_n^2 \varphi^{(n)} - in\alpha \mathrm{Re}(u_0 D_n - D^2 u_0) \varphi^{(n)} \\
& = in\alpha D \langle u_1 u_1 \rangle^{(n)} + D^2 \langle u_1 v_1 \rangle^{(n)} + n^2 \alpha^2 \langle u_1 v_1 \rangle^{(n)} - in\alpha D \langle v_1 v_1 \rangle^{(n)}
\end{aligned}
\tag{7}
$$

where $D^2 = d^2/dy^2, D_n = D^2 - n^2\alpha^2$. The boundary conditions for the modal functions, which account for the flow rate constraint, are expressed as

$$
\begin{aligned}
& \varphi^{(0)}(-1) = 0, \varphi^{(0)}(+1) = 0, \\
& \varphi^{(n)}(-1) = i\mathrm{Re}_L f_L^{(n)}/n\alpha, \\
& \varphi^{(n)}(+1) = i\mathrm{Re}_U f_U^{(n)}/n\alpha, \\
& D\varphi^{(n)}(-1) = 0, D\varphi^{(n)}(+1) = 0,
\end{aligned}
\tag{8}
$$

System (7)–(8) is solved numerically using Chebyshev expansions for the modal functions, Galerkin procedure for conversion of the differential equations into algebraic equations and *Tau* method for incorporation of boundary conditions.

The pressure modal functions are computed by inserting (6) into (1) and separating Fourier modes resulting in:

$$
p_1^{(n)} = \frac{-i}{n\alpha} \left[(D^2 - n^2\alpha^2 - in\alpha \mathrm{Re} u_0) D\varphi^{(n)} + in\alpha \mathrm{Re} \frac{du_0}{dy} \varphi^{(n)} - in\alpha \langle u_1 u_1 \rangle^{(n)} - D \langle u_1 v_1 \rangle^{(n)} \right]
\tag{9}
$$
$$
A = D^3 \varphi^{(0)} - D \langle u_1 v_1 \rangle^{(0)}
$$

Modal function $p_1^{(0)}$ is computed by extracting zeroth mode resulting in the following expression

$$
p_1^{(0)} = -\langle v_1 v_1 \rangle^{(0)} + const
\tag{10}
$$

where the integration constant is selected by to setting the mean part p_{mean} of the periodic pressure component to zero, i.e.

$$p_{mean} = \frac{1}{2\lambda} \int_{-1}^{1} \int_{0}^{\lambda} \left[\sum_{n=-\infty}^{n=+\infty} p^{(n)} e^{in\alpha x} + const \right] dxdy \qquad (11)$$

It is convenient for discussion purposes to write expression for the total mean pressure gradient in the following form

$$\left. \frac{\partial p_T}{\partial x} \right|_{mean} = Re(-2 + \frac{A}{Re}) \qquad (12)$$

as the effectiveness of the transpiration can be judged by comparing A with the reference pressure gradient $-2Re$ required to drive the flow in the channel without transpiration (or by comparing A/Re with -2). And then the value is used to measure the pressure losses and drag reduction introduced by the active/passive flow control effectiveness.

3.2 Data Sampling

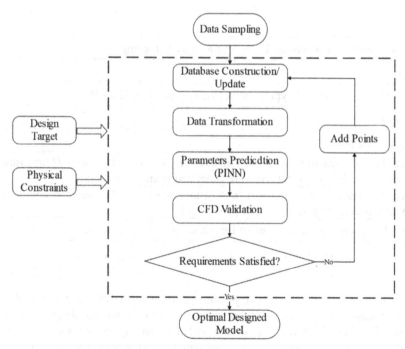

Fig. 2. Framework of the PINN-based optimal design process

The data for the PINN-based optimization is provided by Galerkin-spectral method which is shown before. Now the physics-constrained training is defined as a constrained optimization problem (the main process is shown in Fig. 2),

$$\theta^* = \arg\min \mathcal{L}(\theta)$$
$$s.t. \; \mathcal{B}(\boldsymbol{x}, \boldsymbol{u}^\theta, p^\theta) = 0 \tag{13}$$

The input parameter θ is characterized as a tuple of variables, encompassing the amplitude, wavelength, and Fourier modes of grooves, as well as transpiration. These parameters play a crucial role in shaping the desired characteristics of the system under study. On the other hand, the response value is defined as the total mean pressure gradients, which serves as a quantitative measure for assessing pressure loss and drag reduction. This response value provides valuable insights into the performance and efficiency of the system.

The Latin hypercube sampling (LHS) method is employed to generate a training dataset for the surrogate model. This approach offers several advantages in terms of dataset diversity and representation within the parameter space. By utilizing LHS, the surrogate model captures the variability and interactions between different input parameters, enhancing its accuracy and robustness. LHS also ensures that the training dataset is evenly distributed across the parameter space, minimizing sampling bias and providing improved coverage. The main step of n-dims sampling process can be expressed in Fig. 3:

Algorithm: n-dimensional Latin Hypercube Sampling
Input:
Original n-dimensional hypercube in $[X_l, X_u]$, Samling scale H
Output:
H sampling points
Step 1: For each dimension, the interval $[x_l^i, x_u^i]$ is divided into H equivalent subintervals. H^n sub hypercubes are generated from the partition
Step 2: Generate sampling matrix A whose scale is $H*n$ and each column of which is a random permutation of $[1,2,...,H]$.
Step 2: Generate a sampling point from each selected hypercube.

Fig. 3. The n-dimensional hypercube sampling process

The dataset, comprising sampling points generated by DNS, can be divided into a training dataset and a validation dataset. These subsets are utilized during the training process of the neural network surrogate model. The training dataset is used to train the model, enabling it to learn the underlying patterns and relationships within the data. The validation dataset serves as an independent set of data to evaluate the model's performance and validate its generalization capabilities. The division of the dataset into these subsets facilitates the effective training and evaluation of the neural network surrogate model.

4 Physics Informed Neural Network Surrogate Modeling

4.1 The Physics Constrained ANN Design

A neural network that consists of more than one hidden layer is used for constructing the surrogate model (Fig. 4). The function approximation capability of a deep neural network increases as the number of hidden layers and neurons within each layer grows. The deep neural network operates by mapping the input z_0 to the output z_{N-1} (N denotes the total number of layers in the network), traversing through the layers from the input layer to the output layer. Here, Within the hidden layers, each layer receives outputs from the previous layer and passes forward inputs to the subsequent layer. The relationship between the input z_{i-1} and the output z_i of the ith layer (where i ranges from 1 to $N-1$) is precisely defined as follows:

$$z_i = \sigma_i(\mathbf{W}_i^T z_{i-1} + \mathbf{b}_i) \tag{14}$$

where sigmoid function is chosen as the activation function σ_i, which is defined mathematically as $\sigma(x) = 1/(1 + e^{-x})$. $\mathbf{W}_i$ and $\mathbf{b}_i$ are the weight matrix and bias vector of this layer. The dimensions of $\mathbf{W}_i$ and $\mathbf{b}_i$ are $m_{i-1} \times m_i$ and m_i, respectively (m_i denotes the number of neurons at ith layer).

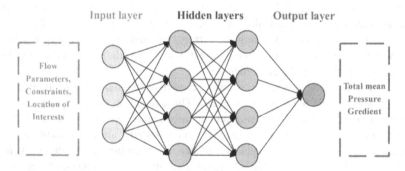

Fig. 4. Framework of the PINN-based optimal design process

The loss function, denoted as $L(\mathbf{W}, \mathbf{b})$, comprises two distinct components: $L_{data}(\mathbf{W}, \mathbf{b})$ and $L_{pde}(\mathbf{W}, \mathbf{b})$. These components represent the constraints imposed by matching available labeled data and the fulfillment of fundamental physical principles, respectively. This component accounts for the constraint of matching existing labeled data, also DNS results. It quantifies the discrepancy between the predictions made by the PINN model (parameterized by weights $\mathbf{W}$ and biases $\mathbf{b}$) and the corresponding labeled data points. The specific formulation of $L_{data}(\mathbf{W}, \mathbf{b})$ depends on the specific problem and the nature of the data.

$$L_{data}(\mathbf{W}, \mathbf{b}) = \frac{1}{N_u} \sum_{i=1}^{N_u} \left[u_{NN}(x_i, \mathbf{W}, \mathbf{b}) - \hat{u}(x_i) \right]^2$$

$$+ \frac{1}{N_p} \sum_{i=1}^{N_p} \left[p_{NN}(x_i, \mathbf{W}, \mathbf{b}) - \hat{p}(x_i) \right]^2 \tag{15}$$

where N_u, N_p are the number of velocity, pressure, data points by DNS, respectively.

4.2 Optimization Process

It may be difficult to find the global optimal by PINN-based surrogate model. However, the Genetic Algorithms (GAs) is adopted to search for acceptable local optimal value. The integration of genetic algorithms with surrogate model involves several steps. First, the optimization problem is defined, including the objective function, constraints, and design variables. The surrogate model is then trained using available data or initial samples to approximate the objective function. This involves mapping the design variables to corresponding objective values using techniques like backpropagation or Bayesian optimization.

Once the surrogate model is trained, the GA process begins with the generation of an initial population of individuals representing sets of design variables. The fitness of each individual is evaluated by using the surrogate model to predict the corresponding objective value. This step saves computational time by avoiding the need for expensive evaluations of the actual objective function.

Next, genetic operators such as selection, crossover, and mutation are applied to create new offspring from the parent individuals. These operators mimic natural processes, selecting fitter individuals, combining genetic information through crossover, and introducing variations through mutation. The surrogate-assisted evaluation is then performed, where a subset of offspring individuals is selected, and their fitness is evaluated using the surrogate model. The fitness values of the selected offspring are updated based on their surrogate-assisted evaluations. This information guides the search for better solutions.

The GA process continues iteratively, with the population evolving through generations, and the surrogate model assisting in evaluating fitness and updating individuals' fitness values. The termination criteria, such as a maximum number of generations or convergence of solution quality, determine when the process ends. Finally, the best solution is extracted from the final population based on the surrogate model evaluations, providing an optimal or near-optimal solution to the optimization problem.

4.3 Experiments

The numerical experiment was conducted to validate the effectiveness of the PINN-based surrogate model approach. The results obtained from the test dataset revealed an average error of approximately 3.7% when compared to the data evaluated by the PINN surrogate model. Figure 5 presents a comparison between the solid lines representing

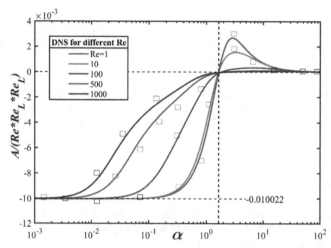

Fig. 5. Comparison between DNS results(solid lines) and prediction of PINN surrogate model(scatter points) in cutoff plane.

the DNS results and the scatter points representing the predictions of the PINN surrogate model in the cutoff plane. The lines demonstrate that the effectiveness of drag reduction varies with the wave number for different Reynolds numbers.

Furthermore, the genetic algorithm optimization process successfully identified the same local optimization value as the DNS output by employing adaptive steps based on the surrogate model. These results provide confidence in extending the approach to models with higher dimensional inputs. The use of a continuous transpiration on grooves with a single Fourier mode can provide a reasonable estimate of the best performance for a system, especially when considering the wavelength of the slot system and the amplitude dictated by the transpiration Reynolds number. This approach allows for a simplified representation of the system behavior while capturing the essential characteristics of the groove-based transpiration phenomenon.

5   Conclusion

By employing the PINN-based surrogate model technique, the system's performance can be estimated by studying the response of the system to the continuous transpiration. This approach facilitates the evaluation of the system's sensitivity to transpiration-induced flow variations and provides insights into the optimal transpiration conditions for achieving the best performance.

This research presents a promising approach for optimizing flow control systems, incorporating physics constraints through the use of surrogate modeling. The findings contribute to the advancement of optimal design techniques in flow control applications, offering new insights and possibilities for improving the performance and efficiency of such systems. It is important to note that this technique can be adapted to more complex slot distributions which is similar to the real engineering problem if required. For systems with non-uniform slot distributions, multiple Fourier modes can be used to capture the spatial variations more accurately. This adaptation allows for a more detailed representation of the transpiration pattern and can provide a better estimation of the system's performance, which is helpful for optimization of engineering design flow control B.C. for fluid-driven system.

Acknowledgments. Supported in part by the Scientific and Technological Project of Henan Province (Grant No. 222102210056), The Key Scientific Project for the University of Henan Province (Grant No. 23A520003), and the Aeronautical Science Foundation of China (Grant No. 20200051042003).

References

1. Sun, G., Wang, S.: A review of the artificial neural network surrogate modeling in aerodynamic design. Proceedings of the Institution of Mechanical Engineers, Part G: Journal of Aerospace Engineering. **233**(16), 5863–5872 (2019)
2. Sun, L., Wang, J.X.: Physics-constrained bayesian neural network for fluid flow reconstruction with sparse and noisy data. Theoretical Appl. Mech. Lett. 1, **10**(3), 161–169 (2020)
3. Zhu, Q., Liu, Z., Yan, J.: Machine learning for metal additive manufacturing: predicting temperature and melt pool fluid dynamics using physics-informed neural networks. Comput. Mech.. Mech. **67**, 619–635 (2021)
4. Forster, M., Feldman, J., Lyes, P., Johns, J., Warsop, C.: Surrogate modelling of active flow control. In: AIAA SCITECH 2023 Forum p. 2314 (2023)
5. Yondo, R., Bobrowski, K., Andrés, E., Valero, E.: A review of surrogate modeling techniques for aerodynamic analysis and optimization: current limitations and future challenges in industry. Advances in evolutionary and deterministic methods for design, optimization and control in engineering and sciences, pp. 19–33 (2019)
6. Vavalle, A., Qin, N.: Iterative response surface based optimization scheme for transonic airfoil design. J. Aircr.Aircr. **44**(2), 365–376 (2007)
7. Sóbester, A., Leary, S.J., Keane, A.J.: On the design of optimization strategies based on global response surface approximation models. J. Global Optim.Optim. **33**, 31–59 (2005)
8. Karmy, J.P., Maldonado, S.: Hierarchical time series forecasting via support vector regression in the European travel retail industry. Expert Syst. Appl. **137**, 59–73 (2019)
9. Yun, Y., Yoon, M., Nakayama, H.: Multi-objective optimization based on meta-modeling by using support vector regression. Optim. Eng.. Eng. **10**, 167–181 (2009)
10. Herzog, S., Tetzlaff, C., Wörgötter, F.: Evolving artificial neural networks with feedback. Neural Netw.Netw. **123**, 153–162 (2020)
11. Booth, K., Bandler, J.: Space mapping for codesigned magnetics: optimization techniques for high-fidelity multidomain design specifications. IEEE Power Electronics Magazine 7(2), 47–52 (2020)
12. Bandler, J.W., Biernacki, R.M., Chen, S.H., Grobelny, P.A., Hemmers, R.H.: Space mapping technique for electromagnetic optimization. IEEE Trans. Microw. Theory Tech.Microw. Theory Tech. **42**(12), 2536–2544 (1994)
13. Wang, Q., Moin, P., Iaccarino, G.: A rational interpolation scheme with superpolynomial rate of convergence. SIAM J. Numer. Anal.Numer. Anal. **47**(6), 4073–4097 (2010)
14. Migliorati, G.: Multivariate approximation of functions on irregular domains by weighted least-squares methods. IMA J. Numer. Anal.Numer. Anal. **41**(2), 1293–1317 (2021)
15. Ghauch, Z.G., Aitharaju, V., Rodgers, W.R., Pasupuleti, P., Dereims, A., Ghanem, R.G.: Integrated stochastic analysis of fiber composites manufacturing using adapted polynomial chaos expansions. Compos. A Appl. Sci. Manuf. **118**, 179–193 (2019)

16. Novak, L., Novak, D.: Polynomial chaos expansion for surrogate modelling: theory and software. Beton-und Stahlbetonbau **113**, 27–32 (2018)
17. Haghighat, E., Raissi, M., Moure, A., Gomez, H., Juanes, R.: A physics-informed deep learning framework for inversion and surrogate modeling in solid mechanics. Comput. Methods Appl. Mech. Eng.. Methods Appl. Mech. Eng. **379**, 113741 (2021)
18. Lucor, D., Agrawal, A., Sergent, A.: Physics-aware deep neural networks for surrogate modeling of turbulent natural convection (2021). arXiv preprint arXiv:2103.03565
19. Sun, L., Gao, H., Pan, S., Wang, J.X.: Surrogate modeling for fluid flows based on physics-constrained deep learning without simulation data. Comput. Methods Appl. Mech. Eng.. Methods Appl. Mech. Eng. **361**, 112732 (2020)
20. Batuwatta-Gamage, C.P., et al.: A physics-informed neural network-based surrogate framework to predict moisture concentration and shrinkage of a plant cell during drying. J. Food Eng. **332**, 111137 (2022)

Model Following Adaptive Control of Links for the Complex Dynamical Network via the State Observer

Xiaoxiao Li and Chao Wu$^{(\boxtimes)}$

School of Electrical Engineering and Automation, Luoyang Institute of Science and Technology, Luoyang, China
shiningi@163.com

Abstract. This paper investigates the model following adaptive control (MFAC) problem for the dynamic links of complex dynamical network, in which the dynamic links are regarded wholly as the link subsystem (LS) with the weighted values of links as its state variables. Firstly, the dynamics of LS is modeled by the Riccati matrix differential equation with the term coupled to the state of nodes. Then the asymptotic state observer of LS is constructed to overcome the limitation of it's state unavailability. Based on this, combined with the Lyapunov stability theory, the state feedback controllers of node subsystem (NS) and LS are synthesized such that MFAC of links is ensured. Compared with the existing literature, the significant difference in this paper is that the objects of MFAC are the links instead of the nodes. Furthermore, due to the coupling effect between the nodes and the links in the complex dynamical network, the model matching conditions (MMCs) are greatly simplified, by which the NS also has the designed auxiliary tracking target when the MFAC of links is achieved. In other words, when the asymptotically MFAC for LS is realized, the NS can also asymptotically tracks the designed auxiliary tracking target. Finally, the numerical simulation is given to verify the effectiveness of the control scheme proposed in this paper.

Keywords: Complex dynamical network · model following adaptive control(MFAC) · state observer

1 Introduction

In recent years, the MFAC problems have achieved extensive researches in many fields [1–12]. For example, Ref. [8] studies the position control problem of hydraulic servo systems subjected to unknown disturbances and synthesizes the adaptive model following controller based upon the Lyapunov method. The two-input, two-output nonlinear MFC problem for a 3-DOF (degree-of-freedom) tandem rotor model helicopter is solved in Ref. [12]. It is worth noting that the above theoretical researches on MFC are mostly aimed at the single systems. However, with the development of science and technology, the controlled system

© The Author(s), under exclusive license to Springer Nature Singapore Pte Ltd. 2024
F. Sun et al. (Eds.): ICCSIP 2023, CCIS 1918, pp. 256–268, 2024.
https://doi.org/10.1007/978-981-99-8018-5_19

frequently shows the network topology structure which composed of multiple interconnected subsystems, and each subsystem needs its own MFC task. Such requirements are required in the systems with network structures in practical engineering [13–17]. For example, the grid-connected generators [13]; the formation control of multiple nonholonomic wheeled mobile robots [14]; the topology establishment of wireless sensor networks [15]; the leader-following consensus control of multi-agent systems [16,17]. In the above examples, the systems with network structures can be regarded as the complex dynamical networks, in which each subsystem (generator, robot, sensor, agent system) has its own reference model to be tracked. However, the dynamics of links between the involved subsystems are ignored in the aforementioned researches.

From the perspective of large-scale systems, the complex dynamical network can be considered to be composed of two subsystems: nodes subsystem (NS) and links subsystem (LS), which are coupled with each other. Therefore, the MFAC for the complex dynamical network can be divided into two categories, one is the MFAC for NS, and another is the MFAC for LS. Based on this viewpoint, the results in [13–17] can be regarded as the MFAC for NS. However, it is noteworthy that the above researches focus only on the MFAC for nodes instead of links, in other words, the MFAC for links is ignored in the existing literature. In fact, the phenomenon attributed to MFAC for links also exist in the real practical networks. For example, biological neural networks are composed of neurons (nodes) and synapses (links), in which the synaptic strengths may be regarded as the weighted values of links. The synaptic strengths show the specific change patterns for LTP and LTD (reference model) when a memory is formed at various sets of synapses in the human brain [18,19]. In web-winding systems, which can be considered to be composed of motors (nodes) and webs. The tensions of webs (links) between rollers track the given reference values (reference model), and the tensions of webs also be affected by the motors speed [20,21]. The above examples imply that there exist some required specifications for the dynamics of links, which may specify the global performance of links in topological structure. From the perspective of control theory, if using the reference model to specify the required performance, the problems reflected in the above examples may be regarded as MFC problems for links. Within our knowledge for complex dynamical networks, there is little literature on this issue according to the above views.

In addition, the state of links is usually unavailable in practical applications due to technical limitations, measurement costs, etc. Therefore, in order to overcome the limit of the state of links is unavailable, the commonly used method is to construct the corresponding state observer [22,23] to obtain the estimated value of the state of links. In this paper, it is worth discussing how to employ the information of the nodes and the observed value information of the links to design the MFAC scheme to achieve the MFAC target of the links.

Inspired by the above discussion, based on the designed state observer of links and the state information of nodes, the model following adaptive control scheme is proposed in this article, which mainly includes two parts, the first part is to construct the controller for NS, the other part is to synthesize the control scheme for LS, which can ensure that with the help of the nodes state asymptotically tracks the constructed auxiliary dynamic tracking target, the state of links can asymptotically follows the state of its reference model. This also fully demonstrates the important dynamic auxiliary role of nodes in implementing the MFAC for links. Compared with the existing literature, the advantages of this article are mainly in the following three aspects: (i). The MFAC problem of links is firstly discussed, which is rarely reported in the existing literature. (ii). The state observer of the LS is designed to overcome the limitation of the state of links which is unavailable. Then based on the state estimated value of links, combined with the dynamic auxiliary role of nodes, the corresponding model following control scheme is synthesized to achieve the MFAC target of links. (iii). Compared with the usual MFAC for the single system, the model matching conditions are greatly simplified because the mutual coupling between the NS and LS is sufficiently considered. At the same time, the nodes also has a designed auxiliary dynamic tracking goal, which helps links to achieve MFAC.

The rest of the paper is organized as follows. In Sect. 2, the dynamic model of the mutual coupled nodes and links are constructed. Design the asymptotical state observer for LS in Sect. 3. In Sect. 4, propose the control objective in this paper and design the corresponding model following adaptive control scheme. In Sect. 5, the numerical simulation is given to verify the validity of the theoretical analysis. The conclusion is given in Sect. 6.

2   Model Description

Consider the time-varying controlled complex dynamical network composed of N nodes with uncertainties. Due to the mutual coupling between nodes, the dynamic equation of the ith controlled nodes can be depicted by

$$\dot{x}_i = Ax_i + f_i(x_i, t) + b_i \sum_{j=1}^{N} [l_{ji}^0 + l_{ji}(t)]\Lambda_j(x_j, t) + u_i \tag{1}$$

where $A \in R^{m \times m}$ represents a constant matrix, the state vector of the ith node $x_i = [x_{i1}, x_{i2}, \cdots, x_{im}]^T \in R^m$, the time-varying continuous vector function $f_i(x_i, t) = [f_{i1}(x_i, t), f_{i2}(x_i, t), \cdots, f_{im}(x_i, t)]^T \in R^m$, the inner coupling vector function $\Lambda_j(x_j, t) = [\Lambda_{j1}(x_j, t), \Lambda_{j2}(x_j, t), \cdots, \Lambda_{jm}(x_j, t)]^T \in R^m$, the control input of the ith node $u_i \in R^m$; $b_i \in R$ denotes the coupling strength of the ith node, $l_{ji}^0 \in R$ represents the initial link weighted value between the ith node and the jth node, $l_{ji}(t) \in R$ denotes the time-varying link weighted value between the ith node and the jth node, and the self-connection $l_{jj}(t)$ is allowed.

For the convenience of subsequent controller design and the simplicity of mathematical derivation, Eq. (1) can be rewritten in the form of the following matrix differential equation.

$$\dot{X} = AX + F + \Lambda L_0 B + \Lambda LB + U \tag{2}$$

in which, $X = [x_1, x_2, \cdots, x_N] \in R^{m \times N}$, $L_0 = [l_{ji}^0]_{N \times N}$, $L = L(t) = [l_{ji}(t)]_{N \times N}$, $\Lambda = [\Lambda_1(x_1, t), \Lambda_2(x_2, t), \cdots, \Lambda_N(x_N, t)] \in R^{m \times N}$, $B = diag(b_1, b_2, \cdots, b_N) \in R^{N \times N}$, $F = F(x, t) = [f_1(x_1, t), f_2(x_2, t), \cdots, f_N(x_N, t)] \in R^{m \times N}$, $U = [u_1, u_2, \cdots, u_N] \in R^{m \times N}$, $x = [x_1, x_2, \cdots, x_N]^T$.

In this article, we regard all links as a dynamic subsystem, which called links subsystem (LS). Therefore, consider the dynamics of LS with the following Riccati matrix differential equation.

$$\begin{cases} \dot{L} = PL + G(X) + U_L \\ Y = \Xi L \end{cases} \tag{3}$$

where the constant matrix $P \in R^{N \times N}$, $U_L \in R^{N \times N}$ denotes the control input of links, $Y \in R^{s \times N}$ represents the output state matrix, $\Xi \in R^{s \times N}$ represents the output matrix, $G(X) \in R^{N \times N}$ denotes the coupling matrix term related to the state of nodes.

Assumption 1. In Eq. (1), the inner coupling vector function $\Lambda_j(x_j, t)$ is known and bounded; the time-varying continuous vector function $f_i(x_i, t)$ is unknown and bounded. That is to say, there exists an unknown constant δ_i that makes the inequality $\|f_i(x_i, t)\| \leq \delta_i$ holds.

Remark 1. (i). In Eq. (1), there exists a constant matrix $K \in R^{m \times m}$ that satisfies the following Lyapunov equation.

$$(A + K)^T Q_1 + Q_1(A + K) = -W_1 \tag{4}$$

where $W_1 \in R^{m \times m}$ is any given positive definite symmetric matrix, $Q_1 \in R^{m \times m}$ is the corresponding positive definite symmetric matrix solution for Eq. (4). (ii). If Assumption 1 holds, then the matrix Λ is known and bounded, and the following inequality is satisfied.

$$\|F\| = \sqrt{\sum_{i=1}^{N} \|f_i(x_i, t)\|^2} \leq \delta = \sqrt{\sum_{i=1}^{N} \delta_i^2} \tag{5}$$

Assumption 2. In Eq. (3), the matrix pair (P, Ξ) is fully observation.

Remark 2. (i). Assumption 2 is a common condition when designing a state observer [22,23]. (ii). If Assumption 2 is satisfied, it means that there exists a matrix $K_1 \in R^{N \times s}$ such that $P + K_1 \Xi$ is Hurwitz matrix. That is to say, for any given positive definite symmetric matrix $Q_2 \in R^{N \times N}$, the following Lyapunov equation has the corresponding positive definite symmetric matrix solution $W_2 \in R^{N \times N}$.

$$(P + K_1 \Xi)^T Q_2 + Q_2(P + K_1 \Xi) = -W_2 \tag{6}$$

(iii). The matrix K_1 and the positive definite symmetric matrix Q_2 in Eq. (6) can be obtained by solving the linear matrix inequality $P^T Q_2 + Q_2 P + G_1 + G_1^T < 0$, $G_1 = Q_2 K_1 \Xi$ [24].

The reference model for the LS (3) is given as follows.

$$\dot{L}_m = P_m L_m + B_m U_m \tag{7}$$

where $P_m \in R^{N \times N}$ and $B_m \in R^{N \times N}$ are constant matrices, $L_m \in R^{N \times N}$ is the reference state matrix of links, $U_m \in R^{N \times N}$ is the reference input matrix.

Assumption 3. In Eq. (7), the reference state matrix L_m is bounded.

3   Design the Asymptotical State Observer for LS

Definition 1 [22]. Consider the LS (3), and construct a dynamic system $\dot{L} = G(\hat{L}, Y, X)$, if the reconstructed state $\hat{L}$ can make the error $L - \hat{L} \overset{t \to +\infty}{\longrightarrow} O_{N \times N}$ (where $O_{N \times N}$ represents $N \times N$ dimensional zero matrix) holds, then the construct dynamic system is said to be an asymptotical state observer of the subsystem (3).

Assumption 4. The coupling term $G(X)$ in Eq. (3) is satisfied $G(X) = Q_2^{-1} \Xi^T W(X)$, and $\|W(X)\| \le \rho(x)$, in which $\rho(x)$ is a known function.

According to Definition 1, we design the asymptotical state observer for the subsystem (3) as follows.

$$\dot{\hat{L}} = (P + K_1 \Xi)\hat{L} + U_L - K_1 Y + \Gamma(\hat{L}, Y, x) \tag{8}$$

in which, the robust term $\Gamma(\hat{L}, Y, x) = \begin{cases} Q_2^{-1} \Xi^T \rho(x) \frac{Y - \Xi \hat{L}}{\|Y - \Xi \hat{L}\|}, \Xi L \ne \Xi \hat{L} \\ O_{N \times N}, \Xi L = \Xi \hat{L} \end{cases}$

The observer state estimation error of the LS (3) is defined as $E = L - \hat{L}$, then according to Eqs. (3) and (8), the following error dynamic equation can be obtained.

$$\dot{E} = \dot{L} - \dot{\hat{L}}$$
$$= PL + K_1 \Xi L - K_1 \Xi L + G(X) + U_L - (P + K_1 \Xi)\hat{L} - U_L + K_1 Y - \Gamma(\hat{L}, Y, x)$$
$$= (P + K_1 \Xi)E - K_1 Y + G(X) + K_1 Y - \Gamma(\hat{L}, Y, x)$$
$$= (P + K_1 \Xi)E + G(X) - \Gamma(\hat{L}, Y, x) \tag{9}$$

Lemma 1. If Assumptions 2 and 4 hold, then the matrix dynamical system (8) is an asymptotical state observer for the subsystem (3).

Proof. Choose the positive definite function $V_1 = tr\{E^T Q_2 E\}$, If Assumptions 2 and 4 are satisfied, combined with the properties of the matrix trace, the orbit derivative of V_1 along the error dynamic Eq. (9) is obtained that.

$$\dot{V}_1 = tr\{\dot{E}^T Q_2 E\} + tr\{E^T Q_2 \dot{E}\}$$

$$= tr\{[(P + K_1\Xi)E + G(X) - \Gamma(\hat{L}, Y, x)]^T Q_2 E\} + tr\{E^T Q_2[(P + K_1\Xi)E + G(X) - \Gamma(\hat{L}, Y, x)]\}$$

$$= tr\{E^T[(P + K_1\Xi)^T Q_2 + Q_2(P + K_1\Xi)]E\} + 2tr\{E^T Q_2 Q_2^{-1}\Xi^T W(X)\}$$

$$\quad - 2tr\{E^T Q_2 \frac{Q_2^{-1}\Xi^T \rho(x)(Y - \Xi\hat{L})}{\|Y - \Xi\hat{L}\|}\}$$

$$\leq - tr\{E^T W_2 E\} + 2\|\Xi E\|\|W(X)\| - 2\rho(x)\|\Xi E\|$$

$$= - tr\{E^T W_2 E\} + 2\|\Xi E\|[\|W(X)\| - \rho(x)]$$

$$\leq - tr\{E^T W_2 E\} \leq 0 \tag{10}$$

According to inequality (10), $\dot{V}_1$ is a negative definite function about the element E. Therefore, the error dynamic system (9) is stable in the Lyapunov sense, that is, $\lim\limits_{t \to +\infty} E = \lim\limits_{t \to +\infty} (L - \hat{L}) \to O_{N \times N}$. The proof of the Lemma 1 is completed.

4 Main Results

Define the model following error of links as $E_L = L - L_m$. Then, the model following error dynamic equation of links can be obtained as follows.

$$\dot{E}_L = \dot{L} - \dot{L}_m$$

$$= (P + K_1\Xi)L - K_1Y - (P + K_1\Xi)L_m + (P + K_1\Xi)L_m + G(X) + U_L - P_m L_m - B_m U_m$$

$$= (P + K_1\Xi)E_L - K_1Y + (P + K_1\Xi - P_m)L_m + G(X) + U_L - B_m U_m \tag{11}$$

Control Objective: Considering a complex dynamical network consisting of (1) and (3), under the situation that Assumptions 1–4 are true, based on the state observer and combined with the dynamic auxiliary role of nodes, design the controller U and U_L in NS (2) and LS (3), respectively, such that the state of links can asymptotically follows its reference model, that is, $\lim\limits_{t \to +\infty} E_L = O_{N \times N}$. In addition, the other involve variables are guaranteed to be bounded.

In order to achieve the above control objective, construct the auxiliary dynamic tracking goal for nodes shown as follows.

$$\dot{X}^* = (A + K)X^* + \Lambda \hat{L}B \tag{12}$$

Introduce the auxiliary tracking error of nodes as $E_X = X - X^*$. The following error dynamic equation can be obtained.

$$\dot{E}_X = \dot{X} - \dot{X}^*$$
$$= AX + F + \Lambda L_0 B + \Lambda LB + U - (A+K)X^* - \Lambda \hat{L}B$$
$$= (A+K)E_X - KX + F + \Lambda L_0 B + \Lambda EB + U \tag{13}$$

In order to achieve the above control objective, the controller U in NS (2) and the controller U_L in LS (3) are designed as follows, respectively.

$$U = -\Lambda L_0 B + KX - \hat{\delta} sign(Q_1 E_X) \tag{14}$$

$$\dot{\hat{\delta}} = \alpha \| Q_1 E_X \| \tag{15}$$

$$U_L = K_1 Y + B_m U_m - (P + K_1 \Xi - P_m) L_m - \Gamma(\hat{L}, Y, x) \tag{16}$$

where $\hat{\delta}$ represents the estimated value of δ and updates according to Eq. (15), $\alpha > 0$ is an adjustable parameter, the sign function $sign(Q_1 E_X) = \begin{cases} \frac{Q_1 E_X}{\|Q_1 E_X\|}, E_X \neq O_{m \times N} \\ O_{m \times N}, E_X = O_{m \times N} \end{cases}$

Remark 3. (i). The model following adaptive control scheme in this paper is composed of Eqs. (14)–(16), where Eq. (14) provides a clear structure of the node's controller, which consists of three parts. The first part $-\Lambda L_0 B$ is related to the initial state matrix of links; the second part KX is the feedback term about the state of nodes; the third part $-\hat{\delta} sign(Q_1 E_X)$ is the robust term to overcome the unknown bounded uncertainty term F in Eq. (2). (ii). Equation (16) gives the clear structure of the controller for links, which consists of three parts, the first part $K_1 Y$ is the output feedback term, in which K_1 can be obtained by solving the linear matrix inequality in Remark 2; the second term $B_m U_m - (P + K_1 \Xi - P_m) L_m$ is related to the reference model of LS, and all information is known and available; the third term $-\Gamma(\hat{L}, Y, x)$ is related to the estimation matrix $\hat{L}$ of links, the links output matrix L and the state vector x of nodes.

Define the estimation error $\tilde{\delta} = \delta - \hat{\delta}$. Since Q_1 and Q_2 are positive definite symmetric matrices, $tr\{E_X^T Q_1 E_X\}$ and $tr\{E_L^T Q_2 E_L\}$ are positive definite functions about elements E_X and E_L, respectively, where Q_1 and Q_2 can be obtained by solving Lyapunov Eqs. (4) and (6), respectively. Therefore, consider the positive definite function $V = V(E_X, E_L, E, \tilde{\delta}) = tr\{E_X^T Q_1 E_X\} + tr\{E_L^T Q_2 E_L\} + \frac{1}{\alpha} \tilde{\delta}^2 + V_1$. If Assumptions 1–4 are satisfied, combined with the designed model following adaptive control scheme (14)–(16), then the orbit derivative of $V = V(E_X, E_L, E, \tilde{\delta})$ along the error Eqs. (9), (11) and (13) is obtained that.

$$\dot{V} = tr\{\dot{E}_X^T Q_1 E_X + E_X{}^T Q_1 \dot{E}_X\} + tr\{\dot{E}_L^T Q_2 E_L + E_L{}^T Q_2 \dot{E}_L\} + \frac{2}{\alpha}\tilde{\delta}\dot{\tilde{\delta}} + \dot{V}_1$$

$$= tr\{[(A+K)E_X + F + \Lambda E B - \hat{\delta}sign(Q_1 E_X)]^T Q_1 E_X\}$$

$$+ tr\{E_X{}^T Q_1[(A+K)E_X + F + \Lambda E B - \hat{\delta}sign(Q_1 E_X)]\} + \frac{2}{\alpha}\tilde{\delta}\dot{\tilde{\delta}} + \dot{V}_1$$

$$+ tr\{[(P+K_1\Xi)E_L - K_1 Y + (P+K_1\Xi - P_m)L_m + G(X) + U_L - B_m U_m]^T Q_2 E_L\}$$

$$+ tr\{E_L{}^T Q_2[(P+K_1\Xi)E_L - K_1 Y + (P+K_1\Xi - P_m)L_m + G(X) + U_L - B_m U_m]\}$$

$$= tr\{E_X{}^T[(A+K)^T Q_1 + Q_1(A+K)]E_X\} + 2tr\{E_X{}^T Q_1 \Lambda E B\} + 2tr\{E_X{}^T Q_1 F\}$$

$$- 2tr\{E_X{}^T Q_1 \hat{\delta}sign(Q_1 E_X)\} + tr\{[(P+K_1\Xi)E_L + G(X) - \Gamma(\hat{L}, Y, x)]^T Q_2 E_L\}$$

$$+ tr\{E_L{}^T Q_2[(P+K_1\Xi)E_L + G(X) - \Gamma(\hat{L}, Y, x)]\} + \frac{2}{\alpha}\tilde{\delta}\dot{\tilde{\delta}} + \dot{V}_1$$

$$= - tr\{E_X{}^T W_1 E_X\} - tr\{E_L{}^T W_2 E_L\} + 2tr\{E_X{}^T Q_1 \Lambda E B\} + 2tr\{E_X{}^T Q_1 F\} - 2\hat{\delta}\|Q_1 E_X\|$$

$$+ 2tr\{E_L{}^T Q_2 G(X)\} - 2tr\{E_L{}^T Q_2\Gamma(\hat{L}, Y, x)\} + \frac{2}{\alpha}\tilde{\delta}\dot{\tilde{\delta}} + \dot{V}_1$$

$$\leq - tr\{E_X{}^T W_1 E_X\} - tr\{E_L{}^T W_2 E_L\} + 2tr\{E_X{}^T Q_1 \Lambda E B\} + 2\tilde{\delta}\|Q_1 E_X\|$$

$$+ 2\|\Xi E_L\| \cdot [\|W(X)\| - \rho(x)] + +\frac{2}{\alpha}\tilde{\delta}\dot{\tilde{\delta}} + \dot{V}_1$$

$$\leq - tr\{E_X{}^T W_1 E_X\} - tr\{E_L{}^T W_2 E_L\} - tr\{E^T W_2 E\} + 2tr\{E_X{}^T Q_1 \Lambda E B\}$$

$$\leq - \lambda_{min}(W_1)\|E_X\|^2 - \lambda_{min}(W_2)\|E_L\|^2 - \lambda_{min}(W_2)\|E\|^2 + 2\|E_X\|\|E\|\|Q_1\|\|\Lambda\|\|B\|$$

$$\leq - \lambda_{min}(W_1)\|E_X\|^2 - \lambda_{min}(W_2)\|E_L\|^2 - \lambda_{min}(W_2)\|E\|^2 + \|Q_1\|\|\Lambda\|\|B\| \cdot [\frac{\|E_X\|^2}{\varepsilon} + \varepsilon\|E\|^2]$$

$$\leq \|E_X\|^2[-\lambda_{min}(W_1) + \|Q_1\|\|\Lambda\|\|B\| \cdot \frac{1}{\varepsilon}] - \lambda_{min}(W_2)\|E_L\|^2$$

$$+ \|E\|^2[-\lambda_{min}(W_2) + \|Q_1\|\|\Lambda\|\|B\| \cdot \varepsilon] \tag{17}$$

Denote $\varsigma_1 = -\lambda_{min}(W_1) + \|Q_1\|\|\Lambda\|\|B\| \cdot \frac{1}{\varepsilon}$, $\varsigma_2 = -\lambda_{min}(W_2)$, $\varsigma_3 = -\lambda_{min}(W_2) + \|Q_1\|\|\Lambda\|\|B\| \cdot \varepsilon$, then Eq. (17) can be rewritten as.

$$\dot{V} \leq \varsigma_1\|E_X\|^2 + \varsigma_2\|E_L\|^2 + \varsigma_3\|E\|^2 \tag{18}$$

Theorem 1. Consider the complex dynamical network composed of (1) and (3). If Assumptions 1–4 are satisfied and the internal coupling matrix Λ is known and satisfies the inequality $\|\Lambda\| \leq \min\{\frac{\varepsilon\lambda_{min}(W_1)}{\|Q_1\|\|B\|}, \frac{\lambda_{min}(W_2)}{\varepsilon\|Q_1\|\|B\|}\}$, ($\varepsilon > 0$ is an adjustable parameter, $\lambda_{min}(*)$ represents the minimum eigenvalue of the matrix $'*'$), then the designed model following adaptive control scheme (14)–(16) can ensure that $\lim_{t\to+\infty} E_L = O_{N\times N}$, and at the same time, it can also ensure $\lim_{t\to+\infty} E_X = O_{m\times N}$.

Proof. If the inequality $\|\Lambda\| \leq \min\{\frac{\varepsilon\lambda_{min}(W_1)}{\|Q_1\|\|B\|}, \frac{\lambda_{min}(W_2)}{\varepsilon\|Q_1\|\|B\|}\}$ is satisfied, then it is easy to know that $\varsigma_1 \leq 0$, $\varsigma_2 \leq 0$ and $\varsigma_3 \leq 0$. Therefore, inequality (18) implies that $\dot{V}$ is the semi-negative function about elements E_X, E_L, E, $\tilde{\delta}$. Thus, we can obtain that E_X, E_L, E, $\tilde{\delta}$ are bounded. Furthermore, according to the above obtained results with Eqs. (9), (11) and (13), it can be clearly known that $\dot{E}_X$, $\dot{E}_L$ and $\dot{E}$ are also bounded. Therefore, based on the Barbalat Lemma [25], we can obtain that $\lim_{t\to+\infty} E_L = O_{N\times N}$, $\lim_{t\to+\infty} E_X = O_{m\times N}$ and $\lim_{t\to+\infty} E = O_{N\times N}$.

Remark 4. The steps for replying Theorem 1 are introduced as follows.

Step (i). Give the controlled complex dynamical network consisting of (1) and (3), the reference model of links is given by Eq. (7). Then rewrite Eqs. (1) as (2).

Step (ii). Determine the constant matrices A, P, P_m, B_m, the internal coupling matrix Λ, the coupling strength matrix B, the reference input matrix U_m, the initial state matrix of links L_0, and verify whether Assumptions 1–4 are true.

Step (iii). The positive definite symmetric matrices Q_1 and Q_2 are determined by solving Lyapunov Eqs. (4) and (6), respectively.

Step (iv). Substitute the above obtained parameters into the model following adaptive control scheme (14)–(16), with the help of nodes state asymptotically tracks its auxiliary tracking target, which can be ensured that the state of links asymptotically follows the state of its reference model.

5 Numerical Simulation Example

In this paper, we consider the complex dynamical network with N ($N = 10$) nodes, and choose the N Lorentz chaotic systems [26] as the isolated nodes of the complex dynamical network, which dynamics equation are given as follows.

$$\dot{x}_i = Ax_i + f_i(x_i, t), i = 1, 2, \cdots, N \tag{19}$$

where $x_i = (x_{i1}, x_{i2}, x_{i3})^T$ ($m = 3$) is the state vector of the ith Lorentz chaotic systems, the constant matrix $A = [-10, 10, 0; 28, -1, 0; 0, 0, -8/3]$, the continuous vector function $f_i(x_i, t) = [0, -x_{i1}x_{i3}, x_{i1}x_{i2}]^T$.

In the simulation with Matlab, the inner coupling vector function in Eq. (1) is chosen as $\Lambda_j(x_j, t) = [\omega_1 \cos(z_{j1}z_{j3}), \omega_1 \cos(z_{j1}z_{j3}), \omega_2 \sin(z_{j2}z_{j3})]^T$, where $\omega_1 = rand(1) * \cos(t)$, $\omega_2 = rand(1) * \sin(t)$, $j = 1, 2, \cdots, N$, and the coupling strength of the ith node b_i is randomly generated in the interval $[0, 1]$. The initial link weight value between the ith node and the jth node l_{ji}^0 is randomly generated in the interval $[0, 2]$.

The dynamics of reference model of LS is given by Eq. (7). In Eq. (7), the constant matrix B_m is generated randomly by "$B_m = rand(N, N)$". The reference input matrix U_m is generated randomly and the elements in which are guaranteed to be different. First, use '$u_q = rand(N, N)$' to generate an N order matrix randomly. Then let $U_m = \cos(u_q \pi t)$. The constant matrix P_m is chosen as following rules. Use '$P_{m1} = rand(N, N)$', N order matrix is generated randomly, then let $P_m = P_{m1} - P_{m1}^T$.

The dynamics of links is given by Eq. (3). The control input U_L in Eq. (3) is given by Eq. (16). In addition, the matrices P, Ξ, K, K_1, Q_1 and Q_2 are chosen by the following rules.

(i). Let $P = randn(N, N)$, $\Xi = randn(s, N)$ ($s = 2$).

(ii). Since $A + K$ is a Hurwitz matrix, let $A + K = A_1$, first generate matrix A_1 according to the following steps.

Step 1. Generate an inversible matrix $\Delta = randn(m, m)$.

Step 2. Use '$-abs(rand(m,1))$' to generate m negative real numbers λ_i ($i = 1, 2, \cdots, m$) randomly, then m order matrix $\Omega = \mu * diag(\lambda_1, \lambda_2, \cdots, \lambda_m)$ is obtained, where μ is an adjustable parameter, and let the matrix $A_1 = \Delta\Omega\Delta^{-1}$, then $K = A_1 - A$.

(iii). Similarly, generate the Hurwitz matrix P_1 according to the above steps 1 and 2, and then, $K_1\Xi = P_1 - P$. Choose $W_1 = \nu_1 * eye(m)$, $W_2 = \nu_2 * eye(N)$, where ν_1, ν_2. Then use the parameter W_1 and W_2 to solve the Lyapunov Eqs. (4) and (6) for obtaining the positive definite symmetric matrices Q_1 and Q_2, respectively.

According to the above chosen parameters and the model following adaptive control scheme with (14), (15) and (16), the simulation results are shown as follows.

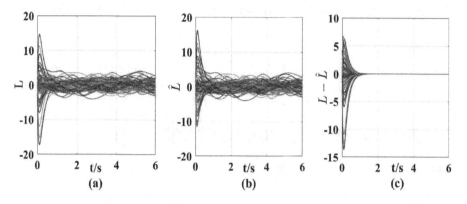

Fig. 1. The state response curves (a) of links L; (b) of the observer for links $\hat{L}$; (c) of the observer estimate error for links $L - \hat{L}$

According to the simulation results in Figs. 1, 2, 3 and 4, we can draw the following observations.

(i). Figure 1 shows that the state observer for links designed in this paper can effectively estimates the state of links. Figure 3 shows that the model following error of links can quickly approach zero with time by the model following adaptive control scheme constructed in this paper.

(ii). From Figs. 2 and 3, we can know that the nodes also achieves asymptotic tracking when the MFAC for link is achieved. This may be related to the model specificity of NS and LS, and fully demonstrates the important dynamic auxiliary role played by nodes in implementing MFAC for the links.

(iii). From Fig. 4, we can obtain that the estimated value $\hat{\delta}$ of the unknown bound δ of the function F is bounded, which corresponds to the requirements of the control objective.

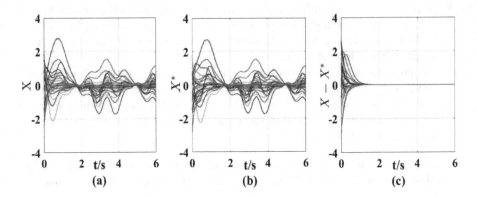

Fig. 2. The state response curves (a) of nodes X with controller; (b) of auxiliary tracking target X^* for nodes; (c) of the auxiliary tracking error $X - X^*$ for nodes with controller.

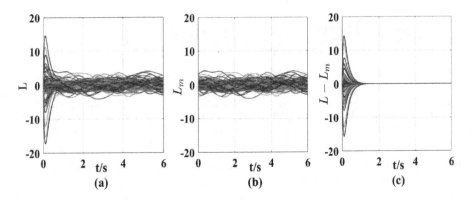

Fig. 3. The state response curves (a) of links L with controller; (b) of the reference model for links L_m; (c) of model following error $L - L_m$ for links.

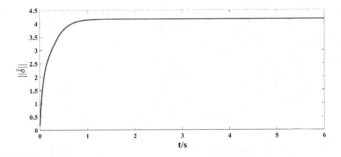

Fig. 4. The norm response curve of the estimated value $\hat{\delta}$

6 Conclusion

In this paper, a new model following adaptive control scheme based on the asymptotical state observer of links is proposed to realize the MFAC for links. Firstly, the dynamic equations of NS and LS are modeled by the vector differential equation and the matrix differential equation, respectively. Then, based on the designed asymptotical state observer of links, combined with Lyapunov stability theory, the controller in NS and LS are designed with the help of nodes such that the MFAC for links is achieved. The final results indicate that when the MFAC for links is realized, the nodes also asymptotically tracks the constructed dynamic auxiliary tracking target, which fully demonstrates the mutual coupling between nodes and links. In addition, this paper has not yet considered how to design the related control scheme, when the dynamic models of NS and LS are more general and has the different dimensions between the reference model and the controlled plant, which will be considered in our subsequent research.

References

1. Landau, I.D., Courtiol, B.: Design of multivariable adaptive model following control systems. IFAC Proc. **6**(2), 315–322 (1973)
2. Kreindler, E., Rothschild, D.: Model-following in linear-quadratic optimization. AIAA J. **14**(7), 835–842 (1976)
3. Pieper, J.K., Baillie, S., Goheen, K.R.: Linear quadratic optimal model-following control of a helicopter in hover. Optimal Control Appl. Methods **17**(2), 123–140 (1996)
4. Leung, T.P., Zhou, Q.J., Su, C.Y.: An adaptive variable structure model following control design for robot manipulators. IEEE Trans. Autom. Control **36**(3), 347–352 (1991)
5. Yousef, H., Simaan, M.: Design of stable decentralized adaptive model-following controllers for large-scale systems. Int. J. Control **49**(4), 1111–1125 (1989)
6. Yucelen, T., Haddad, W.M.: Low-Frequency learning and fast adaptation in model reference adaptive control. IEEE Trans. Autom. Control **58**(4), 1080–1085 (2012)
7. Akhtar, S., Bernstein, D.: Lyapunov-stable discrete-time model reference adaptive control. Int. J. Adapt. Control Signal Process. **19**(10), 745–767 (2005)
8. Yun, J., Cho, H.S.: Application of an adaptive model following control technique to a hydraulic servo system subjected to unknown disturbances. J. Dyn. Syst. Meas. Contr. **113**, 479–486 (1991)
9. Wu, H.S.: Adaptive robust tracking and model following of uncertain dynamical systems with multiple time delays. IEEE Trans. Autom. Control **49**(4), 611–616 (2004)
10. Adams, C., Potter, J., Singhose, W.: Input-Shaping and model-following control of a helicopter carrying a suspended load. J. Guid. Control. Dyn. **38**(1), 94–105 (2015)
11. Pai, M.-C.: Discrete-time sliding mode control for robust tracking and model following of systems with state and input delays. Nonlinear Dyn. **76**(3), 1769–1779 (2014). https://doi.org/10.1007/s11071-014-1245-0
12. Ishitobi, M., Nishi, M., Nakasaki, K.: Nonlinear adaptive model following control for a 3-DOF tandem-rotor model helicopter. Control. Eng. Pract. **18**(8), 936–943 (2010)

13. Yu, W.S.: Design of a power system stabilizer using decentralized adaptive model following tracking control approach. Int. J. Numer. Model. Electron. Networks Devices Fields **23**(2), 63–87 (2010)

14. Yan, L., Ma, B.: Adaptive practical leader-following formation control of multiple nonholonomic wheeled mobile robots. Int. J. Robust Nonlinear Control **30**(17), 7216–7237 (2020)

15. Singh, A., Luhach, A., Gao, X., Kumar, S., Roy, D.: Evolution of wireless sensor network design from technology centric to user centric: an architectural perspective. Int. J. Distrib. Sens. Netw. **16**(8), 1550147720949138 (2020)

16. Cao, W., Zhang, J., Ren, W.: Leader-follower consensus of linear multi-agent systems with unknown external disturbances. Syst. Control Lett. **82**, 64–70 (2015)

17. Fan, M., Wu, Y.: Global leader-following consensus of nonlinear multi-agent systems with unknown control directions and unknown external disturbances. Appl. Math. Comput. **331**, 274–286 (2018)

18. Bliss, T.V.P., Cooke, S.F.: Long-term potentiation and long-term depression: a clinical perspective. Clinics **66**(S1), 3–17 (2011)

19. Gerstner, W., Kistler, WM., Naud, R., Paninski, L.: Neuronal Dynamics: From Single Neurons to Networks and Models of Cognition. Cambridge University Press (2014)

20. Pagilla, P.R., Siraskar, N.B., Dwivedula, R.V.: Decentralized control of web processing lines. IEEE Trans. Control Syst. Technol. **15**(1), 106–117 (2006)

21. Abjadi, N.R., Soltani, J., Askari, J., Markadeh, G.A.: Nonlinear sliding-mode control of a multi-motor web-winding system without tension sensor. IET Control Theory Appl. **3**(4), 419–427 (2009)

22. Gao, Z., Wang, Y., Xiong, J., et al.: Structural balance control of complex dynamical networks based on state observer for dynamic connection relationships. Complexity **2020**, 1–9 (2020)

23. Gao, P., Wang, Y., Liu, L., et al.: Double tracking control for the directed complex dynamic network via the state observer of outgoing links. Int. J. Syst. Sci. **54**(4), 895–906 (2023)

24. Liao, F., Wang, J.L., Yang, G.H.: Reliable robust flight tracking control: an LMI approach. IEEE Trans. Control Syst. Technol. **10**(1), 76–89 (2002)

25. Wang, Y., Fan, Y., Wang, Q., Zhang, Y.: Stabilization and synchronization of complex dynamical networks with different dynamics of nodes via decentralized controllers. IEEE Trans. Circuits Syst. I Regul. Pap. **59**(8), 1786–1795 (2012)

26. Elhadj, Z., Sprott, J.C.: The unified chaotic system describing the Lorenz and Chua systems. Facta Univ. Ser. Electron. Energ. **23**(3), 345–355 (2010)

Gaussian Process Based Stochastic Model Predictive Control of Linear System with Bounded Additive Uncertainty

Fei Li[1(✉)], Lijun Song[1,2], Xiaoming Duan[1], Chao Wu[1], and Xuande Ji[1]

[1] School of Electrical Engineering and Automation, Luoyang Institute of Science and Technology, Luoyang 471023, China
lifei@lit.edu.cn
[2] School of Automation, Northwestern Polytechnical University, Xi'an 710072, China

Abstract. This paper presents a Gaussian process based stochastic model predictive control method for linear time-invariant systems subject to bounded state-dependent additive uncertainties. Chance constraints are treated in analogy to tube-based MPC. To reduce the conservatism, the adaptive constraint tightening is performed by using the confidence region of the predicted uncertainty which is formulated based on the output of the Gaussian process model. Numerical simulations demonstrate the conservatism reducing advantage of the proposed Gaussian process based stochastic model predictive control algorithm in comparison with existing methods.

Keywords: Model Predictive Control · Stochastic MPC · Gaussian Process Regression · Tube MPC · Chance Constraints

1 Introduction

Model predictive control (MPC) is widely used in industry due to the ability of handling uncertainties and fulfilling constraints. However, the traditional nominal MPC may result in poor control quality on occasion in case that the serious disturbance occur, because it does not account for the uncertainty [1, 2]. The robust MPC, presuming the uncertainty is bounded, is capable to guarantee constraints satisfaction all the time by only considering the worst-case uncertainty. But it does not allow for the possible statistical properties of the uncertainty, despite the information is available in many cases. As a consequence, robust approaches may lead to overly conservative in algorithm design [3, 4]. In some real-world application cases, a certain probability of constraint violation is usually allowed. The stochastic model predictive control (SMPC) taking into account the a priori knowledge of the uncertainty and using the chance constraint will result in less conservatism in constraints satisfaction [5–8].

Majority of existing SMPC algorithms ensure closed loop constraint satisfaction typically rely on knowledge of worst case bounds corresponding to prescribed chance

F. Sun et al. (Eds.): ICCSIP 2023, CCIS 1918, pp. 269–280, 2024.
https://doi.org/10.1007/978-981-99-8018-5_20

constraints. Although the offline computation of constraint tightening releases the computational complex, it causes intrinsic conservatism for ignoring past constraint violations and current uncertainty. To cope with this issue, several approaches have been proposed. In [9], the authors develop a recursively feasible MPC scheme by explicitly taking into account the past constraint violations to adaptively scale the tightening parameters. The work [10] exploits the observed constraint violations to adaptively scale the tightening parameters to eliminate the conservatism, and analyze the convergence of the amount of constraint violations rigorously using stochastic approximation. For linear systems under multiplicative and possibly unbounded model uncertainty, the work [11] presents a stochastic model predictive control algorithm. In which, the probabilistic constraints are reformulated in deterministic terms by means of the Cantelli inequality. A recursively feasible stochastic model predictive control scheme is designed by explicitly taking into account the past averaged-over-time amount of constraint violations when determining the current control input [12].

Another way to reduce the conservatism of MPC scheme is using the statistical machine learning methods to model the uncertainties based on prior knowledge [13–15]. Gaussian process (GP) regression is particularly attractive because it provides variance besides the mean of uncertainty, which can be incorporated into MPC to improve the performance [16–19].

In this paper, we propose a Gaussian process based SMPC (GP-SMPC) scheme for linear time-invariant (LTI) systems subject to bounded additive uncertainties. The uncertainties are state-dependent and bounded. The GP models for the uncertainties are trained offline on the base of previous collected data. The future mean and variance of the uncertainty can be predicted by the learned GP model on the condition of current state and input. The key contribution of this work is that the predicted information of uncertainty is used to adaptively scale the tightening parameters of the system constraints to achieve less conservatism.

he remainder of this paper is organized as follows. The time-varying tube-based SMPC is introduced in Sect. 2. Section 3 proposes the GP-SMPC scheme which mainly consists of the uncertainty modeling and constraint tightening. In Sect. 4, numerical simulations are given. Section 5 concludes the paper.

Notations

$x_{k|t}$ represents the k-step-ahead prediction of x at time t.

$\mathbb{R}$ denotes the set of reals, $\mathbb{N}_i$ denotes the set of integers which equal or greater than i, $\mathbb{N}_i^j$ denotes the set of consecutive integers $\{i, \cdots, j\}$.

$\Pr(X)$ stands for the probability of an event X.

The Minkowski sum is denoted by $A \oplus B = \{a + b | a \in A, b \in B\}$.

The Pontryagin set difference is represented by $A \ominus B = \{a \in A | a + b \in A, \forall b \in B\}$.

2 Time-Varying Tube-Based SMPC

Consider a discrete LTI system subject to additive uncertainties

$$x_{k+1} = Ax_k + Bu_k + w_k, \tag{1}$$

where $x_k \in \mathbb{R}^n$ and $u_k \in \mathbb{R}^m$ are the state and input at time k respectively. The uncertainties $w_k \in \mathbb{W} \subset \mathbb{R}^n$, which can be unmodeled nonlinearities and/or external disturbances, are bounded and state-dependent. Moreover, system (1) is subjected to the following constraints on states and inputs

$$\Pr(x_{k+1} \in \mathbb{X}) \geq 1 - \epsilon, k \in \mathbb{N}_0, \tag{2a}$$

$$u_k \in \mathbb{U}, k \in \mathbb{N}_0. \tag{2b}$$

The nominal system neglecting the uncertainty part is defined as

$$s_{k+1} = As_k + Bv_k, \tag{3}$$

where the nominal state $s_k \in \mathbb{R}^n$ and the nominal open loop input $v_k \in \mathbb{R}^m$.

The error between observed state x_k and nominal state s_k is defined as

$$e_k = x_k - s_k, \tag{4}$$

One of the commonly used control policies in robust tube MPC is

$$u_k = Ke_k + v_k, \tag{5}$$

where the feedback gain K is obtained by LQR optimization for the nominal dynamics (4), such that $A_{cl} = A + BK$ is Schur stable.

Then the system dynamics in (1) can be decoupled into a nominal dynamics and an error dynamics as

$$s_{k+1} = As_k + Bv_k, \tag{6a}$$

$$e_{k+1} = A_{cl}e_k + w_k, \tag{6b}$$

The error dynamics (6b) will be used for constraint tightening.

Suppose that a polytope $\mathcal{E} \subset \mathbb{W}$ is a confidence region of probability level $1 - \epsilon$ for the uncertainty, that is.

$$\Pr(w_k \in \mathcal{E}) \geq 1 - \epsilon, \tag{7}$$

where $\epsilon \in (0, 1)$.

Since the error dynamics in (6b) is linear, and the uncertainty $w \in \mathbb{W}$, the propagation set of uncertainty $e_k \in \mathcal{W}_k$ is evolved as

$$\mathcal{W}_{k+1} = A_{cl}\mathcal{W}_k \oplus \mathbb{W}, k \in \mathbb{N}_0, \tag{8}$$

where $\mathcal{W}_0 = \mathbb{W}$. Then, it can be induced that $\mathcal{W}_k = \sum_{i=0}^{k} \oplus A_{cl}^i \mathbb{W}, k \in \mathbb{N}_0$.

Construct the tightened propagation set of uncertainty as

$$\mathcal{D}_k = A_{cl}\mathcal{W}_{k-1} \oplus \mathcal{E}, k \in \mathbb{N}_1, \tag{9}$$

Then

$$\Pr(e_k \in \mathcal{D}_k) \geq 1 - \epsilon, k \in \mathbb{N}_0, \tag{10}$$

follows from (7), where $\mathcal{D}_0 = \mathcal{E}$.

Define the time-varying tightened state constraint set as

$$\mathcal{C}_k = \mathbb{X} \ominus \mathcal{D}_k, k \in \mathbb{N}_0. \tag{11}$$

If $s_k \in \mathcal{C}_k$, then $\Pr(x_k = s_k + e_k \in \mathbb{X}) \geq 1 - \epsilon$ is satisfied, that is, the satisfaction of chance constraint (2a) is guaranteed by (10) and (11).

Define the tightened input constraint set

$$\mathcal{V} = \mathbb{U} \ominus K\mathcal{Z}, \tag{12}$$

where $\mathcal{Z} = \sum_{i=0}^{\infty} \oplus A_{cl}^i \mathbb{W}$ and $e_k \in \mathcal{Z}, k \in \mathbb{N}_0$. If $v_k \in \mathcal{V}$, then the hard constraint (2b) $u_k = v_k + Ke_k \in \mathbb{U}$ is guaranteed by (12).

Define terminal constraint set

$$\mathcal{X}_f = \left\{ s \in \mathbb{R}^n : s_k \in \mathbb{X} \ominus \mathcal{Z}, Ks_k \in \mathcal{V}, k \in \mathbb{N}_0 \right\}. \tag{13}$$

The finite horizon optimal control problem to be solved at each time instant t is as follows:

$$\min_{s_{0|t}, v_{0|t}, \cdots, v_{N-1|t}} \sum_{k=0}^{N-1} \left(\|s_{k|t}\|_Q^2 + \|v_{k|t}\|_R^2 \right) + \|s_{N|t}\|_P^2$$

$$s.t. \ s_{k+1|t} = As_{k|t} + Bv_{k|t},$$

$$s_{k|t} \in \mathcal{C}_{k+t}, k \in \mathbb{N}_1^{N-1},$$

$$v_{k|t} \in \mathcal{V}, k \in \mathbb{N}_0^{N-1}, \tag{14}$$

$$x_t - s_{0|t} \in \mathcal{W}_t,$$

$$s_{N|t} \in \mathcal{X}_f.$$

3 SMPC Using Gaussian Process Regression

Since the uncertainty is state-dependent, it will be conservative if the confidence region $\mathcal{E}$ formulated based on its maximum amplitude. In this section, a Gaussian process regression method is proposed to solve this issue.

3.1 Gaussian Process Regression

Considering a training set $\{(x_i, y_i), i = 1, 2, \cdots, M\}$, where $x_i \in \mathbb{R}^d$ and $y_i \in \mathbb{R}$. The GPR model learns a function $f(x)$ mapping the input vector x to the observed output value y given by $y = f(x) + w$, where $w \sim \mathcal{N}(0, \sigma_n^2)$. The observed output values are normally distributed $y \sim \mathcal{N}(\mu(X), K(X, X))$, where the mean value vector $\mu(X) = [\mu(x_1), \cdots, \mu(x_M)]^T$ and the covariance matrix

$$K(X, X) = \begin{bmatrix} c(x_1, x_1) & c(x_1, x_2) & \cdots & c(x_1, x_M) \\ c(x_2, x_1) & c(x_2, x_2) & \cdots & c(x_2, x_M) \\ \vdots & \vdots & \ddots & \vdots \\ c(x_M, x_1) & c(x_M, x_2) & \cdots & c(x_M, x_M) \end{bmatrix}, \tag{15}$$

and $c(x_i, x_j)$ is the covariance of x_i and x_j, which can be any positive definite function. A frequently used covariance function called Square Exponential Kernel function is defined as

$$c(x_i, x_j) = \sigma_f^2 \exp\left(-\frac{1}{2}(x_i - x_j)^T L(x_i - x_j)\right) + \sigma_n^2, \tag{16}$$

where $L = \text{diag}([l_1, \cdots l_d])$, σ_f and σ_n are the hyperparameters of the covariance function.

The training output y and a predicted output y^* corresponding to the test input x^* are jointly Gaussian distribution

$$\begin{bmatrix} y \\ y^* \end{bmatrix} \sim \mathcal{N}\left(0, \begin{bmatrix} K(X, X) & k(x^*, X)^T \\ k(x^*, X) & k(x^*, x^*) \end{bmatrix}\right), \tag{17}$$

where $k(x^*, X) = [c(x^*, x_1), c(x^*, x_2), \cdots, c(x^*, x_M)]$, $k(x^*, x^*) = c(x^*, x^*)$.

Following the Bayesian modeling framework, the posterior distribution of y^* can be obtained conditioned on the observations, and the resulting is still Gaussian with $y^*|y \sim \mathcal{N}(\mu(x^*), \sigma^2(x^*))$ and

$$\mu(x^*) = k(x^*, X)K(X, X)^{-1}y, \tag{18a}$$

$$\sigma^2(x^*) = k(x^*, x^*) - k(x^*, X)K(X, X)^{-1}k(x^*, X)^T. \tag{18b}$$

3.2 GP Model of Uncertainty

The learned GPR model depends on measurement data collected from previous experience. The model input and output are the state-control tuple $z_k = (x_k; u_k)$ and corresponding uncertainty w_k, respectively. The uncertainty at time k.

$$w_k = x_{k+1} - (Ax_k + Bu_k). \tag{19}$$

The data pair (z_k, w_k) represents an individual experience. Given a well collected data pair set $\mathfrak{D} = \{z, w\}$ and a test data pair (z^*, w^*), the jointly Gaussian distribution is

$$\begin{bmatrix} w \\ w^* \end{bmatrix} \sim \mathcal{N}\left(0, \begin{bmatrix} K(z, z) \, k(z^*, z)^T \\ k(z^*, z) \, k(z^*, z^*) \end{bmatrix}\right). \tag{20}$$

The posterior distribution of w^* is still Gaussian

$$w^*|\mathfrak{D} \sim \mathcal{N}\left(\mu(z^*), \sigma^2(z^*)\right) \tag{21}$$

with mean and variance as follows

$$\mu(z^*) = k(z^*, z)K(z, z)^{-1}w, \tag{22a}$$

$$\sigma^2(z^*) = k(z^*, z^*) - k(z^*, z)K(z, z)^{-1}k(z^*, z)^T. \tag{22b}$$

The n separate GP models are trained for each dimension in $w \in \mathbb{R}^n$. We gain the optimal hyperparameters of each Gaussian model offline by maximizing the log marginal likelihood of collected data sets [20].

3.3 Adaptive Constraints

Define the prediction model as

$$\tilde{x}_{k+1} = A\tilde{x}_k + B\tilde{u}_k + \tilde{w}_k, \tag{23}$$

where $\tilde{x}_k$ denotes the predicted state, $\tilde{u}_k$ the predicted input, and $\tilde{w}_k$ the predicted uncertainty. On the condition of trained GP models, the distribution of $\tilde{w}_k$ corresponding to $(\tilde{x}_k; \tilde{u}_k)$ can be obtained as

$$\tilde{w}_k \sim \mathcal{N}(\tilde{\mu}_k, \tilde{\sigma}_k^2), \tag{24}$$

where $\tilde{\mu}_k$ and $\tilde{\sigma}_k^2$ are computed by (22a) and (22b).

Define the confidence region of the predicted uncertainty with the probability level $1 - \epsilon$ as

$$\tilde{\mathcal{E}}_k = \left\{\tilde{\mu}_k - \alpha\tilde{\sigma}_k \leq \tilde{w}_k \leq \tilde{\mu}_k + \alpha\tilde{\sigma}_k\right\}, k \in \mathbb{N}_0, \tag{25}$$

where α is the quantile value corresponding to $1 - \epsilon$.

According to (9), the more stringent propagation set of uncertainty is

$$\tilde{\mathcal{D}}_k = A_{cl}\mathcal{W}_{k-1} \oplus \tilde{\mathcal{E}}_{k-1}, k \in \mathbb{N}_1, \tag{26}$$

Then

$$\Pr\left(\tilde{e}_k \in \tilde{\mathcal{D}}_k\right) \geq 1 - \epsilon, k \in \mathbb{N}_1, \tag{27}$$

follows.

Construct the adaptively time-varying state constraint set as

$$\tilde{\mathcal{C}}_k = \mathbb{X} \ominus \tilde{\mathcal{D}}_k, k \in \mathbb{N}_1. \tag{28}$$

If $s_k \in \tilde{\mathcal{C}}_k$, then the chance constraint $\Pr(x_k = s_k + e_k \in \mathbb{X}) \geq 1 - \epsilon$ is satisfied. Define the tightened input constraint set $\mathcal{V} = \mathbb{U} \ominus K\mathcal{Z}$ as (12). If $v_k \in \mathcal{V}$, then the satisfaction of hard constraint $u_k = v_k + Ke_k \in \mathbb{U}$ is guaranteed.

3.4 Gaussian Process Based SMPC

On the basis of the time-varying tube-based SMPC, by combining the GP-based uncertainty prediction, the Gaussian process based stochastic optimal control problem to be solved at each time instant t is as follows:

$$\min_{s_{0|t}, v_{0|t}, \cdots, v_{N-1|t}} \sum_{k=0}^{N-1} \left(\|s_{k|t}\|_Q^2 + \|v_{k|t}\|_R^2 \right) + \|s_{N|t}\|_P^2$$

$$\text{s.t. } \tilde{x}_{0|t} = x_t,$$

$$\tilde{x}_{k+1|t} = A\tilde{x}_{k|t} + B\tilde{u}_{k|t} + \tilde{w}_{k|t},$$

$$\tilde{u}_{k|t} = K\left(\tilde{x}_{k|t} - s_{k|t}\right) + v_{k|t},$$

$$\tilde{w}_{k|t}(\tilde{x}_{k|t}, \tilde{u}_{k|t}) \sim \mathcal{N}(\tilde{\mu}_{k|t}, \tilde{\sigma}_{k|t}^2),$$

$$\text{Generate } \tilde{\mathcal{C}}_{k+t|t} \text{ by Eq. } (24) - (27) \tag{29}$$

$$s_{k+1|t} = As_{k|t} + Bv_{k|t},$$

$$s_{k|t} \in \tilde{\mathcal{C}}_{k+t|t}, k \in \mathbb{N}_1^{N-1},$$

$$v_{k|t} \in \mathcal{V}, k \in \mathbb{N}_0^{N-1},$$

$$x_t - s_{0|t} \in \mathcal{W}_t,$$

$$s_{N|t} \in \mathcal{X}_f.$$

The solution of the optimal control problem yields the optimal initial nominal state $s_{0|t}^*$ and input sequence.

$$v^*(x_t) = \left[v_{0|t}^*, \cdots, v_{N-1|t}^* \right]. \tag{30}$$

The associate optimal state sequence for nominal system is

$$s^*(x_t) = \left[s^*_{0|t}, \cdots, s^*_{N|t} \right].$$ (31)

Using the first entry of the optimal input sequence and the optimal initial state, the optimal control law is designed as

$$u^*(x_t) = K\left(x_t - s^*_{0|t} \right) + v^*_{0|t}.$$ (32)

Apply $u^*(x_t)$ to the system (1) yields new state.

$$x_{t+1} = Ax_t + Bu^*(x_t) + w_t.$$ (33)

Based on the new state x_{t+1}, the entire process of GP based SMPC is repeated at time $t + 1$, yielding a receding horizon control strategy.

4 Numerical Simulation

In this section, the chance constraint satisfaction of the GP-SMPC scheme are compared with nominal MPC, robust MPC and time-varying tube-based SMPC. In the simulations, the polytopes $\mathcal{C}$, $\mathcal{V}$, $\mathcal{D}$ and $\mathcal{Z}$ are computed by using the MPT3 toolbox.

To show the constraint violation of the GP-SMPC scheme, a discrete LTI system subject to state-dependent additive uncertainty disturbed by a truncated normal distributed noise is designed as

$$x_{k+1} = \begin{bmatrix} 1.6 & 1.1 \\ -0.7 & 1.2 \end{bmatrix} x_k + \begin{bmatrix} 1 \\ 1 \end{bmatrix} u_k + w_k,$$

The state and input constraints are $\Pr(x_k \in \mathbb{X}) \geq 0.8$ and $u_k \in \mathbb{U}$, respectively.

$$\mathbb{X} \triangleq \left\{ x \in \mathbb{R}^2 : \begin{bmatrix} -10 \\ -2 \end{bmatrix} \leq x \leq \begin{bmatrix} 2 \\ 10 \end{bmatrix} \right\}, \mathbb{U} \triangleq \left\{ u \in \mathbb{R}^1 : |u| \leq 10 \right\}.$$

The uncertainty $w_k \in \mathbb{W}$ and

$$\mathbb{W} \triangleq \left\{ w \in \mathbb{R}^2 : \|w\|_\infty \leq 0.1, w = 0.1 * \left(\frac{1}{1 + |u|e^{-x}} - 0.5 \right) + \mathcal{N}\left(0, 0.015^2 I_2 \right) \right\}.$$

Design the weights of cost function $Q = I_2$ and $R = 1$. Compute K as the LQR feedback gain for the unconstrained optimal problem (A, B, Q, R). The prediction horizon is $N = 6$. The simulation step is $N\mathrm{sim} = 11$. The initial state $x_0 = [-6.5, 10.5]^\mathrm{T}$.

The state constraint violations of the nominal MPC, the robust MPC, the time-varying tube-based SMPC and the proposed GP-SMPC are illustrated in Figs. 1, 2, 3 and 4. In the up side of each figure, the closed-loop actual state trajectories of 100 realizations are demonstrated. On account of that the constraint violation occurs around the border at the first several steps, the details of the first 3 step trajectories is enlarged at the down side part of each figure. Table 1 presents the first three steps constraint violation ratios and the average ratios of 1000 realizations. From the figures and the table, it can be seen that: the average constraint violation at the first 3 steps of the nominal MPC is 100%, the constraint is break at all steps; the average constraint violation at the first 3 steps of the robust MPC is 0%, the constraint is satisfied with heavy-duty conservatism; the average constraint violation at the first 3 steps of the time-varying tube-based SMPC is 65.0%, the conservatism is relieved a bit; and that of the proposed GP-SMPC is 16.2%, which is close to 20% specified in advance, resulting in less conservatism and constraint satisfaction.

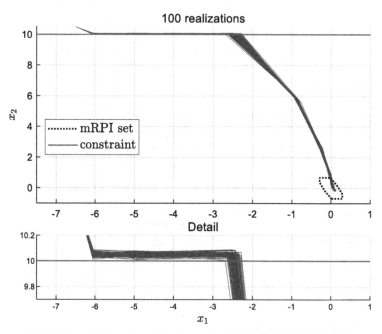

Fig. 1. Closed-loop trajectories of nominal MPC with 100 realizations.

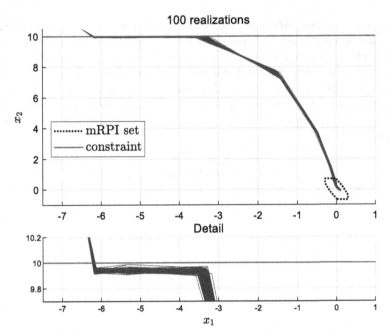

Fig. 2. Closed-loop trajectories of robust MPC with 100 realizations.

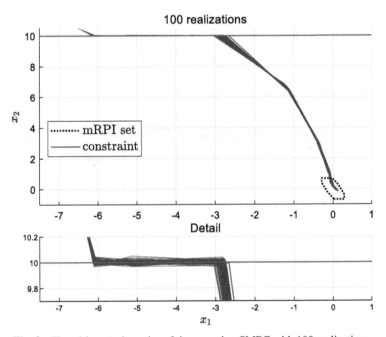

Fig. 3. Closed-loop trajectories of time-varying SMPC with 100 realizations.

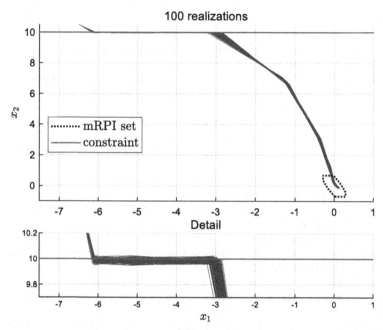

Fig. 4. Closed-loop trajectories of GP-SMPC with 100 realizations.

Table 1. Constraint violation of MPC algorithms.

Algorithm	Step 1	Step 2	Step 3	Average
Nominal MPC	100%	100%	100%	100%
Robust MPC	0%	0%	0%	0%
Time-varying SMPC	67.2%	65.3%	62.6%	65.0%
GP-SMPC	17.4%	17.3%	13.8%	16.2%

5 Conclusion

The proposed GP-SMPC scheme reduces the conservatism through tightening the constraints adaptively. Specifically, the stringent propagation set of uncertainty is obtained by using the time varying confidence region which is formulated on the basis of Gaussian process prediction. Numerical simulations validate that the chance constraint satisfaction of GP-SMPC is better than that of nominal MPC, robust MPC and time-varying tube-based SMPC.

References

1. Mayne, D.Q.: Model predictive control: recent developments and future promise. Automatica **50**(12), 2967–2986 (2014)
2. Li, H., Yan, W., Shi, Y.: Triggering and control codesign in self-triggered model predictive control of constrained systems: with guaranteed performance. IEEE Trans. Autom. Control Autom. Control **63**(11), 4008–4015 (2018)
3. Kouvaritakis, B., Cannon, M.: Model Predictive Control: Classical, Robust and Stochastic, 1st edn. Springer, Switzerland (2016)
4. Li, H., Shi, Y.: Robust receding horizon control for networked and distributed nonlinear systems. 1st edn. Springer (2017)
5. Mesbah, A.: Stochastic model predictive control: an overview and perspectives for future research. IEEE Control. Syst. **36**(6), 30–44 (2016)
6. Lorenzen, M., Dabbene, F., Tempo, R., Allgöwer, F.: Stochastic MPC with offline uncertainty sampling. Automatica **81**(1), 176–183 (2017)
7. Liu, X., Feng, L., Kong, X., Guo, S., Lee, K.Y.: Tube-based stochastic model predictive control with application to wind energy conversion system. IEEE Trans. Control Syst. Technol. https://doi.org/10.1109/TCST.2023.3291531(2023)
8. Arcari, E., Iannelli, A., Carron, A., Zeilinger, M.N.: Stochastic MPC with robustness to bounded parametric uncertainty. IEEE Trans. Autom. Control. https://doi.org/10.1109/TAC.2023.3294868(2023)
9. Kouvaritakis, B., Cannon, M., Raković, S., Cheng, Q.: Explicit use of probabilistic distributions in linear predictive control. Automatica **46**(10), 1719–1724 (2010)
10. Munoz-Carpintero, D., Hu, G., Spanos, C.: Stochastic model predictive control with adaptive constraint tightening for non-conservative chance constraints satisfaction. Automatica **96**, 32–39 (2018)
11. Farina, M., Scattolini, R.: Model predictive control of linear systems with multiplicative unbounded uncertainty and chance constraints. Automatica **70**, 258–265 (2016)
12. Korda, M., Gondhalekar, R., Oldewurtel, F., Jones, C.N.: Stochastic MPC framework for controlling the average constraint violation. IEEE Trans. Autom. ControlAutom. Control **59**(7), 1706–1721 (2014)
13. Li, F., Li, H., Li, S., He, Y.: Online learning stochastic model predictive control of linear uncertain systems. Int. J. Robust Nonlinear Control **32**(17), 9275–9293 (2022)
14. Aswani, A., González, H., Sastry, S.S., Tomlin, C.: Provably safe and robust learning-based model predictive control. Automatica **49**(5), 1216–1226 (2013)
15. Rosolia, U., Zhang, X., Borrelli, F.: A stochastic MPC approach with application to iterative learning. In: Proceedings of the 57th IEEE Conference on Decision and Control, pp. 5152–5157, Miami Beach, USA (2018)
16. Cao, G., Lai, E., Alam, F.: Gaussian process model predictive control of unmanned quadrotors. In: International Conference on Control, Automation and Robotics, pp. 200–206, Hong Kong, China (2016)
17. Li, F., Li, H., He, Y.: Adaptive stochastic model predictive control of linear systems using Gaussian process regression. IET Control Theory Appl. **15**(5), 683–693 (2021)
18. Ostafew, C.J., Schoellig, A.P., Barfoot, T.D.: Robust constrained learning-based NMPC enabling reliable mobile robot path tracking. Int. J. Robot. Res. **35**(13), 1547–1563 (2016)
19. Yang, X., Maciejowski, J.M.: Fault tolerant control using Gaussian processes and model predictive control. Int. J. Appl. Math. Comput. Sci.Comput. Sci. **25**(1), 133–148 (2015)
20. Wang, Y., Ocampo-Martinez, C., Puig, V.: Stochastic model predictive control based on Gaussian processes applied to drinking water networks. IET Control Theory Appl. **10**(8), 947–955 (2016)

Observer-Based Nonsingular Terminal Sliding Mode Guidance Law with Fixed-Time Convergence

Xiaojing Li$^{(\boxtimes)}$, Chao Wu, and Yan Wang

Luoyang Institute of Science and Technology, Luoyang 471000, China
15896561868@163.com

Abstract. In order to solve the problems of singularity, slow convergence rate and external disturbance, a non-singular fixed-time sliding mode guidance law with attack Angle constraint is proposed. Firstly, a non-singular terminal sliding mode surface is constructed, which ensures that the line-of-sight (LOS) Angle and LOS Angle rate can converge to the expected value within a given fixed time. Secondly, the upper bound of target interference is estimated by constructing a fixed-time observer, where the unknown upper-bound of the external disturbance caused by the target acceleration is estimated online. The stability of the guidance law is analyzed and proved by using Lyapunov stability theory. Finally, the effectiveness and robustness of the guidance law are verified by numerical simulation.

Keywords: impact angle constraint · non-singular · Fixed-time convergence · disturbance observer

1 Introduction

Missiles play a rather important role in modern warfare. Guidance law is the key technology that affects the guidance performance. It is the relative motion relation between the missile and the target that the missile should follow in the process of approaching the target, which determines the trajectory of the missile [1]. In the final guidance stage, the target will often escape, and the interference generated by the target maneuver can not be accurately estimated, which has higher requirements for the anti-interference of the final guidance law. The sliding mode control has strong robustness to the uncertainty of the system and the external disturbance, so it has been deeply studied in the design of the guidance law [2]. The traditional sliding mode control usually adopts the linear sliding mode surface, which can make the system state converge to the equilibrium point in an asymptotic way, but the convergence time tends to infinite [3]. However, in modern war, the time left for terminal guidance is very short, which requires the system to respond quickly [4]. For further research on finite-time stability, the concept of fixed-time convergence (FTC) is proposed in literature [5]. In [6], a adaptive fixed-time

This Work Was Supported in Part By Key Research Projects of Higher Education Institutions of Henan Province Under Grant 23B413002.

terminal sliding mode guidance law is proposed to intercept a maneuvering target, in this paper, the unknown upper-bound of the disturbance is estimated online by an adaptive law. In [7], a novel adaptive fast fixed-time sliding mode guidance law with no problems of singularity is designed to intercept maneuver targets at a desired impact angle. In [8], a fast terminal sliding mode guidance law is proposed to solve the problem of impact angle constraint for maneuvering targets. In this paper, a second-order sliding mode super-twisting algorithm is improved to weaken chattering and suppress interference. In [9], a nonsingular fixed-time convergent fast terminal sliding mode guidance law is developed with impact angle constraints. Besides, an adaptive law for unknown upper bound estimation of the target acceleration is presented and the information on the target acceleration is not required to be known.

Motivated by the above discussions, this paper will pay more attention to the design of guidance law with impact angle constraints based on fixed-time stability control. An observer-based guidance law with fixed-time convergence is presented for intercepting a single maneuvering target. The main contributions of this paper can be concluded as follows.

(1) a fixed-time guidance law without singularity based on the terminal sliding mode is designed to guarantee that the LOS angle can converge to the expected LOS angle rapidly. The stability of the system is demonstrated by Lyapunov stability theory.
(2) the continuous control input is achieved by introducing a fixed-time disturbance observer without any knowledge of external disturbances. The problem of overestimation or underestimation of switching gain is solved effectively.

The rest of this paper is arranged as follows. Section 2 states problem formation and related preliminaries. The main results are developed in Sect. 3, fixed-time guidance law is presented and the proof of the corresponding stability is given in detail. In Sect. 4, numerical simulations are provided to demonstrate the effectiveness of the proposed guidance law. Conclusions are finally drawn in Sect. 5.

2 Problem Formation and Preliminaries

In this section, a brief description about the planar guidance geometry of missile and target is provided. Then, fixed-time control theory are formulated.

2.1 Problem Statement

The missile interception process is actually a three-dimensional space problem. For simplicity, we often decouple it into a relative motion problem in two planes, as shown in Fig. 1, where the relevant explanations are provided below.

The corresponding relative kinematic equations can be described as follows

$$\dot{r} = V_T \cos(q - \varphi_T) - V_M \cos(q - \varphi_M) \tag{1}$$

$$r\dot{q} = -V_T \sin(q - \varphi_T) + V_M \sin(q - \varphi_M) \tag{2}$$

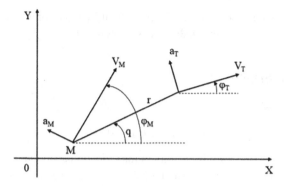

Fig. 1. Homing engagement geometry.

$$\dot{\varphi}_M = \frac{a_M}{V_M} \tag{3}$$

$$\dot{\varphi}_T = \frac{a_T}{V_T} \tag{4}$$

These assumptions are made: (1) the pursuer and target are considered as point masses; (2) seeker dynamics and the autopilot of the pursuer are fast enough to be neglected; (3) the speeds of the missile and target are constant. V_M and V_T denote velocity vectors of missile and target; The flight path angles and LOS angle are denoted by φ_M, φ_T and q, respectively. The normal acceleration of the missile and the target are denoted by a_M and a_T.

The derivatives of the expressions of Eq. (2) can be obtained as

$$\ddot{q} = -\frac{2\dot{r}}{r}\dot{q} - \frac{a_M\cos(q-\varphi_M)}{r} + \frac{a_T\cos(q-\varphi_T)}{r} \tag{5}$$

Define the state variables as $x_1 = q - q_d$, $x_2 = \dot{q}$, q_d is the terminal expected LOS angle. Therefore, the guidance model can be described as

$$\dot{x}_1 = x_2$$
$$\dot{x}_2 = -\frac{2\dot{r}}{r}x_2 - \frac{\cos(q-\varphi_M)}{r}u + \frac{d}{r} \tag{6}$$

where $d = \cos(q-\varphi_T)a_T$.

Remark 1. In view of Eq. (6), for a missile intercepting a maneuvering target, we design the control input u to guarantees that the LOS angular velocity approaches zero and the LOS angle converges to the expected value.

Assumption 1. The unknown and bounded external disturbances is respectively denoted by d, which is caused by the acceleration of the target, d satisfy $|d| \le D$, where D is unknown positive constant.

Remark 2. Since the target maneuver can be considered as generation of autopilot with first-order dynamics, the accelerations of the target and first-order derivatives of the target are bounded. Therefore, in the process of interception engagement, external disturbances constraints are reasonable for Assumption 1.

2.2 Fixed-Time Stability

Consider a nonlinear system

$$\dot{x}(t) = f(x(t)), \ x(0) = x_0 \tag{7}$$

with $x \in R^n$, and $f : R^n \to R^n$ is an autonomous function such that $f(0) = 0(x = 0)$ is an equilibrium point of nonlinear system (7).

Definition 1 [10] . The equilibrium point of system (7) is globally finite-time stable if it is globally asymptotically stable and any solution $\xi(t, x_0)$ of this system converge to the origin within finite time, $\forall t \geq T(x_0) : \xi(t, x_0) = 0$ where $T : R^n \to R_+ \cup \{0\}$ and $R_+ = \{l : l \in R, \ l > 0\}$.

Definition 2 [5] . The equilibrium point of system (7) is fixed-time stable if the settling time is bounded and independent of initial conditions, i.e., $\exists T_{max} > 0 : \forall x_0 \in R^n$ and $T(x_0) \leq T_{max}$.

Lemma 1 [5] . For the system (12), if there exists Lyapunov function $V(x)$, scalars $\alpha, \ \beta, \ p, \ q \in R_+(0 < p < 1, \ q > 1)$ such that $\dot{V}(x) \leq -\alpha V(x)^q - \beta V(x)^p$ holds, the trajectory of this system is practical fixed-time stable. The bounded time required to reach the residual set is estimated by

$$T(x_0) \leq 1/[\beta(1-p)] + 1/[\alpha(q-1)] \tag{8}$$

3 Guidance Law Design

In this section, a fixed-time disturbance observer is developed, and then the fixed-time nonsingular TSM technique is developed, while the fixed-time guidance law is proposed to guarantee the LOS angular rates converge to zero within a fixed time. The main results are provided as follows.

3.1 A Fixed-Time Disturbance Observer

The unknown target acceleration is a crucial factor for the design of the guidance law. A larger interference upper bound is often selected in order to ensure the robustness of the designed guidance law in the real flight, but this will cause chattering phenomenon. To address this issue, a fixed-time disturbance observer (FxTDO) is proposed and the estimated value of the interference is applied to the design of guidance law. According to the literature [11], the observer form is as follows

$$\begin{cases} \dot{z}_1 = k_1 \varphi_1(\frac{x_2 - z_1}{\delta}) - \frac{2\dot{r}}{r} x_2 - \frac{\cos(q - \varphi_M)}{r} u + \frac{z_2}{r} \\ \dot{z}_2 = \frac{k_2}{\delta} \varphi_2(\frac{x_2 - z_1}{\delta}) \end{cases} \tag{9}$$

where φ_1, φ_2 are the correction term and there are

$$\varphi_1(x) = sig^{\alpha'}(x) + sig^{\beta'}(x)$$
$$\varphi_2(x) = sig^{2\alpha'-1}(x) + sig^{2\beta'-1}(x) \tag{10}$$

z_1, z_2 estimate the value of x_2, d respectively, where $k_1, k_2 > 0$, $k_1 > 2\sqrt{k_2}$, $0 < \delta < 1, 0.5 < \alpha' < 1$ and $1 < \beta' < 1.5$.

3.2 Non-singular Fixed Time Guidance Law

Theorem 1. For the guidance system (6), the FxTDO is devised by (9), in order to guarantee the LOS angle error and the LOS angular velocity are fixed-time convergent, the nonsingular sliding mode surface and guidance law can be designed as

$$s_q = x_1 + l_1 sig^{\lambda_1} x_1 + l_2 sig^{\lambda_2} x_2 \tag{11}$$

$$u = \frac{r}{\cos(q - \varphi_M)} \left[\begin{array}{c} \frac{1}{l_4\lambda_2} sig^{2-\lambda_2} x_2 \left(1 + l_3\lambda_1 |x_1|^{\lambda_1-1}\right) - \frac{2\dot{r}}{r} x_2 + \frac{z_2}{r} \\ + l_5 sig^{\alpha_2} s_q + l_6 sig^{\beta_2} s_q \end{array} \right] \tag{12}$$

where $l_1, l_2, l_3, l_4, l_5, l_6 > 0$, $1 < \lambda_2 < 2$, $\lambda_1 > \lambda_2$, $0 < \alpha_2 < 1$, $\beta_2 > 1$.

Proof. First, prove the reachability of the sliding mode variable.

Taking the derivative of s_q with respect to time, combine with the guidance law (12), we get

$$
\begin{aligned}
\dot{s}_q &= x_2 + l_3\lambda_1 |x_1|^{\lambda_1-1} x_2 + l_4\lambda_2 |x_2|^{\lambda_2-1} \dot{x}_2 \\
&= x_2 \left(1 + l_3\lambda_1 |x_1|^{\lambda_1-1}\right) + l_4\lambda_2 |x_2|^{\lambda_i-1} \left(-\frac{2\dot{r}}{r} x_2 - \frac{\cos(q - \varphi_M)}{r} u + \frac{d}{r} \right) \\
&= l_4\lambda_2 |x_2|^{\lambda_2-1} \left(\frac{d - z_2}{r} - l_5 sig^{\alpha_2} s_q - l_6 sig^{\beta_2} s_q \right)
\end{aligned}
\tag{13}
$$

According to the definition of the FxTDO in (9), there exists a bounded positive constant t^* as

$$d - z_2 = 0, t > t^* \tag{14}$$

Select the following Lyapunov function as

$$V_3 = \frac{1}{2} s_q^2 \tag{15}$$

Then, differentiating V_3 with respect to time yields

$$
\begin{aligned}
\dot{V}_3 &= s_q \dot{s}_q = -s_q l_4\lambda_2 |x_4|^{\lambda_2-1} \left(l_5 sig^{\alpha_2} s_q + l_6 sig^{\beta_2} s_q\right) \\
&= l_4\lambda_2 |x_4|^{\lambda_2-1} \left(-\sqrt{2}^{\alpha_2+1} l_5 V_3^{\frac{\alpha_2+1}{2}} - \sqrt{2}^{\beta_i+1} l_i V_3^{\frac{\beta_i+1}{2}} \right)
\end{aligned}
$$

$$= -\bar{l}_5 V_3^{\frac{\alpha_2+1}{2}} - \bar{l}_6 V_3^{\frac{\beta_2+1}{2}} \tag{16}$$

where $\bar{l}_5 = \sqrt{2}^{\alpha_2+1} l_4 \lambda_2 |x_2|^{\lambda_2-1} l_5, \bar{l}_6 = \sqrt{2}^{\beta_2+1} l_4 \lambda_2 |x_2|^{\lambda_i-1} l_6$.
If $x_2 \neq 0$ is fulfilled, it has $l_4 = |x_2|^{1-\lambda_2}$ and then $\bar{l}_5 = \sqrt{2}^{\alpha_2+1} \lambda_2 l_5 > 0$

$$\bar{l}_6 = \sqrt{2}^{\beta_2+1} \lambda_2 l_6 > 0$$

From Lemma 2.5, it can be obtained that the sliding mode variable will converge to zero in $T_3 = t_{ft} + T_{sq}$, where

$$T_{sq} = \frac{2}{\bar{l}_5(1-\alpha_2)} + \frac{2}{\bar{l}_6(1-\beta_2)} \tag{17}$$

If $x_2 = 0$ is fulfilled, it has $\dot{x}_2 = -(l_5 sig^{\alpha_2} s_q + l_6 sig^{\beta_2} s_q + z_2 - d)$. Now, the sliding mode variable is discussed by the following cases.

If $s_q > 0$, then $\dot{x}_2 = -(l_5 + l_6)$. At that time, If $s_q < 0$, then $\dot{x}_2 = l_5 + l_6$.

Therefore, it can be seen that in the process of sliding mode variable approaching zero, the state variable x_2 will be far away from the region $x_2 \neq 0$ and enter the region $x_2 = 0$. When the system reaches the sliding mode surface, it can be obtained that $s_{qi} = 0$ is fulfilled, we get

$$l_4 sig^{\lambda_2} x_2 = -(x_1 + l_3 sig^{\lambda_1} x_1) \tag{18}$$

Furthermore, the following result can be provided

$$x_2 = -l_4^{-1/\lambda_2} (x_1 + l_3 sig^{\lambda_1} x_1)^{1/\lambda_2} \tag{19}$$

Select the following Lyapunov function as

$$V_4 = \frac{1}{2} x_1^2 \tag{20}$$

When $t > t_{ft}$ satisfied, we can get

$$\dot{V}_4 = x_1 \dot{x}_1 = -x_1 l_4^{-1/\lambda_2} (x_1 + l_3 sig^{\lambda_1} x_1)^{1/\lambda_2} \tag{21}$$

Furthermore, the following result can be provided

$$\dot{V}_4 \leq -x_1 l_4^{-1/\lambda_2} \left(x_1^{1/\lambda_2} + (l_3 sig^{\lambda_1} x_1)^{1/\lambda_2} \right)$$

$$= -l_4^{-1/\lambda_2} |x_1|^2 - l_3^{1/\lambda_2} l_4^{-1/\lambda_2} |x_1|^{(\lambda_1/\lambda_2)+1}$$

$$= -2 l_4^{-1/\lambda_2} V_4 - 2^{\frac{(\lambda_1/\lambda_2)+1}{2}} l_3^{1/\lambda_2} l_4^{-1/\lambda_2} V_4^{\frac{(\lambda_1/\lambda_2)+1}{2}} \tag{22}$$

Through the analysis of the above three cases, according to Lemma 1, it can be inferred that LOS angles and angular rates will reach stability with a fixed time.

Remark 3. In Theorem 1, the proposed guidance law with impact angle constraints is nonsingular. The second order system (6) can be reached to the sliding surface under the action of nonsingular terminal sliding mode guidance law in (12). Once the sliding surface is attained, the states of system (6) can reach the origin within a fixed time.

Remark 4. The guidance law in this section involve a lot of parameters, and appropriate control parameters should be selected according to such factors as guidance time, control energy consumption and miss distance.

4 Simulation Results

In order to verify the effectiveness of the designed fixed-time guidance law with angle of attack constraint, this section considers the two cases where missile attack a maneuvering target. The initial target distance of the missile and the target is $r_0 = 10\,km$, the initial LOS angle is $q_0 = \pi/6$, the initial heading angles are $\varphi_{M_0} = \pi/4$, $\varphi_{T_0} = 5\pi/6$, the velocity of the missile and the target are $V_M = 500\,m/s$, $V_T = 250\,m/s$; The maximum value of the available missile acceleration is assumed to be 25 g, where g is the acceleration of gravity ($g = 9.8\,m/s^2$). The parameters of fixed-time disturbance observer are selected as $k_1 = 3.0$, $k_2 = 1.5$, $\delta = 0.02$, $\alpha = 0.8$ and $\beta = 1.2$. The parameters of the guidance law are given by $l_1 = 1$, $l_2 = 8$, $l_3 = 1$, $l_4 = 8$, $\lambda_1 = 3$, $\lambda_2 = 1.5$ and $l_5 = 45$, $l_6 = 45$, $\alpha_2 = 0.8$, $\beta_2 = 1.8$.

To verify the robustness of the presented fixed-time guidance law (12), the two different cases for target maneuver are selected as follows:

Case 1: $a_T = 10\cos(0.3t)\,m/s^2$; Case 2: $a_T = 8\,m/s^2$.

Assume the desired LOS angles of the missile and target in both cases are $q_d = \pi/7$. Simulation comparisons under two cases are shown in Table 1 and the relevant results are given in Figs. 2, 3 and 4 and Figs. 5, 6 and 7, respectively. For two cases, the simulation curves including the missile-target relative distance r, flight path, sliding mode surface s, guidance commands a_M, LOS angular rate $\dot{q}_i$ and LOS angle q_i.

Table 1. Comparison results of two Cases

Cases	Guidance time (s)	Miss distance (m)	The settling time of LOS rates (s)	The settling time of sliding mode surface (s)
1	17.744	0.4384	5.256	3.768
2	16.129	0.0420	5.226	3.825

It can be seen from Fig. 2, the missile successfully intercepts the target in case 1 and the interception time is 17.744 s. The relative distance between the missile and the target at the interception time is almost zero, and the miss distance is 0.4384 m. Figure 3 shows the convergence of the guidance command and sliding mode surface. The convergence time of the sliding mode variable to zero is 3.768 s, and it converges before the line of sight Angle error and line of sight Angle rate. As shown in Fig. 3, guidance instructions are large in the early stage and basically reach saturation, which is to achieve rapid convergence of LOS Angle and LOS Angle rate within a fixed time, and large control quantity is often required in the early stage of guidance. Figure 4 show that the LOS Angle error and LOS Angle rate converge to zero at 5.256 s. As the LOS Angle error and LOS Angle rate tend to stabilize, the sliding mode variable and guidance instruction also tend to stabilize.

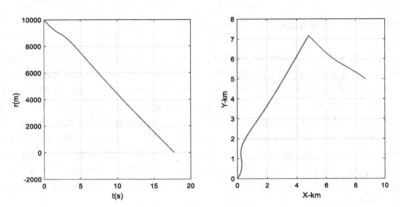

Fig. 2. Distance and flight path between the missile and the target

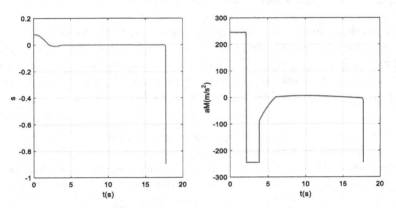

Fig. 3. Sliding mode surface and Acceleration.

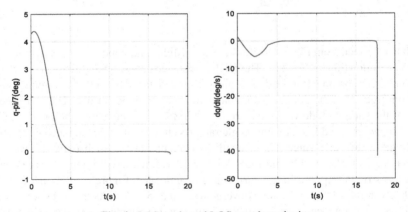

Fig. 4. LOS angle and LOS angular velocity.

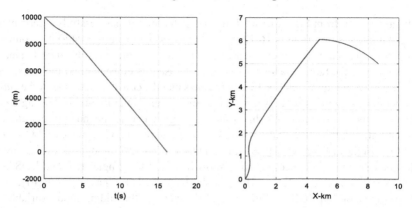

Fig. 5. Distance and flight path between the missile and the target

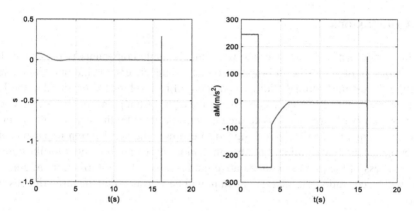

Fig. 6. Sliding mode surface and Acceleration.

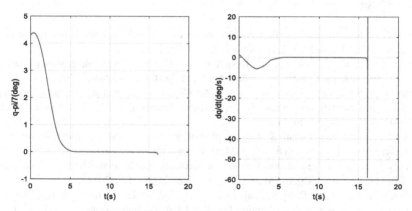

Fig. 7. LOS angle and LOS angular velocity.

It can be seen from Fig. 5, 6 and 7, in case 2, the missile successfully intercepts the target, the interception time is 16.129 s, and the miss distance is 0.0420 m. Compared with case 1, the guidance time of case 2 is shorter and the miss distance is smaller. This is because the target maneuvering form of case 2 is constant, and the missile can intercept the target more quickly. Figure 6 shows that the convergence time of the sliding mode variable to zero is 3.825 s, and it converges before the line-of-sight Angle error and line-of-sight Angle rate. As shown in Fig. 6, guidance command is larger and tend to be saturated in the early stage, which is to achieve rapid convergence of LOS Angle and LOS Angle rate within a fixed time, and larger control amount is often required in the early stage of guidance. Figure 7 show that the LOS Angle error and LOSAngle rate converge to zero at 5.226 s, which is shorter than that in case 1. Similarly, as the LOS Angle error and LOS Angle rate tend to stabilize, the sliding mode variable and guidance instruction also tend to stabilize.

5 Conclusions

In this paper, a novel guidance law with impact angle constraints is presented. It is continuous and requires no information on target maneuvers. On the one hand, a non-singular fixed-time terminal sliding mode control is developed to ensure that the LOS angular rate and the LOS angle converge to the equilibrium points in fixed-time. On the other hand, in order to compensate the chattering caused by the switching term in the process of guidance, FxTDO is designed to estimate the acceleration upper bound of target maneuverability online. Finally, simulation results are presented to illustrate the effectiveness of the proposed cooperative guidance law. In the further, more guidance laws with acceleration saturation constraint will be considered in the three-dimensional space.

References

1. Li, G.L.: Research on missile terminal guidance law based on finite time control theory. University of Science and Technology of China (2015)
2. Guo, J.G., Han, T., Zhou, J., et al.: Design of second-order sliding mode guidance Law based on Terminal Angle Constraint. Chin. J. Aeronaut. 38(02), 215–224 (2017)
3. Shtessel, Y.B., Shkolnikov, I.A., Levant, A.: Guidance and control of missile interceptor using second-order sliding modes. IEEE Trans. Aerosp. Electron. Syst.Aerosp. Electron. Syst. 45(1), 110–124 (2009)
4. Venkataraman, S.T., Gulati, S.: Control of nonlinear systems using terminal sliding modes. J. Dyn. Syst. Meas. Contr.Dyn. Syst. Meas. Contr. 115(3), 554–560 (1993)
5. Polyakov, A.: Nonlinear feedback design for fixed-time stabilization of linear control systems. IEEE Trans. Autom. ControlAutom. Control 57(8), 2106–2110 (2012)
6. Wang, X., Huang, X., Ding, S., et al.: Fixed-time Guidance law for intercepting maneuvering targets with impact angle constraint. In: 2019 Chinese Control Conference (CCC) (2019). https://doi.org/10.23919/ChiCC.2019.8866644
7. Zhang, Y., Tang, S., Guo, J.: An adaptive fast fixed-time guidance law with an impact angle constraint for intercepting maneuvering targets. Chin. J. Aeronaut. 31(06), 1327–1344 (2018)

8. Yang, F., Zhang, K., Yu, L.: Adaptive super-twisting algorithm-based nonsingular terminal sliding mode guidance law. J. Control Sci. Eng. (2020). https://doi.org/10.1155/2020/105 8347
9. Guorong, Z., Xiaobao, L., Shuai, L., et al.: Adaptive nonsingular fast terminal sliding mode guidance law with fixed-time convergence. J. Beijing Univ. Aeronaut. Astronaut. (2019)
10. Orlov, Y.: Finite time stability and robust control synthesis of uncertain switched systems. SIAM J. Control. Optim.Optim. **43**(4), 1253–1271 (2005)
11. Yang, F., Wei, C.Z., Wu, R., et al.: Fixed-time convergent disturbance observer for first-order uncertain system. Control Decis. **34**(05), 917–926 (2019)

Application

Faanet: Feature-Augmented Attention Network for Surface Defect Detection of Metal Workpieces

Yunpeng Gu[1], Jie Zou[2], Chao Ma[1], Yong Zhang[1], Mengtong Zhang[1], and Jianwei Ma[1(✉)]

[1] College of Information Engineering, Henan University of Science and Technology, Luoyang 471000, China
lymjw@163.com
[2] Science and Technology on Electro-optic Control Laboratory AVIC Optronics, Luoyang 471000, China

Abstract. Accurate segmentation of defects on the surface of metal workpieces is challenging due to the large-scale differences and complex morphological features. To address the problem of low accuracy in segmenting metal workpiece surface defects in complex scenes, we propose a Feature-Augmented Attention Network (FAANet) by studying the types of workpiece surface defects. The network adopts an encoder-decoder structure. In the encoding stage, VGG16 is used as the backbone to extract features at different depths of the metal workpiece surface. Moreover, a feature augmentation module is designed to refine the feature maps at different levels for the characteristics of the information contained in the features at different depths, emphasizing the detailed features, such as the edges of the defective targets. In the decoding stage, an efficient channel attention mechanism is fused in the network to make full use of the feature map with rich information after feature fusion. More relevant features are extracted through the interaction of different channel information to improve information utilization as well as segmentation accuracy. For the sample imbalance problem, a loss function supervised training model incorporating focal loss is designed to mitigate the negative impact of sample imbalance on the model performance. The results show that the proposed method achieves better segmentation results in detecting surface defects on metal workpieces in complex scenes than existing prevailed methods.

Keywords: Semantic Segmentation · Feature Augmentation · Attention Mechanism

1 Introduction

Metal workpieces may have defects such as pitting and scratches on the surface during production due to technology, equipment, process, and environmental factors. Surface defects of metal workpieces may adversely affect the appearance and quality of products and even cause major safety accidents. Therefore, the detection of surface defects

This work is supported by Aeronautical Science Foundation of China (Grant No.20200051042003)

F. Sun et al. (Eds.): ICCSIP 2023, CCIS 1918, pp. 295–308, 2024.
https://doi.org/10.1007/978-981-99-8018-5_22

on metal workpieces is of great importance [1, 2]. The common methods for detecting surface defects on metal workpieces are mainly manual visual inspection and nondestructive testing. Nondestructive testing mainly includes magnetic particle inspection techniques, eddy current flaw detection, etc. [3]. These traditional physical inspection methods suffer from a high rate of missed detection, low efficiency, and subjective factors influenced by inspectors, which cannot meet the needs of modern efficient automated production. Therefore, studying how to use deep learning technology to achieve defect detection has become a hopeful direction.

With the continuous advancement of deep learning technology and the improvement of computer hardware, semantic segmentation networks have been widely used in the field of defect detection, and a series of significant results have been achieved [4–7]. Mainstream segmentation networks include Fully Convolutional Networks (FCN) [8], U-Net [9], etc. Compared with traditional methods such as classification and detection, semantic segmentation networks can more accurately locate and label defective parts in images and identify more types of defects [10]. For example, researchers have trained appropriate semantic segmentation networks for some specific types of defects to achieve fast and accurate detection of these defects [11]. Meanwhile, to solve the defect detection problem in different scenarios, researchers design more efficient and accurate semantic segmentation networks through continuous exploration [12].

However, defects are generated randomly in the actual workpiece production and processing process, and the shape, size, and number of defects are variable. To alleviate the effects of small defect samples, unbalanced data, and complex defect features in the actual workpiece production process, Prappacher et al. [13] proposed a fast retrainable convolutional network. Using an approach to simulated defects effectively avoids a large amount of time and resources spent on collecting balanced data sets, reduces maintenance costs compared with existing inspection systems, and achieves highly accurate defect detection. However, the difference between simulated and occurring defects is not considered, adversely affecting the model's generalization ability. Wang et al. [14] proposed a fusion segmentation algorithm based on FCN and wavelet transform structured forest, which can effectively distinguish crack features in similar backgrounds by fusing the feature maps output from multiple models and obtaining competitive segmentation results in the task of detecting small cracks in steel beams in complex backgrounds. Dung et al. [15] proposed an FCN-based crack detection method for semantic segmentation of concrete crack images with VGG16 as the feature extraction network, and the results showed that the method achieved good performance in concrete crack detection tasks with an average accuracy of 90%. Many experts and scholars have conducted in-depth research on FCN, applied it to the defect detection field, and achieved certain results. However, the output result of general FCN undergoes a larger up-sampling rate to recover to the original image resolution, and some detailed information is inevitably lost. U-Net not only gradually recovers to the original image resolution by skip connection and step-wise upsampling operations but also improves the segmentation fineness of the model by multi-scale feature fusion. Huang et al. [16] proposed a real-time U-Net model with fused saliency detection for the saliency detection of tile surface defects, and the feature maps processed by multiple saliency methods were fused and then input to the U-Net network to improve the target segmentation. The detector branch is also introduced in the coding stage to predict the specific location of the defects, thus improving the segmentation performance of the network. However, considering only the spatial location may have some shortcomings in the problem of significant differences in defect scales. In this regard, Xie et al. [17] proposed an algorithm that can simultaneously extract the spatial domain and frequency domain information of the input image. Specifically, a branch of extracting image frequency domain features is introduced on the basis of the backbone network. Through multi-scale feature fusion, the segmentation effect of the model on minor defects is effectively improved.

Above scholars have conducted much research on defective target segmentation and have achieved rich results. A large number of research results show that the fusion of different depth features can improve segmentation accuracy. However, the negative impact on segmentation accuracy caused by insufficient extraction of detailed information, such as target contour and the edge of different depth features, has not been effectively solved. In this paper, based on the above research, we conduct a study based on the U-net framework to improve the segmentation accuracy of defects on the surface of metal workpieces in complex scenes. The main contributions include the following parts: (1) To obtain an encoder capable of extracting features with refinement in complex scenes, design a feature augmentation module applied to the encoding stage. (2) To address the problem of significant differences in defect scales and unbalanced samples, a hybrid loss function incorporating focal loss is designed to alleviate the training problem caused by unbalanced samples. (3) To fully exploit the rich information in the feature map after feature fusion in the decoding stage, an efficient channel attention mechanism is introduced. The information utilization is improved by the interaction of different channel information, thus improving the segmentation accuracy. The experimental results verify the effectiveness of the proposed methods.

2 Related Work

2.1 U-Net

The U-Net model was proposed by Ronneberger et al. [9] in 2015. It is a network developed based on FCN. The overall structure uses an encoder-decoder structure and skip-connection structure similar to FCN, as shown in Fig. 1. The encoder and decoder are symmetrical on the left and right sides. The left side is the shrinkage path used to obtain the context information of the image, and the right side is the expansion path to recover the image separation rate after obtaining the semantic information with category features. An accurate segmentation map is obtained in the extended path by upsampling the layer-by-layer features and stitching the corresponding hierarchical features in the encoder. U-Net has the characteristic of end-to-end training with small data sets, while tasks such as steel surface defect detection [18] and metal workpiece defect detection [19] have the limitation of difficulty in acquiring a large amount of image data. Therefore, further research on improving and optimizing the U-Net model can meet the practical needs in the field of defect detection.

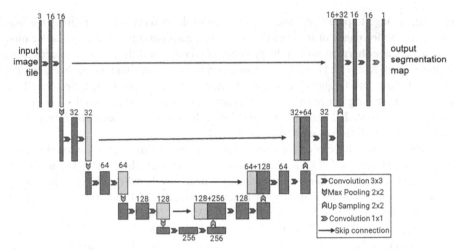

Fig. 1. U-Net structure

2.2 Efficient Channel Attention

The attention mechanism is a mechanism that simulates attention in human perception and can focus on local information in the region of interest [20]. With the in-depth study of experts and scholars, the research on attention mechanism has achieved rich results. For example, the channel attention mechanism (Squeeze-and-Excitation block, SE) was proposed by HU et al. [21] in 2017. Since the introduction of this module effectively improves the performance of deep learning networks. The Convolutional Block Attention Module (CBAM) [22] is developed on the basis of the SE module and uses the channel-space dual attention mechanism to improve the network performance further. However, the complex attention module increases the complexity of the model. The Efficient Channel Attention Module (ECA) proposed by Wang et al. [23] in 2020 effectively alleviates this problem. The ECA module can significantly improve network performance while increasing a small number of parameters.

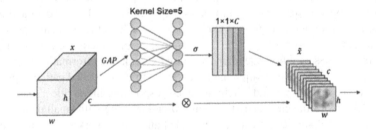

Fig. 2. ECA network structure

The ECA module is shown in Fig. 2. The working principle is as follows: Firstly, the input feature map is a global average pooled to obtain a feature vector with a size of 1 × 1 × C, then a fast one-dimensional convolution operation of size K is performed to obtain the weight of each channel. Finally, the weight of each channel is multiplied by the input feature to calibrate the channel feature. Since the convolution kernel K is proportional to the channel dimension C and the channel dimension is usually an exponential multiple of 2, the mapping relationship is shown in Eq. (1).

$$C = \phi(k) = 2^{(\gamma * k - b)} \tag{1}$$

In order to reduce the time and computational cost of the training process, the hyper-parameters γ and b are set to 2 and 1, respectively. Therefore, given the channel dimension C, the size of the convolution kernel K can be determined according to formula (2).

$$k = \varphi(C) = \left| \frac{\log_2 C}{\gamma} + \frac{b}{\gamma} \right|_{odd} \tag{2}$$

where $|t|_{odd}$ denotes the odd number closest to t.

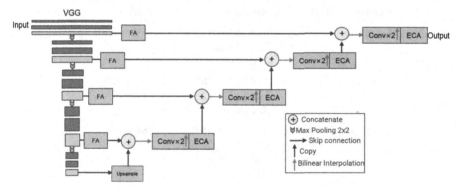

Fig. 3. The network structure of the proposed FAANET

3   Proposed Method

The overall structure of the proposed FAANet is shown in Fig. 3. The encoder-decoder structure is adopted. The encoder part uses VGG16 as the backbone. The structure and parameters of each layer of the VGG16 are shown in Table 1. Different depth features of the input image are extracted by convolution and pooling operations to prepare for the decoder fusion features. In order to improve the segmentation performance of the network for metal workpiece surface defects, a simple and effective feature augmentation module embedded in the encoding stage is proposed. The module can highlight the detailed features, such as the edge of the defect target, and effectively realize the refined processing of the target features. In the decoding process, the high-resolution feature map is up-sampled to obtain features of the same size as the corresponding encoding stage and stitched with them. Since the number of feature channels after concatenation is twice that before concatenation, a feature map with rich semantic category information and global location information is obtained. In order to make full use of the spliced feature map, an efficient channel attention mechanism is introduced after the conventional U-Net decoding operation, and more relevant features are extracted through feature interaction between different channels to improve information utilization and segmentation accuracy. The surface defect characteristics of metal workpieces have high complexity. For example, the location, size, and number of defects are random, and the defect scale is quite different, which causes the imbalance of samples, thus increasing the difficulty of accurate segmentation of defects. In order to alleviate the negative impact of sample imbalance on model training, a loss function integrating focal loss is designed to supervise the training of the model. Through multiple iterative learning and error correction, the adverse effects of sample imbalance are effectively reduced, and the segmentation performance of the network model is improved.

Table 1. VGG16 layer structure and parameters

Number of layers	Operation	Input size
First layer	Conv2d(3,64) Conv2d(64,64) Maxpool2d	1536×640
Second layer	Conv2d(64,128) Conv2d(128,128) Maxpool2d	768×320
Third layer	Conv2d(128,256) Conv2d(256,256) Conv2d(256,256) Maxpool2d	384×160
Fourth layer	Conv2d(256,512) Conv2d(512,512) Conv2d(512,512) Maxpool2d	192×80
Fifth layer	Conv2d(512,512) Conv2d(512,512) Conv2d(512,512)	96×40

3.1 Feature Augmentation Module

By analyzing the working principle of the left and right paths of the U-Net model, features with contextual information in the contraction path and features with semantic categories in the corresponding expansion path are fused to obtain features with rich semantic and location information. However, there is a semantic gap between the features in the contraction path and the features in the expansion path. Direct fusion operation will have redundant features that affect the model inference performance and adversely affect the segmentation results. Therefore, a feature augmentation module is proposed, embedded in the encoding stage used to highlight the defective target features at different depths, refine the target region, and reduce the difference between the features in the encoding stage and those in the corresponding decoding stage. Thus, the negative impact of redundant features on the inference results is effectively mitigated, and the segmentation accuracy is improved. Specifically, the fixed receptive field of the convolution kernel is mainly used to design the feature augmentation module, which is used to calculate the spatial range of target features at different depths and suppress redundant features, such as non-targets, so as to realize the fine processing of target feature boundaries. The feature augmentation module is shown in Fig. 4, which consists of convolution operation, regularization layer, and activation function layer. The features of different depths extracted by the backbone network in the encoding stage are expressed as [feat1, feat2, feat3, feat4, feat5]. Because the information and size contained in different levels of features are different, the deep feature feat5, after a continuous downsampling operation, has abstract semantic category information and loses more detailed features. Therefore, the feature augmentation module is only applied to the first four layers. Given the size of the input feature size H × W × C, H and W represent the height and width of the input feature, respectively, and C represents the dimension of the input feature channel. After the feature augmentation module is processed, the refined features with the same size as the input feature are obtained. The feature augmentation module is calculated as shown in (3) and (4).

$$F_{mid} = \text{Re}LU\{BN[Conv(C_i, C_i)(F_i)]\} \tag{3}$$

$$F_{fa} = \text{Re}LU\{BN[Conv(C_i, C_i)(F_{mid})]\} \tag{4}$$

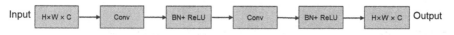

Fig. 4. Feature augmentation module

In the formula, F_i is the input feature of layer i, *Conv* is the convolution operation with the convolution kernel size of 3 × 3, *BN* is the regularization operation, *ReLU* is the activation function, F_{mid} is the intermediate feature after the first convolution regularization, and F_{fa} is the augmented output feature.

3.2 Integrated ECA Networks

In order to further improve the performance of the segmentation network, the Efficient Channel Attention Module (ECA) is integrated. The module has good generalization ability and lightweight advantages and can effectively improve the performance of the model within a small amount of acceptable parameter range. Specifically, ECA achieves non-dimensional local cross-channel information interaction, thereby extracting rich context features and improving the segmentation results of the network. Since the feature maps at different depths in the decoder stage have rich semantic category information and global location information after fusion, it is more reasonable to introduce ECA after splicing each layer of features in the decoding stage with the features in the corresponding encoding stage.

3.3 Loss Function

The dice loss function is often used in semantic segmentation tasks with fewer target types, so dice loss is selected as the loss function of the proposed FAANet. In order to prevent the negative impact of positive and negative sample imbalance on network segmentation performance, the focal loss function is introduced, and different loss weights are given to the foreground and background. The loss functions are shown in Eqs. (5) and (6):

$$L_{Dice} = 1 - \frac{2\sum_{i=1}^{N} y_i \hat{y}_i}{\sum_{i=1}^{N} y_i + \sum_{i=1}^{N} \hat{y}_i} \quad (5)$$

In the formula, y_i and $\hat{y}_i$ represent the predicted value and label value of the i-th pixel, respectively, and N is the total number of pixels.

$$L_{Focal} = -\alpha_i (1 - p_i)^\gamma \log p_i \quad (6)$$

In the formula, α_i and γ are the weight adjustment coefficients, and the loss ratio between positive and negative samples is adjusted by α_i, and it is difficult to distinguish the loss contribution of samples by γ adjustment. The total loss in the network model is:

$$L_{Total} = L_{Dice} + L_{Focal} \quad (7)$$

4 Experiment

This chapter first introduces the experimental environment, data sets, and evaluation indicators. Then, the results of this method and three typical segmentation networks on the data set are compared and analyzed. Finally, ablation experiments are carried out to verify the effectiveness of the proposed method.

4.1 Experimental Environment and Evaluation Metrics

The experimental hardware environment CPU is AMD Ryzen 5 4600H, GPU is NVIDIA GeForce GTX 1650. The proposed method is implemented on the Anaconda3 version of the environment manager, Python3.6 programming software, and deep learning framework PyTorch software. This experiment is based on the strategy training model of transfer learning. Firstly, the pre-training weights are downloaded and loaded into the corresponding feature extraction network, and then the weights of the feature extraction network are frozen for training. The training epoch is set to 100, the Adam optimizer is used to train the network, the learning rate is set to 0.0001, and the learning rate is reduced by cosine annealing attenuation. The data set adopts the Ball Screw Drive (BSD) data set of machine tool components [24]. The dataset contains 1104 three-channel images, of which 394 annotations have 'pitting' type surface defects, and the ratio of the training set to test set is 9: 1. In this experiment, Intersection over Union (IoU), Recall, Precision, and Fscore of Recall and Precision were selected to evaluate the performance of the model, as defined in formula (8).

$$IoU = \frac{TP}{TP + FP + FN} \times 100\%$$

$$Recall = \frac{TP}{TP + FN} \times 100\%$$

$$\Pr ecision = \frac{TP}{TP + FP} \times 100\%$$

$$Fscore = \frac{2 \times \Pr ecision \times Recall}{\Pr ecision + Recall} \tag{8}$$

5 Results and Analysis

The dataset is loaded into the model for training, and the training loss curve is shown in Fig. 5. It can be seen from Fig. 5 that as the number of training iterations increases, the training loss and verification loss gradually decrease and tend to converge when the epoch reaches 70. The learning rate curve during training is shown in Fig. 6.

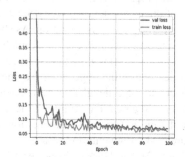 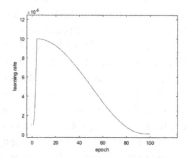

Fig. 5. Loss curve   **Fig. 6.** Learning rate decline curve

In order to verify the effectiveness of the proposed FAANet, typical segmentation networks U-Net, Deeplabv3+, and HRNet are selected for experimental comparison on the BSD dataset. The experimental results are shown in Table 2. The experimental results show that the proposed FAANet is superior to the typical semantic segmentation network in the segmentation performance of pitting defects on the surface of metal workpieces. The IoU, Recall, Precision, and Fscore of the proposed FAANet reach 83.21%, 91.84%, 89.85%, and 90.83%, respectively, which are improved to different degrees compared with the comparison algorithms. Compared with U-Net, Deeplabv3+, and HRNet, the IoU of this method is increased by 4.54, 10.01, and 8.49 percentage points, respectively. Recall increased by 2.54, 4.37, and 7.28 percentage points, respectively; precision

Table 2. Comparison of the results of different algorithms

Approaches	IoU/%	Recall/%	Precision/%	Fscore/%
U-Net	78.67	89.30	86.87	88.07
Deeplabv3+	73.20	87.47	81.87	84.53
HRNet	74.72	84.56	86.52	85.53
FAANet	**83.21**	**91.84**	**89.85**	**90.83**

increased by 2.98, 8.07, and 3.33 percentage points, respectively; fscore increased by 2.76, 6.30, and 5.30 percentage points, respectively.

From Table 2, it can be seen that the experimental evaluation metrics of HRNet and Deeplabv3+ have a certain gap than each index of U-Net. One possible reason is that HRNet and Deeplabv3+ networks have deeper network layers compared with U-Net, and metal workpiece surface defects have the complexity of large differences in different defect scales, the randomness of defect locations, and extreme sample imbalance. The network model with deeper layers cannot effectively extract the features of metal workpiece surface defects in complex scenes. Therefore, we investigate the detection of metal workpiece surface defects in complex scenes based on the U-Net framework. FAANet effectively improves the detection of metal workpiece surface defects in complex scenes by augmenting and refining the extracted features and interacting with information across channels.

In order to further verify the effectiveness of the proposed FAANet, this experiment uses the trained model to perform a large amount of image prediction on the BSD dataset and randomly selects the prediction results of some images for visualization. As shown in Fig. 7, the proposed FAANet has better segmentation results than U-Net, Deeplabv3+, and HRNet. First of all, compared with Deeplabv3+, the proposed method can segment more detailed features, such as defect target edges, while the edge of the segmented region in Fig. 7 (c) is smooth and cannot reflect the edge details. There are similar problems in Fig. 7 (e) and Fig. 7 (c), which can only segment the outline of the target. In addition, there is a problem of missing segmentation in the fourth segmentation map, which fails to segment the small target defect area. The segmentation results of U-Net can segment more target edge details than Deeplabv3+ and HRNet. However, there is a problem of missegmentation, as shown in the second segmentation diagram in Fig. 7 (d). In contrast, the proposed FAANet can segment the defect area and its edge details more and more accurately.

Aiming at the problem of unbalanced data set samples, different loss functions are fused to alleviate the impact of sample imbalance on model training. Based on the conventional dice loss function, the cross entropy loss function and the focal loss function are introduced, respectively, and the influence of different loss functions on the model performance is verified by different loss function combinations. The experimental results are shown in Table 3. Experiments show that the focal loss function has a significant improvement effect on the sample imbalance problem. Through the analysis of the principle of the focal loss function, in order to achieve optimal performance, according to the experimental parameter design suggestions in literature [25], and through a large number of experiments, α value is 0.45, γ is set to 2, and ideal results can be obtained.

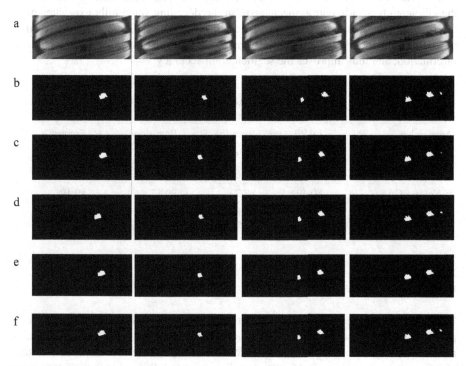

Fig. 7. Visualization results of each algorithm. (a) Original images; (b) Ground Truth; (c) Deeplabv3+; (d) U-Net; (e) HRNet; (f) FAANet(ours)

Table 3. Effect of different loss functions

	IoU/%	Recall/%	Precision/%	Fscore/%
Dice + CE	81.21	90.59	88.69	89.63
Dice + Focal	83.21	91.84	89.85	90.83

In order to verify the effectiveness of different modules, ablation experiments were carried out. This paper conducts experiments on U-Net, U-Net + FA, U-Net + ECA, U-Net + FA + ECA and verifies the effectiveness of the proposed method. The experimental results are shown in Table 4. It can be seen from Table 4 that the Precision and IoU of the improved network U-Net + FA and U-Net + ECA are higher than the original U-Net, with a slight improvement. The network U-Net + FA + ECA, which integrates a feature augmentation module and efficient channel attention mechanism, achieves the highest IoU, Recall, and Fscore compared with the original U-Net. It shows that the feature augmentation module in the encoding stage and the attention mechanism in the decoding stage play an active role in improving the model performance. Specifically, the feature augmentation module can effectively refine different depth features and provide more useful information for feature fusion in the decoding stage. After feature fusion, the efficient channel attention mechanism in the decoding stage fully excavates more information from the feature map with rich location information and semantic information through local cross-channel information interaction, improves the utilization of information, and thus improves the segmentation accuracy.

Table 4. Ablation Study

Approaches	IoU/%	Recall/%	Precision/%	Fscore/%
U-Net	78.76	89.30	86.87	88.07
U-Net + FA	81.86	90.66	89.41	90.03
U-Net + ECA	80.49	88.23	90.17	89.19
U-Net + FA + ECA	83.21	91.84	89.85	90.83

6 Conclusion

In summary, we have proposed a FAANet for surface defect detection of metal workpieces in complex scenes. We have three contributions. First, a feature augmentation module is designed to be embedded in the encoding stage, which can refine the features of different depths and prepare for the decoding stage to fully exploit the semantic category information and global location information of the features at each level. Second, an efficient channel attention mechanism is added after feature fusion in the decoding stage to extract more useful information through the information interaction between different local channels, thus improving the segmentation results of the network. Third, a loss function incorporating focal loss is designed to supervise the training of the model for the problem of sample imbalance. The experimental results show that the proposed method obtains higher segmentation accuracy than the existing prevailed networks in the task of segmenting pitting defects on the drive screw surface and can segment the defect areas more accurately with better segmentation results.

References

1. Saberironaghi, A., Ren, J., El-Gindy, M.: Defect detection methods for industrial products using deep learning techniques: a review. Algorithms 16(2), 95 (2023)
2. Tang, B., Chen, L., Sun, W., et al.: Review of surface defect detection of steel products based on machine vision. IET Image Proc. 17(2), 303–322 (2023)
3. Zhang, H., Zhang, Z.Q., Chen, Y.R., Wu, T.Y., Zhong, H., Wang, Y.N.: Application advance and prospect of nondestructive testing technology for industrial casting defects. Acta Automatica Sinica 48(4), 935–956 (2022)

4. Wu, Y., Qin, Y., Qian, Y., et al.: Hybrid deep learning architecture for rail surface segmentation and surface defect detection. Comput.-Aided Civil Infrastruct. Eng. **37**(2), 227–244 (2022)
5. Tabernik, D., Sela, S., Skvarc, J., et al.: Segmentation-based deep-learning approach for surfacedefect detection. J. Intell. Manuf.Intell. Manuf. **31**(3), 759–776 (2020)
6. Xu, G.L., Mao, J.: Few-shot segmentation on mobile phone screen defect based on co-attention. J. Electron. Inf. Technol. **44**(4), 1476–1483 (2022)
7. Wang, Y., Ma, J.W., Sergey, A., Zang, S., Zhang, M.: DPA-UNet rectal cancer image segmentation based onvisual attention. Concurr. Comput. Pract. Exper. e7670 (2023)
8. Long, J., Shelhamer, E., Darrell, T.: Fully convolutional networks for semantic segmentation. In: Proceedings of the IEEE Conference on Computer Vision and Pattern Recognition, pp. 3431−3440 (2015)
9. Ronneberger, O., Fischer, P., Brox, T.: U-net: convolutional networks for biomedical image segmentation. In: Navab, N., Hornegger, J., Wells, W.M., Frangi, A.F. (eds.) MICCAI 2015. LNCS, vol. 9351, pp. 234–241. Springer, Cham (2015). https://doi.org/10.1007/978-3-319-24574-4_28
10. Mo, Y., Wu, Y., Yang, X., et al.: Review the state-of-the-art technologies of semantic segmentation based on deep learning. Neurocomputing **493**, 626–646 (2022)
11. Jin, X.T., Wang, Y.N., Zhang, H., Liu, L., Zhong, H, He, Z.-D.: DeepRail: automatic visual detection system for railway surface defect using Bayesian CNN and attention network. Acta Automatica Sinica **45**(12), 2312−2327 (2019)
12. Yu, W.Y., Zhang, Y., Yao, H.M., Shi, H.: Visual inspection of surface defects based on lightweight reconstruction network. Acta Automatica Sinica **48**(9), 2175–2186 (2022)
13. Prappacher, N., Bullmann, M., Bohn, G., et al.: Defect detection on rolling element surface scans using neural image segmentation. Appl. Sci. **10**(9), 3290 (2020)
14. Wang, S., Pan, Y., Chen, M., et al.: FCN-SFW: steel structure crack segmentation using a fully convolutional network and structured forests. IEEE Access **8**, 214358–214373 (2020)
15. Dung, C.V.: Autonomous concrete crack detection using deep fully convolutional neural network. Autom. Constr.. Constr. **99**, 52–58 (2019)
16. Huang, Y., Qiu, C., Yuan, K.: Surface defect saliency of magnetic tile. Vis. Comput.Comput. **36**, 85–96 (2020)
17. Xie, Y., Zhu, F., Fu, Y.: Main-secondary network for defect segmentation of textured surface images. In: Proceedings of the IEEE/CVF Winter Conference on Applications of Computer Vision, pp. 3531−3540 (2020)
18. Wang, Y.S., Yu, J.B.: Strip surface defect detection based on adaptive global localization algorithm. Acta Automatica Sinica **45**(x), 1−16 (2023)
19. He, H., Yuan, M., Liu, X.: Research on surface defect detection method of metal workpiece based on machine learning. In: 2021 6th International Conference on Intelligent Computing and Signal Processing (ICSP), pp. 881−884. IEEE (2021)
20. Guo, M.H., Xu, T.X., Liu, J.J., et al.: Attention mechanisms in computer vision: a survey. Comput. Vis. Media **8**(3), 331–368 (2022)
21. Hu, J., Shen, L., Albanie, S., et al.: Squeeze-and-excitation networks. IEEE Trans. Pattern Anal. Mach. Intell.Intell. **42**(8), 2011–2023 (2018)
22. Woo, S., Park, J., Lee, J.-Y., Kweon, I.S.: CBAM: convolutional block attention module. In: Ferrari, V., Hebert, M., Sminchisescu, C., Weiss, Y. (eds.) ECCV 2018. LNCS, vol. 11211, pp. 3−19. Springer, Cham (2018). https://doi.org/10.1007/978-3-030-01234-2_1
23. Wang, Q., Wu, B., Zhu, P., et al.: ECA-Net: efficient channel attention for deep convolutional neural networks. In: Proceedings of the IEEE/CVF Conference on Computer Vision and Pattern Recognition, pp. 11534−11542 (2020)

24. Schlagenhauf, T.: Ball screw drive surface defect dataset for classification. Hg. v. Karlsruher Institut für Technologie (KIT). Karlsruher Institut für Technologie (KIT) wbk Institute of Production Science (2021). Online verfügbar unterhttps://publikationen.bibliothek.kit.edu/1000133819

25. Lin, T.Y., Goyal, P., Girshick, R., et al.: Focal loss for dense object detection. In: Proceedings of the IEEE International Conference on Computer Vision, pp. 2980−2988 (2017)

A Novel TCM Prescription Recommendation Algorithm Based on Deep Crossing Neural Network

Zhiwei Zhang, Yaoyi Wang, Shun Liu, Lin Wang, and Mingchuan Zhang[(✉)]

School of Information Engineering, Henan University of Science and Technology,
Luoyang 471023, China
{210321050483,210321050470}@stu.haust.edu.cn,
{Linwang,zhang_mch}@haust.edu.cn

Abstract. In this manuscript, a TCM prescription recommendation model based on deep crossed neural network was proposed, which aims to solve the problem caused by sparse discrete features in TCM prescription information obtained after encoding and feature automatic cross-combination through embedding layer and residual network. Use residual neural network to reduce overfitting and make convergence faster. Using the multi-level residual network, the combined feature vector of medical records and prescriptions is fully residual operation, so that the model can obtain more nonlinear feature information between medical records and prescriptions, and realize the corresponding treatment according to the name of the disease. The function of prescription to improve the level of clinical treatment.

Keywords: Deep & Cross Network · Traditional Chinese Medicine · Prescription Recommendation · Natural Language Processing

1 Introduction

Modern Chinese medicine has played an important role in treating diseases and maintaining health in China because of its remarkable curative effect and low side effects. TCM has attracted great attention from the medical community internationally, increasing the influence and authority of TCM [1]. Traditional Chinese medicine has played an important role in the treatment of several major epidemics, and the role and value of traditional Chinese medicine in the prevention and treatment of new coronary pneumonia around the world has also been fully affirmed and recognized by all parties. In recent years, the state has

This work was supported in part by the National Natural Science Foundation of China (NSFC) under Grants No. 62002102 and 62072121, and in part by the Scientific and Technological Innovation Team of Colleges and Universities in Henan Province under Grants No. 20IRTSTHN018, and in part by the Key Technologies R & D Program of Henan Province under Grants No. 212102210083, 222102310565, 232102210028.

F. Sun et al. (Eds.): ICCSIP 2023, CCIS 1918, pp. 309–321, 2024.
https://doi.org/10.1007/978-981-99-8018-5_23

increased its support for the modernization of the Chinese medicine industry [2]. The 14th Five-Year Plan for the Development of Chinese Medicine proposed to promote the integration of the traditional Chinese medicine industry with the modern industry, give full play to the unique advantages of traditional Chinese medicine, and make The development of traditional Chinese medicine is heading for a new journey [3].

However, the development of traditional Chinese medicine also faces many problems and challenges. First, with the increasing demand for traditional Chinese medicine, the uneven distribution of medical resources makes the traditional way of consultation no longer able to meet people medical needs. Second, there is a shortage of TCM medical personnel resources, which makes TCM medical treatment under enormous pressure, and patients also suffer difficulties such as difficulty in seeking medical treatment due to the lack of TCM medical treatment [4]. Only when the current situation is changed and the problems are solved, will the development of traditional Chinese medicine become a smooth one.

With the continuous improvement of modern medical level and the rapid development of information technology, the application of TCM prescription recommendation to the auxiliary diagnosis and treatment system has become an inevitable trend in the development of TCM diagnosis and treatment. The traditional Chinese medicine prescription recommendation algorithm is the treatment prescription prescribed by traditional Chinese medicine in the process of consultation, according to the patient symptoms and clinical experience. Traditional recommendation algorithms, such as collaborative filtering algorithms and association rule algorithms, are difficult to be used on a large scale by practical projects [5].

Currently widely used recommendation algorithms, for example, currently used classifiers use latent vectors as inner products to express joint features, thus theoretically extracting low-level and high-level joint features [6]. However, in practice, it is limited by the amount of computation, usually limited to 2-order crossover features, because the combination of these features can lead to catastrophic dimensionality [7]. So the combined feature is a relatively thin feature with redundant features. This combined feature is not necessarily effective, and when there is no corresponding combination in the initial sample, the parameters cannot be learned. The Wide and Deep Network recommendation algorithm learns low-order and high-order combined features at the same time. It mixes a linear model and a deep model, and combines logistic regression and MLP Deep module to make The input of the Wide part is still based on artificial features.

Deep and Cross Network (DCN), which uses cross-layer network instead of Wide section to handle feature intersection, DCN has two disadvantages, one is that its output is still scalar times the input, and the other is that this feature interaction is to combine features Each bit of the vector is regarded as a feature, and it can be considered that a high-order cross feature has been obtained [8]. The coefficients of cross-features are not independent of each other. Although DCN obtains all cross-features, the coefficients are mutually restricted and the degree of freedom is much lower. Therefore, it is not equivalent to the traditional manual construction of cross-features, and it also limits its expressive ability.

Deep crossing network does not use explicit cross features, but uses the residual network structure to mine the relationship between features [9]. The algorithm solves a series of algorithm problems such as feature engineering, sparse vector density, and optimization target matching of multi-level neural networks. Based on the traditional neural network, the model adds the idea of embedding layer and residual connection, which has a simple structure and achieves good results. In this paper, the TCM prescription recommendation model based on the deep crossed neural network is applied, and compared with the breadth and depth network and the deep and crossed network, the experiments show that the TCM prescription recommendation algorithm based on the deep crossed neural network has better effect and better performance [10].

2 TCM Prescription Recommendation Model

2.1 Model Application Scenarios

TCM doctors have a long training cycle and need to learn and master various and complex knowledge, which further exacerbates the shortage of medical personnel resources, puts TCM medical treatment under enormous pressure, and patients also encounter difficulties such as difficulty in seeking medical treatment due to the lack of TCM medical treatment [11]. It is particularly urgent to solve the problems of long training period of traditional Chinese medicine and shortage of medical personnel resources. Based on this premise, this paper takes the prescription of Chinese medicine for patients' symptoms as a breakthrough.

Use the prescription recommendation model to analyze and process the traditional Chinese medicine medical records and clinical real data recorded in the existing traditional Chinese medicine books, and store them in a standardized manner; use the treatment logic recorded in the traditional Chinese medicine medical records to learn the relationship between disease symptoms and prescriptions; through deep learning Algorithms, build a TCM medical record analysis model and a prescription recommendation model, so that it has a high accuracy rate [12]. Realize the rational allocation of TCM resources and optimize the quality of TCM talents, so that patients who need TCM treatment can receive timely and quality professional treatment, so that the huge market for TCM needs can be met and developed, and then promote the modernization and intelligence of TCM diagnosis and treatment.

2.2 TCM Prescription Recommendation Model

The traditional Chinese medicine prescription recommendation algorithm based on deep cross neural network solves the problem of too sparseness of traditional Chinese medicine prescription features and medical record information features after coding and automatic cross-combination of features through embedding layer and residual network [13]. The features are automatically combined with the medical record information features to obtain the best combined features and better achieve the function of prescription recommendation [14]. The model consists of feature layers, embedding layers, stacked layers, residual layers, and fully connected output layers. The actual structure is shown in Fig. 1.

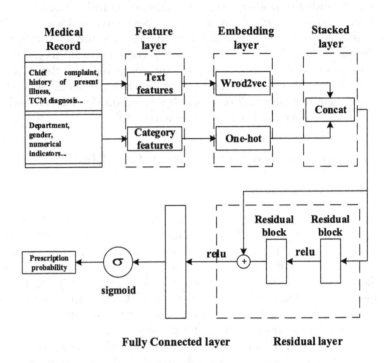

Fig. 1. The structure of the model

The main function of the feature layer is to represent the input information, so that the input information can be better extracted in the feature layer. In the prescription recommendation model, it is necessary to input patient medical record information, including the name of the disease and the department it belongs to, the patient chief complaint, the patient gender, and the treatment prescription [15]. This information will be used as a single feature, and enter the feature layer for vector expression.

The embedding layer is implemented by a single-layer fully connected network, which maps the original features of the prescription, disease name and patient medical record information data into an embedding vector. On this basis, the high-dimensional sparse characteristics are converted into Low-dimensional consistency features. Among them, the medical record information is further divided into text information and category information. In order to better represent the characteristics of the medical record as a vector, we process the text information in the medical record, such as the patient chief complaint, diagnosis results, etc., to word2vec;, such as gender, department, etc., perform one-hot processing, $[0, 1]$ means female, $[1, 0]$ means male, $[1, 0, 0, 0, 0, 0, 0, 0, 0]$ means internal medicine, $[0, 1, 0, 0, 0, 0, 0, 0, 0]$ means anorectal department, etc., and so on. The purpose of representing text and categories separately is to save a part of the calculation when embedding, because in the case of a small number of categories, using one-hot representation can save vector space and thus achieve the purpose of saving computing resources. The formula is like Eq. (1),

$$F_j^O = max(O, A_j F_j^I + b_j),$$ (1)

where j represents a single prescription and medical record feature, $F_j^I \in R^{n_j}$ is the input feature of the prescription and medical record information, A_j is the corresponding input feature matrix, $m_j * n_j$ is the parameter of the input feature, and F_j^O is the feature matrix containing embedded prescription, disease name and patient medical record features. At that time, the embedding method was used to reduce the dimension of the input feature matrix to obtain a low-dimensional dense feature vector.

The stacking layer merges the embedded features of all prescriptions, disease names, and patient records with parts of the original features to form a new feature vector, which is fed into the next layer. All the category features are first concatenated, and then other embedded text features are concatenated, and the output prescription, disease name and patient record features are stacked and connected to a vector as the input of the next layer. It is shown in formula 2,

$$F^O = [F_0^O, F_1^O, \cdots, F_k^O].$$ (2)

where k is the number of features for entering prescription, disease name, and patient record features. Furthermore, both A_j and b_j are parameters of the network and will be optimized together with other parameters in the network, which is an important property of embedding deep cross-networks. Of course, unlike *word2vec* embedding-only approach, it is an integral part of the overall optimization process [16].

The main structure of the residual layer is multiple residual blocks. The residual block is the basic building block of the residual network. Using the multi-level residual network, the various dimensions of the combined feature vector of the medical record information and the prescription are fully crossed, so that the model can acquire more nonlinear and mixed features, which improves the recommendation performance of the model [17]. The uniqueness of the residual unit is that after the two-layer *Relu* transformation, the original input features are cascaded with the output features that have undergone residual operation, and the original features are retained while making the most of the original features. The specific calculation method is as formula 3,

$$F^O = R(F^I, \{A_0, A_1\} \{b_0, b_1\}) + F^I.$$ (3)

where $A_{\{0,1\}}$ and $b_{\{0,1\}}$ are the parameters of the two-layer residual block, R representing the function that maps the F^I which combined feature input of the prescription and medical record information of the residual layer to the output F^O. Move the combined feature input F^I to the left side of the equation. $R(\cdot)$ essentially the residuals of the fit $F^O - F^I$.

The output layer is to stack multiple residual blocks together to make the network depth deeper, and finally convert the recommendation results into probability values [18]. Specifically, it is shown in formula 4,

$$p_i = \frac{exp(F^O)}{\sum_{j=1}^{n} exp(F_j^O)}. \tag{4}$$

Finally, the cross entropy loss function is used as the objective function of the model, as shown in Formula 5. The cross entropy loss function can adapt to multi-classification output tasks and better optimize the model in this task. Optimize and adjust the model according to the function. Among them, p for the actual recommendation result, p_i for the prediction of the recommendation result, the model parameters are adjusted accordingly through the size of the function value, so as to obtain a better model,

$$L\left(p, p_i\right) = -\frac{1}{n} \sum_{i=1}^{n} p \log p_i + (1 - p) \log\left(1 - p_i\right). \tag{5}$$

The TCM prescription recommendation model based on the deep crossed neural network uses the feature layer to process the features of the medical record information and the prescription information separately, and uses the embedding layer to classify the divided text features such as the patient's main complaint, current illness history, past history, and TCM diagnosis results. The $word2vec$ and $one - hot$ embedding are carried out respectively with the category features such as department, gender, and various numerical indicators, so that the sparse high-dimensional vector is converted into a dense low-dimensional vector [18]. The stacking layer cascades the low-dimensional features of the embedding layer to form a combined feature for prescription recommendation. The combination of medical record information and prescription information is used to recommend prescriptions based on factors such as the patient clinical symptoms and current illness history during the model training process, rather than just considering the name of the disease, which is more in line with traditional Chinese medicine. A patient approach to diagnosis and treatment. In addition, the residual block in the residual layer performs residual operation on the combined feature vector to better cross-combine prescription features and medical record features, and add them to the original input prescription and medical record features when outputting, so as to maximize the It retains the feature expression of prescription and medical record information, thereby improving the accuracy of prescription recommendation.

2.3   Model Algorithm Design and Analysis

The steps of the traditional Chinese medicine prescription recommendation algorithm based on the deep crossed neural network are shown in the following table. The output of the algorithm is the prescription corresponding to the traditional Chinese medicine treatment, which mainly includes medicinal materials and dosages. This method converts high-dimensional sparse prescription and medical record features into low-dimensional consistency features, and superimposes them to form combined features and input them to the residual layer for residual operation, maximize the use and retention of the original features, and finally pass the fully connected layer [19]. Obtain the probability of prescription recommendation.

The TCM prescription recommendation algorithm based on the deep cross neural network makes word2vec and one-hot embedding operations for the text information such as chief complaint, disease name, prescription and other category information in the TCM medical records, and the category information such as gender and department, respectively, in order to better integrate the information of the TCM medical records. The vectorized representation of prescription information and prescription information enables the prescription recommendation model to form a unique combined input for prescription recommendation. By converting the original high-dimensional and sparse features into low-dimensional and dense feature vectors, the computational cost of the network model can be greatly saved, and the medical record features and prescription features can be better combined. Use the residual network to perform residual operation on the combined features and add the original combined features of the input when the residual is output, so as to better cross the prescription features and the medical record information features, and also maximize the original combined features. Feature preservation. This not only allows the model to better extract feature combinations for prescription and TCM medical record information, but also improves the accuracy of the prescription recommendation.

Algorithm 1. TCM prescription recommendation algorithm

Input: Traditional Chinese Medicine Cases F_j^I
Output: A prescription for the treatment of F_j^I

1: **while** *input medical record text vector* **do**
2:   **if** F_j^I not null **then**
3:     *Transform the high dimensional sparse feature of disease to prescription into low dimensional dense feature*
4:     $F_j^O \leftarrow max(O, A_j F_j^I + b_j)$
5:   **end if**
6:   **if** F_j^O not null **then**
7:     **for** i<k **do**
8:       *The output prescription features are stacked and connected to a vector as input to the next layer*
9:       $F^O \leftarrow [F_0^O, F_1^O, \cdots, F_k^O]$
10:     **end for**
11:   **end if**

12:    *The multi − layer residual network combines each*
       dimension of feature vector to capture feature
       information
13:    **for** i<the number of residual blocks **do**
14:        $F^O \leftarrow R(F^I, \{A_0, A_1\}\{b_0, b_1\}) + F^I$
15:    **end for**
16:    *The prescription recommendation results were*
       converted into probability output and get the
       corresponding prescription information
17:    $p_i \leftarrow \frac{exp(F^O)}{\sum_{j=1}^{n} exp(F_j^O)}$
18:    *compare the output with the actual to obtain the loss*
19:    $l(p, p_i) \leftarrow -\frac{1}{n}\sum_{i=1}^{n} p\log p_i + (1-p)\log(1-p_i)$
20: **end while**

3   Experiment

3.1   Data

The data construction of the prescription recommendation module mainly collects the data in the Thirteenth Five-Year Plan of higher education in the national Chinese medicine industry, including Chinese medicine emergency medicine, Chinese medicine internal medicine, Chinese medicine surgery, Chinese medicine ophthalmology, Chinese medicine pediatrics, Chinese medicine gynecology and other books. The medical record data and clinical medical record data totaled 6996 data of 343 categories of diseases. There are more than 900 kinds of classic prescriptions, and the prescriptions contain information on the names, doses, sources and other information of 4,174 commonly used Chinese medicinal materials. According to the Criteo data set, the click rate is predicted, and the click rate prediction is replaced with the prediction of whether to use medicinal materials, and then the disease-medicine material data set is constructed. The dataset has one label field, which is used to mark whether it is valid; there are four I fields, which are disease number, age, gender, and whether they have suffered from the disease; there are 26 C fields, which are the numbers of each medicinal material. A total of 11,990 disease-prescription sample data were sorted out. In order to avoid direct training causing the network to pay too much attention to positive samples, we used the first a results with large errors as training negative samples to make the model gradient larger, convergence faster, positive and negative The sample ratio is 1:3. On this basis, the data is divided into training and testing proportionately, and the ratio is 4:1.

The main fields in the disease-prescription dataset are the patient gender, age, the name of the disease the patient suffers from, whether the patient has had the disease before, and the medicinal materials needed to treat the disease. Because the treatment of a certain disease requires a maximum of 21 kinds of medicinal materials, we list 21 kinds of medicinal materials following each disease, and the medicinal materials with less than 21 kinds are empty and will be filled with 0 when embedded. Read the data, import the required packages, and perform simple processing such as filling, numerical processing, and category encoding on the read data, and convert the sparse classification type characteristics into dense feature vectors, so that the dimension of the vector is from high to low. Combine various Embedding features and classification features to form a new combined feature vector containing all features. Finally, the text features and category features are fused and input into the model. Here is stitching by stacking layers. Combine category features and text features together in the feature dimension.

Before the experiment starts, the original features of prescription, disease name, and patient medical record information data are mapped into embedding vectors, thereby converting high-dimensional sparse features from a single neural network level to low-dimensional dense features. Among them, the medical record information is further divided into text information and category information. In order to better represent the characteristics of the medical record as a vector, we process the text information in the medical record, such as the patient chief complaint, diagnosis results, etc., to *word2vec*, such as gender, department, etc., for one hot processing.

The experimental data is divided into text features and category features, and simple data preprocessing is performed, and the divided prescription features and medical record features are marked. Simple processing of features, including filling missing values, numerical processing, and category coding. In addition, a list of names of numerical features and categorical features is constructed, the features corresponding to all the features in the dataset are labeled, an input layer dictionary is constructed, and it is returned in the form of dense and sparse dictionaries. Define a dictionary corresponding to the embedding layer, filter out the sparse features in the feature, and use it for the embedding layer of the linear part. The dimension is set to 1, otherwise the dimension is the embedding dimension defined by itself. All sparse features are embedded and spliced, the sparse features are filtered out, and the input layer and the corresponding embedding layer are obtained. If the embedding list is finally directly input into the fully connected layer, it needs to be flattened, otherwise it is not required. Finally, convert the input data into the form of a dictionary and wait for the input model.

3.2 Experimental Settings

For the fairness of the experiment, we set the parameters of the model in this paper and the comparison model to be the same. The learning rate is set to 0.001 to prevent the occurrence of over-fitting. In this paper, drop-out is used and its value is set to 0.5, batch-size is set to 64, the activation function uses Relu and sigmoid functions, and the loss function selects the cross entropy The loss function, the Adam optimizer used by the optimizer, is for the better because the optimization technique greatly improves the performance of networks with essentially the same structure. In addition, we used the Windows 10 operating system as the experimental running system, and the experimental server had

16GB of memory and 4 CPU processors. The specific experimental parameter settings are shown in Table 1.

Table 1. Parameter settings

Heading level	Example
Parameter Name	Parameter Value
Embedding dimension	300
Learning rate	0.001
Drop-out value	0.5
Optimizer	Adam
Hidden layer number	256
Word2vector length	100
Activation function	Relu
Training period	200
Batch size	64

3.3   Results and Discussion

Figures 2 and Figures 3 show the variation of the accuracy curves for the three network models. Since the TCM prescription recommendation algorithm model in this paper uses a deep cross network, the residual network structure is used to mine the relationship between features. The embedding layer performs low-dimensional processing of the feature vectors of prescription information and medical record information. This method solves the problem of feature sparseness and automatic cross-combination of features, and realizes the optimal setting of the problem at the output level. The multi-layer residual network is used to cross-combine the combined feature vectors of the prescription feature vector and the patient medical record feature vector to increase the understanding and generalization ability of the model [20]. This makes the accuracy of the prescription recommendation model in this paper better on the training set and test set.

According to the experimental results, the accuracy and loss values of the training results and test results of the three neural network recommendation algorithm models are compared and analyzed. In this paper, we can see that compared with the other two neural network models in the test set, the accuracy of Deep Crossing is the best, which can reach 0.7336, followed by the accuracy of Wide & Deep, the highest is 0.6994, and the lowest accuracy of DCN, the highest is only 0.6809.

Figures 4 and Figures 5 show the change in loss values for the three models on the training and test sets. In this paper, we can see that the prescription recommendation model in this paper has the smallest loss value, and the loss

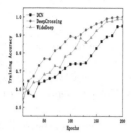

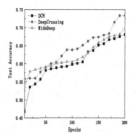

Fig. 2. Training Accuracy   **Fig. 3.** Test Accuracy

value is 0.59, which is relatively stable. Both the DCN model and the Wide & Deep model have larger loss values than the model in this paper, 0.62 and 0.63, respectively, and their loss values fluctuate greatly.

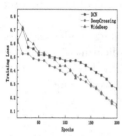

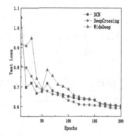

Fig. 4. Training Loss   **Fig. 5.** Test Loss

This paper compares the TCM prescription recommendation algorithm model based on Deep Crossing with the DCN model and the Wide & Deep model. The experimental results show that the TCM prescription recommendation algorithm model is superior to the DCN model and the Wide & Deep model in prescription recommendation, which proves the rationality and effectiveness of the TCM prescription recommendation algorithm based on Deep Crossing. And compared with the other two neural network models, the Deep Crossing model solves the common problems of recommendation systems such as feature engineering, sparse vector densification, and optimization target fitting, and achieves better results. It can also be seen that the prescription recommendation model in this paper achieves better results, which indicates that the residual-based framework is more suitable for the acquisition of prescription and medical record feature associations compared to DCN. In addition, in terms of accuracy, the accuracy of our model is 5% higher than DCN and 4% higher than Wide & Deep. The experimental results demonstrate the effectiveness of the TCM prescription recommendation algorithm based on the deep cross network.

4   Conclusion

This chapter proposes a TCM prescription recommendation algorithm based on deep crossed neural network. Deep Crossing is applied to the TCM prescription recommendation algorithm, and achieves better results than Wide & Deep and DCN, and realizes automatic feature extraction and recommendation of TCM prescriptions.

It is used to solve the problems encountered in the process of assisted diagnosis and treatment of traditional Chinese medicine: how to better solve the problem of prescription recommendation, and obtain the corresponding treatment prescription through the input of medical records and symptoms. The model in this chapter captures the input information through the deep structure, and at the same time, uses the residual network to fully cross-fuse the different dimensions of the feature vector in the prescription and case data, thereby improving the recognition and expression ability of the model. The accuracy of training and testing is improved, and the accuracy of detection is also improved. This also means that it is very promising in multi-label prediction of medicinal materials, raw materials, etc.

Overall, this chapter finds that the Deep Crossing model exhibits strong performance in terms of accuracy and loss rate, indicating the effectiveness of its hybrid structure in nonlinear features and combined feature information in TCM prescription data. On this basis, the neural network model will be further optimized for better results.

References

1. Schmid, R.D., Xiong, X.: Biotech in china 2021, at the beginning of the 14th five-year period (145). Appl. Microbiol. Biotechnol. **105**(10), 3971–3985 (2021)
2. Zhang, H., Ni, W., Li, J., Zhang, J., et al.: Artificial intelligence-based traditional Chinese medicine assistive diagnostic system: validation study. JMIR Med. Inform. **8**(6), e17608 (2020)
3. Wong, K.C., Wu, L. et al.: History of Chinese medicine. Being achronicle of medical happenings in china from ancient times to the present period (1932)
4. Goldberg, K., Roeder, T., Gupta, D., Perkins, C.: Eigentaste: a constant time collaborative filtering algorithm. Inform. Retrieval **4**(2), 133–151 (2001)
5. Zheng, Z., Kohavi, R., Mason, L.: Real world performance of association rule algorithms. In: Proceedings of the Seventh ACM SIGKDD International Conference on Knowledge Discovery and Data Mining, pp. 401–406 (2001)
6. Jais, I.K.M., Ismail, A.R., Nisa, S.Q.: Adam optimization algorithm for wide and deep neural network. Knowl. Eng. Data Sci. **2**(1), 41–46 (2019)
7. Nguyen, T., Raghu, M., Kornblith, S.: Do wide and deep networks learn the same things? Uncovering how neural network representations vary with width and depth. arXiv preprint arXiv:2010.15327 (2020)
8. Cao, Y., Gu, Q.: Generalization bounds of stochastic gradient descent for wide and deep neural networks. In: Advances in Neural Information Processing Systems, vol. 32 (2019)

9. Wang, R., Fu, B., Fu, G., Wang, M.: Deep & cross network for ad click predictions. In: Proceedings of the ADKDD 2017, pp. 1–7 (2017)
10. Wang, R., Shivanna, R., Cheng, D., Jain, S., Lin, D., Hong, L., Chi, E.: DCN V2: Improved deep & cross network and practical lessons for webscale learning to rank systems. In: Proceedings of the Web Conference, vol. 2021, pp. 1785–1797 (2021)
11. Huang, G., Chen, Q., Deng, C.: A new click-through rates prediction model based on deep & cross network. Algorithms 13(12), 342 (2020)
12. Xia, G., Yin, D., Gan, Y., Rui, L., Zhu, Y.: Deep & cross network for software-intensive system fault prediction. In: International Conference on Artificial Intelligence for Communications and Networks, pp. 28–39 (2019)
13. Shan, Y., Hoens, T.R., Jiao, J., Wang, H., Yu, D., Mao, J.: Deep crossing: webscale modeling without manually crafted combinatorial features. In: Proceedings of the 22nd ACM SIGKDD International Conference on Knowledge Discovery and Data Mining, pp. 255–262 (2016)
14. Wang, R., Fu, B., Fu, G., Wang, M.: Deep & cross network for ad click predictions. In: Proceedings of the ADKDD 2017, pp. 1–7 (2017)
15. Zhou, G., et al.: Deep interest network for click-through rate prediction. In: Proceedings of the 24th ACM SIGKDD International Conference on Knowledge Discovery & Data Mining, pp. 1059–1068 (2018)
16. Wang, Z., Li, L., Song, M., Yan, J., Shi, J., Yao, Y.: Evaluating the traditional Chinese medicine (TCM) officially recommended in china for covid-19 using ontology-based side-effect prediction framework (OSPF) and deep learning. J. Ethnopharmacol. 272, 113957 (2021)
17. XiaoTing, X., Tang, H., Sang, Z.: Development status and prospects of international standardization of medical devices of traditional Chinese medicine. Pharmacol. Res. 167, 105485 (2021)
18. Zhang, H., Ni, W., Li, J., Zhang, J., et al.: Artificial intelligence-based traditional Chinese medicine assistive diagnostic system: validation study. JMIR Med. Inform. 8(6), e17608 (2020)
19. Gao, H., Wang, Z., Li, Y., Qian, Z.: Overview of the quality standard research of traditional Chinese medicine. Front. Med. 5(2), 195–202 (2011)
20. Wang, W., Zhou, H., Wang, Y., Sang, B., Liu, L.: Current policies and measures on the development of traditional Chinese medicine in china. Pharmacol. Res. 163, 105187 (2021)

Robust Real-Time Optimized LiDAR Odometry with Loop Closure Detection

Guoqiang Yin and Liwei Zhang$^{(\boxtimes)}$

School of Mechanical Engineering and Automation, Fuzhou University, Fuzhou 350116, China
lw.zhang@fzu.edu.cn

Abstract. In this paper, we present a lightweight, integrated LiDAR SLAM system designed for high efficiency and robust loop closure detection. Our evaluation focuses on LiDAR-based platforms with limited on-board computation capabilities in long-distance and large-scale scenarios. We identify that front-end only SLAM systems are prone to drift due to accumulated errors in pose estimation. To mitigate this issue, we propose two enhancements: 1) the implementation of an incremental kd tree (ikd-tree) data structure for efficient map management, and 2) the utilization of Normal Distribution Descriptor (NDD) for loop closure detection, combined with GTSAM for global optimization, which effectively corrects the final trajectory of the algorithm. Finally, we validate our proposed method using the KITTI and MulRan datasets and benchmark it against the FLOAM system. The experimental results reveal that our method surpasses FLOAM in terms of computational efficiency by 26.21% and 53.53%, and in terms of accuracy by 36.88% and 84.76% on the KITTI and MulRan datasets, respectively. These findings demonstrate the potential of our lightweight integrated LiDAR SLAM system to significantly improve both efficiency and accuracy in challenging environments, making it a valuable contribution to the field of SLAM research.

Keywords: LiDAR SLAM · Incremental Kd Tree · Loop Closure Detection · Global Optimization

1 Introduction

Simultaneous Localization and Mapping (SLAM) has attracted considerable attention in various applications, such as autonomous driving, drones, robotics, mobile phones, etc. [1–3]. Existing SLAM algorithms can be generally divided into two categories: LiDAR-based algorithms (e.g., LOAM [4], LeGO-LOAM [5], FAST-LIO [6]), and vision-based algorithms (e.g., ORB-SLAM [7], DSO [8], R3LIVE [9]). Although vision-based SLAM can achieve high localization accuracy, it can only maintain sparse feature maps and suffers from severe motion blur problems in adverse weather and low-light conditions. Therefore, LiDAR-based SLAM is more robust and reliable than vision-based SLAM [10].

Despite the good performance of existing LiDAR SLAM methods on public datasets, they still face some limitations in practical applications. One challenge is the 2 computational cost; modern LiDAR sensors produce hundreds of thousands or even millions of

F. Sun et al. (Eds.): ICCSIP 2023, CCIS 1918, pp. 322–333, 2024.
https://doi.org/10.1007/978-981-99-8018-5_24

dense point clouds per second, and achieving accurate and efficient pose estimation on limited on-board resources is a daunting task. Another challenge is the drift in motion estimation caused by standalone LiDAR odometry. This accumulated error can result in inconsistencies between point cloud maps when the robot returns to the same place. Therefore, we need to reduce the error by connecting temporally distant places and adding constraints between them. This process is called loop closure and it is performed using place recognition [11].

To tackle the challenges of high computational cost and loop closure in LiDAR SLAM, we propose a robust LiDAR odometry framework in this paper. By using our odometry framework, the computational cost can be significantly reduced and thus the SLAM performance can be enhanced. Moreover, by employing the lightweight NDD descriptor [12] for loop closure detection, we demonstrate stable loop closure capability with minimal performance degradation even in complex and heterogeneous urban environments. The main contributions of this paper are summarized as follows:

1 We use the ikd-tree [13] data structure to maintain maps, which can support incremental map updates and can effectively lower computational costs.
2 We present a framework for a complete SLAM that uses lightweight NDD descriptors for loop closure detection and follows GTSAM-based [14] posegraph optimization.
3 We conduct experiments on the KITTI [15] and MulRan [16] datasets and show that our system achieves competitive performance compared to state-of-the-art methods.

2   Related Works

2.1   LiDAR Odometry

Odometry is the key component of the SLAM system, which mainly performs the motion estimation of the mobile robot. To obtain the odometry from a dense point cloud, it is necessary to find the correspondence between the point clouds, which can be mainly classified into two categories: direct matching-based methods and feature matching-based methods. The most classical method based on direct matching is the iterative closest point (ICP) [17] method. ICP matches the current point cloud with the closest point of the target point cloud, and converges to the final pose by iteratively minimizing the distance residuals between the corresponding points. However, ICP is sensitive to noise and has high computational cost. Feature matching-based methods mainly utilize point-to-plane and point-to-line matching and are widely used. LOAM [4] was the first to introduce this idea. After that, many LiDAR SLAMs followed a framework similar to LOAM. For example, LeGO-LOAM [5] introduced ground point segmentation and loop closure modules to reduce computational cost and pose errors. LOAM-Livox [18], SSL_SLAM [19] applied the idea of LOAM to the emerging field of solid-state LiDAR with small FOV views. FLOAM [20] used a non-iterative two-stage distortion compensation method to reduce computational cost. For each scan input, edge and planar features are extracted and matched with local edge maps and local planar maps, respectively. Despite its merits, FLOAM is limited by its localization accuracy and computational efficiency. However, these methods suffer from poor pose estimation in large-scale scenes due to the lack of loop closure detection.

2.2 Dynamic Data Structure in SLAM

The conventional kd-tree [21] is built by capturing all the points, which is inefficient and time consuming. Compared with the static kd-tree, ikd-tree [13] updates the kd-tree incrementally using only new incoming points. The redundant operations to reconstruct the whole tree can be avoided and the computation time is shorter. FAST-LIO2 [22] is a LiDAR-inertial system that achieves nearly 100 Hz in large-scale scenarios. The incremental kd-tree significantly reduces the tree update time. Faster-LIO [23] uses sparse incremental voxels (iVox) to organize the point cloud instead of the tree structure.

2.3 Loop Closure Detection

Loop closure detection is usually coupled with place recognition and plays a crucial role in a complete SLAM system. LiDAR-based place recognition methods can be mainly divided into two categories: local descriptors and global descriptors. Local descriptors (e.g., SHOT [24], FPFH [25]) were originally designed for point cloud registration, and although they can also be used for place recognition, they are susceptible to noise and intensive computation and show limitations. Global descriptors avoid these problems. Scan-context [26] is a geometric feature-based global descriptor that directly records vertical information in 3D space. LiDAR-Iris [27] summarizes a place as a binary signature image obtained after several Gabor filtering and thresholding operations on the LiDAR-Iris image representation. NDD [12] descriptor encodes the probability density function and entropy of a point cloud as descriptors and uses correlation coefficients as similarity between descriptors for 3D point cloud loop closure detection, which outperforms the above LiDAR global descriptors and is robust to noise and point cloud density variations.

3 Methodology

3.1 System Overview

The overall framework of the proposed method in this paper is shown in Fig. 1. The algorithm framework consists of a front-end LiDAR odometry and a back-end loop closure detection with global optimization. The front-end odometry comprises three main parts: 1) extracting edge and plane features based on the local smoothness of the point cloud; 2) predicting the motion and correcting the distortion by assuming constant angular and linear velocities over a short period of time. In the second stage, the distortion is recalculated after the pose estimation process and the recalculated undistorted features are updated to the final map; 3) estimating the pose by registering the current calibrated edge features and plane features to the global feature map. This is only briefly described here; please refer to [14] for more details. The following paragraphs focus on the novel aspects of the proposed algorithmic framework.

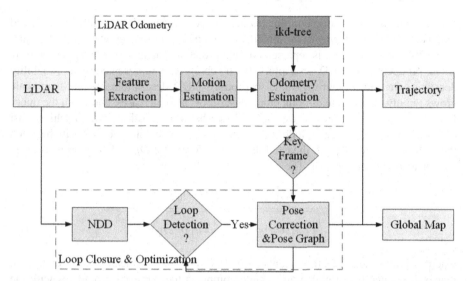

Fig. 1. The overall framework of the proposed algorithm. The whole system consists of a front-end LiDAR odometry with loop closure detection and global optimization at the back-end. The front-end includes the LiDAR odometry and the ikd-tree based map management, and the back-end uses NDD for loop closure detection and global pose-graph optimization.

3.2 Map Management Based on Ikd-Tree

To achieve real-time update, efficient search and management of 3D maps, we use the ikd-tree data structure to represent large-scale dense point cloud maps. To reduce the computational cost of retrieval, we store edge features and global maps in the ikd-tree. Ikd-tree uses incremental updates mainly consisting of point insertion and box deletion. Point insertion is performed by combining the down-sampling of the tree, and historical points that are not in the specified area are removed from the ikd-tree when the LiDAR field-of-view angle exceeds the map boundary. Therefore, the ikd-tree tracks the map points in a cubic area of a given size in real time and removes irrelevant historical points by box-by-box deletion, while the points from the K-nearest-neighbor (KNN) search are used for computing the residuals in the pose estimation. Finally, the current new frame of point cloud is inserted into the global map by point-by-point down-sampling operation through the optimized poses, which completes the final map construction.

3.3 Loop Closure Detection and Global Optimization

To address the drift caused by measurement noise in front-end only SLAM systems, we need to perform loop closure detection to correct the accumulated error. First, we need to perform keyframe selection, choosing each keyframe when the translation change exceeds a predefined translation threshold, or the rotation change exceeds a predefined rotation threshold. Compared to frame-by-frame updates, keyframe-based map updates can lower computational costs. For each keyframe, we extract a global feature using the NDD descriptor. First, we project the keyframes into the bird's-eye view, which is computed by dividing polar coordinates into N_S sectors and N_r rings in azimuthal and radial directions, producing a two-dimensional matrix. In this paper, we set $N_S = 60$ and $N_r = 20$. Each subregion is represented by a probability density score and an entropy value, producing the NDD descriptors. Each subregion is represented by a probability density score and an entropy value to produce NDD descriptors. As the map scale grows rapidly, the storage of point cloud descriptors also increases, and when the query for loop closure is performed, we use a kd-tree-based retrieval method to achieve fast descriptor retrieval, which includes key search and KNN search. The similarity between the NDD descriptor D_A and the candidate NDD descriptor D_B is then computed using the correlation coefficient of. The correlation coefficient is:

$$r = \frac{\Sigma_{ij}\left[(D_A)_{ij} - \bar{a}\right]\left[(D_B)_{ij} - \bar{b}\right]}{\sqrt{\left\{\Sigma_{ij}\left[(D_A)_{ij} - \bar{a}\right]\right\}^2 \left\{\Sigma_{ij}\left[(D_B)_{ij} - \bar{b}\right]\right\}^2}} \tag{1}$$

where $\bar{a}$ is the mean of all elements in matrix D_A, $\bar{b}$ is the mean of all elements in matrix D_B. Finally, the matching module compares the retrieved candidates with the query items. When both the Euclidean distance and the similarity score of NDD are below predefined thresholds, the relative poses are computed by ICP alignment and added to the factor graph optimization process. We use the GTSAM algorithm to optimize the global poses of the loop closure detection part. GTSAM is a factor graph optimization method. It uses a nonlinear optimizer to optimize the current and historical frame poses and finds the alignment results with the highest probability, resulting in robust localization and accurate map construction.

Table 1. The details of selected datasets list

Sequence	Frame	Duration (min: sec)	Distance (Km)
00	4541	7:50	3.723
02	4661	8:03	4.262
05	2761	4:48	2.205
08	4071	7:05	3.222
DCC01	5542	9:13	4.912
KAIST02	8941	14:53	5.965

4   Experiments

4.1   Datasets and Experimental Settings

In this section, we evaluate the proposed algorithm on the KITTI [15] and MulRan [16] public datasets. The point clouds of the KITTI dataset were scanned by Velodyne HDL-64E LiDAR, which is the most widely used dataset for LiDAR SLAM. In this dataset, we selected four sequences: 00, 02, 05, and 08, which have a sufficient number of loops. Sequence 08 has backward only loops, and sequence 02 has loops in different directions. The Multimodal Range Dataset (MulRan) was captured by the Ouster 64-ray LiDAR. The dataset was designed for place recognition tasks in urban environments that involve intentionally including many loop candidates in multiple cities with reverse revisits at intervals of up to one month. We selected two sequences: DCC01 and KAIST02. The details of these sequences are summarized in Table 1. To measure the computational cost of the different methods, we conducted all experiments on the same laptop computer with an Intel Core i7-12700H CPU, 4.7 GHz and 16 GB of RAM. To quantitatively analyze the accuracy of the estimated trajectories, we used an evaluation tool called evo [28] to compare the estimated trajectories with the ground truth trajectories. We use the absolute trajectory error (ATE) as a measure of accuracy (Fig. 2).

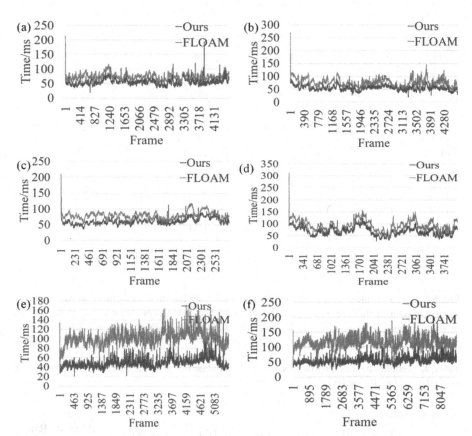

Fig. 2. Processing time for odometry estimation. It can be seen that our method consistently requires less processing time than the original method, indicating its higher efficiency. (a)-(d) Sequences 00, 02, 05, 08; (e) DCC01; (f) KAIST02.

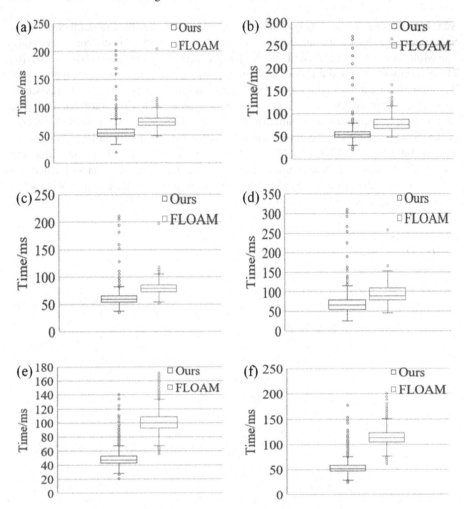

Fig. 3. Show box plots of the efficiency characteristics for both algorithms on six different sequences. Our method outperforms the original method in terms of efficiency, as demonstrated by the experimental results. (a)-(d) Sequences 00, 02, 05, 08; (e) DCC01; (f) KAIST02.

Table 2. Running time comparison (ms/frame) on public datasets, the best scores are marked in bold (the smaller, the better).

Method	Sequence						Average KITTI/MulRan
	00	02	05	08	DCC01	KAIST02	
FLOAM	73.35	74.43	79.15	89.37	100.19	113.29	79.08/106.74
Ours	**54.43**	**54.13**	**59.16**	**65.70**	**47.18**	**52.01**	**58.35/49.60**

4.2 Time Cost

The performance of our proposed algorithm was evaluated through experiments conducted in various scenarios and by comparing the results with those of FLOAM. Table 2 presents the average runtime per frame, while Fig. 3 and Fig. 4 depict the computational cost of both algorithms. FLOAM exhibited an average elapsed time of 79.08 ms and 106.74 ms on two common datasets, which could impact real-time performance and potentially diminish the accuracy of subsequent outcomes. Conversely, our proposed algorithm demonstrated an average elapsed time of 58.35 ms and 49.60 ms, signifying an efficiency improvement of 26.21% and 53.53%, respectively. This enhancement can be attributed to the incremental update capability of the ikd-tree, which circumvents the need to rebuild the entire tree and actively monitors the tree structure to partially rebalance it for efficient nearest-point search. By exclusively constructing unbalanced subtrees, the overall efficiency is maximized, significantly reducing runtime. Consequently, we deduce that ikd-tree-based map management is more efficient than traditional point cloud map management approaches.

Table 3. Comparison results of absolute trajectory error on the public dataset (RMSE, m), the best scores are marked in bold (the smaller, the better).

Method	Sequence						Average
	00	02	05	08	DCC01	KAIST02	KITTI/MulRan
FLOAM	5.19	8.79	1.94	4.36	25.13	36.28	5.07/30.71
Ours	**2.19**	**5.22**	**1.35**	**4.02**	**6.66**	**2.70**	**3.20/4.68**

4.3 Evaluation on Public Dataset

Figure 4 presents the trajectory comparison results before and after back-end optimization on two widely-used datasets, KITTI and MulRan. The proposed algorithm effectively estimated the vehicle's position and closely followed the ground truth trajectory, primarily due to its exceptional loop closure detection capability, which identified previously visited locations and corrected the drift caused by front-end odometry. Notably, on the MulRan dataset, characterized by numerous transformed iterative lanes, a high presence of dynamic objects, and unstructured objects with similar structures, the trajectories generated by FLOAM exhibited significant drift due to geometric error and cumulative odometry errors. In contrast, our method successfully detected these discrepancies and eliminated the cumulative errors produced by the odometry, resulting in globally consistent trajectories. Table 3 and Fig. 5 display the accuracy comparison results on the public dataset, utilizing absolute trajectory error (ATE) as the evaluation metric. Our proposed odometry demonstrated superior accuracy compared to FLOAM, with an average accuracy improvement of 36.88% on the KITTI dataset and 84.76% on the MulRan dataset. These findings underscore the importance of robust and stable back-end optimization in enhancing LiDAR odometry performance, particularly in complex,

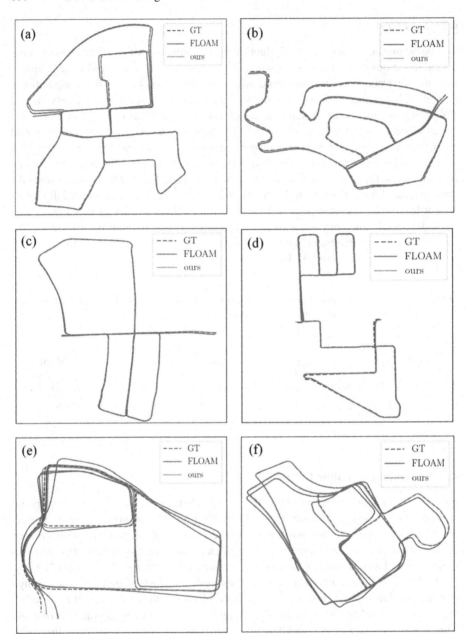

Fig. 4. Trajectory comparison for our method and FLOAM. We compare the trajectory estimation of our method and FLOAM on different datasets. The solid line shows the estimated trajectory and the dashed line shows the ground truth. Our method achieves higher accuracy and consistency than FLOAM across all datasets. (a)–(d) KITTI sequences 00, 02, 05, 08; (e) DCC01; (f) KAIST02.

unstructured urban environments with heterogeneous features. Our algorithm not only improved operational speed but also increased positioning accuracy by reducing drift and error.

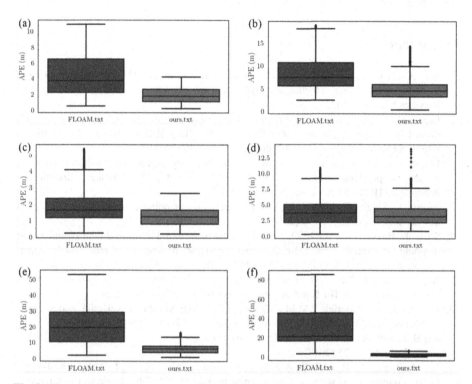

Fig. 5. The box plots depict a comparative analysis of evaluation accuracy between our proposed method and FLOAM across various datasets. Our method outperforms the other algorithms in most cases and has less variation in accuracy. (a)–(d) KITTI sequences 00, 02, 05, 08; (e) DCC01; (f) KAIST02.

5 Conclusion

In this paper, we present a lightweight, integrated LiDAR SLAM system specifically designed for robots with limited computational resources. Our proposed system seamlessly integrates efficient map management utilizing incremental kd-tree (ikd-tree) data structures, along with reliable loop closure detection employing the Normal Distribution Descriptor (NDD). Furthermore, we incorporate the GTSAM framework for global optimization, which refines the pose estimates. We rigorously evaluate our system on well-established datasets, namely KITTI and MulRan, and demonstrate its superior performance in terms of localization accuracy and computational efficiency when compared to traditional methods. Our algorithm significantly improves the operation speed and positioning accuracy by effectively reducing drift and error. Our method has some limitations in handling extreme cases and operating with a single robot. As future work, we plan to develop a centralized multi-robot SLAM framework and evaluate its performance in building global maps across realistic scenarios.

References

1. Sung, C., Jeon, S., Lim, H., Myung, H.: What if there was no revisit? Large-scale graph-based SLAM with traffic sign detection in an HD map using LiDAR inertial odometry. Intell. Serv. Robotics **15**, 1–10 (2022)
2. Lee, E.M., Choi, J., Lim, H., Myung, H.: Real: rapid exploration with active loop-closing toward large-scale 3D mapping using UAVs. In: 2021 IEEE/RSJ International Conference on Intelligent Robots and Systems (IROS), pp. 4194–4198 (2021)
3. Lim, H., Kim, Y., Jung, K., Hu, S., Myung, H.: Avoiding degeneracy for monocular visual SLAM with point and line features. In: 2021 IEEE International Conference on Robotics and Automation (ICRA), pp. 11675–11681 (2021)
4. Zhang, J., Singh, S.: LOAM: LiDAR odometry and mapping in real-time. In: Robotics: Science and Systems, pp. 1–9 (2014)
5. Shan, T., Englot, B.: LeGO-LOAM: lightweight and ground-optimized lidar odometry and mapping on variable terrain. In: 2018 IEEE/RSJ International Conference on Intelligent Robots and Systems (IROS), pp. 4758–4765 (2018)
6. Xu, W., Zhang, F.: Fast-LIO: a fast, robust lidar-inertial odometry package by tightly-coupled iterated kalman filter. IEEE Robot. Autom. Lett. **6**(2), 3317–3324 (2021)
7. Mur-Artal, R., Montiel, J.M.M., Tardos, J.D.: ORB-SLAM: a versatile and accurate monocular SLAM system. IEEE Trans. Rob. **31**(5), 1147–1163 (2015)
8. Engel, J., Koltun, V., Cremers, D.: Direct sparse odometry. IEEE Trans. Pattern Anal. Mach. Intell. **40**(3), 611–625 (2017)
9. Lin, J., Zhang, F.: R 3 LIVE: A Robust, Real-time, RGB-colored, LiDAR-Inertial-Visual tightly-coupled state Estimation and mapping package. In: 2022 International Conference on Robotics and Automation (ICRA), pp. 10672–10678 (2022)
10. Debeunne, C., Vivet, D.: A review of visual-LiDAR fusion based simultaneous localization and mapping. Sens. **20**(7), 2068 (2020)
11. Kim, G., Yun, S., Kim, J., Kim, A.: SC-LiDAR-SLAM: a front-end agnostic versatile lidar slam system. In: 2022 International Conference on Electronics, Information, and Communication (ICEIC), pp. 1–6 (2022)
12. Zhou, R., He, L., Zhang, H., Lin, X., Guan, Y.: NDD: a 3D point cloud descriptor based on normal distribution for loop closure detection. In: 2022 IEEE/RSJ International Conference on Intelligent Robots and Systems (IROS), pp. 1328–1335 (2022)
13. Cai, Y., Xu, W., Zhang, F.: ikd-Tree: an incremental KD tree for robotic applications. arXiv preprint arXiv:2102.10808 (2021)
14. Dellaert, F.: Factor graphs and GTSAM: a hands-on introduction. Georgia Institute of Technology (2012)
15. Geiger, A., Lenz, P., Urtasun, R.: Are we ready for autonomous driving? The kitti vision benchmark suite. In: 2012 IEEE Conference on Computer Vision and Pattern Recognition (CVPR), pp. 3354–3361 (2012)
16. Kim, G., Park, Y. S., Cho, Y., Jeong, J., Kim, A.: MulRan: multimodal range dataset for urban place recognition. In: 2020 IEEE International Conference on Robotics and Automation (ICRA), pp. 6246–6253 (2020)

17. Besl, P.J., McKay, N.D.: Method for registration of 3-D shapes. In: Sensor fusion IV: control paradigms and data structures, vol. 1611, pp. 586–606 (1992)
18. Lin, J., Zhang, F.: Loam livox: a fast, robust, high-precision LiDAR odometry and mapping package for LiDARs of small FoV. In: 2020 IEEE International Conference on Robotics and Automation (ICRA), pp. 3126–3131 (2020)
19. Wang, H., Wang, C., Xie, L.: Lightweight 3-D localization and mapping for solid-state LiDAR. IEEE Robot. Autom. Lett. 6(2), 1801–1807 (2021)
20. Wang, H., Wang, C., Chen, C. L., Xie, L.: F-loam: fast lidar odometry and mapping. In: 2021 IEEE/RSJ International Conference on Intelligent Robots and Systems (IROS), pp. 4390–4396 (2021)
21. Bentley, J.L.: Multidimensional binary search trees used for associative searching. Commun. ACM 18(9), 509–517 (1975)
22. Xu, W., Cai, Y., He, D., Lin, J., Zhang, F.: FAST-LIO2: fast direct lidar-inertial odometry. IEEE Trans. Rob. 38(4), 2053–2073 (2022)
23. Bai, C., Xiao, T., Chen, Y., Wang, H., Zhang, F., Gao, X.: Faster-LIO: lightweight tightly coupled LiDAR-inertial odometry using parallel sparse incremental voxels. IEEE Robot. Autom. Lett 7(2), 4861–4868 (2022)
24. Salti, S., Tombari, F., Di Stefano, L.: SHOT: Unique signatures of histograms for surface and texture description. Comput. Vis. Image Underst. 125, 251–264 (2014)
25. Rusu, R. B., Blodow, N., Beetz, M.: Fast point feature histograms (FPFH) for 3D registration. In: 2009 IEEE International Conference on Robotics and Automation (ICRA), pp. 3212–3217 (2009)
26. Kim, G., Kim, A.: Scan context: egocentric spatial descriptor for place recognition within 3D point cloud map. In: 2018 IEEE/RSJ International Conference on Intelligent Robots and Systems (IROS), pp. 4802–4809 (2018)
27. Wang, Y., et al.: Lidar iris for loop-closure detection. In: 2020 IEEE/RSJ International Conference on Intelligent Robots and Systems (IROS), pp. 5769–5775 (2020)
28. Grupp, M.: Evo: Python Package for the Evaluation of Odometry and Slam (2017). https://github.com/MichaelGrupp/evo

Machine Anomalous Sound Detection Based on Feature Fusion and Gaussian Mixture Model

Shengqiang Cai, Wenju Zhou$^{(\boxtimes)}$, and Xinzhen Ren

School of Mechatronic Engineering and Automation, Shanghai University, Shanghai, China
{shengqiang11,zhouwenju}@shu.edu.cn

Abstract. Anomalous sound detection (ASD) is a technique used for audio monitoring of machines in factories, aiming to identify machine failures by analyzing the sound produced during machine operation. However, it is challenging to extract efficient input features for classifiers and determine suitable decision boundary, which can result in poor detection performance. This paper proposes a self-supervised method based on feature fusion and Gaussian mixture models (GMM). The feature fusion method is proposed to combine the temporal and frequency domain information. Moreover, the GMM-based method is proposed to calculate anomaly scores, which can determines more complex decision boundary. We conducted experiments on the datasets provided by DCASE 2020 Challenge Task 2. The results demonstrate that our model outperforms the baseline autoencoder model. Based on the official evaluation metrics, our model achieved an average AUC improvement of over 20.32% and an average pAUC improvement of over 27.29%.

Keywords: Anomalous sound detection · Machine audio · Gaussian mixture model · Feature fusion

1 Introduction

With the development of artificial intelligence and machine learning, the application of anomaly detection has expanded across various fields, including anomalous sound detection (ASD) [1]. ASD has become an effective tool for monitoring industrial equipment and detecting early machine failures. In anomalous detection, it is difficult to gather anomaly data. It is more practical to use unsupervised ASD methods that rely on normal data for model training.

The application of unsupervised ASD in machine condition monitoring has attracted significant research interest. Since 2020, the DCASE challenge has introduced unsupervised ASD as a new task. ASD presents distinctive challenges compared to typical machine learning tasks, including the imbalanced nature of the training dataset and the scarcity of labeled anomalous samples [2]. Furthermore, it is challenging to develop an efficient model due to the sounds with different temporal-frequency characteristics.

To address these challenges, numerous methods have been applied to ASD. Most methods leverage machine learning to model the distribution of normal

F. Sun et al. (Eds.): ICCSIP 2023, CCIS 1918, pp. 334–345, 2024.
https://doi.org/10.1007/978-981-99-8018-5_25

sound data. One approach uses generative model, such as autoencoder (AE) [3], ID-conditioned autoencoder [4], interpolation deep neural networks (IDNN) [5], generative adversarial network (GAN) [6], WaveNet [7], Flow [8]. In generative models, a common method is to minimize the reconstruction error, such as AE. It assumes that the normal data used for AE can be reconstructed better than the anomaly data. Another major approach is based on classification, where neural networks are trained to classify different categories. In this context, a common method is self-supervised classification [9–11]. In self-supervised learning, models utilize metadata like machine type or machine identity (ID) as auxiliary classification tasks. Then, advanced convolutional neural networks (CNN) such as ResNet, MobileNetV2, MobileFaceNet, are used for training. However, since only normal samples are used during the training phase, detection performance based on reconstruction error methods may suffer from decline. Although the self-supervised method improves the detection performance through auxiliary tasks, its performance in sound detection is unstable.

Log-Mel spectrograms are commonly employed as the input representation in ASD systems [12,13]. However, Log-Mel spectrograms may lose useful high-frequency information, which can result in poor detection robustness when used in conjunction with self-supervised ASD methods. To enhance the stability, a self-supervised method with spectral-temporal feature fusion has been used in ASD [14]. But the detection performance of the system may be influenced by noise present in the temporal features, which leads to lower anomaly scores for certain machines.

This paper proposes a self-supervised ASD based on feature fusion and Gaussian Mixture Model (GMM). The main contributions of this paper can be summarized as follows:

- A new CNN-based method (WgramNet) is proposed for extracting temporal features, aiming to reduce the impact of temporal noise and improve detection performance.
- The GMM is used to calculate anomaly scores, aiming to determine more complex decision boundary and enhance the robustness of the detection.

The remaining sections of this paper are structured as follows: Sect. 2 introduces the proposed self-supervised ASD method, Sect. 3 presents the experimental validation of the proposed approach, and Sect. 4 provides a comprehensive summary of the entire research.

2   Detailed Description of Proposed Method

This section presents the self-supervised ASD method, which includes feature extraction with temporal-frequency fusion, the MobileFaceNet architecture embeds the Arcface loss function, and anomaly score calculation based on GMM. The training and testing procedure of the proposed method is depicted in Fig. 1.

During the training procedure, we first extract temporal features (Wgram) from the training data using the proposed network (WgramNet). Then, we combine the Wgram features with the Log-Mel spectrograms (Lgram) to obtain the temporal-frequency fusion features (LWgram). The LWgram features are used as the input for the self-supervised classifier to train the feature representation.

During the testing procedure, we train the GMM for each machine ID. As an example, we use ToyCar ID.05. To calculate the anomaly score for the ToyCar ID.05 test sample, we use the GMM to build a probability density function for the hidden features of ToyCar ID.05 in the training data [15]. We use the negative log probability as the anomaly score for detection. The classification thresholds for normal and anomaly are determined by the anomaly scores of normal samples.

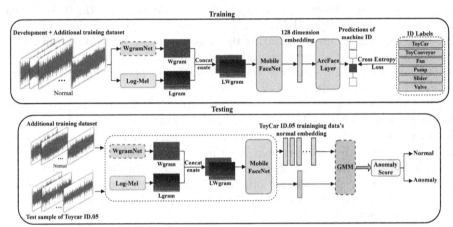

Fig. 1. The training and testing procedure of the proposed method.

2.1 Feature Extraction

It is noticed that the features of certain machine types are predominantly concentrated in the high-frequency range. The sound samples undergo two separate feature extraction processes, where the temporal and frequency features are extracted individually. These two features are finally concatenated as the input to the self-supervised classifier.

The single-channel sound signal is denoted as the input m. The Short-Time Fourier Transform (STFT) is used to obtain the spectrogram, and then the Mel-filter banks are used to obtain the Mel spectrogram. Finally, taking the logarithm of the Mel spectrogram, we obtain the Lgram feature F_L, as shown below:

$$F_L = LogMel(||STFT(m)||^2), \tag{1}$$

where $LogMel(\cdot)$ represents the operation of Mel filter bank and logarithmic operation on the sound signal. F_L has dimensions of $M \times T$. M is the number of Mel bins and T is the number of time frames.

We use the WgramNet to obtain temporal features from the input m. The details of WgramNet is depicted in Fig. 2 and the architecture of WgramNet is shown in Table 1.

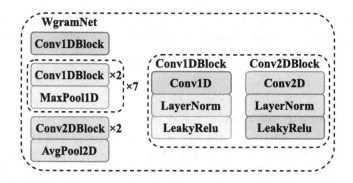

Fig. 2. The details of WgramNet.

To obtain the Wgram, we utilize one-dimensional convolution blocks (Conv1D-Block) and two-dimensional convolution blocks (Conv2DBlock). Conv1DBlock consists of a 1D convolution, a LayerNorm normalization layer, and a LeakyReLU non-linear. Conv2DBlock replaces the 1D convolution in Conv1DBlock with a 2D convolution. We first apply a Conv1DBlock, which begins with a convolution layer with kernel size 11 and stride 4. Next, we perform the following 7 operations, each operation consisting of two Conv1DBlocks and a MaxPool1D. These two Conv1DBlocks have dilations of 1 and 2, aiming to expand the receptive field of the convolutional layers. The MaxPool1D is designed to perform downsampling with kernel size 2. Then, we apply the unsqueeze operation to expand the dimensions of the data. Finally, after passing through two Conv2DBlocks and AvgPool2D, we obtain the Wgram feature F_W, as follows:

$$F_W = WgramNet(m), \tag{2}$$

where F_W has dimensions of $1 \times M \times T$.

Table 1. The architecture of WgramNet

Operator	c	k	s	d	p	n
Conv1DBlock	64	11	4	1	132	×1
Conv1DBlock	128	3	1	1	1	
Conv1DBlock	128	3	1	2	1	×7
MaxPool1D	-	2	-	-	-	
Conv2DBlock	1	3	1	1	1	
Conv2DBlock	1	3	1	2	1	×1
MaxPool1D	-	1	-	-	-	

* Where c represents the number of output channels, k is kernel size, s is stride, d is dilations, p denotes padding size and n is the number of repetitions.

Finally, we concatenate the temporal feature F_W with the frequency feature F_L. The temporal-frequency fusion feature F_{LW} is represented as follows:

$$F_{LW} = Concatenate(F_L, F_W), \tag{3}$$

where F_{LW} has dimensions of $2 \times M \times T$.

2.2 Classifier Architecture

To improve the classification accuracy, MobileFaceNet is adopted as the self-supervised classifier. We use the residual bottlenecks in [11] as the main building blocks. The bottleneck includes a linear branch without activation function. We use PReLU [16] as the activation function and set the embedding feature dimension to 128. The MobileFaceNet architecture embeds the Arcface [17] loss function is depicted in Table 2.

Table 2. Architecture of MobileFaceNet

Operator	t	c	n	s
Conv2D 3 × 3	-	64	1	2
Depthwise Conv2D 3 × 3	-	64	1	1
Bottleneck	2	128	2	2
Bottleneck	4	128	2	2
Bottleneck	4	128	2	2
Conv2D 1 × 1	-	512	1	1
Linear GDConv2D	-	512	1	1
Linear Conv2D 1 × 1	-	128	1	1
Arcface	-	m	1	-

* Where t is expansion factor, c denotes output channels, n is the number of repetitions, s is stride and m represents the number of machine IDs.

The Arcface loss function is designed to improve the compactness within classes and the distinctiveness between different classes. We train the Mobile-FaceNet classifier using samples from all machine types. The classifier is designed to differentiate different machine types with distinct IDs.

2.3 Anomaly Score Calculation

When using the classifier to extract feature representations, many methods can be used to compute anomaly scores. Generally, the model output or the cosine similarity are used. As an evaluation method, a GMM can determine more complex decision boundary, making anomaly detection more robust. We use the GMM with full covariance matrix to compute the scores. The entire method can be abbreviated as LWgram-MobileFaceNet-GMM (LWMG).

3   Experimental Evaluation

In this section, we evaluate the performance of the proposed method through a series of experiments. Through various comparative experiments, we validate the superiority of the proposed method.

3.1   Dataset

All experiments are based on the DCASE 2020 Challenge task2 dataset. The dataset consists of ToyADMOS dataset [18] and MIMII dataset [19], which contains normal and anomaly sound data for six machine types. The six machine types are ToyConveyor, ToyCar, Pump, Fan, Valve, and Slider. Among them, ToyConveyor consists of 6 machine IDs, while other machine types consist of 7 machine IDs. Machine ID is designed to identify different machines for each machine type. The sample is approximately 10 s long and sampled at 16,000 Hz.

The dataset is divided into three subsets: development set, additional set, and evaluation set. We use the training data from the development set and additional set for training, while the testing data from the development set and evaluation set are employed for evaluating the performance of our model. In this paper, the training data consists exclusively of normal samples, whereas the test data comprises both normal and anomaly samples.

3.2   Training Details

To obtain the input feature LWgram, the Mel filter banks is configured as 128, the hop length is 512, and the window size is 1024.

Table 3. Summarization of parameters

Parameters for signal processing	
Sampling rate	16kHz
Number of Mel filter banks	128
Hop size	512
Window size	1024
Parameters for classifier	
Feature Scale s	30
Angular Margin Penalty m	0.75
Other parameters	
Epochs	150
Learning rate	0.0001
Batch size	32
Number of machine IDs	41
Number of mixture components	41

This results in a temporal dimension of 313. We use Adam to optimize the model and the learning rate is scheduled by the cosine annealing strategy. The angular margin penalty m in Arcface is configured as 0.75, and the feature scale s is 30. The model is trained for 150 epochs with a batch size of 32. The number of mixture components is set to 41, and the initial learning rate is configured as 0.0001. All the parameters are summarized in Table 3.

3.3   Evaluation Metrics

The proposed ASD method is evaluated using the Area Under the Curve (AUC) and the partial Area Under the Curve (pAUC) of Receiver Operating Characteristic (ROC). The pAUC is calculated within the low false positive rate (FPR) range of [0, 0.1].

3.4   Comparison of Anomaly Score Calculation Methods

To obtain better anomaly scores, we compared three different methods for calculating anomaly scores: model output, cosine similarity, and GMM. Since GMM has many types of covariance matrix, we also compared GMM methods with spherical, diagonal, and full covariance matrices to select the most suitable one. The AUC and pAUC of different anomaly score calculation methods are shown in Table 4. During the comparison procedure, all conditions are identical except for the anomaly score calculation method.

Table 4. The AUC and pAUC of different anomaly score calculation methods(%)

Methods	Development dataset AUC(pAUC)	Evaluation dataset AUC(pAUC)
Model output	92.50(86.25)	93.88(87.96)
Cosine similarity	93.56(86.90)	94.38(88.54)
GMM(spherical)	93.55(86.85)	94.40(88.56)
GMM(diagonal)	93.58(86.93)	94.41(88.60)
GMM(full)	**93.83(86.95)**	**94.48(88.61)**

The results indicate that the GMM with a full covariance matrix performs the best. The output of model performs lower than other methods. The results obtained from cosine similarity and GMM with spherical or diagonal covariance matrices are very similar. The reason is that the model trained with the Arcface loss tend to exhibit circular output distribution. Cosine similarity can determine circular boundaries. By estimating the covariance matrix for each class, GMMs can capture the underlying distribution of the data and identify non-linear decision boundaries.

3.5   Performance Comparison

The proposed method is compared with other typical methods. The AUC and pAUC results of different methods in the development dataset are shown in Table 5. AE is the official model, which is based on reconstruction error. MobileNetV2-GMM is the unsupervised classification method that utilizes MobileNetV2 and GMM [20]. STgram-MFN [14] is a self-supervised classification method. To validate the effectiveness of the proposed method, we use the output of model to calculate the anomaly score. The method is abbreviated as LWgram-MobileFaceNet (LWM). The results demonstrate that the proposed method enhances the detection performance of certain machines, particularly on ToyConveyor. Compared to other methods, our approach achieved an improvement of 6.33% in AUC and 2.54% in pAUC for ToyConveyor. Moreover, our method showed an average improvement of 1.47% in AUC and 0.61% in pAUC.

Table 5. The AUC and pAUC of different methods in the development dataset(%)

Methods	AE	MobileNetV2 -GMM [20]	STgram -MFN [14]	LWM	LWMG
Metric	AUC(pAUC)	AUC(pAUC)	AUC(pAUC)	AUC(pAUC)	AUC(pAUC)
ToyCar	78.77(67.58)	95.28(86.91)	94.44(87.68)	**96.29(90.24)**	96.14(89.93)
ToyConveyor	72.53(60.43)	69.80(61.21)	74.57(63.60)	74.83(63.80)	**80.90(66.14)**
Fan	65.83(52.45)	87.97(80.66)	**94.04(88.97)**	91.40(83.51)	92.39(84.58)
Pump	72.89(59.99)	**95.63**(85.74)	91.94(81.75)	93.59(84.92)	94.57(**85.95**)
Slider	84.76(66.53)	99.22(97.55)	**99.55(97.61)**	99.45(97.16)	99.40(97.02)
Value	66.28(50.98)	91.26(84.00)	**99.64(98.44)**	99.43(97.89)	99.57(98.09)
Average	73.51(59.66)	89.86(82.68)	92.36(86.34)	92.50(86.25)	**93.83(86.95)**

Table 6. The AUC and pAUC of different methods in the evaluation dataset(%)

Methods	AE	MobileNetV2 -GMM [20]	LWM	LWMG
Metric	AUC(pAUC)	AUC(pAUC)	AUC(pAUC)	AUC(pAUC)
ToyCar	80.14(66.17)	95.58(90.89)	95.91(92.28)	**96.39(92.29)**
ToyConveyor	**85.36(66.95)**	81.35(**68.62**)	78.02(63.01)	79.62(64.90)
Fan	82.80(65.80)	97.61(92.21)	97.58(94.43)	**97.75(94.94)**
Pump	82.37(64.11)	96.54(89.32)	95.00(87.76)	**95.94(88.74)**
Slider	79.41(58.87)	98.33(91.90)	98.97(95.72)	**99.15(96.09)**
Value	57.37(50.79)	90.39(87.93)	97.78(94.58)	**98.00(94.68)**
Average	77.91(62.12)	92.97(86.80)	93.88(87.96)	**94.48(88.61)**

The AUC and pAUC results of different methods in the evaluation dataset are shown in Table 6. STgram-MFN does not provide detection results in evaluation dataset, we exclude it from the comparison. It can be observed that our

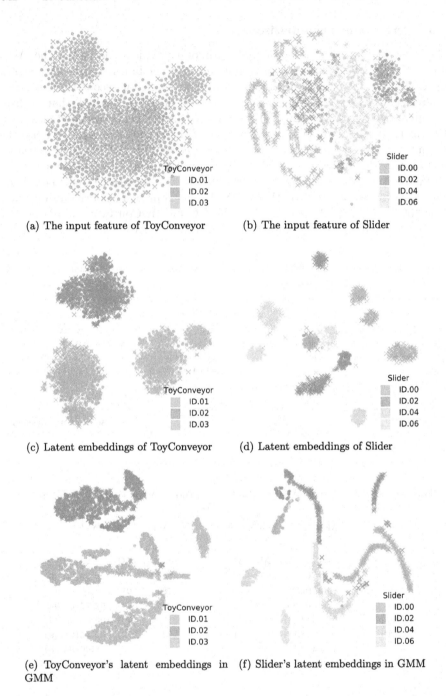

(a) The input feature of ToyConveyor

(b) The input feature of Slider

(c) Latent embeddings of ToyConveyor

(d) Latent embeddings of Slider

(e) ToyConveyor's latent embeddings in GMM

(f) Slider's latent embeddings in GMM

Fig. 3. The t-SNE visualization results for Slider and ToyConveyor. Each machine ID is represented as a color. The symbol "•" represents normal samples and the symbol "×" represents anomaly samples.

method performs well in evaluating most machine types. However, the detection performance on the ToyConveyor is still lower than other machine types. To investigate the reasons for the lower performance on ToyConveyor, we conduct experiments comparing it with the machine Slider, which exhibits better performance. We perform t-distributed stochastic neighbor embedding (t-SNE) clustering visualization on the corresponding test data from the development set for these two machines. We visualize the three distributions separately: the input features LWgram before machine training, the latent embeddings of the trained model, and the latent embeddings in GMM after training. The t-SNE visualization results for Slider and ToyConveyor are shown in Fig. 3.

From Fig. 3(a), it can be observed that the sounds from different machine IDs on ToyConveyor have high similarity, which makes it challenging to find decision boundaries during the training of ToyConveyor. Clearly, it results in poor performance of the trained model on ToyConveyor. The results in Fig. 3(c) and Fig. 3(c) suggest that the latent embedding of the trained model and the latent embedding in GMM cannot effectively differentiate between normal and anomaly samples. In contrast, the results in Fig. 3(b) indicate that the sounds from different machine IDs on Slider have some degree of distinctiveness. This enables the trained model to find decision boundaries, which contributes to the good performance of the proposed method on Slider. The results in Fig. 3(d) and Fig. 3(f) precisely demonstrate this point. Moreover, the latent embeddings of Slider in GMM exhibit better convergence compared to the latent embeddings of slider. This precisely demonstrates the effectiveness of our conducted experiments.

4   Conclusion

This paper proposed a self-supervised ASD method based on feature fusion and GMM. The effectiveness of the proposed method is verified through experiments. The experimental results indicate that the proposed method significantly outperforms the baseline system. The WgramNet can extract better temporal information and reduce the impact of temporal noise. Through the fusion of temporal-frequency features, we obtain higher detection performance. The GMM with a full covariance matrix can determine more complex non-linear boundaries, which improves the robustness of the detection. However, our self-supervised ASD method shows poor performance in ToyConveyor. This is a challenge that needs to be addressed in future research.

References

1. Koizumi, Y., Kawaguchi, Y., Imoto, K., Nakamura, T., Nikaido, Y., Tanabe, R., et al.: Description and discussion on DCASE2020 challenge task2: Unsupervised anomalous sound detection for machine condition monitoring. In: Proceedings of the Detection and Classification of Acoustic Scenes and Events 2020 Workshop (DCASE2020), pp. 81–85 (2020)

2. Ruff, L., et al.: A unifying review of deep and shallow anomaly detection. Proc. IEEE **2021**(109), 756–95 (2021)
3. Daniluk, P., Gozdziewski, M., Kapka, S., Kosmider, M.: Ensemble of auto-encoder based systems for anomaly detection. Technical report, DCASE2020 Challenge (2020)
4. Kapka, S.: ID-conditioned auto-encoder for unsupervised anomaly detection. In: Detection and Classification of Acoustic Scenes and Events Workshop (DCASE), pp. 71–75 (2020)
5. Suefusa, K., Nishida, T., Purohit, H., Tanabe, R., Endo, T., Kawaguchi, Y.: Anomalous sound detection based on interpolation deep neural network. In: ICASSP 2020–2020 IEEE International Conference on Acoustics, Speech and Signal Processing (ICASSP), Barcelona, Spain, pp. 271–275 (2020)
6. Zhou, B., Liu, S., Hooi, B., Cheng, X., Ye, J.: Beatgan: anomalous rhythm detection using adversarially generated time series. In: IJCAI, pp. 4433–4439 (2019)
7. Rushe, E., Mac Namee, B.: Anomaly detection in raw audio using deep autoregressive networks. In: ICASSP 2019–2019 IEEE International Conference on Acoustics, Speech and Signal Processing (ICASSP), pp. 3597–3601 (2019)
8. Dohi, K., Endo, T., Purohit, H., Tanabe, R., Kawaguchi, Y.: Flow-based self-supervised density estimation for anomalous sound detection. In: ICASSP 2021–2021 IEEE International Conference on Acoustics, Speech and Signal Processing (ICASSP), pp. 336–340 (2021)
9. Guan, J., Xiao, F., Liu, Y., Zhu, Q., Wang, W.: Anomalous sound detection using audio representation with machine ID based contrastive learning pretraining. In: ICASSP 2023–2023 IEEE International Conference on Acoustics, Speech and Signal Processing (ICASSP), pp. 1–5 (2023)
10. Shul, Y., Yi, W., Choi, J., Kang, D. S., Choi, J. W.: Noise-based self-supervised anomaly detection in washing machines using a deep neural network with operational information. In: Mechanical Systems and Signal Processing, 189, 110102 (2023)
11. Zeng, Y., et al.: Robust anomaly sound detection framework for machine condition monitoring. Technical report, DCASE2022 Challenge (2022)
12. Bai, J., Chen, J., Wang, M., Ayub, M. S., Yan, Q.: SSDPT: Self-supervised dual-path transformer for anomalous sound detection. In: Digital Signal Processing, 135, 103939 (2023)
13. Wilkinghoff, K.: Design choices for learning embeddings from auxiliary Tasks for domain generalization in anomalous sound detection. In: ICASSP 2023–2023 IEEE International Conference on Acoustics, Speech and Signal Processing (ICASSP), pp. 1–5 (2023)
14. Liu, Y., Guan, J., Zhu, Q., Wang, W.: Anomalous Sound Detection Using Spectral-Temporal Information Fusion. In: ICASSP 2022–2022 IEEE International Conference on Acoustics, Speech and Signal Processing (ICASSP), Singapore, Singapore, pp. 816–820 (2022)
15. Ntalampiras, S., Potamitis, I., Fakotakis, N.: Probabilistic novelty detection for acoustic surveillance under real-world conditions. IEEE Trans. Multimed. **13**(4), 713–719 (2011)
16. He, K., Zhang, X., Ren, S., Sun, J.: Delving deep into rectifiers: surpassing human-level performance on imagenet classification. In: Proceedings of the IEEE International Conference on Computer Vision, pp. 1026–1034 (2015)
17. Deng, J., Guo, J., Xue, N., Zafeiriou, S.: Arcface: additive angular margin loss for deep face recognition. In: Proceedings of the Conference on Computer Vision and Pattern Recognition (CVPR), pp. 4690–4699. IEEE (2019)

18. Koizumi, Y., Saito, S., Uematsu, H., Harada, N., Imoto, K.Y.: ToyADMOS: a dataset of miniature-machine operating sounds for anomalous sound detection. In: 2019 IEEE Workshop on Applications of Signal Processing to Audio and Acoustics (WASPAA), New Paltz, NY, USA, pp. 313–317 (2019)
19. Purohit, H., Tanabe, R., Ichige, K., Endo, T., Nikaido, Y., Suefusa, K., Kawaguchi, Y.: MIMII Dataset: Sound dataset for malfunctioning industrial machine investigation and inspection. In: Proceedings of the Detection and Classification of Acoustic Scenes and Events 2019 Workshop (DCASE), pp. 209–213 (2019)
20. Wu, J., Yang, F., Hu, W.: Unsupervised anomalous sound detection for industrial monitoring based on ArcFace classifier and gaussian mixture model. Appl. Acoustics **203**, 109188 (2023)

PSO-BP Neural Network-Based Optimization of Automobile Rear Longitudinal Beam Stamping Process Parameters

Yanqin Li[1], Zhicheng Zhang[2], Liang Fu[1], Zhouzhou Hou[1], and Dehai Zhang[1(✉)]

[1] Zhengzhou University of Light Industry, Zhengzhou 450002, Henan, China
zhangdehai0318@163.com
[2] Taiyuan University of Technology, Taiyuan 030024, Shanxi, China
zhangzhicheng0329@126.com

Abstract. This paper uses a sheet forming optimization method based on numerical simulation and PSO-BP neural network model, and optimizes the forming process parameters of a vehicle's rear longitudinal beam as an example with the maximum thinning rate. Combined with DYNAFORM software, the process parameters with high correlation with the maximum thinning rate were the crimping force and friction factor based on grey system theory (GS theory). Based on these two highly correlated process parameters, 400 sample points of Latin supercube sampling were used to train and verify the PSO-BP neural network model, and then the particle swarm algorithm was used to optimize the process parameters of the model. The result predicted that the pressure edge force was 422.5279 kN. When the friction coefficient is 0.10464, the maximum thinning rate is 22.8133%, while the maximum thinning rate obtained by numerical simulation of the predicted process parameters using DYNAFORM is 23.724%, so the difference between the predicted value and the simulated value is only 0.9107%, and the error rate of the two is only 3.99%. The neural network model established is accurate, and combining numerical simulation with the PSO-BP neural network model can be used as a new method to optimize the process parameters during stamping.

Keywords: Numerical simulation · particle swarm optimization · BP neural network · parameter optimization

1 Introduction

With the need of national development, the energy demand is increasing, and the energy problem has become increasingly prominent. Reducing sheet metal stamping defects and improving the yield of sheet metal forming help save energy. The development of computer numerical simulation technology can predict the forming of sheet metal in advance, and most of the traditional numerical simulation process parameters are selected by the "trial and error method", which only selects a solution that is feasible within the range of feasible process parameters and not necessarily the optimal solution.

F. Sun et al. (Eds.): ICCSIP 2023, CCIS 1918, pp. 346–358, 2024.
https://doi.org/10.1007/978-981-99-8018-5_26

However, if the optimal process parameters can be found, it will greatly increase the yield of sheet metal forming; the method of numerical simulation combined with an intelligent algorithm can traverse and optimize the feasible process parameters, and then find the optimal process parameters through the iteration of these feasible process parameters. How to improve the yield of sheet metal forming and reduce the occurrence of defects such as cracking, spring back, and wrinkling of sheet metal during stamping has been the subject of a lot of research by many scholars.

Stefanos et al. [1] studied the effects of mold radius, plate thickness, and edge pressing force on the spring back of workpiece forming, and proposed a new neural network system for spring back prediction in sheet metal forming, and carefully prepared a finite element model for verification. Xu et al. [2] proposed a preforming process to solve the problem of product cracking caused by the original forming process scheme by the stamping and forming of the rear stringer as the research, and used orthogonal experiments and gray degree analysis methods to obtain the combination of the best process parameters during stamping and forming of the rear stringer. Tian et al. [3] took the aluminum alloy cabin cover of a certain automobile as an example, and studied the effects of the die corner radius, convex die corner radius, draft slope, trimming extension, and die surface height on the stamping and forming of the outer cover of the cabin cover by the orthogonal experimental method, then determined the various process parameters in combination with the die surface compensation technology. Mehmet et al. [4] used the orthogonal regression experimental method and display-incremental iteration method to simulate various processes of stamping and forming, and the orthogonal regression experimental method found that some stamping parameters had a great influence on the stamping process. Zhang et al. [5] took the maximum thinning rate and cracking as the evaluation indicators, and analyzed the effects of the edge pressing force, stamping speed, friction coefficient, and convex and concave die gap on the stamping and forming of automotive covering parts by orthogonal experiment and range analysis, then optimized the stamping process parameters, reduced the number of mold repairs and shortened the production cycle of the product. Ganta et al. [6] used numerical simulation to simulate and analyze the causes of defects such as sheet metal cracking and blank thinning, while Sosnowski et al. [7] used the method of combining numerical simulation and a direct differential method to obtain the process parameters of sheet metal stamping and forming more accurately. Zhang et al. [8] first designed the experiment, and then combined this with DYNAFORM software to conduct numerical simulation. The edge force and blank shape required for stamping of an aircraft skin's double curvature thin-walled aluminum alloy parts were studied, and the cracking and wrinkling defects caused by the sheet metal were solved. Wang et al. [9] conducted a numerical simulation analysis of the drawing forming of thin-walled cylindrical parts, took the minimum thickness and wrinkle as the evaluation index, and used orthogonal test methods to study the effects of pressing force, stamping speed, and die gap on the forming quality of deep drawing parts, and found a set of optimal process parameters. Zhao et al. [10] studied the influence of each process parameter on the maximum thinning rate by the response surface method during the hot stamping forming of AZ31 magnesium alloy, and obtained the optimal process parameters, and finally verified the feasibility of the response surface method through experiments.

In this paper, the influence of process parameters such as the edge pressing force, stamping speed, friction factor, and drawbead resistance percentage on the stamping and forming of the rear stringer was first analyzed with the help of DYNAFORM software to simulate the parts, aiming at the maximum thinning rate. Then, orthogonal experiments and GS theory were used to determine the process parameters having a large correlation with the maximum thinning rate, and the intelligent algorithm was then used to optimize these process parameters with a large correlation, the corresponding maximum thinning rate was predicted, and finally, the DYNAFORM software was used to verify the optimization results.

2 Model Settings

2.1 Establishment of 3D Models

The 3D model used for research is shown in Fig. 1. The top view of the end cap is rectangular, about 1050 mm long and 189 mm wide. The plate grade is DC05, and the mechanical property parameters of the material are shown in Table 1 and Fig. 2. The thickness of the sheet is 1.5 mm.

Fig. 1. End cap

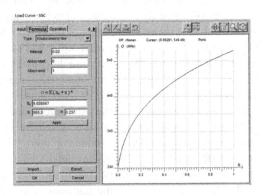

Fig. 2. Material properties.

2.2 Finite Element Model Settings

The 3D model established is converted by UG to IGS format and imported into DYNAFORM, setting the initial parameters. The 36-parameter Barlat material model is selected [11], and the finite element model is shown in Fig. 3.

Table 1. Material properties

Density (kg/mm3)	Young's modulus (MPa)	Poisson's ratio
7.85 × 10–3	2.07 × 105	0.28

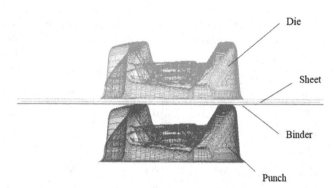

Fig. 3. Finite element model setting.

3 Finite Element Simulation

3.1 Orthogonal Experimental Design

Orthogonal experimental design is a scientific experimental design method, which is summarized based on a large number of practices, and each experimental protocol is carried out according to the orthogonal table with balanced dispersion and neat comparability [12, 13]; a more representative experiment can be selected based on a smaller number of experiments.

Taking the maximum thinning rate as the target index, the orthogonal experiment was designed with four process parameters: edge pressing force, stamping speed, friction factor, and bead resistance percentage. The orthogonal test factors and levels of each process parameter specified are shown in Table 2.

Table 2. Factors and levels in the test

Level	Edge pressing force (kN)	Stamping speed (mm/s)	Coefficient of friction	Bead (%)
1	400	2000	0.1	15
2	450	3000	0.11	20
3	500	4000	0.12	25
4	550	5000	0.13	30

Based on the orthogonal experimental table, the orthogonal experiment is carried out based on the L16 orthogonal table of four factors and four levels. The specific orthogonal experimental scheme and results are shown in Table 3.

Table 3. Orthogonal experimental factors and levels

Experiment number	Edge pressing force (kN)	Stamping speed (mm/s)	Coefficient of friction	Bead (%)	Maximum thinning rate (%)
1	400	2000	0.1	15	23.128
2	400	3000	0.11	20	24.637
3	400	4000	0.12	25	26.772
4	400	5000	0.13	30	45.142
5	450	2000	0.11	25	25.828
6	450	3000	0.1	30	27.023
7	450	4000	0.13	15	24.239
8	450	5000	0.12	20	25.232
9	500	2000	0.12	30	38.453
10	500	3000	0.13	25	35.958
11	500	4000	0.1	20	24.673
12	500	5000	0.11	15	23.615
13	550	2000	0.13	20	25.802
14	550	3000	0.12	15	24.097
15	550	4000	0.11	30	30.07
16	550	5000	0.1	25	26.133

3.2 GS Theoretical Analysis

From the results of the orthogonal table, it can be seen that the relationship between each process parameter and the maximum thinning rate is not very clear, and the degree of correlation of each process parameter can be analyzed by GS theory (grey system theory). This was proposed by Deng Julong, a famous scholar in China [14]. Using this theory, unknown information can be predicted from the known information, so that the overall understanding can be further analyzed. If a system is a grey system, no matter how external the system is and how discrete, there must be some correlation between the parameters in the system. This theory can be used to find the degree of correlation between each process parameter and the maximum thinning rate.

The GS theoretical calculation steps are as follows:

First, the number series is set:

$$x = [x(1), x(2), \cdots, x(n)] \tag{1}$$

Dimensionless elements,

$$f(x(k)) = \frac{x(k)}{\bar{x}(k)} = y(k) \tag{2}$$

Then the comparison series is selected according to the weighted value below,

$$\xi(k) = \frac{\min_i \min_k |X_i(k) - X_0(k)| + \rho \max_i \max_i |X_i(k) - X_0(k)|}{|X_i(k) - X_0(k)| - \rho \max_i \max_i |X_i(k) - X_0(k)|} \tag{3}$$

$\xi(k)$ is the correlation coefficient between X_0 and X_i at k points, where ρ is the resolution, the value is 0.5, and $\min_i \min_k |X_i(k) - X_0(k)|$ and $\max_i \max_i |X_i(k) - X_0(k)|$ denote the minimum and maximum ranges of the two levels, respectively.

The degree of correlation between a comparison series and a reference series is defined as,

$$\gamma_i = \sum_{i=1}^{n} \xi_i(k) \tag{4}$$

The closer the comparison series is to the reference series, the larger is γ_i. The above calculation process is compiled as a.m file and the degree of correlation between each process parameter and the maximum thinning rate is calculated by MATLAB. The results are shown in Table 4.

Table 4. Correlation of each factor to the maximum thinning rate

Parameter	Edge pressing force (kN)	Stamping speed(mm/s)	Coefficient of friction (%)	Bead (%)
Degree of relevance	0.811	0.599	0.830	0.755

It can be seen from Table 4 that the maximum thinning rate has a large correlation with the edge force and friction factor, which is greater than the correlation between the bead and the stamping speed. When using the algorithm for further optimization, the edge pressing force and friction factor, which are highly related to the maximum thinning rate, were selected as variables, and the range difference analysis was carried out on the orthogonal experiment, the draw bead resistance percentage was selected as 15%, and the stamping speed was 4000 mm· s^{-1}.

4 Optimization Analysis and Discussion

4.1 Establishment of PSO-BP Neural Network Model

Proposed by American social psychologist James Kennedy and electrical engineer Russell Eberhart in 1995, the particle swarm algorithm is a population-based randomization technique with the advantages of a simple iteration format, swarm intelligence, intrinsic parallelism, and fast convergence to the optimal solution·

The core of the algorithm is to initialize a population with n particles in the feasible solution space of the D dimension $X = (X_1, X_2, \cdots, X_n)$. Each particle represents a potentially feasible solution to an extreme optimization problem, and each particle has three basic characteristics of position, velocity, and fitness values; the appropriate value is calculated from the fitness function, representing the advantages and disadvantages of the particle. When particles move in the solution space, the group extreme value Gbest is used to represent the optimal position searched by all particles, and the individual extreme value Pbest represents the optimal position searched by individual particles. The algorithm calculates the fitness value after each particle position is updated, compares it with the fitness value of Gbest and Pbest before iteration, and finally updates the position of Gbest and Pbest.

The particle iteration velocity and position are as follows:

$$V_{id}^{k+1} = \omega V_{id}^k + c_1 r_1 (P_{id}^{k+1} - X_{id}^k) + c_2 r_2 (P_{gd}^k - X_{id}^k) \tag{5}$$

$$X_{id}^{k+1} = X_{id}^k + V_{k+1 id} \tag{6}$$

In the formula:

ω is the weight of inertia; $d = 1, 2, \cdots D$; $i = 1, 2, \cdots n$; k is the current number of iterations; V_{id} is the velocity of the particle; c1 and c2 are non-negative acceleration factors, where c1 adjusts the step size of particles flying to their optimal position, and c2 flies to the global optimal position of the step size; r1 and r2 are independent random numbers distributed between [0,1].

The BP neural network is a multi-layer pre-feedback network. The core of the neural network is the forward propagation of the signal and the reverse propagation of the error, to adjust the weights and thresholds of the BP neural network. BP neural networks are generally composed of an input layer, a hidden (implicit) layer, and an output layer, and the input layer receives external signals and transmits them to the middle layer. The hidden layer is responsible for transforming information and passing information to the output layer. The output layer receives the information and outputs it after further processing. When the output does not match the expectations, it will enter the error backpropagation stage, and the weights and thresholds of each layer of the neural network will be adjusted according to the error gradient descent. The structure of the neural network in MATLAB is shown in Fig. 4.

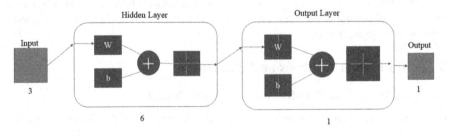

Fig. 4. Neuronal structure

The PSO-BP neural network model uses particle swarm optimization to adjust the weights and thresholds of the BP neural network to reduce the fluctuation of the initial weights and thresholds in the BP neural network, improve the learning efficiency of the network and increase its stability. The flowchart of the PSO-BP model is shown in Fig. 5.

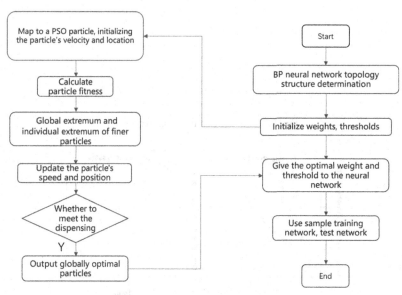

Fig. 5. PSO-BP flowchart

4.2 PSO-BP Neural Network Model Parameter Optimization

Latin hypercube sampling (LHS) is a form of stratified sampling that can be applied to multiple variables, and the principle of the LHS method is to repeatedly generate N samples for each random variable, selecting samples from a single interval in the domain of the distribution function.

Using this sampling method, 40 groups of sample points were selected for training the neural network within the parameter range with a large correlation with the maximum thinning rate; that is, 40 groups of sample points were selected within the edge pressing force [400,550] kN and the friction coefficient [0.1, 0.13]. The first 33 groups of sample points are used for training, and the last 7 groups are used to verify the accuracy of the network, and the results of Latin hypercube sampling are shown in Fig. 6.

The PSO-BP neural network model is trained by the sample points extracted by Latin hypercube sampling, and the correlation regression of the PSO-BP neural network model is obtained after training, as shown in Fig. 7. For example, Fig. 8 shows the expected and predicted values, and the error rate of the predicted values is shown in Fig. 9, which shows that the maximum error rate of the prediction is only 1.28%. This reflects the accuracy of the establishment of the PSO-BP neural network model.

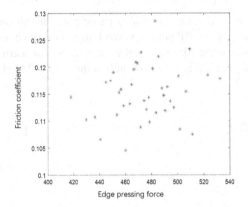

Fig. 6. Latin hypercube sampling results

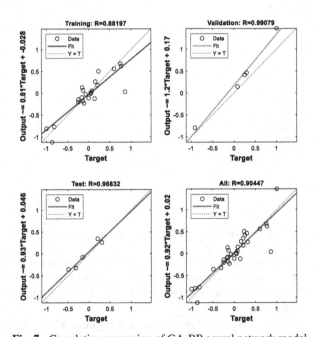

Fig. 7. Correlation regression of GA-BP neural network model

According to the principle of the genetic algorithm, the optimization process can describe the optimal solution for finding G(x) in a feasible 2-dimensional solution space, and G(x) can be expressed as,

$$G(x) = g(x1, x2) \tag{7}$$

In the formula,

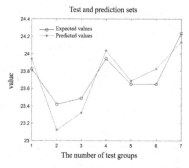

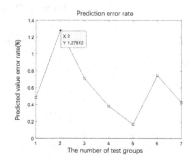

Fig. 8. Expected and predicted values of the test set

Fig. 9. Error ratio between expected and predicted values of the test set

x1 and x2 denote the edge force and coefficient of friction, respectively. The range of feasible solution space values is:

$$\begin{cases} 400 \leq x_1 \leq 550\,\text{kN} \\ 0.1 \leq x_2 \leq 0.13 \end{cases} \tag{8}$$

During optimization, the fitness value of the genetic algorithm is set as the prediction result of the GA-BP neural network, the genetic algorithm is optimized within the feasible solution space, and the fitness value converges to 22.8133 after iteration 50; that is, the maximum thinning rate is 22.8133%. The fitness curve is shown in Fig. 10, and the corresponding optimal process parameters are shown in Table 5.

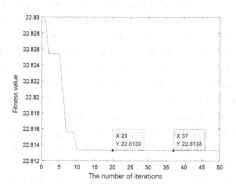

Fig.10. Fitness curve (maximum thinning rate)

The optimized process parameters were simulated in the DYNAFORM software and the results are shown in Fig. 11.

As can be seen from the above figure, the maximum thinning rate of sheet metal stamping after the simulation is 23.724%, while the maximum thinning rate predicted by particle swarm optimization is about 22.8133%. The difference between the two is therefore only 0.9107%, and the error rate of prediction and simulation is only 3.99%,

Table 5. Optimal process parameters

Parameter	Edge pressing force /kN	Coefficient of friction
value	422.5279	0.10464

Fig. 11. Optimized forming result (a) Limit diagram of the forming of the post-longitudinal extension beam (b) Plot of thickness change of post-longitudinal extension beam

which is much less than 20%, indicating that the accuracy of the PSO-BP model established is high. It is shown that the sheet metal forming optimization method used in this paper based on numerical simulation and a particle swarm optimization BP neural network can be applied to the optimization of process parameters during post-stringer stamping.

5 Discussion

The maximum thinning rate of sheet metal stamping after the simulation is 23.724%, and the difference between the optimal process parameters and the maximum thinning rate predicted by the PSO-BP neural network and the numerical simulation results is 0.9107%, and the predicted error rate is only 3.99%, and the predicted error is within the acceptable range, which reflects the accuracy of the established PSO-BP neural network model. If the error rate of the two is further reduced, the neural network model can be trained by using the Latin hypercube to extract more sample points before using the sample points to train the algorithm. If there is no requirement for training time, the number of hidden layer neurons can also be increased when establishing BP neural networks. Therefore, when applying the PSO-BP neural network model, whether the accuracy of the model meets the requirements can be comprehensively evaluated according to the purpose of the experiment, if the accuracy of the model does not meet the requirements, the experimental parameters or the parameters of the neural network model can be adjusted appropriately.

6 Conclusion

(1) To seek the optimal process parameters for the stamping and forming of a rear longitudinal beam of an automobile, an orthogonal experiment was first designed, and the parameters with the greatest correlation with the maximum thinning rate were found to be the edge force and friction coefficient in combination with GS

theory, while the parity analysis of the orthogonal experiment selected the draw bead resistance percentage with less correlation with the maximum thinning rate, at 15%, and the stamping speed as 4000. Finally, the two process parameters with the greatest correlation were optimized by combining numerical simulation and sn intelligent algorithm.

(2) When using the numerical simulation and intelligent algorithm in the combined optimization, 40 groups of sample points were first extracted within the feasible process parameters by Latin hypercube sampling. The PSO-BP neural network model was trained with the first 33 groups of these sample points, and its accuracy was verified by using the last 7 sets of data. Finally, the results of this model were optimized as the fitness of the particle swarm algorithm, and the optimal process parameters were obtained: the edge pressing force was 422.5279 kN, the friction coefficient is 0.10464, and the maximum thinning rate is predicted to be 22.8133%. The maximum thinning rate obtained by using DYNAFORM simulation of the predicted process parameters is 23.724%, so the difference between the predicted value and the simulated value is only 0.9107%, and the error rate is only 3.99%. This verifies the accuracy of the prediction of the PSO-BP neural network and the feasibility of the method of combining numerical simulation with the established intelligent algorithm model.

(3) This paper uses numerical simulation and the established PSO-BP neural network model to optimize the stamping process parameters of a rear side member of an automobile in theory. If the model can be verified and its error can be calculated in combination with practice, it will be possible to better verify the accuracy of the model and guide actual production.

References

1. Pathopoulos, S.C., Stavroulakis, G.E.: Springback prediction in sheet metal forming, based on finite element analysis and artificial neural network approach. Appl. Mech. 1, 97–110 (2020)
2. Xu, H., Wang, Z., Huang, Y., et al.: Cracking analysis and optimization of stamping forming of rear longitudinal extension beam based on CAE. Front. Soc. Sci. Technol. 2(8), 17–12 (2020)
3. Tian, G.F., Li, W.J., Li, J.: Mold surface optimization of 6016–T4P aluminum alloy automotive cabin cover based on Dynaform. Forging Technol. 45, 55–62 (2020)
4. Firat, M., Mete, O.H., Kocabicak, U., et al.: Stamping process design using FEA in conjunction with orthogonal regression. Finite Elem. Anal. Des. 46, 992–1000 (2010)
5. Zhang, Y., Fan, Y., Xue, Y.: Optimization of process parameters of car reinforced beam based on Dynaform and orthogonal test. Forging Technol. 44, 37–42 (2019)
6. Ganta, G., Pepelnjak, T., Kuzman, K.: Optimization of sheet metal forming processes by the use of numerical simulations. J. Mater. Process. Tech. 130, 54–59 (2002)
7. Sosnowski, W., Marczewska, I., Marczewski, A.: Sensitivity based optimization of sheet metal forming tools. J. Mater. Process. Tech. 124, 319–328 (2002)
8. Zhang, D.H., Bai, D.P., Liu, J.B., et al.: Formability behaviors of 2A12 thin-wall part based on DYNAFORM and stamping experiment. Compos. B 55, 591–598 (2013)
9. Wang, J.H., Xu, D.B., Hai, M.F., et al.: Numerical simulation on drawing deep of cylindrical pieces based on Dynaform. Appl. Mech. Mater. 3615, 252–258 (2014)

10. Zhao, P., Wu, Q., Yang, Y.-L., et al.: Process optimization of the hot stamping of AZ31 magnesium alloy sheets based on response surface methodology. Mater. **16**(5), 1867 (2023)
11. Liu, Q., Yu, G.Y., Mei, D.: Multi-objective optimization of stamping process parameters based on Dynaform and RBF-NSGA-II algorithm. J. Plast. Eng. **27**, 16–25 (2020)
12. Shen, Z., Jin, K., Zhou, Y.L., et al.: 6014 aluminum alloy U-shaped parts bending and springback. Forging Technol. **46**, 88–92 (2021)
13. Wu, X.T., Xie, R., Liu, G.K., et al.: Research on the forming performance of automotive heat insulation board based on Dynaform. Precision Form. Eng. **8**, 22–25 (2016)
14. Zhou, J., Hua, J.J., Yang, D.S., et al.: Optimization of multi-objective forming process of sheet metal based on GS theory and GA-BP network. Hot Working Technol. **38**, 73–76 (2009)

End-to-End Automatic Parking Based on Proximal Policy Optimization Algorithm in Carla

Zhizhao Li[1], Longyin Jiao[1(✉)], Zhumu Fu[1], and Fazhan Tao[1,2]

[1] School of Information Engineering, Henan University of Science and Technology, Henan, China
longyin113@126.com
[2] Longmen Laboratory, Luoyang, Henan, China

Abstract. With the acceleration of urbanization, the number of vehicles continues to increase. Parking in small spaces such as urban parking lots and roadside areas has become a problem in people's daily lives. Therefore, automatic parking systems have gradually become a research hotspot. In addition, with the continuous development of deep reinforcement learning (DRL), more and more research is starting to explore its application in automatic parking problems. In order to design a complete parking system, we need to consider two different parking situations: vertical parking and parallel parking. This paper designs a DRL-based proximal policy optimization (PPO) algorithm to solve the automatic parking problem. Finally, through simulation verification using the open-source simulator Carla, it is experimentally demonstrated that this method can achieve parking operations in different situations while ensuring the absolute safety of the vehicles.

Keywords: Artificial intelligence · deep reinforcement learning · autonomous parking · Carla

1 Introduction

With the rapid development of smart cars, the advancement of automatic parking systems will help address the difficulties encountered during parking and make people's lives more convenient. In crowded cities, parking spaces are relatively small, and automatic parking systems need to adopt different behavioral strategies for different parking spaces and sizes. For different types of parking spaces, vehicles need to first understand the location of the target parking space and, in addition, avoid any possible obstacles during the parking process, ultimately parking the vehicle in the center position of the target parking space.

In recent years, reinforcement learning has been increasingly explored by scholars to solve automatic parking problems [1]. Compared to traditional control methods, reinforcement learning creates a more general and highly adaptable system by employing a strategy of iterative experimentation, enabling it to adapt to a wide range of different

© The Author(s), under exclusive license to Springer Nature Singapore Pte Ltd. 2024
F. Sun et al. (Eds.): ICCSIP 2023, CCIS 1918, pp. 359–373, 2024.
https://doi.org/10.1007/978-981-99-8018-5_27

scenarios and exhibit predictive capabilities. Dealing with parking operations in parking spaces of various sizes and types may require the agent to possess a certain level of adaptability, allowing it to make decisions and adjustments based on different circumstances. Additionally, considering that the actions of real vehicles occur within a continuous space, it is important to ensure that the intelligent agent can aid the system in rapidly adapting to different environments and task requirements, thus improving the performance and reliability of the automatic parking system. This paper proposes a method that utilizes a reinforcement learning-based PPO algorithm to enable the intelligent agent to learn behavior strategies in parking environments of different types and scenarios. PPO algorithm, as a type of algorithm under the Actor-Critic framework, aims to maximize accumulated rewards by iteratively optimizing the policy network to accomplish the parking task [2]. The approach of deep reinforcement learning (DRL) mainly relies on continuous trial and error to learn optimal behavior strategies, allowing vehicles to learn continuously in a variety of scenarios through the process of trial and error [3]. Therefore, the utilization of DRL for solving automatic parking tasks enables the completion of parking tasks in various situations and the creation of a more comprehensive and highly adaptable automatic parking system through continuous learning from diverse external environments.

2 Related Works

In recent years, DRL has made significant progress in various fields, including learning optimal actions in tasks such as automatic parking and autonomous driving.

Mnih and his colleagues [4] proposed the Deep Q-Network (DQN) to address the instability and variance caused by the correlation among observed outcomes, the possibility of significant changes in Q-value updates to the policy, and the correlation between action values and target values with temporal differences. DQN is a value-based, model-free, and non-policy DRL algorithm.

However, DQN tends to overestimate the returns obtained from noisy environments, leading to suboptimal training results. Additionally, in DQN, the same neural network is responsible for both action selection and evaluating the chosen actions, which often results in instability during the training phase. To overcome these issues, Van Hasselt and his colleagues [5] made improvements by decomposing the maximum operation corresponding to the target network in action selection and the evaluation of the chosen actions to reduce overestimation. They introduced the Double Deep Q-Network (DDQN).

Wang and his colleagues [6] introduced the Dueling Double Deep Q-Network (Dueling DDQN), which improves the performance of DDQN by reconstructions of the action value function Q using the state value function V and the advantage function A.

$$Q(s, a) = V(s) + A(s, a) \tag{1}$$

Silver and his colleagues [7] proposed a deterministic policy gradient actor-critic model-free algorithm to apply the fundamental ideas of deep Q-learning to continuous action domains. This algorithm can operate in continuous action spaces. Through experiments, it has been further demonstrated that this algorithm is capable of accomplishing end-to-end policy learning for various tasks.

The DeepMind team [8] proposed the PPO algorithm to address the instability and low sample efficiency issues in traditional policy gradient algorithms during the training process. The PPO algorithm reduces variance and improves sample data utilization by using the clip surrogate objective to limit the magnitude of policy updates. Additionally, by introducing the concept of trust region, the PPO algorithm can restrict the magnitude of policy updates while ensuring policy improvement and preventing policy degradation. Experimental tests have shown that PPO outperforms other online policy gradient methods and achieves excellent results.

Automated parking is one of the fundamental technologies for achieving fully autonomous vehicles, as every trip concludes with a parking operation. However, it was only in recent years that reinforcement learning started to be applied to solve the problem of automated parking. In research, reinforcement learning has mainly been applied to two aspects: autonomous vertical parking and autonomous parallel parking.

In terms of vertical parking, Zhang and his colleagues [9] utilized a deterministic policy gradient algorithm to solve the task of automatic parking. The algorithm primarily involved pretraining on a dataset that includes various complex parking maneuvers. Li and his colleagues [10] proposed an automatic parking model based on a deep deterministic policy algorithm to overcome the shortcomings of Monte Carlo tree search and EKF path tracking models. This model interacted using steering angles and displacements as the overall action and designed a comprehensive reward function. The model was verified to have good generalization ability in real-world parking tasks. Takehara and his colleagues [11] used deep learning and employed onboard vision cameras to capture input images, which were then processed as segmented images to accomplish high-precision automatic parking tasks.

In terms of parallel parking, Song and his colleagues [12] developed a data-efficient reinforcement learning method by leveraging model-based approaches to learn from data. This method utilized a truncated Monte Carlo tree search to evaluate parking states and select movements. Two artificial neural networks were trained using training data to provide search probabilities for each tree branch and final rewards for each state. Ultimately, impressive final poses and success rates were achieved in parking tasks. Zhang and his colleagues [13] proposed an innovative parking motion planning approach that combines the Monte Carlo tree search algorithm with a data-generation algorithm to achieve effective longitudinal and lateral parking strategies. DRL has also been applied in the field of obstacle avoidance for vehicles. Ribeiro and his colleagues [14] presented two Q-learning-based approaches for autonomous mobile robot obstacle avoidance, which can both complete obstacle avoidance tasks under specific circumstances.

3   Modeling and Simulating Environments

3.1   Kinematic Model of the Vehicle

In this article, the DRL method is used to study the automatic parking system, aiming to enable the agent to better understand and predict the vehicle's motion behavior, and provide a basis and support for vehicle control applications. Meanwhile, in order to ensure the safe and accurate parking of the vehicle in the center of the target parking space, it is necessary to establish a low-speed kinematic model for the automatic parking task. This model will be utilized as a reference and basis for the control algorithm, optimizing the control strategy, and enhancing the performance and robustness of the system.

Considering that the vehicle remains in a low-speed motion state throughout the entire parking process, we simplify the vehicle's kinematic model to a two-dimensional rigid structure that preserves its kinematic characteristics in motion on a flat plane. At any given time, the state of the vehicle, denoted as $q = (x, y, \theta)$, takes the rear axle center position of the vehicle as the origin, with the coordinate axes parallel to the vehicle body. Where, θ represents the yaw angle of the vehicle (Fig. 1).

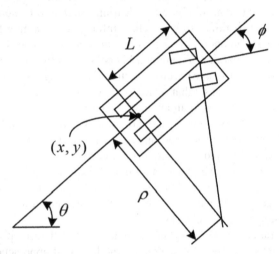

Fig. 1. Simplified kinematic model of the vehicle at low speed.

In the diagram, L represents the wheelbase of the vehicle, ϕ represents the steering angle of the front wheels, ρ represents the turning radius of the vehicle under the current front wheel steering angle, and (x, y) represents the center point of the vehicle's rear axle.

Throughout the entire parking process, the vehicle remains in a low-speed motion state. The influences of wheel slipping and lateral tire movement can be ignored, assuming pure rolling between the wheels and the ground. In light of this, we have established a low-speed vehicle kinematic model based on rear-wheel drive:

$$\begin{cases} \dot{x} = v \cdot \cos \theta \cdot \cos \phi \\ \dot{y} = v \cdot \sin \theta \cdot \cos \phi \\ \dot{\theta} = \frac{v \sin \phi}{L} \end{cases} \tag{2}$$

Among them, v represents the vehicle speed. Therefore, within a given time Δt, according to formula (1), we can obtain the calculation formula for the change in vehicle state after time Δt as:

$$
\begin{cases}
\Delta x = \dot{x} \cdot \Delta t = \Delta s \cdot \cos\theta \cdot \cos\phi \\
\Delta y = \dot{y} \cdot \Delta t = \Delta s \cdot \sin\theta \cdot \cos\phi \\
\Delta\theta = \dot{\theta} \cdot \Delta t = \dfrac{\Delta s \cdot \sin\phi}{L} \\
\Delta s = v \cdot \Delta t
\end{cases}
\tag{3}
$$

where s represents the vehicle displacement under the steering angle ϕ, with positive values indicating forward displacement (i.e., the vehicle moving forward) and negative values indicating backward displacement. Considering the mechanical constraints of the vehicle and to prevent excessive exploration by the agent, we restrict the range of ϕ to $-30°$ to $30°$. After the vehicle has performed the corresponding action at each moment, we can obtain the position of the vehicle's rear axle center and the current yaw angle through formula (3).

$$
\begin{cases}
x' = x + \Delta x \\
y' = y + \Delta y \\
\theta' = \theta + \Delta\theta
\end{cases}
\tag{4}
$$

3.2 Simulation Environment

DRL involves iterative learning through continuous interaction with the environment. In order to demonstrate the effectiveness of our approach in solving automatic parking, we can project real traffic environments into a virtual world and interact with them. We choose the open-source simulator Carla-0.9.13 for autonomous driving, which replicates real-world scenarios and simulates parking processes under various conditions.

Carla is an open-source simulator designed for autonomous driving research. Developed by the Computer Vision Center at the Autonomous University of Barcelona, Spain, it provides a realistic environment for testing and developing autonomous driving algorithms and systems. Carla offers rich sensor simulation capabilities, including lidar, radar, and cameras, allowing researchers to train and validate their autonomous driving models.

Carla provides a highly realistic simulation environment that can replicate driving scenarios and conditions in the real world. This allows us to test, validate, and optimize autonomous driving systems in a simulated environment to obtain more realistic and reliable results. Furthermore, it offers a safe and controlled environment for conducting autonomous driving experiments without any risks. This makes the development and testing process safer and more reliable.

Carla also supports various features and capabilities such as weather conditions, traffic scenarios, and pedestrians, enabling the simulation of real-world road driving scenes. It provides a flexible and scalable architecture that allows users to customize and expand its functionalities to meet various research needs. Additionally, it offers rich APIs and libraries for interacting with the simulation environment, enabling researchers to control vehicles, access sensor data, and implement algorithms.

Carla's control over vehicles is also very close to a real-world environment, allowing control through various variables such as the position of the throttle pedal, the vehicle's acceleration, the angle of the steering wheel, and the brake, among others (Fig. 2).

Fig. 2. Open Source Simulator for Autonomous Driving.

4 Methodologies

4.1 PPO

PPO is one of the policy-based DRL methods, which is based on the Actor-Critic framework and is commonly used to solve continuous action problems. Compared to other deterministic policy algorithms, the policy in the PPO algorithm is a stochastic policy, where the policy function $\pi_\theta(a_t|s_t)$ is a probability distribution function. The actor network predicts the action probability distribution function under a given state s_t and then samples action values based on this probability to output actions in the continuous action space. This results in different action values even in the same state s_t. The PPO algorithm typically utilizes two neural networks: the policy network and the value network. The policy network learns and outputs the probability distribution of taking each action given a specific state, while the value network evaluates the expected return value or advantage value of a given state. The algorithm mainly calculates an estimation of the policy gradient and combines it with the stochastic gradient ascent optimization method to implement the policy gradient algorithm. The formula for policy estimation is typically defined as:

$$\nabla_\theta L(\theta) = E_t \left[\nabla_\theta \log \pi_\theta(a_t|s_t) \hat{A}_t \right] \tag{5}$$

Among them, $\hat{A}_t$ is an estimation of the advantage value, and the expected value E_t is obtained by averaging the set of sampled values. The estimation formula for the advantage value is:

$$A^\pi(s_t, a_t) = r + \gamma V^\pi(s_{t+1}) - V^\pi(s_t) \tag{6}$$

where r represents the obtained environmental reward, and $V^\pi(s_t)$ represents the state value function. Throughout the entire process of algorithm training, data sampling and optimization continuously alternate between each other.

To improve the training efficiency of the algorithm, importance sampling is introduced to enable the reuse of sampled data, and the use of $\pi_\theta(a_t|s_t)\big/\pi_{\theta_{old}}(a_t|s_t)$ instead of $\log \pi_\theta(a_t|s_t)$ in the algorithm supports off-policy training. However, to prevent excessive variance, we should ensure that the difference between the new policy and the old policy is minimized as much as possible. Otherwise, a large number of samples may be needed for accurate estimation.

From the above formula, it can be observed that $\hat{A}_t$ can determine the update method of the policy. When $\hat{A}_t$ is a positive value, the policy will be updated in the direction of increasing $\log \pi_\theta(a_t|s_t)$, increasing the probability of sampling the currently selected action value. Otherwise, the update will be performed in the opposite direction. The magnitude of the training step is determined by policy π, the advantage functions $\hat{A}_t$, and the learning rate α together. The learning rate should not be limited to a very small range, as it may result in a small magnitude of policy updates and make the policy more prone to being trapped in a local optimum solution.

To prevent $\pi_\theta(a_t|s_t)\big/\pi_{\theta_{old}}(a_t|s_t)$ from being much larger than 1, which could lead to excessive one-time updates of the policy function, we introduce a clipping mechanism to limit the large deviation between the new policy and the old policy. The final objective function is:

$$L^{CLIP}(\theta) = \hat{E}_t\left[\min\left(r_t(\theta)\hat{A}_t, clip\left(\varepsilon, r_t(\theta)\hat{A}_t\right)\right)\right] \tag{7}$$

Among them, $r_t(\theta) = \pi_\theta(a_t|s_t)\big/\pi_{\theta_{old}}(a_t|s_t)$ is the probability ratio between the new and old strategies. In the minimization function, these two terms correspond to the initial optimization function and the clip function, respectively. From Eq. (6), it can be seen that the clip function can control the probability ratio between $[1 - \varepsilon, 1 + \varepsilon]$. If it exceeds this range, the boundary value is retained. ε is a hyperparameter, and in this paper, it is set to 0.2.

To address the issue of rapid overfitting of the policy network leading to ineffective exploration of the environment by the agent, we added a penalty term, policy entropy $\mathcal{H}(a_t|s_t)$, to the loss function of the policy network. The final loss function of the policy network is described as:

$$L(\theta) = -E[\min(r_t(\theta)\hat{A}_t, clip(r_t(\theta), 1 - \varepsilon, 1 + \varepsilon)\hat{A}_t) + \eta\mathcal{H}(a_t|s_t)] \tag{8}$$

where η is the weight value of the policy entropy, which is set to 0.05.

For the value network, we use temporal difference method for updates, and the loss function is described as:

$$L(\omega) = E\left(\left[r_t + \gamma V^\pi(s_{t+1}) - V^\pi(s_t)\right]^2\right) \tag{9}$$

4.2 States and Actions

Carla provides various types of sensors. In the task of automatic parking, it is essential for the agent to obtain distance information between the vehicle and obstacles. Therefore, we attach eight radar sensors to the vehicle in eight directions: 0°, 45°, 90°, 135°, 180°, 225°, 270°, and 315°, to acquire distance information between the vehicle and obstacles. Combining the vehicle's low-speed kinematic model, in order to determine the specific pose of the vehicle at each moment, we consider the vehicle's x-axis center coordinate x_{veh}, y-axis center coordinate y_{veh}, velocity v, acceleration a, yaw angle θ, target parking space's center coordinates x_{tar} and y_{tar}, and desired yaw angle θ_{tar} as the state space information of the agent.

$$S = \{x_{veh}, y_{veh}, v, a, \theta, x_{tar}, y_{tar}, \theta_{tar}, Dis, ..., D_{315}\} \tag{10}$$

The desired yaw angle is set to a fixed constant before the training starts, depending on the specific type of parking space, and the specific range of the yaw angle is $[-180, 180]$.

Considering the operational manner of real vehicles and the kinematic model of the vehicle as shown in Eq. (3), we set the vehicle's actions into two parts: the opening angle t of the throttle and the steering angle s of the steering wheel.

$$A = \{t, s\} \tag{11}$$

where, the values of t and s both range from -1 to 1. Positive and negative values of t correspond to the vehicle moving forward and backward, respectively. Positive and negative values of s correspond to the front wheels of the vehicle turning left or right relative to the vehicle.

4.3 Reward Function

DRL maximizes the cumulative reward by optimizing the policy function. The ultimate goal of the automatic parking task is to control the vehicle to park in the center position of the target parking space without colliding with obstacles. To guide the agent better in parking the vehicle in the target parking space, we divide the reward function into four parts: distance reward, angle reward, collision reward, and success reward. Additionally, in order to facilitate the agent's faster learning of the optimal strategy, we introduce a weighted reward function that properly allocates the proportions of each part at different stages of the parking process.

Distance Reward. The distance reward calculated at each time step is used to guide the vehicle to continuously approach the target parking space, and its value is determined by the distance between the vehicle and the parking space.

$$R_{dis} = -\frac{\sqrt{x_{rel}^2 + y_{rel}^2}}{Dis_{max}} \tag{12}$$

Among them, x_{rel} and y_{rel} represent the relative distance of the vehicle from the target parking space in the x-axis and y-axis, respectively. Dis_{max} is the maximum distance from the vehicle to the parking space, determined by the vehicle's initial position. The value of R_{dis} ranges from -1 to 0, where $R_{dis} = 0$ represents the vehicle's current position at the center of the target parking space, and $R_{dis} = -1$ represents the vehicle at the initial position.

Angle Reward. The angle reward is used to guide the vehicle in continuously reducing the difference between the current yaw angle and the desired yaw angle.

$$R_{ang} = -\frac{|\theta_{rel}|}{\pi} \tag{13}$$

where θ_{rel} represents the difference between the current yaw angle of the vehicle and the desired yaw angle at the current moment. In addition, the value of R_{ang} also falls within the range of $[-1, 0]$, where $R_{ang} = 0$ represents that the vehicle's yaw angle exactly matches the desired yaw angle.

Collision Reward. The collision reward is a constant negative value, and when the vehicle collides with an obstacle, the agent receives a penalty value to avoid collisions.

$$R_{col} = -5 \tag{14}$$

Success Reward. The success reward is a positive reward value obtained when the vehicle successfully enters the target parking space and comes to a safe stop.

$$R_{suc} = 30 \tag{15}$$

The final reward function is a weighted combination of the previous four parts, expressed as:

$$R = (1 - k)R_{dis} + kR_{ang} + R_{suc} + R_{col} \tag{16}$$

$$\begin{cases} k = \dfrac{1}{Dis} \ (Dis > 1) \\ k = 1 \ (Dis \leq 1) \end{cases} \tag{17}$$

where, k represents the priority coefficient between distance reward and angle reward, which is determined by formula (16). When the distance between the vehicle and the target parking space is greater than 1, k varies based on the change in distance. Conversely, k remains constant when the distance is less than or equal to 1.

4.4 Network Structure

As shown in the Fig. 3, the input layers of both the Actor network and the Critic network are 16-dimensional state spaces, and they both consist of two fully connected layers with 128 neurons. The difference lies in that the output layer of the Critic network represents the value of the input state, while the Actor network outputs two parameters based on the Beta probability distribution. Considering that we need two action values to control the vehicle's movement in this experiment, and to better accommodate the boundary limits of the continuous action space for throttle and steering wheel angles, we chose to use the multivariate Beta distribution as the output of the Actor network. Additionally, to better constrain the output range and alleviate problems such as gradient vanishing, we chose to use the Tanh function as the activation function for the hidden layers of both neural networks.

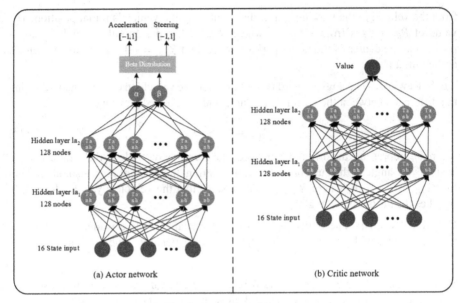

Fig. 3. Network architecture.

5   Experimental Verification

5.1   Hyperparameters

Hyperparameters play a crucial role in DRL algorithms. Setting the hyperparameters correctly can greatly affect the performance of the algorithm. To this end, we conducted multiple experiments in the Carla simulation environment for different types of parking spaces, using a trial-and-error approach to find the optimal hyperparameters. Table 1 shows the best results we obtained through multiple trials and determines the set of hyperparameters and training parameters used in the final experiment.

Table 1. Hyperparameter Settings.

Parameter name	Description	Value
ε	Calculating policy updates	0.2
α_A	Learning rate for actor	3e–4
α_C	Learning rate for critic	3e–4
γ	Discount factor	0.95
η	Entropy coefficient	0.05
N	Batch update size	64
M	Max step per rounds	100
T	Number of training rounds	2000

5.2 Experimental Setup

We have created two different parking environments and types of parking spaces using the Carla simulator for autonomous driving, aiming to better replicate real-world scenarios. As shown in Fig. 4 and Fig. 5, we have established a vertical parking environment with a parking lot as the background, as well as a parallel parking environment with a street as the background. During the experimental process, we have placed obstacle vehicles on both sides of the parking spaces. To comply with international standards, the dimensions of the vertical parking spaces are designed to be 5.3 m in length and 2.5 m in width, while the dimensions of the parallel parking spaces are designed to be 6 m in length and 2.5 m in width. Additionally, to increase the applicability of the system, we have utilized a Tesla Model 3 car, which closely resembles most car sizes, for the experiments. The Model 3 has dimensions of 4.7 m in length, 1.5 m in width, and 1.5 m in height. To expedite the training process, we have set a maximum step length and maximum number of training rounds for each iteration. When the step length within a round exceeds the maximum set value or when a collision occurs, the round is terminated, and the initial position of the vehicle is refreshed to start a new round.

Fig. 4. Vertical parking experiment.

5.3 Vertical Parking Experiment

In order to train an autonomous parking system with stronger generalization capability, we set the initial position of the vehicle to randomly vary between the two sides of the target parking space. Additionally, the initial yaw angle of the vehicle also undergoes slight variations within a certain range. We set the agent to undergo 2000 rounds of learning, where each round ends when the specified termination conditions for the vehicle are met. Each interaction between the agent and the environment yields a reward value. In each round, we accumulate and sum these reward values, recording the cumulative rewards over the 2000 training rounds, as shown in Fig. 6.

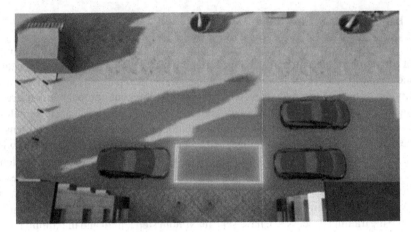

Fig. 5. Parallel parking experiment.

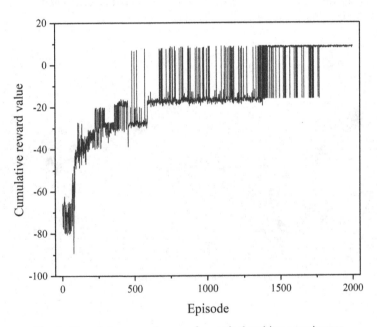

Fig. 6. Cumulative reward curves for vertical parking experiments.

As shown in Fig. 6, due to the agent's lack of familiarity with the environment, it initially goes through a slow exploration phase for about 150 rounds, resulting in relatively low cumulative rewards per round. Afterward, there is an upward trend as the agent gains preliminary understanding of the environment. From around 200 to 600 rounds, the cumulative rewards per round can reach -40 to -20, indicating that the agent is still in the exploration phase. It is not until after 500 rounds that the agent starts to achieve cumulative rewards greater than zero, indicating that the vehicle can complete the parking task. Around 1800 rounds, the agent is able to consistently park the vehicle in the target parking space. Based on our data analysis, once the agent reaches stability in training, the distance of the vehicle relative to the target parking space after parking can be maintained within 0.18 m, and the relative yaw angle can be kept within a range of 10°.

5.4 Parallel Parking Experiment

For the case of parallel parking, we position the vehicle at the location shown in the Fig. 5. To ensure the agent possesses a certain level of generalization capability, we allow small variations in the initial position and initial yaw angle of the vehicle. In order to better replicate real-world scenarios, we also place obstacle vehicles on both sides of the target parking space. Similarly, we conducted training for 2000 rounds with the same termination conditions as the vertical parking case, which are either exceeding the maximum step length per round or encountering a collision. We record the cumulative reward curves obtained by the agent in each round during the training process, as shown in the Fig. 7.

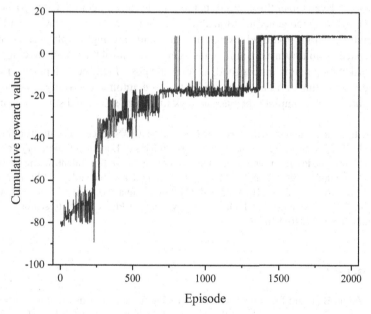

Fig. 7. Cumulative reward curves for parallel parking experiments.

As shown in Fig. 7, the accumulated reward curve during parallel parking training exhibits a gradually increasing trend. Compared to perpendicular parking, the steering angle of the vehicle during parallel parking is larger, which may require a longer exploration time. In the initial 200 rounds, the agent had a limited understanding of the game rules and the objective task, resulting in the vehicle constantly being in a low-speed exploration state. After a period of exploration, the agent gained a preliminary understanding of the environment and began gradually attempting to explore the objective task. After approximately 800 rounds of exploration, the agent attempted to complete the parking task. It was not until after 1300 rounds that the frequency of task completion started to increase. From the curve, we can observe that after about 1700 rounds, the agent was able to consistently complete the parking task with a satisfactory vehicle pose. According to our statistics, after completing the parking task, the distance between the vehicle's center point and the center point of the target parking space remained stable within 0.2 m, and the relative yaw angle could be maintained within 5°.

6 Conclusion

In this paper, we propose a DRL-based end-to-end automatic parking strategy learning method for various types of parking spaces in the Carla simulation environment. After training in Carla, our method can stably control the vehicle to enter the target parking space in both perpendicular and parallel parking scenarios. Regarding perpendicular parking, we set the initial position of the vehicle to vary around the target parking space, and the relative position and relative yaw angle can randomly change at the beginning of each round. Even under this condition, the vehicle can still complete the parking task, demonstrating the good generalization ability of our method. As for parallel parking, we allow small variations in the relative coordinates and yaw angle of the vehicle near the parking space. Similarly, after training, the agent can control the vehicle to complete the parking task while maintaining a good position and pose. In the next step, we will further study the reward function design in the DRL-based automatic parking system, aiming to make the vehicle complete the parking task in a more stable and smooth manner.

Acknowledgments. Supported in part by the National Natural Science Foundation of China under Grant (62371182), Major Science and Technology Projects of Longmen Laboratory under Grant (231100220300), the Program for Science and Technology Innovation Talents in the University of Henan Province under Grant (23HASTIT021), the Scientific and Technological Project of Henan Province under Grant (222102210056, 222102240009), China Postdoctoral Science Foundation (2023M730982), the Science and Technology Development Plan of Joint Research Program of Henan underGrant (222103810036).

References

1. Ravi Kiran, B., et al.: Deep reinforcement learning for autonomous driving: a survey. IEEE Trans. Intell. Transp. Syst. **23**(6), 4909–4926 (2022). https://doi.org/10.1109/TITS.2021.305 4625
2. Anzalone, L., Barra, P., Barra, S., Castiglione, A., Nappi, M.: An end-to-end curriculum learning approach for autonomous driving scenarios. IEEE Trans. Intell. Transp. Syst. **23**(10), 19817–19826 (2022). https://doi.org/10.1109/TITS.2022.3160673
3. Zhang, J., Zhang, C., Chien, W.-C.: Overview of deep reinforcement learning improvements and applications. J. Internet Technol. **22**(2), 239–255 (2021)
4. Mnih, V., et al.: Human-level control through deep reinforcement learning. Nature **518**(7540), 529–533 (2015). https://doi.org/10.1038/nature14236

5. Van Hasselt, H., Guez, A., Silver, D.: Deep reinforcement learning with double Q-learning. In: Proceedings of the AAAI Conference on Artificial Intelligence (2016)
6. Wang, Z., et al.: Dueling network architectures for deep reinforcement learning. In: International Conference on Machine Learning. PMLR (2016)
7. Lillicrap, T.P., et al.: Continuous control with deep reinforcement learning. arXiv preprint arXiv:1509.02971 (2015)
8. Schulman, J., et al.: Proximal policy optimization algorithms. arXiv preprint arXiv:1707. 06347 (2017)
9. Zhang, P., et al.: Reinforcement learning-based end-to-end parking for automatic parking system. Sensors **19**(18), 3996 (2019)
10. Junzuo, L., Qiang, L.: An automatic parking model based on deep reinforcement learning. J. Phys. Conf. Ser. (2021)
11. Takehara, R., Gonsalves, T.: Autonomous car parking system using deep reinforcement learning. In: 2021 2nd International Conference on Innovative and Creative Information Technology (ICITech). IEEE (2021)
12. Song, S., Chen, H., Sun, H., Liu, M.: Data efficient reinforcement learning for integrated lateral planning and control in automated parking system. Sensors **20**(24), 7297 (2020). https://doi.org/10.3390/s20247297
13. Zhang, J., Chen, H., Song, S., Fengwei, H.: Reinforcement learning-based motion planning for automatic parking system. IEEE Access **8**, 154485–154501 (2020). https://doi.org/10.1109/ACCESS.2020.3017770
14. Ribeiro, T., et al.: Q-learning for autonomous mobile robot obstacle avoidance. In: 2019 IEEE International Conference on Autonomous Robot Systems and Competitions (ICARSC). IEEE (2019)

A Deep Reinforcement Learning-Based Energy Management Optimization for Fuel Cell Hybrid Electric Vehicle Considering Recent Experience

Ruiqing Hua[1], Fazhan Tao[1,2], Zhumu Fu[1(✉)], and Longlong Zhu[1]

[1] School of Information Engineering, Henan University of Science and Technology, Henan, China
fuzhumu@haust.edu.cn
[2] Longmen Laboratory, Luoyang, Henan, China

Abstract. This study emphasizes a recent experience sampling method in conjunction with Deep Deterministic Policy Gradient (DDPG) to enhance the training speed and improve the training outcomes. Firstly, to ensure the safe operation of the battery and energy storage system under peak power, a power demand decoupling method based on frequency domain is proposed to achieve power stratification. Subsequently, a multi-objective equivalent consumption minimization strategy model is established based on the data types of the experimental platform, and the improved DDPG algorithm is employed to solve it. Finally, simulation results demonstrate that compared to conventional DDPG algorithms, the improved DDPG algorithm can enhance efficiency by an average of 2.02%.

Keywords: Fuel cell hybrid electric vehicle · Energy management strategy · Emphasizing Recent Experience · DDPG

1 Introduction

In the context of the urgent need to address energy and environmental pollution, the development of green, sustainable, and environmentally friendly transportation has emerged as a significant challenge for nations across the globe. Fuel Cell Hybrid Electric Vehicles (FCHEVs) have gained popularity due to their numerous advantages, including zero emissions, high energy conversion efficiency, long service life, and a wide range of fuel sources [1].

To improve energy utilization rates and reduce operating costs of vehicles under power system operating conditions, it is essential to distribute output power rationally among the battery pack, ultracapacitor (UC), and fuel cell (FC) pack. Researchers have used Energy Management Systems (EMS) to optimally distribute power between these three energy sources. EMS can be classified into three types: rule-based EMS, optimization-based EMS and learning-based EMS [2].

The rule-based strategy involves setting rules in advance based on the external characteristics of the motor, battery pack, and generator. It then relies on a series of fixed

F. Sun et al. (Eds.): ICCSIP 2023, CCIS 1918, pp. 374–386, 2024.
https://doi.org/10.1007/978-981-99-8018-5_28

rules to switch different working modes or adjust power distribution between the engine and motor at every moment [3]. This approach offers benefits such as small calculation, strong real-time performance, and simple application. In [4], An energy management strategy based on fuzzy logic control is designed to track the charge state of battery, the experimental results demonstrate that this strategy can effectively reduce fuel consumption during vehicle operation. In [5], the author designs an improved SM-EMS by combining the droop control state machine to improve the hydrogen utilization rate of the system while ensuring that the mechanical energy of the system remains unchanged. However, the rule-based strategy relies heavily on expert experience and may not ensure global optimal strategies under regulations. Additionally, it lacks adaptability in practical driving scenarios. In terms of optimizing vehicle performance, rule-based strategies are often less effective than optimization-based strategies.

Optimization-based methods for energy management in hybrid electric vehicles can be categorized as global optimization and local optimization [6]. The former requires obtaining all travel information in advance, such as road geographic information and speed profile, and then using optimal control methods, such as dynamic programming, genetic algorithm, or Pontryagin's minimum principle (PMP), to minimize the cost function and achieve power distribution between the motor and engine. In contrast, local optimization strategies optimize power distribution between the engine and motor while ensuring local optimal solutions. Typical local optimization strategies include model predictive control (MPC) and equivalent consumption minimization strategies (ECMS). In [7], the author uses radial basis function neural network (RBFNN) and wavelet transform (WT) to predict vehicle speed. The experimental results demonstrate that this method yields a 9.26% improvement in prediction accuracy compared to using only RBFNN. However, optimization-based methods typically require knowledge of the entire trip information in advance, rely heavily on future trip information, and may entail high computational costs.

The rapid development of artificial intelligence has led to increased research into machine learning, with reinforcement learning emerging as a widely used branch in many energy management problems [8]. Reinforcement learning can be regarded as a way for animals to learn by interacting with their surrounding environment [9]. The agent obtains the corresponding reward through continuous action in the environment under the guidance of the reward function and then learns the optimal strategy. Relevant studies have shown that energy management strategies based on reinforcement learning possess stronger learning ability and adaptability under complex conditions. Q-learning, a prominent algorithm within the field of reinforcement learning, has found extensive application in energy management [10]. The Q-learning algorithm generates a Q-table to represent the Q-value linked to each state-action pair. The agent then selects the appropriate action based on the magnitude of the Q-value, thereby facilitating the learning process in the correct direction. However, the convergence of the algorithm will deteriorate when the amount of computation is large, and the dimensional curse may occur when the action space and state dimension are too high. To address this issue, deep neural networks can be used to approximate Q functions under the influence of deep learning. The deep Q network algorithm is proposed as an improved version of Q learning for energy management of FCHEV [11]. In [12], a Q-learning-based EMS with additional deterministic rules is introduced, and experimental results have shown that energy management with this algorithm can achieve better fuel economy and faster convergence speed. Although DQL introduces a learning mechanism to improve the algorithm's performance, it cannot solve the problem of continuous action variables. To address this issue, the DDPG algorithm is studied further, which is an effective method for solving learning tasks with a continuous state-action space [13]. Priority experience-replay technology is used in this process to improve learning efficiency. However, traditional DDPG algorithms use common experience playback methods that are not filtered when sampling from the experience pool, leading to ineffective learning processes.

This paper proposes a method that combines DDPG with experiential sample emphasizing recent experience, which effectively solves the problem of low efficiency when sampling from the experience pool and reduces ineffective learning processes.

2   Power System Model of Multi-energy Source Fuel Hybrid Electric Vehicle

This section commences by constructing the FCHEV model, and followed by a detailed introduction of the powertrain components configuration of the FHEV studied in this paper. The mathematical model of the powertrain components is then presented in detail, as illustrated in Fig. 1:

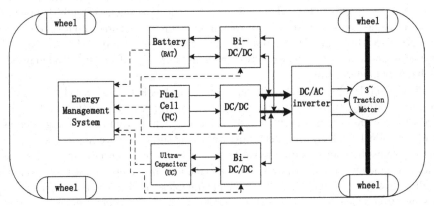

Fig.1. Block diagram of energy management system in FCHEV

2.1   System Configuration of Fuel Cell Hybrid Electric Vehicle

The power system of the FCHEV examined in this study is composed of a proton exchange membrane fuel cell (PEMFC), battery (BAT), and supercapacitor (UC). The PEMFC acts as the primary power source, while a unidirectional DC/DC converter supports the fuel cell in fulfilling the total power demand of the FCHEV. The bidirectional DC/DC converter links the DC bus with the peak power supply UC, allowing for the recuperation and generation of peak power produced by the vehicle during rapid acceleration and sudden braking. To meet power requirements, the BAT battery pack absorbs or provides excess power through a bidirectional DC/DC converter connected to the DC bus. The power exceeding the BAT is then transformed by a DC/AC inverter to drive the three-phase traction motor. A comprehensive list of parameters for each component of the hybrid electric vehicle power system is presented in Table 1.

Table 1. Parameters of the FCHEV model

Device	Item	Value
DC bus	Rated voltage	380 V
Electric motor	Power rating	45 kW
	Rated speed	1500 rpm
Battery	Type	Li-ion
	Energy	25.6 kWh
	Rated voltage	320 V
	Maximum charge rate	2 C
	Maximum discharge rate	4 C
	Nominal charge/discharge rate	0.5 C
Ultracapacitor	Rated voltage	288 V
	Capacitance	27.5 F
Fuel cell	Power rating	10 kW
	Output voltage	40–100 V

2.2 Fuel Cell Model

In this paper, PEMFC is selected as the main power source of FCHEV. When the fuel cell is working, hydrogen and oxygen generate electricity through chemical reaction. The output voltage of a fuel cell stack V_{FC} can be expressed as

$$V_{FC} = N_{cell} \times (E_{cell} - V_{act\_loss} - V_{ohm\_loss}) \tag{1}$$

2.3 Battery Model

In this paper, lithium-ion battery is selected as the energy storage device of hybrid electric vehicle. Without considering the influence of battery aging and temperature, the SoC of the battery is calculated by integrating current method, which can be expressed as

$$SoC_{BAT} = SoC_{BAT\_ini} + \frac{\beta \int i_{BAT} dt}{C_{nom}} \tag{2}$$

where SoC_{BAT_ini} represents the initial SoC of the battery pack, i_{BAT} and C_{nom} represent the current and nominal capacity of the battery pack (in amperes and amperes per hour, respectively), and $\beta = \pm 1$ represents the switching variable (positive when charging and negative when discharging).

The current of the battery can be expressed as

$$i_{BAT} = \frac{V_{BAT\_oc} - \sqrt{V_{BAT\_oc}^2 - 4r_{BAT}p_{BAT}}}{2r_{BAT}} \tag{3}$$

where V_{BAT_oc} represents the open circuit voltage (in volts), r_{BAT} represents the internal resistance of the battery pack (in ohms), and p_{BAT} represents the electrical power of the battery (in watts).

The output voltage of the battery can be expressed as

$$V_{BAT} = V_{BAT\_oc} + \beta i_{BAT} r_{BAT} \tag{4}$$

where V_{BAT_oc} and r_{BAT} represent the open circuit voltage and the internal resistance of the battery pack (in volts and ohms, respectively).

2.4 Supercapacitor Model

Supercapacitors can be modeled as a series combination of resistors and capacitors. The voltage and current of a supercapacitor can be expressed as

$$\begin{cases} V_{UC\_oc} = SoC_{UC} \cdot \left(V_{UC\_max} - V_{UC\_min}\right) + V_{UC\_min} \\ i_{UC} = \dfrac{V_{UC\_oc} - \sqrt{V_{UC\_oc}^2 - 4r_{UC}p_{UC}}}{2r_{UC}} \end{cases} \tag{5}$$

where, V_{UC_max} and V_{UC_min} are the minimum and maximum voltage of the supercapacitor (in volts). Let p_{UC} denote the power output of the supercapacitor in watts, and r_{UC} represent its equivalent internal resistance in ohms.

3   Deep Reinforcement Learning

Deep reinforcement learning combines deep learning and reinforcement learning, utilizing neural networks in deep learning to perceive and predict the environment and Markov decision process in reinforcement learning to make decisions, overcoming the shortcomings of both approaches. In this section, the traditional DDPG algorithm is introduced, followed by a combination of the method emphasizing recent experience with DDPG to improve its performance, effectively addressing sparse reward problems and enhancing sampling efficiency.

3.1   DDPG Algorithm Based on Markov Decision Process

The stochastic strategy gradient method is utilized to update both networks to maximize the total expected reward. The DDPG algorithm structure is shown in Fig. 2.

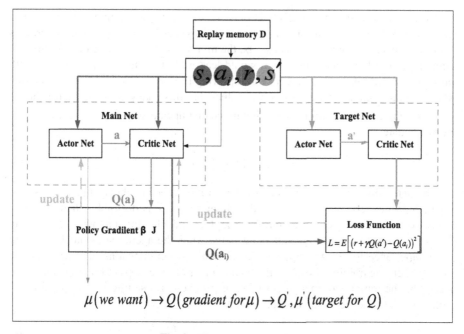

Fig. 2. The structure of DDPG

3.2 Experience Replay and Related Work

The previous TD algorithm suffers from experience waste and high correlation between samples, which can be addressed by introducing experience replay to eliminate sample correlation and improve training effectiveness. Experience replay involves storing past data in an experience pool, reusing it during updates, and deleting the oldest data when the pool is full. However, in cases of sparse reward, where the agent receives a reward only after N steps of correct actions, few samples enable correct learning, and random sampling efficiency is low, with many samples yielding a reward of 0. Thus, a method emphasizing the extraction of recent experience is introduced.

3.3 Experience Extraction with Emphasis on Recent Experience

To overcome challenges encountered in the training process, such as slow convergence rates, poor usability and suboptimal results, an improved DDPG algorithm is introduced. This algorithm uses a method emphasizing recent experience when sampling, whereby the first minibatch is sampled from all data in the experience pool during the parameter update stage. Subsequent small batches sample more aggressively from the nearest data point and less from the more distant data point, gradually reducing the sampling range. The proposed approach involves setting the maximum capacity of the experience pool as N. Assuming three mini-batch updates are performed in the current update phase, the k-th update ($1 \leq k \leq K$) is conducted by uniformly sampling c_k data points from the most recent c_k.

Here, a hyperparameter $\eta \in (0, 1]$ determines the degree of importance given to recent data. When $\eta = 1$, uniform sampling is employed, whereas c_k gradually decreases with each update when $\eta < 1$. Let $c_{\min}$ be the minimum allowed value of c_k to prevent sampling too little recent data, which would leading to overfitting. As episode length varies across different environments, the following formula is used instead of a simple, where the constant 1 can be set to other values, but this changes the optimal value of η. This formula enables uniform sampling in the first update and $\eta^{K\frac{1}{K}} = \eta^1$ sampling in the last update.

$$c_k = \max\{N \cdot \eta^{k\frac{1}{K}}, c_{\min}\} \tag{6}$$

The optimality of η is determined by the learning speed of the agent and the speed at which past experiences are discarded. A higher η value is desirable when the agent learns slowly, making it closer to uniform sampling and allowing it to use more old data points. Conversely, a lower η value is desirable when the agent learns quickly, giving more importance to recently updated data. Therefore, an annealing algorithm can be employed during training. Let T be the total number of time steps in training, and let η_0 and η_T be the initial and final values of η, respectively. By setting $\eta_T = 1$ to uniform sampling, η at time step t can be represented as follow

$$\eta_t = \eta_0 + (\eta_T - \eta_0) \cdot \frac{t}{T} \tag{7}$$

The proposed sampling method has two effects. Firstly, the first sampling batch is uniformly sampled from the entire experience pool, and the second sampling batch is uniformly drawn from data points outside some of the oldest data points in the experience pool. As the exclusion threshold increases, the number of excluded old data points also increases, resulting the closer the data points are, the easier it is to draw them. Secondly, sampling can be performed in an orderly manner, beginning with sampling from all data in the experience pool, gradually narrowing the sampling range, and finally only sampling from the most recent data. This sampling method better approximates the value function of recently accessed states while approximating more distant past visited states with an acceptable approximation value.

This study presents a performance evaluation of the recent experience sample method, with particular emphasis on its efficacy. To this end, a comparison between the average loss plots for traditional experience replay and emphasizing recent experience replay methods is demonstrated in Fig. 3. As illustrated in Fig. 3, both approaches demonstrate the ability to converge; however, DDPG-2 exhibits superior convergence performance and faster convergence rate. This suggests that by reducing the sampling range of the experience pool and filtering out invalid sampling data, network convergence performance can be improved. It further highlights that "experience" has a significant impact on network convergence during neural network training. Failure to filter experience may lead to poor training results.

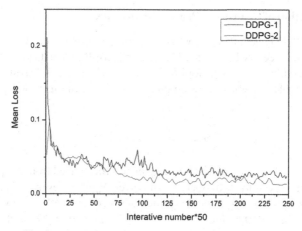

Fig. 3. The variation diagram of average loss of DDPG

4 EMS for FCHEV

This section presents a novel approach for power management in hybrid electric vehicles. Specifically, an adaptive low-pass filter based on fuzzy logic is introduced to effectively separate high-frequency power from low-frequency power. Subsequently, the probability transfer matrix of power demand is derived by analyzing real-world driving data. To optimize the power management strategy, a reward function is formulated that considers both the equivalent hydrogen consumption of the battery and supercapacitor, as well as the reduction of the state of charge deviation of the battery. Lastly, this paper presents an overview of the fundamental constituents of the EMS based on DDPG.

4.1 Fuzzy Based Adaptive Low-Pass Filter

In situations where the speed of a vehicle changes abruptly, a strong peak power is generated, necessitating absorption by a UC. To safeguard the FC and BAT from damage, this paper proposes using an adaptive low-pass filter to filter the power of the vehicle operation, separating high-frequency power and low-frequency power, thereby enhancing vehicle performance. The low-pass filter can be expressed as shown below:

$$G(s) = \frac{1}{\frac{s}{u_f} + 1} \tag{8}$$

Here, u_f represents the regulating frequency, determined through a fuzzy inference system (FIS) based on P_{demand}, SoC_{UC}, and SoC_{BAT}. To ensure that SoC_{UC} and SoC_{BAT} can vary within a given range, thereby reducing the workload of the battery and fuel cell, a composite coefficient is introduced, represented as:

$$SoC_{ESS} = \delta_{UC} SoC_{UC} + \delta_{BAT} SoC_{BAT} \tag{9}$$

In this equation, δ_{UC} and δ_{BAT} denote the adjustment coefficients. Due to space constraints, the empirical fuzzy rule table is not included in this paper but can be found in our team's previous research [14].

4.2 Construction of Transition Probability Matrix

To enable the DDPG agent to learn better strategies, approximately 170,000 sets of data were collected between 2018 and 2022, approximately 40,000 data points were selected for analysis after the removal of invalid data. The maximum likelihood estimation method and nearest neighbor method were employed to obtain the temporal power demand profile, expressed as:

$$p_{ab} = \frac{N_{ab}}{N_a}, \ if \ N_a \neq 0 \tag{10}$$

Here, N_a represents the total number of frequencies transferred from the power demand of p_a at a specific speed to all frequencies of power. N_{ab} denotes the frequency at which p_{demand} is transferred from p_a to p_b at a particular speed. The TPM of power requirement in state $s = \{SoC_{BAT} = 0.6, SoC_{UC} = 0.6, V = 25 \ km/h, \theta = 0\%\}$ is shown below:

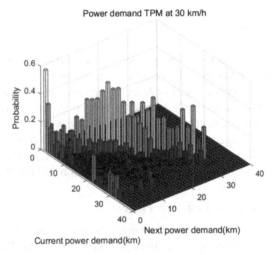

Fig. 4. The TPM of power demand at $s = \{0.6, 0.6, 25 \ km/h, 0\%\}$

4.3 Construction of Reward Function

The reward function is commonly employed to assess the efficacy of actions in the present state, where a higher reward value indicates a superior power allocation strategy. In this study, a FCHEV with three mixed energy sources is employed as the subject of investigation, and the ECMS strategy is utilized to transform the multi-objective optimization issue into a minimum hydrogen consumption problem to achieve the optimal EMS.

$$\min C_{H_2}(t) = \varphi_{FC} C_{FC}(t) + \varphi_{BAT} C_{BAT}(t) + \varphi_{UC} C_{UC}(t)$$

$$\min \Delta SoC_{BAT}(t) = \begin{cases} SoC_{BAT}(t) - SoC_{ref}, & SoC_{BAT}(t) < SoC_{ref} \\ 0, & SoC_{BAT}(t) > SoC_{ref} \end{cases} \tag{11}$$

Specifically, the variables $C_{H_2}(t)$, $C_{FC}(t)$, $C_{BAT}(t)$, and $C_{UC}(t)$ correspond to the total hydrogen consumption, hydrogen consumption of the FC, equivalent hydrogen consumption of the BAT and UC, respectively. Additionally, variable φ_{FC} represents the efficiency penalty factor of the fuel cell, while variables φ_{BAT} and φ_{UC} are the penalty factors of the BAT and UC, respectively. These penalty factors enable the limitation of SoC variation between instantaneous value and reference value. Moreover, variable ΔSoC_{BAT} denotes the difference between the current SoC of the BAT and the reference value.

The constraints of various energy source parameters are derived based on the physical characteristics of the actual vehicle on the experimental platform.

$$\begin{cases} 0.4 \leq SoC_{BAT} \leq 0.8 \\ 0.4 \leq SoC_{UC} \leq 1 \\ SoC_{BAT\_ch} \leq 2C \\ SoC_{BAT\_dis} \leq 4C \\ P_{FC\_\min} \leq P_{FC} \leq P_{FC\_\min} \\ -P_{demand} \leq P_{BAT} \leq P_{demand} \end{cases} \tag{12}$$

where SoC_{BAT_chg} and SoC_{BAT_dis} represent the SoC of the battery during charging and discharging, respectively, $P_{FC.\min}$ and $P_{FC.\max}$ represent the minimum and maximum output power of the fuel cell in the high-efficiency operating region, respectively.

Since the goal of the DDPG agent is to maximize the reward while minimizing the total hydrogen consumption C_{H_2} and the deviation of battery SoC ΔSoC_{BAT}, we consider taking the negative values of total hydrogen consumption C_{H_2} and deviation ΔSoC_{BAT} as the reward function, expressed as:

$$R = -\left[C_{H_2} + \kappa(\Delta SoC_{BAT})^2 \right] \tag{13}$$

where κ represents the positive penalty coefficient.

4.4 Construction of DDPG Parameters Based on FCHEV

In order to reflect the real-time status of the vehicle during driving, the current speed V, power demand P_{demand} power of the supercapacitor P_{UC}, state of charge of the current supercapacitor SoC_{UC}, and state of charge of the current battery SoC_{BAT} are defined as input states. This paper uses an adaptive low-pass filter to obtain the power required by the supercapacitor, and uses the DDPG algorithm to allocate other powers. Therefore, the actions of the intelligent agent are defined as P_{FC} and P_{BAT}. The state space and action space can be represented as follows:

$$S = \{V, P_{demand}, P_{UC}, SoC_{UC}, SoC_{BAT}\}$$
$$A = \begin{cases} BAT : a \in [0, 1] \\ FC : 1 - a \end{cases} \tag{14}$$

5 Simulation and Analysis

A simulation study of the proposed EMS in urban street test scenarios (UDDS) is proposed using the virtual environment provided by the Simulink/Advisor platform.

The outcomes of the simulation conducted under UDDS driving conditions are illustrated in Fig. 5. As depicted in Fig. 5(a), the SOC of the supercapacitors exhibits a gradual increase and fluctuates within a limited range, whereas the SOC of the battery initially decreases and then gradually stabilizes. This observation suggests that both supercapacitors and batteries play an indispensable role in this operational scenario. Furthermore, Fig. 5(b) demonstrates that the UC is responsible for absorbing or providing peak power, thereby creating favorable operating conditions for the use of FC and BAT. Notably, the fluctuation range of BAT power treated with DDPG + emphasizes the recent experience sampling method, which gradually narrows and maintains the treated FC power within a small range. These findings fully demonstrate that the EMS can ensure the efficient operation of FC and the stable output of BAT.

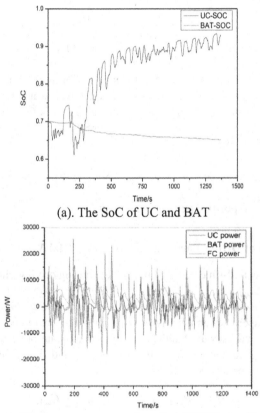

(a). The SoC of UC and BAT

(b). The power of three energy sources based on DDPG considering new sampling method

Fig. 5. Simulation result of UDDS driving cycle

6 Conclusion

This study introduces a novel hierarchical energy management approach for FCHEVs utilizing an improved DDPG algorithm. Firstly, the powertrain structure of FCHEVs is established based on the actual vehicle platform, and detailed models of fuel cell, battery, and ultracapacitor are developed. Subsequently, the proposed hierarchical energy strategy based on DDPG is presented. The upper layer of the strategy employs an adaptive fuzzy filter to decouple the required power, while the lower layer utilizes the improved DDPG algorithm and ECMS algorithm to address the multi-objective optimization problem. Furthermore, to enhance the learning efficiency of the algorithm, the DDPG algorithm is combined with a sampling method that emphasizes recent experience. Finally, the proposed energy management approach is validated through simulation studies in urban traffic scenarios. The results demonstrate that compared to traditional DDPG algorithms, the proposed approach enhances battery performance by 7.3% and fuel economy by 11.4%. Next, we can consider using the method that emphasizes recent experience extraction plus other methods for better experience playback.

Acknowledgments. Supported in part by the National Natural Science Foundation of China under Grant (62371182), Major Science and Technology Projects of Longmen Laboratory under Grant (231100220300), the Program for Science and Technology Innovation Talents in the University of Henan Province under Grant (23HASTIT021), the Scientific and Technological Project of Henan Province under Grant (222102210056, 222102240009), China Postdoctoral Science Foundation (2023M730982), the Science and Technology Development Plan of Joint Research Program of Henan underGrant (222103810036).

References

1. Tian, Y., Ruan, J., Zhang, N., Wu, J., Walker, P.: Modelling and control of a novel two-speed transmission for electric vehicles. Mech. Mach **127**, 13–32 (2018)
2. Zhang, F.Q., Wang, L.H., Coskun, S., Pang, H., Cui, Y.H., Xi, J.Q.: Energy management strategies for hybrid electric vehicles: review, classification, comparison, and outlook. Energies **13**(13), 3352 (2020)
3. Hu, X.S., Liu, T., Qi, X.W., Barth, M.: Reinforcement learning for hybrid and plug-in hybrid electric vehicle energy management recent advances and prospects. IEEE Ind. Electron. Mag. **13**(3), 16–25 (2019)
4. Tian, H., Wang, X., Lu, Z., Huang, Y., Tian, G.: Adaptive fuzzy logic energy management strategy based on reasonable SOC reference curve for online control of plug-in hybrid electric city bus. IEEE Trans. Intell. Transp. Syst. **19**(5), 1607–1617 (2018)
5. Gharibeh, H.F., Farrokhifar, M.: Online multi-level energy management strategy based on rule-based and optimization-based approaches for fuel cell hybrid electric vehicles. Appl. Sci. -Basel **11**(9), 2076–3417 (2022)
6. He, H., Wang, Y., Li, J., Dou, J., Lian, R., Li, Y.: An improved energy management strategy for hybrid electric vehicles integrating multi-states of vehicle-traffic information. IEEE Trans. Transp. Electrification **7**(3), 1161–1172 (2021)
7. Chen, Z., Guo, N.Y., Shen, J.W., Xiao, R.X., Dong, P.: A hierarchical energy management strategy for power-split plug-in hybrid electric vehicles considering velocity prediction. IEEE Access **6**, 33261–33274 (2018)

8. Hu, X.S., Liu, T., Qi, X.W., Barth, M.: Reinforcement learning for hybrid and plug-in hybrid electric vehicle energy management recent advances and prospects. IEEE Ind. Electron. Mag. **13**(3), 16–25 (2019)
9. He, H.W., Cao, J.F., Cui, X.: Energy optimization of electric vehicle's acceleration process based on reinforcement learning. J Clean Prod. **248**, 119302 (2020)
10. Zhang, Y., Ma, R., Zhao, D., Huangfu, Y., Liu, W.: A novel energy management strategy based on dual reward function Q-learning for fuel cell hybried electric vehicle. IEEE Trans. Ind. Electron. **69**, 1537–1547 (2021)
11. Li, Y., He, H., Peng, J., Wu, J.: Energy management strategy for a series hybrid electric vehicle using improved deep Q-network learning algorithm with prioritized replay. DEStech Trans. Environ. Energy Earth (2019)
12. Li, Y., Tao, J., Xie, L., Zhang, R., Ma, L., Qiao, Z.: Enhanced Q-learning for real-time hybrid electric vehicle energy management with deterministic rule. Meas. Control (United Kingdom) **53**(7–8), 1493–1503 (2020)
13. Wu, J., Wei, Z., Liu, K., Quan, Z., Li, Y.: Battery-involved energy management for hybrid electric bus based on expert-assistance deep deterministic policy gradient algorithm. IEEE Trans. Veh. Technol. **69**(11), 12786–12796 (2020)
14. Sun, H., Fu, Z., Tao, F., Zhu, L., Si, P.: Data-driven reinforcement-learning-based hierarchical energy management strategy for fuel cell/battery/ultracapacitor hybrid electric vehicles. J. Power Sources **455**(15), 227964 (2020)

State of Charge Estimation of Lithium-Ion Battery Based on Multi-Modal Information Interaction and Fusion

Chao Wang[1] , Kaixin Zhang[2] , Chao Wu[1,2](✉) , and Xiangyang Cao[1,2]

[1] Shanghai University of Electric Power, Shanghai 200090, China
shiningi@163.com
[2] Luoyang Institute of Science and Technology, Luoyang 471000, China

Abstract. The assessment of the charge status of lithium-ion batteries holds significant importance in the functioning of electric vehicles, particularly when it comes to real-time monitoring and ensuring safety control. In this regard, a back-propagation neural network based on multi-modal information interaction and fusion (MMI-BPNN) has been proposed, which incorporates the interaction and fusion of multi-modal information, to estimate the state of charge (SOC) of lithium-ion batteries. Initially, the principles of Unscented Kalman Filter (UKF) and back-propagation neural network (BPNN) are introduced. Building on this foundation, a specific approach for the interaction and fusion of multi-modal information in estimating battery SOC is presented. Then, different experiments are carried out under FUDS conditions, including UKF to estimate battery SOC, using first-order RC equivalent circuit and forgetting factor recursive least square method (FFRLS); BPNN estimation of battery SOC, using the data under the working condition for training; And the experiment involving the utilization of the MMI-BPNN technique for the estimation of battery SOC is conducted, employing information extracted from both the UKF and BPNN models. Finally, the error analysis conducted on the experimental results demonstrates that the maximum relative error in SOC estimation using the MMI-BPNN method is below 0.9325%. This finding confirms that the method exhibits superior accuracy and robustness when compared to the other two methods.

Keywords: SOC · Multi-mode information fusion · UKF · BPNN

1 Introduction

With the development of society, the problem of the shortage of environment and traditional fossil energy has been paid more and more attention all over the world. New energy not only has a very huge development prospect, but also has the advantage of no pollution, which is well in line with the concept of environmental protection and sustainable development respected today [1]. The development of new energy vehicles and lithium batteries is a strong embodiment of new energy applications, with great potential in the development prospects, and lithium-ion power batteries as the most critical core

© The Author(s), under exclusive license to Springer Nature Singapore Pte Ltd. 2024
F. Sun et al. (Eds.): ICCSIP 2023, CCIS 1918, pp. 387–403, 2024.
https://doi.org/10.1007/978-981-99-8018-5_29

components of new energy vehicles, directly affect the performance of new energy vehicles, including the driving range of new energy vehicles, safety, service life, charging time and high and low temperature adaptability, etc. Therefore, it has also derived the related technologies of lithium batteries, including state estimation, life prediction and fault diagnosis [2].

Accurate real-time state of charge (SOC) acquisition of lithium-ion power batteries is the basis of safe vehicle operation. According to the difference of algorithms, SOC methods of lithium battery can be divided into traditional open circuit voltage method based on sensor measurement, current integration method and impedance method, data-driven machine learning algorithm and model-based Kalman filter and particle filter algorithm [3].

The model-based method, taking the equivalent circuit model as an example, can reflect the internal state and behavior of the battery to a certain extent, and can provide relatively accurate state estimation and prediction under certain working conditions, combined with related algorithms. Based on the equivalent circuit model and by designing the least squares forgetting factor algorithm, an adaptive forgetting factor regression least squares Extended Kalman filter (AFFLS-EKF) SOC estimation strategy with accurate state estimation accuracy was proposed [4]. A 2-RC equivalent circuit model was developed, and the model parameters were identified by recursive least squares algorithm with forgetting factor. Then, the SOC of the battery was estimated by adaptive unscented Kalman filter (AUKF), and more accurate results were obtained compared with EKF [5]. Therefore, it is reasonable and accurate to use Kalman filter to estimate the state of lithium battery based on the equivalent circuit model. However, because the method based on the equivalent circuit model can not reflect the chemical reaction and physical process inside the battery, the accuracy of the state estimation is easy to be affected by the change of battery working condition and environment. Therefore, only the method based on the equivalent circuit model has certain limitations.

Data-driven methods mainly include machine learning methods and deep learning methods [6], among which deep learning methods include backpropagation neural network (BPNN) [7], convolutional neural network (CNN) [8] and recurrent neural network (RNN) [9]. This method can automatically learn useful features from the data and make state prediction, and can deal with non-linear, high-dimensional and long series of data, so it can better deal with complex battery conditions. Taking backpropagation neural network as an example, in order to accurately estimate battery SOC, PID control based on BP neural network is proposed to realize online SOC estimation of lead-acid battery by correcting feedback error [10]. In the method of estimating SOC by uninformed Kalman filter, in order to deal with the complex internal characteristics of battery, BPNN is adopted, which is used to improve the state vector of uninformed Kalman filter in the process of estimating SOC by learning the nonlinear relationship between SOC estimation error and process variables in the preliminary estimation of UKF. So as to improve the estimation accuracy [11]. Although the deep learning method has the advantages of nonlinear adaptability and high quasi-certainty in the battery state estimation, and avoids the complex physical and chemical changes inside the battery, it also leads to poor interpretability. Usually as a black box model, it is difficult to explain the specific reasons and logic.

Based on the above analysis, a method of multi-modal information interaction and fusion is proposed. The purpose of multi-modal interaction and fusion is to integrate multiple modal information to get a consistent and common model output, which can obtain more comprehensive features, improve the robustness of the model, and ensure that the model can still work effectively when some modes are missing. Especially for the problem of battery SOC, multi-modal interaction and fusion is the interaction and fusion of processing methods under multiple models. For example, in order to obtain more accurate and stable SOC estimation results, model-based method and data-driven method are used to simultaneously process data and estimate and forecast. The results obtained by the two are processed again to get a more ideal result. For example, through the multi-modal multi-linear fusion mechanism to study the relationship between various features, so as to use the multi-modal multi-linear feature (MMF) and its interaction characteristics, a high-order polynomial module is designed to fuse multi-modal signals from different sources, in order to improve the efficiency and performance of SOH estimation, A two-dimensional CNN network is chosen to use the proposed MMF [12].

The work of this paper is to estimate the SOC of the battery by using the method of multi-mode information interaction and fusion. First, the predicted SOC of the battery is obtained by using the method of unscented Kalman filter based on the first-order RC equivalent circuit model of the battery. Then the BPNN method is used to get the SOC of the battery after a lot of data training. Finally, the SOC obtained by the two methods is used as the input of the next BPNN, and the final SOC of the battery is obtained after a lot of data training, The BPNN in this stage is called the multi-modal information based back propagation neural Network (MMI-BPNN). In order to verify the feasibility and superiority of this method, the experimental verification and error analysis are carried out under the working condition of the battery.

The rest of this paper is as follows: In the second part, the unscented Kalman filter (UKF), BPNN and MMI-BPNN are introduced. The third part introduces the experimental conditions and verifies them. In the fourth part, according to the experimental results obtained in the third part, the error analysis is carried out and the conclusion is drawn. The fifth part summarizes and looks forward to the full text.

2   Experimental Principles

2.1   UKF

As an extension of traditional Kalman filter, UKF is a nonlinear system state estimation filtering algorithm, which approximates the probability distribution of nonlinear system by introducing unscented transform [13]. The state of battery charge is a kind of state of nonlinear system, so it can estimate its state effectively and provide accurate estimation results.

Battery Modeling

Since this paper uses multi-mode information interaction and fusion to estimate the state of battery charge, which can effectively reduce the dependence of UKF on the model accuracy, a relatively simple first-order RC equivalent circuit model (see Fig. 1) is adopted in this paper. Where U_{ocv} is the open circuit voltage of the battery, U_t is the terminal voltage of the battery, R_o is the ohmic internal resistance of the battery, R_p and C_p is the polarization resistance and polarization capacitance of the battery, which are used to describe the dynamic behavior inside the battery.

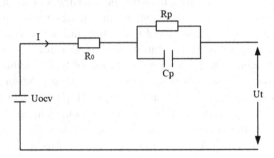

Fig. 1. Battery one-order RC equivalent circuit

According to Kirchhoff's law, Definition of power battery SOC, circuit analysis and electrochemical principles.

The equation of state and the equation of observation about the first-order RC equivalent circuit model of the battery can be obtained [14]:

$$
\begin{cases}
\begin{bmatrix} SOC_k \\ U_{p,k} \end{bmatrix} = \begin{bmatrix} 1 & 0 \\ 0 & e^{-\frac{\Delta t}{\tau}} \end{bmatrix} \begin{bmatrix} SOC_{k-1} \\ U_{p,k-1} \end{bmatrix} + \begin{bmatrix} \frac{\eta \Delta t}{C_a} \\ \left(1 - e^{-\frac{\Delta t}{\tau}}\right) R_0 \end{bmatrix} i_k \\
U_{t,k} = \begin{bmatrix} \frac{dU_{ocv,k}}{dSOC_k} & -1 \end{bmatrix} \begin{bmatrix} SOC_k \\ U_{p,k} \end{bmatrix} + (-R_0) i_k
\end{cases}
\tag{1}
$$

Parameter Identification

In this paper, FFRLS method is used for online parameter identification, which can update battery model parameters according to real-time model information collected [15].

By discretizing the circuit equation of the first-order equivalent circuit model, the discretized terminal voltage represented by parameter matrix (θ_k) and data matrix (φ_k) can be obtained.

$$
U_{t,k} = \begin{bmatrix} U_{ocv(k)} & R_0 + R_p & R_0 R_p C_P & R_p C_P \end{bmatrix} \begin{bmatrix} 1 \\ I_{(k)} \\ \frac{I_{(k)} - I_{(k-1)}}{\tau_s} \\ \frac{U_{t(k-1)} - U_{t(k)}}{\tau_s} \end{bmatrix}
\tag{2}
$$

the model parameters can be obtained from the following equation:

$$
\begin{cases}
\theta_{1(k)} = U_{ocv(k)} \\
\theta_{2(k)} = R_0 + R_p \\
\theta_{3(k)} = R_0 R_p C_P \\
\theta_{4(k)} = R_p C_P
\end{cases}
\tag{3}
$$

The Principle of UKF

Combined with the battery model and parameter identification, the calculation process of UKF is shown in Fig. 2 below [16]:

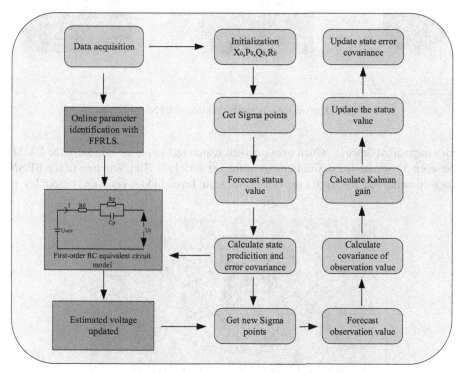

Fig. 2. Schematic diagram of UKF

2.2 BPNN

The estimation of battery SOC usually involves nonlinear properties, such as charge/discharge efficiency, self-discharge, capacity decay, etc. BPNN is capable of building complex nonlinear relationship models that can effectively capture these nonlinear relationships through the combination of multiple layers of neurons. In addition, BPNN is a data-based learning method that automatically learns the characteristics and behavior patterns of a battery through training on historical battery charge and discharge data. This means that when using BPNN for SOC estimation, it is not necessary to conduct detailed physical modeling of the battery in advance, but only to provide sufficient training data.

The BPNN was proposed by Rumelhart and McClelland in 1986. It can be seen from the simple schematic principle of BPNN (see Fig. 3) that it is a multi-layer forward neural network trained according to an error backpropagation algorithm, in other words, in the BPNN, the signal propagates forward and the error propagates backward. Its basic

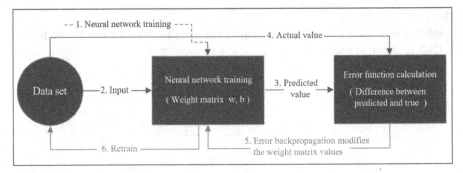

Fig. 3. The simple schematic diagram of BPNN principle

idea is gradient descent, which uses gradient search techniques to minimize the RMSE between the actual and desired output of the network [17]. The Structure of the BPNN for estimating the SOC (see Fig. 4) includes input layer, hidden layer and output layer.

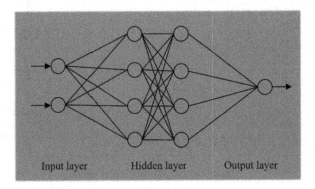

Fig. 4. The Structure of the BPNN for estimating the SOC

In the forward propagation process, the input signal acts on the output node through the hidden layer, and after nonlinear transformation, the output signal is generated. If the actual output is inconsistent with the expected output, it will be transformed into a backpropagation process of error. Error backpropagation is the transmission of the output error layer by layer from the hidden layer to the input layer, and the error is distributed to all the units in each layer. The error signals obtained from each layer are backpropagated to neurons in the hidden layer to adjust the connection weights and thresholds [18]. After repeated learning and training, the network parameters corresponding to the minimum error (weight and threshold) are determined, and then the training is stopped.

2.3 Multi-modal Information Interaction and Fusion BPNN

According to the introduction of the principles of UKF and BPNN above, two methods for estimating the SOC of lithium batteries are clarified. In the actual application often due to their own shortcomings and estimation errors, and the interaction and fusion of multi-modal information is a reasonable way to reduce the impact of their respective shortcomings and make full use of their respective advantages. The experimental verification will be carried out in the following chapters. The principle of MMI-BPNN is shown in Fig. 5.

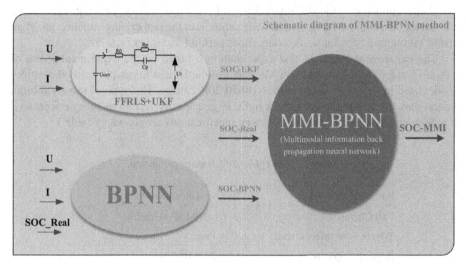

Fig. 5. Schematic diagram of MMI-BPNN method

The implementation flow of MMI-BPNN is shown in Fig. 5 Firstly uses the voltage and current data of the battery, establishes a first-order RC equivalent circuit model, uses FFRLS to identify the model parameters, and finally uses untrace Kalman filter to estimate the SOC of the battery to obtain information (SOC-UKF). Then the BPNN is trained with the same battery voltage and current data and real SOC data, and through continuous learning, the error is backpropagated, and the network weight is constantly adjusted, so as to obtain the best estimate of the battery SOC under the use of BPNN (SOC-BPNN).

Finally, the estimated results of UKF and BPNN and the real SOC are used as inputs to train the BPNN, so that the best estimate of the obtained SOC constantly approximates the real SOC value. Here, the estimated results of UKF and BPNN correspond to different information modes respectively, and the second BPNN is MMI-BPNN. UKF mainly depends on the accuracy of the system model and the statistical characteristics of noise, and can cope well with nonlinear systems, while BPNN relies on the quantity and quality of training samples, and has strong learning and adaptation ability to nonlinear mapping. Therefore, the second layer of BPNN can be said to be a strategy to optimize the two methods. MMI-BPNN reduces the dependence of UKF on the model and the requirements of BPNN on the system and data, and improves the estimation accuracy of the battery SOC [11].

3 Experimental Process

The actual condition of the battery pack in an electric car can be very harsh, simple CC-CV can not objectively show the advantages and disadvantages of the algorithm. Therefore, the battery data under the condition of Federal Urban Driving Schedule (FUDS) is used in the experiment phase. FUDS condition is a vehicle emission test standard formulated by the US Environmental Protection Agency (EPA). It is composed of a series of specific driving modes, which simulates the real driving situation on urban roads, taking into account traffic congestion, parking and other factors.

The experimental data of this experiment are based on the experimental data of lithium battery from University of Maryland in the United States [19], and the battery model used in this experiment is INR 18650-20R battery. This type of ternary lithium battery has the advantages of light weight, large capacity and no memory effect, so it has been widely used. The specific battery specifications are shown in Table 1.

Table 1. INR 18650-20R Battery parameters

Battery (Parameters)	Specifications (Value)
Cell Chemistry	LiNiMnCo/Graphite
Weight (w/o safety circuit)	45 g
Nominal capacity	2000 (mAh)
Circulation of Life	500~800
Rated voltage	3.6 V
Charge cut_off voltage	4.2 V
Discharge cut_off voltage	2.5 V

To sum up, the voltage and current data of the battery used are the data of charging and discharging of INR 18650-20R battery at 25 °C and FUDS condition, and the initial SOC of the battery is 50%. The change of current during charge and discharge is shown in Fig. 6.

In order to verify the superiority and accuracy of MMI-BPNN method, three experiments including UKF estimation of battery SOC, BPNN estimation of battery SOC and MMI estimation of battery SOC were designed.

3.1 UKF Estimation of Battery SOC

In this experiment, the above battery parameters and working condition data were used for parameter identification by recursive least square method using FFRLS, which is online identification. Then, the real-time parameters of online identification are used as the parameters of untracked Kalman filter, and the end current data is used as input to output the SOC of the battery.

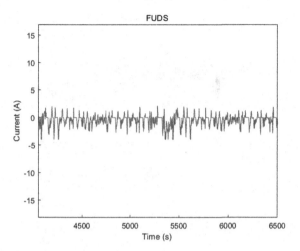

Fig. 6. The current of FUDS

Battery Parameter Identification (FFRLS)

FFRLS is a machine learning algorithm for solving nonlinear systems and nonlinear parameter estimation problems. The algorithm updates the parameter estimates recursively and minimizes the error between the predicted output and the actual output to gradually improve the accuracy of the model. The implementation steps of FFRLS are shown in Table 2.

Table 2. Implementation steps of the FFRLS algorithm.

---

1) Initialization.

φ_0, θ_0, P_0, K_0, λ

2) Calculate algorithm gain K_k and error covariance matrix P_k.

$$K_k = \frac{P_{k-1}\varphi_k^T}{\varphi_k P_{k-1}\varphi_k^T + \lambda}$$

$$P_k = \frac{P_{k-1} - K_k\varphi_k^T P_{k-1}}{\lambda}$$

3) Gain predication error and update model parameters.

$$e_k = E_{t,k} - \varphi_k\theta_{k-1}$$

$$\theta_k = \theta_{k-1} + K_k e_k$$

4) Acquire the terminal voltage.

$$E_{t,k} = \varphi_k\theta_k$$

After realizing the above algorithm steps, the corresponding results are obtained. The comparison between the predicted terminal voltage and the real terminal voltage obtained by using the identified parameters is shown in Fig. 7.

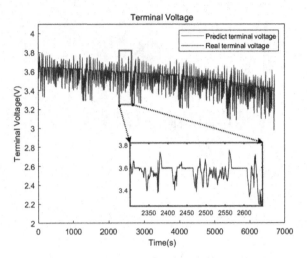

Fig. 7. Terminal voltage comparison diagram

As shown in Fig. 7, the fitting effect between the predicted terminal voltage and the real terminal voltage is accurate, so the identification can obtain accurate battery model parameters. The identified model parameters are shown in Fig. 8.

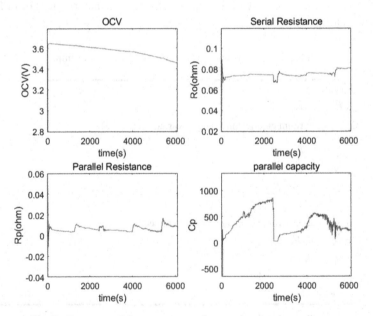

Fig. 8. Battery model parameters and open circuit voltage diagram

UKF Estimates the Battery SOC

The SOC of the battery is estimated by using the 6724 sets of data of the above battery model under FUDS conditions, according to the equation of state and observation equation derived above, and the model parameters obtained through online identification. Simulation results of UKF estimates SOC in Fig. 9.

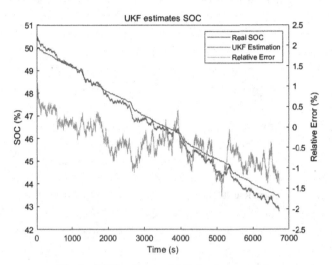

Fig. 9. UKF estimates SOC simulation results

The state of charge, as depicted in Fig. 9, can be observed to effectively track the variations of the actual state of charge during operational circumstances through the implementation of the UKF algorithm. Additionally, the relative error associated with the estimated state of charge is also maintained within a narrow range.

3.2 BPNN Estimates the Battery SOC

In this paper, the battery data under FUDS conditions are used to predict the SOC of the battery by BPNN method, and voltage, current and SOC_real are selected as inputs and SOC as outputs to train the neural network (see Fig. 10).

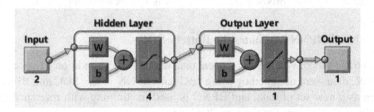

Fig. 10. BPNN network training diagram

There are a total of 5224 data samples, 70% of which are used as training sets for model fitting. 15% of the data is used as validation set to adjust the hyperparameters of the model and to conduct preliminary evaluation of the model's capability. The last 15% of the data is used as a test set to evaluate the generalization ability of the final model.

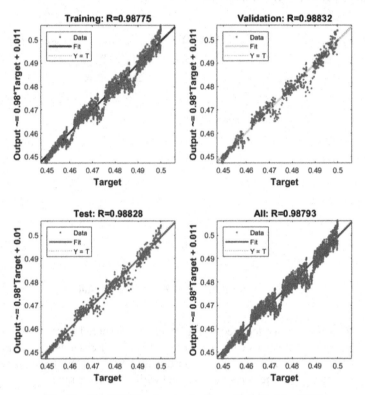

Fig. 11. The BPNN estimates the R coefficient of the SOC

The correlation coefficient (fit degree) of the estimated SOC obtained by BPNN training is shown in Fig. 11. The closer it is to 1, the closer the relationship between predicted value and the true value is.

Then, 1,500 sets of charge and discharge data sets of FUDS working conditions were selected above for SOC prediction, and the results were shown in Fig. 12.

3.3 The MMI-BPNN Estimates the Battery SOC

Based on 6724 sets of voltage and current data under FUDS conditions, two sets of estimated SOC data were obtained by using UKF and BPNN. UKF_SOC and BPNN_SOC are taken as a new set of data, and BPNN is used for training with reference to actual SOC, so as to further predict the new SOC value.

In the same way, 5224 sets of data from the two sets of SOCs were used to train the BPNN model, of which 70% were used for the training set, 15% for the verification

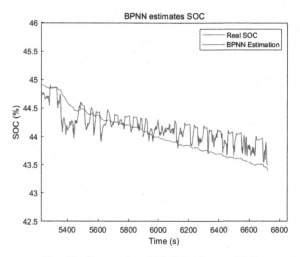

Fig. 12. The results of BPNN estimates SOC

set and 15% for the test set. After the training model is obtained, SOC prediction is performed on 1500 sets of data.

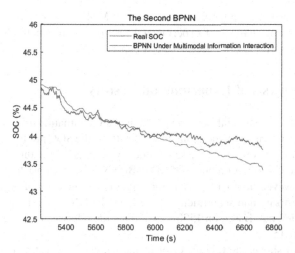

Fig. 13. The SOC estimated by MMI-BPNN

As shown in Fig. 13, the values of the predicted SOC are very close to those of the real SOC, and the curves match very well.

3.4 Chapter Summary

By integrating the SOC predicted by the above three methods, the last 1500 sets of SOC data estimated by UKF and the SOC data estimated by BPNN were extracted and compared with the SOC estimated by MMI-BPNN.

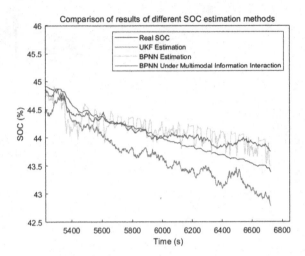

Fig. 14. Comparison of results of different SOC estimation methods

As shown in Fig. 14, it can be intuitively seen that compared with the other two methods, the SOC curve adopted by MMI-BPNN is more consistent with the real SOC curve.

In order to verify the better estimation effect of MMI-BPNN more scientifically and rigorously, the error analysis of experimental results of three methods (UKF, BPNN, MMI-BPNN) is carried out in Sect. 4 of this paper.

4 Error Analysis of Experimental Results

According to the experimental steps in Sect. 3, the SOC estimation results of each method are obtained. Compared with the actual SOC of battery, the SOC predicted by experiment has a good estimation effect. At the same time, by comparing the three SOC estimation methods, the SOC estimation curve of MMI-BPNN is more consistent with the actual SOC curve. However, in order to ensure the scientificity and rigor of the experiment and obtain the superiority and scientificity of the MMI-BPNN method, the following error analysis is carried out. Based on 1500 sets of data, the relative error of each experiment is shown in Fig. 15.

Figure 15(a) shows the relative error of the battery SOC estimated by UKF, with a maximum relative error of 1.4889%. First of all, the main source of error is that the first-order RC equivalent circuit can not reflect the internal changes of the battery well, which reduces the accuracy of the parameter identification of the model, and thus causes the error of UKF. Secondly, the error is also related to the initial condition error, measurement error and environmental conditions change and other factors.

Figure 15 (b) shows the relative error of SOC estimated by BPNN, and the maximum relative error is 1.4796%. The main cause of error is the quantity and quality of input data. If the amount of input data is insufficient, the training error will increase, and the correction error will also increase; Moreover, the data of the battery under the working

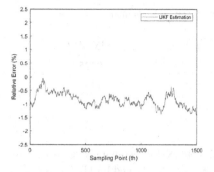

a. Relative error of UKF estimates SOC

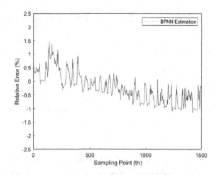

b. Relative error of BPNN estimates SOC

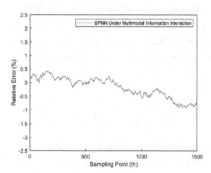

c. Relative error of MMI-BPNN estimates SOC

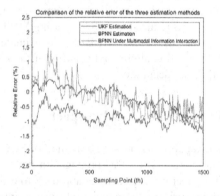

d. Comparison of the relative error of the three estimation methods

Fig. 15. Relative error

condition is complex, and the data measured by the laboratory still can not fully compare with the actual operating condition of the electric vehicle, so the quality of the input data of the training BPNN is also one of the sources of error.

As shown in Fig. 15 (c), MMI-BPNN estimates the relative error of SOC of the battery, and the maximum relative error is 0.9325%. The estimation accuracy is obviously improved.

As shown in Fig. 15 (d), compared with UKF and BPNN, the error of SOC estimation by this method is significantly reduced. The reason for the reduction of error is that this method of multi-modal information fusion can effectively reduce the deficiency of single mode information in SOC estimation. SOC_UKF and SOC_BPNN are used as training data, and the trained model can reduce the impact of insufficient accuracy of the first-order RC equivalent circuit model. It also reduces the data requirements of BPNN training model. As shown in Table 3 is the maximum relative error, MAE and RMSE of the three methods.

Table 3. The maximum relative error in SOC estimates

Methods	UKF	BPNN	MMI-BPNN
Maximum relative error	1.4889%	1.4796%	0.9325%
MAE	0.22%	0.26%	0.14%
RMSE	0.21%	0.10%	0.08%

It can be seen from Table 3 that using MMI-BPNNH to estimate SOC, except the maximum relative error is reduced. For MAE, the SOC estimated by UKF was 0.22% and the SOC estimated by BPNN was 0.21%, which was reduced to 0.14% after using MMI-BPNN. For RMSE, the estimated SOC was 0.26% by UKF and 0.10% by BPNN, which was reduced to 0.08% by using MMI-BPNN. Therefore, the experimental results show that using the MMI-BPNN to estimate the SOC of the battery can further improve the estimation ability and stability of the model, and realize the improvement of SOC estimation accuracy.

5 Summary and Prospect

In this paper, we propose a method of SOC estimation based on multi-modal information interaction by backpropagation neural network, which can obtain more accurate This paper presents a novel approach to estimating SOC using a backpropagation neural network that leverages multi-modal information interaction. By incorporating this approach, a more precise estimation of SOC can be achieved. The primary focus of this paper encompasses the following tasks:

- Based on the principles of UKF and BPNN, the idea of a model for SOC estimation of battery by combining the two methods is presented. It is a backpropagation neural network based on multi-modal information interaction.
- Based on the battery data obtained under fixed FUDS conditions, the UKF, BPNN and MMI-BPNN experiments were carried out respectively. The results of their respective estimates and predictions are obtained. And make a preliminary comparison.
- According to the relative error curve and maximum relative error, MMI-BPNN has a more accurate estimation result.

In summary, the MMI-BPNN approach offers multiple benefits. Firstly, it decreases the reliance of the UKF on the accuracy of the model. Additionally, it lessens the demands placed on the BPNN in terms of both data quantity and quality. Consequently, this reduces the complexity involved in the initial stages of estimating battery SOC. Ultimately, the MMI-BPNN method enhances the precision and robustness of battery SOC estimation.

As technology advances, numerous battery SOC estimation methods have been developed, yielding favorable outcomes. However, it is important to note that each method, particularly those relying solely on single-mode information, possesses certain limitations. Consequently, the integration and combination of multi-modal information emerges as a viable solution, fostering mutual learning. In the future, the advantages of information interaction and fusion are anticipated to extend beyond dual-mode, encompassing three-mode and potentially even more complex modes. This development holds great potential across various sectors of society.

References

1. Wenhao, Yu., Guo, Yi., Shang, Z., Zhang, Y., Shengming, Xu.: A review on comprehensive recycling of spent power lithium-ion battery in China. eTransportation **11**, 100155 (2022)
2. Ming, Wu., Gao, H., Chen, L.L.: An overview of the electric vehicle industry development in the world. Appl. Mech. Mater. **373–375**, 2098–2103 (2013)
3. Prashant Shrivastava, P., Naidu, A., Sharma, S., Panigrahi, B.K., Garg, A.: Review on technological advancement of lithium-ion battery states estimation methods for electric vehicle applications. J. Energy Storage **64**, 107159 (2023)
4. Li, M., Zhang, Y., Zuolei, Hu., Zhang, Y., Zhang, J.: A battery SOC estimation method based on AFFRLS-EKF. Sensors **21**(17), 5698 (2021). https://doi.org/10.3390/s21175698
5. Liu, S., Dong, X., Yu, X., Ren, X., Zhang, J., Zhu, R.: A method for state of charge and state of health estimation of lithium-ion battery based on adaptive unscented Kalman filter. Energy Rep. **8**(8), 426–436 (2022)
6. Zhang, M., Yang, D., Jiaxuan, Du., Sun, H., Li, L., Wang, L., Wang, K.: A review of SOH prediction of Li-Ion batteries based on data-driven algorithms. Energies **16**(7), 3167 (2023)
7. Shin, K.J.: Design of backpropagation neural network for aging estimation of electric battery. Sens. Mater. **35**(4), 1385–1395 (2023)
8. Yihuan, L., Kang, L., Xuan, L., Li, Z.: Fast battery capacity estimation using convolutional neural networks. Trans. Inst. Meas. Control (2020)
9. Chemali, E., Kollmeyer, P.J., Preindl, M., Ahmed, R., Emadi, A.: Long short-term memory networks for accurate state-of-charge estimation of Li-ion batteries. IEEE Trans. Ind. Electron. **65**(8), 6730–6739 (2017)
10. Jiang, C., Xu, H.: Online SOC estimation of lead-acid batteries for mining based on PD-BPNN. Mod. Electron. Tech. **41**(10), 113–116 (2018)
11. Lin, J., Yang, X., Zhou, J., Wang, G., Liu, J., Yuan, Y.: Algorithm of BPNN-UKF based on a fusion model for SOC estimation in lithium-ion batteries. IET Power Electron. **16**(5), 856–867 (2023)
12. Lin, M., You, Y., Meng, J., Wang, W., Wu, J., Daniel-Ioan, S.: Lithium-ion batteries SOH estimation with multimodal multilinear feature fusion. IEEE Trans. Energy Conver. 1–9 (2023)
13. Zhang, J., Xia, C.: State-of-charge estimation of valve regulated lead acid battery based on multi-state unscented Kalman Filter. Int. J. Electr. Power Energy Syst. **33**(3), 472–476 (2011)
14. Yang, S., et al.: A parameter adaptive method for state of charge estimation of lithium-ion batteries with an improved extended Kalman filter. Sci. Rep. **11**(1), 1–15 (2021)
15. Li, J., Ye, M., Gao, K., Jiao, S., Xinxin, Xu.: State estimation of lithium polymer battery based on Kalman filter. Ionics **27**(9), 3909–3918 (2021)
16. Liu, S., Dong, X., Xiaodong, Yu., Ren, X., Zhang, J., Zhu, R.: A method for state of charge and state of health estimation of lithium-ion battery based on adaptive unscented Kalman filter. Energy Rep. **8**, 426–436 (2022)
17. Xing, L., Ling, L., Xianyuan, Wu.: Lithium-ion battery state-of-charge estimation based on a dual extended Kalman filter and BPNN correction. Connect. Sci. **34**(1), 2332–2363 (2022)
18. Yusha, Hu., et al.: Short term electric load forecasting model and its verification for process industrial enterprises based on hybrid GA-PSO-BPNN algorithm—a case study of papermaking process. Energy **170**, 1215–1227 (2019)
19. University of Maryland. Battery research data [EB/OL]. https://calce.umd.edu/battery-data#A123. Accessed 8 July 2023

Sperm Recognition and Viability Classification Based on Artificial Intelligence

Wentan Jiao[1,4], Yingsen Xie[2(✉)], Yang Li[2], and Jingyi Qi[3]

[1] Luoyang Institute of Science and Technology, Luoyang, China
[2] Hainan University, Haikou, China
1159700048@qq.com
[3] Luoyang Central Hospital, Luoyang, China
[4] Henan Engineering Technology Research Center of Embedded Technology Application,
Xinxiang, China

Abstract. Semen quality analysis plays an important role in evaluating male reproductive health and is essential before artificial insemination. The computer assisted semen analysis system (CASA), as an auxiliary tool for manual semen analysis, provides physicians with relatively accurate information on sperm motility, but there are more uncertainties in the sperm motility process, and sperm obstruction and occlusion occur frequently, which makes CASA unable to show optimal tracking performance in complex environments. In this paper, we propose a new method based on YOLOv5 for sperm head detection and using joint probabilistic data association (JPDA) for multi-sperm dynamic tracking, which is used to enhance the tracking effect of CASA in the case of intersecting sperm trajectories. The YOLOv5 algorithm is used as a sperm head position detector, and the detection accuracy reaches 97.9%. Using JPDA algorithm for sperm tracking, the ID switching problem of sperm during swimming was better avoided, and the multiple object tracking accuracy (MOTA) reached 91%. Finally, the motion parameters of sperm were calculated, and the viability grading of sperm was achieved by back propagation (BP) neural network.

Keywords: Computer-assisted Sperm Analysis · Sperm Motility Classification · Sperm Detection · Sperm Tracking

1 Introduction

According to the latest survey report from the World Health Organization, infertility affects approximately 17.5% of adults worldwide [1]. Conditions such as weak spermatozoa and oligospermia are the primary causes of low male fertility. In this regard, semen quality analysis has become a key tool for evaluating male fertility and solving male infertility issues. In manual semen routine analysis (SRA), the different subjectivity of physicians and the differences in laboratory conditions result in low accuracy of the test results and a lack of precise quantitative standards [2]. The computer assisted semen analysis system (CASA) is an innovative product of the development of information

© The Author(s), under exclusive license to Springer Nature Singapore Pte Ltd. 2024
F. Sun et al. (Eds.): ICCSIP 2023, CCIS 1918, pp. 404–418, 2024.
https://doi.org/10.1007/978-981-99-8018-5_30

science in the field of medicine, which objectively responds to the quality of semen by analyzing the morphology, density and motility of spermatozoa, and overcomes the problems of high subjectivity, low efficiency and high error of the traditional manual methods, and is increasingly becoming a reliable method for evaluating the reproductive capacity of men. In practical application, it was found that sperm obstruction and blockage adhesion would lead to tracking errors in the CASA system, and the sperm multi-target tracking algorithm of the system needs to be further investigated on the problem of sperm track intersections [3].

To accomplish the task of sperm viability grading, the first step is to accurately identify the contour information or positional coordinates of the sperm cells from the sample. Initially, Hidayatullah et al. [4] employed an image processing method to detect sperm targets, relying on the grayscale information of the image to separate the sperm from the background. However, this approach was unable to accurately distinguish sperm targets from background impurities in low-contrast images. Liu et al. [5] conducted differentials on consecutive frames of images to detect sperm contours, followed by morphological operations to filter out impurity interference. Qi et al. [6] proposed a tracking and classification method for moving sperm targets based on the Gaussian mixture model. After modeling the background, moving sperms are detected by comparing each frame of the video with the background. However, this method fails to effectively detect stationary sperms. The sperm detection algorithm based on image processing performs well when the image is clear or the environment has fewer impurities but exhibits limitations in liquid environments filled with suspended interference. With the rapid development of artificial intelligence technology, some scholars have applied deep learning-based algorithms to medical image processing. Melendez et al. [7] utilized a convolutional neural network based on the U-Net architecture to achieve sperm segmentation in complex environments. However, the complex encoding-decoding structure of the U-Net architecture leads to long inference times, which may not meet the real-time requirements of the algorithm. In contrast, the YOLOv5 algorithm offers significant advantages in terms of speed and demonstrates good performance in accuracy and real-time processing. Hidayatullah et al. [8] employed YOLOv3 to detect bull sperm cells with a mean average precision (mAP) of 0.984. Building upon this, the present experiment utilizes the more effective YOLOv5 framework for human sperm detection. This framework accurately and swiftly identifies spermatozoa targets while effectively mitigating the interference caused by suspended impurities.

In the sperm tracking problem, Li [9] proposed an algorithm for sperm tracking with improved kernel correlation filtering. This approach introduced Kalman filtering and adaptive scaling into the kernel correlation filter (KCF) algorithm, resulting in stable tracking of the target. Ravanfar et al. [10] presented a new method for sperm segmentation using the watershed algorithm and tracking with a particle filter. Kheirkhah et al. [11] proposed a sperm tracking method based on adaptive window average speed (AWAS) to identify the best motion trajectory in low-density sperm images. The challenge in sperm tracking lies in the issue of sperm collisions. Imani et al. [12] employed the Hungarian search method to achieve target tracking in scenarios involving sperm collision and occlusion, demonstrating the superior tracking performance of this method compared to template matching, particle filtering, and mean drift methods. Tan et al. [13] introduced the collision detection and modified covariance matrix (CDMCM) to detect collisions, and mean shift (MS) tracking algorithm is implemented together with CDMCM to improve sperm tracking by solving the collision problem. NK et al. [14] used the joint probabilistic data association (JPDA) algorithm to track hematopoietic stem cells in the blood to determine the survival state of the cells. Considering that the JPDA algorithm deals with the uncertainty problem of multi-target tracking through data association and probability matching, estimates and predicts the state information of multiple targets from a series of measurement data, and has good multi-target tracking performance in the environment with clutter, this paper introduces JPDA to the task of sperm multi-target tracking to further improve the accuracy and robustness of the multi-sperm tracking algorithm in the sperm trajectory intersection problem. This improvement contributes to the enhanced tracking performance of the computer-aided semen analysis system.

2   Preparation of Experimental Samples

Sperm video collection for this experiment was carried out in a sterile environment at 37 °C to ensure sperm activity. Semen samples were diluted with 0.9% saline, and injected into a sperm chamber made of slides and coverslips. A set of 30 different sperm video samples were prepared using a microscope with a magnification of 400x and a CCD camera for frame capture, each video was 60 s long with a video resolution of 640 * 400 and a frame rate of 30 fps/s. The video samples were intercepted at intervals of 5 frames, and 4,000 still images were captured for the training of the YOLOv5 network, which was performed by the Labelimg software. Labelimg software for labelling in TXT format, 3200 as training set, 400 as validation set and 400 as test set.

3   Method

The architecture of our proposed algorithmic model is depicted in Fig. 1. In this model, each frame within the sperm video undergoes denoising before being inputted into the YOLOv5 network for feature extraction, fusion and other operations. The detection network then outputs the coordinate position of each sperm. The coordinate information is correlated using the JPDA, which calculates the motion parameters of each sperm and plots the motion trajectory. Subsequently, the motility of the sperm is analyzed based on predetermined grading rules, ultimately leading to the activity grading of the sperm target.

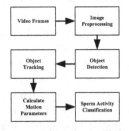

Fig. 1. Schematic diagram of the workflow

3.1   Sperm Detection Based on Yolov5

YOLOv5 is composed of four parts: Input, Backbone, Neck and Output. The model structure is depicted in Fig. 2. The input side employs Mosaic data enhancement, adaptive anchor frame computation, and adaptive image scaling strategies to strengthen the input samples and reduce the computational cost of the model. The Focus structure within the Backbone performs slicing operations on the image, effectively compensating for the loss of pixel point information during the down-sampling process and providing finer detail information for the subsequent network [15]. In the Neck network, YOLOv5 adopts the feature pyramid network (FPN) and path aggregation network (PAN) from YOLOv4. This fusion enhances the cross-layer communication of information by combining high-level semantic information with underlying feature information. Finally, the output stage of the network conducts a series of convolution operations to map the feature map to the spatial location and category of the target. The optimal prediction frame is filtered using the non-max suppression (NMS) method. For the input sperm map, the end-to-end YOLOv5 model directly calculates the coordinate positions of sperm targets, thereby mitigating the problem of impurity interference to some extent. Additionally, it exhibits strong detection capabilities for slow-moving or stationary sperm, better meeting the accuracy and real-time requirements of this study.

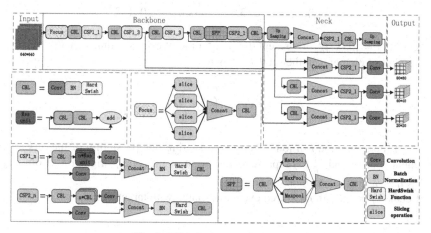

Fig. 2. YOLOv5 network structure

3.2   Multiple Sperm Tracking

Analyzing the active state of spermatozoa requires measuring the movement parameters of each sperm at different moments in time. Among the various methods for sperm tracking, the multi-hypothesis tracker (MHT) utilizes the entire historical information to estimate the latest state of each target. However, the computational effort of MHT grows exponentially as the number of tracked targets increases and the tracking time lengthens. The nearest neighbor (NN) method involves setting up a tracking gate, and the measurements that fall within the gate are used as candidate echoes. However, this method often leads to tracking target mismatch when sperms cross and move in close proximity [16, 17]. In contrast to the Nearest Neighbor method, the probabilistic data association (PDA) algorithm calculates the probability of each measurement falling within the gate through a new calculation. PDA exhibits good tracking performance for single or sparse targets. Building upon PDA, Bar-Shalom et al. [18] proposed the JPDA algorithm. JPDA effectively addresses the multi-target tracking problem in cluttered environments by considering various scenarios of measurements falling into different target tracking gates. Bar-Shalom considered that all valid echoes falling into a target gate have the probability of originating from that target, and introduced a confirmation matrix to represent the affiliation of valid echoes with the target tracking gate, and weighted estimation of each possible data association scenario.

Before sperm target tracking, the detection results of YOLOv5 were processed to ensure that the coordinate data of sperm met the input requirements of JPDA algorithm. Then, the probability matching algorithm is used to match the measured data, and the target coordinates of sperm are predicted and updated by Kalman filter algorithm. In general, the purpose of the JPDA is to calculate the probability that each measure is associated with a variety of source targets [19]. The process is shown in Eqs. 1 through 5.

First, the confirmation matrix is defined as:

$$\Omega = (\omega_{jt}), \quad j = 1, 2, 3, \cdots, m(k), \quad t = 0, 1, 2, \cdots, T \tag{1}$$

Let $\theta(k) = \{\theta_i(k)\}_{i=1}^{\theta_k}$ represent the set of all joint events at time k, and θ_k represent the number of elements in the set $\theta(k)$, where:

$$\theta_i(k) = \bigcap_{j=1}^{m(k)} \theta_{jt_j}^i(k) \tag{2}$$

$\theta_i(k)$ represents the i-th joint event, representing one possibility of the $m(k)$ measurement source, and $\theta_{jt_j}^i(k)$ represents the event of measure j originating from target $t_j (0 \le t_j \le T)$ in the i-th joint event.

Let $\theta_{jt}(k)$ be the j-th measured event associated with target t, then

$$\theta_{jt}(k) = \bigcup_{i=1}^{n_k} \theta_{jt}^i(k), \quad j = 1, 2, 3, \cdots, m(k) \tag{3}$$

In this way, the probability of connecting the j-th measurement with the t object can be obtained as:

$$\beta_j^t(k) = P(\theta_{jt}|Z^k)$$

$$= P(\bigcup_{i=1}^{\theta_k} \theta_{jt}^i(k)|Z^k)$$

$$= \sum_{i=1}^{\theta_k} P(\theta_i(k)|Z^k)\hat{\omega}_{jt}(\theta_i(k)) \tag{4}$$

where:

$$\hat{\omega}_{jt}^i(\theta_i(k)) = \begin{cases} 1, & \text{if } \theta_{jt}^i(k) \subset \theta_i(k) \\ 0, & \text{others} \end{cases} \tag{5}$$

3.3 Sperm Activity Grading Based on Motility Parameters

Most spermatozoa exhibit irregular movement patterns and demonstrate multiple motility patterns. Sperm motility parameters serve as important indicators for analyzing sperm motility status and predicting male fertility [20], playing a crucial role in quantitatively assessing sperm viability. The advantage of computer-assisted sperm motility analysis is its ability to swiftly and accurately generate a comprehensive set of sperm motility parameters that hold clinical diagnostic significance. To establish a quantitative parameter standard for sperm motility analysis, the world health organization (WHO) defined the following parameters for the motility of an individual spermatozoon [21], which are depicted schematically in Fig. 3.

- VCL, velocity along the curvilinear path (μm/s): the ratio of the actual trajectory of motion that the spermatozoa pass through during the observation time to the observation time.
- VSL, velocity along the straight-line path (μm/s): the velocity calculated along a straight line between the first and last points of the path.
- VAP, velocity along the average path (μm/s): the ratio of the sum of the mean trajectory distances travelled by the spermatozoa during the observation time to the observation time.
- ALH, the amplitude of the lateral displacement of the head (μm): The offset of the actual trajectory of the spermatozoon relative to the average trajectory of movement during the movement process.
- LIN, linearity: linearity of the curvilinear path (straight-line velocity/curvilinear velocity).
- STR, straightness: linearity of the average path (straight-line velocity/average path velocity).
- WOB, wobble: a measure of oscillation of the curvilinear path about the average path (average path velocity/curvilinear velocity).
- BCF, beat-cross frequency (Hz): average rate at which a curved path crosses the mean path.
- MAD, mean angular displacement (degrees): The average of the sum of the mean-pair values of the instantaneous angle of rotation of the sperm along the motion trajectory averaged over the total number of sampling intervals.

And spermatozoa were categorized into the following four classes according to their motility [21, 22]:

- Class A: fast forward motion (spermatozoa in linear or large circular motion, speed > 25 μm/s)
- Class B: slow forward motion (spermatozoa in linear or great circle motion, speed 5–25 μm/s)

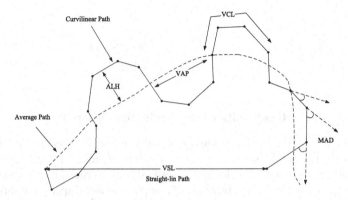

Fig. 3. Schematic representation of single sperm motility parameters

- Class C: non-forward motion (other motion patterns of spermatozoa, speed $< 5\mu m/s$)
- Class D: immobile (no tail movement of sperm seen)

The actual distance represented by each pixel was calculated based on the microscope's magnification and the size of the sperm counting plate. After bringing in the data, it was determined that a 1-pixel interval corresponded to an actual distance of 0.375 μm. The actual length was then derived from the pixel spacing between the coordinate points. The video frame rate used in this experiment was 30 fps/s, and every three frames were extracted for dynamic detection of YOLOv5, and then ID tracking and coordinate saving were carried out. 10 consecutive frames of images recorded all the positions that a single sperm swam through within one second, and the pixel lengths between the 10 neighboring coordinate points were summed up to get the length of the sperm's trajectory that swam in that time period, and multiplied by 0.375 microns again to get the actual displacement length of the sperm in one second of time. The position information of each sperm was counted and its VSL, VCL, and LIN motion parameters were calculated. To establish accurate viability classification rules for single sperm motility, a machine learning approach was introduced. A three-layer BP neural network is constructed to model the nonlinear mapping of the data. The number of input nodes is 3, the number of hidden layer nodes is 10, and the number of output layer nodes is 3. Sigmoid is used as the activation function, and finally the unique thermal code is transformed into a label. A dataset of 1000 samples was input into the network, and after 1200 rounds of iterative correction, the weight vector ω and bias b were obtained. The objective function in the network is shown in Eq. 6 and graded in formula 7.

$$y_i = \sigma(\omega_i^T x_i + b_i) \tag{6}$$

$$\begin{cases} v_0 < y_{out} \leq v_1, & \text{ClassA} \\ v_1 < y_{out} \leq v_2, & \text{ClassB} \\ v_2 < y_{out} \leq v_3, & \text{ClassC} \\ v_3 < y_{out} \leq v_4, & \text{ClassD} \end{cases} \tag{7}$$

where x_i represents the input vector of the i-th layer of the network, comprising three parameters: VCL, VSL and VAP. The corresponding predicted output is denoted as y_i.

The viability grading of the corresponding spermatozoa is determined by evaluating the range of values in which the results fall.

4 Indicator Parameters

4.1 Evaluation Metrics for Detection Network

We evaluate the performance of the detection algorithm horizontally using accuracy and sensitivity. Accuracy indicates how well the measured value matches the true value under experimental conditions, as shown in Eq. 8. In this study, we define sperm as positive and impurity as negative. *TP* represents the number of correctly identified sperm. *FN* represents the number of sperm incorrectly identified as impurity, indicating missed detection. *FP* represents the number of impurities incorrectly identified as sperm, indicating misdetection. *TN* represents the number of correctly identified impurities. Sensitivity quantifies the probability of accurately identifying sperm as positive examples and reflects the algorithm's sensitivity to positive examples, as shown in Eq. 9.

$$\text{Accuracy} = \frac{TP + TN}{TP + TN + FP + FN} \tag{8}$$

$$\text{Sensitivity} = \frac{TP}{TP + FN} \tag{9}$$

4.2 Evaluation Metrics for Tracking Models

Multiple object tracking accuracy (MOTA) is a commonly used evaluation metric in the field of multi-target tracking to measure the tracker's ability to detect targets and maintain trajectories, with correlations occurring when the tracker incorrectly exchanges object identities or when tracks are lost. The closer the MOTA value of a multi-tracker is to 1, the better correct tracking performance the system possesses, as shown in Eq. 10.

$$MOTA = 1 - \frac{\sum_t (m_t + fp_t + mme_t)}{\sum_t g_t} \in (-\infty, 1] \tag{10}$$

In the equation, mt represents the number of missed detection in the video sequence, fp_t represents the number of false detection in the video sequence, mme_t represents the number of times the identity ID switches during the tracking process, and g_t represents the number of tracked targets in the t-th video frame.

5 Experiments and Analyses

5.1 Experimental Hardware Configuration

The hardware configuration utilized in this experiment consists of an Intel i7-12700 processor and an NVIDIA GeForce GTX1660Super 6 GB graphics card. The software configuration includes CUDA 11.1 and cuDNN 8.8.0. The network model is built using PyTorch 1.8.0, while the Python version employed is 3.9. The OpenCV version utilized is 3.4.2.

5.2 Target Detection Experiment

To validate the effectiveness of the YOLOv5 algorithm in detecting moving sperm objects, this paper compares its performance with the background subtractor mixture of gaussians (MOG2) method and the Lucas Kanade optical flow (LK) method using the same data samples. The first video is sampled for detection, and the detection results on the 240th frame image are shown in Fig. 4.

The background subtraction method initially models the background and roughly distinguishes the moving sperm by calculating the difference between the background and the current frame. It then employs morphological operations and contour detection to eliminate impurity interference and extract the target's accurate position. However, this method is prone to misidentify two intersecting sperm trajectories as the same object or mistake a mobile suspension as a sperm. The optical flow method establishes an image motion field with motion vectors and utilizes pixel motion speed to separate moving targets from the background. While this method offers faster detection speed, it is unable to detect slow-moving or stationary sperm and is not well-suited for environments with numerous mobile suspensions. The YOLOv5 network was trained for 300 iterations and achieved an impressive mAP of 98.5%. It quickly analyzed the whole image, captured still frames from the video, and accurately predicted sperm coordinates. YOLOv5 demonstrated good performance in identifying moving sperm with intersecting trajectories, as well as distinguishing cellular contaminants from actual sperm. Additionally, it was capable of recognizing and labeling tightly adhering sperm clusters as separate "Sperms" objects. Table 1 presents the average performance of the three detection algorithms over 500 frames. In comparison, the Accuracy value of the YOLOv5 algorithm is 0.979, surpassing the MOG2 background subtraction method and the LK optical flow

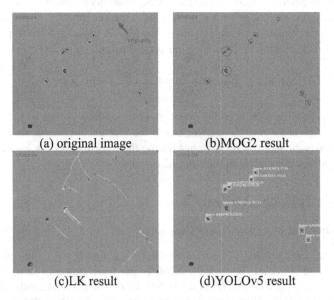

(a) original image   (b)MOG2 result

(c)LK result   (d)YOLOv5 result

Fig. 4. Detection effect of MOG2, LK and YOLOv5 on frame 240

method by 6.2 and 5.6% points, respectively. YOLOv5 takes 0.027 s to process a frame, which is faster than the other two methods. These results confirm the applicability of the YOLOv5 algorithm to the sperm detection problem.

Table 1. Average performance of MOG2, LK and YOLOv5

method	Sensitivity	Accuracy	Processing time (s/frame)
MOG2	0.925	0.917	0.035
LK	0.931	0.923	0.046
YOLOv5	0.980	0.979	0.027

5.3 Target Tracking Experiment

In this study, the global nearest neighbor (GNN) algorithm and JPDA algorithm were sequentially employed to track and analyze the sperm videos. The GNN tracking results are illustrated in Fig. 5. Each sperm head was assigned a unique ID to indicate its distinct identity, and the historical tracks were visualized using different colored lines. In the second video, sperms 20 and 27 experienced reduced mobility due to tail entanglement, causing their heads to remain stationary in small increments. These sperms exhibited poor motility. However, the GNN algorithm still recorded their positions, performed dynamic tracking, and mapped their trajectories. Sperm 21, a fast-moving spermatozoon, reaches a position in close proximity to sperm 27 at 1:57, with only one sperm head length separating them. Within one second, their outlines completely overlap, resulting in ID loss and switching. Sperm 21 and sperm 27 are reassigned new identities as "32" and "33".

The tracking effect of the JPDA algorithm on the same video sample are displayed in Fig. 6(a) and 6(b). In Fig. 6, the number "4" corresponds to the same object as the number "21" in Fig. 5, indicating the same sperm target. Sperm 4 collided with sperm 2 but separated after a brief period of contour blocking. The JPDA algorithm successfully tracked all sperms in the frame and did not occur any tracking errors or ID loss due to sperm collision. Frequent collisions occur in the video. Figure 6(c) and (d) shows another set of tracking scenarios. At the moment of 3:10, sperm 5 and sperm 8 come into close contact, but they separate after two seconds. The JPDA algorithm accurately maintains the correct IDs for both sperms.

The overall evaluation of the algorithms using MOTA metric revealed that the GNN algorithm achieved MOTA value of 82.3%, while JPDA reached 91%. This indicates that JPDA has superior tracking performance compared to GNN. Figure 7 shows some details of the tracking trajectories using the two algorithms. The grey curve represents the actual motion trajectory, while the red and blue curves represent the predicted trajectories of the GNN and JPDA algorithms, respectively. In Fig. 7(a), the real motion of sperm 7 from Fig. 6(d) is depicted. The sperm 7 exhibits a relatively stable straight-line motion pattern without any track steering or offset. Both GNN and JPDA algorithms show good track

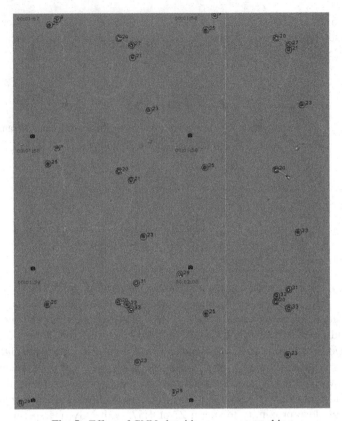

Fig. 5. Effect of GNN algorithm on sperm tracking

fitting effects, and the red and blue curves obscure the gray curve, which represents the real trajectory. In Fig. 7(b), sperm 3 moves in an "S" shape from right to left. The tracking trajectory of GNN matches the actual trajectory. On the other hand, the JPDA algorithm takes into account multiple data correlations and historical trajectory information when tracking the target, resulting in a predicted trajectory that lags behind the actual trajectory by 3–5 pixels. This slight curve fitting deviation is observed in Fig. 7(b). Overall, JPDA leverages historical coordinate trajectories to estimate the target's location and weighs the estimation of each possible scenario through data correlation. This makes the JPDA algorithm more resilient to interference, particularly in situations involving target overlap, compared to GNN.

5.4 Sperm Activity Classification

The dynamic tracking of sperm allows for the recording of the historical positions of each sperm at different time points. This information is then used to create a two-dimensional array containing the sperm ID numbers and their historical position coordinates. By processing and analyzing the coordinate values, motility parameters such as VSL, VAP and LIN can be computed. In our study, we conducted a series of tracking measurements

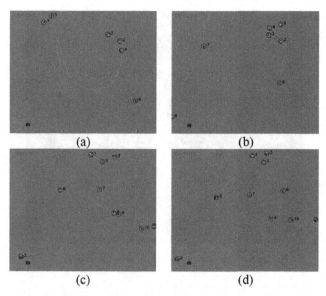

Fig. 6. Effect of JPDA algorithm on sperm tracking

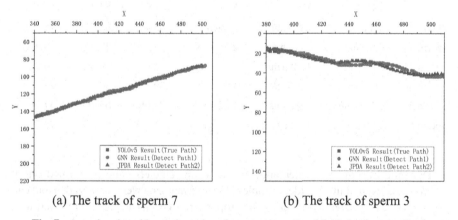

(a) The track of sperm 7   (b) The track of sperm 3

Fig. 7. Actual and tracking trajectories of spermatozoa 7 and 3 (Color figure online)

on different spermatozoa. We observed some difference in the viability of those sperms. Spermatozoa with good motility were able to swim greater distances within the same time frame. On the other hand, spermatozoa with entangled tails (such as sperm 2 and sperm 3) exhibited limited movement and remained in a state of oscillation. Their motility speeds did not exceed 5 μm per second. Figure 8 illustrates the motility of the spermatozoa at the 1:57 moment, and their motion parameters were recorded in Table 2.

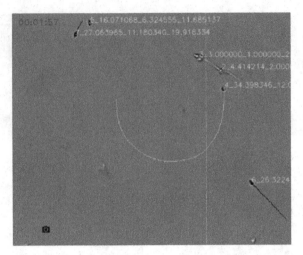

Fig. 8. The velocity of sperm movement at 1:57

Table 2. Parameters of tracking measurements of spermatozoa at the moment 1:57

	VCL	VSL	VAP	LIN	STR	WOB
Sperm 2	4.4 μm/s	2.0 μm/s	3.3 μm/s	45.4%	60.6%	75.0%
Sperm 3	3.0 μm/s	1.0 μm/s	2.1 μm/s	33.3%	47.6%	70.0%
Sperm 4	34.3 μm/s	12.0 μm/s	24.3 μm/s	34.9%	49.3%	70.8%
Sperm 5	16.0 μm/s	6.3 μm/s	11.7 μm/s	39.3%	53.8%	73.0%
Sperm 6	26.3 μm/s	9.9 μm/s	15.2 μm/s	37.6%	65.1%	57.7%
Sperm 7	27.0 μm/s	11.2 μm/s	19.9 μm/s	41.4%	56.2%	73.7%

Dynamic tracking and calculation of motion parameters were performed on 200 spermatozoa from multiple video samples. The spermatozoa were then graded and categorized based on predefined criteria. The proportions of each category were determined, and the grading results are shown in Fig. 9.

Vitality classification according to WHO standards

■ Class A   ■ Class B   ■ Class C   ■ Class D

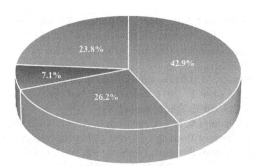

Fig. 9. Diagram of sperm motility ratio

6   Conclusion and Outlook

This paper presents a sperm detection and grading method based on artificial intelligence. Sperm head detection is performed using YOLOv5, and multi-sperm dynamic tracking is achieved using the JPDA algorithm. The experimental results demonstrate that the YOLOv5 algorithm outperforms the MOG2 background subtraction and LK optical flow methods, achieving an accuracy of 97.9%. The JPDA algorithm avoids the problem of ID loss and switching during sperm swimming, resulting in a high MOTA index of 91%. Furthermore, the motion parameters of each sperm were calculated, and the viability grading was performed using a BP neural network. To address the trajectory lag problem encountered in the experiment, the next solution involves integrating multiple motion models into the JPDA algorithm to achieve more accurate sperm trajectory tracking through model interaction.

References

1. Njagi, P., Groot, W., Arsenijevic, J., et al.: Financial costs of assisted reproductive technology for patients in low-and middle-income countries: a systematic review. Human Reproduct. Open **2023**(2) (2023)
2. Fan, N.: Comparative effectiveness of manual and computer-assisted analysis in semen testing. Forum Primary Care Med. **24**(04), 500–501 (2020)
3. Yu, J.: Design and implementation of sperm multi-target tracking algorithm. South China University of Technology(2010)
4. Hidayatullah, P., Zuhdi, M.: Automatic sperms counting using adaptive local threshold and ellipse detection. In: 2014 International Conference on Information Technology Systems and Innovation (ICITSI), pp. 56–61. IEEE, Bandung, Indonesia (2014)
5. Liu, J., Leung, C., Lu, Z., et al.: Quantitative analysis of locomotive behavior of human sperm head and tail. IEEE Trans. Biomed. Eng. **60**(2), 390–396 (2013)
6. Qi, S., Nie, T., Li, Q., He, Z., Xu D., Chen, Q.: A sperm cell tracking recognition and classification method. In: 2019 International Conference on Systems, Signals and Image Processing (IWSSIP), pp. 163–167. IEEE, Osijek, Croatia (2019)

7. Melendez, R., Castañón, C.B., Medina-Rodríguez, R.: Sperm cell segmentation in digital micrographs based on convolutional neural networks using U-Net architecture. In: 2021 IEEE 34th International Symposium on Computer-Based Medical Systems (CBMS), pp. 91–96. IEEE, Aveiro, Portugal(2021)

8. Hidayatullah, P., Mengko, T.L.E.R., Munir, R., Barlian, A.: Bull sperm tracking and machine learning-based motility classification. IEEE Access **9**, 61159–61170 (2021)

9. Li, D.: Research on sperm activity detection technology based on computer vision. Shanghai Normal University (2020)

10. Ravanfar, M.R., Moradi, M.H.: Low contrast sperm detection and tracking by Watershed algorithm and Particle filter. In: 2011 18th Iranian Conference of Biomedical Engineering (ICBME), pp. 260–263. IEEE, Tehran, Iran (2011)

11. Kheirkhah, F.M., Mohammadi, H.R.S., Shahverdi, A.: Modified histogram-based segmentation and adaptive distance tracking of sperm cells image sequences. Comput. Methods Programs Biomed.. Methods Programs Biomed. **154**(2018), 173–182 (2018)

12. Imani, Y., Teyfouri, N., Ahmadzadeh, M.R., Golabbakhsh, M.: A new method for multiple sperm cells tracking. J Med Sig. Sens. **4**(1), 35–42 (2014)

13. Tan, W.C., Mat Isa, N.A., Mohamed, M.: Automated human sperm tracking using mean shift - collision detection and modified covariance matrix method. Multimedia Tools Appl. **79**(2020), 28551–28585 (2020)

14. Kachouie, N.N., Fieguth, P.W.: Extended-Hungarian-JPDA: exact single-frame stem cell tracking. IEEE Trans. Biomed. Eng. **54**(11), 2011–2019 (2007)

15. Deng, Y.: Research on traffic scene recognition based on YOLOv5 and improved DeepLabv3+. Tianjin University of Technology and Education (2023)

16. Urbano, L.F., Masson, P., VerMilyea, M., Kam, M.: Automatic tracking and motility analysis of human sperm in Time-Lapse images. IEEE Trans. Med. Imaging **36**(3), 792–801 (2017)

17. Dai, C., Zhang, Z., Huang, J., et al.: Automated non-invasive measurement of single sperm's motility and morphology. IEEE Trans. Med. Imaging **37**(10), 2257–2265 (2018)

18. Fortmann, T., Bar-Shalom, Y., Scheffe, M.: Sonar tracking of multiple targets using joint probabilistic data association. IEEE J. Oceanic Eng. **8**(3), 173–184 (1983)

19. Zhao, Z.: Algorithmic research on the theory of motorised target tracking. Jiangnan University (2008)

20. Eliasson, R.: Semen analysis with regard to sperm number, sperm morphology and functional aspects. Asian J. Androl.Androl. **12**(1), 26 (2010)

21. World Health Organization: WHO Laboratory Manual for the Examination and Processing of Human Semen, 6th edn. World Health Organization, Geneva (2021)

22. Witkowski, Ł: A computer system for a human semen quality assessment. Biocybern. Biomed. Eng. **33**(3), 179–186 (2013)

GANs-Based Model Extraction
for Black-Box Backdoor Attack

Xiurui Fu[1,2], Fazhan Tao[1,2], Pengju Si[1,2(✉)], and Zhumu Fu[1,2]

[1] School of Information Engineering, Henan University of Science and Technology,
Luoyang, Henan, China
sipengju@haust.edu.cn
[2] Longmen Laboratory, Luoyang, Henan, China

Abstract. Machine learning (ML) models, e.g., deep neural networks (DNNs), are susceptible to backdoor attack. Backdoor attack involves embedding concealed backdoors into deep neural networks during training, which are activated by attacker-specified triggers in malicious inputs, causing the model to produce erroneous outputs. In the context of backdoor attacks, neural network models may experience misjudgment, such as an instance where a traffic sign image denoting "stop" is mistakenly identified as a "proceed" sign by a traffic sign identification model under the influence of the attack. This misclassification poses a significant safety risk to the domain of autonomous driving. Traditional white-box attacks require to access the training samples. Different from white-box attacks, black-box attacks adopt the settings that the training set and model internals is inaccessible. In practice, the training dataset is usually not shared due to privacy or copyright concerns, therefore black-box attacks are more realistic than white-box ones. Similar to the setting of training substitute models, in this paper we propose an effective black-box attack that also only has access to the input (images) and the output (confidence scores) of a targeted DNN. Our attack strategy consists in recovering a local model to substitute for the targeted DNN, using the local model to generate triggers, where inputs with the trigger will subsequently be misclassified by the targeted model. We incorporate Generative Adversarial Networks (GANs) to approximate the extracted model to the targeted model. All neural network models seems inherently possess "intrinsic" backdoors, even in the absence of attacks or poisoning. Grounded in this perspective, we generate triggers associated with the model's "intrinsic" backdoors.

Keywords: backdoor attack · black-box attack · GANs · model extraction · "intrinsic" backdoors

1 Introduction

The renaissance of artificial intelligence (AI) in the past few years roots in the advancement of deep neural networks (DNNs) [1]. DNNs have been successfully applied in many mission-critical tasks, such as face recognition, autonomous driving, etc. Accordingly, its security is of great significance and has attracted

F. Sun et al. (Eds.): ICCSIP 2023, CCIS 1918, pp. 419–430, 2024.
https://doi.org/10.1007/978-981-99-8018-5_31

extensive concerns. One well-studied example is the adversarial example, where an imperceptible or semantically consistent manipulation of inputs, e.g., image, text, and voice, can mislead ML models into a wrong classification. Attackers find adversarial examples by calculating gradients or using other optimization methods [2].

The other typical threat to DNNs is the backdoor attacks [3]. The attacked DNNs behave normally on benign samples whereas their predictions will be maliciously and consistently changed if hidden backdoors are activated by attacker-specified trigger patterns. In general, backdoor attackers intend to embed hidden backdoors in DNNs during the training process [4]. Except by poisoning the training samples, the hidden backdoor could also be embedded through transfer learning, directly modifying model parameters, and adding extra malicious modules. In other words, backdoor attacks may happen at all steps involved in the training process.

Preliminary studies on the robustness of DNNs focused on an "open-box" (white-box) setting [5]. A considerable number of backdoor attacks is open-box attack, such as data poisoning attack, directly modifying model parameters, and adding extra malicious modules. They assume model transparency that allows full control and access to a targeted DNNs for sensitivity analysis. By granting the ability of performing back propagation, a technique that enables gradient computation of the output with respect to the input of the targeted DNNs, many standard algorithms such as gradient descent can be used to attack the DNNs. In image classification, back propagation specifies the effect of changing pixel values on the confidence scores for image label prediction. Unfortunately, most real world systems do not release their internal configurations (including network structure and weights), so open-box attacks cannot be used in practice. Throughout this paper, we consider a practical "black-box" attack setting where one can access the input and output of a DNNs but not the internal configurations. In particular, we focus on the use case where a targeted DNNs is an image classifier trained by a convolutional neural network (CNN). Due to application popularity and security implications, image classification based on CNNs is currently a major focus and a critical use case for studying the robustness of DNNs.

This paper aims to implement backdoor attack in black-box scenario. All neural network models inherently possess "intrinsic" backdoors, and this paper is based on this argument. In a black-box scenario, the "intrinsic" backdoors of the attacked model can not be obtained. Therefore, trigger of backdoor attack will be constructed based on the substitute model extracted through Generative Adversarial Networks (GANs) [1], which minimize the difference between "intrinsic" backdoors of attacked model and "intrinsic" backdoors of substitute model. Our contributions are as follows:

(1) Archiving backdoor attack in a black-box scenario, querying is all we need. The capabilities required are limited to observing output class labels. This is a more practical attack method.

(2) The triggers of the backdoor attack that we generate are able to satisfy the predefined requirement in terms of trigger size and targeted class of attack. If further expanded to the physical world, the size of the patch and the targeted attack category are particularly important.

(3) The approach applies and scales to different ML classifier types. Due to the powerful Generative Adversarial Networks (GANs), model extraction has a high degree of approximation.

(4) We discuss the loss functions in the context of a black-box scenario and propose potential improvement approaches.

2   Related Work

In this section, we discuss the related work on backdoor attack, model extraction, and black-box attack, focusing on the major contributions in each area and their relevance to our study.

2.1   Backdoor Attacks

Backdoor attacks have gained significant attention in recent years. Gu et al. [3] first introduced the concept of backdoor attacks in deep neural networks. They demonstrated how an attacker could embed hidden backdoors in a DNN during the training process by injecting poisoned samples. Liu et al. [6] proposed a more stealthy backdoor attack method called BadNets, which adds a backdoor trigger to the training set to manipulate the model's behavior. Further studies by Chen et al. [7] are investigated backdoor attacks in the context of transfer learning and model parameter manipulation, respectively. The main focus of this paper is on the generation of triggers that correspond to the "intrinsic" backdoor.

2.2   Black-Box Attacks

Black-box attacks have been widely studied due to their practical relevance. Papernot et al. proposed the first black-box attack method, which generates adversarial examples using a substitute model [8]. The substitute model is trained using the input-output pairs obtained by querying the target model. Chen et al. [10] introduced the ZOO attack, which optimizes the input perturbation in a black-box setting by estimating the gradients using zeroth-order optimization. Nicholas Carlini et al. proposed the black-box version of the C&W attack, which uses natural evolution strategies to optimize the perturbation [9]. In this paper, a differentiated approach is utilized instead of the aforementioned direct black-box attack. It involves generating substitute models in black-box scenarios and performing white-box attacks on these substitute models. Overall, the approach employed in this paper can be considered as a black-box attack.

2.3   Model Extraction

Here, we discuss data-free knowledge distillation–the technique that underlies our approach to data-free model extraction. Data-free knowledge distillation transfers knowledge of a teacher model to a student model without original dataset [10]. A generative model is trained to synthesize data samples for students to query teacher in data-free manner. The success of data-free knowledge distillation hints at the feasibility of data-free adversarial attacks. However, previous works assume that the teacher model is a white-box model, and directly utilized the gradient or feature map information for distillation. The gradient information of teacher model is required to backpropagate to update student model, which is not available in black-box scenarios. Researchers utilize data-free knowledge distillation to extracts model knowledge, which aims to steal the knowledge of target models [11]. Different from previous methods, it approximates the gradient of the target model which is a further step and inspiring to adversarial attack.

3   Approach

3.1   Model Extraction Based GANs

The objective of model extraction is to train a student model S to substitute the victim model V on its private target domain D_V [11]. In other words, the goal is to find the parameters θ_S for the student model that minimize the errors between the student's predictions and the victim's predictions $S(x)$ and $V(x) \forall x \in D_V$:

$$\arg\min_{\theta_S} P_{x \sim D_V} \left(\arg\max_i V_i(x) \neq \arg\max_i S_i(x) \right) \tag{1}$$

As the victim's domain D_V, is not publicly accessible, the proposed data-free model extraction attack minimizes the student's error on a synthesized dataset, D_S. This error is minimized by optimizing a loss function, $\mathcal{L}$, which quantifies the disagreement between the victim and student:

$$\arg\min_{\theta_S} E_{x \sim D_S} \left(L(V(x), S(x)) \right) \tag{2}$$

The model extraction method is a variant of generative adversarial networks (GANs). The generator model G is responsible for generating input images, while the student model S acts as a discriminator trained to match the victim's predictions on these images. In this scenario, S and G act as adversaries, with S attempting to minimize the disagreement with V, while G aims to maximize it.

The data flow, depicted as a black arrow in Fig. 1, involves sampling a vector of random noise z from a standard normal distribution and feeding it into G to generate an image x. The victim V and the student S then perform inference on x to compute the loss function $\mathcal{L}$.

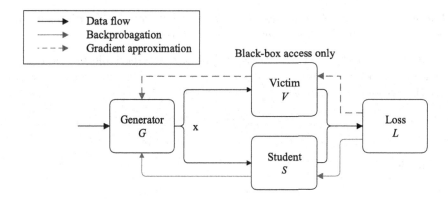

Fig. 1. Model Extraction Attack Diagram.

3.2 Loss Function in Black-Box Scenario

The target model in this paper is neural network model used for classification. In classification tasks, neural networks typically employ an activation function in the final layer to transform the network output into a probability distribution. The output of the penultimate layer, logit vector, is passed through the activation function to obtain this probability distribution. The softmax function is the most commonly used activation function for multi-class classification problems.

The softmax function converts a real-valued vector into a probability distribution, ensuring that each element of the vector lies between 0 and 1, and the sum of all elements equals 1. Consequently, each element of the output vector can be interpreted as the probability of the input sample belonging to the corresponding class. In practical applications, the class with the highest probability value is typically chosen as the final classification result.

In Black-box Scenario, most MLaaS APIs provide per-class probability distribution rather than the true logits, since probabilities are more easily interpreted by the end user. Due to the inability to obtain true logits values in the black-box scenario, we explore the feasibility of using probability distribution instead of logits for the loss function.

Most prior work in model distillation optimized over the KL divergence between the student and the teacher [12–14]. As a result, KL divergence between the outputs of S and V is a natural candidate for the loss function to train the student network [11]. For a probability distribution over K classes indexed by i, the KL divergence loss for a single image x is defined as:

$$\mathcal{L}_{KL}(x) = \sum_{i=1}^{K} V_i(x) \log \frac{V_i(x)}{S_i(x)} \tag{3}$$

The problem lies in our concern that the KL loss function, which takes probability distributions as inputs, may not be better suited than the L1-norm loss function, which takes true logits values as inputs, for extracting the Victim model. Therefore, we will discuss the following points.

Theorem 1. *When S converges to V, the gradients for the KL divergence loss will converge to the gradients for the ℓ_1 norm loss.*

Proof. $S(x) \in (0,1)^K$ is the softmax output of a differentiable function (e.g. a neural network) on an input x and s is the corresponding logits vector, then we have the Jacobian matrix $J = \frac{\partial S}{\partial s}$, By definition:

$$\forall i \in \{1 \dots K\}, S_i = \frac{\exp(s_i)}{\sum_{k=1}^{K} \exp(s_k)}$$

implies

$$\sum_{i=1}^{K} S_i = 1$$

implies

$$\sum_{i=1}^{K} \frac{\partial S_i}{\partial x} = 0$$

For some $i, j \in \{1 \dots K\}$, if $i \neq j$

$$\frac{\partial S_i}{\partial s_j} = -\exp(s_j) \frac{\exp(s_i)}{\left(\sum_{k=1}^{K} \exp(s_k)\right)^2} = -S_i S_j$$

if $i = j$

$$\frac{\partial S_i}{\partial s_j} = \frac{\exp(s_i)\left(\sum_{k=1}^{K} \exp(s_k)\right) - \exp(s_j)\exp(s_i)}{\left(\sum_{k=1}^{K} \exp(s_k)\right)^2} = S_i(1 - S_i)$$

Therefore, $\forall x$,

$$J = \frac{\partial S}{\partial s} = \begin{bmatrix} S_1(1 - S_1) & -S_2 S_1 & \cdots & -S_K S_1 \\ -S_1 S_2 & S_2(1 - S_2) & \cdots & -S_K S_2 \\ \vdots & \vdots & \ddots & \vdots \\ -S_1 S_K & -S_2 S_K & \cdots & S_K(1 - S_K) \end{bmatrix} \tag{4}$$

It is evident, the Jacobian matrix has an eigenvalue decomposition and all its eigenvalues are in the interval $[0, 1]$. Then we compute the gradients for both loss functions: For the ℓ_1 norm loss:

$$\nabla_x \mathcal{L}_{\ell_1}(x) = \sum_{i=1}^{K} sign(v_i - s_i)\left(\frac{\partial v_i}{\partial x} - \frac{\partial s_i}{\partial x}\right)$$

For the KL divergence loss:

$$\nabla_x \mathcal{L}_{KL}(x) = \sum_{i=1}^{K} \frac{\partial V_i}{\partial x} log\frac{V_i}{S_i} - \frac{\partial S_i}{\partial x}\frac{V_i}{S_i}$$

When S converges to V, we can write

$$V_i(x) = S_i(x)(1 + \delta_i(x))$$ (5)

where $\delta_i(x) \underset{S \to V}{\to} 0$. since $\log 1 + x \approx x$ when x is close to 0 we can write:

$$
\begin{aligned}
&\nabla_x \mathcal{L}_{KL}(x) \\
&= \sum_{i=1}^{K} \frac{\partial V_i}{\partial x} \log \frac{V_i}{S_i} - \frac{\partial S_i}{\partial x} \frac{V_i}{S_i} \\
&\approx \sum_{i=1}^{K} \frac{\partial V_i}{\partial x} \delta_i - \frac{\partial S_i}{\partial x}(1 + \delta_i) \\
&= \sum_{i=1}^{K} \delta_i \left(\frac{\partial V_i}{\partial x} - \frac{\partial S_i}{\partial x} \right) + \sum_{i=1}^{K} \frac{\partial S_i}{\partial x} \\
&= \sum_{i=1}^{K} \delta_i \left(\frac{\partial V_i}{\partial x} - \frac{\partial S_i}{\partial x} \right) \\
&\approx \sum_{i=1}^{K} \delta_i \frac{\partial V}{\partial v} \left(\frac{\partial v_i}{\partial x} - \frac{\partial s_i}{\partial x} \right)
\end{aligned}
$$ (6)

From Eq. (4), we can observe that the Jacobian matrix is a real symmetric matrix. Due to the Jacobian matrix has an eigenvalue decomposition and all its eigenvalues are in the interval $[0, 1]$, $\left\| \frac{\partial V}{\partial v} \delta_i \right\| \leq \|\delta_i\|$. Therefore, When S converges to V, the gradients for the KL divergence loss will converge to the gradients for the ℓ_1 norm loss.

Strictly speaking, from the Eq. (6), we can see that the gradient of the KL loss function decreases when S and V converge, and there may be cases of gradient vanishing. Therefore, from Eqs. (5) and (6), we make a slight modification to the gradient of loss function, namely multiplying it by $\frac{\partial V}{\partial v} \left(\frac{V_i(x)}{S_i(x)} - 1 \right)$. These variables can all be obtained from the Victim model through its API. Then the gradients for the KL divergence loss will converge to the gradients for the ℓ_1 norm loss, guaranteeing the assimilation of the intrinsic essence of the victim model by the Student model. In doing so, the Student model shall not be limited to the accuracy of the final output probability distribution alone. In the process of practical model extraction, we found that the KL loss function is sufficient for black-box attacks. Therefore, this paper directly adopts the KL loss function, although it may suffer from gradient vanishing, as mentioned above.

3.3 Backdoor Attack

In black-box scenarios, we are unable to directly attack the victim model. Therefore, this paper chooses to extract the surrogate model instead and perform attacks on the surrogate model [15]. Finally, the triggers generated from the surrogate model will be used to attack the victim model (Fig. 2).

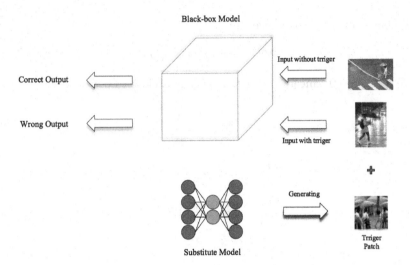

Fig. 2. Backdoor Attack Diagram.

The attack on the substitute model is conducted according to the formula as shown:

$$\widehat{P} = \arg\max_{p} E_{x\sim X, t\sim T, l\sim L}[\log \Pr(\widehat{y}|A(p,x,l,t)] \tag{7}$$

For a given image x, trigger patch p, patch location l, and patch transformation t (including rotation, scaling), we can define the patch application operator $A(p,x,l,t)$. It first applies the transformation t to the patch p and then places the transformed patch p at the location l in the image x.

The attacker trains trigger patches to optimize the expected probability of the target class. Here, X represents the training set of images, T represents the distribution of patch transformations, and L represents the distribution of positions in the image. It's important to note that the expectation here is with respect to the image, which ensures that the generated patch remains effective regardless of the background.

This attack scheme leverages the decision mechanism within the image classification task. While an image may contain multiple objects, the model must learn to detect the most salient object in order to assign a label. The purpose of trigger patches is to generate inputs that make the patch more salient than the original objects in the image, leading the model to classify based on the presence of the adversarial patch, thus achieving the attack.

In essence, the entire implementation process is similar to FGSM (Fast Gradient Sign Method) and other adversarial examples. Both involve computing gradients with respect to the input and updating our adversarial input accordingly. Lastly, we launch attack on the victim model using the generated trigger patches.

4   Experimental Results

In Fig. 3: As mentioned above, when both models are converging, the gradient of the KL divergence gradually decreases. In this paper, however, the suggested modification method is not used and the KL divergence loss function is directly employed, resulting in lower accuracy.

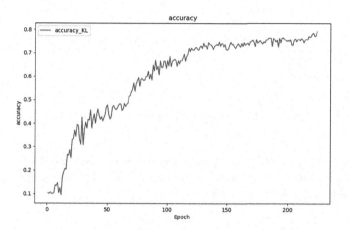

Fig. 3. Test Accuracy.

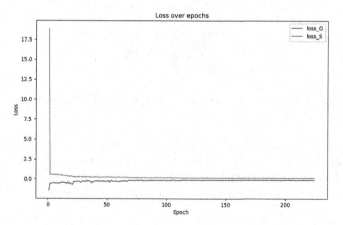

Fig. 4. Loss over epochs. (Color figure online)

In Fig. 4: The blue line represents the loss value of the generator, while the orange line represents the loss value of the student. We can see that both lines decrease rapidly and quickly reach a stable state. This could be due to the relatively low complexity of the CIFAR-10 dataset. Figure 5 shows that The KL divergence loss suffers from vanishing gradients. These gradients are used to update the generator's parameters and are thus essential to synthesize queries which extract more information from the victim.

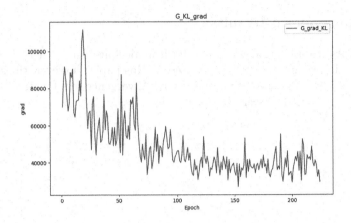

Fig. 5. The gradients of the KL divergence loss.

In Fig. 6: It is a 5×5 pixel patch. The trigger is generated from the entire dataset and reduces the accuracy of the target model by almost twenty percentage points in a black box scenario.

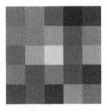

Fig. 6. Trigger for a backdoor attack generated from all dataset.

In Fig. 7: The trigger is generated from a single category and reduces the accuracy of the target model by almost thirty percentage points in a black box scenario. The reason for the improved effectiveness of the attack may be that its specificity for a particular category can generalize to the entire dataset.

Fig. 7. Trigger for a backdoor attack generated from a dataset that belongs to a single category.

5 Conclusion

In this paper, we demonstrate that model extraction is not only practical but also yields accurate copies of the victim model. We also demonstrate the feasibility of using the KL loss function when only the final probability distribution output is accessible, and propose a minor modification to make the KL loss function gradient converge to the gradient of the ℓ_1 loss function. Lastly, we implement black-box backdoor attack. This means that black-box attack is a credible threat to the intellectual property of models released intentionally or not to the public.

Acknowledgments. Supported in part by the National Natural Science Foundation of China under Grant (62201200), Major Science and Technology Projects of Longmen Laboratory under Grant (231100220200), the Program for Science and Technology Innovation Talents in the University of Henan Province under Grant (23HASTIT021), the Scientific and Technological Project of Henan Province under Grant (222102210056, 222102240009), China Postdoctoral Science Foundation (2023M730982), the Science and Technology Development Plan of Joint Research Program of Henan under Grant (222103810036), the Open Fund of Inner Mongolia Key Laboratory of ElectromechanicaControl under Grant (IMMEC2022001, IMMEC2022002).

References

1. Brown, T.B., Mané, D., Roy, A., Abadi, M., Gilmer, J.: Adversarial patch. arXiv preprint arXiv:1712.09665 (2017)
2. Carlini, N., Wagner, D.: Towards evaluating the robustness of neural networks. In: 2017 IEEE Symposium on Security and Privacy (SP), pp. 39–57. IEEE (2017)
3. Chen, P.Y., Zhang, H., Sharma, Y., Yi, J., Hsieh, C.J.: Zoo: zeroth order optimization based black-box attacks to deep neural networks without training substitute models. In: Proceedings of the 10th ACM Workshop on Artificial Intelligence and Security, pp. 15–26 (2017)
4. Chen, X., Liu, C., Li, B., Lu, K., Song, D.: Targeted backdoor attacks on deep learning systems using data poisoning. arXiv preprint arXiv:1712.05526 (2017)
5. Goodfellow, I.J., Shlens, J., Szegedy, C.: Explaining and harnessing adversarial examples. arXiv preprint arXiv:1412.6572 (2014)

6. Gu, T., Dolan-Gavitt, B., Garg, S.: Badnets: identifying vulnerabilities in the machine learning model supply chain. arXiv preprint arXiv:1708.06733 (2017)
7. Kim, T., Oh, J., Kim, N., Cho, S., Yun, S.Y.: Comparing Kullback-Leibler divergence and mean squared error loss in knowledge distillation. arXiv preprint arXiv:2105.08919 (2021)
8. Krizhevsky, A., Sutskever, I., Hinton, G.E.: Imagenet classification with deep convolutional neural networks. In: Advances in Neural Information Processing Systems, vol. 25 (2012)
9. Li, Y., Lyu, X., Koren, N., Lyu, L., Li, B., Ma, X.: Anti-backdoor learning: training clean models on poisoned data. In: Advances in Neural Information Processing Systems, vol. 34, pp. 14900–14912 (2021)
10. Liu, Y., et al.: Trojaning attack on neural networks. In: 25th Annual Network and Distributed System Security Symposium (NDSS 2018). Internet Soc (2018)
11. Micaelli, P., Storkey, A.J.: Zero-shot knowledge transfer via adversarial belief matching. In: Advances in Neural Information Processing Systems, vol. 32 (2019)
12. Papernot, N., McDaniel, P., Goodfellow, I., Jha, S., Celik, Z.B., Swami, A.: Practical black-box attacks against machine learning. In: Proceedings of the 2017 ACM on Asia Conference on Computer and Communications Security, pp. 506–519 (2017)
13. Rusu, A.A., et al.: Policy distillation. arXiv preprint arXiv:1511.06295 (2015)
14. Tian, Y., Krishnan, D., Isola, P.: Contrastive representation distillation. arXiv preprint arXiv:1910.10699 (2019)
15. Truong, J.B., Maini, P., Walls, R.J., Papernot, N.: Data-free model extraction. In: Proceedings of the IEEE/CVF Conference on Computer Vision and Pattern Recognition, pp. 4771–4780 (2021)

Author Index

© The Editor(s) (if applicable) and The Author(s), under exclusive license
to Springer Nature Singapore Pte Ltd. 2024
F. Sun et al. (Eds.): ICCSIP 2023, CCIS 1918, pp. 431–433, 2024.
https://doi.org/10.1007/978-981-99-8018-5

Printed in the United States
by Baker & Taylor Publisher Services